MOON

U.S. & CANADIAN ROCKY MOUNTAINS

Road Trip

BECKY LOMAX

CONTENTS

Although every effort was made to make sure the information in this book was accurate when going to press, research was impacted by the COVID-19 pandemic and things may have changed since the time of writing. Be sure to confirm specific details, like opening hours, closures, and travel guidelines and restrictions, when making your travel plans. For more detailed information, see p. 606.

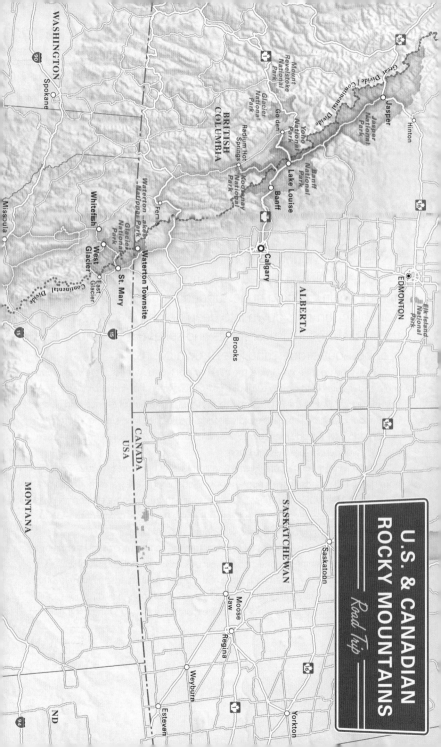

DISCOVER
the Rockies

The Rocky Mountains dominate this continent. Shifting tectonic plates collided here, shoving the landscape up, up, and up again, creating huge, rugged mountains that sweep from high summits down into deep gorges. Glaciers scoured the peaks into fantastical spines and spires cut by long valleys, scooped-out cirques, and lake-strewn basins.

This is the Continental Divide, the backbone of North America. Here year-round snow and glaciers feed cloudy turquoise lakes, their waters flowing into clear blue rivers that make their way to the Pacific and Atlantic Oceans, the Gulf of Mexico, and Hudson Bay. But our changing climate is rapidly altering the Rockies. Many glaciers from just a century ago have already melted into oblivion. Traveling to the Rockies now is to see these icy wonders before they are gone.

This environment harbors diverse wildlife. Herds of bison graze in meadows, bighorn sheep butt heads, bull elk bugle, moose plod through lakes, and mountain goats trot on cliffs. Meanwhile, the chirps of pikas resound through high-elevation rockfalls and short-tailed weasels skitter after mice. This is also the home of top-of-the-food-chain predators: grizzly bears, wolves, wolverines, and bald eagles.

A drive through the Rockies takes you across the continent, crosses international borders, and brings nine national parks in reach. As your car snakes through valleys, craggy mountains tower overhead. Some of the best moments are on high-elevation passes, when you find yourself surrounded by a sea of summits in all directions.

The Rocky Mountains are indeed a place that kindles awe. It's time to hit the road to see them.

14 TOP EXPERIENCES

1 **Drive the Icefields Parkway:** This scenic road runs through Banff (page 123) and Jasper National Parks (page 76), boasting some of the largest glaciers and icefields remaining in the Rocky Mountains.

∨
∨
∨

2 **Set your watch by Old Faithful:** The famous geyser in Yellowstone National Park erupts on a predictable schedule (page 383).

3 **Reach new heights on Trail Ridge Road:** Rocky Mountain National Park is bisected by this scenic road that climbs to over 12,000 feet in elevation (page 526).

4 **Paddle glacier-fed lakes:** Hop in a kayak to absorb the turquoise waters of Moraine Lake (pictured; page 133) in Banff and Maligne Lake (page 96) in Jasper.

<<<

5 **Hike to Grinnell Glacier:** Walk up to the edge of a glacier—while you still can—in Glacier National Park (page 287).

>>>

6 **Gape at Takakkaw Falls:** The second highest waterfall in Canada spills from the upper elevations of Yoho National Park (page 187).

<<<

7 **Watch wildlife:** Feast your eyes on bison, bears, and wolves in Yellowstone's Lamar Valley (page 380) and spot moose, elk, and bighorn sheep in Rocky Mountain National Park (page 521).

>>>

^^^
^

8 **Tour Going-to-the-Sun Road:** This engineering marvel crosses stunning Logan Pass in Glacier National Park. Drive it yourself or hop on a tour bus (page 278).

9 **Spend the night at a grand park lodge:** The Fairmont Chateau Lake Louise (pictured; page 133) in Banff has a classic storybook appeal. In Glacier, enjoy a historic Swiss chalet vibe at the Many Glacier Hotel (page 276).

<<<

10 Cruise across an international border: Ride a tour boat over the U.S.-Canada border in Waterton Lakes National Park (page 237).

>>>

11 Motor down Teton Park Road: There's no better way to see the Teton Mountains than on this scenic drive (page 438).

>>>

12 Go backpacking: Head into the backcountry for a few days by hiking Kootenay's Rockwall (page 219) or the Teton Crest Trail (pictured; page 445) in Grand Teton National Park.

>>>

13 Go stargazing: Watch the Milky Way spread out across the night sky from Jasper (page 93) or Glacier (page 293).

<<<

14 Marvel at Grand Prismatic Spring: Absorb the radiance of the largest and most colorful hot spring in Yellowstone (page 383).

>>>

PLANNING YOUR TRIP

Where to Go

Calgary
Tucked along the Bow River, Calgary is western Canada's interior hub of and the third largest city in the country. This one-time **cowboy town** turned oil kingdom hosts the **Calgary Stampede,** one of the largest rodeos and outdoor shows on the continent.

Jasper National Park
From **glaciers** spilling off the **Columbia Icefield** to **Maligne Lake,** Jasper National Park is filled with raw beauty. Here you can hike to high mountain passes or enjoy easy adventures via trams and snow coaches. Then relax with a soak in **Miette Hot Springs.**

Banff National Park
The crown of the Canadian Rockies, Banff National Park is filled with **icy summits, wildflower meadows,** and mesmerizing **turquoise lakes.** Historic hotels, ski resorts, and **backcountry lodges** offer base camps for once-in-a-lifetime escapades.

Yoho National Park
Yoho National Park is tiny compared to the neighboring Canadian parks, but it holds dramatic water features: **Emerald Lake** sparkles a vivid blue-green, remote **Lake O'Hara** is tucked into a sculpted basin, and immense **Takakkaw Falls** tumble 1,250 feet (373 m).

Kootenay National Park
Often ignored in favor of the larger parks, Kootenay is a place to escape the crowds. Hiking trails climb to stunning **glaciers** that tumble from alpine bowls. Cap any day with the soothing waters of **Radium Hot Springs.**

Waterton Lakes National Park
The tiniest park in the Canadian Rockies, Waterton Lakes is where **glacier-carved peaks** meet the prairie. It shares an international boundary with Glacier National Park; together they form the world's first **International Peace Park.**

Glacier National Park
Alpine **meadows,** tiny melting **glaciers,** and **turquoise lakes** flank the serrated peaks of Glacier National Park, a main draw for hikers and backpackers. The engineering marvel that is **Going-to-the-Sun Road** climbs through cliffs to reach the Continental Divide.

Flathead Valley to Bozeman
Flathead Valley serves as the **gateway to Glacier.** To the southwest, Bozeman and Big Sky provide the **gateways to Yellowstone.** These year-round recreation hubs provide bases for hiking, skiing, bicycling, and paddling.

Yellowstone National Park
Yellowstone National Park is known for outstanding **wildlife watching.** Bighorn sheep, bison, wolves, bears, and eagles number among its many residents. But because it's located on North America's largest supervolcano, Yellowstone's biggest attractions are **geysers, mud pots,** and **hot springs.**

Grand Teton National Park
The peaks of Grand Teton National Park rise like jagged teeth, dominating the landscape around **Jackson Hole.** They can be admired from **lake hikes, scenic drives,** and **boat tours.**

Salt Lake City and Central Utah
Squeezed between Great Salt Lake and the Wasatch Mountains, Salt Lake City derives much of its identity from its Mormon heritage. But the sprawling metropolis has evolved into an **outdoor center** with year-round recreation:

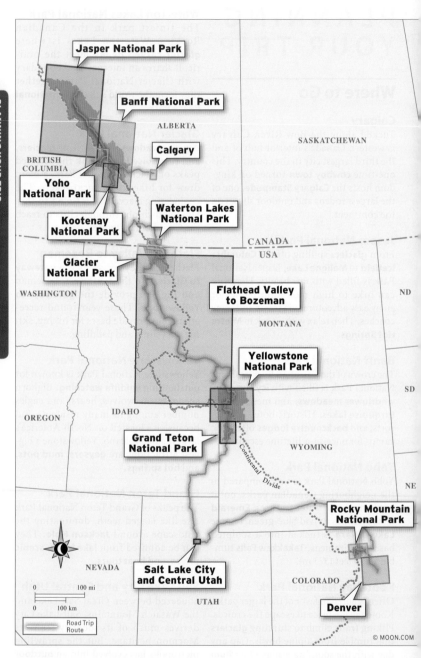

Jasper National Park

Banff National Park

ALBERTA

SASKATCHEWAN

Calgary

BRITISH
COLUMBIA

Yoho
National Park

Kootenay
National Park

Waterton Lakes
National Park

CANADA
USA

Glacier
National Park

WASHINGTON

Flathead Valley
to Bozeman

ND

MONTANA

Yellowstone
National Park

SD

OREGON

IDAHO

Grand Teton
National Park

WYOMING

Continental Divide

NE

Rocky Mountain
National Park

NEVADA

Salt Lake City
and Central Utah

COLORADO

0   100 mi

0   100 km

UTAH

Denver

Road Trip
Route

© MOON.COM

Clockwise from top left: lupine growing in the Rocky Mountains; driving in Yoho National Park; Bear Lake in Rocky Mountain National Park

hiking, boating, mountain biking, and world-class skiing.

Rocky Mountain National Park

Sporting some of the highest peaks of the Rocky Mountains, this national park offers prime **scenic drives,** scads of **hiking trails,** and the ambitious climb of towering **Longs Peak.** In fall, bull elk bugle as they fight for dominance against a backdrop of autumnal color.

Denver

Sprawling Denver is a vibrant city in the **foothills** of the Rockies. Lively downtown contains pedestrian zones perfect for **shopping, dining, theater-going,** and **museum-hopping.** Nearby **Boulder** is a funky, recreation-loving city nestled below the **Flatirons.**

When to Go

High Season

Summer (early June-mid-Sept.) is high season in the Rockies, with the warmest weather, **highest prices,** and **biggest crowds.** That's when the most hiking trails and visitor services are accessible, tours run most frequently, and seasonal roads and hotels are open. Daytime temps range 65-85°F (18-29°C) and nights range 35-50°F (2-10°C).

Shoulder Seasons

In **spring** (Apr.-early June), lower-elevation trails are accessible, though **snow lingers** in the high country through June. **Seasonal scenic roads** often open in late May, but some take longer for snow removal, even into July. Temperatures during the day run 30-65°F (0-18°C), while nights are much cooler, ranging -4°F to 23°F (-20°C to 5°C) nights.

In **fall** (mid-Sept.-early Nov.), the weather often yo-yos between **warm days** and **wintry storms.** High mountain elevations can see snow, which may turn trails and roads icy, sometimes requiring temporary closures. Daytime and nighttime temperatures run about the same as they do in spring.

Low Season

Winter (early Nov.-Mar.) sees **fewer crowds** and **lower prices**—except for **ski resort areas,** which are usually open early November-April. Visitor services mostly close down, except for year-round park regions and towns. **Seasonal roads are closed;** plowing is only maintained on major roadways. Closed roads often permit **cross-country skiing** and **snowshoeing.** Temperatures range 0-28°F (-18°C to -2°C) during the day. Nightly temperatures run -5°F to 10°F (-21°C to -12°C).

Before You Go

Reservations

The popularity of the Canadian and U.S. national parks has skyrocketed in recent years, resulting in increased visitation. Reservations are **mandatory** for **inside-park lodging** in the Rockies. Lodging outside the national parks also fills up quickly in summer. While it's possible find a room at the last minute due to cancellations, it's better to **book one year ahead** to ensure you get your top choice.

CANADIAN NATIONAL PARKS

Inside the Canadian national parks, **hotels, cabins, and lodges** are run by independent operators. For reservations, contact the individual lodging. Most accept reservations a year in advance.

Camping reservations (877/737-3783, 519/826-5391 from outside North America, https://reservation.pc.gc.ca) inside the park open in **early January** for the year ahead. Some campsites are first come, first served and don't accept reservations.

U.S. NATIONAL PARKS

Many of the U.S. parks have designated

concessionaires that operate the in-park lodges. Contact these operators **12-13 months** in advance for reservations:

- Glacier: **Xanterra** (855/733-4522, 303/265-7010 outside U.S., www.glaciernationalparklodges.com) or **Pursuit Collection** (844/868-7474, www.glacierparkcollection.com)

- Yellowstone: **Xanterra** (307/344-7311, www.yellowstonenationalparklodges.com)

- Grand Teton: **Grand Teton Lodging Company** (307/543-3100, www.gtlc.com) or **Signal Mountain Lodge** (307/543-2831, www.signalmountainlodge.com)

For **camping** in Glacier, Grand Teton, Rocky Mountain, and four of Yellowstone's campgrounds, make **reservations** (877/444-6777, www.recreation.gov) **six months** in advance. Book campsites for Yellowstone's five other campgrounds **12-13 months** in advance through **Xanterra** (307/344-7311, www.yellowstonenationalparklodges.com).

TICKETING
You'll need **advance reservations** to enter Glacier's **Going-to-the-Sun Road** and **timed entry** reservations for **Rocky Mountain National Park.** Check the parks' websites for specific ticketing policies several months before your trip.

Fees and Passes

Daily entry fees in **Canadian national parks** cost C$10 for adults, C$9 for seniors, or C$20 per family or vehicle. Kids 17 and younger are free. Annual **Discovery Passes** to all of the parks and historic sites in the Canadian Rockies cost C$70 for adults, C$60 for seniors, or C$140 per family or vehicle. Entry is free on Canada Day (July 1).

Entry fees to **U.S. national parks** in the Rocky Mountains cost $35 per vehicle for seven days (motorcycles $30, individuals

$20). Rocky Mountain National Park also sells a **one-day pass** for $25 per vehicle. Winter fees are lower at Glacier ($25 per vehicle, $20 motorcycle, $15 individual) and Grand Teton ($15 per vehicle, motorcycle, or individual).

Annual passes for Glacier, Yellowstone, Grand Teton, or Rocky Mountain cost $70. Annual **America the Beautiful Passes,** which give admittance to all U.S. national parks, cost $80. (The pass is free for U.S. military personnel, veterans, gold star families, and U.S. fourth graders.) For U.S. citizens and permanent residents over 62, a **lifetime pass** costs $80. The **annual Senior Pass** is $20 per year. U.S. citizens and permanent residents with permanent disabilities can also get a free lifetime pass.

The U.S. national parks have several **fee-free days:** January 21 (Dr. Martin Luther King Jr.'s birthday); the first day of National Park Week in April; August 25 (National Park Service's birthday); September 28 (Public Lands Day); and November 11 (Veterans Day).

Passports and Visas
ENTERING CANADA
International travelers entering Canada must have **passports.** The one exception is travelers from the United States and Western Hemisphere Travel Initiative countries, who may use **passport cards, enhanced driver's licenses,** or **NEXUS cards** instead. **Visas** are not required for visitors from about 50 countries, including the United States. All others must apply for visas. Find the list of visa-exempt countries and visa requirements at www.cic.gc.ca.

ENTERING THE UNITED STATES
International travelers entering the United States must have **passports.** One exception applies to travelers from Canada and countries in the Western Hemisphere Travel Initiative, who may use a **passport card, enhanced driver's license,** or **NEXUS card** instead. **Visas** may

also be required for some countries; check https://travel.state.gov for countries with visa waivers and visa applications.

Driving Tips

Weather and Safety

Because snowfall is possible any time of year in the Rocky Mountains, especially over high mountain passes, roads might be unexpectedly icy or wet. Luckily, ice often melts within a day or two. During hail and lightning storms, which are common in summer, pull over, turn your hazard lights on, and wait it out. Most mountain squalls move on in 20 minutes or so.

Winter driving requires **snow tires** or **all-weather tires.** Carry **chains** for traveling over high-elevation passes if you don't have studded snow tires. Many back roads, dirt and gravel roads, and several scenic drives close in winter. These include Going-to-the-Sun Road in Glacier, Trail Ridge Road in Rocky Mountain, most of Grand Loop Road in Yellowstone, and a portion of Teton Park Road in Grand Teton.

Cell Service and Internet Access

In the large cities of Calgary, Salt Lake City, and Denver, cell and internet service are ubiquitous. But in the other parts of the Rocky Mountains, cell service is spotty to nonexistent. Do not depend on cell service on **mountain roads, hiking trails,** and in the **backcountry.** You may need to handle emergencies on your own. If necessary, flag down a passing car to get help or, if possible, get to the nearest lodge to make a phone call.

Inside the **national parks,** you'll find wireless internet in most lodges but only in a handful of visitors centers. Internet speeds are often slow and clogged with users. Plan to download park apps, maps, and media before you leave home.

Maps and GPS

Road maps are available for members through the **Canadian Automobile Association** (CAA, www.caa.ca) and **American Automobile Association** (AAA, www.aaa.com). They are also available through federal, provincial, and state tourism bureaus of British Columbia (www.helloBC.com), Alberta (www.travelalberta.com), Montana (www.visitmt.com), Wyoming (www.travelwyoming.com), Utah (www.visitutah.com), and Colorado (www.colorado.com), plus Destination Canada (www.canada.travel). National parks also have road maps on their websites. U.S. national parks hand out maps at entrance stations. For hiking, plan on purchasing more detailed **topographical maps** from the **U.S. Geological Survey** (https://store.usgs.gov). For the Canadian national parks, **Gem Trek Maps** (www.gemtrek.com) publishes driving and hiking maps.

Don't rely solely on GPS to reach destinations. Seasonal road closures, rugged dirt roads, and weather can affect routes, but not all GPS devices will have the most current data. Many drivers have gotten stranded on back roads following GPS instructions. Always use a **road map** in addition to GPS. Be sure to check for **road status updates** from national park websites before embarking on your adventure.

Conscientious Travel Tips

Your visit can have an impact on the mountain parks and local communities. Make it a positive one by following these tips:

Planning

♦ Bring a **refillable water bottle** instead of disposable plastic bottles.

♦ Always have a **backup plan** in case of crowds or full parking lots.

♦ Check national park websites in advance of your trip for information on **road construction, closures,** and **alerts.**

♦ Get all **necessary permits** in advance.

Traveling

♦ Buy **locally made** products.

♦ Take **tours** with local, park-approved guide companies.

♦ Limit your **consumable waste;** many mountain communities have limited trash and recycling services.

♦ Visit crowded sites at **less popular times** or seasons.

Driving and Parking

♦ Park only in **designated parking areas** and trailheads, not on roadsides.

♦ **Minimize driving** by hiking, biking, paddling, and skiing to experience the parks. Ride shuttles where available.

♦ **Turn off the car engine** rather than idling when you stop to watch wildlife or take in sights.

♦ Observe posted **speed limits** to keep wildlife safe.

Wildlife Watching and Photography

♦ Bring **binoculars** to watch wildlife; this helps maintain a safe distance for you and the animals. Use **telephoto lenses** to photograph wildlife and scenery from safe distances and perches.

♦ Stay **100 yards** (100 m) or **10 bus lengths** away from bears, wolves, bison, and cougars. Stay **25 yards** (30 m) or three bus lengths from other large animals (moose, elk, deer, sheep, and goats). If you cause an animal to move, you are too close. Do not disturb or harass wildlife by making noise or in any other way.

♦ **Do not approach wildlife,** even if you're separated by a fence. If you are pulling over to see wildlife, stay in your car, and move on quickly. Use established paved or gravel **pullouts** for wildlife-watching rather than stopping in or on the side of a road.

♦ Leave **drones** home; they are prohibited in all Canadian and U.S. national parks.

♦ **Keep wildlife wild:** Do not feed them. Dispose of all organic waste and other litter in proper receptacles.

Hiking and Backpacking

♦ Follow **Leave No Trace** (www.lnt.org) principles at all times.

♦ Get **required permits** for wilderness camping and backpacking.

♦ Stay on **established trails, paths,** and **boardwalks** to avoid damaging fragile ecosystems.

♦ Build fires (if permitted) only in **designated fire rings.**

HIT THE ROAD

Best of the Rockies in 21 Days

This three-week adventure starts in Calgary and continues south to Denver, packing in the best of the Rocky Mountains along the way. The route takes in big scenery filled with turquoise lakes, plunging waterfalls, rushing rivers, frozen icefields, and rugged pinnacles across nine national parks. Wildlife sightings punctuate the thrills in between idyllic mountain towns where outdoor recreation is a way of life. This is a once-in-a-lifetime road trip that covers over 2,500 miles (4,000 km). If you prefer to drive south to north, you can start in Denver and follow this itinerary in reverse.

Day 1
CALGARY TO JASPER
250 miles/400 km; 5 hours
Fly into the **Calgary airport.** From the city, it's only about an hour's drive to reach the mountains. Bypassing Banff and Lake Louise for a later day, head north on the stunning **Icefields Parkway.** At **Bow Summit,** walk to **Peyto Lake Overlook.** Tour **Athabasca Falls** before reaching the **Jasper Townsite.** Check into **Jasper Park Lodge** for two nights.

Day 2
JASPER NATIONAL PARK
62 miles/100 km; 2 hours
Drive to **Maligne Lake** for a **boat tour** followed by lunch in the lodge. After returning to the Jasper Townsite, take in the scenery from the **Jasper Sky Tram** and hike to the summit of **Whistlers Summit.** Afterward, tour the town and enjoy the evening on the shore of Beauvert Lake at Jasper Park Lodge.

Day 3
JASPER TO LAKE LOUISE
145 miles/235 km; 3 hours
Get an early start to enjoy multiple stops on the Icefields Parkway. Begin with **Wabasso Falls,** then continue to the **Icefield Centre.** From there, walk the **Toe-of-the-Glacier Interpretive Trail** and take a guided **glacier tour.** Stop at **Bow Lake** for views before descending to **Lake Louise.** Stay at the **Fairmont Chateau Lake Louise** for three nights.

Day 4
LAKE LOUISE
24 miles/39 km; 1.5 hours
Start the day by driving south to turquoise **Moraine Lake.** Follow the **Rockpile Trail** for classic lake photos. Afterward, head to **Lake Louise Ski Area** to catch the **scenic lift** for exceptional views of Temple Mountain, the Fairmont Chateau Lake Louise, and possibly grizzly bears. In the afternoon, **paddle Lake Louise** and walk the lakeshore. Cap off the day with dinner at the Fairmont and admire the tableside views of the lake.

Day 5
LAKE LOUISE TO YOHO NATIONAL PARK
84 miles/135 km; 3 hours
Yoho National Park yields unparalleled scenery. Stop at **Kicking Horse Pass** for views and interpretive displays. Descend to **Emerald Lake** for a walk along the shoreline followed by lunch. In the afternoon, drive up the scenic **Yoho Valley Road** to walk to the base of **Takakkaw Falls** spilling in a white ribbon from the Waputik Icefield. (It takes about an hour each way to drive Yoho Valley Road.) Return to Lake Louise for the night.

Day 6
LAKE LOUISE TO BANFF
37 miles/60 km; 1 hour
Start the morning off with a drive down the **Bow Valley Parkway** along Bow River. The route takes you below the parapets of **Castle Mountain** before reaching the

Epic Drives

♦ **Icefields Parkway** (pages 76 and 123): Dripping with more than 100 glaciers, this parkway (144 mi/232 km) threads through Jasper and Banff National Parks, with views of turquoise lakes and plummeting waterfalls along the way.

♦ **Banff-Windemere Highway** (page 215): From the Great Divide in the north to hot springs in the south, this scenic highway (58 mi/94 km) through Kootenay National Park follows the Vermilion and Kootenay Rivers between two stunning mountain ranges.

♦ **Going-to-the-Sun Road** (page 278): This historic route over Logan Pass (50 mi/80 km) in Glacier National Park is anchored by long, finger-like crystalline lakes. The engineering on this cliff-cut road uses arches and tunnels that show off the rugged mountain landscape.

Icefields Parkway, Banff National Park

♦ **Grand Loop Road** (page 390): This figure-eight loop (142 mi/229 km) through Yellowstone National Park takes in mountains, canyons, waterfalls, and broad meadows filled with wildlife, all in a volcanic landscape full of geyser basins.

♦ **Teton Park Road** (page 438): This short scenic road (20 mi/32 km) in Grand Teton National Park showcases views of the Grand Teton and Mount Moran, which still harbor small glaciers.

♦ **Trail Ridge Road** (page 526): The highest road in the Rocky Mountains, this route (48 mi/77 km) climbs above the tree line through alpine tundra for a top-of-the-world vista, where you can see for miles.

Banff Townsite. Spend the rest of the day touring the **Cave and Basin National Historic Site,** shopping downtown, or taking a **boat tour** on nearby **Lake Minnewanka.** Spend the night in the historic **Fairmont Banff Springs.**

Day 7
BANFF TO RADIUM HOT SPRINGS
85 miles/137 km; 2.5 hours
A drive along the **Vermilion** and **Kootenay Rivers** on the Banff-Windemere Highway cuts through **Kootenay National Park.** The orange- and yellow-hued **Paint Pots** and the red walls of **Sinclair Canyon** add colorful surprises to the mountainous

terrain. When you reach the **Radium Hot Springs pool complex,** stop for a dip in the refreshing pools. Continue into the **town of Radium Hot Springs** to spend the night.

Day 8
RADIUM HOT SPRINGS TO WATERTON LAKES NATIONAL PARK
250 miles/400 km; 5 hours
From Radium Hot Springs, follow the Kootenay and Columbia Rivers south through a series of small towns, then head east to **Fernie** to stop for lunch and a scenic chairlift ride. Continue to the **Frank Slide Interpretive Centre** at Crowsnest

Clockwise from top left: Athabasca Falls in Jasper National Park; wildflowers along the Vermilion River in Kootenay National Park; Lake Minnewanka in Banff National Park

Pass, where you can walk around the site of a colossal landslide. Follow the highway to **Waterton Lakes National Park** and check into your lodging in the **Waterton Townsite** for two nights.

Day 9
WATERTON LAKES NATIONAL PARK
42 miles/68 km; 2 hours
In the morning, take the **boat tour** down **Waterton Lake** and across the Canadian-U.S. border to reach **Goat Haunt, USA.** In the afternoon, drive **Akamina Parkway** to **Cameron Lake** for paddling and a lakeshore walk. After dinner in Waterton Townsite, drive **Red Rock Parkway** to look for wildlife and walk the **Red Rock Canyon loop trail.**

Day 10
WATERTON LAKES TO GLACIER NATIONAL PARK
71 miles/115 km; 2 hours
After a leisurely morning, take **Chief Mountain Highway** across the border between Canada and the United States. As you approach **Many Glacier** in **Glacier National Park,** watch for moose and bears on the entrance road. Stretch your legs on the trail to **Red Rock Lake and Falls.** Check into the historic **Many Glacier Hotel** for two nights.

Day 11
GLACIER NATIONAL PARK
No driving today! Hike to **Grinnell Lake,** go **horseback riding,** and sit on the hotel deck watching for wildlife. For a full-day hike, go to **Grinnell Glacier.**

Day 12
GLACIER NATIONAL PARK TO FLATHEAD VALLEY
97 miles/156 km; 3 hours
Of all the mountain roads you've driven so far, **Going-to-the-Sun Road** stands in a class of its own. Stop at overlooks as it climbs to **Logan Pass.** Hike to **Hidden**

Lake Overlook to enjoy the meadows and mountain goats. Wade in **Lake McDonald** before exiting the park at **West Glacier** to reach **Whitefish** in the **Flathead Valley.**

Day 13
FLATHEAD VALLEY
14 miles/23 km; 30 minutes
Have a leisurely morning, then take the scenic chairlift at **Whitefish Mountain Resort** to eat lunch with a view of Glacier and Flathead Valley below. Go **paddling** on **Whitefish Lake** for a spell. In the evening, enjoy the small-town scene: Eat dinner at **Tupelo Grille,** listen to live music, and go bar-hopping.

Day 14
FLATHEAD VALLEY TO YELLOWSTONE NATIONAL PARK
424 miles/682 km; 6.5 hours
Get an early start today. You'll drive through **Missoula** and **Butte** before crossing Pipestone Pass, surrounded by rock spires. After passing **Bozeman,** a **scenic drive** tours **Paradise Valley,** ascending along the Yellowstone River to Gardiner. Enter **Yellowstone National Park,** climb the winding road to **Mammoth Hot Springs Hotel,** where you'll spend the night. Be sure to walk through the travertine terraces.

Day 15
YELLOWSTONE NATIONAL PARK
113 miles/183 km; 3.5 hours
Head to **Lamar Valley** in the morning for wildlife-watching. Then drop down to the **Grand Canyon of the Yellowstone** to see the thundering **Upper and Lower Falls** from the **North Rim.** Swing west to **Norris Geyser Basin** and then south to **Lower and Midway Geyser Basins,** stopping to walk the boardwalks at each. At **Upper Geyser Basin,** see **Old Faithful** erupt. Spend the night in historic **Old Faithful Inn.**

Clockwise from top left: Grand Teton; Norris Geyser Basin in Yellowstone National Park; Many Glacier Hotel in Glacier National Park

Day 16
YELLOWSTONE TO GRAND TETON NATIONAL PARK
65 miles/105 km; 2 hours

In the morning, make your way to **West Thumb Geyser Basin** to walk the boardwalk loop along immense **Yellowstone Lake.** Stop to see **Lewis Falls** before exiting Yellowstone and driving to **Grand Teton National Park.** Pop by **Colter Bay** to tour the Indigenous arts exhibit at the visitors center and hike to **Heron Pond.** End your day at **Jackson Lake Lodge,** watching the sun set over the Tetons.

Day 17
GRAND TETON NATIONAL PARK
35 miles/56 km; 1 hour

Tour **Teton Park Road** for closeup views of the Grand Teton and **Teton Glacier.** En route, stop at **Jenny Lake** for a **boat tour** and hike to **Hidden Falls and Inspiration Point** for views out over Jackson Hole. Dine in downtown **Jackson** and finish the night at the famed **Million Dollar Cowboy Bar.** Spend the night at one of the hotels in town.

Day 18
JACKSON TO SALT LAKE CITY
280 miles/450 km; 4.5 hours

Hit the road bright and early. Follow the **Snake River** as it cuts south through Hoback Canyon and Bridger Teton National Forest. At Alpine, turn south through Star Valley to reach Freedom, where a jaunt westward and south leads to glimpses of **Great Salt Lake.** Stop to stretch your legs in **Ogden** and walk down **historic 25th Street,** or push onward to **Salt Lake City,** where you'll spend the night. Unwind with a walk along **City Creek Canyon** and delicious Mexican food at the **Red Iguana.**

Day 19
SALT LAKE CITY TO ROCKY MOUNTAIN NATIONAL PARK
440 miles/710 km; 8 hours

Cross northern Utah, taking a break at **Dinosaur National Monument** to visit the **Quarry Visitor Center,** where you can see the dinosaur fossils dotting the landscape. Next, you'll make the trek across Colorado. After passing through the resort town of Steamboat Springs, pull into **Grand Lake,** the quiet western gateway to **Rocky Mountain National Park.**

Day 20
ROCKY MOUNTAIN NATIONAL PARK
48 miles/77 km; 2 hours

Today will take to you the top of the world along the windswept **Trail Ridge Road,** where you may see elk, bighorn sheep, and alpine wildflowers. The road climbs to **Alpine Visitor Center,** the highest national park visitors center in the country. Hike up the short **Alpine Ridge Trail** to get a picture next to the sign reading "Elevation 12,000 feet." Stop at pullouts like **Forest Canyon Overlook** to soak up the views and walk interpretive trails. Roll into **Estes Park,** Rocky's eastern gateway, in time for dinner.

Day 21
ESTES PARK TO DENVER
64 miles/103 KM; 1.5 hours

Do some sightseeing in Estes Park, making sure to stop at the allegedly haunted **Stanley Hotel.** Take the scenic drive to **Boulder** and stop there for lunch. Then, tackle the final miles to **Denver.** Celebrate your trip in the vibrant downtown area, enjoying the bustle of the city.

Canadian Road Trip: Calgary to Jasper

A week in the Canadian Rockies gives you a lifetime of memorable experiences. You can fly into Calgary and reach the first national park that same day. Famed mountain scenery fills the route, and there are plenty of hiking trails to alpine lakes and vistas along the way.

Day 1
CALGARY TO WATERTON LAKES NATIONAL PARK
175 miles/280 km; 3 hours
Drive south from **Calgary** to land at the shore of **Upper Waterton Lake** in **Waterton Lakes National Park.** Take a hike up **Bear's Hump** to enjoy the view. Take in **Cameron Falls** and overnight in the historic **Prince of Wales Hotel.**

Day 2
WATERTON TO KOOTENAY NATIONAL PARK
245 miles/395 km; 4.5 hours
Enjoy a scenic drive across Crowsnest Pass and through **Fernie** and the Columbia Valley to reach the southern tip of **Kootenay National Park** at the town of **Radium Hot Springs.** Enter the park and drive to the parking lot of the **Radium Hot Springs pools,** then hike through **Sinclair Canyon** via the **Juniper Loop Trail.** Be on the lookout for bighorn sheep. When you return to the trailhead, you can reward yourself with a soak in the pools. Have dinner and stay in town overnight.

Day 3
KOOTENAY TO BANFF NATIONAL PARK
81 miles/130 km; 1.5 hours
As you drive through Kootenay today, stop at roadside overlooks to enjoy views of Kootenay Valley, tucked between two rugged mountain ranges. Walk through the ochre mineral springs of the **Paint Pots,** then follow the self-guided trail along **Marble Canyon.** At the **Continental Divide,** you'll cross into **Banff National Park.** Stop to take a photo at the sign. Head north to **Lake Louise** to see the famed turquoise lake below glaciated peaks. Check into the historic **Fairmont Chateau Lake Louise** for three nights.

Day 4
LAKE LOUISE TO BANFF TOWNSITE
75 miles/120 km; 2 hours
In the morning, drive **Bow Valley Parkway** to the **Banff Townsite.** Hop on the **Banff Gondola** to ascend to the summit of Sulphur Mountain for top-of-the-world views. Afterward, tour the **Banff Park Museum** and the **Whyte Museum of the Canadian Rockies** before finishing with dinner and a romp through the Townsite's shops.

Day 5
DAY TRIP TO YOHO NATIONAL PARK
65 miles/104 km; 2.5 hours
Take a day trip on the dramatic Trans-Canada Highway, which cuts through **Yoho National Park.** The route is lined with views of forests, mountains, and the **Kicking Horse River.** Listen to the thundering roar of **Wapta Falls** and see if you can spot a train coming through the **spiral tunnels.** With advance reservations, you can join a tour of the **Burgess Shale fossil beds** or take the shuttle to **Lake O'Hara** for scenic hiking. Return to Lake Louise for the night.

Day 6
LAKE LOUISE TO JASPER NATIONAL PARK
144 miles/232 km; 3 hours
From Lake Louise, the **Icefields Parkway** shoots north over **Bow Summit.** The views from the car are spectacular: turquoise lakes, braided rivers, and glacier-topped peaks. Hike **Parker Ridge** to look out over Saskatchewan Glacier before entering **Jasper National Park** to check out the **Athabasca Glacier** and rest up at the **Icefield Centre.** Spend two nights in the **Jasper Townsite.**

Top: Parks Canada interpretive guide with hikers on the way to the Burgess Shale fossil beds;
Bottom: Parker Ridge in Jasper National Park

Hiking and Biking the Continental Divide

The Rocky Mountains form the crest of North America—the apex that divides the flow of water to the Pacific and Atlantic Oceans. This spine is the Continental Divide or Great Divide. For hikers and bikers, grand adventures await.

Continental Divide National Scenic Trail
One of the most spectacular long-distance trails in the United States, the 3,100-mile (4,989-km) **Continental Divide National Scenic Trail** runs from Mexico to Canada. Backpackers usually take around six months to thru-hike the trail, starting in the south and working north. The CDT travels through Rocky Mountain (28 mi/45 km), Yellowstone (71 mi/114 km), and Glacier (110 mi/177 km) National Parks.

Great Divide Trail
The 698-mile (1,123-km) **Great Divide Trail** is a romp through the wilderness of the Canadian Rockies. It goes from Waterton Lakes, Alberta (where the U.S. CDT ends) to Kakwa Provincial Park, British Columbia. It passes through Kootenay, Yoho, Banff, and Jasper National Parks en route, crossing more than 30 mountain passes. Portions outside the national parks follow dirt roads and unsigned cross-country regions, where navigation skills are a must.

Great Divide Bike Route
Mountain biking the Great Divide is an epic North American adventure that takes most riders two months or so. The 3,084-mile (4,962-km) **Great Divide Bike Route** follows gravel and dirt roads, old railroad beds, and single-track trails with a few segments on paved road or bike trails. It connects Jasper, Alberta, and Antelope Well, New Mexico, traveling mostly outside the national parks. It does cut briefly through Banff and Grand Teton National Parks.

Best Hiking and Backpacking Options
For most hikers or backpackers, exploring the Continental Divide on shorter trails is the way to go. Check out these top trails:

BEST DAY HIKING

♦ Sunshine Meadows, Banff National Park (page 155)

♦ Highline Trail and Granite Park Chalet, Glacier National Park (page 282)

♦ Swiftcurrent Valley and Lookout, Glacier National Park (page 288)

BEST BACKPACKING

♦ Skyline Trail, Jasper National Park (page 101)

♦ The Rockwall, Kootenay National Park (page 219)

♦ Dawson-Pitamakin Loop, Glacier National Park (page 292)

♦ Continental Divide Trail, Rocky Mountain National Park (page 541)

Day 7
JASPER NATIONAL PARK
73 miles/118 km; 4 hours
Start with a quick, rugged drive and a short hike to **Cavell Meadows.** Afterward, drive to **Maligne Lake** for an afternoon **boat tour.** On the return, stop for a walk over several bridges to see limestone **Maligne Canyon** and its waterfalls. Toast your adventure at dinner in downtown Jasper. Tomorrow you'll head back to Calgary, a five-hour drive.

Montana and Wyoming Road Trip: Grand Teton to Glacier

This week-long U.S. adventure links the three national parks of Montana and Wyoming: Glacier, Yellowstone, and Grand Teton. The route leads you to glaciated mountains, hots springs, fumaroles, and geysers. Bring binoculars: You might spot grizzly bears, mountain goats, bison, pronghorn, and wolves. Fly into Jackson, Wyoming; fly home from Kalispell or Great Falls, Montana.

Day 1
GRAND TETON NATIONAL PARK
78 miles/126 km; 2.5 hours
From **Jackson,** head into **Grand Teton National Park,** following the highway north to **Moran,** then looping around south onto the scenic **Teton Park Road.** Be sure to stop at interpretive turnouts along the way. Stop at **Jenny Lake** for a **boat tour** or a self-guided paddle. Hike to **Taggart Lake,** then drive the narrow **Moose-Wilson Road** to **Jackson Hole Mountain Resort.** Ride the **tram** to the top of the Tetons and admire the views. Spend tonight at a hotel in town.

Day 2
JACKSON TO YELLOWSTONE NATIONAL PARK
120 miles/193 km; 3 hours
Head directly to **Colter Bay** on **Jackson Lake** for a **horseback ride** or to hike the **Lakeshore Trail.** Then continue north into **Yellowstone National Park.** Drive along **Lake Yellowstone,** walk the boardwalk at **Mud Volcano,** and stop for wildlife-watching in **Hayden Valley.** Stay at **Canyon Lodge and Cabins** for two nights.

Day 3
YELLOWSTONE NATIONAL PARK
100 miles/160 km; 3 hours
Today you'll drive the scenic **Upper Grand Loop Road.** Climb north over Dunraven Pass to **Tower Fall.** Next, head toward the park's Northeast Entrance for wildlife-watching in **Lamar Valley.** Return the way you came, then continue north on the loop road.

Make stops to visit **Petrified Tree** and **Undine Falls** before walking the boardwalk around **Mammoth Hot Springs,** near the park's North Entrance. Follow the loop south, passing **Swan Lake Flat** and **Roaring Mountain.** Stretch your legs at **Norris Geyser Basin,** then return to **Canyon Lodge and Cabins.**

Day 4
YELLOWSTONE NATIONAL PARK
90 miles/145 km; 2.75 hours
Today's route traces the park's **Lower Grand Loop Road.** Make your way to South Rim Drive at the **Grand Canyon of the Yellowstone.** Walk out to the famed **Artist Point** overlook or climb down the stairway to **Uncle Tom's Overlook.**

Continue south past **Yellowstone Lake** before crossing Craig Pass to the **Upper Geyser Basin,** where you can see

Clockwise from top left: Teton Park Road in Grand Teton National Park; Great Fountain Geyser in Yellowstone National Park; historic red tour bus in Glacier National Park

Old Faithful erupt. From here, fit in as many stops as you can: the blue pools of **Biscuit Basin,** the colorful rays of **Grand Prismatic Spring** in **Midway Geyser Basin,** the geyser-filled **Firehole Lake Drive,** and **Fountain Paint Pots,** where you'll find geysers, mud pots, and hot springs. Watch for bison and elk along the **Madison River** en route to **West Yellowstone** for the night.

Day 5
WEST YELLOWSTONE TO EAST GLACIER
360 miles/580 km; 6 hours
It's a full day's drive to reach **Glacier National Park** from West Yellowstone. The route runs through small towns in central Montana before sweeping along the Rocky Mountain Front. Overnight in **East Glacier.**

Day 6
GLACIER NATIONAL PARK
93 miles/150 km; 2.5 hours
You can sleep in a bit today. In the late morning, head to **Two Medicine** to catch the **tour boat** across the lake and hike to **Twin Falls.** After returning to East Glacier, follow US 2 west across **Marias Pass** and along the Middle Fork of the Flathead River to **West Glacier.** From here, head back inside the park. Enjoy the drive along **Lake McDonald** and bed down at **Lake McDonald Lodge** for the night.

Day 7
GLACIER NATIONAL PARK
49 miles/79 km & 2 hours
The week ends with the dramatic cliffside ride along **Going-to-the-Sun Road** in one of the parks historic **red buses** or the Blackfeet-led **Sun Tours.** The road climbs the west side to **Logan Pass.** Add in walks on **Trail of the Cedars** or **Hidden Lake Overlook.** The road crosses the Continental Divide and ends in **St. Mary.** Tomorrow, you'll head to Kalispell or Great Falls for your flight home.

Rocky Mountain High: Denver to Yellowstone

A quick zip from Denver launches this week-long adventure. In Rocky Mountain National Park, you'll enjoy the drama of mountaintop Trail Ridge Road. Just a few days later, you'll stare up at craggy peaks in Grand Teton National Park. The grand finale comes at Yellowstone before you loop back to Denver.

Day 1
DENVER TO ROCKY MOUNTAIN NATIONAL PARK
81 miles/130 km; 2 hours
It's just a quick scoot from **Denver** to the east side of **Rocky Mountain National Park.** Tour the interactive exhibits in **Moraine Park Discovery Center** and walk the **nature trail.** Drive or catch the shuttle up **Bear Lake Road** to walk the loop around idyllic **Bear Lake.** Watch for wildlife on the descent to **Estes Park,** where you can enjoy the town and spend two nights. Get a good night's sleep for your big day tomorrow.

Day 2
TRAIL RIDGE ROAD DAY TRIP
100 miles/160 km; 4 hours
Today, you'll climb to the highest road-accessible elevation in the Rockies. Drive up **Trail Ridge Road,** stopping for photos at spots like **Lava Cliffs Overlook.** Stretch your legs and walk the short **Alpine Communities Trail.** At Fall River Pass, tour **Alpine Visitor Center.** Drop down to the west side of the park to see the **Kawuneeche Valley** before retracing your route back to Estes Park.

Day 3
ESTES PARK TO JACKSON
490 miles/790 km; 8 hours
Get an early start for this long day of driving through Colorado and Wyoming. Head to Fort Collins and then Laramie, crossing prairieland to Rock Springs before cutting north. After passing along

Best Views

♦ **Columbia Icefield** (Jasper National Park): The largest and most accessible glacial area along the Icefields Parkway has incredible views of the Athabasca Glacier.

♦ **Lake Louise** (Banff National Park): Soak up the beauty of this glacial lake rimmed by icy peaks.

♦ **Bow Lake** (Banff National Park): On still days, the translucent water reflects the snowy peaks and their sheer cliffs.

♦ **Takakkaw Falls** (Yoho National Park): You'll need to crane your neck to admire this tall ribbon of plunging water, the biggest waterfall in the Canadian Rockies.

Artist Point, Yellowstone National Park

♦ **Sinclair Canyon** (Kootenay National Park): Drive through this narrow canyon of red-orange walls and watch for bighorn sheep.

♦ **Prince of Wales Hotel** (Waterton Lakes National Park): Walk out on the bluff beyond the hotel for the best views of Waterton Lake.

♦ **Logan Pass** (Glacier National Park): Sitting atop the Continental Divide between hulking mountains, Logan Pass boasts colorful wildflowers in summer.

♦ **Artist Point** (Yellowstone National Park): This overlook offers a classic view of the Grand Canyon of the Yellowstone and its Lower Falls.

♦ **Teton Glacier Turnout** (Grand Teton National Park): At this viewpoint, you'll get the closest possible look at Grand Teton itself.

♦ **Forest Canyon Overlook** (Rocky Mountain National Park): This viewpoint on Trail Ridge Road overlooks a glacier-formed canyon and surrounding peaks.

---

the Wind River Range, cut through the Gros Ventre Mountains to reach **Jackson.** Have a hearty meal in town and check into the **Hotel Jackson** for one night.

Day 4
GRAND TETON NATIONAL PARK
58 miles/93 km; 2.5 hours
Leave early for the **Laurance S. Rockefeller Preserve Center** so that you can get a parking space. Tour the sensory exhibits in the center and hike to **Phelps Lake,** keeping an eye out for moose. From the preserve, head to **Teton Park Road,** working your way north. Stop at **Jenny Lake Overlook** for the great view, then climb **Signal Mountain Road** for sweeping views of the Teton Mountains at **Jackson Lake Overlook.** Overnight at **Signal Mountain Lodge.**

Day 5
GRAND TETON TO YELLOWSTONE NATIONAL PARK
112 miles/180 km; 3.5 hours
From the lodge, continue north into **Yellowstone National Park.** Tour the **Lower and Middle Geyser Basins** first to see **Fountain Paint Pot, Great Fountain Geyser,** and **Grand Prismatic Spring.** Save the **Upper Geyser Basin** for after you have checked into **Old Faithful Inn** for the night. Since you'll be here through the evening, you'll have several chances to see **Old Faithful** erupt.

Day 6
YELLOWSTONE NATIONAL PARK
185 miles/300 km; 5 hours
Head north on **Grand Loop Road,** stopping at **Gibbon Falls** en route to **Norris Geyser Basin** and **Mammoth Hot Springs.** Continue east to **Calcite Springs,** where you can stroll the boardwalks to viewpoints over the Yellowstone River. From here, the route turns south. Follow it to **North Rim Drive,** where you can walk to overlooks of the **Grand Canyon of the Yellowstone.** Drive slowly through the inevitable **bison jams** in Hayden Valley, then exit the park via **Fishing Bridge** and continue east to **Cody,** where you'll spend the night.

Day 7
CODY TO DENVER
490 miles/790 km; 7 hours
After sightseeing in the cowboy town of Cody, head south through Thermopolis, Casper, and Cheyenne to drop straight into Denver to complete the loop and head home.

Best Hikes

Tackle these trails to experience the best hike in every national park covered in this guide. With the exception of the three that require significant elevation gain and a full day of hiking, you can do most of these easy and moderate trails in 2-4 hours.

Wilcox Pass, Jasper National Park
5.9 miles/9.5 km round-trip
A climb to Wilcox Pass yields huge ridgetop views of the Columbia Icefield, Mount Athabasca, and the Snow Dome (page 83).

Plain of the Six Glaciers, Banff National Park
6.6 miles/10.6 km round-trip
Starting at turquoise Lake Louise, you'll follow the trail to Plain of the Six Glaciers, a rubble-strewn basin below Mount Victoria and the hanging Victoria Glacier (page 135).

Iceline, Yoho National Park
8 miles/14 km round-trip
Spectacular barely describes this high-elevation hike through a string of glacial basins filled with ice (page 191).

Stanley Glacier, Kootenay National Park
5.2 miles/8.4 km round-trip
Cross the Vermillion River to ascend through an area where a wildfire once burned. You'll be rewarded with views of hanging Stanley Glacier (page 215).

Crypt Lake, Waterton Lakes National Park
10.6 miles/17 km round-trip
A boat ride and climb past waterfalls is only part of the drama. Reaching this lake, which is tucked in a hanging cirque, requires scrambling up a ladder, through a tunnel, and around a cliff (page 243).

Grinnell Glacier, Glacier National Park
7.8-11 miles/12.6-17.7 km Round-trip
Use the tour boats to whittle down the mileage to reach Grinnell Glacier, which is melting into the icy Upper Grinnell Lake (page 287).

Top: Wilcox Pass in Jasper National Park; **Bottom:** Grinnell Glacier Trail above Grinnell Lake in Glacier National Park

Off-Route Detours

♦ **Mount Robson Provincial Park** (page 112): On the eastern border of Jasper National Park, spectacular Mount Robson Provincial Park protects a vast wilderness of steep canyons, wide forested valleys, icy lakes, and rugged mountain peaks permanently blanketed in snow and ice.

♦ **Mount Assiniboine Provincial Park** (page 174): This provincial park is sandwiched between Kootenay National Park to the west and Banff National Park to the east. It's inaccessible by road; you can only get there on foot or by helicopter. It's a haven for experienced hikers and skiers, with alpine meadows, lakes, glaciers, and high peaks.

♦ **Kicking Horse Mountain Resort** (page 201): West of Yoho National Park, you can hop onto the gondola to the summit of Kicking Horse Mountain Resort, where you can hike and take in impressive views of the Purcell Mountains.

♦ **Panorama Mountain Resort** (page 226): Southwest of Kootenay National Park, this year-round resort known for its skiing also features an open-air gondola, a water park, and an extensive complex of hot springs pools.

♦ **Head-Smashed-In Buffalo Jump** (page 259): Learn about the early life of Indigenous people, namely the Blackfoot, who depended on bison for survival. Located between Calgary and Waterton Lakes National Park, this interpretive center is laid out so you can follow the entire process of bison harvesting. Outside, follow trails to archaeological cliff jump sites.

♦ **Blackfeet Reservation** (page 312): This reservation extends across rolling plains from the Canadian border to East Glacier, adjacent to Glacier National Park. Here you can visit museums and art galleries that showcase the stories and artwork of the Blackfeet people.

♦ **Bison Range** (page 348): One of the oldest national wildlife refuges in the United States preserves herds of bison on rare intermountain grasslands. The refuge is south of Flathead Valley, on Qlispé, Sélis, and Ksanka land.

♦ **Craters of the Moon National Monument and Preserve** (page 419): Three hours southwest of Yellowstone's western entrance, this preserve contains evidence of eight major volcanic eruptions.

♦ **Beartooth Highway** (page 422): This 68-mile (109-km) highway is the most dramatic road to reach Yellowstone National Park. Flanked by deep snowbanks in early summer and wildflowers in late August, the route yields 360-degree views of more than 20 gray granite peaks.

♦ **Dinosaur National Monument** (page 508): Straddling the Utah-Colorado border is one of the world's most productive sites for dinosaur bones. Here you can see fossils that are still in the ground where they were discovered.

Top: Iceline Trail, Yoho National Park; **Bottom:** ladder to reach the tunnel on Crypt Lake Trail, Waterton Lakes National Park

Fairy Falls and Grand Prismatic Overlook, Yellowstone National Park
6.8 miles/10.9 km round-trip

On the trail to Fairy Falls, a side loop climbs to an overlook of Grand Prismatic Spring, which appears like a blue pool with orange radiating arms (page 395).

Hidden Falls and Inspiration Point, Grand Teton National Park
2 miles/3.2 km Round-trip

Hop on a boat shuttle to make the hike to Hidden Falls and Inspiration Point a breeze. You'll reap double the rewards, too: a gushing waterfall and knoll overlooking Jenny Lake (page 444).

Nymph, Dream, and Emerald Lakes, Rocky Mountain National Park
3.6 miles/5.8 km Round-trip

This popular trail takes you to three idyllic lakes flanked by rugged peaks. Emerald Lake is the crown jewel (page 534).

Highlights

★ **Visit the Glenbow Museum:** Dive into the largest public collection of art and historical artifacts in Western Canada, with incredible exhibits on First Nations of the area (page 48).

★ **Climb Calgary Tower:** Marvel at the city and Rocky Mountains from on high (page 48).

★ **Jump back in time at Heritage Park:** This living history museum offers interactive experiences with costumed interpreters (page 52).

★ **Cheer on your favorite horse at Spruce Meadows:** Admire the skills of world-class show jumpers at this immense equestrian facility (page 53).

★ **Walk or bike the Bow River Pathways:** These paths parallel the scenic Bow River (page 53).

★ **Uncover fossils in Dinosaur Valley:** Take a side trip from Calgary to see a massive collection of fossils at **Royal Tyrrell Museum** or take a guided tour to fossil beds at **Dinosaur Provincial Park** (page 54).

★ **Saddle up at the Calgary Stampede:** Join in Calgary's annual celebration of its ranching roots with one of the biggest rodeos in the world (page 58).

Calgary

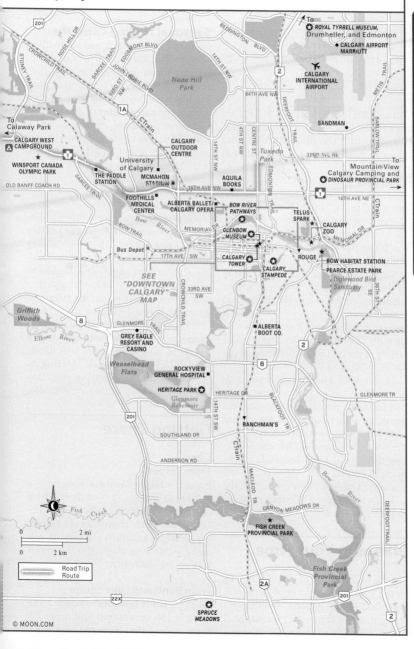

To ROYAL TYRRELL MUSEUM,
Drumheller, and Edmonton

CALGARY AIRPORT
MARRIOTT

CALGARY INTERNATIONAL AIRPORT

201

NOSE HILL DR

STONEY TRAIL

CROWCHILD TRAIL

SARCEE TRAIL

53RD ST NW

EDGEMONT BLVD

JOHN LAURIE BLVD

BEDDINGTON BLVD

14TH ST NW

2

MELIS TRAIL

BARLOW TRAIL

Nose Hill Park

84TH AVE NW

SANDMAN

1A

CTrain

To Calaway Park

CALGARY WEST CAMPGROUND

WINSPORT CANADA OLYMPIC PARK

OLD BANFF COACH RD

SARCEE TR

University of Calgary

CALGARY OUTDOOR CENTRE

4TH ST NW

CENTRE ST

14TH ST NW

Tuxedo Park

32ND AVE NE

To Mountain View Calgary Camping and DINOSAUR PROVINCIAL PARK

THE PADDLE STATION

MCMAHON STADIUM

AQUILA BOOKS

16TH AVE NW

FOOTHILLS MEDICAL CENTER

ALBERTA BALLET CALGARY OPERA

BOW RIVER PATHWAYS

16TH AVE NE

CTrain

Bow Trail

MEMORIAL DR

Bow River

TELUS SPARK

CALGARY ZOO

MEMORIAL DR

36TH ST SE

GLENBOW MUSEUM

Bus Depot

17TH AVE SW

CALGARY TOWER

CALGARY STAMPEDE

ROUGE

BOW HABITAT STATION

PEARCE ESTATE PARK

Inglewood Bird Sanctuary

SEE "DOWNTOWN CALGARY" MAP

CROWCHILD TRAIL

33RD AVE SW

Griffith Woods

8

GLENMORE

GLENMORE TRAIL

Elbow River

GREY EAGLE RESORT AND CASINO

ALBERTA BOOT CO.

2

8

Weaselhead Flats

ROCKYVIEW GENERAL HOSPITAL

HERITAGE PARK

HERITAGE DR

BLACKFOOT TR

GLENMORE TR

Glenmore Reservoir

14TH ST SW

SOUTHLAND DR

RANCHMAN'S

BLACKFOOT TR

CTrain

ANDERSON RD

MACLEOD TR

201

Bow River

DEERFOOT TRAIL

Fish Creek

CANYON MEADOWS DR

0   2 mi

0   2 km

FISH CREEK PROVINCIAL PARK

Fish Creek Provincial Park

2A

201

2

Road Trip Route

22X

SPRUCE MEADOWS

© MOON.COM

A cowboy town turned oil kingdom, Calgary is the interior hub of western Canada and the leap-off point for visiting the Canadian Rockies. It's filled with museums, international restaurants, and sights all clustered around the Bow River coming from its headwaters in Banff National Park.

Calgary's nickname, Cowtown, is cherished by the city's one million residents. Once a North West Mounted Police post and later run by ranchers, the city is still an important cattle market. It's known for its production of AAA Alberta beef.

Calgarians prefer that modest vision of their beloved home to the city's more modern identity as a world energy and financial center. The city's rapid growth to a large and vibrant metropolis in little more than a century can be credited largely to the oil and gas bonanzas of the 1940s, 1950s, and 1970s.

Downtown is a massive cluster of modern steel-and-glass skyscrapers. Set in this futuristic mirage on the prairie are banks, insurance companies, investment companies, and the head offices of hundreds of oil companies. But not forgetting its roots, the city sets aside all the material success each July to put on the "Greatest Outdoor Show on Earth," the Calgary Stampede, a Western extravaganza second to none.

Planning Your Time

For the vast majority of visitors arriving by air, Calgary International Airport is their first stop in Alberta, and then it's straight off to the mountain national parks of Banff and Jasper. But you can easily spend **2-3 days** in Calgary enjoying the city life, especially if you visit during the Calgary Stampede.

Seasonal Driving Concerns

Calgary can have slick and icy roads in winter. Plus, Chinook winds in winter quickly warm up conditions and then turn them to freezing again, often causing **black ice.** Have **snow tires** on your vehicle and **carry chains** to deal with icy and snowy conditions. After snowstorms, major highways are plowed first with secondary roads later. Call 511 or check online (https://511.alberta.ca) for current updates on road conditions.

Reservations

If you're visiting Calgary in July, advance planning is necessary due to **Canada Day** (July 1) and the annual 10-day **Calgary Stampede.** You will need to make lodging reservations about nine months in advance if you want to stay at a particular spot, especially near the stampede grounds. If you don't care about proximity, you can find something a month in advance. You'll also need to purchase tickets to stampede events well in advance. Tickets go on sale starting in September for the following year. Buy your tickets as soon as they are available.

Getting There

Car
From Jasper
From the **Jasper Townsite,** Calgary is a 410-km (255-mi), five-hour drive. Drive south on the Icefields Parkway to Lake Louise and catch Trans-Canada 1 heading to Banff and then Calgary. If you make sightseeing stops, this drive can take up to eight hours.

From Banff and Lake Louise
From the **Banff Townsite** to Calgary, the drive is 130 km (80 mi) and takes 1.5 hours. From **Lake Louise** to Calgary, it's

One Day in Calgary

Many visitors plan their trip to Calgary to coincide with the **Calgary Stampede** in early July. If this includes you, you'll spend the entire day on the grounds, having bought advance tickets for the **rodeo** and **chuckwagon races.** But if you're not Stampede-bound, explore these Calgary icons:

Morning

Spend the morning walking in the downtown core, taking in the **Calgary Tower** to get the grand view of town and visiting the **Glenbow Museum.** Stop to admire the *Wonderland* sculpture en route to the pathways that parallel the **Bow River.** Then, stroll to **River Café** on **Prince's Island Park** for a leisurely lunch.

Afternoon

Opt to spend the afternoon at **Heritage Park** to leap back in time via living history exhibits or at the **Calgary Zoo** to whirl around the world through its animal exhibits.

Evening

Serious foodies should head to **Rouge** for dinner, while those wanting to taste Alberta's very best beef could make a reservation at **Caesar's.**

a 185-km (115-mi) drive that takes two hours. From either origin point, go east on the Trans-Canada Highway.

From Kootenay National Park

From the north entrance of **Kootenay National Park** to Calgary is a 165-km (105-mi) drive that takes almost two hours. Take Highway 93 north through Banff National Park to Castle Junction and then east on Trans-Canada 1.

From Glacier National Park

From **St. Mary** at the eastern entrance of Glacier National Park to Calgary is a 290-km (180-mi) drive, which usually takes a little over three hours. Drive north on US 89 to the **Piegan-Carway international border crossing.** In Canada, the road becomes AB 2. Stay on that highway through Fort MacLeod and continue north to Calgary.

Air

Northeast of downtown, **Calgary International Airport** (YYC, 403/735-1200 or 877/254-7427, www.yyc.com) bustles with flights. Served by 25 airlines, including Air Canada, WestJet,

and several U.S. airlines, YYC is Canada's fourth-busiest airport. Arrivals is on the lower level, where passengers are greeted by volunteers who are dressed in traditional Western attire and can answer questions about the airport, transportation, and the city. Across from the baggage carousels is an information desk. Airport shuttles connect with downtown, hotels, car rental agencies, and the Greyhound bus terminal. The desks for all major rental car companies are across the road.

Downtown Calgary is 17 km (11 mi) from the airport, a 15-minute drive. Taxis are available, or you can hop on the **Calgary Transit bus** (403/537-7777, www.calgarytransit.com, 5am-midnight daily, C$11). Once you reach downtown, your ticket includes unlimited transit network rides for the remainder of the day. The airport bus runs every 30 minutes.

Bus and Shuttle

Two shuttle services connect Banff with the Calgary airport; reserve seats in advance. The **Banff Airporter** (403/762-3330 or 888/449-2901, www.banffairporter.com) runs multiple times daily. **Brewster**

Express (403/762-6700 or 866/606-6700, www.banffjaspercollection.com) goes twice daily, and also connects with Lake Louise.

Red Arrow (403/531-0350 or 800/232-1958, www.redarrow.ca) provides bus service to Calgary from Lethbridge, Edmonton, Red Deer, and Fort McMurray.

Sights

★ Glenbow Museum

With the largest public art and artifacts collection in Western Canada, the **Glenbow Museum** (130 9th Ave. SE, 403/268-4100, www.glenbow.org, 9am-5pm Mon.-Sat., noon-5pm Sun., adults C$18, seniors C$12, children C$11) displays permanent and special exhibitions in its three floors. Canadian artists make up most of the collection, which covers a breadth of historical and contemporary works and many mediums.

The second-floor gallery, *Niitsitapiisinni: Our Way of Life,* is the best part of the museum. Developed under the watchful eye of Blackfoot elders, it details the stories and traditions of Indigenous peoples through interpretive panels and displays of ceremonial artifacts, jewelry, and a full-size tepee. The third floor presents *Mavericks: An Incorrigible History of Alberta,* telling the story of prominent Albertans from various local perspectives, like those involved in the fur trade, the North West Mounted Police, settlement, ranching, and the oil industry.

Wonderland

Designed by Jaume Plensa, a Spanish artist, *Wonderland* is a huge sculpture made from wire. The mesh head of a young girl stands an impressive 11.9 meters (39 ft) tall, and photographers enjoy capturing its reflection in the glass of the Bow, Calgary's tallest tower, which serves as a backdrop. Walking around the sculpture

yields different views, and two entrances allow you to go inside the head. At night, the sculpture takes on a different life when it lights up. Find the sculpture at the base of the Bow Tower (110 6th Ave. SE).

★ Calgary Tower

While the **Calgary Tower** (101 9th Ave. SW, www.calgarytower.com, 9am-10pm June-Aug., 9am-9pm Sept.-May, C$18 adults, C$16 seniors, C$9 children) is no longer the tallest building in the city, it still offers outstanding views from 191 meters (627 ft) above. It has been one of the city's landmarks since it was built in 1968. Its space-age shape makes it stand out from other downtown skyscrapers. The tower lights up each morning and evening with changing LED light shows. It is topped with a giant torch, lit up for the 1988 Olympics, that gets turned on for special events.

At the top of the tower is a glass-floored **viewing platform.** Take a self-guided tour of the sights below with an interactive smartphone app, which points out what you're seeing. From this height, you can survey the city below and see west to the Rocky Mountains jutting up from the plains. The tower also houses a rotating restaurant and a theater, which shows a film on the concrete-and-steel construction.

To visit the tower, park in the Palliser Parkade (120 10th Ave. SW), which is accessible from 9th and 10th Avenues. You can also get to the tower by taking the C-Train or a city bus, or you can walk to the tower on a Plus 15 walkway.

Studio Bell

Music fans will enjoy **Studio Bell** (850 4th St. SE, 403/543-5115, www.studiobell.ca), a concert venue and home to the **National Music Centre.** It's the best place to learn about Canadian music history, with exhibits containing an impressive collection of musical artifacts, including rare instruments, an Elton John piano, and a mobile recording studio from the Beatles. The huge building also contains several Canadian halls of fame for music, songwriters, and country music. You can take a guided tour and go backstage to try out your musical skills on several instruments.

Prince's Island Park

Calgary's downtown is rimmed by city parks along the Bow River. **Prince's Island Park** (4th St. and 1st Ave. SW, www.calgary.ca, 5am-11pm daily) isn't a natural island; it was created when a channel was dug to transport logs to a lumber mill. That channel today is the centerpiece of the park, a lagoon with a fountain surrounded by walkways, trees, and flowers and crossed by three pedestrian bridges. In winter, the lagoon becomes an outdoor skating rink. The **Chevron Learning Pathway** on the island's east end tours a constructed wetland that attracts birds and wildlife while naturally filtering out sediments from the Bow River; the gravel trail has interpretive signs. Walking and bicycle paths loop around the park; in winter, cross-country skiers can use them.

The island has grassy areas, shade trees, water fountains, gardens, a playground, restrooms, and picnic tables, and the park hosts festivals throughout the year, including the annual **Canada Day celebration** (July 1) and **Calgary Folk Music Festival** (www.calgaryfolkfest. com, late July). The park is also home to the River Café restaurant.

Fort Calgary

In 1875, the North West Mounted Police built Fort Calgary at the confluence of the Bow and Elbow Rivers in fewer than six weeks. The site has been transformed into **Fort Calgary historic park** (750 9th Ave. SE, 403/290-1875, www.fortcalgary. com, 9am-5pm daily, adults C$12, seniors C$11, children C$7). Most of the focus is on the interpretive center, which houses a replica of 1880s barracks and

has volunteer Royal Canadian Mounted Police veterans on hand to answer questions. The lives of Canada's famous "Mounties," the legacy of the province's Indigenous inhabitants, and the stories of hardy pioneers are brought to life through convincingly costumed interpreters. Various shops and businesses from Calgary's earliest days, including an entire 1930s streetscape, are inside the center.

Outside is an exact replica of the original fort, built using tools and techniques of the time. History comes alive through a variety of activities and programs, including carpenters at work, a room especially for kids that is filled with games of a bygone era, and a museum shop styled on an old Hudson's Bay Company store.

Calgary Zoo

The **Calgary Zoo** (210 St. George's Dr. NE, 403/232-9300 or 800/588-9993, www.calgaryzoo.com, 9am-5pm daily, adults C$35, seniors C$33, children C$25, parking C$12) is home to about 1,000 animals of 120 different species, all of whom reside in realistic simulations of their natural habitats. In Destination Africa, giraffes tower over a huge glass-walled pool that provides a home to two hippos, with sunken stadium seating allowing visitors a fish-eye view of the hippos' often-relaxing day. Other highlights include an exhibit on Australia's nocturnal animals, habitats with lions and tigers, and conservatories filled with tropical flowers, butterflies, and birds. In winter, king penguins go on supervised walks through the zoo, an up-close experience that delights visitors.

One of the zoo's largest display areas is Canadian Wilds, devoted to endemic mammals such as black bears and grizzly bears. In the Prehistoric Park section, the world of dinosaurs is experienced via full-size replicas, including a tyrannosaur, set amid plant life, ponds, and rock. Find the zoo on St. George's Island east of downtown. To get there via public transit,

Downtown Calgary

Riley Park

5TH AVE NW

LAZY DAY RAFT RENTALS

SHAKESPEARE BY THE BOW

BOW RIVER PATHWAY (north)

Prince's Island Park

RIVER CAFÉ

PEACE BRIDGE (pedestrians and cyclists only)

BOW RIVER PATHWAY (south)

PAGES ON KENSINGTON

DEVILLE COFFEE

KENSINGTON RD

EAU CLAIRE AVE

1886 BUFFALO CAFE

HOTEL ARTS KENSINGTON

West Eau Claire Park

2ND AVE SW

JOE'S GARAGE MOBILE BICYCLE SHOP

ALFORNO CAFE

3RD AVE SW

Bow River

To Bus Depot

4TH AVE SW

CAESAR'S

INTERNATIONAL HOTEL

4TH AVE SE

5TH AVE SW

MAP TOWN

CEILI'S

5TH AVE SE

SUSHI HIRO

6TH AVE SW

6TH AVE SE

Shaw Millennium Park

CALGARY TRANSIT CUSTOMER SERVICE CENTRE

JAMES JOYCE IRISH PUB

8TH AVE SW

HUDSON'S BAY COMPANY

STEPHEN AVENUE WALK

9TH AVE SW

LAMMLE'S

HOTEL LE GERMAIN CALGARY

TRANSFORMATION FINE ART

MOUNTAIN EQUIPMENT CO-OP

FAIRMONT HOTEL PALLISER

ATMOSPHERE

CALGARY TOWER

11TH AVE SW

TWISTED ELEMENT

BONTERRA TRATTORIA

10TH AVE SW

THAI SA-ON

THE BACKLOT

BRIGG'S KITCHEN AND BAR

12TH AVE SW

HABITAT SOUND LOUNGE

Central Memorial Park

BEST WESTERN PLUS SUITES DOWNTOWN

13TH AVE SW

HOTEL ARTS/ YELLOW DOOR BISTRO/ RAW BAR/ POOLSIDE BAR

14TH AVE SW

HOTEL ELAN

15TH AVE SW

16TH AVE SW

THE COUP

PHILOSAFY

MODEL MILK

17TH AVE SW

CAFFE BEANO

18TH AVE SW

18TH AVE SW

19TH AVE SW

Lindsay Park

20TH AVE SW

© MOON.COM

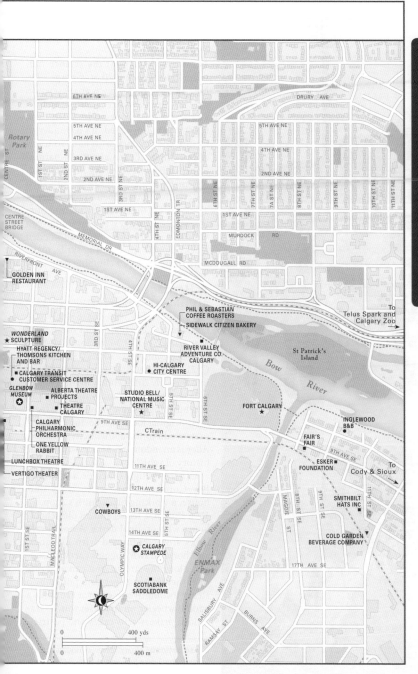

6TH AVE NE
5TH AVE NE
4TH AVE NE
3RD AVE NE
2ND AVE NE
1ST AVE NE

DRURY AVE
5TH AVE NE
4TH AVE NE
2ND AVE NE
1ST AVE NE

Rotary Park

CENTRE ST
1ST ST NE
2ND ST NE
3RD ST NE
4TH ST NE
EDMONTON TR
6TH ST NE
7TH ST NE
7A ST NE
8TH ST NE
9TH ST NE
10TH ST NE
11TH ST NE

CENTRE STREET BRIDGE

MEMORIAL DR
MURDOCK RD
MCDOUGALL RD

RIVERFRONT AVE

GOLDEN INN RESTAURANT

To Telus Spark and Calgary Zoo

PHIL & SEBASTIAN COFFEE ROASTERS
SIDEWALK CITIZEN BAKERY

WONDERLAND ★ SCULPTURE
HYATT REGENCY/ THOMSONS KITCHEN AND BAR
CALGARY TRANSIT CUSTOMER SERVICE CENTRE
GLENBOW MUSEUM ✪

3RD ST SE
4TH ST SE

RIVER VALLEY ADVENTURE CO. CALGARY
HI-CALGARY CITY CENTRE

St Patrick's Island
Bow River

ALBERTA THEATRE PROJECTS
THEATRE CALGARY
STUDIO BELL/ NATIONAL MUSIC CENTRE ★

5TH ST SE
6TH ST SE

FORT CALGARY ★

INGLEWOOD B&B

CALGARY PHILHARMONIC ORCHESTRA
ONE YELLOW RABBIT
9TH AVE SE
CTrain

FAIR'S FAIR
9TH AVE SE
ESKER FOUNDATION

To Cody & Sioux

LUNCHBOX THEATRE
VERTIGO THEATER
11TH AVE SE
12TH AVE SE

MAGGIE ST
8TH ST SE
9TH ST SE
11TH ST SE

SMITHBILT HATS INC

COWBOYS
13TH AVE SE
14TH AVE SE
5TH ST SE

CALGARY STAMPEDE ✪

Elbow River

COLD GARDEN BEVERAGE COMPANY

1ST ST SE
MACLEOD TRAIL
OLYMPIC WAY

ENMAX Park
17TH AVE SE

SCOTIABANK SADDLEDOME

SALISBURY AVE
BURNS AVE
RAMSAY ST

0   400 yds
0   400 m

you can jump aboard the 202 CTrain running east along 7th Avenue.

Telus Spark

The main displays at the science museum **Telus Spark** (220 St. George's Dr. NE, 403/817-6800, www.sparkscience. ca, 9am-4pm Sun.-Fri., 9am-5pm Sat., adults C$26, seniors C$24, children C$19) are kid-oriented. It's a wonderful facility chockablock with hands-on science exhibits. Learn about the natural world in *Earth & Sky,* dig into technology in *Energy & Innovation,* and then get creative in the Open Studio. Part of Telus Spark is the Creative Kids Museum, where children ages 10 and under can build a structure using oversized wooden blocks, hone their painting skills, make music, and explore a climbing structure.

★ Heritage Park

At **Heritage Park Historical Village** (1900 Heritage Dr. SW, 403/268-8500, www. heritagepark.ca, 10am-5pm daily mid-May-early Sept., 9:30am-5pm Sat.-Sun. early Sept.-mid-Oct., adults C$26, seniors C$21, children C$14), you can leap back into the early 20th century in this pioneer village. The village contains more than 100 buildings, some moved here from their original locations; costumed interpreters add to the authenticity. *Gasoline Alley* is an indoor exhibit showcasing the history of vehicles.

Other highlights include a Hudson's Bay Company fort, a two-story outhouse, a working blacksmith's shop, an 1896 church, a tepee, and an old schoolhouse with original desks. A boardwalk links stores crammed with antiques, and horse-drawn buggies carry passengers along the streets. You can also ride in authentic passenger cars pulled by a steam locomotive or enjoy a cruise in a paddle wheeler on the reservoir. A traditional bakery sells cakes and pastries,

Top to bottom: Calgary Tower; penguins at the Calgary Zoo; horse jumping at Spruce Meadows

and full meals are served in the on-site Wainwright Hotel.

★ Spruce Meadows

Calgary is home to the world's premier horse show-jumping facility, **Spruce Meadows** (18011 Spruce Meadows Way SW, 403/974-4200, www.sprucemeadows.com). The immense facility has six grassed outdoor rings, two indoor arenas, seven stables holding 700 horse stalls, 90 full-time employees, thousands of volunteers, and its own television station that broadcasts worldwide.

Spruce Meadows hosts a packed schedule of annual tournaments that attract the world's best riders and up to 40,000 spectators a day. The four big tournaments are the **National,** the first week of June; **Canada One,** the last week of June; the **North American,** the first week of July; and the **Masters,** the first week of September. The Masters is the world's richest show-jumping tournament, with C$1 million up for grabs on the Sunday afternoon ride-off. During the major tournaments, browsing through the on-site agricultural fair, arts and crafts booths, and a large marketplace promoting Alberta attractions rounds out a busy day following the competitions from ring to ring.

The atmosphere at Spruce Meadows is more casual than you might expect. Visitors spread out picnic lunches on grassy embankments, wander through the stables, and watch the horses and riders up close and personal.

Admission to Spruce Meadows costs C$5 during an outdoor tournament, but it's otherwise free. On tournament weekends, the covered rush or reserved seating (C$30-55) is the best way to watch the action. To get to Spruce Meadows on public transit, take the CTrain south to Fish Creek-Lacombe Station, from which bus transfers to the grounds are free. By car, take Macleod Trail south to Highway 22X and turn right toward the mountains along Spruce Meadows Way.

Recreation

Multiuse Trails

Calgary maintains 1,000 km (620 mi) of **paved trails** (www.calgary.ca) within the city. Most are designated for pedestrian and bicycle use. Maps are available on the city's website. Some of these path segments link up several parks and sites such as Fort Calgary, the Calgary Zoo, Bow Habitat Station, and Heritage Park. Paths are plowed in winter.

★ Bow River Pathways

Walk or cycle the pathways on either side of the **Bow River.** To cross the river, use the **Peace Bridge,** which is for pedestrians and cyclists only (no motor vehicles). Near downtown, the longest unbroken segment is on the north side of the Bow River paralleling **Memorial Drive and Parkdale Boulevard.** On the river's south side, shorter paths go both east and west from the Peace Bridge. Heading east connects you with Prince's Island Park, where you can add on some of the park's trails along the river.

Bike rentals (from C$15/hr, C$5 helmet) are available near the pathway. Look for **Joe's Garage Mobile Bicycle Shop** (403/874-5637, joesgarage.mobi), a truck renting cruiser bikes, on the south side of the Bow River, just east of the 10th Street bridge. Along the river, north of 656 Confluence Way, **River Valley Adventure Company** (403/970-7347, www.rivervalleyadventure.com) also rents bikes.

Prince's Island Park

At the north end of downtown, along the Bow River, you can pop over three bridges onto the trail system at picturesque **Prince's Island Park** (698 Eau Claire Ave. SW, www.calgary.ca). Running, walking, and bicycling paths tour the park, and one section has an interpretive trail.

★ Side Trip: Dinosaur Valley

East of Calgary, the Red Deer River has carved a deep valley through the otherwise flat prairie, and in doing so has unearthed one of the world's most significant paleontological areas, known as the Badlands or Dinosaur Valley. Some 75 million years ago, this arid desert-like area was a wetter, more tropical landscape. It was home to dinosaurs and a diverse number of vertebrates, including fish, amphibians, reptiles, and even a few mammals. Evidence of those former residents remains today.

In Dinosaur Valley are two major destinations: The town of **Drumheller** and **Dinosaur Provincial Park.** They are two hours apart from each other, so it's best to pick just one, or visit each separately, on a day trip from Calgary.

Dinosaur Provincial Park

Drumheller

Drumheller, in the northern part of Dinosaur Valley, is so crazy for dinosaurs that they built the world's biggest tyrannosaur at the visitors center. Drumheller has lodging, campgrounds, and restaurants. Check on options via **Travel Drumheller** (60 1st Ave W., 403/823-1331 or 866/823-8100, traveldrumheller.com).

The **Royal Tyrrell Museum** (North Dinosaur Trl., 403/823-7707 or 888/440-4240, www.tyrrellmuseum.com, 9am-9pm daily mid-May-Aug., 10am-5pm Tues.-Sun. Sept.-mid-May, C$19 adults, C$14 seniors, C$10 children) is the world's largest museum devoted entirely to paleontology. It integrates display areas with fieldwork done on its doorstep, with specimens transported to the museum for research and cataloging. Even for visitors with little interest in dinosaurs, it's easy to spend half a day in the massive complex. The museum holds more than 80,000 specimens, including 50 full-size dinosaur skeletons, the world's largest such display.

To get to Drumheller, drive 145 km (90 mi) northeast of Calgary, which takes just under

Fish Creek Provincial Park

The huge **Fish Creek Provincial Park** (15979 Bow Bottom Trl. SE, albertaparks.ca), located in Calgary's south end, has forested and creekside walking and bicycling trails. It attracts scads of birds and hence, bird-watchers. The **Stream Changes Trail** (1.3 km/0.8 mi) is a wheelchair-accessible loop near the Bow Valley Ranch Visitors Center. The **Paved Path** (66 km/41 mi) runs on two out-and-back spurs along Fish Creek and the Bow River, with multiple access points.

Mountain Biking

In the summer, **WinSport Canada Olympic Park** (88 Canada Olympic Rd. SW, 403/247-5452, www.winsport.ca, May-Oct.) caters to mountain bikers with 14 trails, a skills loop, pump track, and lift-accessed downhill flow trails with banked turns and jumps. Trails are labeled similarly to ski runs with different degrees of difficulty from easy, family-friendly green to challenging black. Bike rentals (from C$60) are available. Chairlift passes are required (from C$32).

two hours. From downtown, take AB 2 north to Airdrie and head east on Highway 567, then north and east on AB 9 to Drumheller. Go northwest on Dinosaur Trail (AB 838) to the museum.

Dinosaur Provincial Park

Dinosaur Provincial Park (403/378-4344, albertaparks.ca) is in the southern segment of Dinosaur Valley. It's more rustic than Drumheller and has fewer services. If you want to stay overnight, you can set up in the park campground. The town of Brooks has the closest accommodations and restaurants; contact **Brooks Region Tourism** (201 1st Ave. W., 403/794-2262, brooksregiontourism.com) for options. Located on Trans-Canada 1, Brooks is 45 km (30 mi) from the visitors center in the park, a drive of about 35 minutes.

At the park, you'll discover one of the world's most important dinosaur fossil beds. Fifty species of dinosaurs have been unearthed here, along with the skeletal remains of crocodiles, turtles, fish, lizards, frogs, and flying reptiles. Not only is the diversity of specimens great, but so is the sheer volume; more than 300 museum-quality specimens have been found, including 150 full skeletons.

Access to sites is only via **guided tour,** as the entire park is protected as a UNESCO World Heritage Site. More than 20 interpretive programs, bus tours, and walks are offered from late May to mid-October. You can work in the paleontology lab, go on a dig or fossil safari, and even see an excavation. The range of programs allows for people with different levels of ability to participate. Some programs are great for kids. Dates, duration, physical requirements, and costs are outlined on the website. Reservations are highly recommended for these popular programs; make them online or by phone. For all outdoor programs, sturdy footwear is required with closed toes and heels.

There are five **self guided interpretive trails** in the park, which tour three different habitats. The **visitors center** (9am-4pm daily Apr.-Oct., Wed.-Sun. Nov.) has an information desk, tour ticket pick up desk, amphitheatre, fossil preparation lab, and gift shop. The exhibit gallery (C$3-4 adults, C$1 youths, C$10 family) has interactive displays.

The park has one **campground** with electrical hookups for RVs, tent camping, and canvas tents with beds. Make **reservations** (877/537-2757, reserve.albertaparks.ca) up to three months in advance.

It's a 235-km (145-mi) drive to the park from Calgary, which takes 2.5 hours. From Calgary, head east on Trans-Canada 1, then take AB 544 north and east followed by Highway 876 north. Turn east onto Township Road 210A to reach the park.

Paddling

Most Calgarians float the fast-moving **Bow River** in rubber rafts, kayaks, or on paddleboards. Kayakers often hone their skills along the artificial rapids near **Pearce Estate Park** (1440 17A St. SE). The slower moving **Elbow River** is more relaxing for novices.

The **Paddle Station** (5227 13th Ave. NW, 403/456-2418, www.paddlestation. ca, May-Sept., C$50-220) sets you up for 2-4 hours of self-guided floating down the Bow River from Shouldice Athletic Park to St. Patrick's Island. You either need to set up a car shuttle or taxi back to your car parked at the start. The company rents single and double kayaks, inflatable paddleboards, and four types of rubber rafts. You can also hire a guide.

Lazy Day Raft Rentals (720 3rd St. NW, 403/258-0575, www.lazydayraftrentals. com, 9am-7pm Wed.-Mon., C$55-125) rents four sizes of rafts and offers a shuttle service for floating. **AQ Outdoors** (8435 Bowfort Rd. NW #300, 403/288-9283 or 877/440-9283, aqoutdoors.com, 10am-6pm Tues.-Fri., 9am-5pm Sat., 11am-5pm Sun., C$40-55 for 24 hours) rents inflatable paddleboards and single or double kayaks.

Skiing and Snowboarding

WinSport Canada Olympic Park (88 Canada Olympic Rd. SW, 403/247-5452, www.winsport.ca, hours and days vary May-Oct., 9am-5pm daily mid-Nov.-late Mar., lift tickets C$32-60) was developed especially for the Paralympics and the ski jumping, luge, bobsled, and freestyle skiing events of the 1988 Winter Olympic Games. Now the park offers public activities year-round.

In winter, the beginner and intermediate skiing and snowboarding runs are filled with locals riding three chairlifts and a T-bar. The resort also has night skiing (weeknights until 9pm), a lodge, rentals, and lessons. The **tube park** (10am-5:30pm Sat.-Sun. and holidays, C$20-25) has eight lanes accessed via a magic carpet. You can also ice-skate at an indoor rink.

In summer, thrill sports take front stage. You can ride wheeled **downhill carts** on a track, fly on **a zipline** tour, or leap in a **free-fall.** But the most unique thrill is racing at 80 kph (50 mph) down the Olympic track on a **bobsleigh.** Rates and hours vary by activity.

Equipment Rental

If you need outdoor gear, **Calgary Outdoor Centre** (2500 University Dr. NW, 403/220-7749, https://outdoor-centre.ucalgary.ca) rents equipment for camping, backpacking, boating, bicycling, fishing, snowshoeing, climbing, and skiing. Part of the University of Calgary, the rental shop charges daily rates for tents, backpacks, GPS units, stoves, sleeping bags, clothing, hiking boots, climbing gear, and rain gear. The shop also rents rafts, kayaks, skis, canoes, mountain bikes, and car racks. Reserving equipment ahead of time is a must during midsummer; a nonrefundable credit card deposit is required. When picking up gear, try it on to be sure it fits, and have the staff demonstrate how to use unfamiliar equipment. You'll need a driver's license or photo ID to rent gear.

Spectator Sports
Hockey

There's no better way to spend a winter's night in Calgary than by attending a home game of the **Calgary Flames** (403/777-4646, www.calgaryflames.com, from C$99), the city's National Hockey League franchise. The **Saddledome** (555 Saddledome Rise SE) in Stampede Park fills with 20,000 hockey fans who follow every game with an electrifying passion. The regular season runs October-April.

Football

The **Stampeders** (403/289-0205, www.stampeders.com, C$50-110) are Calgary's franchise in the Canadian Football League, an organization similar to the United States' NFL. The team's popularity fluctuates with its performance, but crowd levels have been high in recent years. Near the end of the July-November season, weather can dictate both the games' results and attendance at the 35,500-seat **McMahon Stadium** (1817 Crowchild Trail NW): Temperatures can drop far below freezing, with wind chills adding to the frigid conditions.

Entertainment and Events

The Arts
Music and Dance

Calgary Opera (403/262-7286, calgaryopera.com) performs October-April in a restored church (Mamdani Opera Centre, 1315 7th St. SW). The 2,000-seat Jack Singer Concert Hall at Arts Common is home to the **Calgary Philharmonic Orchestra** (403/571-0270, www.calgary-phil.com), one of Canada's top orchestras. **Alberta Ballet** (403/245-4549, www.albertaballet.com) performs at locations throughout the city.

Theater

Calgary has about 10 professional theater

companies. The main season for performances is September-May.

Alberta Theatre Projects (403/294-7402, albertatheatreprojects.com) is a well-established company based in the downtown **Arts Common** (225 8th Ave. SE). Usual performances are of contemporary material. Also based at Arts Common is **Theatre Calgary** (403/294-7440, www.theatrecalgary.com), which performs modern and classic plays and musicals.

Lunchbox Theatre (115 9th Ave. SE, 403/265-4292, www.lunchboxtheatre. com, mid-Sept.-early May), in a custom-built theater at the base of the Calgary Tower, runs especially for the lunchtime crowd. For adult-oriented experimental productions, consider a performance by **One Yellow Rabbit** (Big Secret Theatre, 225 8th Ave. SE, 403/264-3224, www.oyr. org).

Art Galleries

The city has a remarkable number of galleries displaying and selling work by local artisans. Unfortunately, they are not concentrated in any one area, and most require some effort to find. The **Esker Foundation** (1011 9th Ave. SE, 403/930-2490, eskerfoundation.com) specializes in modern visual arts. **Moonstone Creation** (1219 10th Ave. SE, 403/261-2650, moonstonecreation.ca) carries works of First Nations artists. **Transformation Fine Art** (The Grain Exchange Bldg., 815 1st St. SW #202, 403/615-2038, www.transformationfineart.com) features Inuit art. **Collectors' Gallery** (1332 9th Ave. SE, 403/245-8300, www.collectorsgalleryofart.com) features the works of about 30 Canadian contemporary artists.

Nightlife
Country-Music Bars

With a nickname like Cowtown, it's not surprising that some of Calgary's hottest nightspots play country music. **Ranchman's** (9615 Macleod Trail SW, 403/253-1100, 4pm-2am Wed.-Sat.) is

the place, especially during Stampede Week. Some of country's hottest stars have played this authentic honky-tonk. The space features a large dance hall that is also a museum of rodeo memorabilia, with a chuck wagon hanging from the ceiling.

At **Cowboys** (421 12th Ave. SE, 403/265-0699, www.cowboysnightclub. com, 8pm-2am Wed.-Sat.), a hip bar near Stampede Park, the crowd is cool. When country music plays, they all seem to know every word.

Other Bars and Dance Clubs

Thomsons Kitchen and Bar (Hyatt Regency, 700 Centre St., 403/537-4449, 2pm-midnight daily) stands out for its central location, classy surroundings, and extensive drink selection. **Raw Bar** (Hotel Arts, 119 12th Ave. SW, 403/206-9565, www.rawbaryyc.ca, 4pm-midnight Mon.-Sat.) is an ultramodern lounge that extends to seating around an outdoor pool. In an old bank building, **James Joyce Irish Pub** (114 8th Ave. SW, 403/262-0708, www.jamesjoycepub. com, 11am-1am Mon., 11am-2am Tues.-Sat., 11am-midnight Sun.) has Guinness on tap and a menu of traditional British dishes. Another Irish pub, **Ceili's** (351 4th Ave. SW, 403/262-0080, www.ceilisdt. ca, 11am-2am Mon.-Fri., 6pm-2am Sat.) has over 60 beers on tap. **Habitat Sound Lounge** (1217 1st St. SW 403/263-5447, www.habitatlivingsound.com, 10pm-2am Wed.-Sun., cover C$10-18) is the place to go if you are serious about hearing the best DJs in a smaller, intimate setting.

LGBTQ

To find current LGBTQ events and shows around town, check *Gay Calgary magazine* (www.gaycalgary.com). Otherwise, head to **The Backlot** (209 10th Ave. SW, 403/265-5211, thebacklotbar.com, 3pm-2am daily), which is one of the oldest gay bars in Calgary. Owned and operated by a gay Black man, The

Backlot has music, dancing, an outdoor patio, and sometimes drag shows. **Twisted Element** (1006 11th Ave. SW, 403/802-0230, twistedelement.club, 2pm-midnight Sun.-Tues., 2pm-2am Wed.-Sat.) is an inclusive nightclub and cabaret lounge with karaoke, music, dancing, and drag shows. It serves pub food and sells jars of their artisan pickled vegetables.

Festivals and Events
★ Calgary Stampede

For 10 days every July, the city's cowtown image is thrust to the forefront. During the annual **Calgary Stampede** (403/261-0101 or 800/661-1767, www.calgarystampede.com), business leaders don Stetsons, bankers wear boots, and half the town walks around in tight denim outfits. Stampede is a celebration of the city's past when life was broncos, bulls, and steers and cowboys rode through the streets and posted up in saloons on every corner. Flapjacks and bacon are served free of charge around the city, normally staid citizens shout "Yahoo!" for no particular reason, and there's drinking and dancing every night until dawn.

The epicenter of the action is **Stampede Park** (555 Saddledome Rise SE), immediately south of the city center, where more than 100,000 people converge each day. The park hosts the world's richest outdoor rodeo and just-as-spectacular chuck wagon races, where professional cowboys from all over the planet compete. Stampede Park offers a staggering number of attractions, displays, and entertainment included with gate admission, a glittering grandstand show, and fireworks. Stampede Park opens on Thursday evening for **Sneak-a-Peek,** an event that attracts approximately 40,000 eager patrons.

Stampede Parade
Stampede Week officially begins Friday morning with a spectacular **parade** (9am) through the streets of downtown Calgary. With 150 floats, 4,000 parade participants, and 700 horses, the procession takes two hours to pass any one point. More than 250,000 people line the streets to cheer Alberta's oldest residents, Stampede royalty, members of Calgary's professional sports teams, politicians, and street sweepers. From the starting intersection (2nd St. E. and 6th Ave.), the parade proceeds west along 6th Avenue, south on 10th Street, and east on 9th Avenue. Crowds start claiming front-row spots at 6am.

Rodeo
The pinnacle of any cowboy's career is walking away with the C$100,000 winner's check on the last day of competition in the Calgary Stampede. For the first eight days, 20 of the world's best cowboys and cowgirls compete in two pools for the right to ride on the final Sunday. Saturday is a wild-card event. The **rodeo** (1:30pm daily, ticket required) features competitions for cowboys in bronc riding, bareback riding, bull riding, calf roping, and steer wrestling, and cowgirls compete in barrel racing. Bull fighting and nonstop chatter from hilarious rodeo clowns keep the action going.

Chuck Wagon Races
The **Rangeland Derby chuck wagon races** include nine intense heats each evening (8pm daily, ticket required). Team drivers must steer the chuck wagons through an initial figure eight before bursting onto the track for the Half-Mile-of-Hell to the finish line. The first team across the finish line does not always win the race; drivers must avoid 34 penalties, ranging 1-10 seconds, which are added to their overall times. At the week's end, the top four drivers compete in a C$100,000 dash-for-the-cash final.

Other Highlights
Once you've paid gate admission, all entertainment is free, except the rodeo and chuck wagon races. The cavernous

Roundup Centre holds various commercial exhibits and demonstrations, like the Kitchen Theatre showcasing Calgary's culinary scene, and the Western Showcase, with art and photography. The center's **Stampede Corral** hosts dog shows, the Calgary Stampede Show Band, and a talent show for seniors. At the western edge of the park, **amusement rides** offer thrills, such as the reverse bungee, drawing as many spectators as paying customers.

Agricultural displays are situated in the center of Stampede Park. **Centennial Fair** is an outdoor stage with children's attractions such as duck races and magicians. In the **Agricultural Building**, livestock is displayed. The World Blacksmith's Competition and horse shows take place next door in the **John Deere Show Ring.**

At the far end of Stampede Park, across the Elbow River, is **Indian Village.** Here, members of the Blackfoot, Blood, Piegan, Sarcee, and Stoney First Nations set up camp for the duration of the Stampede. Each tepee has its own colorful design. Behind the village is a stage which features First Nations dance competitions.

Well-known Canadian performers appear at the outdoor **Coca-Cola Stage** (11am-midnight). **Nashville North** (until 2am) is an indoor venue with a bar, live country acts, and a dance floor.

Tickets

You can purchase two types of tickets to the Stampede. **Advance tickets** (403/269-9822 or 800/661-1767, www.calgarystampede.com) are available for the afternoon rodeos and evening chuck wagon races and grandstand shows; these include general admission to the Stampede grounds. Advance tickets go on sale in September for the next year's event, and the best seats sell out fast.

The grandstand is divided into

Top to bottom: bronc riding; calf roping; barrel racing

sections, each with a different price tag. The best views are from the "A" section, closest to the infield yet high enough not to miss all the action. To either side are the "B" and "C" sections, also with good views. Above the main level is the Clubhouse level, divided into another four glass-enclosed, air-conditioned sections; these seats don't have the atmosphere of the lower or higher levels, but are protected from the elements, and patrons have access to a bar, full-service restaurant, and lounge area. Ticket prices for the first eight days of rodeo competition range C$25-110. The evening chuck wagon races and grandstand shows run C$50-140. Tickets for the final two days of competition cost more.

General admission tickets (11am-midnight, adults C$18, seniors and children C$9) are available at the gate; these get you into the grounds. From here, you can purchase rush tickets for the rodeo or chuck wagon races 90 minutes prior to show time. You'll only have access to either an area of the infield with poor views or seats well away from the action.

Getting There and Parking
The CTrain runs at least every 10 minutes eastbound along 7th Avenue downtown to one of two Stampede stations. Many hotels and campgrounds run shuttle services to downtown for the Friday parade and then to Stampede Park for the rest of the week.

Parking close to the grounds is possible, but roads can be chaotic. The official Calgary Stampede parking lots immediately north of Stampede Park usually charge C$25-50 per day, depending on how busy they are.

Calgary Folk Music Festival
The family-friendly **Calgary Folk Music Festival** (www.calgaryfolkfest.com, late July) attracts locals and visitors alike to Prince's Island Park. Running for more than 40 years, the annual four-day event brings in musicians and entertainers

from Alberta plus national and international artists. Big names have included Emmylou Harris, Joe Jackson, Elvis Costello, Lucinda Williams, and k.d. lang. Performances occur across eight different stages.

Shopping

Western Wear
Alberta Boot Co. (50 50th Ave. SE, 403/263-4623, 9am-6pm Mon.-Sat.) is Alberta's only Western-boot manufacturer. The boots are made on-site, and the factory shop has thousands of pairs for sale in all shapes and sizes, all made from leather. Boots start at C$250 and go all the way up to C$2,000 for alligator hide.

Downtown on Stephen Avenue Walk, **Lammle's Western Wear** (211 8th Ave. SW., 403/266-5226, www.lammies.com, 9:30am-6pm Mon.-Wed., 9:30am-8pm Thurs.-Fri., 9:30am-5:30pm Sat., noon-5pm Sun.) carries the Western-style shirts, jeans, hats, boots, and accessories needed for the Calgary Stampede.

Camping Gear
Mountain Equipment Co-op (830 10th Ave. SW, 403/269-2420, www.mec.ca, 10am-6pm Mon.-Wed. and Sat., 10am-7pm Thurs.-Fri., 10am-5pm Sun.) is Calgary's largest camping store. This massive outlet boasts an extensive range of high-quality clothing, climbing and mountaineering equipment (and a climbing wall), tents, sleeping bags, kayaks and canoes, books and maps, and other accessories. The store is a cooperative, owned by its members; to purchase anything you must be a member (a onetime C$5 charge). Across the road, a similar supply of equipment is offered at **Atmosphere** (817 10th Ave. SW, 403/264-2444, www.atmosphere.ca, 9am-9pm Mon.-Fri., 9am-7pm Sat., 11am-6pm Sun.) with a smaller selection and some name-brand items are perpetually sale priced.

Bookstores

For an extensive collection of Canadian Rockies maps, as well as city and wall maps, travel guides, and atlases, **Map Town** (400 5th Ave. SW, 403/266-2241 or 877/921-6277, www.maptown.com, 10am-4pm Mon.-Fri.) should have what you're looking for. Tech-savvy travelers will be impressed by the selection of GPS units and related software, as well as the scanning service, which allows you to have topo maps sent directly to your email inbox.

Pages (1135 Kensington Rd. NW, 403/283-6655, www.pageskensington. com, 11am-6pm Mon., 11am-9pm Tues.-Fri., 10am-6pm Sat., noon-5pm Sun.) offers a thoughtful selection of Canadian fiction and nonfiction titles in the suburb of Kensington, immediately northwest of downtown.

Fair's Fair (907 9th Ave. SE, 403/237-8156, 9am-6pm Mon.-Sat., 10am-5pm Sun.) is the biggest of Calgary's second-hand and collector bookstores. It's remarkably well organized, with a solid collection of well-labeled Canadiana filling more than one room. On the north side of downtown, **Aquila Books** (826 16th Ave. NW, 10am-7pm Mon.-Sat., 11am-6pm Sun.) has one of the world's best collections of antiquarian Canadian Rockies and mountaineering books.

Food

In Calgary, you can find international restaurants and cuisine that goes far beyond burgers, pizza, and poutine (fries smothered in gravy and cheese curds). Southwest of downtown, along 17th Avenue and 4th Street, is a focal point for Calgary's restaurant scene, with cuisine to suit all tastes.

Canadian

In Prince's Island Park, ★ **River Café** (25 Prince's Island, 403/261-7670, river-cafe. com, 11am-10pm Mon.-Fri., 10am-10pm Sat.-Sun. Feb.-Dec., C$36-52) is a cozy, rustic dining room serving some of Calgary's finest cooking. More of a restaurant than a café, it features extensive produce and ingredients sourced from across Canada in seasonal menus. Standouts include top-quality Alberta beef and salmon dishes, with the latter often incorporating maple syrup. Lunch runs from a leek tart to duck confit, while weekend brunch (11am-4pm Sat.-Sun.) does eggs Benedicts with creamed kale, wild boar bacon, or herbed goose sausage.

Near Prince's Island Park, the **1886 Buffalo Café** (187 Barclay Parade SW, 403/269-9255, www.1886buffalocafe. com, 6am-2pm Mon.-Fri., 7am-3pm Sat.-Sun., C$9-15) is named for the year its building was constructed, and it oozes authentic Old Calgary ambience. The café only serves breakfast, but portions are generous, coffee refills are free, and when you've finished your meal, ask to see the museum downstairs.

A few blocks out of the main downtown core, **Briggs's Kitchen & Bar** (317 10th Ave. SW, 587/350-5015, briggskandb.com, 11:30am-10pm Tues.-Thurs., 11:30am-midnight Fri.-Sat., C$17-36) is in a restored wooden warehouse, where the original floor has been polished and the massive beams exposed. The history of the building starkly contrasts with the modern open kitchen and presentation of top-notch Canadian ingredients. Dishes include lobster gnocchi and a variety of beef offerings. Their massive 48-ounce rib eye is designed for sharing.

Atop the Calgary Tower, the **Sky 360** (101 9th Ave. SW, 403/532-7966, www. sky360.ca, 11:30am-close Tues.-Fri., 10:30am-close Sat.-Sun., C$15-60) will be memorable for more than the view. As the restaurant rotates, making one revolution per hour, you can take in the scenery surrounding town. The kitchen serves healthy, modern dishes that use Canadian produce. Small plates, pasta, fish, and steaks comprise the menu. Brunch is served on weekends.

★ **Rouge** (1240 8th Ave. SE, 403/531-2767, rougecalgary.com, 11:45am-2pm Mon.-Fri., 5pm-close daily, C$30-46) is one of Calgary's best restaurants and regarded by many as one of the best in Canada. It is ensconced in an 1890s residence that was once home to one of the founders of the Calgary Stampede. Extensive renovations have created a refined dining experience, but one that is not overly pretentious. The home is surrounded by a beautiful garden that is planted with herbs and vegetables each summer. But the main focus is inside, where high-quality, locally sourced ingredients are prepared with a Provençal French flair.

In a converted dairy, ★ **Model Milk** (308 17th Ave. SW, 403/265-7343, www.modelmilk.ca, 5pm-11pm Tues.-Sun., C$16-42) showcases local game and produce through simple yet creative dishes, including many that are perfect for sharing. While the menu changes regularly, one staple is Sunday Supper (C$42 pp), a multicourse set menu that shows off the kitchen's best seasonal choices. Wines are organic.

Steakhouses

Caesar's (512 4th Ave. SW, 403/264-1222, www.caesarssteakhouse.com, 11am-9pm Mon.-Fri., 5pm-9pm Sat., C$30-72) elegant room is decorated in a Roman-style setting with dark woods, leather seating, and dim lighting, just what you expect from a steakhouse. It's known for juicy prime cuts of Alberta beef. Most cuts can be ordered in a smaller or a larger size.

Charcut (899 Centre St. SW, 403/984-2180, www.charcut.com, 11am-10pm Mon.-Fri., 7:30am-2pm and 5pm-10pm Sat.-Sun., C$22-50) is a slick urban spot with an open kitchen and a dining room that's warmed up with local barnwood. House-butchered steak is the big draw, along with their own preserves, with the

Top to bottom: cowboy hats for sale; top of the Calgary Tower; Hyatt Regency Calgary

emphasis on Alberta-sourced game and seasonal produce. Brunch is served on weekends.

Vegetarian

Typifying creative vegetarian food is ★ **The Coup** (924 17th Ave. SW, 403/541-1041, www.thecoup.ca, 11am-8pm Sun.-Thurs., 11am-9pm Fri.-Sat., C$17-24), where the emphasis is on local, sustainable, seasonal ingredients prepared in simple and tasty ways. Many diners concentrate on small plates, shared nibbles, and unique cocktails as starters before moving on to house specialties such as the Magic Dragon Bowl, a build-your-own sautéed vegetable dish. The space itself is appealing, with slick decor and a few streetside tables. Brunch is served until 3pm on weekends.

Asian

Chinatown, along 2nd and 3rd Avenues east of Centre Street, naturally has the best assortment of Chinese restaurants. The long-time **Golden Inn Restaurant** (107 2nd Ave. SE, 403/269-2211, www.goldeninn.ca, 4pm-3am Mon.-Sat., 4pm-2am Sun., C$13-23) is popular with local Chinese Canadians as well as visitors, and the late hours can top off a night of fun. It's known for its Cantonese-style dishes.

At **Sushi Hiro** (727 5th Ave. SW, 403/233-0605, 11:30am-2pm and 5pm-10pm Mon.-Fri., 5pm-10pm Sat., C$14-22), don't be put off by the drab exterior; the food is delicious. Sushi choices change regularly but generally include red salmon, yellowtail, sea urchin, and salmon roe. If you sit at the oak-and-green-marble sushi counter, you'll be able to ask the chef what's best.

Tucked away across the railway tracks from downtown is ★ **Thai Sa-On** (351 10th Ave. SW, 403/264-3526, www.thai-sa-on.com, 11:30am-2pm and 5pm-10pm Mon.-Fri., 5pm-10pm Sat., C$13-25), a small space that's big on the tastes of Thailand. The extensive menu offers a great variety of red and green curries, beef and seafood dishes, vegetarian options, and, of course, classic pad Thai.

Italian

Bonterra Trattoria (1016 8th St. SW, 403/262-8480, www.bonterra.ca, 3pm-8pm Sun.-Thurs., 3pm-9pm Fri.-Sat., C$25-44) has a stylish dining room with a vaulted ceiling and lots of exposed woodwork. Tables out on the Mediterranean-style patio are in great demand through summer. The menu is modern upscale Italian, with classic starter courses, pastas, and meat dishes such as osso buco. The Canadian-centric wine list has only a couple of bottles under C$60, but many wines are available by the glass.

Alforno Café (222 7th St. SW, 403/454-0308, alforno.ca, 8am-8pm daily, C$15-22) has a huge breakfast menu that includes several eggs Benedicts, and you can order breakfast on weekends until 2pm. Lunch and dinner menus contain creative dishes, many with Italian twists. You can also get pastas and pizzas.

Coffee and Cafés

Most of the best coffee haunts are along 17th Avenue and in Kensington. **Deville Coffee** (1122 Kensington Rd., 403/764-2669, www.devillecoffee.ca, 7am-7pm daily) serves up all the expected espresso variations. You can also get fresh-made breakfast or lunch pastries. On the eastern edge of downtown, coffee connoisseurs will want to search out **Phil & Sebastian's** (618 Confluence Way SE, 587/353-2268, 6:30am-9pm Mon.-Fri., 7:30am-9pm Sat.-Sun.) in a riverfront converted warehouse. The coffeehouse shares the building with a bakery that serves up delicious soups and sandwiches, but coffee is the star here, prepared to order, with the entire roasting process in full view of the public.

For gourmet coffees, hot cocoa made with local chocolate, and exotic teas, join the crowds at **Caffé Beano** (1613 9th St. SW, 403/229-1232, www.caffebeano.ca,

7am-8pm Mon.-Sat., 8am-8pm Sun.), who have been enjoying brews here since 1990. They also serve fresh-baked goodies and, in summer, a chocolate espresso milkshake. **Philosafy** (632 17th Ave. SW, 403/454-3177, www.philosafy.com, 9am-9pm daily) is a rustic-chic café where coffee is the main draw, but they also have baked goods.

Accommodations and Camping

Accommodations in Calgary vary from budget motels to high-quality hotels. Most are brand-name hotels which you can locate via **Tourism Calgary** (800/661-1678, www.visitcalgary.com). The majority of downtown hotels offer drastically reduced rates on weekends with Friday and Saturday nights sometimes half the regular room rate. During Stampede Week, expect prices to be significantly higher than the usual rates listed here; accommodations are booked often nine months in advance.

The Calgary airport terminal houses the extremely convenient **Calgary Airport Marriott In-Terminal Hotel** (2008 Airport Rd. NE, 403/717-0522 or 844/631-0595, www.marriott.com) for those flying in late at night or out early in the morning.

Hostels
Part of the worldwide Hostelling International, **HI-Calgary City Centre** (520 7th Avenue SE, 403/269-8239 or 866/762-4122, www.hihostels.ca, dorms C$39-45 members, C$43-49 nonmembers) serves budget travelers with a convenient location and wide variety of facilities. It has six-bed dormitories with shared bathrooms; dorms are men only, women only, or mixed gender. Private rooms (C$116-125 members, C$129-139 nonmembers) with en suite bathrooms include family rooms for 4-5 people. Other amenities include a fully equipped kitchen, laundry facilities, a large common room, an outdoor barbecue, lockers, and free parking. It's one block east of the City Hall CTrain station.

Hotels
A few blocks west of the downtown shopping district and near the CTrain, the **Sandman Hotel** (888 7th Ave. SW, 403/237-8626 or 800/726-3626, www.sandmanhotels.com, C$100-255) is convenient for ditching the car and touring by train or on foot. The high-rise features an indoor pool, fitness room, a family-style restaurant, and modern spacious rooms. If you'd rather be close to the airport, there is a second **Sandman** (25A Hopewell Way NE, 403/234-7255).

★ **Hotel Arts** (119 12th Ave. SW, 403/266-4611, www.hotelarts.ca, C$219-325) is a modern 12-story accommodation on the south side of the railway tracks, within easy walking distance of Stampede Park. The rooms are contemporary-slick, with luxurious bathrooms and plush beds with goose-down duvets. Amenities include a fitness room, an outdoor heated pool surrounded by a beautiful patio, and a bistro.

It's difficult to beat the ★ **Hotel Arts Kensington** (1126 Memorial Dr. NW, Kensington, 403/228-4442 or 877/313-3733, www.hotelartskensington.com, C$229-345), surprisingly the city's only boutique hotel. From the moment you're tempted by a homemade cookie from the jar at the reception to the time you slide between the Egyptian cotton sheets that top out ultra-comfortable mattresses, the inn has a captivating atmosphere that is unlike any other city accommodation. Each of the 19 guest rooms has a slightly different feel, ranging from bold contemporary to warmly inviting. Some have a private balcony; others have a gas fireplace or jetted tub. In-room niceties include heated towel racks. The on-site restaurant, Oxbow, opens for a delicious breakfast each morning; plan on a weekend stay, when a memorable brunch is offered. The hotel is across the Bow River from downtown in Kensington, one of Calgary's hippest neighborhoods.

One block north from the Calgary Tower is the ★ **Hyatt Regency Calgary** (700 Centre St. S., 403/717-1234, www. hyatt.com, C$255-390). Incorporating a historic building along Stephen Avenue Walk in its construction, this 21-story hotel features an indoor swimming pool, a refined lounge, over 500 pieces of original art, and a renowned restaurant specializing in Canadian cuisine. The hotel's Stillwater Spa is the premier spa facility in Calgary. The up-to-date guest rooms won't take your breath away, but they have a wide range of amenities, luxurious bathrooms, and views of the city lights.

Calgary's best-known hotel, the graceful ★ **Fairmont Palliser** (133 9th Ave. SW, 403/262-1234 or 800/257-7544, www.fairmont.com, C$250-2,500) was built in 1914 by the Canadian Pacific Railway for the same clientele as the company's famous properties in Banff and Jasper. The rooms may seem smallish by modern standards, and the hotel lacks certain recreational facilities, but the elegance and character of the grande dame of Calgary accommodations are priceless. The cavernous lobby has original marble columns and staircases, a magnificent chandelier, and solid-brass doors that open onto busy 9th Avenue. As you'd expect, staying at the Palliser isn't cheap, but it's a luxurious way to enjoy the city.

On the Tsuut'ina First Nation, on the west side of Calgary, the **Grey Eagle Resort and Casino** (3777 Grey Eagle Dr., 403/719-8883, reservations 403/719-8777 or 844/719-8777, www. greyeagleresortandcasino.ca, C$106-330) has modern spacious rooms in four main styles. Amenities include a fitness facility, indoor heated pool, and outdoor hot tub. The complex includes the large casino with 36 gaming tables and 970 slot machines, plus five eateries including a buffet.

Bed-and-Breakfasts

The bed-and-breakfast scene in Calgary is alive and well. Most are located off the main tourist routes. The **Bed & Breakfast Association of Calgary** (www.bbcalgary. com) represents around 40 B&Bs. The association doesn't offer a reservation service (although they do have a handy online availability calendar) but is simply a grouping of properties that meet certain standards.

The most central bed-and-breakfast is **Inglewood B&B** (1006 8th Ave. SE, 403/262-6570, www.inglewoodbedandbreakfast.com, C$120-180), named for the historic neighborhood in which it lies. Its location is close to the Bow River and Stampede Park, as well as a 10-minute stroll from downtown. The three rooms within this modern Victorian-style home each have private bathrooms, and rates include a cooked breakfast of your own choosing.

Camping

No camping is available within the Calgary city limits, although campgrounds can be found to the east and west along the Trans-Canada Highway. The only Calgary campground with an outdoor swimming pool is **Calgary West Campground** (221 101st St. SW, 403/288-0411 or 888/562-0842, calgarycampground.com, mid-Apr.-mid-Oct., unserviced sites C$35-37, hookups C$44-52), on a north-facing hill a short way west of Canada Olympic Park. In addition to the pool, facilities include showers, a laundry room, a grocery store, and free basic Wi-Fi. Around 320 sites are laid out on terraces, so no one misses out on the views.

West of Calgary, **Calaway Park** (245033 Range Rd. 33, 403/240-3822 or 403/249-7372, www.calawaypark.com, Fri.-Sun. early-mid-June, daily mid-June-early Sept., tent sites C$32, hookups C$38-44) is farther out along the Trans-Canada Highway. It offers a large, open camping area, coin-operated showers (C$2),

Wi-Fi (C$5 for 24 hours), and a laundry room. The campground is part of a family amusement park with rides, a big attractant for kids.

East from Calgary, **Mountain View Calgary Camping** (244024 Range Rd. 284, 403/293-6640, www.calgarycamping.com, year-round, C$43-55) is on the Trans-Canada Highway. The 180 sites for RVs are lined up in parking lot fashion, with no privacy. Facilities include coin-operated showers, a grocery store, and a laundry room. No water or sewer hookups are available in winter.

Tranportation and Services

Emergency Services
For medical emergencies, call **911** or go to **Foothills Medical Centre** (1403 29th Ave. NW, 403/670-1110, www.albertahealthservices.ca) or **Rockyview General Hospital** (7007 14th St. SW, 403/943-3000, www.albertahealthservices.ca).

Gas
Near downtown Calgary, find gas at **Gas Plus** (204 11th Ave. SE) or **Petro-Canada** (1438 Kensington Rd. NW). On the west side of town near Trans-Canada 1, find two locations of **Esso,** one on the west side of town (4700 16th Ave. NW) and the other on the east side of town (1440 52nd St. NE).

Tours
Calgary Walks and Bus Tours (855/620-6520, calgarywbtours.com) provides guided ways to see the city, getting insider views from long-time Calgarians. They have five different van tours and two walking tours.

Getting Around
Skyways
Calgary's **Plus 15** (www.calgary.ca) is a public system of **elevated pedestrian walkways** in the city's downtown. The mostly glass-enclosed skyways have more than 60 bridges that connect buildings in the downtown core, including some hotels. All of the skyways are wheelchair-accessible and are reached via elevators in connecting buildings. You can access a map of the system online.

Bicycle
Bicycle-friendly Calgary has designed ways for cyclists to easily travel around town. In addition to the miles of pathways in the downtown core and connecting parks, some urban streets have special bike lanes that separate bicyclists from traffic. The paved, two-lane **Mattamy Greenway** (138 km/86 mi) completely circles Calgary and connects to bike paths radiating from the downtown core.

Public Transit
Calgary Transit (403/262-1000, www.calgarytransit.com, from C$3.50) goes just about everywhere in town by combining two light-rail lines with extensive bus routes. You can get schedules online or download an app with schedules and routes. A **day pass** (adults C$11, children C$8) is valid for unlimited bus and rail travel. The best place for information and schedules is the **Customer Service Centre** (Centre Street Platform, 125 7th Ave. SW, 403/262-1000, 10am-5:30pm Mon.-Fri.).

All light-rail trains and stations are wheelchair-accessible. Low-floor buses are employed on many bus routes; call ahead for a schedule. Passengers can take bikes on the CTrains except during rush hours (6:30am-9am and 3pm-6pm Mon.-Fri.); many buses are outfitted with bike racks.

Bus
There are more than 150 bus routes running through the city. Pay fare (C$3.50 adults, C$2.40 children) by depositing exact change in the fare box beside the driver. If you need a transfer, request one

from the driver. Transfers are valid for 90 minutes.

Light-Rail

CTrain, the city's light-rail transit (LRT) system, has two lines, Red and Blue, that stop at more than 40 stations. The lines converge on **7th Avenue,** running parallel for the entire distance through downtown. Tickets are valid for 90 minutes and can be purchased from kiosks at the stations.

Taxi

Calgary taxi companies include **Associated Cabs** (403/299-1111, www.associatedcab.ca), **Checker Cabs** (403/299-9999, www.thecheckergroup.com), and **Mayfair Taxi** (403/255-6555). Uber and Lyft are also available.

RV Rental

Two RV-rental companies are near the Calgary Airport: **Canada RV Rentals** (877/778-9569, canada-rv-rentals.com) and **CanaDream** (888/480-9726 or 925/2558383, www.canadream.com) RV rentals start at C$100 per day.

Jasper
National
Park

Highlights

★ **Get close to a glacier on the Columbia Icefield:** See the Athabasca Glacier via trail (page 83) or by taking a tour right onto the ice (page 76).

★ **Admire Athabasca Falls:** Witness the sheer power of nature at this roaring cascade that spans the Athabasca River (page 81).

★ **See Mount Edith Cavell:** Gawk at this icy mountain with its hanging glacier from **roadside viewpoints** (page 82) or by hiking to **Cavell Meadows** (page 84).

★ **Hike to Wilcox Pass:** Escape to a sweeping panorama of several glaciers

tumbling from the Columbia Icefield (page 83).

★ **Go backpacking in Tonquin Valley:** This high-elevation valley is home to Amethyst Lakes, the sky-scraping Ramparts, two backcountry lodges, and several campgrounds (page 85).

★ **Take a ride on the Jasper Skytram:** Get views from on high, then hike to **Whistlers Summit** (page 98) for immense mountain vistas in all directions (page 91).

★ **Traverse Maligne Canyon:** Follow the twists, turns, and plunging waterfalls of this impressive canyon by **trail** (page 100) in

summer and on an **ice walk** (page 93) in winter.

★ **Cruise or paddle Maligne Lake:** Take a boat tour or paddle around this glacial blue lake rimmed with snow-laden peaks (page 96).

★ **Soak in Miette Hot Springs:** Relax and relieve sore muscles in the developed pools at this hot spring (page 97).

★ **Go rafting:** Navigate the glacial meltwaters of the Athabasca or Sunwapta Rivers—or take a scenic float, if that's more your style (page 101).

Jasper National Park

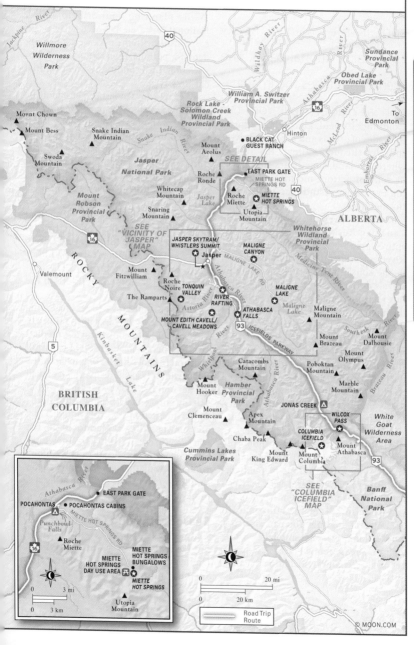

Jasper National Park commands the northernmost spot in the chain of Rocky Mountain national parks. The scenery stretches the imagination, as glaciers spill from the Columbia Icefield, glacial lakes glitter in shades of greens and blues, and rivers thunder through valleys. It's a place where the landscape bears the marks of eons of action: mountains thrusting ever upward and glaciers carving through rock.

Lying on the Albertan side of the Canadian Rockies, Jasper protects the entire upper watershed of the Athabasca River, extending to the Columbia Icefield in the south. The Continental Divide travels down the west side of the park. But running smack down the middle, the north-south Icefields Parkway slices through big, rugged scenery on one of the world's best mountain drives.

Hiking gets you to high passes with stunning surroundings. But trails aren't the only way to experience this rugged place. Take a tram up a mountain or a coach onto an icefield. After any activity, soaking in Miette Hot Springs provides all the relaxation you could hope for.

Almost twice the size of neighboring and more popular Banff National Park, Jasper's raw wilderness is prime habitat for grizzly bears and wolves. Keep your eyes open for resident herds of elk and listen in fall for the bulls that fill the air with bugling. You can also spot moose along riverways and lakes, while bighorn sheep frequent areas along the Yellowhead Highway, including the town of Jasper.

Planning Your Time

While planning your trip to **Jasper National Park** (780/852-6176, www.pc.gc.ca), consult with the park website on updates for permits, reservations, road construction, trail conditions, and potential closures.

With **two days** in Jasper, you should be able to see most of the park's highlights, but you won't have time for long hikes or adventures. With **three days,** you'll be able to fit in a hike, rafting, or some paddling time, or just experience the park at a more leisurely pace. For hikers, backpackers, and those looking for immersive adventures, you'll want to spend **4-5 days** in Jasper. If you're traveling up from Lake Louise, plan on spending the first day along the **Icefields Parkway.** Aim to arrive at the **Columbia Icefield** by midmorning before the crowds. The best choices for accommodations are in the Jasper Townsite.

Summer is the crowded season. Spring and fall offer slightly less hectic times to travel, albeit with cooler and less predictable weather. Late August and early fall bring on the gold shades of larch needles. But in **winter** Jasper is delightful. It's much quieter and less crowded than Banff, but equally gorgeous with snow. Most of the wintertime action revolves around skiing and snowboarding at **Marmot Basin,** but you can also cross-country ski, snowshoe, ice skate, or take a sleigh ride. A guided winter ice walk through **Maligne Canyon** should top your list. Plan for at least a three-day stay in winter.

Seasonal Driving Concerns

The park is open year-round, including Icefields Parkway, the Yellowhead Highway, and the roads to Miette Hot Springs and Maligne Lake. However,

One Day in Jasper National Park

Jasper is a huge park, so trying to see the highlights in just one day is ambitious. For a slower-paced day, opt for either the glacier tour at the Icefield Centre or the Maligne Lake boat tour.

Morning
Get an early start driving the **Icefields Parkway,** aiming first for the **Columbia Icefield.** Tour the displays in the Glacier Gallery of the **Icefield Centre** and walk the **Toe-of-the-Glacier Interpretive Loop.**

If you've never set foot on a glacier, then take one of the **glacier tours** by foot or bus instead. After your adventure, picnic outside at one of the tables (wear layers, as it can be chilly) or grab lunch in the cafeteria.

Afternoon
Drive farther north on the Icefields Parkway, stopping to see **Athabasca Falls.** Then, after passing through **Jasper Townsite,** tour the trails around the waterfalls and gorge of **Maligne Canyon** on the way to **Maligne Lake** for a **boat tour** to famously photogenic Spirit Island.

Evening
End your day at the **Fairmont Jasper Park Lodge,** with a memorable dinner on the balcony overlooking scenic Lac Beauvert.

road closures do occur, especially on the Icefields Parkway during winter months due to avalanche-control work and snowstorms. After heavy storms, sometimes plowing snow takes a little longer on the secondary roads off the highways. For **road conditions,** tune into **Jasper National Park Radio** at 1490 AM. For **weather conditions** in the park, call 780/852-6176.

Alberta does not require snow tires. Driving the Icefields Parkway does require **snow tires or chains** (Nov.-Mar.). All-season or winter tires are best, but chains may be needed in slick, icy conditions. Expect to find snowy roads October until mid-May, and snowstorms can even come in June.

Best Route Through the Park
The best route through Jasper National Park year-round is the **Icefields Parkway** (Hwy. 93). Driving it both directions yields different views and allows the option of stopping at more sights on the return.

Reservations and Where to Stay
Most visitors to the park base themselves in **Jasper Townsite.** Reservations are the best way to ensure you will have a place to sleep. For summer, make reservations **9-12 months in advance** if your heart is set on a certain style of room in a certain lodge. For winter, make reservations 6-9 months in advance. You can usually find last-minute rooms, but you may not have many choices. If you're flying into Edmonton or Calgary, plan to book your spot on an airport shuttle once you know your flight arrival time and at least one month in advance.

Both front- and backcountry **camping reservations** (877/737-3783, reservation. pc.gc.ca) usually open for the year in January. Competition for frontcountry sites is high, as only 4 of the 11 campgrounds have reservable campsites. Plan to be online as soon as bookings open. Reservations for **backcountry permits** are equally competitive, especially for the Skyline Trail and Tonquin Valley.

Getting There

Car
From Calgary

From **Calgary,** drive west on Trans-Canada Highway 1 and continue on the highway through Banff National Park. Just north of Lake Louise, exit onto Icefields Parkway (Hwy. 93), heading north to Jasper. The 400-km (250-mi) drive to the Jasper Townsite takes five hours without stopping. It'll be an eight-hour trip if you add in sightseeing stops.

From Edmonton

From **Edmonton,** Alberta's capital, the route to Jasper National Park is on the wide Yellowhead Highway (Hwy. 16). The 345-km (225-mi) drive takes four hours to reach the Jasper Townsite.

From Banff and Lake Louise

From **Banff,** drive west on Trans-Canada Highway 1 through Banff National Park to just past Lake Louise. Exit onto Icefields Parkway (Hwy. 93), heading north to Jasper. The 285-km (175-mi) drive to the Jasper Townsite takes four hours. Sightseeing stops will add on more time.

From **Lake Louise,** hop on Trans-Canada heading northwest and promptly exit onto the Icefields Parkway. From there, the 235-km (145-mi) drive to the Jasper Townsite will take about three hours without stops.

Air

The closest airport handling Canadian domestic flights is **Edmonton International Airport** (YEG, 1000 Airport Rd., Nisku, flyeia.com), just southwest of Edmonton. Edmonton-bound international flights may be routed through Vancouver, BC, or Toronto, ON. From the airport, you can rent cars or catch a bus to Jasper. It's a four-hour drive west to reach the Jasper Townsite.

The closest airport with international passenger flights is **Calgary International Airport** (YYC, 2000 Airport Rd. NE, Calgary, 403/735-1200, www.yyc.com). You can also fly from Calgary to the Edmonton airport. Shuttles to Jasper and car rentals are available. It's a five-hour drive to Jasper from Calgary without stops.

Train

Jasper lies on the only remaining transcontinental passenger rail service in Canada. **VIA Rail** (800/561-8630, www.viarail.ca) trains run through Jasper three times weekly. To the west the line divides, going northwest to Prince Rupert or southwest to Vancouver; to the east it passes through Edmonton, but not Calgary. The journey from Edmonton to Jasper takes about six hours.

The Jasper Townsite hosts a **VIA Rail station** (607 Connaught Dr., 888/842-7245, 24 hours daily in summer, 7:30am-10:30pm Mon.-Sat., 7:30am-11am and 6:30pm-10:30pm Sun. fall-spring). Lockers are available for C$1 per day. Car-rental agencies and a café are here, too.

Bus and Shuttle

Sun Dog Tours (414 Connaught St., Jasper, 780/852-4056 or 888/786-3641, www.sundogtours.com, year-round) runs several shuttle routes. One goes between the Edmonton International Airport, Edmonton, and Jasper. This shuttle also extends from Edmonton to Calgary International Airport. Plan to book your spot on the shuttle once you know your flight's arrival time, at least one month in advance. The company also operates a shuttle between Banff, Lake Louise, and Jasper.

Visiting the Park

Entrances and Fees

Jasper has several **entrance stations** where you can buy park passes. Coming from Edmonton, the **east gate station,** the busiest entrance to the national park, is located west of Hinton, Alberta, on the Yellowhead Highway (Hwy. 16). Try to enter early in the morning or later in the evening to avoid line-ups. The **west gate station** is located near Yellowhead Pass, on the Yellowhead Highway (Hwy. 16). Two entrance stations are on the **Icefields Parkway.** One is on the southern end of the parkway near Lake Louise and the other is at the parkway's northern end, just south from the town of Jasper. Entrances are open 24/7 but may be unstaffed; if so, you can purchase park passes in campground kiosks or at the park visitors center in Jasper.

A daily or annual national park pass is required for entry into Jasper National Park. Passes are also valid in the neighboring national parks in the Canadian Rockies (Banff, Yoho, and Kootenay).

A **one-day pass** (C$20 family/vehicle, C$10 adults, C$9 seniors, kids 17 and younger free) is good until 4pm the day following purchase. You can buy as many days as you need. It may be more economical to get an annual **Discovery Pass** (C$140 family/group, C$70 adults, C$60 seniors), which allows admittance to all of Canada's national parks and historic sites for one year. The Discovery Pass can be purchased in advance online or in person.

Visitors Centers
Jasper Park Information Centre
The residence of Jasper's first superintendent, now a National Historic Site, is a beautiful old stone building with a red-tiled roof dating to 1913. It is used by Parks Canada as the **Jasper Park Information Centre** (500 Connaught Dr., Jasper, 780/852-6176, www.pc.gc.ca, 9am-5pm daily year-round). The staff provides general information on the park and can direct you to hikes in the immediate vicinity. You can also get maps, brochures, visitors guides, and program schedules for nightly amphitheater presentations in some of the campgrounds. Kids can pick up an Xplorer booklet for Jasper and the Icefields Parkway.

For backpackers, information and permits are available at the **Backcountry Office** (780/852-6177). You can also get information from **Tourism Jasper,** which has a desk inside the visitors center. Also inside, an outlet of **Friends of Jasper National Park** (780/852-4767) sells maps, books, bear spray, and souvenirs.

The visitors center has no parking lot, so you'll need to park on a side street or near the train depot. If you are staying in town, it's better to walk from your lodge.

Columbia Icefield Centre
At the **Columbia Icefield Centre,** opposite the Columbia Icefield along the Icefields Parkway, Parks Canada operates an **information desk** (780/852-6288, 9am-5pm daily mid-May-Sept.) on the main floor, where you can learn about trail conditions in the immediate area. The several-story structure also includes a theater that shows films on glacial history. Located on the lower level, the **Glacier Gallery** has exhibits on glacial recession, ice studies, time-lapse photography of the glacier's toe, and how crevasses form. Displays also cover local wildlife and wildflowers. On the second floor, the center has a patio with outstanding views of Athabasca Glacier. A telescope offers close-up views of crevasses, tour groups on the glacier, and sometimes mountain climbers on Mount Athabasca. The Parks Canada desk has booklets about the Icefields Parkway for kids. The building shares space with restaurants, tour desks, a gift shop, and an inn.

Icefields Parkway

Laden with scenery, the Icefields Parkway runs north-south through the Canadian Rockies with limited services. The total parkway spans between Jasper and Banff National Parks at 230 km (143 mi). The Jasper Townsite anchors the north portion of the parkway; the southern portion is in Banff National Park, running to Lake Louise. The attractions, restaurants, and lodgings in this section are listed from south to north. (For more information about the southern half of the Icefields Parkway, see page 123.)

TOP EXPERIENCE

Driving the Icefields Parkway

From the Columbia Icefield Centre in the south to the town of Jasper in the north, the **Jasper National Park portion** (105 km/65 mi) of the Icefields Parkway (Hwy. 93) takes in colossal scenery and takes about an hour to drive without stops. The spectacular scenery along this stretch of road is equal to the southern half through Banff National Park, and it's easy to spend a full day en route. Most of the route follows the **Athabasca** the **Sunwapta Rivers,** passing powerful waterfalls on both rivers.

Around the parkway's halfway point, the long, steep grade of 8-11 percent that you've been driving up tops out at **Sunwapta Pass** (2,040 m/6,690 ft), which marks the boundary between Jasper and Banff National Parks. The highlight of the drive is the **Columbia Icefield.** You'll see the eastern rim of the icefield and the myriad of glaciers plunging from it, including **Dome** and **Athabasca Glaciers,** rather than the immense icefield towering unseen above, which feeds them. But the sheer size of what you do see speaks to eons of glacial activity, despite the glacial recession from a warming climate.

As an alternative for the northernmost section of the Icefields Parkway, you can take curvier **Highway 93A** (25 km/16 mi), which was the original Icefields Parkway until the more direct route was built. This route follows the western bank of the Athabasca River. Catch 93A about 5 km (3 mi) south of Jasper on the Icefields Parkway, and it rejoins the parkway just after **Athabasca Falls** (32 km/20 mi south of Jasper).

Sights
★ Columbia Icefield

At the south end of Jasper National Park, the largest and most accessible of 17 glacial areas along the Icefields Parkway is the **Columbia Icefield.** The 325-square-kilometer (125-square-mile) icefield perches atop the Continental Divide, where 34 glaciers spill down in all directions, including major ones toward the Icefields Parkway. The icefield is a remnant of the last major glaciation that covered most of Canada 20,000 years ago, and it has survived because of its high elevation (1,900-2,800 m/6,230-9,190 ft), cold temperatures, northern latitude, and heavy snowfalls.

From the main body of the ice cap astride the Continental Divide, six glaciers creep down three main valleys. Of these, **Athabasca Glacier** is the most accessible and visible from the Icefields Parkway; it is one of the few glaciers in the world that you can drive right up to. It is an impressive 600 hectares (1,480 acres) in area. While the speed at which glaciers advance and retreat varies, in a little more than 100 years, Athabasca Glacier has retreated from across the highway to its current position, a distance of about 1.6 km (1 mi). It also has lost about half of its volume. Currently, the glacier is thinning by about 5 meters (16 ft) each year. While gravity and the glacier's mass push the ice downhill at a rate of 15-25 meters (49-82 ft) annually, melting of the ice still causes the total length of the glacier to shrink back uphill about 2 meters (6 ft) yearly. The rubble between the toe of Athabasca Glacier and the

Icefields Parkway in Jasper National Park

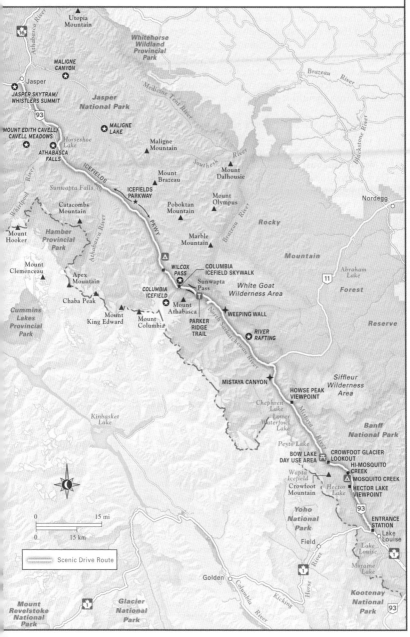

highway is a mixture of rock, sand, and gravel known as **till,** deposited by the glacier as it retreats.

Dome Glacier is also visible from the highway to the northwest of Athabasca. Although Dome is part of the Columbia Icefield, it is not actually connected to it. Instead, the glacier is made of ice that breaks off the icefield above, supplemented by large quantities of snow each winter.

The icefield is made more spectacular by the impressive peaks that surround it. As you face Athabasca Glacier, to the left is **Mount Athabasca** (3,491 m/11,450 ft). Dominating the skyline, it has three glaciers clinging to its flanks. Above the right side of Athabasca Glacier, the **Snow Dome** (3,451 m/11,322 ft) is capped with ice that spills down both sides of the Continental Divide. In fact, this point is a triple divide because it feeds the waters of three oceans: the Arctic, Atlantic, and Pacific.

The icefield is about 130 km (80 mi) north of Lake Louise, a drive of around 1.5 hours. To reach the Columbia Icefield from the Jasper Townsite, drive Icefields Parkway south from for about 105 km (65 mi), which takes around one hour.

Icefield Centre

On the opposite side of the highway from the Columbia Icefield, the **Icefield Centre** (Icefields Pkwy., 9am-10pm daily July-Aug., reduced hours May-June and Sept.-mid-Oct.) is nestled at the base of Mount Wilcox, overlooking the Athabasca Glacier. This multi-story building holds a plethora of services and attractions.

On the main floor of the center, you'll find a **Parks Canada desk** (780/852-6176, 9am-5pm daily early May-late Sept.). Go here for information on road and trail conditions, maps, and brochures. This floor also contains restrooms, a gift shop, and the Ice Explorer and Columbia Icefield Skywalk ticketing desk.

On the lower floor, the **Glacier Gallery** is a large exhibit area that details all aspects of the frozen world, including the story of glacier formation and movement. The centerpiece is a scaled-down fiberglass model of the Athabasca Glacier, which is surrounded by hands-on displays and audiovisual presentations.

On the upper floor, two restaurants are run by **Pursuit** (966/606-6700, www.banffjaspercollection.com, daily May-mid-Oct.). One is a self-serve café with indoor and outdoor seating. The other has table service with outstanding views of the glaciers and mountains.

The building is environmentally friendly in many ways: Lights work on motion sensors to reduce electricity, some water is reused, and suppliers must take their packaging with them after deliveries. Be aware that you are at high elevation (1,984 m/6,509 ft). The air is thinner here, so you may feel a shortness of breath while walking stairs or inclines. Take it slowly.

Toe-of-the-Glacier interpretive Trail

This wide rock-and-pebble **interpretive trail** (1.8 km/1.1 mi, 1 hr) climbs to a viewpoint, where it loops around the moraine and bedrock below the toe of Athabasca Glacier. It's the closest you can walk to the glacier without going on a guided ice walk or ice coach tour. You'll pass markers with dates on them, such as 1996 or 2006; these mark how large the glacier was in those years, which gives you a visual picture of how much ice has melted since then. You'll peer up at the ice at the toe of Athabasca Glacier and its outflow streams.

Bring binoculars for closer looks at crevasses. Do not go out onto the ice; it is dangerous due to unseen crevasses and snow bridges that can collapse. Wear sturdy shoes as the rock can be wet and slippery. Also, wear layers, as temperatures are cooler with breezes blowing off the ice.

To find the trailhead, turn toward the icefield across from the Icefield Centre on the unpaved Snocoach Road. Take the

Columbia Icefield

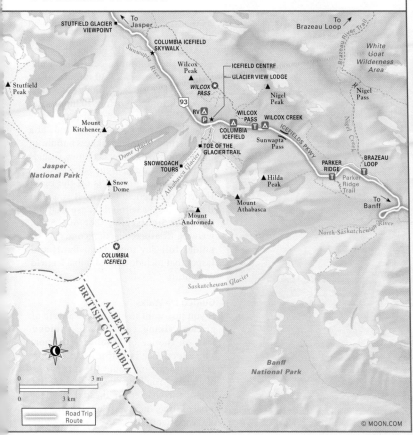

right fork down the Glacier Road through piles of till left by the retreating glacier to a potholed and sometimes muddy parking area beside Sunwapta Lake. En route, watch for the signs that denote where the Athabasca Glacier reached in preceding years. The farthest marker is across the highway beside the stairs leading up to the Icefield Centre.

Glacier Tours

It's only possible to step onto the glacier via guided tour, due to hazards like crevasses. If you want to experience the glacier firsthand, sign up for the three-hour **Columbia Icefield Adventure** (877/423-7433 or 866/606-6700, www. banffjaspercollection.com, 9am-6pm daily, adults C$87, children C$44). On the tour, an Ice Explorer coach, takes passengers out onto the Athabasca Glacier, thanks to special tires that can travel over the crevassed surface. Out on the glacier, you'll be able to walk within a designated area. The adventure is wheelchair-accessible (but you'll want to make reservations 72 hours in advance). Early in the season, the glacier

is still covered in a layer of snow and is therefore not as spectacular as during the summer. Crevasses and ice are revealed as the winter snows melt off throughout the summer.

After departing the glacier, the coach goes to the Columbia Icefield Skywalk. Trips depart every 15-30 minutes from the Icefield Centre. To dodge the most crowded times, go before 10am or after 3pm. Make reservations at least a few days in advance if you want a tour at a certain time. Combo packages bundle up glacier tours with other activities, including boat tours on Maligne Lake.

The ticketing office is on the main floor of the Icefield Centre. If you're in Banff or Jasper without transportation, **Brewster Sightseeing** (866/606-6700, www.banffjaspercollection.com, C$281) guides full-day tours from Banff and Jasper that include the Columbia Icefield Adventure.

Guided Ice Walks

If you just want to experience a taste of glacier walking, you can take a **guided trek** on the ice of **Athabasca Glacier.** The experience is half ice-exploration and half learning about the intricacies of glaciers. You'll meet your guide at the Toe-of-the-Glacier Trailhead at the designated time, then, walk up onto the toe of the glacier in between crevasses, snow bridges, and moulins. The guides know where to go to avoid dangerous crevasses. No previous glacier-walking experience is required to participate; however, you need to be fit enough to climb uphill on uneven surfaces for the duration of the walk and be ready to handle inclement weather that may roll in.

Ice Walk (icewalk.com, late May-early Oct., C$115-185) guides two excursions onto the glacier. One walk tours the lower parts of the glacier (3 hrs, departs 2-4 times daily). The other option hikes to

---

Top to bottom: Jasper Park Information Centre; Icefield Centre; glaciers at Mount Edith Cavell

the Athabasca Icefall (6 hrs, select dates). The company supplies boots, if needed, and spikes for walking on the ice.

Rockaboo Mountain Adventures (610 Patricia St., Jasper, 780/820-0092, rockaboo.ca, daily June-Sept., C$175) guides a four-hour walking tour onto the glacier. They supply crampons, mountain boots, and hiking poles. The company also guides a similar trip for those itching to try rock climbing.

Columbia Icefield Skywalk

The architecturally impressive **Columbia Icefield Skywalk** (866/606-6700 or 866/816-2758, www.banffjaspercollection.com, 10am-5pm daily May-mid-Oct., adults C$36, children C$18, reservations accepted) arcs out into the Sunwapta Canyon above the valley floor. A short interpretive trail leads along the canyon edge and then out onto the wheelchair-accessible glass-floored skywalk, where you can stare down a dizzying 280 meters (918 ft). Looking upstream from the skywalk, you can see the massive, ice-draped slopes of Mount Athabasca (3,491 m/11,450 ft) framed by the walls of the valley. Directly across the valley is the ice-capped east face of Mount Kitchener. The skywalk is located on the Icefields Parkway just north of the Icefield Centre; however, no passenger vehicles are allowed to stop there. Access is only by shuttle bus from the Icefield Centre, where tours depart about every 15 minutes. Purchase tickets on the main floor of the Icefield Centre.

Tangle Creek Falls

Tangle Creek Falls is picturesque year-round, as it splits into ribbons and plunges over multiple shelves. But it is extra special in winter, when it freezes solid into an icy sculpture. This roadside waterfall sits on the east side of Icefields Parkway (on the right for northbound drivers and left for southbound drivers), but parking is on the opposite side of the road. Be very careful when crossing the road, both to park and to view the falls. Locate the falls 7 km (4 mi) north of the Icefield Centre and 97 km (60 mi) south of the Jasper Townsite.

Sunwapta Falls

As the Sunwapta River churns toward its confluence with the Athabasca River, it changes direction sharply and drops into a deep canyon, creating **Sunwapta Falls.** Fed by the Athabasca Glacier, the river churns up a froth spilling around a boulder and squeezing into a narrow slot with multiple drops. The best viewpoint is from the bridge across the river, but it's also worth following the path on the parking lot side of the river downstream along the rim of the canyon. A trail (2.6 km/1.6 mi rt) also leads downstream to Lower Sunwapta Falls, where the river widens to spill down several slots.

Sunwapta Falls is located 50 km (31 mi) north of the Icefield Centre and 56 km (35 mi) south of Jasper. Turn west off the Icefields Parkway at Sunwapta Falls Rocky Mountain Lodge, then follow a spur road west for a short distance to reach the parking lot for Sunwapta Falls.

★ Athabasca Falls

When the Athabasca River is forced through a narrow gorge and over a cliff into a cauldron of roaring water below, the result is **Athabasca Falls.** It's not the height of the falls that creates an impression, but the sheer force at which the water from the Columbia Icefield propels through the gorge. The water splits into several spillways and hits multiple tiers, creating a visible spray. As the river slowly erodes the center of the riverbed, the falls will move upstream. Trails lead from a day-use area to various platforms and interpretive sites for viewing above and below the falls. A trail branching under Highway 93A follows an abandoned river channel before emerging at the bottom of the canyon. In winter, the falls are a frozen spectacle. Facilities at

Athabasca Falls include picnic tables and restrooms.

The fastest way to reach Athabasca Falls is via the Icefields Parkway. Turn west onto the southern end of Highway 93A to reach the falls, which are 73 km (45 mi) north of Icefield Centre and 32 km (20 mi) south of the town of Jasper.

★ Mount Edith Cavell

The peak of **Mount Edith Cavell** (3,363 m/11,033 ft) is the most distinctive and impressive in the park. Known to local Indigenous people as the "White Ghost" for its snowcapped summit, the mountain was given its English name in honor of a British nurse who was executed for helping prisoners of war escape German-occupied Belgium during World War I. The peak was first climbed in 1915.

Today, the most popular route to the summit is up the east ridge (to the left of the summit), but the imposing north face above the parking lot is the most dramatic, with its impressive glacier. The mountain's massive north face rises in a vertical wall (1,500 m/4,920 ft). Below the mountain's summit is a hanging valley rounded into a basin by the glacier; on its lip, **Angel Glacier** perches with wings outstretched and its body draping down the cliff face. Below Angel Glacier, **Cavell Glacier** melts into a cloudy green glacial lake known as **Cavell Pond.** Sometimes, you may see icebergs that calved off the glacier in the pond.

While you can see the mountain from downtown Jasper, including the golf course, the most impressive place to marvel at it is from directly below the **north face.** The paved **Mount Edith Cavell Road** (14.5 km/9 mi, mid-June-mid-Oct.) winds up the Astoria River Valley from Highway 93A, ending right below the face. This steep, narrow road has many switchbacks; big RVs (over 7 m/22 ft) are not recommended, and trailers must be left in the designated area at the bottom. The parking lot at the end of the road is 28 km (17 mi) south of the

Athabasca Falls

Jasper Townsite via Highway 93A, about a 45-minute drive. To avoid the large July and August crowds, aim to arrive before 9am or after 3pm.

From the parking lot, you must crane your neck to take in the sight of Mount Edith Cavell and Angel Glacier. On warm days, those who are patient may witness an avalanche tumbling from the glacier, creating a roar that echoes across the valley. Up the stairs above the parking area, a few picnic tables offer places to gaze up at the scenery while eating lunch. The **Path of the Glacier Trail** (1.6 km/1 mi, 70 m/230 ft elevation gain, 1 hr rt) departs to a couple viewpoints. The first part of the trail is paved to the junction that turns off to Cavell Meadows; continue straight on the rocky path to the overlooks.

Recreation
Hiking

Hikers are always surprised at how few day hikes are in the Jasper section of the Icefields Parkway. Nevertheless, some top-notch trails are in the Jasper section of the parkway, so set aside some time to hit the trail.

★ Forefield and Toe-of-the-Glacier Interpretive Loop

Length: 5.4 km (3.4 mi) rt
Duration: 2 hours
Elevation gain: 60 meters (197 ft)
Effort: moderate
Trailhead: Across the highway from the Icefield Centre

Instead of driving to the trailhead for Toe-of-the-Glacier, you can leave your vehicle beside the highway or in the Icefield Centre parking lot to hike the **Forefield** through the lunarlike landscape. It's a rubbly field of moraines, boulders, and other detritus left helter-skelter as the glacier melted and deposited rocks and glacial till it carried. You'll find a few hardy alpine plants gaining a foothold. Don sturdy footwear to handle the rocky trail, and wear layers for the chilly temperatures and often breezy open field. A word of caution: This field of debris contains many meltwater streams that can swell and become impassable on warm days. Hike in the morning for lower water levels.

When you reach the parking lot near the glacier and Sunwapta Lake, cross the lot to head uphill on the Toe-of-the-Glacier Interpretive Loop. Circle the loop for close-up views of the glacier and its outflow streams. Then retrace your steps back across the Forefield to your starting point.

★ Wilcox Pass

Length: 9.5 km (5.9 mi) rt
Duration: 3.5 hours
Elevation gain: 439 meters (1,440 ft)
Effort: moderate
Trailhead: Wilcox Creek Campground access road

Views of the Columbia Icefield from the Icefields Parkway pale in comparison with those achieved along this trail, on the same side of the valley as the Icefield Centre. This trail was used by Indigenous

people and other travelers more than a century ago because the impassable Athabasca Glacier covered the valley floor; Wilcox Pass provided the only way around the obstacle. The complete **Wilcox Pass Trail** goes from the campground trailhead over Wilcox Pass to a second trailhead at Tangle Falls (11.2 km/7 mi one way) but requires a self-shuttle to return to the original trailhead. Snowfields can linger at Wilcox Pass until late July, and you'll need snowshoes in winter.

This out-and-back route goes to Wilcox Pass and a stunning viewpoint of the Columbia Icefield. Beginning from the Wilcox Creek Campground trailhead, the path climbs through a stunted forest of Engelmann spruce and subalpine fir to a ridge with big views of the Columbia Icefield from a pair of red chairs. But the scenery only gets better at the upper viewpoint. Ascending gradually from there, the trail enters a fragile environment of alpine meadows to reach **Wilcox Pass.** Look for small herds of bighorn

sheep in these meadows. Near the pass, take a left spur trail back towards the icefields to reach the **Wilcox Viewpoint,** opting for left routes at junctions instead of the climbers' trails up Wilcox Peak. The trail rounds through several small basins as it climbs to its high point and drops to the edge of the ridge for the biggest panoramic view of Athabasca Glacier, the Columbia Icefield, Mount Athabasca, and the Snow Dome.

★ Cavell Meadows

Length: 6 km (3.8 mi) rt
Duration: 2.5 hours
Elevation gain: 380 meters (1,250 ft)
Effort: moderate
Trailhead: parking lot at the end of Mount Edith Cavell Rd. (open mid-June-mid-Oct.)

This trail, beginning from the parking lot beneath Mount Edith Cavell, provides access to an alpine meadow and panoramic views of Angel Glacier. The hike starts by following the paved Path of the Glacier Trail. At the junction, branch left and

Wilcox Pass Trail and Mount Athabasca

leave the pavement, climbing steadily along a rocky ridge deposited by the huge Cavell Glacier, which is now quite small. Departing the ridge, the trail weaves on switchbacks through a subalpine forest of Engelmann spruce and then stunted subalpine fir to emerge facing the northeast face of **Mount Edith Cavell.** Climb on the trail through the meadows, which fill with wildflowers by mid-July. Avoid going off trail and disturbing the fragile wildflowers. At the top is a flat knoll. The view of **Angel Glacier** from this point is stunning, as the ice spills out of the hanging valley, clinging to the cliff face.

From here, the trail continues climbing eastward across the meadows, gaining a little more elevation before dropping around the other side of the meadows to meet up with the main trail back in the trees. Retrace your steps to get back to the trailhead.

Backpacking

Jasper is renowned for long, remote

wilderness backpacking routes that ford streams and climb high passes. **Athabasca Pass** (98 km/61 mi rt) or the two-pass **South Boundary Trail** (120 km/75 mi one-way) require 7-10 days. But there are trips you can do for 3-5 days that will introduce you to some of Jasper's iconic backcountry.

Permits and Campsites

Permits (C$10 pp/night) are required for backcountry camping in Jasper. While you can walk into the backcountry office in the **Jasper Park Information Centre** (500 Connaught Dr., Jasper, 780/852-6176, www.pc.gc.ca, 9am-5pm daily year-round) to see what's available, it's better to try to make reservations in advance, especially for popular backpacking routes in July and August. **Reservations** (877/737-3783, 519/826-5391 from outside North America, reservation.pc.gc.ca, C$12) open usually in January; many routes book up fast for July to early September.

For planning, download Jasper's **Backcountry Guide** (www.pc.gc.ca/en/pn-np/ab/jasper). Before heading out, check trail conditions with the **Backcountry Office** (780/852-6177, www.pc.gc.ca/jaspertrails). Many backcountry campgrounds have bear poles provided for hanging food, water accessible nearby, pit toilets, cooking tables, and tenting sites.

★ Tonquin Valley
44 kilometers (27 miles)
The high-elevation Tonquin Valley is a sight to behold. The stunning Amethyst Lakes splay out below The Ramparts, a series of pinnacles and spires that rake the sky. The lakes attract wildlife, especially moose, and the valley is home to mountain caribou. (The area closes Nov.-mid-Feb. for caribou conservation.) By setting up a car shuttle, the route can be done point-to-point; most hikers enter via Astoria Trailhead, opposite the Cavell Hostel, for less elevation gain, and then exit via the

bigger descent along Portal Creek. But you can also go in the reverse direction or enter and exit at the same trailhead.

Due to mosquitoes and mud, Tonquin Valley is best in late summer and fall; you can also make it a ski destination in winter. To have time to explore Eremite Valley and hike to Maccarib Pass if you aren't exiting via the Portal, plan for four days and three nights. Seven campgrounds are on the route, with four in the central Tonquin Valley area; the best views of the Ramparts are from **Amethyst** and **Surprise Point Campgrounds.** As an alternative to camping, you can stay in the **Wates-Gibson Hut** (403/678-3200, www.alpineclubofcanada.ca, year-round, C$30 members, C$40 nonmembers) run by Alpine Club of Canada.

Fryatt Valley
43 kilometers (27 miles)
This three-day, out-and-back trail is best done by hiking into one of the backcountry campgrounds and spending two nights in the same site. Midway campgrounds include **Lower Fryatt** (12 km/7.5 mi one way) or **Brussels** (18.1 km/11.3 mi one way). On your second day, hike the remaining distance into Fryatt Lake, Headwall Campground, and Headwall Waterfall. Find the trailhead on Geraldine Road (2 km/1.2 mi north from southern end of Hwy. 93A).

The **Sydney Vallance/Fryatt Hut** (403/678-3200, www.alpineclubofcanada. ca, year-round, C$30 members, C$40 nonmembers), run by the Alpine Club of Canada, sits on a scramble route to the top of the headwall. Just bring food and a sleeping bag. You can also ride **mountain bikes** as far as Lower Fryatt Campground to chop off half the walking distance to Headwall Campground.

Brazeau Loop
81 kilometers (50 miles)
For experienced backpackers, this high-elevation route loops through the southern mountains of Jasper. It's a strenuous route that climbs over five passes (1,878 m/6,161 ft elevation change), fords streams, and may have snowfields until mid-July, as well as snowstorms in summer. Most hikers take at least five days and four nights, though some prefer to add another night or two.

The route starts from the Nigel Pass Trailhead south of the Icefield Centre on the Icefields Parkway in Banff National Park. The trail goes up and over Nigel Pass into Jasper National Park. Along the **Brazeau River,** you meet the junction for the loop at Four Point, the first night's destination for most hikers. You can go either direction to complete the circuit over Jonas Pass, Jonas Shoulder, and Pobotkan Pass. Six campsites are en route: **Brazeau Lake** is the most prized one, on the shore of the eponymous turquoise lake.

Mountaineering

Jasper is renowned for mountaineering, rock climbing, glacier and ice climbing, and ski mountaineering. You can scramble to the top of a few peaks, such as Mount Wilcox, Sunwapta Peak, or Pyramid Mountain. But you'll need technical know-how, experience, and gear to climb something like Mount Edith Cavell. Jasper is home to 10 of the 20 highest peaks in the Canadian Rockies, and several are big climbing attractants rimming the Columbia Icefield area: Mount Athabasca, Mount Columbia, Mount Alberta, Mount Andromeda, and the Snow Dome.

Permits are not required for climbing, but you will need a **permit** (C$10 pp/night) to **bivouac** or spend the night at a **backcountry camp.** Daily **avalanche bulletins** (avalanche.pc.gc.ca) and the **Mountain Conditions Report** (mountainconditions.ca, subscription required) are useful tools for mountaineering.

ACC Huts
Alpine Club of Canada (403/678-3200, www.alpineclubofcanada.ca, C$30

members, C$40 nonmembers) manages four user-maintained shared **huts** in the Jasper backcountry. The huts have mattress pads, stoves, and outhouses; bring your own food and sleeping bags. They are mostly used by mountaineers and climbers, but hikers may use some of them, too, to avoid hauling a tent and stove.

The **Wates-Gibson Hut** (closed Nov.-mid-Feb. for caribou conservation) is a two-story log cabin in the Tonquin Valley that appeals to hikers, scramblers, ski tourers, and mountaineers. In winter, the approach takes two days.

The small single-story **Sydney Vallance Hut,** also known as the **Fryatt Hut,** is located up the Fryatt Valley after a scramble up to the top of a headwall surrounded by ski mountaineering, scrambling, and climbing routes, but hikers can use it as a destination accessed via the trail. The **Lloyd Mackay-Mount Alberta Hut** (summer only) is a tiny metal hut used solely by climbers on Mount Alberta. The small **Mount Colin Centennial Hut** (summer only) is used by rock climbers on Mount Colin.

Biking
Road Biking
Bicycling the **Icefields Parkway** is a world-class cycling trip. While avid road cyclists ride from Jasper to Icefield Centre and back in one day (210 km/130 mi rt), most touring riders take more time, staying in hostels or campgrounds en route. Some cyclists prefer to take the hilly **Highway 93A** route to get off the major thoroughfare, but be ready for shoulders that are skimpy and not too firm. The campgrounds have bear food storage containers for bike campers to use.

Top to bottom: Cavell Meadows Trail and Angel Glacier; patio at Icefield Centre; Glacier View Lodge

Mountain Biking

Along the Icefields Parkway, there are just a few trails that allow bikes (including e-bikes). They make excellent biking-hiking combo trips, so you can get further into the backcountry. Tucked between Mount Christie and Mount Fryatt, the **Fryatt Valley Trail** (43 km/27 mi rt) travels an old fire road along the Athbasca Valley floor with views of Mount Kerkeslin. Bikes are allowed to reach the **Lower Fryatt Campground** (12 km/7.5 mi one way) on Fryatt Creek. You can spend the night here, hike further up the glaciated valley into the more open area of **Brussels Campground** (6.1 km/3.8 mi farther), or continue on to Fryatt Lake and the **Headwall Campground** (3.4 km/2.1 mi farther) below a waterfall. More than half of the total distance of the adventure is via mountain bike. **Permits** (C$10 pp/night) are required for camping at all locations. **Reservations** (877/737-3783, 519/826-5391 from outside North America, reservation.pc.gc. ca, C$12) usually open for the year in January. Find the trailhead on Geraldine Road (2 km/1.2 mi north from southern end of Hwy. 93A).

Food

Restaurants

Above the main floor in the **Icefield Centre** are two restaurants (966/606-6700, www.banffjaspercollection.com) that offer dining with outstanding views of the glaciers. The **Chalet** (9am-5pm daily May-mid-Oct., C$9-15) is a casual, self-serve café with hot drinks, sandwiches, pizza, burgers, and salads, plus grab-and-go items. Seating is inside or out, with the outside tables offering unparalleled glacier views. Across the hallway is the modern and stylish **Altitude Restaurant** (7:30am-9:30am, 10:45am-2:45pm, and 6pm-9pm daily May-mid-Oct.). Breakfast is a buffet or à la carte (C$14-26). Lunch and dinner have a Canadian-oriented menu (C$22-45) with beer, wine, and cocktails. Vegan,

vegetarian, gluten-free, and kids' meals are available.

The dining room at **Sunwapta Falls Rocky Mountain Lodge** (Icefields Pkwy., 55 km/34 mi south of Jasper Townsite, 50 km/31 mi north of Icefield Centre, 780/852-4852 or 888/828-5777, www. sunwapta.com, 8am-9pm daily May-mid-Oct.) serves breakfast and lunch with grab-and-go items in the morning. Hot lunch meals are served 11am-5pm. In the evening this same room is transformed into a restaurant featuring simply prepared Canadian game and seafood (6pm-9pm daily, C$25-45). Dinner reservations, available online or by phone, are required.

Picnic Areas

With limited dining options on the Icefields Parkway, your time may be better served packing a picnic lunch to enjoy more of the scenery. Picnic tables are at several locations along the parkway. The picnic tables at the **Icefield Centre** have incredible views of Athabasca Glacier. Some tables and a picnic shelter are located at the lower end of the parking lot opposite the highway. You can also use the second-floor deck tables at the Icefield Centre. Toilet facilities are available. Plan on bundling up as temperatures can be chillier here.

Athabasca Falls has about 10 picnic tables with a shelter, and toilet facilities. It's the perfect place to picnic before or after touring the trails around the falls. Between these two sightseeing locales on the parkway, you can find picnic tables and toilets at **Mount Christie/Goat Lick Picnic Site, Bubbling Springs,** and **Tangle Falls.**

Accommodations and Camping

Hostels

HI-Canada (778/328-2220 or 866/762-4122, www.hihostels.ca, members C$36, nonmembers C$40) runs three **wilderness hostels** in the Icefields Parkway region, either on the main highway or off Highway 93A. Check-in is 5pm-11pm, but the main lodges are open all day. Make advance reservations for staying in these rustic hostels as they are a long way from other options. As wilderness hostels, they do not have electricity, running water, or showers; you'll be off the grid. Toilets are outhouses.

★ **HI-Mount Edith Cavell** (13 km/8 mi up Mt. Edith Cavell Rd. off Hwy. 93A, mid-June-mid-Oct.) offers a million-dollar view for the price of a dorm bed. Opposite the hostel are trailheads for hiking in the Tonquin Valley, and it's just a short walk to the base of Mount Edith Cavell and the Cavell Meadows Trail. The hostel has a kitchen, dining area, eight bunks in a mixed-gender cabin, and an outdoor wood sauna. You can stay in winter by cross-country skiing in 12 km (7.5 mi). The hostel is about 45 minutes from Jasper Townsite.

HI-Athabasca Falls (Icefields Pkwy., 32 km/20 mi south of Jasper Townsite, 73 km/45 mi north of Icefield Centre, May-Oct. and Dec.-Apr.) has limited solar-powered electricity and well water. Athabasca Falls is only a few minutes' walk away. It has three mixed gender sleeping cabins, a couple private rooms, and the cooking cabin has a huge kitchen and lounge.

HI-Beauty Creek (Icefields Pkwy., 88 km/55 mi south of Jasper Townsite, 17 km/10.5 mi north of Icefield Centre, May-early Oct.) is nestled in a small stand of Douglas fir between the Icefields Parkway and the Sunwapta River. Each of its two mixed gender sleeping cabins has a woodstove and propane lighting. A third building holds a kitchen and dining area. Due to virtually no light pollution, you'll have outstanding stargazing on clear moonless nights.

Lodges

Historic **Sunwapta Falls Rocky Mountain Lodge** (Icefields Pkwy., 780/852-4852 or 888/828-5777, www.sunwapta.com, May-mid-Oct., C$170-330) features 52 comfortable motel-like units, with various bed configurations that include queens, kings, and twins. Some rooms have a fireplace or balcony. Amenities include a restaurant and gift shop, and you can walk to Sunwapta Falls. The lodge is located about halfway along Jasper's segment of the Icefields Parkway: 55 km (34 mi) south of the town of Jasper, and 50 km (31 mi) north of the Icefield Centre.

Glacier View Lodge (Icefields Pkwy., 888/770-6914, www.banffjasper collection.com, May-mid-Oct., from C$279), comprising the top story of the Icefield Centre, lies in a stunning location high above the tree line and overlooking the Columbia Icefield. It features 29 standard rooms, 17 of which have glacier views, and 3 larger, more luxurious corner rooms. All units have satellite TV and phones. Because of the remote location, dining options are limited to the in-house café and restaurant. You can get a room only or package up the experience with meals and an evening skywalk tour. The lodge is 105 km (65 mi) south from the Jasper Townsite, a drive of one hour, and 132 km (82 mi) north of Lake Louise, a drive of 1.5 hours.

Backcountry Lodges

The Tonquin Valley is home to two **lodges.** But you must hike, ride horseback, or ski in to reach them, as they are not accessible by road. These lodges make outstanding base camps for hiking to Eremite Valley and Maccarib Pass, as well as elsewhere around scenic Tonquin Valley. All meals are included: breakfast, lunch, dinner, and snacks. Horse trips include the guided trail ride in and out, plus daily rides to scenic locales around Tonquin Valley. Most hikers launch from the Astoria Trailhead across from the Edith Cavell Hostel (12 km/7.5 mi up Mt. Edith Cavell Rd.), but you can also hike in the steeper route from Portal Creek Trailhead over Maccarib Pass.

Sitting on the north shore of Amethyst Lake with stunning views of

The Ramparts, the ★ **Tonquin Valley Backcountry Lodge** (780/852-3909, www.tonquinvalley.com, mid-July-mid-Sept.) offers comforts in the wilderness without electricity. Lodging is in private cabin rooms with wood-burning stoves and beds with down duvets. Canoes and fishing rowboats are provided for enjoying the lake. To reach the lodge, you must hike, ride horseback, or ski (23 km/14 mi). Hikers (C$325 pp/night) must carry in their own gear. Horse trips (C$4,000 per rider for 5 days/4 nights) include the ride in and daily horseback tours to different destinations. In winter, you can ski in (mid-Feb.-Mar., C$185 pp/night) to the lodge to overnight.

On a knoll overlooking Amethyst Lake, the ★ **Tonquin Amethyst Lake Lodge** (780/852-1188, tonquinadventures.com, late June-early Oct.) is operated by Tonquin Valley Adventures. Lodging is in private heated cabins, which sleep up to four people. The historic Brewster Cabin provides the dining room and a place to sit in front of the fire. Fishing boats are available for the lake. Reaching the lodge is shortest via the Astoria River Trail (18.6 km/11.6 mi). Hiking trips (C$250 pp/night) include horse support for carrying gear. Horseback trips are for 4 days/3 nights (C$1,600) or 3 days/2 nights (C$1,275). In winter, skiers can do self-guided, self-catered trips (mid-Feb.-early Apr., C$380 per cabin per night, two-night minimum).

Camping

Six first-come, first-served campgrounds line the Icefields Parkway near the southern junction with Highway 93A. These campgrounds do not have hookups for RVs. With the exception of the Icefield Centre RV campground, facilities include picnic tables, fire pits, cooking shelters, potable water, bear-proof food storage, and flush or vault toilets. Fire permits (C$9) include firewood. None of these campgrounds take reservations. In July

and August, you'll want to claim a campsite early in the day.

Mount Kerkeslin Campground (42 sites, late May-late Sept., RV limit 27 ft, C$25) enjoys the ambience of the nearby Athabasca River. Spruce and fir trees shade the campsites, so to see rugged Mount Fryatt, you'll need to walk to the river. Due to minimal light pollution, stargazing is spectacular on moonless nights, also at the river. The campground is 36 km (22 mi) south of Jasper and 69 km (43 mi) north of the Icefield Centre.

On the east side of the parkway, the forested **Honeymoon Lake Campground** (35 sites, late May-late Sept., RV limit 27 ft, C$25) is set below the mountains of the Endless Chain. You can paddle Honeymoon Lake and hike the short trail to Buck and Osprey Lakes. On clear, moonless nights, stargazing is outstanding. The campground sits halfway between Jasper (53 km/33 mi) and the Icefield Centre (52 km/32 mi).

Along the cascading Jonas Creek, **Jonas Campground** (25 sites, early June-early Sept., RV limit 25 ft, C$25) has campsites near the water and on a hillside. Due to tight sites and road curves, this campground is better suited to tents and is popular with cyclists. Although it's close to the parkway, it does have dark enough skies for seeing the Milky Way. The campground is south of Jasper (78 km/49 mi) and north of the Icefield Centre (27 km/17 mi).

Three campgrounds cluster at the extreme southern end of Jasper National Park around the **Icefield Centre** (105 km/65 mi south of Jasper, 125 km/78 mi north of Lake Louise). Despite small sites, the attraction is the proximity to the Columbia Icefield and views of Athabasca Glacier from many of the campsites and cook shelters, plus trailheads and ice tours within close proximity. The **Icefield Centre RV Campground** (100 sites, mid-May-late Sept., C$16), an asphalt parking lot north of the day-use lot, is only for trailers and RVs; no tents are permitted. The campground has no hookups, water, or fire pits. Sites can accommodate large RVs. The **Columbia Icefield Tent Campground** (33 sites, early June-mid-Oct., C$25) has small sites only for tents; RVs are not allowed. With stunning views from the campground, sites can go fast, especially in the mornings of July and August. Get here early to claim a campsite before going hiking or on tours. Two minutes south of the Icefield Centre, **Wilcox Creek Campground** (46 sites, early June-late Sept., RV limit 27 ft, C$25) has small, tight sites clustered on a forested hillside, but it's advantageously positioned right at the trailhead for Wilcox Pass. It's great for night-sky watching.

Information and Services
Emergency Services
In case of emergency, call **911.** In the town of Jasper, **Seton-Jasper Healthcare Centre** (518 Robson St., 780/852-3344, www.albertahealthservices.ca) has a 24-hour emergency center.

Gas
No gas is available along this stretch of the Icefields Parkway. The nearest gas stations are at **Saskatchewan River Crossing** (Banff National Park) and in the town of **Jasper,** 150 km (93 mi) apart, so top up your tank before driving the parkway.

Cell Service and Internet Access
Cell reception is not available along the Icefields Parkway on the entire route from Lake Louise to Jasper. Neither will you have cell service while hiking. However, the Icefield Centre and a few campgrounds have pay phones for emergencies. You can get cell service and Wi-Fi in the Jasper Townsite.

Jasper Townsite and Environs

The town of Jasper, the national park's main service center, has half the population of Banff but an equally dramatic setting. It's located at the confluence of the Athabasca and Miette Rivers and surrounded by rugged, snowcapped peaks. The town is also less commercialized than Banff.

July and August are especially busy, and they come with accompanying parking woes. Connaught Drive, the town's main street, parallels the rail line as it curves through town. You'll also find the bus depot, train terminal, restaurants, and motels. Behind Connaught Drive is Patricia Street (one-way eastbound), lined with more restaurants and services, which leads to a string of hotels on Geikie Street. Behind this main core are rows of neat houses and all the facilities of a regular town, including a library, school, civic center, post office, museum, swimming pool, and hospital.

Getting There
The Jasper Townsite anchors the north end of the Icefields Parkway. It sits at the junction of the Icefields Parkway and the Yellowhead Highway (Hwy. 16), which runs east-west between Edmonton and Mount Robson Provincial Park. From Lake Louise, it's 235 km (145 mi) to Jasper via the Icefields Parkway, a drive that takes three hours without stops.

Sights
★ Jasper Skytram
The **Jasper Skytram** (end of Whistlers Rd., 780/852-3093 or 866/8508726, www.jasperskytram.com, 8am-9pm daily summer, shorter hours late Mar.-June and Sept.-Oct., adults C$52, children 6-15 C$28) climbs up the steep north face of **The Whistlers,** named for the hoary marmots that live on the summit. Two 30-passenger cars take seven minutes to whisk up 1,000 meters (3,280 ft) to the upper terminal, during which time the conductor provides information about the mountain and its environment. The best views are on the downhill sides of

92

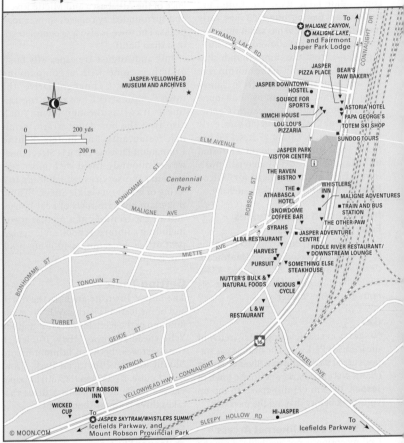

Jasper Townsite

the tram, but if low clouds hang around the mountain, you won't get any views at all. Take layers, as the top often has winds and chillier temperatures. At the top, a short boardwalk tours the area and platforms allow for overlooking Jasper far below.

Both the lower and upper tram stations house food services, gift shops, and restrooms. The upper terminal has a restaurant with wrap-around windows for big views. From the upper terminal, a trail (2.8 km/1.8 mi rt) climbs to the true summit. On a clear, crowded day, you should

allow for two hours at the top and two more hours in line to return down the tram. Make tram reservations online in summer.

In fall, the Jasper Planetarium hosts **astronomy nights** (dates vary, 6:15pm-10:30pm, C$130 adults, C$82 youth, reservations required) that combine the tram ride, dining, and stargazing.

The Jasper Skytram is about 10 minutes from town. Drive 3 km (1.9 mi) south on the Icefields Parkway, turn right onto Whistlers Road, and go to the end. RV parking is available.

Jasper Planetarium

As an International Dark Sky Preserve, the **Jasper Planetarium** (Fairmont Jasper Park Lodge, 1 Old Lodge Rd., 780/921-3275, jasperplanetarium.com, evenings year-round, days and times vary) offers the best introduction to the night sky in Jasper National Park. Inside the planetarium dome, interactive tours of the Jasper skies fly you through the universe (40 min.); you will want to download their recommended stargazing smartphone apps before arriving. The outdoor **Telescope Experience** includes an interactive tour of powerful telescopes and live **sky-viewing** if weather permits. You may also be able to see the northern lights. (Fall, winter, and spring are when you'll have the best chance of seeing them, but they also appear in summer.)

The best deal is the package (C$59 adults, C$25 youth) that combines the planetarium show and the outdoor Telescope Experience. Book your activities online and then check-in at the planetarium desk in the lobby of the Fairmont Jasper Park Lodge. The planetarium experts also guide tours of the night sky on special astronomy nights in fall at the top of the Jasper Skytram.

Jasper-Yellowhead Museum

At the back of town is the excellent **Jasper-Yellowhead Museum and Archives** (400 Bonhomme St., 780/852-3013, jaspermuseum.org, 10am-5pm daily mid-May-mid-Oct., 10am-5pm Thurs.-Sun. winter, adults C$7, seniors and children C$6), as unstuffy as any museum could possibly be. The main gallery features colorful, modern exhibits that take visitors along a timeline of Jasper's human history, from the Indigenous people that lived here, the fur trade, the coming of the railway, and the creation of the park. Documentaries are shown on demand in a small television room. The museum also features a gallery of local and regional artists.

East of Jasper

Wildlife-Watching

The Jasper Townsite and the fields along the Yellowhead Highway north of town are common places to spot wildlife, especially in the early morning and evening. (Note that these are often no-stopping zones to prevent disruption of the wildlife.) **Elk** are particularly easy to spot and hear in fall when big-antlered bulls bugle to round up harems of cows. Sometimes they spar with usurpers. Elk often hang out around the Fairmont's golf course, too.

Bighorn sheep, which usually inhabit alpine meadows in summer, migrate down to the town and open fields for winter. You may also spot them at Miette Hot Springs.

Look for **moose** around lakes, especially Maligne Lake, Medicine Lake, Annette Lake, and Lac Beauvert. For spotting **grizzly** or **black bears,** drive the Maligne Lake Road just after dawn or at dusk. In spring, you can see bears around the Fairmont's golf course.

Maligne Adventures (604 Connaught Dr., 780/852-3331 or 844/808-7177, maligneadventures.com, July-early Oct., 3 hrs, C$69 adults, C$49 youth) leads early morning wildlife tours. **SunDog Tours** (414 Connaught Dr., 780/852-4056 or 888/786-3641, www.sundogtours.com, year-round, 3-3.5 hrs, C$69 adults, C$35 children) leads evening wildlife tours in summer and morning tours in winter.

★ Maligne Canyon

Formed from the fast-flowing steep gradient of the Maligne River, **Maligne Canyon** is one of nature's works of art, carved in limestone. Maligne Lake, which was originally known by the area's Indigenous people as Chaba Imne (Beaver Lake), feeds the Maligne River.

Vicinity of Jasper

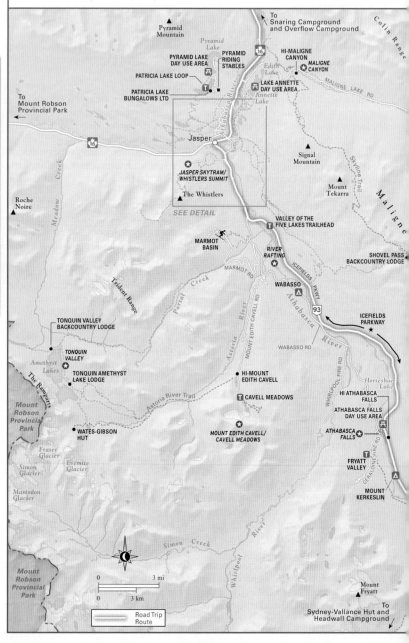

To
Snaring Campground
and Overflow Campground

Colin Range

Pyramid
Mountain

Pyramid
Lake

PYRAMID LAKE
DAY USE AREA

PYRAMID
RIDING
STABLES

HI-MALIGNE
CANYON

MALIGNE
CANYON

Edith
Lake

PATRICIA LAKE LOOP

PATRICIA LAKE
BUNGALOWS LTD

LAKE ANNETTE
DAY USE AREA

MALIGNE LAKE RD

Annette
Lake

To
Mount Robson
Provincial Park

Jasper

JASPER SKYTRAM/
WHISTLERS SUMMIT

Signal
Mountain

Skyline Trail

Roche
Noire

Meadow Creek

The Whistlers

SEE DETAIL

Mount
Tekarra

Maligne

VALLEY OF THE
FIVE LAKES TRAILHEAD

MARMOT
BASIN

RIVER
RAFTING

SHOVEL PASS
BACKCOUNTRY LODGE

Trident Range

MARMOT RD

Portal Creek

WABASSO

ICEFIELDS PKWY

Athabasca

ICEFIELDS
PARKWAY

93

TONQUIN VALLEY
BACKCOUNTRY LODGE

Astoria River

MOUNT EDITH CAVELL RD

WABASSO RD

River

TONQUIN
VALLEY

Amethyst
Lakes

TONQUIN AMETHYST
LAKE LODGE

The Ramparts

Mount
Robson
Provincial
Park

Fraser
Glacier

WATES-GIBSON
HUT

Astoria River Trail

HI-MOUNT
EDITH CAVELL

CAVELL MEADOWS

WHIRLPOOL FIRE RD

Horseshoe
Falls

HI ATHABASCA
FALLS

ATHABASCA FALLS
DAY USE AREA

Simon
Glacier

Evemite
Glacier

MOUNT EDITH CAVELL/
CAVELL MEADOWS

ATHABASCA
FALLS

Mastodon
Glacier

FRYATT
VALLEY

GERALDINE FIRE RD

MOUNT
KERKESLIN

Mount
Robson
Provincial
Park

Simon Creek

River

Whirlpool River

Mount
Fryatt

To
Sydney-Vallance Hut and
Headwall Campground

0   3 mi

0   3 km

Road Trip
Route

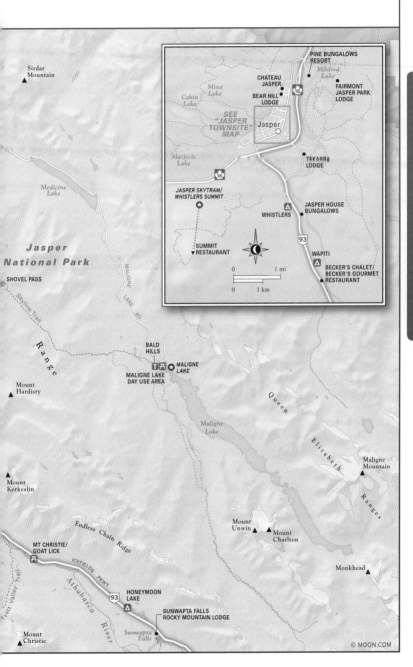

© MOON.COM

The river mostly disappears underground from Medicine Lake to surface with ferocity in Maligne Canyon.

The canyon is up to 50 meters (165 ft) deep, yet so narrow that squirrels often jump across. At the top of the canyon, you'll see large potholes in the riverbed. These potholes are created when rocks and pebbles become trapped in what begins as a shallow depression; under the force of the rushing water, they carve jug-shaped hollows into the soft bedrock.

An **interpretive trail** winds down from the parking lot, crossing the canyon six times via **bridges.** The most spectacular sections of the canyon can be seen from the first two bridges, at the upper end of the trail. To avoid the crowds at the upper end of the canyon, an alternative would be to park at Sixth Bridge, near the confluence of the Maligne and Athabasca Rivers, and walk up the canyon.

By late December, the torrent that is the Maligne River has frozen solid. Where it cascades down through Maligne Canyon, the river creates remarkable ice formations, including frozen waterfalls, through the deep limestone canyon. **Jasper Adventure Centre** (306 Connaught Dr., 780/852-5595 or 800/565-7547, www.jasperadventurecentre.com, 3-3.5 hrs, 10am and 2pm, C$70 adults, C$35 kids) offers guided **ice walks** into the depths of the canyon throughout winter. They also sometimes guide evening tours by headlamp.

In summer, the **Maligne Canyon Wilderness Kitchen** (780/820-2256, www.banffjaspercollection.com, 9:30am-9pm daily) has a sit-down restaurant, grab-and-go foods, and a gift shop at the top of the canyon.

To get here, head northeast from town on the Yellowhead Highway (Hwy. 16) and turn right across the bridge onto Maligne Lake Road and turn left into the canyon parking lot. The canyon is 11 km (6.8 mi) from Jasper, a drive of about 10-15 minutes.

Medicine Lake

From Maligne Canyon, Maligne Lake Road climbs to **Medicine Lake,** which does a disappearing act each year. The water level fluctuates due to a network of underground passages that emerge downstream at Maligne Canyon. At the northwest end of the lake, beyond where the outlet should be, the riverbed is often dry. In fall, when runoff from the mountains is minimal, the water level drops, and by November the lake comprises a few shallow pools. Local Indigenous people believed that spirits were responsible for the phenomenon, hence the name. You can stop at two **interpretive exhibits,** one at the north end of the lake near the boat ramp and the other near the south end of the lake.

TOP EXPERIENCE

★ Maligne Lake

One of the world's most photographed lakes, **Maligne Lake** is the largest glacier-fed lake in the Canadian Rockies and second largest in the world. The first paying visitors were brought to the lake in the 1920s, and it has been a draw for camera-toting tourists from around the world ever since. Once at the lake, activities are plentiful.

You can get out on the water in two ways. The narrated **Maligne Lake Boat Cruises** (780/852-3370, www.banffjaspercollection.com, 10pm-5pm daily late May-mid-Oct., 1.5-2 hrs, C$75-110 adults, C$38-55 kids) go to oft-photographed **Spirit Island,** where you debark onto a short loop path. The longer two-hour cruise adds on **Pincushion Bay.** Cruises leave in summer every hour on the hour with fewer sailings in spring and fall. Reservations are highly recommended to avoid long waits; book online or at the **boat tour office** (616 Patricia St., 8am-6pm daily). The other way to enjoy the water requires a little more work on your part: **Maligne Lake Boat Rentals** (9am-5pm daily June-mid-Sept.,

C\$40-100/hr) rents rowboats, single and double kayaks, and canoes on an hourly, first-come, first-served basis from the **Boat House,** a provincial historic site dating to 1929. Full-day rentals are available, too. The lake also has excellent trout fishing; guided fishing tours are available.

All commercial operations around the lake are run by **Pursuit** (403/762-6700 or 866/606-6700, www.banffjaspercollection.com, late May-mid-Oct.). **Maligne Lake Lodge,** a day-use facility, has a souvenir shop. Dining is available at three restaurants. **Lakehouse Café** (8:30am-6pm daily June-Aug., 10am-4pm daily Sept., lunches C\$9-17) has loads of windows for indoor dining with a view, a huge area of tiered outdoor seating overlooking the lake, and an outdoor **Waffle Hut.** The **View Restaurant** (780/852-3370, 11am-7pm daily June-Aug., shorter hours in Sept., C\$23-34) serves Canadian cuisine on an outdoor patio with lake views.

The 48-km (30-mi) drive to Maligne Lake from Jasper takes one hour without stops. Though the lake is southeast of Jasper, you must drive north on the Yellowhead Highway (Hwy. 16) to cross the bridge onto Maligne Lake Road. The road ends at the lake.

★ Miette Hot Springs

With the warmest springs in the Canadian Rockies, **Miette Hot Springs** (800/767-1611, www.hotsprings.ca, 10:30am-9pm daily mid-May-mid-Oct., C\$7-10 adults, C\$6-9 youth and seniors) were one of the park's biggest attractions the early 1900s. In 1910, a packhorse trail was built up the valley, and the government constructed a bathhouse. The original hand-hewn log structure was replaced in the 1930s with pools that remained in use until new facilities were built in 1985. Water that flows into the outdoor pools is artificially cooled from 54°C (128°F) to

Top to bottom: Maligne Canyon; Maligne Lake cruise boat; Miette Hot Springs

a soothing 39°C (100°F). Also part of the complex is a smaller, cool plunge pool. You can buy a one-time entry or an all-day pass. (Stay as long as you wish with the one-time entry, but there are no in-and-out privileges, which the all-day pass does afford.) The complex has changing rooms, a gift shop, and a café. Many hiking trails begin from the hot springs; the shortest goes from the picnic area to the source of the springs, a five-minute walk each way.

To get to the hot springs from Jasper, drive north on the Yellowhead Highway (Hwy. 16) for 44 km (27 mi) and turn right onto Miette Hot Springs Road, then continue for 17 km (11 mi) to its terminus. RV parking is available. The drive takes about an hour.

Scenic Drives
Yellowhead Highway
From Jasper to the park's eastern boundary, the **Yellowstone Highway** (Hwy. 16, 50 km/31 mi) follows the Athabasca River the entire way. Beyond the turnoff to Maligne Lake, the road enters a wide valley flanked to the west by The Palisade and to the east by the Colin Range. The valley is a classic montane environment, with open meadows and forests of Douglas fir and lodgepole pine. After crossing the Athabasca River, the highway parallels **Jasper Lake,** which is lined by sand dunes along its southern edge. At the highway, a plaque marks the site of **Jasper House** (the actual site is on the opposite side of the river). Less than 5 minutes north, **Disaster Point** offers a great spot for viewing bighorn sheep, which gather at a mineral lick for the exposed mineral salts. Disaster Point is on the lower slopes of Roche Miette, a distinctive peak that juts out into the Athabasca River Valley. Across the highway, the braided Athabasca River is flanked by wetlands alive with migrating birds in the spring and fall. The road exits the park near Hinton. The drive will take about 45 minutes to an hour, depending on the length of stops.

Miette Hot Springs Road
From the Yellowhead Highway, **Miette Hot Spring Road** (17 km/11 mi) cuts southeast below the Miette Range. Its turnoff junction (43 km/27 mi east of Jasper) marks the site of **Pocahontas,** a coal-mining town in existence between 1910 and 1921. The mine itself was high above the township, with coal transported to the valley floor by cable car. Most buildings have long since been removed, but a short **interpretive walk** leads through the remaining foundations.

Continue 1 km (0.6 mi) farther down the road and pull over to walk a short trail leading to photogenic **Punchbowl Falls.** Here Mountain Creek cascades through a narrow crevice in a cliff to a pool of turbulent water. From here, the road curves, swerves, rises, and drops many times. Stop at a viewpoint of **Ashlar Ridge** on a sharp switchback and follow the Fiddle River upstream until you reach Miette Hot Springs, where the road terminates. With stops, you'll need about 40 minutes each way.

Recreation
Hiking
★ **Whistlers Summit**
Length: 2.8 km (1.8 mi) rt
Duration: 1.5 hours
Elevation gain: 246 meters (805 ft)
Effort: strenuous
Trailhead: Top of the Jasper Skytram (fee to access)

A steep, rocky trail leads to **Whistlers Summit** (2,470 m/8,104 ft). This trail is named for hoary marmots that burrow under the rock piles along the trail. They have a loud whistle that functions as a warning call. The trail climbs several rocky, steep pitches with views the entire way due to the open alpine tundra. Short alternative routes allow for more gradual ascents. The view from the summit takes in so much more than from the top of the tram that it's worth the climb. Mountains splay out in all directions. On clear days, you can spot the Columbia Icefield to the south and Mount Robson, the highest peak in the Canadian Rockies, to the northwest.

Lac Beauvert

Length: 4 km (2.4 mi) loop
Duration: 1.5 hours
Elevation gain: minimal
Effort: easy
Trailhead: Lac Beauvert south end parking lot

This strolling trail loops around the clear waters of **Lac Beauvert,** mostly along the lakeshore, and you can go in either direction. Head eastward along the lake toward the golf course, following the yellow Trail 4a diamond markers through the course and then back to the lakeshore for views of Pyramid Mountain. At the Fairmont Jasper Park Lodge, the trail swings west, passing cabins, the boat house, the main lodge, and more cabins. To the south, Mount Edith Cavell rises above the valley. The trail continues through the woods, crossing the lake's outlet creek on a bridge to trot along the lake back to the parking lot.

Annette Lake

Length: 2.6 km (1.6 mi) loop
Duration: 1 hour
Elevation gain: 8 meters (25 ft)
Effort: easy
Trailhead: Annette Lake picnic area at the yellow Trail 4d signs

This wheelchair-accessible interpretive trail loops around **Annette Lake** on a paved route with one hill on the west side. From the picnic area, aim for the beach to pick up the trail, which you can walk in either direction to arc around the lake's three bays. Heading east to go clockwise, the trail passes across a narrow spit of land between the turquoise Annette Lake and the smaller brownish **Ochre Lake.** Most of the trail then

Top to bottom: Whistlers Summit; Maligne Canyon; Annette Lake

follows through the forest with periodic views of Pyramid Mountain and Mount Edith Cavell.

Valley of the Five Lakes

Length: 4.8 km (3 mi) loop
Duration: 2 hours
Elevation gain: 104 meters (340 ft)
Effort: moderate
Trailhead: east side of the Icefields Parkway, 9 km (5.5 mi) south of Jasper

Favored by families with kids, this forested trail has so much to see that it keeps the kids hiking. Starting on Trail 9a, the wide path goes over a ridge to cross **Wabasso Creek** and then another ridge to a junction. Turn left here to go to the first and largest lake (the lakes are named by order of appearance). At the next junction on the southwest end of **First Lake**, turn right to pass the tiny **Second, Third,** and **Fourth Lakes.** A short spur trail leads to **Fifth Lake.** The main trail returns to the first junction where a left turn goes back to the parking lot. The lakes vary in blue-green shades, based on the amount of glacial flour and depth of each.

Bald Hills

Length: 11.4 km (7 mi) rt
Duration: 5 hours
Elevation gain: 500 meters (1,640 ft)
Effort: strenuous
Trailhead: picnic area at the end of Maligne Lake Rd.

This trail (23) follows an old road for its entire distance to the site of a fire lookout that has long since been removed. Alpine meadows above the tree line bloom with wildflowers in late July. From the top, the sweeping view takes in the jade-green waters of Maligne Lake and the grandeur of the Queen Elizabeth Ranges, plus the twin peaks of Mount Unwin and Mount Charlton. The **Bald Hills** extend up into the Maligne Range.

★ Maligne Canyon

Length: 7.4 km (4.6 mi) rt
Duration: 3 hours
Elevation gain: 125 meters (410 ft)
Effort: moderate
Trailhead: turnoff to Sixth Bridge, 2.5 km (1.6 mi) along Maligne Lake Rd. from Hwy. 16

Maligne Canyon is one of the busiest places in the park, yet few visitors hike the entire length of the canyon trail. By beginning from the lower end of the canyon, at the confluence of the Maligne and Athabasca Rivers, you'll avoid starting your hike alongside the masses, and you'll get to hike downhill on your return when you're tired. To access the lower end of the canyon, follow the spur (1 km/0.6 mi) off Maligne Lake Road to Sixth Bridge.

You will cross the **Maligne River** six times on six bridges on this hike up the canyon. Crowds will be minimal for the first hour as you hike upstream to **Fourth Bridge,** where the trail starts climbing. By the time you get to **Third Bridge,** you'll start encountering adventurous hikers coming down the canyon. Soon thereafter, you'll meet the real crowds. This is where the canyon is deepest and most spectacular, with frothing water and plunging waterfalls. Continue climbing and cross the last two bridges. At the top, you can grab a snack or lunch at the restaurant before descending back through the canyon, which will give you an alternate view from the way up.

Backpacking

Permits

Permits (C$10 pp/night) are required for backcountry camping in Jasper. **Reservations** (877/737-3783, 519/826-5391 from outside North America, reservation.pc.gc.ca, C$12) usually open for the year in January, and the Skyline books fast. For planning, download Jasper's **Backcountry Guide** (www.pc.gc.ca/). Backcountry campgrounds have bear poles provided for hanging food, water accessible nearby, cooking tables, and tenting sites. **Totem Ski Shop** (408 Connaught Dr., 780/852-3078 or 800/363-3078, totemskishop.com) rents backpacking gear.

Skyline Trail

45 kilometers (28 miles)

The **Skyline Trail** is a top-of-the-world route that crosses three high passes and the Continental Divide, with peaks in every direction. Due to the high elevation, snow lingers through most of July and wildflowers burst forth in August. Doing this route in late July to September offers the best conditions. The trail is best hiked in 3-4 days, spending 2 or 3 nights at assigned backcountry camps. While the trail maintains a fairly gentle uphill grade, it does have significant elevation change (1,411 m/4,628 ft), and the passes can be windy and cold, with conditions changing quickly to snowstorms in summer. Six backcountry camps line the route, with the middle four the best: **Little Shovel, Snowbowl, Curator,** and **Tekarra.**

It's easy to make the trail a point-to-point hike with a shuttle from **Maligne Adventures** (604 Connaught Dr., 780/852-3331 or 844/808-7177, maligneadventures.com, C$35). It runs from Jasper to the North Skyline/Signal Mountain Trailhead, where you leave your car, then to the Maligne Lake Trailhead, where your trip begins.

Mountain Biking

In addition to paved roads, many designated unpaved **bicycle trails** radiate from town. These trails also permit e-bikes. One of the most popular is the **Athabasca River Trail** (8.8 km/5.5 mi one-way), which begins at Old Fort Point and follows the river downstream to a point below Maligne Canyon. Cyclists are particularly prone to sudden bear encounters; make noise when passing through heavily wooded areas.

The **Lake Edith Shoreline Loop** (4.4 km/2.7 mi) on Trails 4e, 7, and 4g, is great for families and beginner riders. Intermediate riders often head to **Pyramid Bench** for a network of technical mountain bike trails.

The park produces the **Mountain Biking Trail Guide,** which describes designated trails; pick it up at the information center and all local sport shops or download it from the Parks Canada website (www.pc.gc.ca).

Bike rental outlets include **Vicious Cycle** (630 Connaught Dr., 780/852-1111, www.visciouscanada.com, 9am-6pm Sun.-Thurs., 9am-7pm Fri.-Sat.), **The Bench Bike Shop** (606 Patricia St., 780/852-7768, www.thebenchbikeshop.com, 10am-6pm daily), and **The Boathouse** at the **Fairmont Jasper Park Lodge** (780/852-3301, 10am-8pm daily). Expect to pay C$20-50 per hour or C$50-100 for a full day; rates include a helmet and lock.

★ **Rafting**

Within the park, the **Athabasca** and **Sunwapta Rivers** make for splashy whitewater experiences. On the Athabasca River, the **Mile 5 Run** is a gentle **scenic float** anyone can enjoy. Further upstream, some guides offer a trip that begins below Athabasca Falls, on a frothy family-friendly stretch of **Class II** river that passes through a narrow canyon. For **Class III** thrills, the boulder-strewn rapids of the Sunwapta provide a roller-coaster ride, with the biggest water in early summer.

Most rafting companies transport you to and from downtown hotels. Trips last 2-4 hours, run mid-May to September, and cost C$74-120. Here are a few recommended outfitters:

- **Maligne Rafting Adventures** (604 Connaught Dr., 780/852-3331 or 844/808-7177, www.raftjasper.com)

- **Rocky Mountain River Guides** (618 Connaught Dr., 780/852-3777, rmriverguides.com)

- **Jasper's Whitewater Rafting Co.** (618 Connaught Dr., 780/852-7238, whitewaterraftingjasper.com)

- **Jasper Raft Tours** (611 Patricia St.,

780/852-2665 or 888/553-5628, www.jasperrafttours.com)

Paddling

Several lakes make for good paddling destinations. **Lake Annette** and adjacent **Lake Edith** are good for beginning paddlers and families due to their protected waters. You can launch **kayaks, canoes,** and **paddleboards** from their picnic area beaches. Several larger lakes also work for paddling, although they aren't as protected: **Medicine Lake, Pyramid Lake,** and **Maligne Lake.**

Maligne Lake Boat Rentals (www.banffjaspercollection.com, 9am-5pm daily June-mid-Sept., C$40-75/hr, C$165-200/day) rents single or double kayaks and canoes on a first-come, first-served basis from the Boat House on Maligne Lake. The **Fairmont Jasper Park Lodge** (Old Lodge Rd., 780/852-3301, www.jasper-park-lodge.com, 10am-6pm daily May-mid-Oct., C$45-75/hr) rents single and double kayaks, canoes, paddleboards, and pedal boats from the Boathouse on Lac Beauvert. **Pure Outdoors** (632 Connaught Dr., 708/852-4717 or 888/852-4717, pureoutdoors.ca, 8am-8pm daily May-Oct., shorter hours in winter, C$40-80 for half- to full-day) rents paddleboards, kayaks, and canoes. They offer delivery to select lakes for an extra fee.

Paddlers can tour Maligne Lake and overnight at four **backcountry shoreline campgrounds.** The campgrounds are equipped with bear food storage lockers, firepits, picnic tables, pit toilets, and tent sites. Beginner paddlers and families may want to overnight at the campground at **Hidden Cove** (4 km/2.5 mi). Stronger experienced paddlers can stay at **Fisherman's Bay** (13 km/8 mi); it's only 2 km (1.2 mi) farther to Spirit Island. **Permits** (C$10 pp/night) are required. Pick them up at the backcountry office in the information center in Jasper or better yet, apply for an advanced reservation. **Reservations** (877/737-3783,

519/826-5391 from outside North America, reservation.pc.gc.ca, C$12) usually open for the year in January.

The lake is 22 km (13.7 mi) long, so you'll need to keep an eye on the weather. Sudden winds can crop up, bringing large waves to the lake. Plan to stay along the shoreline for the safest route, and paddle in early morning for calmer water.

Swimming

On warm summer days, the sandy beach at **Annette Lake**'s picnic area attracts swimmers. **Lake Edith** is also good for swimming near the picnic area. Due to the smaller size of these lakes, the water warms up more than in the larger ones, but they are still chilly.

Golfing

The world-famous **Fairmont Jasper Park Lodge Golf Course** (1 Old Lodge Rd., 780/852-3301, www.jaspermountaingolf.com, daily June-Sept., greens fee C$209-225) was designed by golf-course architect Stanley Thompson. It is consistently ranked as one of the top 10 courses in Canada. The 18-hole, 6,670-yard course takes in the contours of the Athabasca River Valley as it hugs the banks of turquoise-colored Lac Beauvert. Facilities include a driving range, club rentals, a restaurant, and a café.

Horseback Riding

On the benchlands immediately behind the town of Jasper is **Jasper Riding Stables** (1 Pyramid Lake Rd., 780/852-7433, jasperstables.com, May-mid-Oct., C$57-148). The stables offer one-, two-, and three-hour guided rides with views of the Athabasca River Valley. **Jasper Park Stables** (Fairmont Jasper Park Lodge, Old Lodge Rd., 780/852-6476, jasperparkstables.com, mid-May-mid-Oct., C$57-104) offers 1-, 1.5-, and 2-hour rides. Wear long pants and sturdy shoes.

In summer, **overnight pack trips** consist of 4-6 hours of riding per day in the mountains combined with backcountry lodge stays. Contact **Skyline Trail Rides** (780/852-4215, www.skylinetrail.com), **Tonquin Valley Backcountry Lodge** (780/852-3909, www.tonquinvalley.com), or **Tonquin Amethyst Lake Lodge** (780/852-1188, tonquinadventures.com) for details on available pack trips.

Winter Sports
Winter is a quiet time in the park, when hotels reduce rates by 40-70 percent. But the snow fun comes alive with alpine skiing and snowboarding, cross-country skiing on groomed trails, ice skating on frozen lakes, horse-drawn sleigh rides, and tours through the enchanting ice in Maligne Canyon.

Marmot Basin
The skiing at **Marmot Basin** (780/852-3816 or 866/952-3816, www.skimarmot.com, Dec.-late Apr., C$105 adults, C$85 kids) is highly underrated. The resort has nine lifts, including the longest detachable quad in Alberta. The modern facilities are in great shape. Groomed runs, open bowls, and tree glades provide the fun across two mountain faces. Marmot doesn't get the crowds of the three alpine resorts in Banff National Park, so lift lines are rare. Rentals are available at the resort or in town at **Totem Ski Shop** (408 Connaught Dr., 780/852-3078 or 800/363-3078, totemskishop.com).

Cross-Country Skiing and Snowshoeing
An extensive network (300 km (185 mi) of summer hiking trails is designated for skiers, with about one-third of it groomed. The four main areas of trails are along **Pyramid Lake Road,** around **Maligne Lake,** in the **Athabasca Falls area,** and at **Whistlers Campground.** A booklet available at the park information center and online (www.pc.ga.ca) details each trail and its difficulty. Weather forecasts and avalanche-hazard reports are also posted.

Rental packages are available from the rental shop at the **Fairmont Jasper Park Lodge** (780/852-3301, www.fairmont.com/jasper) and **Totem Ski Shop** (408 Connaught Dr., 780/852-3078 or 800/363-3078, totemskishop.com).

Entertainment and Events
Nightlife
The most popular nightspot in town is the **Atha-B** (Athabasca Hotel, 510 Patricia St., 780/852-3386, www.athabascahotel.com, 11am-2am daily), which hosts bands some nights and attracts all the seasonal workers. The hotel that houses it also has a large **sports bar** with a big screen TV and a pool table. The **De'd Dog Bar and Grill** (Astoria Hotel, 404 Connaught Dr., 780/852-4328, www.deddog.com, noon-1am daily) is a large, dimly lit sports bar with pool tables that's frequented by locals who drink copious amounts of beer.

Right downtown, the **Whistle Stop Pub** (Whistlers Inn, 105 Miette Ave., 780/852-3361, www.whistlersinn.com, 11am-1am daily) has a great atmosphere, with a classic wooden bar, big screen TVs, and sometimes live music. The **Downstream Lounge** (620 Connaught Dr., 780/852-9449, www.downstreamjasper.ca, 5pm-2am daily) has live music Friday and Saturday.

Festivals and Events
Celebrate **National Indigenous Peoples Day** in late June. The one-day festival features drumming and traditional dances. It takes place on the lawn in front of the information center.

Canada Day (July 1) celebrations begin with a pancake breakfast followed by a flag-raising ceremony in front of the information center and a parade along Connaught Drive. Live entertainment and fireworks end the day.

The **Jasper Heritage Rodeo,** on the second or third weekend of August, attracts pro cowboys from across Canada. Apart from the seven traditional rodeo events, the fun includes the ever-popular stick-pony parade and a kids' rodeo. Most of the action takes place at the Jasper

Heritage Rodeo Grounds, at the base of the road up to the Jasper Skytram.

For nine days in October, Jasper celebrates the **Dark Sky Festival** (jasperdarksky.travel) with astronomy-themed talks and events that highlight Jasper's status as an International Dark Sky Preserve. In late January, **Jasper in January** (jasperinjanuary.com) is a two-week celebration that includes fireworks, special evenings at local restaurants, a street party, discounted lift tickets at Marmot Basin, and all the activities associated with winter.

Food

Connaught Drive and Patricia Street are lined with cafés and restaurants. Menus are reasonably priced. Make reservations for dinner in summer.

Canadian

★ **Harvest** (616 Patricia St., 780/852-9676, harvestfoodanddrink.ca, 9am-9pm daily, C$14-25) is a casual, contemporary restaurant that serves up excellent food.

Breakfasts include mashed avocado on toast, Belgian waffles, and a delicious kale and potato hash topped with a poached egg and hollandaise sauce. Lunch has inventive bowls. The dinner menu is loaded with tapas-style choices designed for sharing: cheese boards and charcuterie. Ingredients are fresh and simply prepared, making for a tasty night out.

International

For Greek fare such as charbroiled chicken or lamb souvlaki, head to **Something Else Steakhouse** (621 Patricia St., 780/852-3850, somethingelsejasper. com, 11am-10pm daily, C$20-40) where portions are generous. The large menu includes a lineup of signature steaks and Greek-style pizza.

Italian specialties are the mark of the **Alba Restaurant** (610 Patricia St., 780/852-4002, albarestaurant.ca, 5pm-9pm daily, C$20-32), upstairs in the Patricia Centre Mall. Sit in the bright, breezy interior or on a narrow terrace

ceremony with Sunchild First Nation at National Indigenous Peoples Day

bedecked in flowers. Look for contemporary pastas made fresh, braised lamb shank, and a dark chocolate cheesecake to finish.

Directly behind the park information center, **Raven Bistro** (504 Patricia St., 780/852-5151, theravenbistro.com, 5pm-10pm Mon.-Fri., 9am-1pm and 5pm-10pm Sat.-Sun., C$26-46) is a small eatery that covers all the bases, with dishes showing influences from around the world. Vegetarian choices include a delicious curried vegetable strudel. If a daily feature is offered, you're in for a treat, with the chef sourcing seasonal seafood and game to create a memorable dish. Adding to the appeal is the fact that most bottles of wine are under C$60.

★ **Syrahs** (606 Patricia St., 780/852-4559, www.syrahsofjasper.com, 5:30pm-9pm daily, C$26-49) is an elegantly casual eatery offering a wide range of uncomplicated dishes using Canadian game and produce prepared with Swiss-influenced cooking styles. Start with portobello

mushroom and red wine bisque, then choose between dishes such as elk tenderloin or grilled sturgeon. Syrahs also has one of Jasper's most impressive wine lists.

The Korean family who runs **Kimchi House** (407 Patricia St., 780/852-5022, kimchihousejasper.com, noon-8pm daily, C$15-28) is always friendly and welcoming, whether you are sitting down for a meal or popping in for takeout. The menu is traditionally Korean, with almost everything made from scratch in-house and plenty of vegetarian entrées.

Seafood

Fiddle River Restaurant (upstairs at 620 Connaught Dr., 780/852-3032, fiddleriverrestaurant.com, 5pm-9:30pm daily, C$24-43) is a long way from the ocean and not particularly coastal in feel, but it offers a wide variety of seafood. Trout, arctic char, red snapper, lobster, and halibut all make regular appearances on the blackboard menu. For non-seafood lovers, there are choices such as bison lasagna and wild game meatloaf.

Casual and Family-Style Dining

One of the original family-style restaurants in Jasper is the **L&W Restaurant** (701 Patricia St. at Hazel Ave., 780/852-4114, landwjasper.ca, 11am-10pm daily, C$13-32). It features a small outside patio facing the street and plenty of greenery that brings to life an otherwise ordinary spot. Lunch has salads, burgers, and sandwiches, while dinner serves steak, fish, and pizza. Both menus have a few classic Greek dishes, too.

Pizza lovers congregate at **Jasper Pizza Place** (402 Connaught Dr., 780/852-3225, www.jasperpizza.ca, 3pm-midnight daily, C$16-27). It's a large and noisy restaurant with bright furnishings, a concrete floor, exposed heating ducts, and walls lined with photos from Jasper's earliest days. The wood-fired oven produces thin-crust pizzas with adventurous toppings. On the same side of town, but one street back, **Lou Lou's Pizzeria** (407 Patricia St.,

780/852-3373, loulous.ca, 9am-9pm daily, C$15-25) is a more casual, family-friendly place with long rows of tables inside and another outside on a covered patio. It's an order-at-the-counter place with excellent pizza, breakfast served until 2pm, poutine variations, and a few Chinese dishes.

Jasper's oldest restaurant, **Papa George's** (Astoria Hotel, 404 Connaught Dr., 780/852-2260, www.papageorgesjasper.com, 7:30am-2pm and 4pm-10pm daily, C$10-38) has been dishing up hearty fare to park visitors since 1925. The setting is old-fashioned, with east-facing windows taking in the panorama of distant mountain peaks.

Coffeehouses and Cafés

You'll smell the wonderful aroma of freshly baked bread even before entering ★ **Bear's Paw Bakery** (4 Pyramid Rd., 780/852-3233, www.bearspawbakery.com, 6am-6pm daily, C$10). The European-style breads (the muesli loaf is a delight) are perfect for a picnic lunch, but not as tempting as the cakes, pastries, and oversized scones. Operated by the same owners, **The Other Paw** (610 Connaught Dr., 780/852-2253, 7am-6pm daily, C$8-12) has a slightly more contemporary feel but more of the same great baked goods, as well as delicious salads.

SnowDome Coffee Bar (607 Patricia St., 780/852-3852, snowdome.coffee, 7am-8pm daily) is tucked away downstairs in the Coin Clean Laundry but still manages to pour what many locals claim is the best coffee in town. The muffins and banana bread are baked daily on-site.

Well worth searching out is **Wicked Cup** (Maligne Lodge, 912 Connaught Dr., 780/852-1942, www.wickedcup.ca, 7am-2:30pm daily, C$9-12), on the west side of downtown, for the extensive selection of coffee drinks, teas, and breakfast and lunch items. Seating is inside or out on a heated deck, and the café is far

---

Top to bottom: Bear's Paw Bakery; L&W Restaurant; Syrahs

enough from downtown that it is usually crowd-free.

Fairmont Jasper Park Lodge

Across the river from downtown, the **Fairmont Jasper Park Lodge** (1 Old Lodge Rd., 780/852-3301, www.fairmont.com/jasper) offers a choice of casual or elegant dining in several restaurants and lounges. Across from the reception area is a dedicated dining **reservation desk** (780/852-6052, 11am-8pm daily summer); reservations are required for ORSO Trattoria

Downstairs in the lower promenade, **ORSO Trattoria** (7am-11am and 5pm-10pm daily, reservations required, C$68-98) is a stylish room open for a breakfast buffet (C$35) throughout summer that gets very busy. ORSO's personality really shines in the evening, when the menu turns Italian, and you can select seasonal specialties from a three-course menu that includes gnocchi and steaks.

On the Beauvert Promenade, the tiny **Oka Sushi** (4pm-9pm daily) rolls fresh fish into delectable morsels of sushi. **The Emerald Lounge** (11am-midnight daily, C$16-40) has table settings of various configurations; seating also sprawling along an outdoor deck, from where you can gaze over picturesque Lac Beauvert to Whistlers Mountain over cocktails. The all-day menu features a wide range of choices, including appetizers, light meals, and entrées. Adjacent to the lounge, the **Great Hall Gastropub** (7am-11pm daily, C$13-44) serves breakfast, lunch, and dinner à la carte. Seating is available around the lobby and, in summer, on the patio.

Outside Downtown

With so many dining choices in downtown Jasper, it may be surprising to know that there are a couple fine restaurants scattered elsewhere in the park.

One of Jasper's best restaurants, ★ **Becker's Gourmet Restaurant** (Becker's Chalets, 780/852-3535, beckerschalets.com, 8am-11am and 5:30pm-9pm daily May-mid-Oct., C$28-45) has seating in a cozy dining room, where the atmosphere is intimate, and in the adjacent enclosed conservatory, with views of Mount Kerkeslin and the Athabasca River. This restaurant is a throwback to days gone by, with an ever-changing menu of seasonal game and produce, including vegetarian entrées. At C$16 per person, the breakfast buffet is one of the best dining deals in the park. The restaurant sits south of town (6 km/3.7 mi) along the Icefields Parkway.

The dining room at historic **Tekarra Lodge** (780/852-4624, tekarrarestaurant.ca, 8am-10:30am and 5pm-9:30pm daily mid-May-early Oct., C$13-40) specializes in local and seasonal foods. The setting may be mountain-style rustic, but the cooking appeals to modern preferences with small plates, shared plates, and homestyle main courses. Located on Highway 93A, the lodge is a five-minute drive from downtown Jasper.

Accommodations and Camping

Summer is the busiest season, especially July and August. Rooms are at their highest prices during this time, and advanced reservations are strongly advised if you want something specific. Booking 9-12 months ahead for lodge rooms and cabins is imperative; make your reservations at least a year in advance for stays in July or August.

Hostels

Jasper Downtown Hostel (400 Patricia St., 780/852-2000, www.jasperdowntownhostel.ca, dorm beds C$35-65, private rooms C$90-260) is perfectly located one block from the bus depot/train station. It has been custom built for backpackers, with lots of common space including a kitchen, lounge area, and outdoor seating. Dorms range from two beds to eight, and each bed has its own privacy curtain, light, locker, and charging station. Private rooms have shared bathrooms or en suite bathrooms and range from two bunk beds to a two-bedroom unit.

HI-Canada (778/328-2220 or 866/762-4122, www.hihostels.ca) operates two hostels in the Jasper Townsite area. Within walking distance of downtown, **HI-Jasper** (708 Sleepy Hollow Rd., 587/870-2395, C$30-58 members, C$33-62 nonmembers, private rooms from C$116) opened in 2019. It's a three-story facility with a maximum of four beds in any dorm, with some set aside as women-only. Private and family rooms have en suite bathrooms. Communal facilities include a kitchen, two dining areas, a lounge with fireplace, a café, a game room, and an outdoor area with a barbecue and firepit. The rustic **HI-Maligne Canyon** (Maligne Lake Rd., June-Sept., members C$36, nonmembers C$40) is beside the Maligne River and a short walk from the canyon. The 24 dorm beds are in two cabins; other amenities include electricity, a kitchen, and a dining area.

Cabins

★ **Becker's Chalets** (6 km/3.7 mi south of Jasper on Icefields Pkwy., 780/852-3779, www.beckerschalets.com, May-mid-Oct., C$180-515) is spread along a picturesque bend of the Athabasca River. This historic lodging took its first guests in the 1940s and continues to be a park favorite for many guests who make staying here an annual ritual. Chalets each have a kitchenette, gas fireplace, and double bed; a few are located on the riverfront. Deluxe log duplexes feature all the modern conveniences, and one unit sleeps eight. Becker's also boasts one of the park's finest restaurants.

★ **Alpine Village** (780/852-3285, www.alpinevillagejasper.com, late Apr.-mid-Oct., C$250-550) is laid out across well-manicured lawns, and all its buildings are surrounded by colorful gardens of geraniums and petunias. You can soak away your cares in the outdoor hot tub or kick back on Adirondack chairs scattered along the Athabasca River, directly opposite the resort. Some of the cabins have a kitchen and fireplace; the larger deluxe cabins feature open plans, stone fireplaces, luxurious bathrooms, and decks with private forested views. Family cabins sleep up to five, with two beds in an upstairs loft, a fireplace, and a full kitchen. The Whistler cabins have vaulted ceilings, full kitchens, and king beds. The resort is at the junction of Highway 93A and the Icefields Parkway, south of town (3 km/1.9 mi).

Typifying a cabin camp of the 1950s, **Pine Bungalows** (2 Cottonwood Creek Rd., 780/852-3491, pinebungalows.com, May-mid-Oct., C$250-400) lies on a secluded section of the Athabasca River opposite the northern entrance to town. The least expensive units are wooden cabins with kitchens and fireplaces (most cabins face the river; numbers 1 and 3 enjoy the best views). More modern two-bedroom log cabins have heated bathroom floors and gas fireplaces. None of the cabins has TV, Wi-Fi, or telephones. A three-night minimum applies in July and August.

Patricia Lake Bungalows (Pyramid Lake Rd., 780/852-3560 or 888/499-6848, www.patricialakebungalows.com, early May-mid-Oct., C$235-550) sits beside the lake of the same name. Older cottages have kitchens and TVs; some have either a lake view or fireplace. The newest units have separate bedrooms and a balcony or patio with barbecue. Resort amenities include an outdoor hot tub. The bungalows are a five-minute drive north from Jasper (2 km/1.2 mi).

Flanking the Athabasca River, **Jasper House Bungalows** (Icefields Pkwy., 3.5 km/2.1 mi south of town, 780/852-4535 or 888/217-6939, www.jasperhouse.com, early May-mid-Oct., C$230-350) is an old-style resort complex with 56 cedar log cabins. Those at the upper end of the price range are fully self-contained and overlook the river; woodsy motel-style units have kitchenettes. Also on-site is a rustic restaurant open through the summer season for a breakfast buffet and inexpensive à la carte dinner.

Hotels and Inns

In downtown Jasper, the historic three-story brick **Athabasca Hotel** (510 Patricia St., 780/852-3386 or 877/542-8422, www. athabascahotel.com, C$100-350) dates to 1928, replacing the original structure of the same name, which was the town's first hotel. The cheapest of its 61 rooms share bathrooms and are above a noisy bar. This hotel also has more expensive rooms with vaguely Victorian decor and private bathrooms.

Also downtown, the **Astoria Hotel** (404 Connaught Dr., 780/852-3351 or 800/661-7343, www.astoriahotel.com, C$160-180 winter, C$265-285 summer) is a European-style lodge built in 1925 and has been run by the same family ever since. It was extensively renovated in 2017, but still lacks an elevator to the second story. Rooms are brightly furnished, and each has a small fridge and TV.

Southwest of downtown, **Mount Robson Inn** (902 Connaught Dr., 780/852-3327 or 855/552-7737, www. mountrobsoninn.com, C$120-450) has 80 air-conditioned rooms reminiscent of generic city hotels. On the plus side, a light breakfast is included, and the suites are a good deal relative to other Jasper accommodations; they have a fireplace or a jetted tub, sometimes both.

Pursuit (866/606-6700, www. banffjaspercollection.com) operates two hotels, both on the northern edge of town. The **Sawridge Inn** (76 Connaught Dr., C$128-400) offers 154 air-conditioned rooms built around a large atrium and indoor pool. **Chateau Jasper** (96 Geikie St., C$118-380) has 119 spacious rooms with a cozy feel. Amenities include an indoor pool, hot tub, heated underground parking, and on-site restaurant.

Top to bottom: Fairmont Jasper Park Lodge pool and deck; Alpine Village; Becker's Chalets

Lodges and Resorts

With a variety of cabin layouts and a central location, ★ **Bear Hill Lodge** (100 Bonhomme St., 780/852-3209, www. bearhilllodge.com, C$180-1,200) makes a great base camp for travelers who want the cabin experience within walking distance of downtown services. The original cabins are basic with bathrooms and gas fireplaces. Cottages and chalets are larger and more modern, and each has a wood-burning fireplace but no kitchen. The three Homestead suites, which can accommodate eight adults in private bedrooms, are more spacious and have a full kitchen. Lodge rooms are standard motel-type rooms; some come with gas fireplaces, whirlpool baths, and kitchenettes. Other on-site resort amenities include a sauna, a barbecue area, laundry facilities, and internet access.

The lure of **Tekarra Lodge** (Hwy. 93A, 1.6 km/1 mi south from downtown, 780/852-3058 or 877/532-5862, www. tekarralodge.com, mid-May-early Oct., C$240-520) is its historic log cabins and forested setting on a plateau above the confluence of the Miette and Athabasca Rivers. Each cabin has been totally modernized yet retains a cozy charm, with comfortable beds, fully equipped kitchenettes, wood-burning fireplaces, and smallish but adequate bathrooms. The spacious Tekarra Cabins are best suited for small families. Lodge rooms have queen or king beds. Amenities include an on-site restaurant open for breakfast and dinner, bike rentals, and a laundry room. From the lodge, hiking trails lead along the Athabasca River in both directions.

On Pyramid Lake north of town, **Pyramid Lake Resort** (6 km/3.7 mi up Pyramid Lake Rd., 866/606-6700, www. banffjaspercollection.com, C$148-460) has motel-style accommodations. Amenities include on-site access to water activities, with rentals for kayaks, canoes, and paddle boats. You can also rent mountain bikes, snowshoes, and ice skates to glide across the frozen lake in winter. The resort boasts a restaurant with lake views and a large barbecue area.

Fairmont Jasper Park Lodge

The ★ **Fairmont Jasper Park Lodge** (1 Old Lodge Rd., 780/852-3301 or 866/540-4454, www.fairmont.com/jasper, from C$280 winter, from C$739 summer) lies along the shore of Lac Beauvert across the Athabasca River from downtown. This is the park's original resort and its most famous. It's a sprawling property offering plenty of activities: golf, walking trails, horseback riding, canoeing, tennis, and swimming in an outdoor heated pool that remains open year-round. The main lodge features stone floors, carved wooden pillars, and a high ceiling; it also contains multiple restaurants and lounges, an activity booking desk, a fitness room, a game room, and Jasper's only covered shopping arcade.

The 441 rooms vary in configuration and are linked by paths and green space. The least expensive Fairmont Rooms are smallish and offer limited views. Set away from the lake are larger Deluxe Rooms; each has a patio or balcony. Junior Suites have a distinct country charm, and each has either a sitting room and balcony or patio with lake views. One of the most expensive options, the Lakeview Suites overlook Lac Beauvert and are backed by the 18th fairway of the golf course. Each features a patio or balcony and a fireplace.

The historic luxury cabins provide the Fairmont Jasper Park Lodge's premier accommodations. Starting from C$1,600 per night, they are among the most exclusive guest rooms in all of Canada. They have hosted true royalty (Elizabeth II) and movie royalty (Marilyn Monroe, during the filming of *River of No Return*). The smallest is the secluded and cozy Athabasca Cottage. The historically charming Point Cabin, built in 1928, features five en suite bedrooms, a kitchen with outdoor barbecue, lake views, and a massive living area anchored by a stone fireplace.

Backcountry Lodges

If you want to hike the Skyline Trail with only a day pack, then an overnight stay at **Shovel Pass Backcountry Lodge** (250/838-0972, skylinetrail.com, mid-July-Aug.) is the way to do it. This historic lodge, operated by Skyline Trail Rides, provides dinner, breakfast, and bag lunches and overnight stays in cabins with bedding, washstands, and heat. Hikers (C$280 pp/night) walk 20 km (12.6 mi) on their way to the lodge from Maligne Lake and 25.4 km (15.8 mi) on the way out to Maligne Canyon.

Miette Hot Springs Area

Miette Hot Springs Bungalows (17 km/11 mi up Miette Hot Springs Rd., 780/866-3750, miettebungalows.com, May-Sept., C$150-270) is within walking distance of the park's only hot springs. Here, lodging options consist of 1960s motel-style rooms, historic cabins, and suites in the Chalet Building. All of the cabins have kitchenettes; some of the motel rooms and chalet apartments do as well. Guest facilities include a covered barbecue area, restaurant, and laundry room.

Located at the site of a once-bustling coal-mining town, **Pocahontas Cabins** (Hwy. 16 E. and Miette Rd., 866/606-6700, www.banffjaspercollection.com, from C$99 winter, from C$359 summer) is at the bottom of the road that leads to Miette Hot Springs. Cabins come in eight styles varying from basic sleeping rooms to kitchen-equipped units; some have separate bedrooms. Each is equipped with a full kitchen and fireplace. Amenities include an outdoor pool, hot tub, playground, and barbecue area.

Hinton

Hinton is a medium-size town that lies along Yellowhead Highway (Hwy. 16) east of Jasper National Park. Staying here provides an inexpensive alternative to lodging in the park. Its highway strip is filled with motels, restaurants, fast-food places, and gas stations. Hinton is 20 km (12 mi) east of the park's east gate, about a 15-minute drive, and 70 km (43 mi) east of the town of Jasper, about a 45-minute drive.

The best value is **Pines Motel** (709 Gregg Ave., 780/865-2624 or 780/865-3125, pinesmotel.business.site, from C$130) with 22 updated rooms adjacent to the local golf course. Each room has a microwave, fridge, coffeemaker, and wireless internet.

Hinton's main street is lined with mid-priced chain motels with reliable rooms, including the **Hinton Super 8** (284 Smith St., 780/817-2228, www.wyndhamhotels.com, C$115-235) and the **Holiday Inn Express & Suites Hinton** (462 Smith St., 780/865-2048, www.ihg.com, C$135-180). Both have an indoor pool and free breakfast.

The mountain retreat ★ **Black Cat Guest Ranch** (50508 Range Rd. 271A, Hinton, 780/865-3084 or 800/859-6840, www.blackcatguestranch.ca, May-Oct., C$170-185) lies on the eastern edge of the park, surrounded by mountain wilderness. All 16 rooms have private baths and views of the mountains. Horseback riding from a nearby operator is offered during the day, and in the evening guests can relax in the large living room or hot tub. Breakfast is included.

Camping

You can reserve campsites at **Whistlers, Wapiti, Wabasso,** and **Pocahontas Campgrounds** through the **Parks Canada Campground Reservation Service** (877/737-3783, www.reservation.pc.gc.ca, C$12). Bookings usually open for the year in January, with summer dates for most of the electrical sites at Whistlers, Wapiti, and Wabasso getting snapped up fast. These three campgrounds also have less privacy due to lack of trees. Standard amenities include picnic tables, fire pits, cooking shelters, bear-proof food storage

✿ Side Trip: Mount Robson Provincial Park

At the northern end of the Canadian Rockies, spectacular **Mount Robson Provincial Park** (bcparks.ca) protects a vast wilderness of steep canyons and wide forested valleys; icy lakes, rivers, and streams; and rugged mountain peaks permanently blanketed in snow and ice. Towering over the park's western entrance is **Mount Robson** (3,954 m/12,970 ft), the highest peak in the Canadian Rockies. The park shares its eastern boundary with Jasper National Park.

The park is west of the town of Jasper along the Yellowhead Highway (Hwy. 16). At the park's western entrance is the **Mount Robson Visitor Centre** (250/566-9174, 8am-7pm daily mid-June-early Sept., 8am-5pm daily mid-May-mid-June and early Sept.-mid-Oct.).

Berg Lake

Tours
From the Jasper Townsite, you can hop on a tour with **Jasper Adventure Centre** (306 Connaught Dr., 780/852-5595 or 800/565-7547, www.jasperadventurecentre.com, 5-7 hrs, C$115-130), which combines guided train and van travel to visit Mount Robson Provincial Park.

Roadside Sights
Highway 16 enters the park from the east at **Yellowhead Pass** (1,066m/3,500 ft), on the British Columbia-Alberta border. From the pass, it's 60 km (37 mi) to the park's western boundary and the visitors center. Just west of the pass, a rest area beside picturesque **Portal Lake** is a good introduction to the park.

Continuing west, the highway passes narrow **Yellowhead Lake** at the foot of **Yellowhead Mountain,** then crosses the **Fraser River.** The Moose River drains into the Fraser at **Moose Marsh,** a good spot for watching wildlife at the southeast end of **Moose Lake.** Moose often feed here at dawn and dusk, and waterfowl are present throughout the day.

As the road descends steeply to a wide, open section of the valley, it passes the main park complex, where you'll find the visitors center, campgrounds, a gas station, and a restaurant. The sheer west face of **Mount Robson** slices skyward across a flower-filled meadow. This is as close as you can get to the peak in your car.

Backpacking Berg Lake Trail
Berg Lake Trail (19.5 km/12 mi one-way, 725 m/2,380 ft elevation gain, moderate/strenuous) is the most popular overnight hike in the Canadian Rockies. Aqua-colored **Berg Lake** lies below the north face of Mount Robson. Glaciers regularly calve into the lake, resulting in the icebergs that give the lake its name. The trailhead is 2 km (1.2 mi) north of the park's visitors center.

The trail begins by following the Robson River through dense forest to glacially fed **Kinney Lake** (4.5 km/2.8 mi), an excellent destination with picnic tables at the south end.

From the lake, the trail narrows, crossing the fast-flowing river about an hour later and climbing alongside it. The next segment, touring through the **Valley of a Thousand Falls,** is the most demanding. Views of several spectacular waterfalls, including **White Falls, Falls of the Pool,** and **Emperor Falls,** ease the relentlessly steep climb. The first glimpses of Mount Robson come soon after reaching the head of the valley, from where it's about a 20-minute walk to the outlet of turquoise **Berg Lake** (17.5 km/10.9 mi). **Berg Lake Campground** (19.5 km/12 mi) is 2 km (1.2 mi) farther. The trail continues to the **Robson Pass Campground** (23 km/14.3 mi) and up to **Robson Pass** (29 km/18 mi) on the border with Jasper National Park.

Along the route, seven **primitive campgrounds** hold 98 sites. Of these, Marmot, Berg Lake, and Rearguard Campgrounds rim Berg Lake with tremendous views of Berg Glacier and Mount Robson. Reservations for sites can be made usually starting in October for the upcoming mid-June to mid-September season; advance permits are required. Make reservations through **Discover Camping** (800/689-9025 from Canada and the U.S., 778/371-0607 from other countries, www.discovercamping.ca); the booking fee ranges C$6-18 per night. Book early, because the quota fills quickly.

Accommodations

Two lodges lie just outside the park's western boundary. **Mount Robson Mountain River Lodge** (4 km/2.5 mi west of the visitors center at the junction of Hwy. 16 and Swift Current Rd., 250/566-9899 or 888/566-9899, mtrobson.com, C$150-250) has lodge rooms and cabins alongside the Fraser River. Further west is **Mount Robson Lodge** (Hwy. 16, 250/566-4821, mountrobsonlodge.com, May-late Sept., C$140-190), home to freestanding cabins (some with kitchens) and rooms in rows of cabins.

Camping

Within the park are three auto-accessible **campgrounds** (mid-May-early Sept.), all of which have first-come, first-served sites. Robson River and Robson Meadows Campgrounds also have some reservable sites, which can be booked through **Discover Camping** (800/689-9025 from Canada and the U.S., 778/371-0607 from other countries, www.discovercamping.ca). All sites have fire pits and picnic tables, and each campground has paved wheelchair-accessible sites.

♦ **Robson River Campground** (40 sites, RV limit 32 ft, C$28-36) has 22 electrical hookup sites. Trails lead down to the river for a view of Mount Robson. Amenities include flush toilets, potable water, and hot showers.

♦ **Robson Meadows Campground** (125 sites, C$28) has an outdoor theater that hosts evening interpretive programs throughout the summer. Amenities include flush and pit toilets, potable water, and hot showers.

♦ **Lucerne Campground** (36 sites, C$22) is a primitive campground with pit toilets and hand pumps for potable water. The campground flanks the east end of Yellowhead Lake, convenient for launching nonmotorized watercraft.

Just outside the park, **Robson Shadows Campground** (Mount Robson Lodge, 5 km/3.1 mi west of the visitors center, 50 sites, 250/566-4821, mountrobsonlodge.com, May-late Sept., C$28-33) has unobstructed views of Mount Robson; some sites are riverside. The campground has flush toilets and showers but no hookups.

containers, potable water, and flush or vault toilets. Fire permits (C$9) include firewood.

Whistlers Campground (Icefields Pkwy., 2.4 km/1.5 mi south of Jasper, 781 sites, May-mid-Oct., C$23-50 tent and RV sites, C$120 oTENTiks) is the largest campground in the Canadian Rockies. It is divided into four sections: walk-in tent sites, unserviced tent and RV sites, electrical sites, sites with full hookups, and oTENTiks—large six-person tents with beds, heaters, and wooden floors. The campground has updated washroom and hot shower buildings, wide two-way roads, and hookups with electricity at 50 amps. Parks Canada puts on interpretive shows in the evenings.

At **Wapiti Campground** (Icefields Pkwy., 4.4 km/2.7 mi south of Jasper, 363 sites, year-round, C$33-44), 86 of the sites have electrical hookups, and facilities include heated bathrooms and hot showers. Sites can fit most RVs. Some sites are near the Athabasca River. Wapiti is partially open throughout winter (75 sites, mid-Oct.-early May).

Sites at **Wabasso Campground** (Wabasso Rd., 16 km/10 mi south of Jasper, 231 sites, late May-late Sept., RV limit 35 ft, C$31-40) are set among stands of spruce and aspen with some prizeworthy options along the Athabasca River. Loop D has electrical sites, and at the opposite end of the campground are 46 sites for tents only.

North of Jasper, two campgrounds sit off Yellowhead Highway (Hwy. 16) on Snaring Road, 17 km (11 mi) from town. Secluded **Snaring River Campground** (62 sites, mid-May-late Sept., RV limit 27 ft, C$25) has first-come, first-served sites that range from forested to open with views, including options along the Snaring River. Nine sites are walk-ins for tenters. Two minutes further north, the **Overflow** (late May-late Sept., C$16) is a large parking-lot zone with vault toilets, potable water, and no firepits. Most RVs can fit here. Twelve walk-in sites are for tenters only, and reservations are available for some sites.

Pocahontas Campground (Miette Hot Springs Rd., 140 sites, mid-May-early Sept., RV limit 27 ft, C$31) has easy access to Miette Hot Springs. It is located just south of Punchbowl Falls, accessed by trail from the back of B Loop. Five sites are walk-ins for tenters only. The campground is 45 km (28 mi) northeast of town, about an hour's drive.

Transportation and Services
Tourist Information
At the **Jasper Park Information Centre** (500 Connaught Dr., 780/852-6176, www.pc.gc.ca, 9am-7pm daily mid-May-mid-Sept., 10am-5pm Wed.-Sun. mid-Sept.-Oct. and Dec.-mid-May), the Parks Canada staff can answer your park questions and direct you to hikes in the immediate vicinity. Within the same building, the **Parks Canada Trail Office** (780/852-6177) has trail reports and information on backcountry camping. **Tourism Jasper** (780/852-6236, www.jasper.travel) also has a desk in the building for info on activities, where to stay, and events in town.

Emergency Services
Seton-Jasper Healthcare Centre (518 Robson St., 780/852-3344, www.albertahealthservices.ca) has a 24-hour emergency center. For other emergencies, contact the **Royal Canadian Mounted Police** (RCMP, 600 Bonhomme St., 780/852-4421).

Gas and Vehicle Charging Stations
Find gas in the Jasper Townsite along Connaught Driver: **Petro-Canada** (300 Connaught Dr.), **Shell** (638 Connaught Dr.), and **Esso** (702 Connaught Dr.). The **Jasper Train Station** (611 Connaught Dr.) and **Jasper Public Library** (500 Robson Dr.) have **electric vehicle charging stations.**

Cell Service and Internet Access

Cell service is available in the Jasper Townsite, but not for long on the Yellowhead Highway (Hwy. 16). For free Wi-Fi, you can go to the Jasper National Park Information Centre or the train station; however, plan on downloading anything you'll need before leaving home as the system can be slow.

Parking

Street-side parking is difficult to find in Jasper and limited to 15 minutes or two hours during the day—but it is free. Head east on Connaught Drive to find several parking lots on the train track side between Hazel Avenue and Aspen Avenue.

RV parking is not allowed in downtown Jasper on Connaught Drive and Patricia Street between Hazel Avenue and Pyramid Lake Road. RVs can park on **Sleepy Hollow Road** (near the off-leash pet area) and use the pedestrian underpass to walk into downtown.

Car Rentals

Several rental car companies have local agencies in Jasper: **Avis** (414 Connaught Dr., 780/852-3970, www. avis.com), **Budget** (414 Connaught Dr., 780/852-3222, www.budget.com), and **National** (607 Connaught Dr., 780/852-1117, www.nationalcar.com).

Tours

Pursuit (403/762-6700 or 866/606-6700, www.banffjaspercollection.com, C$80-130) offers a three-hour morning Discover Jasper tour that takes in Maligne Canyon with select hotel pickups in Jasper. Their eight-hour tour goes to Maligne Canyon and for a boat cruise on Maligne Lake. This is a way to visit these two destinations if you don't have a car.

Jasper Adventure Centre (611 Patricia St., 780/852-5595 or 800/565-7547, www. jasperadventurecentre.com, C$70-170) runs several summer tours. They guide wildlife-watching, sunrise photography, and Maligne Valley sightseeing experiences.

From Vancouver, **Rocky Mountaineer Vacations** (604/606-7245 or 877/460-3200, www.rockymountaineer.com, from C$1,350 pp) operates luxurious summer-only rail tours to Jasper, with an overnight en route. Glass-domed windows allow for big views of the scenery. Two of their train tours go to Jasper, one via Whistler and the other via Kamloops.

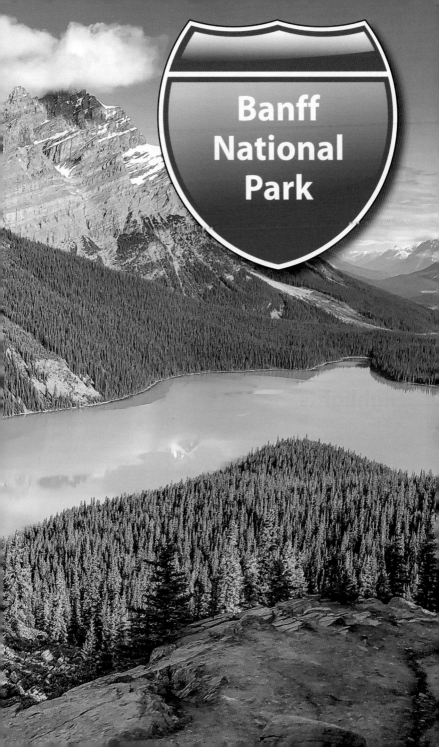

Banff
National
Park

Highlights

★ **Drive Icefields Parkway:** Cruise down the Banff section of this famed road for a mountain experience you'll never forget (page 123).

★ **Enjoy the views at Bow Summit:** From this high pass, you can walk to overlooks of turquoise **Peyto Lake** (page 125).

★ **Hike to Parker Ridge:** Climb through wildflowers on this trail overlooking the Saskatchewan Glacier as it spills from the Columbia Icefield (page 127).

★ **Snap photos at Lake Louise:** Capture the beauty of this glacial lake rimmed by icy peaks (page 131).

★ **Overnight at Fairmont Chateau Lake Louise:** Spend the night in this storybook hotel whose windows look out on captivating scenery (page 133).

★ **Admire Moraine Lake:** This cloudy blue body of water is tucked at the base of the serrated Ten Peaks (page 133).

★ **Climb Fairview Mountain and Saddleback:** Revel at the spectacular views on one of the few walk-up summits in the park (page 136).

★ **Visit Fairmont Banff Springs:** This elegant hotel is reminiscent of a castle—but with the added perk of hot spring pools (page 150).

★ **Take a ride on the Banff Gondola:** Whisk your way up to mountaintop views overlooking Banff (page 150).

★ **Stop and smell the flowers at Sunshine Meadows:** Stroll through these alpine wildflower meadows in mid-summer to relish their fragile blossoms (page 152 and 155).

Banff National Park

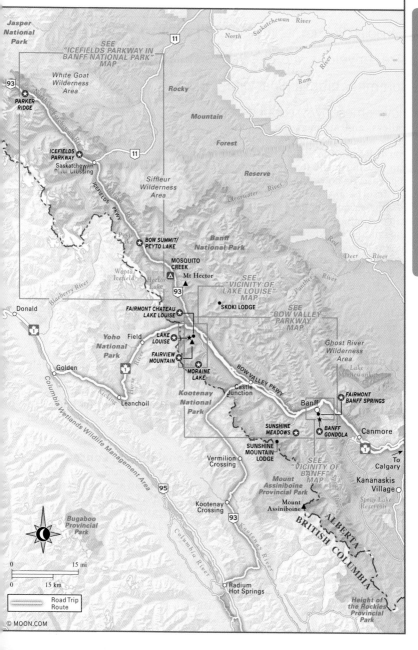

Jasper National Park

White Goat Wilderness Area

93

PARKER RIDGE

11

North Saskatchewan River

Rocky

Mountain

Forest

Reserve

North Saskatchewan River

Ram River

Clearwater River

ICEFIELDS PARKWAY

Saskatchewan River Crossing

ICEFIELDS PKWY

Siffleur Wilderness Area

Peyto Lake

BOW SUMMIT/ PEYTO LAKE

Banff National Park

Deer River

Red Deer River

Wapta Icefield

Blueberry River

Hector Lake

MOSQUITO CREEK

Mt Hector

93

SEE "VICINITY OF LAKE LOUISE" MAP

Panther River

Donald

1

FAIRMONT CHATEAU LAKE LOUISE

SKOKI LODGE

SEE "BOW VALLEY PARKWAY" MAP

Yoho National Park

Field

LAKE LOUISE

FAIRVIEW MOUNTAIN

Ghost River Wilderness Area

Golden

1

MORAINE LAKE

BOW VALLEY PKWY

Castle Junction

Lake Minnewanka

Columbia Wetlands Wildlife Management Area

Kicking Horse River

Leanchoil

Kootenay National Park

FAIRMONT BANFF SPRINGS

Banff

Canmore

SUNSHINE MEADOWS

BANFF GONDOLA

1

Vermilion Crossing

SUNSHINE MOUNTAIN LODGE

SEE "VICINITY OF BANFF" MAP

To Calgary

95

Mount Assiniboine Provincial Park

Kananaskis Village

Kootenay Crossing

93

Mount Assiniboine

Spray Lake Reservoir

ALBERTA

BRITISH COLUMBIA

Bugaboo Provincial Park

Columbia River

Kootenay River

Radium Hot Springs

Height of the Rockies Provincial Park

0   15 mi

0   15 km

Road Trip Route

© MOON.COM

Banff National Park is the crown of the parks in the Canadian Rockies. Its immense size envelops ice-chewed summits, high alpine wildflower meadows, scooped-out valleys, and mesmerizing turquoise lakes. Mountaineering and hiking get you to divine scenery, and road-tripping can take in equally stunning sightseeing. Historic hotels, mountain towns, ski resorts, and backcountry lodges offer base camps for once-in-a-lifetime explorations. Before the development, though, the Blackfoot, Tsuut'ina, and Stoney Nakoda First Nations ventured into this area seasonally to hunt, fish, and marvel at the landscapes.

Two roadways, the spectacular Icefields Parkway and the scenic Bow Valley Parkway, escort visitors to incomparable sights of mountains and glacial lakes. This accessibility is one of the park's assets, for anyone can enjoy its roadside wonders. For those looking to explore the wilds, massive sections of the park can only be explored by trail or mountaineering, which is often the way to see grizzly bears, bighorn sheep, mountain goats, and wolves.

Hikers especially get treated to Banff's wonders. Tendrils of trails trot along thundering rivers and climb into alpine wildflower meadows. They top out on high passes or ridges where rugged icy peaks spread in all directions. In winter, world-class resorts attract skiers and snowboarders for the seasonal beauty that snow delivers.

The famed mountain towns of Banff and Lake Louise attract visitors for their amenities: historic hotels, hot springs, and dining for all palates. But it's their surroundings that keep people coming back, year after year: the blue-green lakes, the wildlife, and the peaks soaring above.

Planning Your Time

While planning your trip to **Banff National Park** (403/762-1550 or 403/522-3833, www.pc.gc.ca), consult with the park website on updates for permits, reservations, road construction, trail conditions, and potential closures.

A visit of **3-5 days** will give you a taste of Banff; hikers especially will leave wanting more. In three days, you'll be able to drive the Icefields Parkway, go on a couple of short hikes, see Lake Louise and Moraine Lake, and enjoy Banff Townsite. One or two more days will give you enough time to do longer hikers while still taking in the highlights.

Summer packs in crowds with nearly half of Banff's four million annual visitors coming in July and August. Lodging rates are at their highest and **dinner reservations** are imperative. Early fall brings ideal hiking temperatures and the yellows of the larch needles. Late spring is the time to see grizzly sows with cubs, spotted elk fawns, and young gangly moose followed by the early blossoms of wildflowers. In winter, world-class resorts crank up their lifts for skiing and snowboarding, but the area is magical even for non-skiers.

Seasonal Driving Concerns

The park's main roads, including the Icefields Parkway, are open year-round; however, expect snow October through May. (The park roads are plowed during winter.) All-season or snow tires are best for travel here, and you should carry chains for icy conditions, when they may be required.

The Icefields Parkway is often closed for short periods in winter for avalanche control. Check road conditions in Banff or Lake Louise before setting out. The Parks Canada website has current

One Day in Banff National Park

Morning

Starting from the town of **Banff,** rise before dawn and head to **Moraine Lake.** Plan on arriving before 6am to ensure a parking spot. Watch the first rays of light hit the surrounding mountains. Then head up to **Lake Louise.** Lace up your hiking boots for a **hike** to **Lake Agnes,** where you can enjoy a snack at the delightful teahouse.

Afternoon

Drive north up the **Icefields Parkway,** stopping at **Bow Lake** for the view. Continue to **Bow Summit** to overlook turquoise **Peyto Lake.** Return to Banff to wander through the shops of **Banff Avenue.** Explore local history at the **Whyte Museum of the Canadian Rockies.**

Evening

Enjoy dinner at the iconic **Fairmont Banff Springs hotel** by splurging at **1888 Chop House.** After dinner, take advantage of the long days of summer to enjoy a late evening stroll or drive along **Vermilion Lakes.**

---

weather conditions and road reports. You can also call **Alberta Roads** (855/391-9743) or check online (511.alberta.ca). And be sure to fill up with gas; no services are available on the parkway between November and April.

Best Route Through the Park

The curvy **Bow Valley Parkway** in southern Banff and **Icefields Parkway** in northern Banff are the best scenic routes in the park. Icefields Parkway is the only way to travel through the northern section of the park.

Reservations and Where to Stay

The park has two year-round towns to make your base camp. **Banff** is the larger of the two and is big and busy enough to seem urban if not for the surrounding mountains. The smaller **Lake Louise** is closer to the Icefields Parkway, but both locations are convenient for visiting the park. A smattering of lodges and cabins are sprinkled in between. You can book one accommodation for your entire stay or spend an equal number of nights in Banff and Lake Louise.

Make lodging reservations for July and August trips a **year** in advance. For off-season visits, make reservations **6-9 months** in advance if your heart is set on staying at a specific place. Otherwise, you can usually get reservations a week to a month in advance. Plan to book tours at the same time you make reservations.

Getting There

Car

From Calgary

From **Calgary,** it's 128 km (80 mi) west to the town of Banff on the Trans-Canada Highway, a drive of 1.5 hours. Lake Louise is 56 km (35 mi) northwest of Banff along the Trans-Canada Highway 1, a 45-minute drive. It's a little bit longer if you take the quieter Bow Valley Parkway (Hwy. 1A).

From Jasper

From the town of **Jasper,** the Icefields Parkway leads 230 km (145 mi) south to Lake Louise, a three-hour drive without stops. At the end of the parkway, merge onto Trans-Canada heading south for a short while to the exit for Lake Louise. To reach Banff, stay on Trans-Canada south for 56 km (35 mi), another 45 minutes. Driving between the town of Jasper and the town of Banff, a distance of 290 km (180 mi), usually takes four hours without stops.

From Golden and Yoho National Park

From **Golden,** the town to the west of **Yoho National Park,** take the Trans-Canada Highway east for 134 km (83 mi) to the town of Banff, a drive of 1.5 hours. En route, you'll pass Lake Louise, which is 83 km (52 mi) from Golden, or just under an hour's drive.

From Kootenay National Park

From **Kootenay National Park,** take Highway 93 north to Castle Junction and go east on the Trans-Canada Highway to reach the Banff Townsite. From the eastern park boundary (along the Continental Divide), it's a 35-km (22-mi), 30-minute drive. From **Radium Hot Springs,** the 136-km (85-mi) drive takes a little less than two hours.

To reach Lake Louise, turn north at Castle Junction onto Trans-Canada. From Kootenay's east boundary, the 36-km (22-mi) drive will take 30 minutes. From Radium Hot Springs, the 133-km (83-mi) drive will take just under two hours.

Air

The closest airport with international service is **Calgary International Airport** (YYC, 2000 Airport Rd. NE, Calgary, 403/735-1200, www.yyc.com). Car rentals are available. Additionally, two **shuttle services** connect with Banff National Park from the Calgary airport, running multiple trips daily. The **Banff Airporter** (403/762-3330 or 888/449-2901, www.banffairporter.com, adults from C$138 rt) goes to Canmore and Banff Townsite. **Brewster Express** (403/762-6700 or 866/606-6700, www.banffjaspercollection.com, daily May-Oct., adults from C$148 rt) stops in Banff, then continues to Lake Louise. This shuttle delivers guests to all major

Banff hotels as well as the **Brewster Transportation Centre** (100 Gopher St.), a five-minute walk from downtown Banff. For either shuttle, be sure to reserve seats in advance.

Bus and Shuttle

The Banff-based **Brewster Express** (403/762-6700 or 866/606-6700, www.banffjaspercollection.com, daily May-Oct., adults from C$148 rt) is the main carrier from Calgary International Airport, to Calgary, Banff, and Lake Louise. You can get picked up or dropped off at many lodges along the way.

Sun Dog Tours (414 Connaught St., Jasper, 780/852-4056 or 888/786-3641, www.sundogtours.com, year-round) runs a shuttle between Banff, Lake Louise, and Jasper. One-way adult rates start at C$30 to go between Banff and Lake Louise; between Lake Louise and Jasper starts at C$70. Discounted rates are available for children.

Visiting the Park

Entrances and Fees

Banff National Park has two **entrance stations.** The **eastern entrance** is on the Trans-Canada Highway, about 5 km (3 mi) west of Canmore. The **southern entrance,** officially named the Niblock Gate, is at the south end of the Icefields Parkway (Hwy. 93), 4 km (2.5 mi) north of Lake Louise. If you are coming to Banff via Jasper, Yoho, or Kootenay, your pass from those parks is also valid for Banff.

A **one-day pass** (C$20 family/vehicle, C$10 adults, C$9 seniors, kids 17 and younger free) is required. It is valid until 4pm the day following its purchase; you can purchase as many days as you will need for your trip. The pass is valid also for Kootenay, Yoho, and Jasper National Parks.

It may be more economical to purchase an annual **Discovery Pass** (C$140 family/vehicle, C$70 adults, C$60 seniors). It is good for entry into national parks and national historic sites across Canada for one year.

The Discovery Pass can be purchased in advance from the Parks Canada website or in person. All passes can be bought at park gates, the visitors centers in Banff and Lake Louise, and at campground kiosks.

Visitors Centers

Banff Visitor Centre

In the Banff Townsite, the **Banff Visitor Centre** (224 Banff Ave., Banff, 403/762-1550, www.pc.gc.ca, 9am-5pm daily) has information on the park and activities in the town of Banff. You can also pick up maps and brochures. Free slideshows and videos about the park are shown. On the right-hand side of the large room is a row of desks staffed by Parks Canada employees, who can answer queries regarding Banff's natural wonders, trail closures, and road conditions. **Banff & Lake Louise Tourism** (www.banfflakelouise.com) also has staff on hand to answer questions.

If you haven't already done so, you can purchase a park pass here, or check for available backcountry campsites. A parking lot is on the south side of the building, but the visitors center is within walking distance of many hotels in town.

Lake Louise Visitor Centre

In Lake Louise, the **Lake Louise Visitor Centre** (201 Village Rd., Lake Louise, 403/522-3833, www.pc.gc.ca, 9am-5pm daily) has park information, exhibits, maps, and brochures. The center's theater shows videos and slideshows. **Banff & Lake Louise Tourism** (www.banfflakelouise.com) also has a desk for information inside. Look for the taxidermy female grizzly and read her fascinating but sad story. Backpacking permits are available, and you can get updates on trail and road conditions. Parking is in the Samson Mall parking lot or across the street behind the gas station; the latter is best for RVs.

Icefields Parkway

The **Icefields Parkway** (230 km/143 mi), which runs between Lake Louise and Jasper, is one of the most scenic, exciting, and inspiring mountain roads ever built. From Lake Louise this paved route parallels the Continental Divide, following in the shadow of the highest, most rugged mountains in the Canadian Rockies. The attractions, restaurants, and lodgings in this section are listed from south to north.

Although the road is steep and winding in places, it has a wide shoulder, making it ideal for an extended bike trip. Allow seven days to pedal north from Banff to Jasper, staying at hostels or camping along the route. This is the preferable direction to travel by bike because the elevation at the town of Jasper is more than 500 meters (1,640 ft) lower than either Banff or Lake Louise. (For more information on the northern half of the Icefields Parkway, see page 76.)

(For more information on the northern half of the Icefields Parkway, see page 76.)

TOP EXPERIENCE

★ Driving the Icefields Parkway

From Lake Louise in the south to Sunwapta Pass in the north, the **Banff National Park portion** (125 km/78 mi) of the Icefields Parkway (Hwy. 93) occupies just over half of the entire distance of the parkway. The road continues to the Columbia Icefield in Jasper National Park. It takes about two hours to drive straight through, but it's likely you'll want to spend at least a day, probably more, stopping at the viewpoints, hiking the trails, watching the abundant wildlife, and just generally enjoying one of the world's most magnificent landscapes. Along the section within Banff National Park are two lodges, three hostels, three campgrounds, and one gas station.

BANFF NATIONAL PARK

Icefields Parkway in Banff National Park

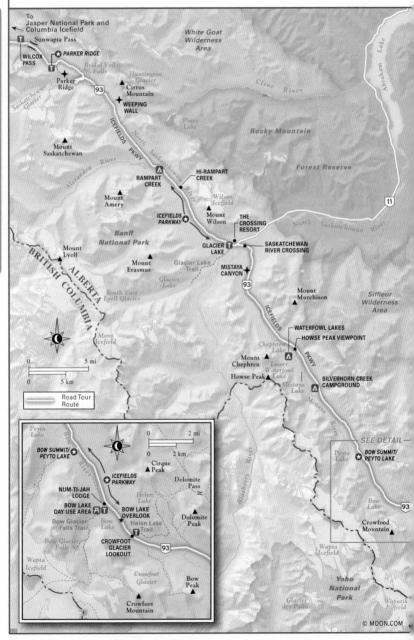

© MOON.COM

Sights
Wapta Icefield

High along peaks on the west side of the of the Icefields Parkway, you can get glimpses of the **Wapta Icefield,** which is shared by Banff and Yoho National Parks. Located on the Continental Divide, this sheet of ice in the Waputik Mountains feeds several outlet glaciers and the Bow River. From the **Hector Lake viewpoint** (22 km/11 mi north of Lake Louise), you can see **Vulture Glacier** spill from the icefield down the eastern slope toward the parkway. Farther up the parkway, be on the lookout for two other spots to see glaciers dropping from the icefield: **Bow Glacier** from the parking lot at the turnoff to Num-Ti-Jah Lodge and **Peyto Glacier** at the Peyto Lake viewpoint.

Crowfoot Glacier

The aptly named **Crowfoot Glacier** sits on a wide ledge near the top of Crowfoot Mountain, from where its glacial claws cling to the mountain's steep slopes. The retreat of this glacier has been dramatic. In the 1960s, two of the claws extended to the base of the lower cliff. Today they are a shadow of their former selves, barely curling over the cliff edge. There's a pullout on the west side of the parkway, 36 km (22 mi) north of Lake Louise, with views of the glacier.

Bow Lake

As you drive toward **Bow Lake,** its turquoise color is visible. But at the lakeside pullout 1.4 km (0.9 mi) north from the Crowfoot Glacier viewpoint, the sparkling waters of Bow Lake become more translucent. The lake was created when moraines deposited by retreating glaciers dammed subsequent meltwater. On still days, the water reflects the snowy peaks, their sheer cliffs, and the scree slopes that run into the lake. You don't need photography experience to take good pictures here!

At the upper end of the lake, you'll find the historic Num-Ti-Jah Lodge and a trailhead that leads to Bow Glacier Falls. (To reach the lodge, continue north from the Bow Lake pullout for 1.3 km/0.8 mi. Turn left and continue to the end of the road.) A quarter-mile south of the viewpoint, a day-use area offers waterfront picnic tables overlooking the lake's outlet, the beginning of the Bow River.

★ Bow Summit and Peyto Lake

Bow Summit is one of the highest points crossed by a public road in Canada. From the parking lot at the summit, a short but steep paved trail leads to overlooks of **Peyto Lake,** a lake whose hues change according to season. Before heavy melting of nearby glaciers begins in June or early July, the lake is dark blue. As summer progresses, meltwater flows across a delta and into the lake carrying finely ground particles of rock debris, known as glacial flour, suspended in the water. These particles reflect the blue-green sector of the light spectrum; as the amount of suspended rock flour changes, so does the color of the lake. To reach the summit parking lot, continue north on the parkway for 6 km (3.7 mi). Turn left, following the signs, and continue a short distance until you reach the signed vehicle lot.

Mistaya Canyon

The Mistaya River created the curvy **Mistaya Canyon** by cutting through limestone rock. But rather than a straight slot, the result is a series of narrow twisting turns. There's a trail (1 km/0.6 mi rt) that allows you to see the canyon; although it's short, there's a steep descent and climb back up to see the canyon. A bridge crosses over the canyon, and you can walk out on several rock slabs to peer down at the churning water in the middle and at the top. Be cautious of your footing as there are no guardrails. From Bow Summit, it's 30 km (19 mi) to the signed trailhead parking lot.

North Saskatchewan River

The swift and huge **North Saskatchewan**

River, a Canadian Heritage River, drains from Banff across the continent into Hudson Bay. The Icefields Parkway crosses over the river at Saskatchewan Crossing. The **Howse River viewpoint** is 1 km (0.6 mi) past the bridge that crosses the river (and 35 km/22 mi north of the turnoff for Bow Summit); it's before the junction with David Thompson Highway (Hwy. 11) and The Crossing Resort.

A short path tours around the bluff to see the silt-laden delta of braided channels where the Howse and Mistaya Rivers converge with the North Saskatchewan. To the west, look for two sharp peaks: The farther is Mount Forbes (3,630 m/11,975 ft), the highest peak in Banff National Park.

Weeping Wall

Admire the sheer, gray limestone face on Cirrus Mountain that's known as the **Weeping Wall.** The wall takes on a different character in different seasons. In early summer, it drips with waterfalls, one ribbon after another. In winter, this wall of water freezes, becoming a mecca for ice climbers. There's a signed viewpoint for the Weeping Wall on the east side of the parkway, 27 km (17 mi) north of the Howse River River viewpoint. Admire the wall from your car due to the dangerous avalanche-prone terrain.

Sunwapta Pass

A signed cairn at **Sunwapta Pass** on the Continental Divide marks the boundary of Jasper National Park's south end and Banff's north end. It also marks a division of watersheds: To the north, streams feed the Sunwapta River that flows to the Arctic while to the south waters go into the North Saskatchewan heading to the Atlantic. The westside pullout next to the cairn is 18 km (11 mi) northwest of the Weeping Wall viewpoint.

Bow Lake on the Icefields Parkway

Recreation
Hiking
★ Parker Ridge
Length: 4.8 km/3 mi rt
Duration: 2 hours
Elevation gain: 210 m/690 ft
Effort: moderate
Trailhead: Icefields Parkway, 4 km/2.5 mi south of Sunwapta Pass

From the trailhead on the west side of the highway, this wide path gains elevation quickly through open meadows and scattered stands of subalpine fir. This fragile environment is easily destroyed, so it's important that you stay on the trail. During the short alpine summer, these meadows are carpeted with wildflowers like red heather, white mountain avens, and blue alpine forget-me-nots. From the summit of **Parker Ridge,** you look down on the 2-km-wide (1.2-mi) **Saskatchewan Glacier** spreading out between Castleguard Mountain and Mount Athabasca.

Bow Glacier Falls
Length: 6.8 km/4.2 mi rt
Duration: 2 hours
Elevation gain: 130 m/430 ft
Effort: easy
Trailhead: public parking lot in front of Num-Ti-Jah Lodge, at the north end of Bow Lake

This hike skirts **Bow Lake** before ending at a narrow but spectacular waterfall. Follow the shore to a gravel outwash at the northwest end of the lake and begin a short but steep climb up the rim of a canyon before leveling out at the edge of a vast moraine of gravel, scree, and boulders. Pick your way through the rough ground to reach the base of **Bow Glacier Falls.** While you can't see **Bow Glacier** from the waterfall named for it, you can see it from the trailhead.

Peyto Lake
Length: 2.8 km/1.8 mi rt
Duration: 1 hour
Elevation loss: 100 m/330 ft
Effort: easy
Trailhead: unmarked pullout on the Icefields Parkway, 2.4 km (1.5 mi) north of Bow Summit

The easiest way to access the shoreline of **Peyto Lake** is via this short trail, which starts farther north on the Icefields Parkway from the Bow Summit overlook of the lake. A pebbled beach, strewn with driftwood, is the perfect setting for picnicking, painting, or just admiring the lake's quieter side.

As an alternative, departing from the lake overlook at Bow Summit, a rough trail plunges to the lake's west end (4.8 km/3 mi rt, 300 m/980 ft, 2 hrs). It lets you survey the inlet streams pouring glacial flour into the lake that gives it such an intense color. But you will have to climb back up afterward.

Helen Lake
Length: 12 km/7.4 mi rt
Duration: 4 hours
Elevation gain: 455 m/1,500 ft
Effort: moderate
Trailhead: across the Icefields Parkway from Crowfoot Glacier overlook south of Bow Lake

The trail to Helen Lake is one of the easiest ways to access a true alpine environment. The path climbs steadily through a forest of Engelmann spruce and subalpine fir to an avalanche slope to reach the tree line and the first good **viewpoint** with Crowfoot Glacier visible to the southwest. As the trail crests a ridge, it turns sharply and passes through extensive meadows of wildflowers that are at their peak in late July and early August. The trail then crosses a photogenic stream and climbs to the glacial cirque where **Helen Lake** lies. Listen and look for hoary marmots along the last section of trail and around the lakeshore.

For those with the time and energy, the route continues on to **Dolomite Pass,** for an additional 6 km (3.8 mi) roundtrip. The trail switchbacks steeply and then descends to Katherine Lake and beyond to the broad pass.

Backpacking
Permits
Permits (C$10 pp per night) are required for backcountry camping in Banff. Permits are available at visitors centers. **Reservations** (877/737-3783, 519/826-5391 from outside North America, reservation.pc.gc.ca, C$12) usually open for the year in January. Many routes book up fast for July to early September.

Glacier Lake
19 kilometers (12.4 miles)
A two-day/one-night backpacking route goes to **Glacier Lake** (19 km/12.4 mi rt), one of the park's largest lakes. The trail crosses the North Saskatchewan River to climb gradually to a viewpoint overlooking the Howse River; then it climbs through a thick forest to the lake tucked at the base below the north sides of Mount Outram and Mount Forbes, the highest peak in the park. Campsites

Top to bottom: ice climbers on the frozen Weeping Wall; Parker Ridge; Peyto Lake

enjoy the lake shore, and the lower elevation often means the campsites are snow-free by June. Find the trailhead just west of the Crossing Resort at Saskatchewan Crossing.

Mountaineering

For skilled rock and ice climbers, the **Weeping Wall** has oodles of routes on the lower and upper walls. Some routes have fixed bolts, but Parks Canada does not maintain them, so use at your own risk. In winter, the wall of frozen waterfalls attracts ice climbers. **Canadian Rockies Alpine Guides** (www.cdnalpine.com) leads ice climbing ascents.

Wapta Traverse

Skilled alpinists on foot or skis can travel the strenuous **Wapta Traverse** (45 km/28 mi) across glaciers, basins and cols of the Wapta and Waputik Icefields that drape the Continental Divide. This classic multi-day route begins at **Peyto Lake** off the Icefields Parkway and ends at **Sherbrook Lake** near the Trans-Canada Highway. The exposed route requires technical gear and expertise in glacier travel, alpine navigation, assessing rock fall and avalanche hazards, and monitoring weather. Surrounding peaks invite mountaineers to climb or ski while staying at the route's four huts run by the **Alpine Club of Canada** (403/678-3200, www.alpineclubofcanada.ca): Peyto, Bow, Balfour, and Scott Duncan. Varying in size, the huts have bunks, propane stovetops, and outhouses; bring your own food and sleeping bag.

Sawback Alpine Adventures (403/707-9996, sawback.com) and **Yamnuska Mountain Adventures** (403/768-4164 or 866/678-4164, yamnuska.com), both located in Canmore, guide ski mountaineering trips.

Food, Accommodations, and Camping
Lodges and Restaurants
The historic red-roofed, rock-and-timber

Num-Ti-Jah Lodge (40 km/25 mi north of Lake Louise, 403/522-2167, www.num-ti-jah.com, late May-mid-Oct., from C$375) sits on the north shore of Bow Lake. The octagonal main lodge has a roaring log fire and the library is filled with historical mountain literature. The lodge has 25 rooms (some share bathrooms) without TVs, phones, Wi-Fi, or cell service. Open for breakfast and dinner, the **Elkhorn Dining Room** (C$28-45), which serves Canadian cuisine, is lined with memorabilia. Or warm up with bison chili in the **Bow Lake Café** (C$10-20). The trail to Bow Glacier Falls departs outside.

The Crossing Resort (403/761-7000, www.thecrossingresort.com, early May-mid-Oct., C$160-370) is a highway motel with an interpretive site absorbing the scenery. Rooms come in different sizes with varied bed configurations. Each of the 66 units has a phone and TV. The Crossing has the only gas station between Lake Louise and Jasper, a self-serve **cafeteria**, a **restaurant**, a **pub**, and a supersized gift shop. The large complex is just north of Saskatchewan Crossing (87 km/54 mi north of Lake Louise, 45 km/28 mi south of the Columbia Icefield).

Hostels
On the Banff National Park segment of the Icefields Parkway, three wilderness **hostels** (778/328-2220 or 866/762-4122, hihostels.ca, mid-June-Mar., from C$36 members, from C$40 nonmembers) offer rustic places to stay. Beds should be reserved as far in advance as possible due to the hostels' popularity. Facilities include kitchens, shared cabins, wood-heated saunas, and outhouses, but no showers. Near Mosquito Creek Campground south of Bow Lake, **HI-Mosquito Creek** (24 km/15 mi north of Lake Louise) has drinking water and one cabin with two private family rooms in addition to shared rooms. Located north of Saskatchewan Crossing near Rampart Creek Campground, **HI-Rampart Creek** (13 km/8 mi north of The Crossing

Resort) has no electricity and no running water. Located closest to Jasper National Park and 8 km (5 mi) from the Icefield Center, the bare-bones **HI-Hilda Creek** (0.8 km/0.5 mi north of Parker Ridge Trailhead) sleeps six.

Camping

Four campgrounds sit on Icefields Parkway between Lake Louise and the Icefield Centre. Amenities include picnic tables, firepits, potable water, kitchen shelters, food lockers, and vault or flush toilets. Fire permits (C$9) include firewood.

Two campgrounds are first come, first served: Despite its name, the forested **Mosquito Creek Campground** (32 sites, early June-mid-Oct., RV limit 10.7 m/35 ft, C$18) doesn't really have more mosquitoes than anywhere else. Sites are next to a tumbling creek separating the campground from a hostel of the same name. Mosquito Creek is 24 km (15 mi) north of Lake Louise. Further north, **Waterfowl Lakes Campground** (116 sites, mid-June-early Sept., RV limit 9 m/30 ft, C$22) sits between Upper and Lower Waterfowl Lakes, with a few sites in view of the lower lake. It has flush toilets and an RV dump station. Waterfowl Lakes is 57 km (35 mi) north of Lake Louise.

Two campgrounds take reservations for the summer months. The **Parks Canada campground reservation service** (877/737-3783, reservation.pc.gc.ca, C$12) accepts bookings usually launching in January for the upcoming year. A bare-bones campground, **Silverhorn Creek** (45 sites, June-late Sept., RV limit 20 m/70 ft, C$16) has only pit toilets and no potable water or kitchen shelters. Silverhorn Creek is 52 km (32 mi) north of Lake Louise. North of Saskatchewan Crossing is **Rampart Creek Campground** (50 sites, early June-mid-Oct., RV limit 10.7 m/35 ft, C$18). Two of its loops restrict RVs to a maximum length of 7.5 m (25 ft). It is 88 km (55 mi) north of Lake Louise.

Num-Ti-Jah Lodge on Bow Lake

Information and Services

Emergency Services

In an emergency, call **911.** The closest hospitals are **Mineral Springs Hospital** (305 Lynx St., Banff, 403/762-2222, www.covenanthealth.ca) in Banff and **Seton-Jasper Healthcare Centre** (518 Robson St., Jasper, 780/852-3344, www.albertahealthservices.ca) in Jasper. Both have 24-hour emergency services.

Gas

The only gas on this portion of the Icefields Parkway is available at **The Crossing Resort** (403/761-7000, www.thecrossingresort.com, early May-early Oct.).

Cell Service and Internet Access

Cell reception is not available along the Icefields Parkway on the entire route from Lake Louise to Jasper. You'll have cell service in the towns of Lake Louise and Banff. There's a pay phone in the general store at **The Crossing Resort** (403/761-7000, www.thecrossingresort.com, early May-early Oct.).

Lake Louise

The hamlet of Lake Louise, composed of a small mall, hotels, and restaurants, is in the Bow Valley on the west side of the Trans-Canada Highway. The lake itself is above the valley floor, along a winding, paved road. Overlooking the magnificent scene, the Fairmont Chateau Lake Louise is one of the world's most photographed hotels. Only a short distance away is beautiful Moraine Lake.

Lake Louise is 56 km (35 mi) northwest of Banff along the Trans-Canada Highway, about a 45-minute drive. The distance is a little bit longer if you take the quieter Bow Valley Parkway. The town is conveniently located for exploring the Icefields Parkway and neighboring Yoho National Park.

Sights

★ Lake Louise

In summer, about 10,000 visitors per day make the journey up to **Lake Louise,** famous for its stunning turquoise color. Several paved trails lead to the lake's eastern shore, from where you can gain dramatic views of the lake surrounded by rugged peaks and backed by glacier-draped Mount Victoria. The lake, which freezes in winter, has frigid waters that reach only 4°C (39°F) in August. In winter, you can ice skate or cross-country ski on the lake; in summer you can rent a canoe from the lakeshore boathouse. Most people enjoy a stroll along the **paved lakeshore trail** to soak up the lake color, mountains, and the **Chateau Lake Louise,** the grand Fairmont property that sits on the lake's northern shore.

By **sunrise** in summer, the **Lake Louise Lakeshore parking lot** (C$12 7am-7pm daily June-mid-Oct., free after 7pm but no overnight parking) fills to capacity. Write down or take a photo of your car's

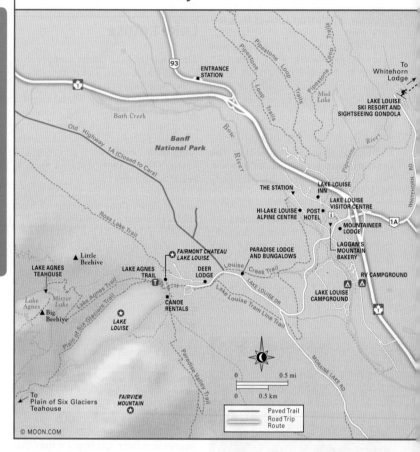

Lake Louise Village

To Whitehorn Lodge

LAKE LOUISE SKI RESORT AND SIGHTSEEING GONDOLA

ENTRANCE STATION

Pipestone Loop Trails

Mud Lake

Pipestone River

WHITEHORN RD

Bath Creek

Bow River

Banff National Park

Old Highway 1A (Closed to Cars)

THE STATION

LAKE LOUISE INN

LAKE LOUISE VISITOR CENTRE

HI-LAKE LOUISE ALPINE CENTRE

POST HOTEL

MOUNTAINEER LODGE

Ross Lake Trail

FAIRMONT CHATEAU LAKE LOUISE

PARADISE LODGE AND BUNGALOWS

LAGGAN'S MOUNTAIN BAKERY

Little Beehive

LAKE AGNES TEAHOUSE

LAKE AGNES TRAIL

DEER LODGE

Louise Creek Trail

RV CAMPGROUND

Lake Agnes Trail

CANOE RENTALS

LAKE LOUISE DR.

LAKE LOUISE CAMPGROUND

Mirror Lake

Lake Agnes

LAKE LOUISE

Lake Louise Tram Line Trail

Big Beehive

Plain of Six Glaciers Trail

To Plain of Six Glaciers Teahouse

Paradise Valley Trail

FAIRVIEW MOUNTAIN

MORAINE LAKE RD

0   0.5 mi

0   0.5 km

Paved Trail
Road Trip
Route

© MOON.COM

license plate number for when you pay for parking at the kiosks on the trailhead. **Shuttles** (every 20 min., 8am-6:20pm daily June-mid-Oct., 7:50pm last return bus from lake, roundtrip C$8 adults, C$4 seniors, C$2 youth, free under 6) to the lakeshore run from the Park-and-Ride along the Trans-Canada Highway east of town; make **reservations** (reservation.pc.gc.ca, C$3) **48 hours** in advance starting at 8am. Electronic signage along the highway will direct you to the Park-and-Ride when parking at the lake is full. You can also use the **connector shuttle**

(first come, first served, fee included in shuttle ticket) to get to Lake Louise from Moraine Lake. Or you can walk to the lake from Lake Louise Village by ascending two hiking trails, both of which cover 195 meters (640 ft) of elevation through forest. The more direct trail is **Louise Creek** (5.6 km/3.5 mi rt), though it's steeper; the **Tramline** (9 km/5.6 mi rt) follows the old tram route to the lake at a lesser grade.

The snow-covered peak at the back of Lake Louise is **Mount Victoria** (3,459 m/11,350 ft), which sits on the

Continental Divide. First climbed in 1897, Victoria remains one of the park's most popular peaks for mountaineers, with the easiest route to the summit along the southeast ridge, approached from Abbot Pass. You can hike up the Plain of Six Glacier Trail for closer views of Victoria Glacier and the Death Trap ice fall, Abbot Pass, and Abbot Pass Hut. For a more sedate activity, nothing beats seeing the first flush of morning sun hitting **Victoria Glacier,** and the impossibly steep northern face of Mount Victoria reflected in the sparkling waters of the lake.

TOP EXPERIENCE

★ Fairmont Chateau Lake Louise

The **Fairmont Chateau Lake Louise** is a tourist attraction in itself. Built by Canadian Pacific Railway in 1890 to take the pressure off the popular Fairmont Banff Springs hotel, the chateau has seen many changes over the years, yet it remains one of the world's great mountain resorts. Hordes of camera- and phone-toting tourists traipse through the building each day, gawking at the lobby and admiring the view through the floor-to-ceiling windows in the Lakeview Lounge. Manicured gardens between the chateau and the lake make an interesting foreground for the millions of Lake Louise photographs taken each year. In winter ice sculptures enliven the frozen landscape.

TOP EXPERIENCE

★ Moraine Lake

Although less than half the size of Lake Louise, **Moraine Lake** is just as spectacular. Its rugged setting, nestled in the Valley of the Ten Peaks below towering mountains, is punctuated by the lake's turquoise waters. Trails explore the northern shoreline and the large rock pile at its foot, deposited by major rockfalls from the Tower of Babel to the south. The **Rockpile Trail** climbs rock steps

to reach several viewpoints at the top, where you'll get the best photos of the lake's color. The **lakeshore trail** goes to short waterfalls with benches at the inlet en route to enjoy the view. The lake often remains frozen until June, and the access road is closed all winter. You can rent a canoe to paddle its waters.

Moraine Lake is accessed via a winding road (13 km/8 mi, open mid-May-mid-Oct.) off Lake Louise Drive. Check with the visitors center or online on the opening date; some years, snow precludes access until mid-June. The lake's **parking lot** fills by **sunrise** in summer. If you arrive after 6am, expect the road to the lake to be closed. **Shuttles** (every 20-30 min., 6am-5:30pm daily June-mid-Oct., 7:50pm last return bus from lake, roundtrip C$8 adults, C$4 seniors, C$2 youth, free under 6) to Moraine run from the Park-and-Ride along the Trans-Canada Highway east of town; make **reservations** (reservation.pc.gc.ca, C$3) **48 hours** in advance starting at 8am. (Look for destination signs on the bus.) You can also use the **connector shuttle** (first come, first served, fee included in shuttle ticket) to go between Moraine Lake and Lake Louise.

Lake Louise Ski Area Scenic Lift

The main ski lift at the **Lake Louise Ski Resort** (1 Whitehorn Rd., 403/522-3555 or 877/956-8473, www.skilouise.com, 9am-5pm daily May-Sept., from C$38 adults, C$17 children) is for more than just winter sports enthusiasts. The lift whisks visitors up the face of Mount Whitehorn to Whitehorn Lodge in either open chairs or enclosed gondola cars. The view from the top, across the Bow Valley, Lake Louise, and the Continental Divide, is among the most spectacular in the Canadian Rockies. Short trails lead through the forests, across open meadows, and drop to the lodge where you can tour the Wildlife Interpretive Centre and dine on the deck. Due to the resort's location in prime grizzly bear habitat, you

Vicinity of Lake Louise

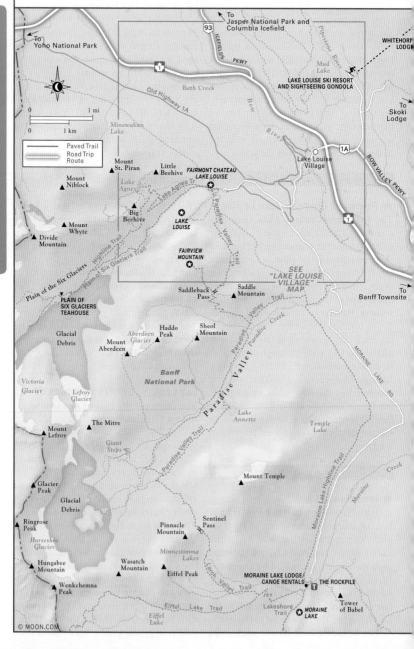

To Jasper National Park and Columbia Icefield

To Yoho National Park

WHITEHORN LODGE

93

ICEFIELDS

PKWY

Bath Creek

Old Highway 1A

Mud Lake

LAKE LOUISE SKI RESORT AND SIGHTSEEING GONDOLA

1

Bow River

To Skoki Lodge

Minewakun Lake

0   1 mi
0   1 km

Paved Trail
Road Trip Route

Lake Louise Village

1A

BOW VALLEY PKWY

Mount St. Piran

Little Beehive

FAIRMONT CHATEAU LAKE LOUISE

Mount Niblock

Lake Agnes

Lake Agnes Tr.

Big Beehive

LAKE LOUISE

Paradise Valley Trail

Mount Whyte

Divide Mountain

Highline Trail

Plain of Six Glaciers Trail

FAIRVIEW MOUNTAIN

SEE "LAKE LOUISE VILLAGE" MAP

To Banff Townsite

Plain of the Six Glaciers

Saddleback Pass

Saddle Mountain

Paradise Valley Trail

MORAINE LAKE RD

PLAIN OF SIX GLACIERS TEAHOUSE

Aberdeen Glacier

Haddo Peak

Sheol Mountain

Paradise Creek

Glacial Debris

Mount Aberdeen

Banff National Park

Paradise Valley

Victoria Glacier

Lefroy Glacier

Lake Annette

Temple Lake

Mount Lefroy

The Mitre

Paradise Valley Trail

Giant Steps

Moraine Lake Highline Trail

Moraine Creek

Glacier Peak

Glacial Debris

Mount Temple

Ringrose Peak

Horseshoe Glacier

Pinnacle Mountain

Sentinel Pass

Hungabee Mountain

Wasatch Mountain

Minnestimma Lakes

Larch Valley Trail

Wenkchemna Peak

Eiffel Peak

MORAINE LAKE LODGE/ CANOE RENTALS

THE ROCKPILE

Eiffel Lake Trail

Lakeshore Trail

MORAINE LAKE

Tower of Babel

Eiffel Lake

© MOON.COM

can often spot bears from the lift, lodge deck, or trails. Free shuttles run between Lake Louise hotels and the resort.

Mount Temple

Hulking over the western side of the Trans-Canada Highway, the striking **Mount Temple** (3,544 m/11,627 ft) is the highest peak in the Lake Louise area and one of the 10 highest in the Canadian Rockies. The blocky peak is capped with a glacier that spills off its eastern ridge. For the best views, hike up Mount Fairview or take the main lift at the Lake Louise Ski Resort. Experienced mountaineers can also scramble the southwestern ridge to Temple's summit.

Recreation
Hiking

Parks Canada leads **guided educational hikes** (877/737-3783, reservation.pc.gc. ca, dates vary, C$70 adults, C$60 seniors, C$35 youth) where you'll learn about the local ecosystem. Rates include a shuttle ride to the trailhead. Reservations are required.

Plain of the Six Glaciers

Length: 10.6 km (6.6 mi) rt
Duration: 3.5 hours
Elevation gain: 370 meters (1,215 ft)
Effort: moderate
Trailhead: Lake Louise

Hikers along this trail are rewarded with panoramic views of glaciated peaks and a rustic teahouse serving homemade goodies baked on a wooden stove. From the foot of Lake Louise, the trail follows the Louise Lakeshore Trail to the west end of the lake, where it begins a steady climb through a forest. An open slope containing a colorful carpet of wildflowers interrupts the forest before reaching a vast wasteland of moraines produced by the advance and retreat of Victoria Glacier. Views of surrounding peaks continue to

Top to bottom: lakeshore trail at Lake Louise; Lake Louise canoe dock; Lake Louise Ski Area

Backcountry Teahouses

At Lake Louise, two **backcountry teahouses** (daily June-mid-Oct., C$4-15, cash only) offer unique places to eat due to their hiking-only access. Instead of hauling a lunch on the trail, you can eat at these rustic restaurants instead. They serve sandwiches on fresh-baked bread, hot drinks, homemade soups, and desserts. With tables indoors and outdoors, seating is first come, first served, so you may have a wait.

The **Plain of Six Glaciers Teahouse** (p6teahouse.com, 9am-5pm), located on the Plain of Six Glaciers Trail, is tucked in the trees with partial views of Mount Victoria. On the Lake Agnes Trail, the **Lake Agnes Teahouse** (www.lakeagnesteahouse.com, 8am-5pm) enjoys views of Lake Agnes.

improve until the trail enters a stunted forest. After switchbacking up through this forest, the trail arrives at the **Plain of Six Glaciers Teahouse** (9am-5pm daily June-mid-Oct.), where you can rest and refuel.

From the teahouse, an unmaintained trail climbs on the narrow ridge of a lateral moraine where the path fizzles amid the rocks on a steep hillside. Six glaciers are visible: Aberdeen, Upper Lefroy, Lower Lefroy, Upper Victoria, Lower Victoria, and Pope's. Between Mount Lefroy and Mount Victoria is Abbot Pass, where it's possible to make out the stone Abbot Hut on the skyline above the Death Trap ice fall.

Lake Agnes

Length: 7.2 km (4.4 mi) rt
Duration: 3 hours
Elevation gain: 400 meters (1,312 ft)
Effort: moderate
Trailhead: Lake Louise

This popular and ultra-crowded hike begins in front of the Lake Louise chateau, branching right at the first junction. It switchbacks up steeply through Engelmann spruce and subalpine fir, crossing a horse trail, passing beneath a lookout, and leveling out at tiny **Mirror Lake.** Here the old, traditional trail veers right (use it if the ground is wet or snowy), while a more direct route veers left to the Plain of the Six Glaciers. The final elevation gain along both trails is made easier by a flight of steps beside

Bridal Veil Falls. The trail ends at idyllic **Lake Agnes,** nestled in a hanging valley. Near the outlet, the rustic **Lake Agnes Teahouse** (8am-5pm daily June-mid-Oct.) has homemade soups, healthy sandwiches, and teas.

From the teahouse, you can return the way you came or explore more. A trail leads to **Little Beehive** (2 km/1.2 mi rt) and impressive views of the Bow Valley. Another trail arcs around Lake Agnes, climbing to **Big Beehive** (3.4 km/2.1 mi rt) to look down at the chateau and Lake Louise. Return the way you came or drop south to the Plain of the Six Glaciers Trail to loop back to the trailhead.

Louise Lakeshore

Length: 4 km (2.4 mi) rt
Duration: 1 hour
Elevation gain: none
Effort: easy
Trailhead: Lake Louise

Probably the busiest trail in all the Canadian Rockies, this wide strolling path follows the **north shore of Lake Louise** to the west end. Along the trail's length are benches for sitting to soak up the views. At the lake's head, numerous braided glacial streams empty their silt-filled waters into Lake Louise, contributing to its color.

★ Fairview Mountain and Saddleback

Length: 7.4 km (4.6 mi) rt
Duration: 3 hours
Elevation gain: 600 meters (1,970 ft)

Effort: moderate-strenuous
Trailhead: Lake Louise boathouse

From the boathouse on Lake Louise, this trail climbs the lower slopes of **Fairview Mountain** ending in a sparsely forested alpine meadow with a view of Mount Temple across Paradise Valley. Shortly after starting, the trail forks. Keep left and follow the steep switchbacks through a spruce and fir forest to reach the flower-filled meadow, which is the **Saddleback,** a pass between Fairview Mountain to the northwest and Saddle Mountain to the southeast. Trees are beginning to crowd out the meadows; many hikers are content here and return along the same trail.

But the scenery from the summit of Fairview Mountain is far more impressive, and the peak is one of the few in the park with a trail to the top. From the pass, strong hikers can tackle the steep rough rock trail that climbs above the alpine larch, switchbacking steeply north up the face to the summit (add on 2.3 km/1.4 mi rt, 400 m/1,310 ft, 1.5 hrs). Views in all directions take in scads of peaks, including Mount Temple and Mount Victoria, plus Lake Louise directly below. Return the way you came.

Larch Valley and Sentinel Pass

Length: 5.8-11.6 km (3.6-7.2 mi) rt
Duration: 2-4 hours
Elevation gain: 400-727 meters (1,310-2,380 ft)
Effort: moderate-strenuous
Trailhead: Moraine Lake

In mid- to late September, when the larch trees have turned a magnificent gold and the sun is shining, few spots in the Canadian Rockies can match the beauty of this valley—but don't expect to find much solitude. It's equally outstanding in summer, when the meadows are filled with colorful wildflowers.

The trail begins just past Moraine Lake Lodge and climbs fairly steeply through **Larch Valley,** with occasional glimpses

Top to bottom: Plain of the Six Glaciers; Lake Agnes; trail to Sentinel Pass

of Moraine Lake below. After reaching the junction of the Eiffel Lake Trail, keep right, passing through an open forest of larch. The range of larch is limited in the park; this small, high-elevation valley is one of the few areas where they are prolific. To the south, **Mount Fay** dominates the skyline, rising above the other mountains that make up the **Valley of the Ten Peaks.** Continue up through alpine meadows to the two **Minnestimma Lakes,** where views back to the Ten Peaks are unforgettable. This route is 5.8 km (3.6 mi) round-trip.

Sentinel Pass (2,608 m/8,560 ft) is one of the park's highest trail-accessible passes. From the lakes, the trail switchbacks up a steep scree slope to the pass, sandwiched between Pinnacle Mountain and Mount Temple. Views extend down into Paradise Valley. From the pass most hikers opt to return along the same trail (for a total hike of 11.6 km/7.2 mi), although with a car shuttle, you can continue into Paradise Valley and back to the Moraine Lake access road (17 km/10.6 mi one-way).

Due to the risk of human-bear conflicts in Larch Valley, hikers may be required to be in groups of four or more; often you can hook up with others at the trail junction near Moraine Lake Lodge.

Paradise Valley

Length: 19 km (12 mi) loop
Duration: 6 hours
Elevation gain: 380 meters (1,250 ft)
Effort: moderate-strenuous
Trailhead: Moraine Lake Rd.

This loop trail passes multiple signed junctions; stay on the Paradise Valley Trail and use a map. The path climbs slowly for the first 5 km (3 mi), crossing Paradise Creek numerous times to reach the valley entrance. At the junction of the loop through Paradise Valley, go left (counterclockwise on the loop) for the steep ascent to **Lake Annette** (5.7 km/3.5 mi, 245 m/804 ft, 4 hrs rt), a subalpine lake tucked against the immense,

near-vertical north face of ice-capped **Mount Temple.** The lake is a worthy destination in itself. To continue the loop up valley, go beyond the lake into a boulder-filled avalanche slope resounding with pika and marmot screeches. From this vantage above the valley floor, views extend across **Paradise Valley** to the Horseshoe Glacier cirque tucked below Mount Hungabee. At the valley head, you'll pass several junctions. Take the side spur that descends steeply to reach the series of cascading tiers of the **Giant Steps.** Return to the main trail and follow Paradise Creek downstream until you reconnect your starting point on the loop below Lake Annette and then retrace your steps to exit the valley and descend back to the trailhead.

Backpacking
Permits
Permits (C$10 pp per night) are required for backcountry camping in Banff. **Reservations** (877/737-3783, 519/826-5391 from outside North America, reservation.pc.gc.ca, C$12) usually open for the year in January, when many routes book up fast for July to early September.

Paradise Valley Loop
19 kilometers (12 miles)
Paradise Valley makes an easy two-day/one-night backpacking trip to enjoy the splendor of Mount Temple, Horseshoe Glacier, and Mount Hungabee. The Paradise Valley backcountry campground (10 sites) is at the far western end of the loop on a side spur (0.6 km/0.4 mi) between the junctions with Sentinel Pass and Giant Steps.

Skoki Mountain Loop
39 kilometers (24 miles)
This loop through Skoki Valley, with numerous side trips to lakes and scenery-laden viewpoints, is best done as a four-day/three-night trip. Take a good map to navigate the maze of side trip

options and myriad trail junctions. Plan to camp one night each on the Hidden Lake trail spur, Merlin Meadows west of Skoki Lodge, and Baker Lake The route crosses three passes: Boulder, Deception, and Cotton Grass. Add on mileage for side trips to Hidden Lake, Merlin Lake, Skoki Mountain, Tilted Lake, and Redoubt Lake.

Mountaineering

Rock climbers enjoy the cliffs at the head of Lake Louise. Short pitches allow plenty of options to hone skills on faces with varying degrees of technical difficulty. Bring your own gear for these unmaintained routes and climb responsibly.

A challenging, strenuous scramble ascends from Sentinel Pass up the southwest ridge to the summit of **Mount Temple**. It is for experienced mountaineers who can handle exposure on a steep crux, falling rocks from other climbers (wear a helmet), ice, and whiteouts. Route-finding and weather assessment skills are a must. You can hire a guide at the visitors center or from the Parks Canada website (www.pc.gc.ca). If you are tentative about your skills, hire **Yamnuska Mountain Adventures** (403/768-4164 or 866/678-4164, yamnuska.com) to guide you.

TOP EXPERIENCE

Paddling

While many lakes in the Canadian Rockies have scenic paddling, two lakes around Lake Louise offer exceptional scenery and exquisite waters colored turquoise by glacial flour. Rimmed with huge peaks and glaciers, these lakes will shape an experience you'll never forget. You can launch your own kayaks, paddleboards, or canoes by carrying them to the shore (but you must complete a self-certification for aquatic invasive species. Clean, drain, and dry crafts before launching). You can also **rent canoes** onsite. Paddles and life jackets are included

with rentals, and each canoe holds 2-3 adults. No reservations are taken; rentals are first come, first served, so you may have to wait in line. Rentals close down when conditions are windy or rainy. Take a shoreline route for safety, so you can easily return if the weather sours. The water in these lakes is frigid, so use caution and wear layers.

Lake Louise

Despite scads of other canoes on **Lake Louise,** you can still feel off in the wilds with Mount Victoria and Victoria Glacier providing the backdrop. The immensity of the scenery and the silty turquoise waters elevate the paddling far beyond most other lakes. Skilled paddlers can go to shallows at the end of the lake and back in about 1.5 hours. At the **Lake Louise Boathouse** (111 Lake Louise Dr., 403/522-3511, www.fairmont.com/lake-louise, 11am-7pm daily mid-June-early Oct.), you can rent canoes (C$125-130/hr).

Moraine Lake

On a glassy day, **Moraine Lake** begs to be paddled, with glaciers and the serrated Ten Peaks reflecting in the turquoise water. Paddling to the head of the lake and back takes about one hour. From the concession below **Moraine Lake Lodge** (1 Moraine Lake Rd., 877/522-2777, morainelake.com, 9:30am-5pm daily mid-June-mid-Sept.), you can rent canoes (C$95-100/hr).

Winter Recreation

Lake Louise is an immense winter playground with one of the world's premier alpine resorts, plus cross-country skiing and snowshoeing. You can ice skate on frozen Lake Louise and go for sleigh rides, too.

Lake Louise Ski Resort

Opposite Lake Louise and Mount Temple, **Lake Louise Ski Resort** (1 Whitehorn Rd., 403/522-3555 or

877/956-8473, www.skilouise.com, daily early Nov.-mid-May, C\$125 adults, C\$95 seniors, C\$37-95 kids), Canada's second-largest winter resort, has skiing and snowboarding on gentle trails, mogul fields, long cruising runs, steep chutes, and vast bowls filled with famous Rocky Mountain powder. The front side is served by eight lifts, including four high-speed quads and one six-passenger chairlift. Four backside bowls are each as big as many midsize resorts and are all well above the tree line. Two mid-mountain lodges have restaurants and bars, and the Lodge of the Ten Peaks, a magnificent post-and-beam day lodge in the base area, stares at the mountain's front face. It has restaurants, a cafeteria, rentals, clothing, and souvenirs.

Free shuttle buses run regularly from Lake Louise accommodations to the ski area, as well as from Banff. For information on packages, shuttles, and multiday tickets that cover all three Banff ski resorts, go to www.skibig3.com.

Cross-Country Skiing

The most popular cross-country skiing areas are on **Lake Louise,** along **Moraine Lake Road,** and in **Skoki Valley,** at the back of the Lake Louise ski area. For details and helpful trail classifications, pick up a copy of *Cross-Country Skiing— Nordic Trails in Banff National Park* from the Lake Louise Visitor Centre. Before heading out, check the weather forecast at the visitors center or call 403/762-2088. For avalanche reports, call 403/762-1460.

In Lake Louise village, **Wilson Mountain Sports** (Samson Mall, 201 Village Rd., 403/522-3636, www.wmsll.com) rents classic and skate skis (C\$25-40) and snowshoes (C\$10).

Entertainment and Events

Every January, the **Ice Magic International Ice Carving Competition** (Fairmont Chateau Lake Louise, www.banfflakelouise.com, 12 days starting mid-Jan.) comes to Lake Louise. Between the chateau and the lake, you can watch

skiing back bowls at Lake Louise

the carvers create ice castles and sculptures within 30 hours of the event's start. Tickets (C$6-13, C$35 family) are required for specific time slots to view the sculptures on weekends. Free shuttles run on weekends from Samson Mall to Lake Louise. Viewing is free on weekdays and for guests of the chateau. Several lodges also include admission with an overnight stay. The creations stay up often through February, as weather allows; they are best in early February before melting and snowstorms take a toll.

Food
Canadian
Laggan Station used to serve as the area's train depot, but today visitors dine in **The Station Restaurant** (200 Sentinel Rd., 403/522-2600, www.lakelouisestation. com, 5pm-9pm daily, C$24-42). Although the menu is not extensive, it puts an emphasis on imaginative dishes with a combination of Canadian produce and Asian ingredients. Expect entrées

like pan-seared salmon smothered in basil pesto.

Well worth the drive, **Baker Creek Bistro** (Baker Creek Mountain Resort, 403/522-3761, bakercreek.com, 7am-10pm daily, C$28-52), which is 10 km (6.2 mi) south of Lake Louise on Bow Valley Parkway, serves up Canadian game and produce from its log cabin. Dining is in an intimate room, an adjacent lounge, or out on a small deck decorated with pots of colorful flowers. The compact menu has favorites such as beer-pork ribs, duck breast, and bison tenderloin.

Family-Friendly
Crowds attest to the goodness at ★ **Laggan's Mountain Bakery** (101 Village Rd., 403/552-2017, www.laggans. com, 7am-7pm daily, C$8-12), *the* place to hang out with a coffee and a freshly baked croissant, pastry, or breads. You can also get breakfast sandwiches, meat pies, chili, poutine, pizza bagels, and salads. If the tables are full, order takeout and enjoy your feast on the riverbank behind Samson Mall.

For a casual meal, head to **Bill Peyto's Cafe** (203 Village Rd., 403/522-2200, 7am-10pm daily, C$13-23) in the Lake Louise Alpine Centre, where the food is consistent: elk burgers, poutine, pasta, and stir-fries.

At Lake Louise Ski Area, the **Lodge of the Ten Peaks** (1 Whitehorn Rd., 403/522-3555 or 877/956-8473, www.skilouise. com, 8am-4pm daily early Nov.-early Oct., C$12-25) serves a large and varied breakfast buffet. There's also lunch station service, pub dining, and a cafeteria. Food is best enjoyed out on the covered balcony. The lodge also has a café where you can grab coffee and muffins.

International
In 1987, the ★ **Post Hotel** (200 Pipestone Dr., 403/522-3989 or 800/661-1586, posthotel.com, 6:30pm-10pm daily, C$34-60) renovated their original log building into a rustic, timbered dining room

linked to the rest of the hotel by an intimate lounge. The chef specializes in European cuisine, preparing several Swiss dishes such as veal *zurichoise*. He's also renowned for his presentation of Alberta beef, Pacific salmon, and Peking duck. The 32,000-bottle wine cellar is one of the finest in Canada. Reservations are essential. While jackets are not required, most diners dress with casual elegance. No athletic attire is permitted.

Fairmont Chateau Lake Louise

Within the famous lakeside **Fairmont Chateau Lake Louise** (111 Lake Louise Dr., 403/522-1818, www.fairmont.com/lake-louise) is a choice of eateries and an ice-cream shop. The **Poppy Brasserie** has obscured lake views and is the most casual place for a meal. Breakfast (6:30am-10am daily, C$34) is a buffet. Dinners (5:30am-9pm daily, C$34-52) are à la carte.

The **Walliser Stube** (5:30pm-9pm daily, C$38-55) is an elegant two-story wine bar decorated with rich wood paneling and solid oak furniture. It offers a simple menu of German dishes as well as a number of classic fondues. The **Lakeview Lounge** (11am-10pm daily, C$24-36) has floor-to-ceiling windows with magnificent lake views. Choose this dining area for lunch or afternoon tea (noon-3pm daily, reservations required, C$56-66). The **Fairview Dining Room** (5:30pm-9:30pm daily, C$42-62) has a lot more than just a fair view. As the chateau's signature dining room, it enjoys the best views and offers the most elegant setting.

Accommodations and Camping

Summer sees the highest rates. Fall and spring rates are lower, with winter rates the lowest. Reservations are imperative for summer and winter holidays.

Top to bottom: Ice Magic International Ice Carving Competition; Laggan's Mountain Bakery; Baker Creek Bistro

Huts and Hostels

You'll need hiking boots to reach ★ **Skoki Lodge** (403/522-1347 or 888/997-5654, skoki.com, late June-early Oct. and late Dec.-mid-Apr., C$200-250 pp per night), north of the Lake Louise Ski Resort and far from the nearest road. Getting there requires an 11-km (6.8-mi) hike or ski. A National Historic Site, the lodge is an excellent base for exploring nearby valleys and mountains. It has a main lodge with mostly twin beds in rooms, cabins that sleep up to five, outhouses, and a wood-fired sauna. There's propane heat but no electricity. Rates include three meals daily, including a picnic lunch that guests build from a buffet-style layout before heading out hiking or skiing. The dining room and lounge center on a wood-burning fire, where guests come together each evening to swap tales from the trail.

The 164-bed **HI-Lake Louise Alpine Centre** (203 Village Rd., 403/522-2201 or 866/762-4122, hihostels.ca, year-round, dorms C$52-63, private rooms C$110-250) is popular. Of timber-frame construction, the building has large windows and high vaulted ceilings. Upstairs is a large lounge area and guide's room, a quiet place to plan your next hike or browse through the large collection of mountain literature. Other amenities include Wi-Fi, a laundry, a game room, and a wintertime ski shuttle. Most shared rooms have 4-5 beds, and private room options include two singles, doubles with en suites, and family rooms. Make reservations six months in advance for summer and weekends during the winter season. Bill Peyto's Café is on-site.

Hotels and Inns

Aside from the chateau, the **Lake Louise Inn** (210 Village Rd., 403/522-3791 or 800/661-9237, www.lakelouiseinn.com, C$150-680) is the village's largest lodging, with more than 200 units spread throughout five buildings. Across from the lobby, in the main lodge, is a gift shop and an activities desk, and beyond is a pizzeria, restaurant, bar, and indoor pool. Most online bookings include breakfast.

The **Post Hotel** (200 Pipestone Dr., 403/522-3989 or 800/661-1586, posthotel. com, C$510-950) is one of only a handful of Canadian accommodations that have been accepted into the prestigious Relais & Châteaux organization. Bordered to the east and south by the Pipestone River, the hotel may lack views of Lake Louise, but it boasts a modern, woodsy elegance. Each bungalow-style room is furnished with Canadian pine and has a balcony. Many rooms have whirlpools and fireplaces, while some have kitchens. Other facilities include the upscale Temple Mountain Spa, an indoor pool, steam room, and library. The hotel has 17 different room types, including four sought-after cabins, each with a wood-burning fireplace.

Surrounded by exquisite scenery, the ★ **Fairmont Chateau Lake Louise** (111 Lake Louise Dr., 403/522-3511 or 866/540-4413, www.fairmont.com/lake-louise, from C$799) is an elegant historic 500-room hotel on the shore of Lake Louise. Smaller, older rooms in the lakefront building have outstanding views. But larger, more modern rooms are in the Mountain View building. All this historic charm comes at a price. Rooms on the Fairmont Gold Floor come with a private concierge and upgraded everything for a little over C$1,000 a night. Off-season, you can pick up a room for C$400. Children younger than 18 sharing with parents are free.

Lodges

Historic **Deer Lodge** (109 Lake Louise Dr., 403/410-7417 or 800/661-1595, crmr.com, C$339-499) began life in 1921 as a teahouse, with rooms added later. Facilities include a rooftop hot tub with glacier views, a game room, a restaurant (serving breakfast and dinner), and a bar. The least-expensive rooms are older and don't have phones. Larger

heritage-themed Tower Rooms are higher end. The lodge is a five-minute walk from Lake Louise.

On the valley floor, **Mountaineer Lodge** (101 Village Rd., 403/522-3844 or 855/556-8473, mountaineerlodge.com, C$150-5400) offers large guest rooms, many with mountain views. On the downside, the rooms have no phones or air-conditioning, and there is no elevator. Amenities include an indoor hot tub.

An excellent option for families and those looking for old-fashioned mountain charm is **Paradise Lodge and Bungalows** (105 Lake Louise Dr., 403/522-3595, www.paradiselodge.com, mid-May-early Oct., from C$345). This family-operated lodge spreads out around well-manicured gardens with 21 attractive cabins in four configurations. Each has a rustic yet warm and inviting interior, a separate sitting area, and an en suite bathroom. Each cabin has a small fridge, microwave, and coffeemaker, while the larger ones have full kitchens and separate bedrooms. You can walk to Lake Louise, which is about 10 minutes away.

At Moraine Lake, the super-luxurious **Moraine Lake Lodge** (1 Moraine Lake Rd., 403/522-3733 or 877/522-2777, www.morainelake.com, June-Sept., from C$1,100) rivals the scenery. Designed by renowned architect Arthur Erickson, the lodge is a bastion of understated charm, partially obscured from the masses of day-trippers who visit the area and yet taking full advantage of its location beside one of the world's most photographed lakes. The decor reflects the wilderness location, with an abundance of polished log work and solid, practical furnishings in heritage-themed rooms. The rooms have no TVs or phones; instead, guests take guided nature walks, have unlimited use of canoes, and are pampered with gourmet breakfast and afternoon tea.

Top to bottom: HI-Lake Louise Alpine Centre; Post Hotel; Fairmont Chateau Lake Louise

Resorts

★ **Baker Creek Mountain Resort** (10 km/6.2 mi south from Lake Louise on Bow Valley Pkwy., 403/522-3761, bakercreek.com, C$470-800) has a small village of log chalets with a kitchenette, separate bedroom, fireplace, and outside deck complete with cute wood carvings of bears climbing over the railings. The Trapper's Cabin is a huge space with a log bed, antler chandelier, wood-burning fireplace, double-jetted tub, and cooking facilities. A lodge wing has eight upscale suites, each with richly accented log work, a deck, a microwave and fridge, and a deluxe bathroom. A bistro serves meals on-site.

Camping

Lake Louise has one campground within easy walking distance of the village. **Lake Louise Campground** (C$35) is divided into two sections by the Bow River but is linked by the Bow River Loop hiking trail, which leads into the village along either side of the river. Amenities include picnic tables, hot showers, potable water, flush toilets, a dump station, and accessible campsites. Fire permits (C$9) include firewood. Interpretive programs run nightly at the outdoor theatre. The east side (189 sites, year-round, RV limit 22 m/75 ft) is for hard-sided vehicles only and has electrical-only hookups; some loops have fire pits while others do not. The west side is the tent and soft-sided campground (206 sites, mid-May-Sept., RV limit 6 m/21ft), which is enclosed inside an electric fence to deter bears, and most sites have fire pits. Walk to Lake Louise Village to catch shuttles to various locales.

Book sites as soon as the **Parks Canada Campground reservation service** (877/737-3783, reservation.pc.gc.ca, C$12) opens for the year, usually in January. Campsites go fast, especially for July and August.

Transportation and Services

Emergency Services

Call **911** for emergencies. The closest hospital is **Mineral Springs Hospital** (305 Lynx St., Banff, 403/762-2222, www.covenanthealth.ca) in Banff. It has 24-hour emergency services.

Gas and Vehicle Charging Stations

Two gas stations are in Lake Louise village: **Petro-Canada** (100 Village Rd.) and **Husky** (200 Village Rd.). There are **electric vehicle charging stations** in the village, in the **parking lot** across from the visitors center and at **Lake Louise Campground.**

Cell Service

Lake Louise has good cell phone reception in the village and at the lake. Most trails and Moraine Lake do not have service.

Getting Around

Wilson Mountain Sports (Samson Mall, 201 Village Rd., 403/522-3636 or 866-929-3636, www.wmsll.com) has mountain and e-bikes for rent. Rentals include a helmet and bike lock.

Parking

Lake Louise Village, Lake Louise, and Moraine Lake are super crowded from **May to October.** Arrive early to be assured a parking spot.

In **Lake Louise Village,** the parking at the visitors center and Samson Mall fills up, though most people don't park here for a full day. Additional parking is behind the gas station across the street, including a section for large RVs. If you are staying in the campground, hostel, or nearby hotels, walk to this area instead of driving.

Along the Trans-Canada Highway, the **Lake Louise Park-and-Ride** (8 km/5 mi south of Lake Louise Village) is a huge parking lot with shuttle pickups for Lake Louise Village, Lake Louise, and Moraine

Lake. RVs will find plentiful parking here.

In summer, plan on arriving at **Lake Louise** or **Moraine Lake** by **sunrise;** both lots fill by 6am. When the parking lots are full (indicated by electronic signage on the highway), go to the Park-and-Ride lot to catch a shuttle.

Shuttles

Lake Louise and **Moraine Lake shuttles** (roundtrip C$8 adults, C$4 seniors, C$2 youth, free under 6) depart from the **Lake Louise Park-and-Ride lot** (8 km/5 mi south of Lake Louise Village) along the Trans-Canada Highway. **Reservations are required** (reservation.pc.gc.ca, C$3) and are available **48 hours** in advance starting at 8am. If you have tickets to one lake, you can take the first-come, first-served **connector shuttle** (free) to the other lake. Shuttles run daily to **Lake Louise** (every 20 min., 8am-6:20pm mid-May-mid-Oct., 7:50pm last return bus from lake) and **Moraine Lake** (every 20-30 min., 6am-5:30pm daily June-mid-Oct., 7:50pm last return bus from lake).

Roam Transit (www.roamtransit.com) runs **Banff-Lake Louise buses** (daily mid-May-mid-Sept., one-way C$10 adults, C$5 youth and seniors, free under 12) about 10 times each day in summer (hours and number of runs shorten in spring and fall). Purchase tickets with exact cash when you board or via the smartphone app. The **Lake Louise Express** (route 8X) goes from Banff to Lake Louise village and lakeshore. The **Lake Louise Scenic** (route 8S, reserve online) departs from Banff to go up the Bow Valley Parkway to Lake Louise with stops at Johnston Canyon and Protection Mountain Campground. A special bus also runs in fall from **Banff to Moraine Lake** (route 10, daily late Sept.-mid-Oct., C$20 round-trip) to see the larch trees changing colors.

Lake Louise Ski Resort (403/760-1222, www.skilouise.com) runs a free shuttle between Samson Mall in Lake Louise Village, Lake Louise Inn, Mountaineer Lodge, and the ski area. It coincides with the winter ski season and summer sightseeing gondola season.

Hop On Banff (www.hoponbanff.com, daily early June-late Sept., C$60 adults, C$45 kids) is half bus tour, half shuttle. This hop-on, hop-off service connects Banff, Lake Louise sightseeing gondola, Lake Louise Village, Lake Louise, and Moraine Lake. Schedules are online. Make reservations in advance to guarantee a seat.

Banff Townsite

Many visitors planning a trip to the national park don't realize that the town of Banff is a bustling commercial center. It is spread out along the Bow River, between Sulphur Mountain and Tunnel Mountain. In one direction is the towering face of Mount Rundle, and in the other, framed by the buildings along Banff Avenue, is Cascade Mountain. Hotels and motels line the north end of Banff Avenue, while a profusion of shops, boutiques, cafés, and restaurants hugs the south end. Also at the south end, just over the Bow River, the road forks to the historic Cave and Basin Hot Springs and the historic Fairmont Banff Springs hotel and Banff Gondola. Some people are happy walking along the crowded streets or shopping in a unique setting; those more interested in some peace and quiet can easily slip into pristine wilderness just a five-minute walk from town.

Sights
Whyte Museum of the Canadian Rockies

The Whyte Foundation, established in the mid-1950s by local artists Peter and Catharine Whyte, preserves artistic and historical artifacts relating to the Canadian Rockies. Their **Whyte Museum of the Canadian Rockies** (111

Bear St., 403/762-2291, www.whyte.org, 10am-5pm daily, C$9-10 adults, C$5 kids) houses the world's largest collection of Canadian Rockies literature and art. Included in the archives are more than 4,000 volumes, oral tapes of early pioneers and outfitters, antique postcards, old cameras, manuscripts, and a large photography collection. The highlight is the photography of Byron Harmon, whose black-and-white studies of mountain geography have shown people around the world the beauty of the Canadian Rockies. The downstairs gallery features changing art exhibitions. The museum also houses the library and archives of the Alpine Club of Canada. On the grounds are several heritage homes and cabins formerly occupied by local pioneers. **Heritage Homes Tours** (11:30am daily summer, C$10) allow an opportunity for visitors to take a closer look at these.

Banff Park Museum National Historic Site

The **Banff Park Museum National Historic Site** (91 Banff Ave., 403/762-1558, www. pc.gc.ca, daily year-round, C$3-4 adults, free for youth, included with Discovery Pass) is a walk into the past, as Canada's oldest natural history museum and oldest national park building (1903). It contains over 5,000 historic specimens, including plants, minerals, fish, birds, and wildlife—everything from bees to taxidermy bighorn sheep.

Buffalo Nations Luxton Museum

The **Buffalo Nations Luxton Museum** (1 Birch Ave., 403/762-2388, www. buffalonationsmuseum.com, 10am-7pm daily summer, 11am-5pm daily fall-spring, C$5-10) is the best place in Banff to learn about the First Nations of the Canadian Rockies and the Northern Plains. The museum shares the cultural heritage of Indigenous people through displays, art, demonstrations, dancing and drumming classes, films, speakers, and events like an annual powwow. The museum's four sections are inside a fort-like exterior. Displays contain beaded regalia, hunting tools, art, ceremonial objects, and arrowheads, plus an ornate tepee, relating the elements of daily life from historic to modern times. Interpretive tours by local elders are available. The gift shop sells handmade arts and crafts made by First Nations artisans.

Cave and Basin National Historic Site

The birthplace of Banff National Park and the Canadian National Parks system, **Cave and Basin National Historic Site** (end of Cave Ave., 403/762-1566, www.pc.gc.ca, 10am-5pm daily summer, shorter hours off-season, C$7-8 adults, free for youth) is where three Canadian Pacific Railway employees stumbled on the hot springs in 1883. They built a fence around the springs, constructed a crude cabin, and began the process of establishing a claim to the site. But the government beat them to it, settling their claims for a few thousand dollars and acquiring the hot springs.

Bathhouses were installed in 1887, and bathers paid C$0.10 for a swim. The pools were eventually lined with concrete, and additions were built onto the original structures. Ironically, the soothing minerals in the water that had attracted millions of people to bathe here eventually caused the pools' demise. The minerals, combined with chlorine, produced sediments that ate away at the concrete structure until the pools were deemed unsuitable for swimming in 1993. Although the pools are now closed to swimming, the site is still one of Banff's most popular attractions. You can tour interpretive displays, go through a narrow tunnel into the dimly lit cave, and walk short trails leading to the cave entrance and through a unique environment created by the hot water from the springs.

Vicinity of Banff

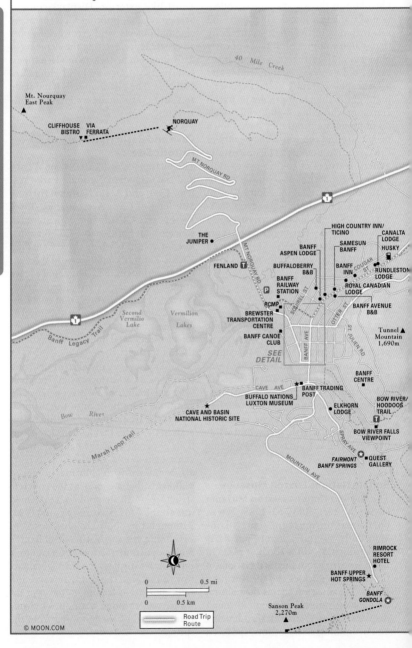

Mt. Nourquay East Peak

CLIFFHOUSE BISTRO VIA FERRATA

40 Mile Creek

NORQUAY

MT NORQUAY RD

THE JUNIPER

FENLAND

BANFF ASPEN LODGE

BUFFALOBERRY B&B

BANFF RAILWAY STATION

HIGH COUNTRY INN/ TICINO

SAMESUN BANFF

BANFF INN

CANALTA LODGE

HUSKY

COUGAR ST

RUNDLESTON LODGE

ROYAL CANADIAN LODGE

BANFF AVENUE B&B

SQUIREL ST

OTTER ST

ST JULIEN RD

BANFF AVE

Tunnel ▲ Mountain 1,690m

RCMP

BREWSTER TRANSPORTATION CENTRE

BANFF CANOE CLUB

SEE DETAIL

Second Vermilio Lake

Vermilion Lakes

Banff Legacy Trail

BANFF CENTRE

CAVE AVE

BANFF TRADING POST

BUFFALO NATIONS LUXTON MUSEUM

CAVE AND BASIN NATIONAL HISTORIC SITE

Bow River

ELKHORN LODGE

BOW RIVER/ HOODOOS TRAIL

BOW RIVER FALLS VIEWPOINT

Marsh Loop Trail

SPRAY AVE

MOUNTAIN AVE

FAIRMONT BANFF SPRINGS

QUEST GALLERY

RIMROCK RESORT HOTEL

BANFF UPPER HOT SPRINGS

BANFF GONDOLA

Sanson Peak 2,270m

0   0.5 mi

0   0.5 km

Road Trip Route

© MOON.COM

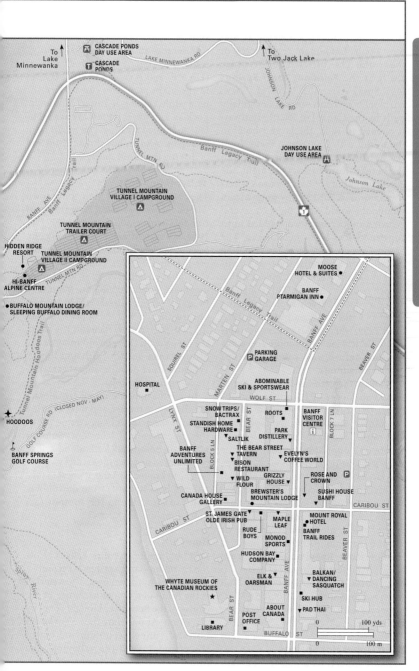

To Lake Minnewanka

CASCADE PONDS DAY USE AREA

CASCADE PONDS

LAKE MINNEWANKA RD.

To Two Jack Lake

JOHNSON LAKE RD

Banff Legacy Trail

JOHNSON LAKE DAY USE AREA

Johnson Lake

TUNNEL MOUNTAIN VILLAGE I CAMPGROUND

TUNNEL MOUNTAIN TRAILER COURT

BANFF AVE

Banff Legacy Trail

TUNNEL MTN Trail

HIDDEN RIDGE RESORT

TUNNEL MOUNTAIN VILLAGE II CAMPGROUND

HI-BANFF ALPINE CENTRE

TUNNEL MTN RD

BUFFALO MOUNTAIN LODGE/ SLEEPING BUFFALO DINING ROOM

Tunnel Mountain Hoodoos Trail

HOODOOS

GOLF COURSE RD (CLOSED NOV - MAY)

BANFF SPRINGS GOLF COURSE

Spray River

Banff Legacy Trail

MOOSE HOTEL & SUITES

BANFF PTARMIGAN INN

BANFF AVE

BEAVER ST

PARKING GARAGE

HOSPITAL

ABOMINABLE SKI & SPORTSWEAR

WOLF ST

SOURREL ST

MARTEN ST

BEAR ST

BLOCK 7 LN

SNOW TRIPS/ BACTRAX

ROOTS

BANFF VISITOR CENTRE

STANDISH HOME HARDWARE

PARK DISTILLERY

SALTLIK

LYNX ST

BLOCK 5 LN

THE BEAR STREET TAVERN

EVELYN'S COFFEE WORLD

BANFF ADVENTURES UNLIMITED

BISON RESTAURANT

GRIZZLY HOUSE

ROSE AND CROWN

WILD FLOUR

SUSHI HOUSE BANFF

CANADA HOUSE GALLERY

BREWSTER'S MOUNTAIN LODGE

CARIBOU ST

CARIBOU ST

ST. JAMES GATE OLDE IRISH PUB

MAPLE LEAF

MOUNT ROYAL HOTEL

RUDE BOYS

BANFF TRAIL RIDES

MONOD SPORTS

BANFF AVE

BEAVER ST

HUDSON BAY COMPANY

BALKAN/ DANCING SASQUATCH

WHYTE MUSEUM OF THE CANADIAN ROCKIES

ELK & OARSMAN

SKI HUB

PAD THAI

BEAR ST

POST OFFICE

ABOUT CANADA

0   100 yds

LIBRARY

BUFFALO ST

0   100 m

★ Fairmont Banff Springs

On a terrace above a bend in the Bow River is one of the largest, grandest, and most opulent mountain resort hotels in the world. This turreted 20th-century castle is the **Fairmont Banff Springs** (405 Spray Ave., 403/762-2211, www.fairmont.com/banff-springs), originally built by the Canadian Pacific Railway. It opened in 1888, the largest hotel in the world, with 250 rooms. Water from the nearby hot springs was piped into the hotel's steam baths. Overnight, the quiet community of Banff became a destination resort for wealthy guests from around the world. Over the next several decades, more rooms were added until construction of a new hotel began. The original design, an 11-story tower joining two wings in a baronial style, was reminiscent of a Scottish castle mixed with a French country chateau. This concrete-and-rock-faced, green-roofed building stood as it did at its completion in 1928 until 1999, when ambitious renovations created a new lobby in a more accessible location, refurbished rooms, and upgraded restaurants.

Wander through the hotel to admire the 5,000 pieces of furniture and antiques (most in public areas are reproductions), paintings, prints, tapestries, and rugs. Take in the medieval atmosphere of **Mount Stephen Hall**, with its lime flagstone floor, enormous windows, and large oak beams; take advantage of the luxurious spa facility; or relax in one of 12 eateries or four lounges.

The hotel is a 15-minute walk southeast of town, along Spray Avenue or via the trail along the south bank of the Bow River. **Roam buses** (C$2) leave Banff Avenue for the hotel twice an hour. **Horse-drawn buggies** (Banff Trail Riders, 138 Banff Ave., 800/661-8352, horseback.com, C$240) can also take you to the hotel.

Banff Upper Hot Springs

At **Banff Upper Hot Springs** (1 Mountain Ave., 800/767-1611, www.hotsprings.ca, 9am-11pm daily mid-May-mid-Oct., shorter hours off season, C$9 adults, C$8 seniors and youths, C$27 family), water flows out of the bedrock at 47°C (116.6°F) and is cooled to 40°C (104°F) in the main pool. You can soak in the pool while looking at Tunnel Mountain. Lockers and towel rentals are available. Due to limited parking, you might want to hop on a Roam bus (Route 1) instead of driving to the hot springs.

★ Banff Gondola

The easiest way to get high above town without breaking a sweat is on the **Banff Gondola** (end of Mountain Ave., 866/756-1904, www.banffjaspercollection.com, 8:30am-9pm daily summer, shorter hours off-season, C$37-70). Four-person cars rise 700 meters (2,300 ft) in eight minutes to the summit of **Sulphur Mountain.** From the wheelchair-accessible **rooftop observation deck** at the upper terminal, the 360-degree view includes the town, the Bow Valley, Cascade Mountain, Lake Minnewanka, and the Fairholme Range. When weather permits, sunsets are outstanding from the top.

Inside the upper terminal are interactive displays, a theater, and three eateries. Bighorn sheep often hang around below the upper terminal. The short **Sulphur Mountain Boardwalk** leads along a ridge to a restored weather observatory.

Due to limited parking, it's best to take a Roam bus (Route 1) from downtown. You can also hike to the summit (5.5 km/3.4 mi one-way).

Bow Falls

Small but impressive **Bow Falls** is below the Fairmont Banff Springs hotel, only a short walk from downtown. The waterfall is the result of a dramatic change in the course of the Bow River brought about by glaciation. At one time the river flowed north of Tunnel Mountain and out of the mountains via the valley of Lake Minnewanka. As the glaciers retreated, they left terminal moraines, forming natural dams and changing the course of the river. Eventually the backed-up water found an outlet here between Tunnel Mountain and the northwest ridge of Mount Rundle. The falls are biggest in late spring when runoff from the winter snows fills every river and stream in Bow Valley.

To reach the falls on foot from town, cross the bridge at the south end of Banff Avenue, scramble down the grassy embankment to the left, and follow a pleasant trail (2 km/1.2 mi, 40 min) along the Bow River to a point above the falls. By car, cross the bridge and follow the signs for the golf course. From the falls, a paved road crosses the Spray River and passes through the golf course.

Lake Minnewanka

Lake Minnewanka, or "Lake of the Water Spirit," is the largest body of water in Banff National Park. Mount Inglismaldie and the Fairholme Range form an imposing backdrop for the reservoir. Go for a short walk along the lakeshore. You'll pass a concession selling snacks and drinks and the tour boat dock before entering an area of picnic tables and covered cooking shelters. Children will love exploring the rocky shoreline and stony beaches in this area, but you should continue farther around the lake, if only to escape the crowds. An easy walking **trail** leads past a number of picnic spots and rocky beaches to **Stewart Canyon.**

Banff Lake Cruise (403/762-3473, www.banffjaspercollection.com, 9am-7pm daily summer, shorter hours spring and fall, C$60-75 adults, C$30-38 children) has 1- and 1.5-hour cruises on the lake, departing multiple times daily. You can also rent canoes, and single or double kayaks (C$40-75/hr) and aluminum boats with small outboard engines (C$105-285).

Top to bottom: Cave and Basin National Historic Site; Fairmont Banff Springs; Lake Minnewanka

From Lake Minnewanka, the road continues along the reservoir wall, passing a lookout point. You'll likely have to slow down along this stretch of road for bighorn sheep. The road then descends to **Two Jack Lake** and a lakefront day-use area. Take the turnoff to **Johnson Lake** to access a lakeside trail, Banff's busiest swimming and sunbathing spot on the warmest days of summer. It has picnic facilities with views across to Mount Rundle.

Mount Norquay

One of the best views of town accessible by vehicle is on the road that switchbacks steeply to the base of **Mount Norquay,** the local winter hangout for skiers and snowboarders. On the way up are several **overlooks,** including one near the top where bighorn sheep often graze.

Where the road ends, the North American chairlift at **Mount Norquay** (2 Mt. Norquay Rd., 403/762-4421, banffnorquay.com, 9am-7pm daily mid-June-mid-Oct., C$40 adults, C$25 children, C$115 family) lifts visitors even higher for immense views across the town and Bow Valley. Also at the top is the **Cliffhouse Bistro** (11am-5:50pm daily, C$10-36), ensconced in a stone building clinging to the mountain slope.

★ Sunshine Meadows

Perched on the boundary of Alberta and British Columbia along the Continental Divide, **Sunshine Meadows** (end of Sunshine Village Rd., 403/705-4000 or 877/542-2633, www.banffsunshinemeadows.com) is a ski area and summer resort west of Banff. You cannot reach it by car; instead, you'll take a **gondola** (8am-6pm daily late June-mid-Sept., C$42-45 adults, C$23 youths, C$110 family) up to the Sunshine Village resort, which has an overnight lodge, restaurants, and a day lodge and interpretive center. In the winter, ski lifts run up the resort's slopes; in summer, hiking trails crisscross the area.

The terrain around the resort is famed for the eponymous meadows that burst with spectacular wildflower displays in summer. Large amounts of precipitation create a lush cover of vegetation where over 300 species of wildflowers have been identified, including pink fireweed, glacier lilies, mountain avens, white mountain heather, and forget-me-nots. Blooms usually peak mid-July to early August. Take a **sightseeing lift** (closes at 5pm) to go even higher and walk to the **Standish sightseeing deck** (0.8 km/0.5 mi rt) to survey the meadows and mountains. Longer trails tour the meadows and loop to scenic alpine lakes.

Dining, overnight lodging, and guided walks of various lengths are available. You can get a free shuttle from Banff to the Sunshine gondola base with the gondola and chairlift ticket; otherwise, drive 8 km (5 mi) west of Banff on Trans-Canada to reach the access road to Sunshine Village.

Scenic Drive
Bow Valley Parkway and Trans-Canada Highway Loop

Two roads run through Bow Valley, linking Banff and Lake Louise: **Trans-Canada** (Hwy. 1) and **Bow Valley Parkway** (Hwy. 1A). Together, they create a loop route that allows you to drive both sides of the Bow River. The two roads connect in three locations: Lake Louise in the north, Castle Junction in the middle, and 5 km (3 mi) west of Banff.

Both roads are 51 km (32 mi) long between the north and south connections. However, Trans-Canada has faster speeds at 90 kph (56 mph) and is a straighter road, allowing for a drive of under 45 minutes without stops. Bow Valley Parkway is narrower, curvier, and has slower speed limits at 60 kph (37 mph), so it will take around an hour to drive this route without stops.

Along Bow Valley Parkway, the original road through the area, are several impressive viewpoints, interpretive displays,

Bow Valley Parkway

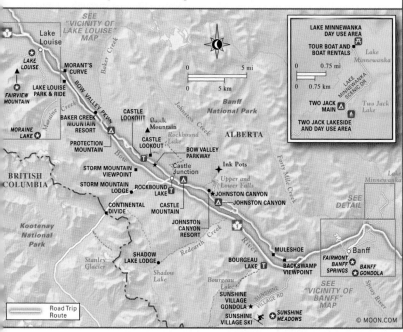

picnic areas, hiking trails, opportunities for wildlife-watching, three lodges, and campgrounds. Parks Canada is piloting a popular program during spring (Mar.-late June) that closes the area between **Johnston Canyon and the Fireside Picnic Area** to cars, so **bicyclists** can enjoy the road while many trails are still buried under snow. During this time, the same area closes overnight (8pm-8am) for wildlife.

Lake Louise to Castle Mountain
Starting on the **Bow Valley Parkway** (Hwy. 1A) at **Morant's Curve**, the rail line, river, and mountains combine for perfect symmetry. Farther south, the road passes **Baker Creek Mountain Resort,** where you can grab a snack.

As you continue south, look to the west as the dramatic **Castle Mountain** comes into view. The mountain consists

of 500-million-year-old rock sitting atop much younger 200-million-year-old rock. This unusual formation occurred as the mountains were forced upward by pressure below the earth's surface, thrusting the older rock up and over the younger rock in places. At **Castle Mountain village** (which has gas, groceries, and lodging), the parkway continues straight ahead, or you can turn right (west) to cross the bridge over the Bow River to Castle Mountain Junction. From the junction, you can hop on Trans-Canada north to Lake Louise or Banff or continue onto Highway 93 to reach Kootenay National Park.

Castle Mountain Junction to Banff
On the southern half of Bow Valley Parkway, a small plaque marks the site of **Silver City** at a pullout on the west end of **Moose Meadows.** At its peak in the

mid-1800s, this boomtown had a population of 2,000, making it bigger than Calgary at the time. Five mines extracted ore rich in copper and lead, not silver. The demise of Silver City happened when two men salted their mine with gold and silver ore to attract investors, sold 2,000 shares at C$5 each, and then vanished, leaving investors with a useless mine. Investment in the town ceased, mines closed, and people left. Look for wildlife around Moose Meadows.

Johnston Canyon (arrive by 8am), the most popular stop on Bow Valley Parkway, is a chasm carved in limestone where Johnston Creek drops over a series of spectacular **waterfalls.** An elevated catwalk within the canyon leads to the **lower falls** (2 km/1.2 mi rt). It's illegal to veer off the designated route. Portions of the canyon are closed May 1-November 15 to protect black swift nesting areas.

South of Johnston Canyon, wetlands abound. Look for wildlife at **Muleshoe,** where oxbow lakes formed when the Bow River abandoned its meanders for a more direct path. At **Backswamp Viewpoint,** you can look upstream to the site of a former dam, now a swampy wetland filled with aquatic vegetation.

Lastly, you'll pass a short side road to the **Fireside picnic area,** adjacent to a creek, before joining Trans-Canada. To circle back north to Lake Louise, follow Trans-Canada northwest. To continue to Banff, follow Trans-Canada eastward.

Recreation
Hiking
Tunnel Mountain
Length: 4.6 km (2.8 mi) rt
Duration: 1.5 hours
Elevation gain: 300 meters (990 ft)
Effort: easy-moderate
Trailhead: St. Julien Rd.

Accessible from town, this short hike is an easy climb to one of the park's lower peaks. It ascends the western flank of **Tunnel Mountain** through a forest of lodgepole pine, switchbacking past

viewpoints before reaching a ridge just below the summit. Here the trail turns northward, climbing through a forest of Douglas fir to the partially treed summit with partial views.

Bow River and Hoodoos
Length: 4.8 km (3 mi) one-way
Duration: 1.5 hours
Elevation gain: minimal
Effort: easy
Trailhead: Bow River Viewpoint, Tunnel Mountain Dr.

From an overlook famed for its view of the **Fairmont Banff Springs hotel,** this trail descends to the **Bow River,** passing under the sheer east face of Tunnel Mountain. It then follows the river a short distance before climbing into a meadow where deer and elk often graze. From this perspective, the north face of Mount Rundle is particularly imposing. As the trail climbs, you'll hear the traffic on Tunnel Mountain Road long before you see it. The trail ends at a viewpoint above

hoodoos, strange-looking limestone-and-gravel columns jutting mysteriously out of the forest. To return to the trailhead, catch the Banff Transit bus from Tunnel Mountain Campground. Or return the way you came for a 9.6 km (6 mi) round-trip hike.

Cascade Amphitheatre
Length: 13.2 km (8.2 mi) rt
Duration: 4 hours
Elevation gain: 610 meters (2,000 ft)
Effort: moderate-difficult
Trailhead: day lodge at the top of Mount Norquay Rd.

This enormous cirque and the subalpine meadows directly behind Cascade Mountain are one of the most rewarding destinations in the Banff area. The demanding trail begins by passing the day lodge, then skirting the base of several lifts and following an old road to the floor of **Forty Mile Valley.** Keep right at all trail junctions. After crossing Forty Mile Creek, the trail begins switchbacking up the western flank of **Cascade Mountain** through a forest of lodgepole pine. Along the way are views of Mount Louis's sheer east face. After the trail levels off, it enters a U-shaped valley, and the amphitheater begins to define itself. The trail becomes indistinct in the subalpine meadow, which is carpeted in colorful wildflowers during summer. Farther up the valley, vegetation thins out as boulder-strewn talus slopes cover the ground. If you sit still long enough on these rocks, marmots and pikas will slowly appear, emitting shrill whistles before disappearing again.

★ Sunshine Meadows
Length: 3.6-18.6 km (2.2-11.6 mi) rt
Duration: 1.5-6 hours
Elevation gain: 121-777 meters (397-2,550 ft)
Effort: moderate-strenuous
Trailhead: day lodge, top of Sunshine Gondola

Sunshine Meadows, straddling the Continental Divide, is best known for Sunshine Village, an alpine winter and

trail to Sunshine Meadows

summer resort accessible only by gondola from the valley floor. But for a few months each summer, the area is snow-free and becomes a hiking wonderland noted for wildflower meadows that peak mid-July to early August. From Sunshine Village, trails radiate across the alpine meadows, several looping to lake destinations.

The most popular destination is **Rock Isle Lake** (3.6 km/2.2 mi rt, 121 m/397 ft, 2 hrs), a jaunt that crosses the Continental Divide without too much climbing. Mount Assiniboine, known as the "Matterhorn of the Rockies," is visible to the southeast. Various viewpoints punctuate the descent to an observation point overlooking the lake. From Rock Isle Lake Junction, you can add on a loop around **Larix and Grizzly Lakes** (3.6 km/2.2 mi rt, 146 m/479 ft, 2.5 hrs). The trail drops to the lakes and climbs up on the return.

A longer, more strenuous excursion goes from Sunshine Village to **Citadel Pass** (18.6 km/11.6 mi rt, 6 hrs). The route starts uphill to the junction with Rock Isle Lake, where a left turn aims for the pass. The path crosses above Rock Isle Lake through intermittent meadows and glaciated rock rubble and drops into a basin on the north side of Quartz Hill. The trail passes **Howard Douglas Lake** and climbs again by **Citadel Lake** before reaching Citadel Pass (2,360 m/7,743 ft), between Citadel Peak and Fatigue Mountain. The pass is the boundary with Mount Assiniboine Provincial Park.

To access the trailheads, take the **Sunshine Meadows Gondola** (end of Sunshine Village Rd., 403/705-4000 or 877/542-2633, www.banffsunshinemeadows.com, 8am-6pm daily late June-mid-Sept., C$42-45 adults, C$23 youths, C$110 family). To get to the base of the gondola from Banff, follow the Trans-Canada 8 km (5 mi) west to Sunshine Village Road, which continues a similar distance along Healy Creek to the Sunshine Village parking lot.

Bourgeau Lake

Length: 15.2 km (9.4 mi) rt
Duration: 5 hours
Elevation gain: 730 meters (2,400 ft)
Effort: moderate
Trailhead: signposted parking lot, Trans-Canada Highway, 3 km (1.9 mi) west of Sunshine Village Junction

This trail follows Wolverine Creek to a small subalpine lake nestled at the base of an impressive limestone amphitheater. Although the trail is moderately steep, plenty of distractions along the way are worthy of a stop to rest. Back across the Bow Valley, the Sawback Range is easy to distinguish. As the forest of lodgepole pine turns to spruce, the trail passes under the cliffs of Mount Bourgeau and crosses Wolverine Creek below a spot where it tumbles photogenically over exposed bedrock. After strenuous switchbacks, the trail climbs into the cirque containing **Bourgeau Lake** below the immense cliff face of Mount Borgeau. As you explore the lake's rocky shore, you'll hear the colonies of noisy pikas, even if you don't see them. For those looking for more, circle the lake's west side to pick up a rough trail ascending further to **Harvey Lake and Harvey Pass** (add 5 km/3.1 mi rt) for views of Sunshine Meadows and Mount Assiniboine in the distance.

Shadow Lake

Length: 28.6 km (17.8 mi) rt
Duration: 8 hours
Elevation gain: 440 meters (1,445 ft)
Effort: moderate
Trailhead: Redearth Creek Parking Area, Trans-Canada Highway

Shadow Lake is one of the many impressive subalpine lakes along the Continental Divide. This trail follows an abandoned fire road for 11 km (6.8 mi) before forking right and climbing into the forest. The Shadow Lake **backcountry campground** (5 sites) is 2 km (1.2 mi) beyond this junction; just 0.3 km (0.2 mi) farther is **Shadow Lake Lodge.** The lake is huge, but it cowers below the blocky

Mount Ball. On a calm day, you'll catch its image reflected in Shadow Lake. From the lake's eastern shore, trails lead further to Ball Pass, Gibbon Pass, and Haiduk Lake.

Johnston Canyon

Length: 2-5.2 km (1.2-3.2 mi) rt
Duration: 1-2 hours
Elevation gain: 30-120 meters (98-394 ft)
Effort: easy-moderate
Trailhead: Bow Valley Parkway, 31 km (19 mi) northwest of Banff

Johnston Canyon sees tremendous crowds from May to September. People come to see the series of waterfalls deep within the chasm carved through limestone. Plan to get here well before 8am or go after 6pm to avoid crowds on the trail. You can also hop a bus from Banff (route 8S or 9, www.roamtransit.com), which runs several times throughout the day to the canyon. It's possible to hike this trail year-round; however, you'll need ice cleats (spikes) in winter. During other seasons, the trail can be wet, muddy, and sometimes slippery. Portions of the canyon are closed May 1-November 15 for black swift nesting. By law, hikers are required to stay on the designated trail at all times.

An easy trail leads to an elevated catwalk with railings within the lower canyon. The walk follows Johnston Creek upstream, with the canyon's walls stretching above and below you. You can spot the **lower falls** before the bridge that crosses the creek. Across the bridge, the trail cuts through a short, drippy tunnel to gain a better view of the falls. In winter, the canyon is filled with fantastical ice formations—including the falls themselves. Wheelchairs can go most of the way to the lower falls, but the catwalk is narrow at times and assistance may be required for inclines and declines.

The **upper falls** are farther upstream via a steep climb. The trail ascends out of the lower canyon, goes through the forest, and then follows the creek past small plunges of water and scenic pools. At the top, the trail forks to two different overlooks: one at the bottom of the falls and one at the top.

Castle Lookout

Length: 7.4 km (4.6 mi) rt
Duration: 3 hours
Elevation gain: 520 meters (1,700 ft)
Effort: moderately strenuous
Trailhead: Bow Valley Parkway, 5 km (3.1 mi) northwest of Castle Junction

However you travel through the Bow Valley, you can't help but be impressed by **Castle Mountain,** rising proudly from the forest floor. This trail takes you above the tree line on the mountain's west face to the site of the **Mount Eisenhower fire lookout,** burned in the 1980s. From the Bow Valley Parkway, the trail follows a wide pathway to an abandoned cabin in a forest of lodgepole pine and spruce. It then becomes narrower and steeper, switchbacking through a meadow before climbing through a narrow band of rock and leveling off near the lookout site. Panoramas of the Bow Valley spread out before you in both directions with Storm Mountain perched directly across the valley.

Rockbound Lake

Length: 16.8 km (10.4 mi) rt
Duration: 5-6 hours
Elevation gain: 760 meters (2,500 ft)
Effort: strenuous
Trailhead: Castle Junction, Bow Valley Parkway, 30 km (18.6 mi) northwest of Banff

For the first 4.8 km (3 mi), the trail follows an old fire road along the southern flanks of Castle Mountain. Early in the season or after heavy rain, this section can be boggy. Glimpses of surrounding peaks ease the pain of the steady climb as the trail narrows. Soon, after 2.4 km (1.5 mi) more, you'll come to **Tower Lake,** which the trail skirts to the right before climbing a steep slope. From the top of the ridge, **Rockbound Lake** comes into view, surrounded by golden larch in early fall and backed by vertical cliff walls. A scramble up any of the nearby slopes will reward you with good views.

Backpacking
Permits
Permits (C$10 pp per night) are required for backcountry camping in Banff. **Reservations** (877/737-3783, 519/826-5391 from outside North America, reservation.pc.gc.ca, C$12) open usually in January; many routes book up fast for July to early September. You can also get reservations for trail shelters at Bryant Creek and Egypt Lake (C$17).

Egypt Lake
25 kilometers (16 miles)
This out-and-back trip launches from the parking lot at the Sunshine Village ski area. It's best done over three days so you have time to explore further from Egypt Lake, where you'll camp or stay in the trail shelter for two nights. You'll cross through the wildflower meadows and, in September, stands of golden larch climbing over Healy Pass. On your middle day, go to Scarab and Mummy Lakes or the three tiny lakes along the base of the Pharoah Peaks.

Great Divide
41 kilometers (25 miles)
From the Sunshine Village parking lot or the Vista Lake Trailhead (Hwy. 93), go either direction on this strenuous point-to-point route that trots along the Continental Divide/Great Divide, linking up several high passes and alpine lakes with stunning scenery of the Ball Range dripping with glaciers. The trail has lots of ups and downs between sections that climb above the tree line over Healy, Whistling, and Gibbon Passes, and several side trips may lure you to add distance. The route is best from July to September with wildflowers hitting their peak mid-July to early August. As a four-day/three-night trip, camp at Egypt Lake, Ball Pass Junction, and Twin Lakes. To extend your time in the high country, add a night at Shadow Lake after the side trip climbing Ball Pass (5.4 km/3.5 mi rt).

Mountaineering
Rundle Mountain
It's hard to look at **Rundle Mountain** (2,949 m/9,675 ft) from downtown Banff and ignore the urge to climb it. The **scramble route** climbs up the lower-angled side (the right-hand side if you are looking at it from Banff Ave.), which is still steep. Stop in the visitors center for a route description guide or look online (www.pc.gc.ca) to avoid pitfalls of veering off the scramble route onto something more technical.

Cascade Mountain
After following the trail to Cascade Amphitheatre, experienced scramblers can pluck their way up to the summit of **Cascade Mountain** (2,998 m/9,840 ft). The most popular route climbs along the southern ridge of the amphitheater wall, a long scramble up **scree slopes** and beyond the false summit to the top. Pick up a guide to the route from the visitors center or online (www.pc.gc.ca).

Castle Mountain
The distinctive **Castle Mountain,** so prominent from Bow Valley Parkway and Trans-Canada, is a lure for rock climbers despite the crumbly limestone. The **Goat Plateau** runs horizontally across the mountain between its upper and lower cliffs. The upper cliffs have the **Brewer Buttress** and the **Eisenhower Tower,** two of the mountain's most popular routes.

On the Goat Plateau, climbers can stay in the tiny **Castle Hut** run by **Alpine Club of Canada** (ACC, 403/678-3200, www.alpineclubofcanada.ca). To go on guided climbs on Castle Mountain, contact **Canadian Rockies Alpine Guides** (www.cdnalpine.com).

Norquay Via Ferrata
The North American chairlift at **Mount Norquay** (2 Mt. Norquay Rd., 403/762-4421, banffnorquay.com) goes to the **Norquay Via Ferrata** (2.5-6 hrs, C$175-375). There you'll find four European-style climbing routes in which even visitors without mountaineering experience can try out climbing.

Biking
Whether you have your own bike or you rent one from the many bicycle shops in Banff, cycling options abound. The roads to **Lake Minnewanka, Mount Norquay,** through the **golf course,** and along the **Bow Valley Parkway** are all popular cycling routes. To avoid vehicle traffic, the **Banff Legacy Trail** (29 km/18 mi one-way) is a paved bike path that runs from Bow Valley Parkway west of Banff to Canmore. It takes in the Bow River and wildlife-rich Vermillion Lakes that reflect peaks like Mount Rundle, passes Cascade Ponds, and has picnic areas en route. Access to the trail is from five trailheads: Valleyview, Cascade Ponds, Vermilion Lakes day-use area, Fireside day-use area, and the east end of Banff Avenue.

Several hiking trails radiating from Banff and ending deep in the backcountry permit bicycles. These include **Sundance** (3.7 km/2.3 mi one-way), **Rundle Riverside to Canmore** (15 km/9.3 mi one-way), **Spray River via Goat Creek** (19 km/12 mi one-way), and **Redearth Creek** (10 km/6.2 mi one-way). Before heading into the backcountry, pick up a mountain biking guide from the visitors center or online (www.pc.gc.ca). Riders are particularly susceptible to sudden bear encounters, so be alert and make loud noises when passing through heavy vegetation.

Bactrax (225 Bear St., 403/762-8177, snowtips-bactrax.com) and **Banff Adventures Unlimited** (211 Bear St., 403/762-4554, www.banffadventures.com) rent front- and full-suspension mountain bikes for C$25-45 for half day or C$50-80 full day. Rates include a helmet, lock, and biking map.

Boating, Paddling, and Fishing
Just west of town, **Vermillion Lakes** are a series of small lakes, many connected by the slow-moving water of the **Bow River.** For paddlers, they offer loads of places to explore and maybe spot wildlife and birds. At the launch dock on the river, **Banff Canoe Club** (corner of Wolf St. and Bow Ave., 403/762-5055, banffcanoeclub. com, 9am-8pm daily summer, shorter hours in fall) rents canoes, kayaks, and paddleboards (C$30-45/hr) for paddling upstream to the lakes.

A much larger body of water that can whip up with winds and white caps, **Lake Minnewanka** has a boat launch and the dock has rentals at the **boathouse** (403/762-3473, www. banffjaspercollection.com, 10:30am-5pm daily mid-May-early Oct.). You can rent aluminum motorboats (C$115/hr, C$295 half day) or canoes, single kayaks, or double kayaks (C$45-85/hr). Rentals are first come, first served, but you can call the boathouse in advance to check on availability. The boathouse also has fishing guides, permits, and gear.

To launch your own watercraft (including inflatables and paddleboards), you must complete a self-certification for aquatic invasive species. Clean, drain, and dry all craft before launching.

Horseback Riding
Banff Trail Riders (138 Banff Ave., 403/762-4551 or 800/661-8352, www. horseback.com, C$69-246) offers a great variety of trips: 1- to 4-hour rides, plus trail rides with barbecue cookouts. You can even get pony rides for kids (C$25). The company also runs 18-km (11.5-mi) trips to their backcountry **Sundance Lodge** (C$730 pp one night, C$1,140 pp two nights), which has 10 guest rooms, a large living area, and hot showers. All meals are included. Trail rides depart

from either **Warner Stables** (Sundance Rd., 403/762-2832), behind the recreation grounds off Cave Avenue, or **Spray River Corrals** (Spray Ave., 403/762-2848), below the Fairmont Banff Springs.

Golf

One of the world's most scenic golf courses, the **Banff Springs Golf Course** (403/762-6801, www.fairmont.com/banff-springs, May-early Oct.) spreads out along the Bow River between Mount Rundle and Tunnel Mountain. The first course, laid out in 1911, was revamped by Stanley Thompson in 1928 to take advantage of the area's natural contours. It features elevated tees, wide fairways, treacherous fescue grass rough, and holes aligned to distant mountains. There's always the chance of seeing elk feeding on the fairways, or bears scurrying across. This 18-hole course (C$210-260) is supplemented by the Tunnel Mountain 9-hole course (C$100-110). The course has club rentals, putting greens, a driving range, pro shop, and restaurant.

Winter Recreation

From November to May, the entire park transforms itself into a winter playground covered in a blanket of snow. Activities include downhill skiing and snowboarding, cross-country skiing, ice-skating, snowshoeing, dogsledding, and sleigh rides.

The **Ski Hub** (114 Banff Ave., 403/762-4754, www.skibig3.com, 9am-8pm daily) represents three ski resorts in Banff National Park: Lake Louise, Sunshine Village, and Mount Norquay. Joint multi-day tickets are good at all three areas, and the hub has shuttles that go to all three resorts so you don't have to drive. It also has rentals on-site.

Mount Norquay

Mount Norquay (403/762-4421, banff-norquay.com, daily Dec.-early Apr., C$94 adults, C$37-73 kids and seniors) has two distinct faces—literally and figuratively. The mountain sports great cruising runs and a well-respected ski school, as well as the North American Chair's experts-only double-black-diamond Lone Pine run. The post-and-beam day lodge nestled below the main runs is flanked on one side by a wide deck that catches the afternoon sun. Inside you'll find a cafeteria, restaurant, and bar. The resort offers lessons, rentals, and has a shuttle bus that makes pickups at Banff hotels. It also has loads of ticket options: full days, half days, nights, and last hour.

Sunshine Village Ski Resort

Accessed via gondola, **Sunshine Village Ski Resort** (403/762-6500 or 877/542-2633, www.skibanff.com, daily mid-Nov.-late May, C$128 adults, C$49-100 kids and seniors) piles up more than 6 meters (20 ft) of snow without using snowmaking machines. Its claims to fame are dry powder, wide-open bowls, a heated chairlift, and the only slopeside

accommodations in the park. The area is best known for its outstanding beginner and intermediate terrain, which covers 60 percent of the mountain. For experts only, Delirium Dive drops off the northeast-facing slope of Lookout Mountain; to ski or board this up-to-50-degree run, you must be equipped with a transceiver, shovel, probe, and partner, but you'll have bragging rights that night at the bars. The resort has restaurants and bars, in addition to lessons and ski, snowboard, and clothing rentals.

Cross-Country Skiing and Snowshoeing
Many summer hiking trails are groomed for winter cross-country skiing (Dec.-Mar.). The most popular areas near town are **Johnson Lake, Golf Course Road, Spray River, Sundance Canyon,** and upstream from the **canoe docks.** You can get info on groomed trails and current weather forecasts at the visitors center and online (www.pc.gc.ca). Rental packages are available from **Snow Tips** (225 Bear St., 403/762-8177, snowtips-bactrax. com). **White Mountain Adventures** (403/678-4099 or 800/408-0005, whitemountainadventures.com) offers snowshoeing tours.

Ice Walks
In winter, **Johnston Canyon** on Bow Valley Parkway is a wonderland of frozen waterfalls. Two companies offer guided canyon ice walks to the **Upper Falls** (C$82, includes transportation from Banff). They provide ice cleats for your shoes and hot drinks to take the chill off. Make reservations through **Discover Banff Tours** (403/760-5007 or 877/565-9372, www.banfftours.com) or **White Mountain Adventures** (403/678-4099 or 800/408-0005, whitemountainadventures.com).

Shopping
Canadiana and Clothing
Founded in 1670, **Hudson's Bay Company** (HBC) established trading posts

chairlift at Sunshine Village Ski Resort

throughout western Canada, many of which attracted settlers, forming the towns and cities that survive today. **Banff's HBC** (125 Banff Ave., 403/762-5525, www.thebay.com) carries clothing, footwear, and home goods, including the classic HBC striped blanket.

Another Canadian store, this one famous for its fleeces, sweaters, and leather goods and for its role as supplier to the Canadian Olympic teams, is **Roots** (227 Banff Ave., 403/762-9434, www.roots.com). **About Canada** (105 Banff Ave., 403/760-2996) sources Canadian-made gifts.

Camping and Outdoor Gear

Inexpensive camping equipment and supplies can be found in **Standish Home Hardware** (223 Bear St., 403/762-2080, www.homehardware.ca). **Monod Sports** (129 Banff Ave., 403/762-4571, www.monodsports.com) has ski touring, skiing, and climbing gear. Locally owned **Abominable Sports** (229 Banff Ave., 403/762-2905, abominablesports.ca) has a good selection of hiking boots, outdoor clothing, and winter gear, including skis and snowboards. **Rude Boys** (205 Caribou St., 403/762-8211, www.rudeboys.com) is *the* snowboarder and skateboarder hangout.

Gifts and Galleries

Banff's numerous galleries display the work of mostly Canadian artists. **Canada House Gallery** (201 Bear St., 403/762-3757, canadahouse.com) features a wide selection of Canadian landscape and wildlife works and First Nations art. In the Fairmont Banff Springs, the **Quest Gallery** (405 Spray Ave., 403/762-4422, thequestgallery.com) offers a diverse range of Canadian paintings and crafts, as well as more exotic pieces such as mammoth tusks from prehistoric times and Inuit carvings from Nunavut. Browse through First Nations arts and crafts at the **Banff Trading Post** (101 Cave Ave., 403/762-2456, www.banfftradingpost.

com), across the Bow River from downtown.

Entertainment and Events
Nightlife

Like resort towns around the world, Banff has a deserved reputation as a party town, especially among seasonal workers, the après-ski crowd, and young Calgarians. Given the location and vacation vibe, drink prices are as high as you may expect.

One of Banff's most distinctive bars is **Park Distillery** (219 Banff Ave., 403/762-5114, www.parkdistillery.com, 11am-2am daily), a two-story space that reflects the history of the park through the use of wood and stone and features such as a huge canvas tent that rolls over one section of the upstairs seating area. Beer choices represent many local breweries, while spirits such as gin are distilled in-house using glacial water and local Alberta grains. Their kitchen (11am-midnight daily, C$18-33) combines classic campfire cooking with modern dining trends: sides of rotisserie chicken chowder or corn bread smothered in maple-rum butter followed by mains such as pork-and-beans or the AAA T-bone.

The **Elk & Oarsman** (119 Banff Ave., 403/762-4616, elkandoarsman.com, 11am-1am daily) serves up beer and more in a clean, casual atmosphere that is as friendly as it gets in Banff. The **Rose and Crown** (202 Banff Ave., 403/762-2121, roseandcrown.ca, 11am-2am daily) serves local and British beers plus hearty pub fare. It also features a rooftop patio and rock-and-roll bands a few nights a week, but without much room for dancing.

Off the main drag, the **St. James Gate Olde Irish Pub** (207 Wolf St., 403/762-9355, stjamesgatebanff.com, 11am-1am daily) is an Irish-style bar with British-style meals and occasional appearances by Celtic bands. Relative to other town drinking spots, prices are better at the **Bear Street Tavern** (Bison Courtyard, 211 Bear St., 403/762-2021, www.bearstreettavern.ca, 11:30am-10pm daily), with funky surroundings and a sunny courtyard.

The **Fairmont Banff Springs** (405 Spray Ave., 403/762-2211, www.fairmont.com/banff-springs) has three notable places to get a drink or nightcap. For old-world atmosphere, nothing in town comes close to matching **Grapes** (5pm-9:30pm daily, reservations required), a casual wine bar noted for its fine cheeses, cured meats, and pâtés. The mezzanine-level **Rundle Lounge** (11am-1am daily) has an outdoor patio with views extending down Bow Valley. Below the hotel is the **Waldhaus Pub** (11am-11pm daily summer) with the best deck in town for sweeping mountain views.

Banff's most popular nightclub is **Dancing Sasquatch** (120 Banff Ave., 403/762-4002, 9pm-2am Fri.-Wed., cover charge varies), a modern, intimate space that gets very loud, especially when a celebrity DJ is in town spinning discs.

Festivals and Events

One of the year's biggest events is the **Banff Centre Mountain Film and Book Festival** put on at the **Banff Centre** (St. Julien Rd., 403/762-6100, www.banffcentre.ca) over the first weekend of November. Mountain-adventure filmmakers from around the world submit films to be judged by a select committee. Films are then shown throughout the weekend to an enthusiastic crowd of thousands. Exhibits and seminars are also presented, and top climbers and mountaineers from around the world are invited as guest speakers. Tickets go on sale one year in advance from the **Banff Centre box office** (403/762-6301 or 800/413-8368, www.banffcentre.ca, from C$50) and sell out quickly. Films are shown in the center's two theaters. (If you miss the actual festival, it hits the road on the Best of the Festival World Tour; venues and dates are online.) Starting in the days leading up to the film festival, then running in conjunction with it, is the book component (C$15-40) of the festival, which showcases publishers, writers, and photographers whose work revolves around the world's great mountain ranges.

Food

Whether you're in search of an inexpensive snack for the family or silver service, you can find it in the town of Banff. It has more than 80 restaurants, more per capita than any other town or city across Canada.

Canadian

For a moderate splurge, **Sleeping Buffalo Dining Room** (Buffalo Mountain Lodge, 700 Tunnel Mountain Dr., 403/762-4484, crmr.com, 7am-11am, noon-5pm, and 5:30pm-10pm daily, C$24-46) features a modern mountain interior with vaulted ceiling, a stone fireplace, and an elk antler chandelier. The cuisine reflects an abundance of Canadian game and seafood combined with native berries and fruits.

The food at ★ **Storm Mountain Lodge** (Hwy. 93, 403/762-4155, stormmountainlodge.com, 8am-10:30am, 11:30am-3pm, and 5pm-9pm daily May-mid-Oct., 5pm-9pm Fri.-Sun. early Dec.-Apr., C$29-45) is excellent and the ambience blends historic appeal and rustic mountain charm. The chef uses mostly organic produce with seasonally available Alberta game and seafood to create tasty dishes well suited to the Canadian wilderness surroundings. To reach the lodge, drive 25 minutes northwest from Banff via Trans-Canada and west at the Castle Mountain junction.

On one of Banff's busiest corners is the **Maple Leaf** (137 Banff Ave., 403/760-7680, www.banffmapleleaf.com, 11am-10pm daily, C$28-47). The décor features exposed river stone, polished log work, a two-story interior rock wall, and a moose head. The menu has an abundance of Canadian game and produce. Lunch serves a bison burger, along with lighter salads and gourmet sandwiches. Dinner brings on Canadian favorites such as stuffed halibut and bacon-wrapped bison tenderloin. Treat yourself to a glass of Canadian ice wine to accompany dessert.

Bison Restaurant and Terrace (Bison Courtyard, 211 Bear St., 403/762-5550, www.thebison.ca, 5pm-10pm daily, C$25-66) is an upstairs eatery featuring farm-to-table Canadian ingredients. Tables are inside or out in this dining room that blends a chic-industrial and mountain rustic look with views of the open kitchen. The food is solidly Canadian, with a menu that takes advantage of wild game, seafood, and Alberta beef.

Juniper Bistro (The Juniper Hotel, 1 Juniper Way, thejuniper.com, 403/762-2281, 7am-1:30pm and 5pm-10pm daily, C$17-35) is worth searching out for its views of Mount Rundle, especially from the outside patio. The menu blends traditional tastes of AAA ribeye or lamb with Canadian produce.

International

The **Balkan** (120 Banff Ave., 403/762-3454, www.banffbalkan.ca, 11:30am-9pm Sun.-Thurs., 11:30am-10pm Fri.-Sat., C$24-37) is run by a local Greek family, and the menu blends their heritage with the cuisines of Italy, China, and Canada. Greek flavors enhance the pork ribs, the chow mein, and spaghetti. But the most popular dishes are souvlaki and an enormous Greek platter for two.

★ **Ticino** (High Country Inn, 415 Banff Ave., www.ticinorestaurant.com, 403/762-3848, 5:30pm-10pm daily, C$19-38) reflects the heritage of the park's early mountain guides, with lots of peeled and polished log work, old wooden skis, huge cowbells, and an alpenhorn decorating the walls. It's named for the southern province of Switzerland, where Italian cuisine influences dishes. The Swiss chef is best known for a creamy wild mushroom soup, beef and cheese fondues, juicy cuts of Alberta beef, and veal dishes.

At the back of the Clock Tower Mall, **Pad Thai** (110 Banff Ave., 403/762-4911, www.padthaibanff.com, noon-9pm daily, C$13-20) has inexpensive Thai cuisine, including the namesake pad Thai, curries, and delicious spring rolls. You can eat in or take your food to-go.

Sushi House Banff (304 Caribou St., 403/762-4353, www.sushihousebanff.ca, 11:30am-10pm daily, C$16-22) is a tiny space with a dozen stools set around a moving miniature railway that has diners picking sushi and other delicacies from a train as it circles the chef, who is loading the carriages as quickly as they empty.

Fine Dining

The ★ **Grizzly House** (207 Banff Ave., 403/762-4055, www.banffgrizzlyhouse. com, 11:30am-midnight daily, C$48-80 pp for four courses) provides Banff's most unusual dining experience amid twisted woods, a motorbike hanging from the ceiling, and a melted telephone on the wall. Each table has a phone for across-table conversation, or you can put a call through to your server, the bar, a cab, diners in the private booth, or even those who spend too long in the bathroom. Most dining revolves around traditional Swiss fondues, but with non-traditional dipping meats such as rattlesnake, alligator, shark, ostrich, scallops, elk, and wild boar. Lunch features Canadian game: wild game meatloaf and an Alberta-farmed buffalo burger.

★ **Saltlik** (221 Bear St., 403/762-2467, www.saltlik.com, 11am-midnight daily, C$27-52) is the perfect choice for serious carnivores with cash to spare. At one of Banff's most fashionable restaurants, the dining room is big and bold, and the concrete-and-steel split-level interior is complemented by modish wood furnishings. Facing the street, glass doors in the street-level lounge fold back to a terrace for warm-weather dining. The specialty is AAA Alberta beef, finished with grain feeding to enhance the flavor, then flash-seared at 650°C (1,200°F) to seal in the juices, and served with a side platter of seasonal vegetables. Entrées are priced comparable to a city steakhouse, but the cost creeps up as you add side dishes.

Coffee and Cafés

Whitebark (Banff Aspen Lodge, 401 Banff Ave., www.whitebarkcafe.com, 403/760-7298, 6:30am-7pm daily), a few blocks north of the main shopping strip, is well worth searching out for the best coffee in town. It's one of the only places in Banff that serves Americanos. Indoor seating is limited to a few window-facing stools, but the outside patio is a great place to soak up summer sun.

Modern **Evelyn's Coffee World** (Sundance Mall, 215 Banff Ave., 403/762-2000, www.evelynscoffeebar.com, 7am-9pm daily, sandwiches C$8-12) has a very central location pouring good coffee sourced from around the world and serving breakfast and huge sandwiches. The few outside tables on the busiest stretch of the busiest street in town are perfect for people-watching.

Banff's lone bakery is **Wild Flour** (Bison Courtyard, 211 Bear St., 403/760-5074, www.wildflourbakery.ca, 8am-4pm daily, C$7-12). Organic ingredients are used whenever possible, and everything is freshly baked daily. The result is an array of healthy breads, gluten-free choices, mouthwatering cakes and pastries, and delicious meat pies. Eat inside or out in the courtyard for breakfast or lunch.

Fairmont Banff Springs

The **Fairmont Banff Springs** (405 Spray Ave., 403/762-6860, www.fairmont.com/banff-springs) has more eateries than most small towns, from a deli serving coffee and muffins to the finest of fine dining in the 1888 Chop House. Make reservations for evening dining.

Ensconced in an octagonal room of the Manor Wing, **Castello Ristorante** (6pm-9:30pm daily, C$36-53) is a seductive dining room with a modern, upscale ambience. The menu is dominated by Italian favorites, with traditional pastas and specialties such as veal tenderloin.

The **Vermillion Room** (www.vermillionroom.com, daily) is a huge, pleasantly laid out dining room. At breakfast (7am-11am, C$14-35) order à la carte or choose from an expansive buffet of hot and cold delicacies, including freshly baked bread and seasonal fruits. Lunch (11:30am-3pm, C$14-35) offers a wide-ranging menu featuring everything from salads to seafood. The evening menu (5:30pm-9pm, C$30-48) is decidedly French. The weekend brunch (11am-3pm Sat.-Sun., adults C$54, children C$27) is legendary, with chefs working at numerous stations scattered around the dining area and an enormous spread unequaled in variety anywhere in the mountains.

The hotel's most acclaimed restaurant is **1888 Chop House** (www.1888chophouse.com, 6pm-9:30pm daily, C$42-165). This fine-dining restaurant is a bastion of elegance, apparent once you arrive through a gated entrance. Inside, extravagantly rich wood furnishings, perfectly presented table settings, muted lighting, and professional staff create an atmosphere as far removed from the surrounding wilderness as is imaginable. Local ranches and farms provide the ingredients for the menu rich in beef and fish, and the wine cellar contains over 2,000 labels. Reservations are required.

The **Waldhaus Restaurant** (6pm-9pm daily, C$23-34) is nestled in a forested area directly below the hotel. The big room is dominated by dark woods and is warmed by an open fireplace. The menu features German specialties, such as fondues.

Accommodations and Camping

Finding a room or campsite in Banff in summer is hard, and you'll pay handsomely for any available rooms. To guarantee yourself a place to stay, make **reservations a year in advance** for summer and holidays. In summer, room rates will be at their highest; off-season, from October to May, sees the lowest rates.

Banff has a few accommodations right downtown, but most are strung out along Banff Avenue, within easy walking distance from the shopping and dining district. For lodgers staying farther afield on Tunnel Mountain, leave your car and hop the Roam bus into town to avoid parking hassles.

Hostels

HI-Banff Alpine Centre (801 Hidden Ridge Way, 778/328-2220 or 866/762-4122, hihostels.ca, C$54-58 members, C$60-66 nonmembers) is just off Tunnel Mountain Road which is serviced by Roam buses. This large, modern hostel sleeps 216 in small two-, four-, and six-bed dormitory rooms as well as four-bed cabins. The large lounge area has a fireplace, and other facilities include a recreation room, public internet access, a bike and ski/snowboard workshop, large kitchen, self-service café/bar, and laundry. Private rooms (C$180-200) are available. During July and August, reserve at least a couple of months in advance to be assured a bed.

Along the main strip of accommodations and a five-minute walk to downtown is **Samesun Banff** (433 Banff Ave., 403/762-4499 or 877/972-6378, www.samesun.com/banff, C$33-60), which offers clean and comfortable lodgings. As converted motel rooms, each 8- or 16-bed dormitory has its own bathroom, and some are for women only. Private rooms (C$70-180) are available. Guest amenities include a pub with daily food and drink specials, wireless internet, free continental breakfast, guest kitchen, laundry, and underground (but not heated) parking.

Hotels and Inns

Since opening in 1908, the centrally located **Mount Royal Hotel** (138 Banff Ave., 866/606-6700, www.banffjaspercollection.com, C$119-540) has seen various expansions and revamps.

Fairmont Banff Springs

Today, guests are offered more than 130 tastefully decorated rooms with queen or king beds. One-bedroom suites have sitting rooms and kitchenettes. Guests have the use of a large health club with hot tub. Also on the premises is a family-style chain restaurant and small lounge that serves cocktails and small plates.

The 99 guest rooms at the **Banff Inn** (501 Banff Ave., 403/762-8844, www. banffinn.com, C$165-380) are modern, but no frills in appearance. Families can get rooms with three beds. Pluses include underground heated parking and a steam room, sauna, and a large indoor whirlpool. The guest lounge has a fireplace and serves breakfast daily (C$20). A pizzeria is also on-site.

Two blocks from downtown is **Moose Hotel & Suites** (345 Banff Ave., 403/762-2638 or 800/563-8764, www. moosehotelandsuites.com, C$170-790). Even the standard rooms are air-conditioned and come with luxuries such as rain showers. The one- and two-bedroom suites all have balconies, gas fireplaces, and basic cooking facilities. Other features include outdoor and indoor hot pools, a day spa with a private outdoor hot pool, a central courtyard with lots of outdoor seating and a fire pit. A classy family-style Italian restaurant is on-site.

Lodges

The intimate, heritage **Elkhorn Lodge** (124 Spray Ave., 403/762-2299, elkhorn-banff.ca, C$120-300) is good for travelers on a budget. The four small rooms have been renovated, and each has one queen or two twin beds, a private bathroom, TV, and small fridge. Likewise, the four suites have been revamped with fireplaces, equipped kitchens, and bedrooms, perfect for families.

More than 100 years since Jim and Bill Brewster guided their first guests through the park, their descendants are still actively involved in the tourist industry, operating ★ **Brewster's Mountain Lodge** (208 Caribou St., 403/762-2900, www.brewstermountainlodge.com, C$100-380). The building features an eye-catching log exterior with an equally impressive lobby with log furniture and historic family photos. The Western theme is continued in the 77 upstairs rooms. Standard rooms feature two queen-size beds, deluxe rooms offer a jetted tub and sitting area, and loft suites are designed for families. Amenities include a sauna, fitness facility, heated underground parking, and complimentary continental breakfast. The downtown location is prime for walking to restaurants and shopping.

The **Rundlestone Lodge** (537 Banff Ave., 403/762-2201 or 800/661-8630, rundlestonelodge.com, C$100-450) features mountain-style architecture with an abundance of raw stonework and exposed timber inside and out. At street level, a comfortable sitting area centers around a fireplace. The lodge also has an indoor pool, a lounge-style bar, and a restaurant. Furniture and fittings in the 96 rooms are elegant, and many of the 11 styles of rooms have small balconies, lofts, jetted tubs, and gas fireplaces; some are wheelchair-accessible.

Canalta Lodge (545 Banff Ave., 403/762-2112, www.canaltalodge.com, C$132-590) is a modern mountain-style lodge where the 120 guest rooms are spacious and come in a variety of bed configurations. Some options include kitchens, fireplaces, bunk beds, and loft suites that sleep four. A hot breakfast buffet is included in the room rates, and underground park is available. The outdoor patio has hot tubs, a glacier plunge tub, and fire pit, in addition to being a place to just sit and enjoy the ambience.

The **Banff Aspen Lodge** (401 Banff Ave., 403/762-4401 or 877/886-8857, www.banffaspenlodge.com, C$140-400) has three styles of rooms. Smaller economy rooms with one queen bed are on the ground floor. Superior rooms have one queen bed and a balcony. The premium rooms can sleep four and have a balcony or patio. Rates include a full breakfast buffet, use of two outdoor hot pools, a steam room, and a sauna.

The best rooms along the motel strip are at **Royal Canadian Lodge** (459 Banff Ave., 403/762-3307 or 888/778-5050, www.royalcanadianlodge.com, C$170-500), which features an elegant stone-and-timber lobby as a precursor to the 99 luxuriously appointed rooms and suites. Amenities include heated underground parking, a lounge, a dining room where upscale Canadian specialties are the highlight, a spa, a pool complex, and a landscaped courtyard.

Buffalo Mountain Lodge (700 Tunnel Mountain Rd., 403/762-2400 or 800/661-1367, crmr.com, C$120-500) takes its name from Tunnel Mountain, which early park visitors called Buffalo Mountain for its shape. Impressive timber-frame construction marks this lodge, as well as the hand-hewn construction of the lobby with its vaulted ceiling and eye-catching fieldstone fireplace. The 108 rooms, chalets, and bungalows all have fireplaces, balconies, large bathrooms, and comfortable beds topped by feather-filled duvets; many also have kitchens. It's a 15-minute walk from town on Tunnel Mountain Road or you can catch the bus.

Bed-and-Breakfasts

Banff Avenue B&B (430 Banff Ave., 403/762-5410, www.banffavenuebb.com, C$160-290) offers three simple yet inviting guest rooms, each with a queen bed and private bathroom. Guests enjoy a cooked breakfast, free wireless internet, a lounge area, and a deck overlooking a flower-filled garden. Its location, just three blocks from the heart of downtown, gives quick walking access to restaurants and shopping. A two-night minimum stay is required May-September.

Bed-and-breakfast connoisseurs will fall in love with **Buffaloberry B&B** (417 Marten St., 403/762-3750, www.buffaloberry.com, C$485), a purpose-built lodging within walking distance of downtown. The home itself is a beautiful timber-and-stone structure, while inside, guests soak up mountain-style luxury in the vaulted living area in front of a stone fireplace on super-comfortable couches surrounded by a library of local-interest books. The spacious rooms come with niceties such as pillow-top mattresses, heated bathroom floors, and bathrobes. Breakfast, which changes daily, is equally impressive. Buffaloberry is also the only Banff bed-and-breakfast with heated underground parking.

Resorts

On Mountain Avenue, a short walk from the Upper Hot Springs, is **Rimrock Resort Hotel** (300 Mountain Ave., 403/762-3356 or 888/746-7625, www.rimrockresort.com, C$175-1,200). The original hotel was constructed in 1903 but was fully rebuilt and opened as a full-service luxury resort in the mid-1990s. Guest amenities include two restaurants, two lounges, a health club, an outdoor patio, spa, pool, hot tub, and a multistory heated parking garage. Each of the 345 well-appointed rooms is decorated with earthy tones offset by brightly colored fabrics. They also feature picture windows, a king-size bed, a comfortable armchair, a writing desk, and a minibar. Since the hotel is set high above the Bow Valley, views for the most part are excellent, most notably from Suite Infinity (C$3,000).

Hidden Ridge Resort (901 Hidden Ridge Way, 403/762-3544 or 800/661-1372, www.banffhiddenridge.com, C$130-840) sits on a forested hillside away from the main buzz of traffic. Choose from modern condo-style units that can sleep up to eight people to much larger king whirlpool tub suites. All units have wood-burning fireplaces, balconies or patios, and the condos have washer/dryer combos. Some are loft units. In the center of the complex is a barbecue area and a large, boulder-rimmed outdoor hot tub which overlooks the valley.

The 770-room ★ **Fairmont Banff Springs** (405 Spray Ave., 403/762-2211 or 800/257-7544, www.fairmont.com/banff-springs, from C$430-3,200) is Banff's best-known accommodation, originally built in 1888. Even though the rooms have been modernized, many date to the 1920s and are small. But room size is only a minor consideration when staying in this elegant historic gem. Rooms and suites have luxury furnishings, some of which are antiques. With 12 eateries, four lounges, a luxurious spa facility, a huge indoor pool, elegant public spaces, a 27-hole golf course, tennis courts, horseback riding, and enough twisting, turning hallways, towers, and shops to warrant a detailed map, you won't want to spend much time in your room…unless, of course, you're in the eight-room presidential suite. Packages can include breakfast, while others will have you golfing, horseback riding, or relaxing in the spa.

Backcountry Lodges

Anyone can experience the remote ★ **Sunshine Mountain Lodge** (Sunshine Village, 1 Sunshine Access Rd., 403/762-6500 or 877/542-2633, 403/705-4000 outside North America, www.sunshinemountainlodge.com, late June-mid-Sept. and mid-Nov.-late May, from C$465 pp) since it's accessed via gondola. At 2,200 meters (7,200 ft), the experience after day-time skiers or hikers depart is quiet. It's especially exquisite on clear nights for seeing brilliant stars or the full moon. The stone-and-timber buildings have modern mountain-style rooms in the main lodge or the newer west wing. Loft rooms have giant views of the mountains and ski resort from extra-tall windows. The inn has a restaurant, lounge, and large outdoor hot tub.

Only trails go to remote **Shadow Lake Lodge** (403/678-3200, shadowlakelodge.com, weekends only late Jan.-late Mar., daily late June-late Sept., C$375-850) where cozy private log cabins, warm beds, and fresh meals await. The Alpine Club of Canada (ACC) now owns and operates the historic lodge. Access is via three trails that require 14-26 km (8-16 mi) of hiking; the shortest is via Redearth Creek. Trails from the lodge lead to Ball Pass, Gibbon Pass, and Haiduk Lake.

Camping

Sites at most campgrounds can be reserved through the **Parks Canada Campground reservation service** (877/737-3783, reservation.pc.gc.ca, C$12). The booking window usually opens for the year in January, when reservations go fast, especially for July and August. If you require electrical hookups or want to stay at one of the more popular campgrounds, such as Two Jack Lakeside, make reservations as soon as bookings open.

Although some sites are available without a reservation, they fill fast each day, especially in July and August. The official checkout time is 11am, so if you don't have a reservation, plan on arriving at your campground of choice earlier than this to claim a site. On summer weekends, a line often forms, waiting for sites to become vacant.

Campgrounds have flush toilets, potable water, picnic tables, fire pits, kitchen shelters, and bear-proof food storage. Fire permits (C$9) include firewood.

Banff Townsite

Although the town of Banff has five campgrounds with more than 1,500 sites, most fill by early afternoon. The three largest campgrounds are strung out along Tunnel Mountain Road, with the nearest sites 2.5 km (1.6 mi) from town. Reservations are accepted for all five campgrounds.

Closest to town is **Tunnel Mountain Campground,** which is three campgrounds rolled into one. It's almost like a small city, with over 1,000 campsites, many of them lined up in parking lots with no privacy. The location is a lightly treed ridge east of downtown, with views north to Cascade Mountain and south to Mount Rundle. In addition to the standard campground amenities, all three have hot showers, wheelchair-accessible sites, and dump stations for RVs. To get to downtown Banff, hop a bus and leave your car at the campground to avoid parking hassles.

To reach the campground from the Trans-Canada Highway, you'll take different exits depending on whether you are coming from the west or east. From the east, take the first Banff exit and turn left at the stop sign, then left again onto Tunnel Mountain Road. From the west, take the third Banff exit and turn left onto Tunnel Mountain Road. Once on Tunnel Mountain Road, continue to the signed entrance for your specific campground and the registration booth.

- **Tunnel Mountain Village I** (618 sites, mid-May-early Oct., RV limit 7 m/24 ft, C$28) is located 8 km (5 mi) from downtown Banff. Most campsites are

A family enjoys breakfast at their campsite at Two Jack Lakeside Campground.

forested with some privacy. None of the sites have hookups. No kitchen shelters are available.

- **Tunnel Mountain Village II** (188 sites, year-round, RV limit 15 m/50 ft, C$33) has electrical hookups at many reservable sites. There are 34 walk-in tent sites. You can also rent an oTENTik (mid-May-mid-Oct., C$123), a half-tent/half-cabin with raised floors and beds with mattresses; bring your own bedding or sleeping bags.

- **Tunnel Mountain Trailer** (321 sites, mid-May-early Oct., RV limit 18 m/60 ft, C$40) has full hookups for power, water, and sewer, but it lacks fire pits and cooking shelters.

Northeast of town, along **Lake Minnewanka Road,** are two campgrounds offering fewer services than at Tunnel Mountain, but with more private sites.

- **Two Jack Lakeside Campground** (64 sites, mid-May-early Oct., RV limit 8

m/27 ft, C$28) has sites tucked into trees at the south end of Two Jack Lake, an extension of Lake Minnewanka. There's a designated parking area for 23 walk-in tent sites. You can also rent an oTENTik (C$123), a half-tent/half-cabin with raised floors and beds with mattresses; bring your own bedding or sleeping bags. This campground has showers.

- **Two Jack Main Campground** (380 sites, late June-early Sept., RV limit 8 m/27 ft, C$22) is a short distance farther along the road, with sites spread throughout a shallow valley. This is the one Banff-area campground without showers, but it does have equipped campsites (C$72) that come with a tent, camping stove with propane, and lantern. If you arrive in Banff without reservations, Two Jack Main is probably your best chance of getting a campsite, but there are no guarantees.

Bow Valley Parkway

Bow Valley Parkway has three rustic campgrounds that tent to be quieter and more relaxed than the busy campgrounds in town. They are located 22-40 km (14-25 mi) from the town of Banff.

- **Johnston Canyon Campground** (132 sites, RV limit 8 m/27 ft, C$28) has showers, wheelchair-accessible sites, and an RV dump station. It is the closest to the town of Banff, with the trail to Johnston Canyon departing nearby. Reservations are available.

- **Castle Mountain Campground** (43 sites, RV limit 7 m/24 ft, C$22) is first come, first served. It is near the trailhead to Rockbound Lake and Castle Village, where you can pick up a few supplies.

- **Protection Mountain Campground** (72 sites, RV limit 22 m/75 ft, C$22) is the farthest from Banff and closest to Lake Louise (17 km/11 mi). The once thickly forested campground now has more views due to thinning. It is first come, first served and has wheelchair-accessible sites.

Transportation and Services
Emergency Services
For emergencies, call **911. Mineral Springs Hospital** (305 Lynx St., 403/762-2222, www.covenanthealth.ca) has 24-hour emergency service.

Gas and Vehicle Charging Stations
Find gas stations in Banff near the Trans-Canada Highway: **Shell** (435 Banff Ave. and 230 Lynx St.) and **Petro-Canada** (302 Squirrel St.). There are **electric vehicle charging stations** at the **Banff Visitor Centre** (224 Banff Ave.) and **Banff Park Museum** (91 Banff Ave.).

Cell Service
The town of Banff gets good cell reception; however, you will not have cell service on most hiking trails.

Tours
Pursuit (866/606-6700, www.banffjaspercollection.com, C$135-160 adults, C$80-85 children) runs several tours in the park. The **Explore Banff bus tour** (4.5 hrs, departs 8:30am daily summer) takes in downtown Banff, Tunnel Mountain Drive, the hoodoos, Bow Falls, and Banff Gondola (fare included). The **winter tour** (5 hrs, departs 1pm winter, days vary) does a slight variation by adding snowshoeing on Lake Minnewanka and visiting Cave and Basin. During summer, the company also guides **bus tours** (C$184-281) from the town of Banff to Lake Louise and Yoho National Park or the Icefields Parkway, the Columbia Icefield, and Jasper. Days and durations vary as well as activities that are included in the tours.

Discover Banff Tours (215 Banff Ave., 403/760-5007 or 877/565-9372, www.banfftours.com) is a smaller company than Pursuit, with smaller buses and more personalized service. The **Discover Banff tour** (3 hrs, departs 8:30am summer, days vary, C$80) visits Lake Minnewanka, Cave and Basin, the Fairmont Banff Springs, and the hoodoos. The same tour adds on a gondola option (C$156) and a winter option (C$130). The company also leads summer tours from Banff to Lake Louise, Moraine Lake, and the Columbia Icefield (C$90-278).

The days when horse-drawn buggies transported wealthy visitors around the area have long since passed, but the **Trail Rider Store** (132 Banff Ave., 403/762-4551, horseback.com, 9am-5pm daily, C$82-240) offers visitors rides around town in a beautifully restored carriage. You can do a short loop around downtown, head out to the Bow River, or go to the Fairmont Banff Springs.

Getting Around
On Foot
Along Banff Avenue, there are three intersections with **scramble crosswalks,** where pedestrians can cross straight or diagonally. The crosswalks are at Wolf Street, Caribou Street, and Buffalo Street.

Walking trails weave through town. You can use these to travel by foot between your lodging or campground and downtown. Pick up a map at the visitors center or see the town of Banff's website (banff.ca).

Driving and Parking
The downtown core of Banff is busy year-round, but especially so between May and September. It's nearly impossible to find an RV parking spot. If you're staying along Banff Avenue or on Tunnel Mountain, don't drive into town. Instead, walk or catch a Roam bus; these depart every 30 minutes from the Tunnel Mountain campgrounds to downtown.

If you do drive into downtown, prepare to pay to park (8am-8pm daily year-round, $3/hr May-Oct., $2/hr Nov.-Apr.) in the eight square blocks that make up the downtown core. Parking options include streetside, lots, and the Bear Street garage. Pay at the machines, online, or via the Blinkay app. Some areas, like the train station, offer free parking. The city's website offers detailed information and a map of parking areas and fees.

Plan on renting a vehicle before you reach the park. In addition to high pricing for walk-in customers, local companies don't always offer unlimited mileage, especially for larger and premium vehicles. It's best to rent at the airport. If you need to rent in town, **Avis** and **Budget** share a desk at street level in Cascade Shops (317 Banff Ave., 403/762-3222). The other agency represented in Banff is **Hertz** (Fairmont Banff Springs, 405 Spray Ave., 403/762-2027). Reservations for vehicles in Banff should be made well in advance, especially in summer.

Bus

Roam Transit (403/762-0606, www. roamtransit.com) operates **bus service** along two routes through the town of Banff: one from the Banff Gondola north along Banff Avenue, the other from the Fairmont Banff Springs to the Tunnel Mountain campgrounds. From mid-May to September, buses run twice an hour between 7am and midnight. You can pay one-way fares (C$2 adults, C$1 youths and seniors, free kids 12 and under) or get passes for one day, three days, or 10 rides. Passes are available from select locations in towns and by smartphone app. You can also download a smartphone app to track bus arrivals.

In summer, buses run out to Lake Minnewanka and to Cave and Basin. An **express bus** (route 8X, 7:30am-10pm daily summer, shorter hours fall-spring, C$5-10 one-way) runs to Lake Louise. Reservations are available online for two buses (9am-6:30pm daily summer, shorter hours fall-spring, C$5-10 one-way): the **route 9** bus to Johnston Canyon and the **route 8S** scenic bus to Lake Louise Village and the lakeshore via Bow Valley Parkway.

Taxi

Cabs around the town of Banff are reasonably priced, but far more expensive if you need to go outside town. A ride from the Banff bus depot to the Fairmont Banff Springs will run around C$12, more after midnight. Call **Banff Taxi** (403/762-4444).

Canmore

Long perceived as a gateway to the Canadian Rockies national parks, the town of Canmore is a destination in itself; the surrounding mountains provide additional opportunities for recreation. Canmore lies in the Bow Valley, 100 km (64 mi) west of Calgary and 30 km (19 mi) southeast of Banff.

Sights
Canmore Museum

Inside the Civic Centre complex is the **Canmore Museum and Geoscience Centre** (902B 7th Ave., 403/678-2462, www.canmoremuseum.com, 10am-4:30pm daily summer, shorter hours and days off-season, C$5 adults, C$4 seniors, youth 17 and under free). This facility highlights the region's rich geological history and its importance to the growth of the town and related industries. Geological formations along three local trails are described, which, along with a small fossil display, microscopes, and computer resources, make this facility a good rainy-day diversion.

Recreation
Canmore Nordic Centre Provincial Park

Canmore Nordic Centre Provincial Park (1988 Olympic Way, 403/678-2400, www.albertaparks.ca) once held the Nordic events for the Olympic Games in 1988, so it's not surprising that its 100 km of groomed trails are outstanding for **skate-** or **classic skiing** (Nov.-Mar., C$15 adults, C$11 seniors, C$9-11 kids) in winter. The

Side Trip: Mount Assiniboine Provincial Park

winter at Mount Assiniboine

Named for one of the Canadian Rockies' most spectacular peaks, **Mount Assiniboine Provincial Park** is sandwiched between Kootenay National Park to the west and Banff National Park to the east. It's inaccessible by road; access is on foot or by helicopter only. A haven for experienced hikers and skiers, the park offers alpine meadows, lakes, glaciers, and high peaks. The park's highest peak, Mount Assiniboine (3,618 m/11,870 ft) is named for the Assiniboine people, who ventured into the Canadian Rockies thousands of years before European exploration. The name Assiniboine means "stone boilers," a reference to their preferred cooking method.

Getting There

Four trails provide access to the park's huts, campgrounds, and lodge, as well as Lake Magog. All are lengthy treks and have backcountry campgrounds en route. The most popular starts from **Sunshine Village** in Banff National Park and goes over **Citadel Pass** (29 km/18 mi). From the east, at the Mount Shark staging area in **Spray Valley Provincial Park,** the shortest trail climbs up Bryant Creek to cross over **Assiniboine Pass** (27 km/16.8 mi); a longer route goes via Marvel Lake over **Wonder Pass** (26 km/17 mi). The longest and least-used trail departs Highway 93 at Simpson River in **Kootenay National Park** to ascend the Simpson River and Surprise Creek drainages to cross **Ferro Pass** (32 km/20 mi).

You can fly in by helicopter (C$190-220), too, from the **Mount Shark Heliport** (40 km/25 mi southwest of Canmore) at the southern end of Spray Valley Provincial Park, or from the **Canmore Municipal Heliport** (91 Bow Valley Trl., Canmore). **Alpine Helicopters** (403/678-4802, www.alpinehelicopter.com) operates the flights, but all bookings must be made through **Mount Assiniboine Lodge.** You can also pay to have your gear flown in while you hike.

Sights and Recreation

Once you hike, ski, or take a helicopter into the park, there are many options for what to see and do amid Assiniboine's spectacular scenery.

- ◆ **Lake Magog:** The park's largest lake is the destination of most park visitors. Its locale has the park's only facilities and trailheads for several hikes.

- ◆ **Sunburst Valley/Nub Ridge Trail:** From Assiniboine Lodge, this loop trail (11 km/6.8 mi rt) and ski route links Sunburst Lake, Cerulean Lake, and Elizabeth Lake before climbing Nub Ridge to a viewpoint overlooking Lake Magog and Mount Assiniboine.

- ◆ **Wonder Pass:** From Assiniboine Lodge, a path (6.2 km/3.8 mi rt) heads east, passing Gog Lake to ascend through larch alternating with wildflower meadows and leading to this scenic pass on the boundary of Banff National Park. Skiers need to have avalanche gear.

- ◆ **Mount Assiniboine:** Known as the "Matterhorn of the Rockies" for its resemblance to that famous Swiss landmark, this peak is visible from much of the park. Climbers stay in the small Hind Hut to ascend the peak, which requires technical rock, snow, or ice climbing. For guided climbs, hire **Yamnuska Mountain Adventures** (403/768-4164 or 866/678-4164, yamnuska.com).

Accommodations and Camping

The rustic log **Mount Assiniboine Lodge** (403/678-2883, www.assiniboinelodge. com, early Feb.-Mar. and late June-early Oct., C$325-555 pp, two-night minimum) is on a meadow flanking Lake Magog with phenomenal views of Mount Assiniboine. The historic main building holds six double rooms that share bathroom facilities and a dining area where hearty meals are served around a huge table. Scattered in the surrounding trees are six one-room cabins that sleep 2-5 people. Each has propane for heat and lights. Outhouses, showers, and the sauna are shared. Rates include lodging, all meals (including bag lunches), and daily guided adventures. You can reach the lodge on foot or fly in by helicopter.

Near the lodge, the five **Naiset Huts** (C$25 pp per night) are primitive shared cabins without running water or electricity. They contain bunk beds with mattresses and a wood stove (bring your own linens and wood). Amenities include the equipped Wonder Lodge cooking shelter, food storage bins, and outhouses. Beds fill very quickly, so book through Mount Assiniboine Lodge as soon as reservations open, which is usually January for the upcoming summer season.

Backcountry campgrounds (C$10 pp per night) in the core of the park are at **Lake Magog,** which is the largest of the three with 40 sites, **Og Lake,** and **O'Brien Meadows.** The campgrounds have tent pads, bear-proof food storage, and pit toilets. Fires are not allowed. **Reservations** (800/689-9025, discovercamping.ca) are required from late June to September for the two lake campgrounds. Bookings open four months in advance.

ski area also has a day lodge, rentals, and lessons.

In summer, the trails convert to **mountain biking** and **trail-running** routes. You can download the summer trail maps or purchase them at the day lodge (C$2). Mountain bike rentals, lessons, and guided tours are on-site, and a **mountain bike skills park** has drops, bridges, and a wall ride. Other summer activities include an **orienteering course** and **disc golf course.**

Hiking

Grassi Lakes

Length: 4 km (2.4 mi) rt
Duration: 1.5 hours
Elevation gain: 300 meters (980 ft)
Effort: easy-moderate
Trailhead: Spray Village, beyond the Nordic center, off Spray Lakes Rd.

This trail climbs to two small lakes below Ha Ling Peak. From the parking lot just off Spray Lakes Road, take the left fork soon after starting. It climbs steadily to stairs cut into a cliff face before leading up to a bridge over Canmore Creek and to the lakes. Interpretive signs along the trail point out interesting aspects of the Bow Valley and detail the life of Lawrence Grassi, who built the trail in the early 1920s. With Ha Ling Peak as a backdrop, these gin-clear, spring-fed lakes are a particularly rewarding destination. Behind the upper lake, an easy scramble up a scree slope leads to four ancient pictographs of human figures. They are on the first large boulder in the gorge. An alternate return route is down a rough access road between the hiking trail and Spray Lakes Road, passing a broken-down log cabin along the way.

Rock Climbing

Mount Yamnuska has become a notable rock-climbing site, with scads of cliff routes on the limestone face. It's full of mostly traditional climbs, including challenging multi-pitch routes. To hire a guide, go with the local **Yamnuska**

Mountain Adventures (403/678-4164 or 866/678-4164, yamnuska.com). They also teach rock climbing courses, from beginner to advanced.

Rafting and Fishing

The **Bow River** runs right through Canmore with relatively tame water that is best for **scenic floating.** Early morning and evening floats offer the best times for potential wildlife sightings. **Guided scenic float trips** (late spring-early fall, C$30-60) take 1-2.5 hours. Several companies guide float trips:

- **Canmore Raft Tours** (702 8th St., 403/688-1775, www.canmorerafttours.com)

- **Canmore River Adventures** (Rundle Dr. and Bridge Rd., 403/981-4544 or 844/621-7238, www.canmoreriveradventures.com)

- **Canadian Rockies Rafting and Adventure Center** (909A Railway Ave., 403/678-6535, rafting.ca)

Golf

Stewart Creek Golf Club (4100 Stewart Creek Dr., 403/609-6099 or 877/993-4653, www.stewartcreekgolf.com, greens fees C$160-215) has relatively wide fairways but positioning of tee shots is important, and the course is made more interesting by hanging greens, greenside exposed rock, and historic mineshafts. Rates include use of a power cart and practice facility.

Food

Canmore has many top-notch restaurants, and one of the best is **Tavern 1883** (709 9th St., 403/609-2000, www.tavern1883.com, 11:30am-10pm daily, C$17-33), a family-friendly venue that is part pub and part restaurant. Earthy tones, hardwood floors, rustic furniture, and a large deck out front create a modern Western ambience. The menu takes its roots from across Canada, with an emphasis on freshly prepared Canadian produce. Choose from dishes such as elk burger, grilled bison and prawns, or poutine.

Crazyweed Kitchen (1600 Railway Ave., 403/609-2530, www.crazyweed.ca, 5pm-9pm Mon.-Wed., 11:30am-3pm and 5pm-9pm Thurs.-Sun., C$25-38) dishes up creative culinary fare. From the busy open kitchen, creative dishes served in healthy portions include beef short ribs in curry, truffle and mushroom gnocchi, and Alaskan king crab risotto.

Communitea Cafe (1001 6th Ave., 403/688-2233, thecommunitea.com, 8am-7pm daily, C$9-15) is a bright, welcoming space with lots of comfortable seating. As the name suggests, tea is the specialty, with over 80 blends to choose from, but the coffee is also good and the food outstanding. The menu features many creative, healthy choices, including pad Thai, an organic Indian-spiced chicken burger, and a goat cheese and beet quesadilla.

Accommodations
The Alpine Club of Canada (ACC, 403/678-3200, www.alpineclubofcanada. ca) operates the **Canmore Clubhouse** (Indian Flats Rd., C$30 members, C$40 nonmembers), a hostel-like lodge with outstanding mountain views. It has an equipped kitchen and shared dorm rooms. Bathrooms and showers are down the hall. Bedding and towels are included. The property also has two cabins with family rooms and dorm-style rooms.

Clique Hotels operates several lodges in Canmore. These upscale properties feature modern mountain designs and classy rooms starting from C$210.

The Malcolm Hotel (321 Spring Creek Dr., 403/812-0680, www.malcolmhotel. ca) takes advantage of the Spring Creek scenery with rooms and suites plus an outdoor heated pool and two hot tubs. **Falcon Crest Lodge** (190 Kananaskis Way, 403/678-6150 or 866/609-3222, www.falconcrestlodge.ca) has hotel rooms, condominiums, and two outdoor hot tubs. **Blackstone Mountain Lodge** (170 Kananaskis Way, 403/609-8098 or 888/830-8883, www.blackstonelodge. ca) has hotel rooms plus one- to three-bedroom suites.

South of Canmore, the road to remote and quiet **Mount Engadine Lodge** (1 Mount Shark Rd., 587/807-0570, mount-tengadine.com, C$385-600) sits along Spray Lakes Reservoir. The rustic, cozy lodge caters to year-round outdoor recreationists: cross-country skiers, hikers, and climbers. Accommodations include lodge rooms, cabins, glamping tents, and a yurt with all meals included.

Information and Services
Emergency Services
For emergencies, call **911. Canmore General Hospital** (1100 Hospital Pl., 403/678-5536, www.albertahealth services.ca) has 24-hour emergency services.

Gas and Vehicle Charging Stations
For fuel, head to **Shell** (1714 Bow Valley Trl.) or **Fas Gas Plus** (510 Bow Valley Trl.). There's an electric vehicle charging station at **Canmore Supercharger** (1719 Bow Valley Trl.).

Cell Service
Canmore has cell reception, but it disappears outside of town and in Spray Valley.

Yoho
National
Park

Highlights

★ **Soak up the scenery at Lake O'Hara:** Relish the exquisite mountains surrounding this idyllic alpine lake—if you're lucky enough to get reservations to visit for a day hike (page 186).

★ **Gaze up at Takakkaw Falls:** You'll need to crane your neck to admire this tall ribbon of plunging water, the biggest waterfall in the Canadian Rockies (page 187).

★ **Admire Natural Bridge:** This bridge has been carved out of rock by the sheer force of the Kicking Horse River (page 189).

★ **Hike or paddle Emerald Lake:** Circle this forest-rimmed lake by trail (page 193), canoe its placid green water (page 197), or simply soak up the views of the craggy peaks that tower overhead (page 189).

★ **Hike the Iceline Trail:** Trek through rocky moraines on this high-elevation trail that skirts the base of several glaciers (page 191).

★ **Go on a guided hike to the Burgess Shale fossil beds:** Jump back 500 million years at one of the world's most important paleontological sites, which holds ancient sea-bed fossils (page 194).

Yoho National Park

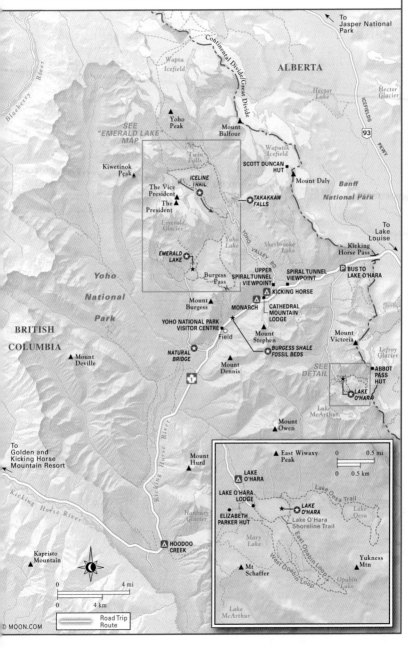

To Jasper National Park

Continental Divide/Great Divide

ALBERTA

Wapta Icefield

Hector Lake

Hector Glacier

ICEFIELDS

93

Yoho Peak

Mount Balfour

Waputik Icefield

SCOTT DUNCAN HUT

Mount Daly

Banff

Kiwetinok Peak

SEE "EMERALD LAKE" MAP

Twin Falls

ICELINE TRAIL

TAKAKKAW FALLS

National Park

The Vice President

The President

Emerald Glacier

Emerald Lake

Yoho Lake

Sherbrooke Lake

To Lake Louise

Kicking Horse Pass

Burgess Pass

YOHO VALLEY RD

UPPER SPIRAL TUNNEL VIEWPOINT

SPIRAL TUNNEL VIEWPOINT

BUS TO LAKE O'HARA

Yoho

Mount Burgess

KICKING HORSE

CATHEDRAL MOUNTAIN LODGE

National

MONARCH

YOHO NATIONAL PARK VISITOR CENTRE

Field

Mount Stephen

BURGESS SHALE FOSSIL BEDS

Mount Victoria

Lefroy Glacier

Park

BRITISH COLUMBIA

Mount Deville

NATURAL BRIDGE

Mount Dennis

SEE DETAIL

ABBOT PASS HUT

LAKE O'HARA

Lake McArthur

Kicking Horse River

Mount Owen

To Golden and Kicking Horse Mountain Resort

Mount Hurd

East Wiwaxy Peak

0   0.5 mi

0   0.5 km

LAKE O'HARA

Lake Oesa Trail

Hanbury Glacier

LAKE O'HARA LODGE

LAKE O'HARA

Lake O'Hara Shoreline Trail

Lake Oesa

Kapristo Mountain

ELIZABETH PARKER HUT

Mary Lake

East Opabin Loop

West Opabin Loop

Opabin Lake

Yukness Mtn

HOODOO CREEK

Mt Schaffer

Lake McArthur

0   4 mi

0   4 km

Road Trip Route

© MOON.COM

Yoho National Park may be smaller than its neighbor Banff, but it fits one-of-a-kind sights and potent experiences within its borders. The water features alone are dramatic. Up high, glaciers line the Wapta Icefield and the Iceline Trail. At lower elevations, Emerald Lake splays out, a vivid blue-green below rugged peaks, and Lake O'Hara tucks into a sculpted basin. Spewing from the Wapta Icefield, Takakkaw Falls outranks all other waterfalls with sheer immense height.

Glaciated water pours from the icefields through creeks and rivers that swell the milky Kicking Horse River. Its route cuts the path for the Trans-Canada Highway and the rail tracks that split the park into north and south sections. The north contains the vibrant Emerald Lake and wild Yoho Valley. The south has the famed Lake O'Hara. Kicking Horse Pass sits on the Continental Divide on the east side of the park. All of this mountainous land was originally crossed by the Ktunaxa people, heading to hunting grounds on the east side of the area.

As part of the Canadian Rockies UNESCO World Heritage Site, Yoho contains fossil beds full of trilobites and other ancient sea creatures. You can only see these via guided hikes. Spectacular hiking trails also await. Some climb to glaciers, tripping through rocky moraines, while others circle stunning lakes of vivid colors. Hovering above it all are the rugged peaks that define the park.

Don't underestimate Yoho. Its mountainous landscape holds great beauty and wildness that will stick with you long after you return home.

Planning Your Time

Yoho National Park (403/522-1186, www. pc.gc.ca) is tucked on the Continental Divide west of Banff National Park, connected by the Trans-Canada Highway. Yoho also borders Kootenay National Park to the south, but only connects via trails. The park can be a **day trip** from Banff or the northern part of Kootenay. In **one day,** you'll have enough time to drive to **Takakkaw Falls,** hike the loop trail around **Emerald Lake,** and explore stops on the **Trans-Canada Highway.** Consult with the park website on updates for permits, reservations, road construction, trail conditions, and potential closures.

Hikers will want to spend at least **three days** here. The highlight of a visit to Yoho is **Lake O'Hara,** one of the most special places in the Canadian Rockies. You can't simply drive up to O'Hara. Instead, you must make **advance reservations** for a shuttle bus that trundles up a restricted-access road to the lake or reserve space in the lake's campground, lodge, or rustic hut.

The **summer tourist season** in Yoho is shorter than in the other national parks. Emerald Lake doesn't become ice-free until early June, and the road to Takakkaw Falls remains closed until mid- or late June. While July and August are the prime months to visit, September is also pleasant, both weather- and crowd-wise. Lake O'Hara doesn't become completely snow-free until early July, but the best time to visit is during the last two weeks of September, when the forests of larch have turned a brilliant gold color.

You will need to have your own **transportation** or **rental car,** as Yoho does not have public transportation to and around the park. However, you can take **organized day tours** from Banff that hit some of the highlights in Yoho.

Despite being in British Columbia,

Yoho is in the **Mountain Time Zone,** which means it's in the same time zone as the other national parks in the Canadian Rockies.

Seasonal Driving Concerns

Yoho is open year-round, although road conditions in winter can be treacherous. Occasional weather related closures occur on Kicking Horse Pass, on the Trans-Canada Highway, which cuts through the park. The Emerald Lake Road also stays open year-round. The **Yoho Valley Road** to Takakkaw Falls closes from mid-October until mid- or late June.

Through 2025, a section of Trans-Canada Highway 1 through Yoho National Park is undergoing construction. The section spans 5 km (3 mi) near Golden. There may be long waits or detours along this stretch of highway, affecting visitors driving between Banff and Golden. (Access to Field, Emerald Lake, and Yoho Valley Road from the east will not be affected.) The **Kicking Horse Canyon Project** (844/815-6111, www. kickinghorsecanyon.ca) has information on closures and delays.

Trans-Canada Highway 1 also sees **avalanche control work** October to mid-June. Do not stop in signed avalanche zones. From October through March, **snow tires** are required on vehicles. Carry chains in case of more difficult winter conditions. For **road reports,** check with **Drive BC** (800/550-4997, www.drivebc.ca) or **511 Alberta** (511, 511.alberta.ca).

Wildlife can also be a hazard when driving, as park roads go through seasonal migration routes. If you spot wildlife that you want to watch, pull completely off the road and remain at a distance.

Best Route through the Park

Trans-Canada Highway 1 slices roughly east-west across the park. It takes in many classic Yoho views, but you'll want to head north off the highway onto the **Yoho Valley Road** or the **Emerald Lake Road** to take in some of the best sights.

Reservations and Where to Stay

Because lodging and dining options are limited inside the national park, you may want to base yourself outside the park. The town of **Golden** is about 20 minutes beyond the park's western boundary; above it, **Kicking Horse Mountain Resort** provides even more lodging choices. You can also base yourself in **Banff National Park.** The **Banff Townsite** is 45 minutes southeast, and **Lake Louise** is right around the corner, just 10 minutes away from Yoho. The town of **Field,** located in the middle of the park across from the visitors center, also has lodging options.

For staying inside Yoho, make **lodging reservations 9-12 months in advance.** You will also need **advance reservations** for **Lake O'Hara.** Reservations start on different dates, and some are by lottery. For the day visitors **shuttle bus,** reservations for the random draw usually start in January; **camping reservations** also open in January. For the **Elizabeth Parker Hut,** the lottery opens usually in October for the following summer and fall. Reservations for guided **Burgess Shale** trips also open in January.

Getting There

Car
From Banff and Lake Louise

Trans-Canada Highway 1 connects Banff National Park with the east entrance to Yoho National Park. From the town of **Lake Louise,** it's a 10-km (6-mi), 10-minute drive northwest on the highway. Once inside Yoho, it's 17 km (11 mi) west on the highway, a 15-minute drive, to reach the town of Field, also the location of the park's visitors center.

From the town of **Banff,** it's a 66-km (41-mi), 45-minute drive to Yoho's eastern entrance via **Trans-Canada Highway**

One Day in Yoho National Park

If you have one day in Yoho National Park, spend it hiking at **Lake O'Hara.** To do so, you will need to plan ahead by booking your **shuttle bus reservations** in advance. If you did not make a shuttle reservation for Lake O'Hara, you can still experience top-notch locales.

Morning
Drive up **Yoho Valley Road,** negotiating the steep switchbacks, and stop to admire **Takakkaw Falls.** Then climb the **Iceline Trail** to get up close and personal with glaciers.

Afternoon
Next, head out to **Emerald Lake.** Relax over a late lunch and a cool drink on the lake-side patio of **Emerald Lake Lodge.** Then go **canoeing** on the placid green water.

Evening
Drive across the **Kicking Horse River** and into the village of **Field,** where dinner at **Truffle Pigs Bistro** is a must.

1, which travels north on the west side of Bow River. You can also take the **Bow Valley Parkway** (Hwy. 1A), east of the river. Though the mileage is similar, at 67 km (42 mi), the narrower road and heavy summer traffic makes for a longer drive at 1.5 hours or more.

From Jasper
From the town of **Jasper,** take Highway 93 south, also called the **Icefields Parkway.** At the intersection with the Trans-Canada Highway 1, merge to go west on the highway to Yoho's east entrance. Without stops, which is really hard to do on this ultra-scenic road, the 235-km (145-mi) drive takes a little less than three hours.

From Calgary
From **Calgary International Airport,** the 210-km (130-mi) drive to Yoho's east entrance takes two hours going west on Highway 201 and Trans-Canada Highway 1. From **downtown Calgary,** it's 190 km (120 mi) via the Trans-Canada Highway, a drive of just under two hours.

From Kootenay National Park
From **Radium Hot Springs,** there are two

routes to Yoho, both of which take around 1.5 hours. To go through **Kootenay National Park,** take Highway 93 north to Trans-Canada Highway 1, then follow it north through Banff National Park to the east entrance of Yoho. This route is 140 km (85 mi). If you are staying inside Kootenay, it will take less time to reach Yoho.

To go to the **west entrance of Yoho** from Radium Hot Springs, drive north on BC 95 and then turn east on Trans-Canada Highway 1. This route is 130 km (80 mi).

From Golden, Cranbrook, or Revelstoke
From **Golden,** hop on Trans-Canada Highway 1 heading east to reach the west entrance of Yoho. It's only 30 km (19 mi), a 20-minute drive. Add on another 30 km (19 mi), a drive of 25 minutes, to continue farther west to the visitors center at Field, BC.

From **Revelstoke,** it's a mountain-ous 170-km (105-mi), two-hour shot east to Yoho via Trans-Canada. From **Cranbrook,** drive north on BC 3/95 to join BC 93/95 north to Radium Hot Springs. From there, stay on BC 95 to

Golden, then head east on Trans-Canada to Yoho. This route is 275 km (170 mi) and takes three hours to drive.

Air

Calgary International Airport (YYC, 2000 Airport Rd. NE, Calgary, 403/735-1200 or 877/254-7427, www.yyc.com) is the closest airport to Yoho National Park, a 210-km (130-mi), two-hour drive from the park's east entrance. About 12 airlines, including many U.S. and Canadian carriers, service the airport. Car rentals are available. Shuttles from the airport only go as far as Lake Louise; from there, you'll need a car to tour Yoho on your own. Otherwise, you can take a bus tour from Banff or Lake Louise for a day to visit Yoho.

You can also fly into Cranbrook, BC. **Canadian Rockies International Airport** (YXC, 1-9370 Airport Access Rd., Cranbrook, 250/426-7913, flyyxc.com) has flights from Vancouver, BC. The drive to Yoho from the Cranbrook airport is 280 km (175 mi), which takes three hours.

Bus

The bus service **Rider Express** (rider-express.ca) stops in **Golden** (Husky Gas Station, 1050 Hwy. 1), **Lake Louise** (Husky Gas Station, 200 Village Rd.), and **Banff** (Brewster Sightseeing, 100 Gopher St.). While Rider Express buses do travel on the highway through Yoho, they make **no stops inside the park.** You can rent cars in Golden, Lake Louise, or Banff.

Visiting the Park

Entrances and Fees

Yoho has two entrances, both on the Trans-Canada Highway 1. The **east entrance** is at Kicking Horse Pass and the Continental Divide; the **west entrance** is 27 km (17 mi) east of Golden. Neither has an official entrance station, but you will see signs welcoming you to the park.

Unless you're traveling straight through and not stopping at any overlooks, a daily or annual national park pass is required for entry into Yoho National Park. Passes are available from the Yoho National Park Visitor Centre and at campground kiosks.

A **one-day pass** (C$20 family/vehicle, C$10 adults, C$9 seniors, kids 17 and younger free) is valid until 4pm the following day. You can add on as many days as you need. The pass is also valid in Kootenay, Banff, and Jasper, so you can purchase a single pass for your whole trip.

The **Discovery Pass** (C$140 family/vehicle, C$70 adults, C$60 seniors) is good for entry into all of Canada's national parks and is valid for one year from purchase. It may be a more economical option for your Canadian Rockies road trip if you're visiting several parks. The Discovery Pass can be purchased in advance online or in person.

Visitors Centers
Yoho National Park Visitor Centre

In the middle of the park, **Yoho National Park Visitor Centre** (250/343-6783, 8:30am-7pm daily June-Sept., 9am-5pm May and early Oct.) sits on the Trans-Canada Highway in Field. Inside you'll find helpful staff, information boards, and interpretive exhibits, including one on the Burgess Shale fossils. The on-site Friends of Yoho bookstore sells topographical maps, books, and souvenirs. This is also the place to ask about trail closures and road conditions and to find out schedules for campground interpretive programs. Travel Alberta has a staffed desk inside the building with brochures, maps, and other information.

Outside the visitors center, you can stroll along the banks of the Kicking Horse River or walk across the bridge toward Field to enjoy its milky blue hue. Picnic tables are also available.

To reach the visitors center from the east entrance of Yoho, drive west on Trans-Canada for 17 km (11 mi; 15

minutes). From the west entrance of Yoho, drive east on Trans-Canada for 30 km (19 mi; 25 minutes).

Sights

★ Lake O'Hara

Nestled in a high bowl of lush alpine meadows, **Lake O'Hara** is surrounded by dozens of smaller alpine lakes and framed by spectacular peaks permanently mantled in snow. As if that weren't enough, the entire area is webbed by a network of **hiking trails** that radiate from the lake in all directions through wildflower meadows, to mountain passes, along scenic ledges, and around lakes. What makes this destination all the more special is that a quota system limits the number of visitors to protect the sensitive area and wildlife. Its distance from the nearest public road (11 km/6.8 mi) means that is it accessible only by foot or shuttle bus (or skis, in the winter). This is an ideal destination for hikers, but also for anyone who wants to enjoy the idyllic scenery. Day visitors can have lunch or tea at the Lake O'Hara Lodge, then walk part of the trail the circles the lake.

Overnighting at Lake O'Hara is a treat, especially seeing the stars overhead or the peaks light up under a full moon. You can **camp** (mid-June-early Oct.), stay at **Elizabeth Parker Hut** (year-round, but ski-in only during winter), or check into the **Lake O'Hara Lodge** (mid-June-early Oct. and Feb.-Apr.). All three require **reservations.**

Shuttle Bus

You can hike into Lake O'Hara, but most visitors take the **day-use shuttle bus** (daily mid-June-early Oct., roundtrip C$15 adults, C$8 youth). Seats on the shuttle are issued via **lottery** (877/737-3783, outside North America 519/826-5391, reservation.pc.gc.ca, C$10 per application, C$12 per reservation) in February for that year's season. In the

model of the spiral tunnels at the Yoho visitors center

lottery application, you'll pick up to six dates and times for your inbound bus trip. (You do not need a reservation for an outbound bus.) If you have a reservation for camping, the hut, or the lodge, you do not need to enter the lottery; you'll book your shuttle seats with your overnight reservation.

Inbound buses depart from a signed parking lot on the south side of Trans-Canada Highway 1, located 15 km (9.3 mi) east of Field and 3 km (1.9 mi) west of the Continental Divide. O'Hara-bound buses leave at 8:30am and 10:30am (daily mid-June-early Oct.). Outbound buses depart Lake O'Hara at 9:30am, 11:30am, 2:30pm, 4:30pm, and 6:30pm.

After the 20-minute bus ride to the lake, day trippers are dropped off at **Le Relais,** a log shelter where books and maps are sold. The *Lake O'Hara* Gem Trek map (C$6) is the best one for hiking here. Hot drinks and light snacks are available. Meet back in the afternoon at Le Relais for the outbound bus.

Spiral Tunnel Viewpoints

The joy that Canadian Pacific Railway president William Van Horne must have felt upon completion of his transcontinental rail line in 1886 was tempered by massive problems along a stretch of line west of Kicking Horse Pass. Big Hill was less than 5 km (3.1 mi) long, but its grade was so steep that runaway trains, crashes, and other disasters were common. Nearly 25 years after the line opened, railway engineers and builders finally solved the problem. By building two **spiral tunnels** down through 2 km (1.2 mi) of solid rock to the valley floor, they lessened the grade dramatically, and the terrors came to an end. The tracks do not continuously spiral down, but rather follow a sweeping loop through each tunnel with some of the cross-over sections on the hillsides in between.

Today, the Trans-Canada Highway follows the original railbed. On the north side of the highway, between Wapta Lake and Yoho Valley Road, is the **Lower Spiral Tunnel Viewpoint.** It has interpretive displays telling the story of Big Hill and a relief map depicting the spirals, so you can get an idea of what's inside the tunnels. On Yoho Valley Road, after crossing the Yoho River, is the **Upper Spiral Tunnel Viewpoint.** From both viewpoints you can see wee bits of train passing through the trees. If the train is especially long, you might be able to see one end going in the first tunnel as the other ends exits the second tunnel. Trains pass through frequently, about 25-30 per day. From Kicking Horse Campground, the interpretive **Walk in the Past Trail** (3 km/1.8 mi rt, 1.5 hrs) takes you past the wreckage of one of the doomed trains that didn't survive Big Hill.

★ Takakkaw Falls

The most impressive waterfall in the Canadian Rockies, **Takakkaw Falls** is fed

by the Daly and Des Poilus Glaciers of the Waputik Icefield, which straddles the Continental Divide. Meaning "wonderful" in the language of the Cree people, Takakkaw tumbles 254 meters (830 ft) over a sheer rock wall at the lip of the Yoho Valley, creating a spray bedecked by rainbows. While it is not Canada's tallest waterfall, its drop is unbroken, which raises the wow factor. You can see it from the parking lot, but you'll get much closer via an easy 10-minute stroll over the Yoho River to appreciate Takakkaw in all its glory.

To see this wonder, drive to the end of Yoho Valley Road (14 km/8.7 mi, open mid-June-mid-Oct.) from Trans-Canada Highway 1. The road is only passable for cars and small RVs due to very tight switchbacks.

Kicking Horse River

Starting at Wapta Lake near Kicking Horse Pass, the clear-watered **Kicking Horse River** descends to bisect the park from east to west. Lined with pink fireweed in summer, the river glints with bluish milky water coming from the Yoho River. You can stop to admire the varied colors of the **confluence** at a pullout near the beginning of Yoho Valley Road. Between there and Field, the milky water cuts a wide braided swath through the forest and along the highway. The water is highest in June due to snowmelt. By August, the river splits around islands full of cobble.

Field

Located across the Kicking Horse River from the Trans-Canada Highway and the Yoho National Park Visitor Centre, **Field** (www.field.ca) is a tiny mountain town built on a hillside. Its year-round population of about 200 residents balloons in summer. The town has hotels,

Top to bottom: Takakkaw Falls; Kicking Horse River; Natural Bridge hostels, and lots of guest houses to support the influx, plus restaurants and a few shops. Field was once a mining town, and its heritage is evident in a few places, including its historic railway and telegraph buildings and its location on the Canadian Pacific Railway line.

★ Natural Bridge

While the mighty Kicking Horse River is just gaining steam at **Natural Bridge,** it still has enough power that it's been able, over time, to scour through rock itself. As the river churned against the rock, it eventually cut its way under and through, creating the bridge-like formation that exists today. The accompanying roar of the water is also a testament to its power.

You can view the bridge from the rocky shore and from the human-built bridge that crosses the river to a viewing platform. As water spews from below Natural Bridge, it churns in a sculpted basin before rushing down the valley. More of the bridge and undercut is exposed when the waterflow decreases in fall. Natural Bridge is located less than five minutes (2.4 km/1.5 mi) up Emerald Lake Road.

★ Emerald Lake

The largest of the lakes in the Canadian Rockies, beautiful **Emerald Lake** sparkles with various hues of blue-green. It is surrounded by a forest of Engelmann spruce, as well as many peaks more than 3,000 meters (9,840 ft) high. It is covered in ice most of the year but comes alive with activity for a few short months in summer when hikers, canoeists, and horseback riders take advantage of the magnificent surroundings. **Emerald Lake Lodge** is the grandest of Yoho's accommodations, offering a restaurant, café, lounge, and recreation facilities for guests and non-guests alike. Find the lake at the end of Emerald Lake Road (9.4 km/5.8 mi, open year-round).

Scenic Drives

Trans-Canada Highway

From east to west, **Trans-Canada Highway 1** (128 km/80 mi) yields big mountain views in a 1.5-hour drive. In eastern Yoho, **Kicking Horse Pass** is the highest pass (1,650 m/5,340 ft) on the cross-Canada highway. It's on the Continental Divide, which sheds water through Banff to the Atlantic Ocean and through Yoho to the Pacific Ocean. The pass also marks the boundary between Alberta and British Columbia. After crossing Kicking Horse Pass, you'll spend the remainder of the drive going through **Kicking Horse Canyon.**

A bit farther west, you'll drive past **Wapta Lake,** the headwaters for the **Kicking Horse River,** which you'll follow for much of the drive. Stop at the **Upper Spiral Tunnel Viewpoint** to learn about the struggles and solutions for a safe railway route through the steep pass.

Just before the **Yoho Valley Road,** you'll cross over the Kicking Horse River to follow it through the flats to **Field,** a tiny mountain hamlet that houses the park's visitors center and a good place to stop for lunch. After passing **Emerald Lake Road,** the forested highway squeezes through a canyon with huge swaths cut through cliffs in its final descent to the **Columbia Valley** and the park's western boundary, where the Kicking Horse River grows in size with the addition of many tributaries. From here to Golden is another 27 km (17 mi), which takes less than 25 minutes to drive.

Yoho Valley Road

Take a tour of Yoho Valley with a scenic drive up **Yoho Valley Road** (28 km/17.4 mi rt, open mid-June-mid-Oct.). The road starts at a signed turnoff from Trans-Canada 1 and follows the cloudy **Kicking Horse River** upstream, crossing two bridges en route. Stop at the **Upper**

Emerald Lake

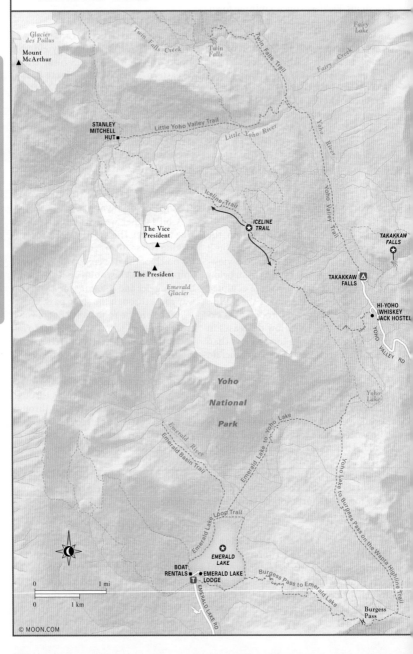

© MOON.COM

Spiral Tunnel Viewpoint to watch trains on the steep pass. Then swing into a pull-out to view the **confluence of the Yoho and Kicking Horse Rivers,** a particularly impressive sight as the Yoho is glacier-fed and therefore silty, while Kicking Horse is lake-fed and clear.

Next, you'll climb two *very* tight switchbacks (where tour buses must reverse through the mid-section). Due to these tight switchbacks, vehicles with trailers and RVs aren't suited for this drive. The climb continues into the narrow **Yoho Valley,** surrounded by huge walls. The road ends at the trailhead to **Takakkaw Falls,** an awe-inspiring sight. Some years, Yoho Valley Road won't be snow-free until late June. You'll need 45 minutes or so to do this drive.

Recreation

Hiking
Yoho Valley
To reach trailheads in Yoho Valley, drive the Yoho Valley Road (14 km/8.7 mi, open mid-June–mid-Oct.) north from Highway 1. For all hikes, park in the Takakkaw Falls parking lot at the end of the road.

★ Iceline Trail
Length: 12.8 km (8 mi) rt
Duration: 5 hours
Elevation gain: 690 meters (2,260 ft)
Effort: moderate-strenuous
Trailhead: HI-Yoho (Whiskey Jack Hostel)

The Iceline is one of the most spectacular day hikes in the Canadian Rockies. This route goes from the HI-Yoho hostel to the highest point along the trail (2,250 m/7,380 ft). From the hostel, the trail begins a steep and steady ascent of switchbacks to a point where two options present themselves: The Iceline Trail is to the right, and Yoho Lake is to the left. As the climb changes from forest to rocky rubble, the Iceline Trail enters its highlight: a traverse of the moraine below

Emerald Glacier. Views across the valley to the **Waputik Icefield** improve as the trail climbs to its crest and passes a string of small lakes filled with glacial meltwater, the point of return.

Instead of hiking out and back, many day hikers succumb to the lure of hiking the Iceline as a longer **circuit** (21 km/13.5 mi, 710m/2,329 ft elevation gain, 8 hrs). From the trail junction at the small lakes on the Iceline, go left to finish out the moraine heading north, where the trail drops into wildflower meadows of **Little Yoho River Valley.** Below Stanley Mitchell Hut, the trail descends east through forest along the **Little Yoho River** to link with the **Yoho Valley Trail.** Follow the **Yoho River** back to the trailhead. Another option is to take the right trail at the Iceline lakes junction for a forested descent to **Celeste Lake** (18 km/11.2 mi, 6 hrs) to a lower junction on the Little Yoho River Valley Trail and loop back to the trailhead.

Yoho Lake
Length: 7.4 km (4.6 mi) rt
Duration: 2.5 hours
Elevation gain: 300 meters (990 ft)
Effort: moderate
Trailhead: HI-Yoho (Whiskey Jack Hostel)

The trail to Yoho Lake begins along the HI-Yoho hostel access road. After ascending a few switchbacks to a junction with the Iceline Trail, go left. Soon you'll reach the picturesque, spruce-encircled **Yoho Lake,** located on forested Yoho Pass. There are campsites and picnic tables at the lake.

From Yoho Pass, you can extend your hike to other destinations: descend to **Emerald Lake** (5.5 km/3.4 mi, 530 m/1,740 ft elevation loss), climb to spectacular **Burgess Pass** (6 km/3.7 mi, 300 m/985 ft elevation gain), or intersect with the **Iceline Trail** (2 km/1.2 mi) via a different trail than the one you hiked up.

Twin Falls
Length: 16 km (10 mi) rt
Duration: 5 hours

Elevation gain: 300 meters (980 ft)

Effort: moderate

Trailhead: Takakkaw Falls parking lot

This hike follows the **Yoho Valley Trail** in a northerly direction up the Yoho River to **Twin Falls,** passing many other waterfalls along the way, including **Laughing Falls.** At Twin Falls, water from the Wapta Icefield divides in two before plunging off an 80-meter-high (262-ft) cliff. Mother Nature may work in amazing ways, but sometimes she needs a helping hand, or so the Canadian Pacific Railway thought. In the 1920s, the company dynamited one of the channels to make the falls more symmetrical.

Lake O'Hara

To hike Lake O'Hara's trails requires taking the day-use **shuttle bus** into the area or staying overnight in the Lake O'Hara campground, Elizabeth Parker Hut, or Lake O'Hara Lodge. All four options **require reservations.** Across from Le Relais, where the shuttle bus drops you off, behind the warden's cabin, interpretive boards lay out the hiking options throughout the area and explain local history. Most Lake O'Hara trails have multiple junctions; take a map to aid with route-finding.

Lake O'Hara Shoreline

Length: 2.8 km (1.7 mi) loop

Duration: 1 hour

Elevation gain: minimal

Effort: easy

Trailhead: warden's cabin, across from Le Relais

Most people use sections of this easy loop around Lake O'Hara to access other trails, but it is an enjoyable walk in its own right, especially in the evening. Heading in a clockwise direction, the trail crosses **Cataract Creek,** the lake's outlet. Next, it passes along the north shoreline, crossing gullies, and then reaches **Seven Veil Falls,** a wide series

Top to bottom: Yoho Valley Road; hiker on the Iceline Trail; Emerald Lake Loop

of ribbons. Traversing the cool, damp, southern shoreline, the route passes trails that branch off to the Opabin Plateau and a short detour to Mary Lake. After passing **Lake O'Hara Lodge,** it's a short stroll back along the road to Le Relais.

Lake Oesa

Length: 8.2 km (5.1 mi) rt
Duration: 3 hours
Elevation gain: 240 meters (787 ft)
Effort: moderate
Trailhead: warden's cabin, across from Le Relais

Walk around the north shore of Lake O'Hara to the trail junction for Lake Oesa. Switchback up the slope that's been sheered of trees by avalanches, gaining bigger views of Lake O'Hara. The route climbs past the tiny **Yukness, Victoria,** and **Lefroy** pocket lakes as it works its way up a beautifully engineered trail of slabs and rock steps. You'll pass one scenic outcrop after another in between fragile wildflower meadows. The route crests through bedrock into the rocky alpine basin cradling the blue **Lake Oesa** with peaks of the Continental Divide towering overhead.

Opabin Lake Loop

Length: 7.4 km (4.6 mi) loop
Duration: 3 hours
Elevation gain: 250 meters (820 ft)
Effort: moderate
Trailhead: warden's cabin, across from Le Relais

Also called the **Opabin Plateau Circuit,** this trail links the Lake O'Hara Shoreline Trail with the West Opabin and East Opabin Trails. Start by walking around the south shore of Lake O'Hara to the junction with the West Opabin Trail. Turn right to start climbing to **Mary Lake,** swinging around the east shore. Here, the trail pitches steeper across talus slopes, stunted trees, and meadows to reach the **Opabin Plateau,** a hanging valley of lakes, meadows, and rock knolls tucked below Mount Hungabee. You'll pass junctions with alpine routes, but stay on the path passing on the south side of **Hungabee**

Lake, surrounded by wildflower meadows. The trail climbs farther up into an alpine basin holding **Opabin Lake,** where views extend up to Opabin Glacier and Opabin Pass.

To descend, take the East Opabin Trail under Mount Yukness, passing the north side of Hungabee Lake and the Yukness Ledge Alpine Route. The trail wanders through meadows before plunging down switchbacks to the Lake O'Hara Shoreline Trail. Turn left to return to the trailhead.

Emerald Lake

To reach the trailheads for Emerald Lake, drive north from Highway 1 on Emerald Lake Road (9 km/5.6 mi, open year-round). Park in the large lot at the end of the road. From late May to September, plan for an early arrival, around 8am, as the parking lot fills up fast.

★ Emerald Lake Loop

Length: 3.7 km (2.3 mi) loop
Duration: 1.5 hours
Elevation gain: minimal
Effort: easy
Trailhead: Emerald Lake parking lot

One of the easiest yet most enjoyable walks in Yoho is around the park's most famous lake. The interpretive trail encircles **Emerald Lake** and can be hiked in either direction. The best views are from the western shoreline, where a massive avalanche has cleared away the forest of Engelmann spruce. Across the lake from this point, you'll see Mount Burgess rising with its massive rock spires. Traveling in a clockwise direction, stay right at the trail junction to Emerald Basin and cross a small bridge. At this point, you are walking across the alluvial fan of rocky debris washed down from the President Range. Views extend back across the lake to the lodge, backdropped by the Ottertail Range.

Beyond the lake's inlet, the vegetation changes dramatically. A lush forest of towering western red cedar creates a canopy, protecting moss-covered fallen trees, thimbleberry, and bunchberry extending to the water's edge. Watch your footing on slippery tree roots and rocks. At the next junction the left fork leads back to the parking lot via a small forest-encircled pond, or you can continue straight ahead through the grounds of Emerald Lake Lodge.

Emerald Basin

Length: 9 km (5.6 mi) rt
Duration: 3 hours
Elevation gain: 280 meters (920 ft)
Effort: easy-moderate
Trailhead: Emerald Lake parking lot

Follow the west shore of Emerald Lake to the junction for Emerald Basin. Turn left to ascend along the edge of the alluvial fan full of rocky rubble. The trail ascends a narrow valley on a steady climb through a dense subalpine forest. Soon, the trail leaves the tree cover behind to ascend along a creek into the rocky cirque. Towering overhead are the humungous peaks and impressive vertical walls of The President and Vice President, part of the President Range. You can poke around the basin before returning, where the view south takes in Mounts Wapta and Burgess.

Wapta Highline

Length: 16.1 km (10 mi) loop
Duration: 5-6 hours
Elevation gain: 889 meters (2,917 ft)
Effort: moderate-strenuous
Trailhead: Emerald Lake parking lot

This route makes a large loop linking Emerald Lake, Yoho Pass, the Wapta Highline, and Burgess Pass. While you can go either direction, a clockwise route gains the ascent more moderately. If you want less knee pounding on the descent, reverse to hike counter-clockwise. This trail can hold steep snowfields into July.

Hike the west shore of Emerald Lake to the junction with the Yoho Pass Trail, then head uphill across multiple creeks in the alluvial fan to ascend talus slopes and along waterfalls to the forested **Yoho**

Pass, where a right turn launches you onto the **Wapta Highline.** This traverse skirts across Mount Wapta, rising above the tree line with outstanding views of peaks, glaciers, and waterfalls in the President Range. The trail crosses scree and talus slopes en route as you hike straight toward the rocky cliffs of Mount Burgess. From **Burgess Pass,** the trail plunges into the forest, down switchbacks on a fast descent to the south shore of Emerald Lake, where a left turn completes the loop.

★ Burgess Shale Fossil Beds Guided Hikes

High on the rocky slopes above Field is a layer of sedimentary rock known as the **Burgess Shale,** which contains what are considered to be the world's finest fossils from the Cambrian period. Discovered by Charles Walcott in 1909, the 500-million-year-old fossils here are from marine invertebrates. These soft-bodied animals, such as trilobites,

brachiopods, and bristle worms, were preserved completely. Today paleontologists continue to uncover perfectly preserved fossils here. They've also uncovered additional fossil beds, similar in makeup and age, across the valley on the north face of Mount Stephen. The fossil sites are only accessible via **guided tour.** On a tour, you'll get to pick up fossils to admire and photograph.

Reaching the Fossil Sites

The trails to both fossil sites are steep, challenging, strenuous, and unrelenting in their elevation gain. To visit the sites, you must be fit enough to hike to **Walcott's Quarry** (22 km/14 mi rt, 825 m/2,710 ft elevation gain, 11 hrs) or the **Mount Stephen Trilobite Beds** (8 km/5 mi rt, 795 m/2,610 ft elevation gain, 7 hrs).

Reservations

Protected by UNESCO as a Canadian Rockies World Heritage Site, the two research areas are open only to those accompanied by a licensed guide. **Reservations are required.**

Guides working with **Parks Canada** lead hikes to both sites. Make your reservations (877/737-3783, outside North America 519/826-5391, reservation.pc.gc. ca, C$12 per party) as soon as bookings open for the year, usually in January. **Mount Stephen trips** (C$55 adults, C$47 seniors, C$28 youth) run from mid-June to late June (Fri.-Mon.) and from early July to early September (Fri.-Sun.). The **Walcott Quarry trips** (C$70 adults, C$60 seniors, C$35 youth) go out from early July through August (Thurs.-Tues.) and from early September until mid-September (Fri.-Sun.).

The **Burgess Shale Geoscience Foundation** (800/343-3006, www. burgess-shale.bc.ca) also guides trips to both sites. **Mount Stephen trips** (C$95 adults, C$65 ages 13-18, C$44 ages 6-12) are offered in June (Sat.-Sun.) and from July to mid-Sept. (Sat.-Mon.). **Walcott**

A Parks Canada interpretive guide shows off a fossil specimen at the Burgess Shale.

Trips (C$126 pp) go out from late June to mid-September (Fri.-Sun.).

Backpacking
Permits and Campsites

For backpacking, **wilderness camping permits** (877/737-3783, reservation pc.gc.ca, C$10 pp per night) are required. While you can pick up a last-minute permit, most of the top destinations and backcountry campsites are filled as soon as **reservations** open in January. Competition is stiff for July and August.

Yoho has only a handful of **backcountry campgrounds.** Each has picnic tables, tent pads, pit toilets, and food lockers or cables. The best campgrounds, **Laughing Falls, Twin Falls,** and **Little Yoho,** are sprinkled across Yoho Valley, accessible via Yoho Valley Road and with trailhead parking at Takakkaw Falls. **Yoho Lake Campground** is located at Yoho Pass, accessible from the Takakkaw Falls parking lot or from the west side at Emerald Lake.

Iceline Backpacking Loop
25 kilometers (15.5 miles)

Tackle this loop in either direction for a leisurely stroll of the Iceline Trail. For a three-day backpacking route, spend one night at **Yoho Lake** at the south end and the other at **Little Yoho** on the north end of the traverse. In between, you'll cross through rocky moraine at the base of glaciers with outstanding views of Yoho Valley. This route has options for side day-trip explorations onto the Wapta Highline from Yoho Lake, and you can add on another night at Laughing Falls to take a side trip up to Twin Falls.

Mountaineering
Lake O'Hara Alpine Routes

The Lake O'Hara area has gorgeous but challenging routes, populated with scrambles, scree fields, and exposed ledges, best accomplished by experienced, strong hikers. Access is only via the Lake O'Hara day-use shuttle

bus or by overnighting at Lake O'Hara Campground, Elizabeth Parker Hut, or Lake O'Hara Lodge; **reservations are required** for all four. Many routes are marked by cairns or with a splotch of blue paint with yellow stripes. There are multiple trail junctions and areas of scrambling, so use a map for route-finding. To calculate the full mileage for each route described here, you'll need to add on the distance of the **access trails** that funnel you to the start of these alpine routes. Note that avalanche hazards often keep these routes closed into July.

One of the best alpine routes skitters along the steep **Yukness Ledges** (2.2 km/1.4 mi one-way) on Yukness Mountain. The route links Lake Oesa with Hungabee Lake on the Opabin Plateau, looping from the Lake O'Hara Shoreline Trail. An optional side spur climbs aggressively up a scree slot to **Sleeping Poet Pool** (0.4 km/0.3 mi rt) on a higher alpine bench.

From Lake Oesa, the climb to **Abbot Pass** (3.8 km/2.4 mi rt) goes to a knife-like col on the Continental Divide between Mount Lefroy and Mount Victoria. Although the distance isn't much, the final portion climbs straight up a steep, loose scree field (460 m/1,500 ft) on the south side of the pass, while the north side drops precipitously into the Death Trap icefall. The stone hut at the pass is a National Historic Site. Helmets are required. The total trip will take 8-10 hours.

From the north shore of Lake O'Hara, the trail to **Wiwaxy Gap** and **Huber Ledges** (3.2 km/2 mi one-way) create a loop to Lake Oesa with a return via the Lake Oesa Trail. Steep switchbacks climb out of the forest, where the relentless route sometimes goes straight uphill. After reaching Wiwaxy Gap, a pass between Wiwaxy Peaks and Mount Huber, the route traverses Mount Huber via a narrow goat trail on skimpy ledges. Be prepared for extreme exposure through cliffs and crossing loose scree fields.

ACC Huts

In Yoho, the **Alpine Club of Canada** (403/678-3200, www.alpineclubofcanada. ca) has several shared rustic, wood-heated **huts** with outhouses. They are user-maintained. Bring your own food, sleeping bag, and personal gear. With the exception of the Elizabeth Parker Hut at Lake O'Hara, the huts are in locations only accessible by hiking trail or mountaineering routes. Most are open year-round, but in winter require long ski ascents in avalanche-prone terrain.

The log **Stanley Mitchell Hut** sits in Little Yoho Valley at the north end of the Iceline, a base for climbing in the President Range. Above Lake O'Hara, the historic stone **Abbot Pass Hut** is for summer mountaineering only (check on its status ahead of time, as it has been closed for slope stabilization). On the north shoulder of Mount Daly, the small, boxy **Scott Duncan Hut** is most often accessed by glacier travel (with ropes, harnesses, crampons, and ice axes) or winter skiing as part of the hut-to-hut Wapta Traverse that starts in Banff National Park.

★ Paddling

During summer, especially when **Emerald Lake** calms into a glassy surface, it begs for paddlers to enjoy the scenery. You can launch your own **kayak, canoe,** or **paddleboard** near the parking lot. No motorized boats are allowed. The **Emerald Lake Boathouse** (250/343-6000, 9am-7pm daily mid-May-mid-Oct., rentals C$75/hr) is based in a small boat shed on the shore of Emerald Lake and rents out canoes only. Rates include life jackets.

Be sure your vessel (including inflatables and paddleboards) is properly cleaned, drained, and dry before launching. You'll also need to complete the required self-certification at the visitors center before getting in the water.

Top to bottom: Stanley Mitchell Hut; canoeing on Emerald Lake; Cilantro Cafe

Rafting Kicking Horse River

If you're hoping for some white-water rafting action, look no further than the Kicking Horse River—as long as you're outside the boundaries of Yoho National Park, that is. The town of Golden, on the west side of the park, is the local rafting capital, where you'll find all the outfitters. If you're looking to start your rafting trip from Lake Louise or Banff, though, you're in luck: There are outfitters here that run guided trips that include transportation.

The **Lower Canyon,** immediately upstream of Golden, offers the biggest thrills, including a stretch of huge Class IV-plus continuous rapids. In the **Middle Canyon,** the river is tamer but still has splashy Class III rapids that are great for families. Farther upstream, near the western boundary of the national park, **scenic float trips** offer a calmer experience.

The rafting season runs **mid-May to mid-September,** with river levels at their highest in late June. Outfitters run half-day (C$90-130) or full-day (C$160-200) trips on various sections of the river. Some trips include lunch. Heli-rafting trips (C$350) allow you to run the entire river or double your trips down the whitewater.

Here are a few outfitters based in Golden that offer guided Kicking Horse rafting trips:

♦ **Wet 'n' Wild Adventures** (250/344-6521 or 877/344-7238, www.wetnwild.bc.ca)

♦ **Glacier Raft Company** (1509a Lafontaine Rd., 250/344-6521 or 877/344-7238, glacierraft.com)

♦ **Alpine Rafting** (1509c Lafontaine Rd., 250/344-6521 or 877/344-7238, alpinerafting.com)

Food

Emerald Lake

Emerald Lake Lodge (403/410-7417, crmr.com) offers several options for dining at Emerald Lake. On the waterfront, ★ **Cilantro Cafe** (250/343-6321, 1pm-9pm daily mid-May-mid-Sept., C$9-23) is a casual spot featuring magnificent views from tables inside an open-fronted, log chalet-style building or out on the lakefront deck. You can sip a coffee or have a full meal, such as chili with a cornbread muffin. The main lodge houses the more formal **Mount Burgess Dining Room** (8am-11am and 5pm-9pm daily mid-May-mid-Sept., C$32-45), where dinner dishes include elk striploin and halibut. Make reservations for dinner. The more casual **Kicking Horse Lounge** (noon-close daily mid-May-mid-Sept.) has comfy couches and an abbreviated but still appealing menu.

Yoho Valley Road

Cathedral Mountain Lodge (1 Yoho Valley Rd., 250/343-6442 or 866/619-6442, www.cathedralmountainlodge.com, 7am-10:30am and 5:30pm-9pm daily late May-early Oct., C$34-55) offers upscale dining in its **Riverside Dining Room** overlooking the Kicking Horse River. The menu changes daily but can feature dishes such as Alberta beef ribeye or duck breast. Elegantly casual dinner attire is required, and reservations are highly recommended.

Field

★ **Truffle Pigs Bistro** (100 Centre St., 250/343-6303, www.trufflepigs.com, 11am-3:30pm and 5pm-9pm daily, C$24-40) is one of those unexpected finds that makes traveling such a joy. In the evening this place really shines, with dishes as meaty as bacon-wrapped beef tenderloin and as simple as seared salmon served with local vegetables. The bistro also has a coffee shop and tiny grocery (9am-5pm daily).

In a relaxed, friendly atmosphere, **The Siding Café** (318 Stephen Ave., 250/343-6002, thesidingcafe.ca, noon-9pm daily, shorter days and hours in winter, C$10-20) serves up breakfast, lunch, and dinner. You can get bowls, sandwiches, fresh salads, Friday night fish and chips, and Saturday night pizza. If you just want to stop in for an espresso and dessert, that's okay, too. It also has a tiny liquor store.

Accommodations and Camping

Huts and Hostels

Marvel at the wonder of Takakkaw Falls from the deck at **HI-Yoho National Park** (Yoho Valley Rd., 778/328-2220 or 866/762-4122, www.hihostels.ca, late June-Sept., HI members C$31, nonmembers C$34), also known as Whiskey Jack Hostel. It has three mixed gender dorm rooms for nine people each in bunks stacked three-high. A communal kitchen and showers are available. The trail to the Iceline is right out the door.

In a meadow near Lake O'Hara, the historic log **Elizabeth Parker Hut** has rustic, wood-heated accommodations owned by the **Alpine Club of Canada** (403/678-3200, www.alpineclubofcanada.ca, year-round, C$30 pp ACC members, C$40 pp nonmembers) and user-maintained. The main cabin holds the communal kitchen and two giant bunks that sleep people lined up next to each other. The smaller cabin has additional bunks. Guests bring their own sleeping bags, food, and personal items. What sets this accommodation apart from other ACC huts is the ease of reaching it: It's just a 10-minute walk from the shuttle bus drop-off point at Le Relais. For summer reservations, you must enter the lottery system during the preceding October; the lottery gets you a place in line for choosing dates for your trip. If you are successful in the lottery, your reservation includes a guaranteed seat on the shuttle bus to Lake O'Hara. In winter, you'll need to ski 3-4 hours through avalanche terrain to reach the hut.

Trail hikers, even families, can also stay in the log **Stanley Mitchell Hut**, also owned by the **Alpine Club of Canada** (403/678-3200, www.alpineclubofcanada.ca, year-round, C$30 pp ACC members, C$40 pp nonmembers), midway on the loop connecting the Little Yoho Valley and Iceline Trails (21 km/13.5 mi). From the Takakkaw Falls parking lot on Yoho Valley Road, the hike to the hut takes 3-4 hours.

Lodges

Along the Kicking Horse River, ★ **Cathedral Mountain Lodge** (1 Yoho Valley Rd., 250/343-6442 or 866/619-6442, www.cathedralmountainlodge.com, late May-early Oct., C$405-900) has upscale, spacious log chalets with modern amenities. With an eye to comfort, the chalets have log beds topped by down duvets, stone fireplaces, bathrooms with soaker tubs and bathrobes, and private decks. Rates include a continental breakfast, naturalist program, and the use of canoes at Banff's Moraine Lake. The timber-frame lodge in the center of the complex has a stylish restaurant and lounge.

★ **Emerald Lake Lodge** (250/343-6321 or 800/663-6336, crmr.com, year-round, C$250-900 winter, C$470-1,070 summer) is a luxury-class accommodation along the southern shore of Emerald Lake. Guests lap up luxury in 24 richly decorated duplex-style cabins. Each spacious unit is outfitted in a heritage theme and has a wood-burning fireplace, private balcony, luxurious bathroom, and comfortable bed topped by a plush duvet. Other lodge amenities include an outdoor hot tub and sauna, swimming pool, restaurant, lounge, and café. Guests can

also go horseback riding or canoeing on Emerald Lake.

Spending a night at ★ **Lake O'Hara Lodge** (250/343-6418, www.lakeohara. com, Feb.-Apr. and mid-June-early Oct., C$555-770 lodge rooms, C$1,095 cabins) is a special experience. On a practical level, it allows hikers not equipped for overnight camping the opportunity to explore one of the finest hiking destinations in the Canadian Rockies. The 15 one-bedroom cabins, each with a private bathroom, are spread around the lakeshore, while within the main lodge are eight rooms, most of which have twin beds and share bathrooms. Rates include all meals and transportation to the lake. To get to the remote lake, you'll take a 20-minute ride on a shuttle bus (included in your reservation) from a parking lot adjacent to the Trans-Canada Highway, which climbs up a road that's closed to private vehicles.

Field

In the hamlet of Field, you can find varied lodging at inns, as well as loads of private homes offering reasonably priced overnight accommodations in rooms of varying privacy and quality. Summer is the busiest season, when rates are highest; winter has the low rates.

The simple yet elegant **Truffle Pigs Lodge** (100 Centre St., 250/343-6303, www.trufflepigs.com, C$105-300) offers modern, well-furnished rooms with private bathrooms. A couple rooms have kitchen facilities, and most have mountain views.

For a room in a private home, the **Alpine Guesthouse** (313 2nd Ave., 250/939-9110, alpineguesthouse.ca, C$125-250) has a modern two-bedroom suite with a kitchen, cable TV, outdoor patio, and private entrance.

Don't be put off by the dull redbrick

Top to bottom: Cathedral Mountain Lodge; cabin at Emerald Lake Lodge; Kicking Horse Campground

Side Trip: Golden and Kicking Horse Mountain Resort

Golden, the rafting capital of the region, flanks the Kicking Horse River and the mighty Columbia River. The town has fewer than 4,000 residents, but bustles in summer and winter with tourism. It has restaurants, motels, shops, and a local brewery.

Whether it's summer or winter, as you descend into Golden from Yoho National Park, it's easy to make out the ski slopes of **Kicking Horse Mountain Resort** (1500 Kicking Horse Trl., 250/439-5425 or 800/259-7669, www.kickinghorseresort. com, late June-Sept. and mid-Dec.-early Apr.) across the valley. It offers lodging in the form of condos, townhomes, and vacation homes, including upscale options. The most convenient lodging is right at the base of the gondola: The Glacier

hiking at Kicking Horse Mountain Resort

Mountaineer Lodge (C$110-450) has hotel rooms with queen or king beds and one- to two-bedroom suites (some of which have lofts). Summer rates are substantially lower than winter rates.

Skiing and **snowboarding** are the main attractions in winter for both resort guests and day visitors. With an impressive vertical rise of 1,260 meters (4,134 ft), almost half its terrain is steep pitches for experts, and it piles up dry powder snow. Lift tickets cost C$125 adults and C$50-95 for children. Overnight guests can get lodging packages with lift tickets included.

Summer features an assortment of adventures, ranging from easy to challenging. The resort's eight-person detachable **Golden Eagle Express gondola** (C$46 adults, C$24-40 children) transports visitors high into the alpine in just 18 minutes. The 360-degree panorama at the summit is equal to any other accessible point in the Canadian Rockies, with the Purcell Mountains immediately to the west and the Columbia Valley laid out below.

At the summit, graded **hiking trails** lead from the upper terminal through a fragile, treeless environment with stunning views. Here, **mountain bikers** revel in challenging descents. You can also test your mountaineering skills on the **via ferrata.** On the lower mountain, you can visit the **Grizzly Bear Interpretive Centre,** where sightings of Boo, the resident grizzly bear, are almost guaranteed.

In the summit lodge, **Eagle's Eye** (250/439-5425 or 866/754-5425, lunch daily, dinner weekends only, C$28-42) is Canada's highest restaurant. The views are set off by a stylish timber-and-stonework interior, including a floor-to-ceiling fireplace and a wide wraparound deck protected from the wind by glass paneling. Dinner choices are more adventurous than lunch, but the food remains distinctly Canadian. Check out the gondola/lunch combos before purchasing your ticket, as they are a very good deal.

Getting There

Golden is west of Yoho National Park on the Trans-Canada Highway. It is 58 km (36 mi) west of Field. It's a 14-km (8.7-mi), 20-minute drive from Golden to Kicking Horse Mountain Resort. Turn west onto 7th Street North and veer right as the road becomes Kicking Horse Drive, crosses over the Columbia River, and climbs up Kicking Horse Trail.

exterior of the **Canadian Rockies Inn** (308 Stephen St., 250/343-6046, www.fieldcanadianrockiesinn.com, from C$255), housed within what was once the local police station. Inside, the three adults-only guest rooms are spacious and filled with contemporary styling and kitchenettes.

Camping

Yoho has five campgrounds with potable water. Only Kicking Horse Campground accepts reservations; the other four are first come, first served. Campsites have picnic tables, and some have food storage boxes. None have hookups for RVs. Using firepits where available requires a fire permit (C$9) that includes firewood.

Yoho Valley Road

Flanking the Kicking Horse River, **Kicking Horse Campground** (88 sites, mid-June-early Oct., C$29) has firepits, flush toilets, coin showers, a dump station, and kitchen shelters. It is the only campground that takes **reservations** (877/737-3783, reservation.pc.gc.ca) for some campsites from late June to mid-September. Due to the extreme popularity of this campground, make your reservations as soon as bookings open for the year in January.

Near the entrance to Yoho Valley Road, the primitive **Monarch Campground** (44 sites, mid-May-early Sept., C$18) has pit toilets and some walk-in tent sites. At the end of Yoho Valley Road, **Takakkaw Falls Campground** (35 tent-only sites, late June-Sept., C$18) has outstanding views from most campsites. At the parking lot, load your gear in the supplied carts for

a 10-minute walk to the campground, which has pit toilets and fire pits.

Trans-Canada Highway

Located 23 km (14 mi) southwest of Field, **Hoodoo Creek Campground** (30 sites, mid-June-Aug., C$23) has campsites among the trees. Facilities include pit toilets and fire pits.

Lake O'Hara

The ultra-popular **Lake O'Hara Campground** (30 tent-only sites, mid-June-Sept., 3 nights max., C$10 pp per night) is surrounded by some of the region's finest hiking. Campsites have small tent pads and fire pits. Other facilities include pit toilets, two small kitchen shelters with woodstoves, and food storage lockers.

Access is via shuttle bus; no private vehicles are permitted on the road into Lake O'Hara. Meet your inbound bus at the signed parking lot on the south side of Trans-Canada Highway 1, located 15 km (9.3 mi) east of Field and 3 km (1.9 mi) west of the Continental Divide. Treat the trip as one into the backcountry; passengers are limited on what they can bring (find the list on Yoho's website). The bus drops you off at Le Relais, within a short walk of the campground.

The very popular campground requires **advance reservations** (877/737-3783, reservation.pc.gc.ca, C$12 per reservation), which are hard to get. Book your reservations as soon as they open for the year in January. Getting a campsite reservation guarantees you a seat on the shuttle bus (C$15 adults, C$8 kids); you will not need to enter the lottery for the day hiker shuttle bus.

Transportation and Services

Emergency Services

For emergencies, contact **911**. You can also call the **park wardens** (888/927-3367) 24 hours a day. The **Lake Louise Medical Clinic** (200 Hector Rd., 403/522-2184, www.llmc.ca) is in Lake Louise, Alberta, east of the park. **Golden and District Hospital** (835 9th Ave. S., 250/344-5271, www.interiorhealth.ca) is in Golden, British Columbia, west of the park.

Gas and Vehicle Charging Stations

Field has a gas station at the **Yoho Trading Post** (101 Field Access Rd.), the only one inside the park. Outside the park, the nearest gas stations are in Lake Louise, Alberta, and Golden, British Columbia. There's an electric vehicle charging station at the **Yoho National Park Visitor Centre** in Field.

Cell Service and Internet Access

Cell service in Yoho is intermittent at best and non-existent at Lake O'Hara, on Yoho Valley Road, at Emerald Lake, and in the backcountry. You can get some service in Field; however, plan to download everything you need before you arrive because Wi-Fi will be slow. The Yoho National Park Visitor Centre has **pay phones.**

Tours

The **Rocky Mountaineer** (877/460-4200 Canada and U.S., 604/606-7245 international, www.rockymountaineer.com, mid-Apr.-mid-Oct.) offers luxury train travel with glass-domed viewing cars from Vancouver to Lake Louise or Banff. It is a guided touring experience, with gourmet meals and overnights in hotels. On the trip's second day, the train chugs through the famed spiral tunnels in Yoho National Park.

Discover Banff (877/565-9372 or 403/760-5007, www.banfftours.com, from C$184 adults) runs a tour highlighting the area's lakes and waterfalls from Banff Townsite. Stops include the spiral tunnels, Emerald Lake, and Takakkaw Falls.

Getting Around

Parking

Two of Yoho's **parking lots** fill quickly in the day, especially from mid-June to September. Plan to arrive around 8am to park in the lots for **Takakkaw Falls** and **Emerald Lake.**

Public Transportation

The park has no public transportation, except for the lottery-based shuttle bus into Lake O'Hara (C$15 adults, C$8 youth, by reservation only).

Kootenay
National
Park

Highlights

★ **Admire Marble Canyon:** This water-carved canyon features several gushing falls and turquoise pools (page 211).

★ **Walk to Paint Pots:** These natural ponds are colored different shades by ocher (page 212).

★ **Drive through Sinclair Canyon:** Watch for bighorn sheep as you cruise through the canyon's narrow red-orange walls (page 214).

★ **Soak at Radium Hot Springs:** The mineral waters of this developed hot spring are rejuvenating after a long day of hiking or sightseeing (page 214).

★ **Hike Stanley Glacier Trail:** See the glacier tumbling down from its high cirque (page 215).

★ **Backpack the Rockwall:** Follow this craggy mountain spine to admire glaciers, waterfalls, and subalpine wildflower meadows (page 219).

★ **Spot Bighorn Sheep:** They're a common sight in Radium Hot Springs (page 224).

Kootenay National Park

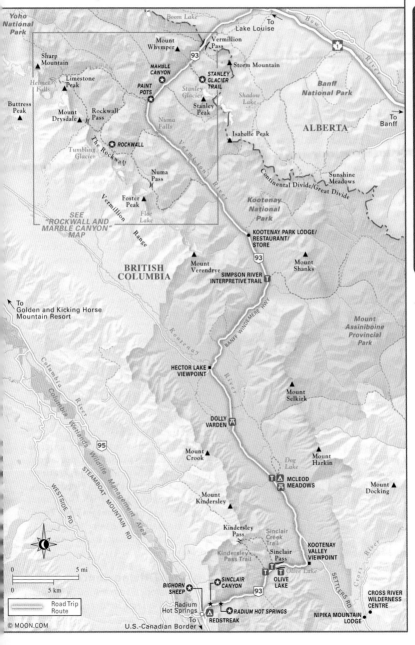

© MOON.COM

Often ignored in favor of Banff and Jasper, Kootenay National Park is a place to get away from the pervasive crowds that fill the other large Canadian parks. But it still has the hallmarks you'd want to see in a national park: rugged peaks, glaciers, rivers, and wildlife. Despite its lesser renown, Kootenay is recognized as part of the UNESCO World Heritage Site that includes the four national parks of the Canadian Rockies.

Roadside stops take you into narrow canyons, along the silty Vermillion River, and to unique ochre beds. Trails lead to glittering lakes, while backpacker destinations such as the Rockwall rival almost any other area in the Canadian Rockies. In summer when trails melt out, paths travel to large glaciers tumbling from alpine bowls. No matter what adventures you choose, Radium Hot Springs caps any day with a soak in soothing waters.

Once lands of the Ktunaxa and Secwepemc First Nations, this narrow park lies on the British Columbia side of the Canadian Rockies. Kootenay is bordered by Banff National Park to the northeast and Yoho National Park to the northwest; Mount Assiniboine Provincial Park lies to the east.

Kootenay has the fewest services of the four contiguous Canadian Rockies national parks. Day-use areas, a lodge, and three campgrounds are the only roadside services inside the park. Near the park's southwest tail, the small town of Radium Hot Springs has a permanent population of under 1,000 people, but it offers a range of visitor services—and the chance to see bighorn sheep.

Planning Your Time

While planning your trip to **Kootenay National Park** (250/347-9505, www. pc.gc.ca), consult with the park website for updates on permits, reservations, road construction, trail conditions, and potential closures. In Kootenay, just one road, **BC 93** (Banff-Windemere Hwy.), travels north-south through the park. You can travel BC 93 in under two hours, but plan to spend at least a **full day** in the park. You can hit all the short hikes and roadside highlights, basing yourself out of Banff or Radium Hot Springs. Pack a picnic lunch to enjoy along the way. You'll enjoy Kootenay more by staying at least **2-3 days** in a **lodge** or spending **3-5 days backpacking.**

Tourism in Kootenay is at its peak in **summer,** seeing the most visitors from **mid-June through August.** The crowds here are fewer than at Banff, Jasper, and Yoho. Most low-elevation trails are melted out by late May, but snow can remain on trails above the tree line until mid-July. The **best hiking season** is from July through mid-September. **September** visitors enjoy pleasant weather, fewer crowds, and fall colors—though there's sometimes early snow. In **winter,** most visitors do the scenic drive through the park without stopping due to snow-buried trails and avalanche danger.

Plan to do all your own driving, as Kootenay has **no public transportation.** Additionally, there are no **gas stations** between Banff and Radium Hot Springs.

Despite being in British Columbia, Kootenay is in the **Mountain Time Zone,** which means it's in the same time zone as the other national parks in the Canadian Rockies.

Seasonal Driving Concerns

The park is open year-round, although you should check road conditions in winter, when avalanche-control work and snowstorms can close BC 93 for short periods. Kootenay's road is loaded with avalanche zones. Heed the signs that mark them and avoid stopping in these dangerous zones. The **snow and avalanche season** in Kootenay is long: **October into June.**

Snow tires are required October-March; carrying **chains** is recommended, as they may be required in certain conditions. The speed limit through the park is 90 kph (56 mph), but you may need to slow down for snowy and icy roads in winter. For road reports, check with **Drive BC** (800/550-4997, www.drivebc.ca) or **511 Alberta** (511, 511.alberta.ca). Get conditions before you go, as no cell service is available inside the park.

Best Route Through the Park

The best route through Kootenay National Park is the only route. Slicing through the park's heart, **BC 93** goes from the northeast to the southwest, traveling through mountain passes and valleys.

Reservations and Where to Stay

Accommodations within the park are limited and book up early. For summer or winter holidays, make reservations **9-12 months** in advance at **park lodges.** Three **park campgrounds** take reservations for stays between **mid-June and mid-September.** Competition for these can be tough, so make your reservation when bookings open for the year in January.

If you can't get lodging or camping inside the park, your best options are to stay in **Banff** or in the town of **Radium Hot Springs.** Radium has a broad selection of accommodations: cabins, condos, roadside motels, resorts, and a couple of campgrounds. Since the town is on one of the main thoroughfares to Banff and draws heavy visitation in summer and winter from Calgary, plan to make reservations in advance. For summer, the busiest season, and winter holidays, make reservations **six months** ahead.

Getting There

Kootenay National Park is on the west side of the Continental Divide between Banff National Park and the Columbia River Valley. Radium Hot Springs is at the junction of BC 93 and BC 95.

Car
From Calgary

The route from **Calgary** goes on Trans-Canada Highway 1 west through Banff and then on the Bow Valley Parkway to Castle Junction before turning southeast to climb to the Continental Divide and Kootenay National Park's **north entrance.** The entrance of Kootenay, which is on the Continental Divide, does not have an entrance station, but you'll see a monument and a sign. (You'll pass an entrance station before entering Banff National Park.) To the north entrance of Kootenay the drive is 165 km (103 mi), a drive of almost two hours.

From Banff

To get to Kootenay from the town of **Banff,** head northwest on the Trans-Canada Highway for 29 km (18 mi) to Castle Junction and then southwest on BC 93 for 6 km (3.7 mi) to the **north entrance** along the Continental Divide (no entrance station, but look for the sign marking the Divide). The 35-km (22-mi) drive takes about 30 minutes.

From Golden or Cranbrook

From locales in the Columbia River Valley, distances to the **west entrance** of Kootenay National Park (just beyond the town of **Radium Hot Springs**) vary. From **Cranbrook** to the west entrance of Kootenay, follow BC 93 for 144 km (87 mi) north, a drive of a little less than two hours. From **Golden** to the west entrance of Kootenay, take BC 95 south for 105 km

(65 mi), a drive of a little more than an hour.

From Waterton Lakes National Park

From **Waterton Lakes National Park** in southeastern Alberta, the **west entrance** of Kootenay at **Radium Hot Springs** is 382 km (237 mi). The drive takes a little over four hours. From Waterton, take AB 6 north to Pincher Creek, then take AB 3 west to merge with BC 93 heading north.

From Whitefish and Glacier National Park

From **Whitefish,** Montana, the drive to the **west entrance** for Kootenay at **Radium Hot Springs** takes you north on US 93 and BC 93. The route is 323 km (201 mi) and takes about 3.5 hours to drive. En route, you will cross the U.S.-Canadian border at **Roosville.** Most of the year, the wait time at the border is minimal, but from mid-June to September there can be lines, especially midday. Avoid the lines by crossing earlier or later in the day.

If you're starting from **West Glacier** in Glacier National Park, that increases the travel distance to 364 km (226 mi), which will take about four hours. Take US 2 and MT 40 west to Whitefish, then connect with US 93.

Air

The two closest airports sit almost the same distance from Kootenay National Park. **Calgary International Airport** (YYC, 2000 Airport Rd. NE, Calgary, 403/735-1200, www.yyc.com), east of the Canadian Rockies, is the largest airport in the area, with flights coming in from cities across North America and international locations. The airport sits 183 km (114 mi) east of Kootenay's north entrance, a little less than a two-hour drive. You can catch shuttles to Banff, but they do not continue west to Kootenay. The drive from the airport to Radium Hot Springs, outside the west entrance of

Kootenay, is 269 km (167 mi) and takes 3.5 hours. Car rentals are available at the airport and in Banff.

In Cranbrook, the small **Canadian Rockies International Airport** (YXC, 1-9370 Airport Access Rd., Cranbrook, 250/426-7913, flyyxc.com), which is serviced by two airlines, connects with flights from Vancouver and Calgary. The drive to the west entrance of Kootenay, at Radium Hot Springs, is 153 km (95 mi) and takes just under two hours. Car rentals are available from the Cranbrook airport.

Visiting the Park

Entrances and Fees

Kootenay National Park has two entrances, which are 94 km (58 mi) apart on BC 93 (Banff-Windemere Highway). The **north entrance** is located at the Continental Divide day-use area, marked by a sign and a monument. It does not have an entrance station. The **west entrance station,** on the southwest end of the park, is on BC 93 between the town of Radium Hot Springs and the Radium Hot Spring pools.

You'll need to purchase a park pass when entering through Radium Hot Springs. Those entering from Banff will already have a pass that's also good for Kootenay. **One-day passes** (C$20 family/vehicle, C$10 adults, C$9 seniors, kids 17 and younger free) can also be used in Banff, Yoho, and Jasper National Parks. They are valid until 4pm the day following purchase, but you can add on as many days as you need.

If you are touring multiple Canadian Rockies national parks for multiple days, a **Discovery Pass** (C$140 family/vehicle, C$70 adults, C$60 seniors) may be more economical than purchasing day passes. It is valid for entry into all Canadian national parks for one year from purchase. Both types of passes are available from the western park entrance station, park

One Day in Kootenay National Park

Morning

Starting from Banff, leave early in the morning and be the first on the trail to **Stanley Glacier.** Climb up through the forest to view the receding glacier and the rocky rubble it left behind. After returning to your car, continue south to stop at **Marble Canyon,** where a walk over Tokumm Creek will let you peer into the colorful canyon with turquoise water. Stop next at the **Paint Pots,** where you'll walk across the Vermillion River to the ochre beds.

Afternoon

After your morning exertions, relax with a late lunch at the **Numa Falls picnic area,** followed by a short walk to the bridge to see the falls. Then spend the afternoon leisurely making your way south along the **Vermillion River,** stopping at **Hector Gorge** and **Olive Lake.**

On the descent from Sinclair Pass into **Sinclair Canyon,** settle into a long soak at the pools at **Radium Hot Springs.**

Evening

Drive back north over Sinclair Pass and descend onto Settler's Road to **Nipika Mountain Resort** for your own private cabin for the night. Curl up in front of the toasty wood stove and enjoy your dinner. After dark, walk outside to see a sky filled with stars.

---

information centers, and campground kiosks. The Discovery Pass can also be purchased online.

Visitors Centers

Kootenay National Park Visitor Centre (7556 Main St. E., Radium Hot Springs, 250/347-9505, 9am-5pm daily Apr.-early June and early Sept.-mid-Oct., 9am-7pm daily early June-early Sept.) is outside the park in the town of Radium Hot Springs, at the base of the access road to Redstreak Campground. Here you can peruse exhibits, collect a free map with hiking trail descriptions, find out about trail closures and campsite availability, get the weather forecast and road conditions, buy park passes and fishing licenses, and pick up permits for overnight backcountry trips. The gift shop has books, maps, souvenirs, and apparel. Kids ages 6-12 can also register here for the educational Junior Naturalist Program.

Sights

★ Marble Canyon

A self-guided trail (1.6 km/1 mi rt, 30 minutes) leads along **Marble Canyon** and through the remains and regrowth of a forest destroyed by wildfires in 2003. The walk takes you back more than 500 million years, with interpretive signs that highlight the geology and explain how water carved the canyon.

From the parking lot, the trail follows a fault in the limestone and marble bedrock through this marble-streaked canyon, which has been eroded to depths of 37 meters (130 ft) by the fast-flowing Tokumm Creek. Bridges cross the chasm, allowing for views of the marbled rock, deep pools, and turquoise water, colored from glacial silt. As the canyon narrows, water roars down through it in a series of falls. The trail ends at a splendid **viewpoint** where a natural rock arch spans a gorge.

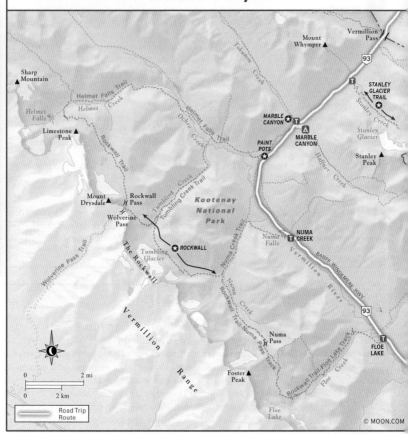

Rockwall and Marble Canyon

★ Paint Pots

A scenic trail (2 km/1.6 mi rt, 40 minutes) leads over the Vermilion River to a unique natural wonder known as the **Paint Pots:** three circular ponds stained red, orange, and mustard yellow by oxide-bearing springs. For hundreds of years, the Kootenay people, who believed that animal spirits resided in these springs, collected ocher from around the pools. They mixed it with animal fat or fish oil and then used it in ceremonial body and rock painting. The ocher had a spiritual association and was used in important rituals. European settlers, seeing an economic opportunity, mined the ocher in the early 1900s and shipped it to paint manufacturers in Calgary. You'll also see some mining artifacts along the trail.

Vermilion River

Since the parkway parallels the glacial-fed **Vermilion River** for 30 km (19 mi) through Kootenay, you'll have several opportunities to stretch your legs at scenic riverside stops. The water changes color throughout the summer, appearing silty

Spotting Wildfire Zones

Since 2001, Kootenay National Park has seen a rash of large wildfires due to a combination of a warming climate and pine beetle infestations killing trees. In some locations, you'll see entire mountainsides that have been burned. Some spots are generating a new forest of trees, while others are just starting to come back and are marked by wildflowers. One of the largest wildfires burned much of Kootenay Valley east of the highway in 2003. The most recent **wildfire zones** are on both sides of the highway around the **Simpson Creek Trailhead.** To the east, flanking Mount Shanks, you'll see the largest from the 2017 **Verdant Creek Fire** that occurred in one of BC's biggest fire seasons. To the west on Mount Wardle, the **Wardle Creek Fire** burned in 2018.

At the Simpson River Trailhead, you can walk the self-guided **Simpson River Interpretive Trail** (3 km/1.9 mi rt, 1 hr) to learn about wildfires. The interactive exhibits are good for families with kids. At the start, the trail crosses the Vermilion River via a bridge. After the interpretive segment, the trail continues to Assiniboine Provincial Park.

and gray in June, but often settling into turquoise pools in late summer.

At **Numa Falls,** the Vermilion River tumbles over exposed bedrock. Enjoy the picnic area and walk the short path from the south end of the parking lot to the bridge over the river. Here you can get the best view of the frothy falls and enjoy the roar of the water.

At Vermillion Crossing, where the highway crosses the river over a bridge, the **Vermillion Crossing picnic area** offers a place to view the river and enjoy its sounds. While water comes up to its banks in early summer, later in summer you can explore the large, exposed river bar that's full of cobble.

Several overlooks let you admire the power of the river cutting through the landscape. In late summer, the river braids with multiple channels through exposed cobble bars. South of the Simpson River Trailhead, look for a pullout on the east side as the road rises for a good view of the **confluence of Simpson River with the Vermillion River** and later at the viewpoint for **Hector Gorge.**

Kootenay River

South of Kootenay Crossing, a confluence of creeks and rivers, including Vermilion River, forms the large **Kootenay River**

that eventually joins the Columbia River flowing through Canada and the United States. You can get views of the waterway at **Dolly Varden Creek picnic area** and **McLeod Meadows picnic area.** The river also follows along the roadway between the two.

Dolly Varden Creek

The day-use area at **Dolly Varden Creek** near the Kootenay River is the best stop for children. A small **self-guided interpretive park** here offers interactive exhibits with facts about wildlife. There's also a miniature version of a wildlife underpass that the kids can run through. On the highway, you'll see a stretch of wildlife fencing that funnels animals to the full-scale versions of underpasses where they can safely cross. These underpasses have significantly reduced wildlife mortalities. The picnic area also has restrooms and picnic tables.

Olive Lake

At Sinclair Pass, the tiny roadside **Olive Lake** is a picnic area with a **wheelchair-accessible boardwalk trail** (0.5 km/0.3 mi rt) that tours the forest along the lake's shoreline. You can sit on benches and listen to birds, look for brook trout, and admire the emerald color of this shallow lake.

★ Sinclair Canyon

On the southwest end of BC 93, the highway squeezes through narrow **Sinclair Canyon,** descending steeply to the town of Radium Hot Springs. The red-orange color of the canyon comes from iron in the Redwall Fault, the source of hot water for Radium Hot Springs. Over time, the fast-flowing waters of Sinclair Creek easily eroded the canyon. But the canyon wasn't wide enough for a two-lane highway—nothing a stick of dynamite couldn't fix. In addition to widening the canyon, road builders constructed the highway over the top of the creek where it flows through a narrow gap. Small parking lots above and below the canyon provide an opportunity to pull over and walk through the canyon. The pullout at the bottom end of the canyon lets you admire the creek as it spills out of the canyon via **Sinclair Falls.** Drive slowly through the canyon to admire its walls and look for bighorn sheep that climb on the cliffs. You may also see sheep right on the roadway.

★ Radium Hot Springs

The soothing **Radium Hot Springs pool** (5420 BC 93, 800/767-1611, www.hotsprings.ca, 9am-11pm daily summer, noon-9pm daily off-season, adult C$8, senior C$7, youth C$6, family C$23) lies inside the park but just 3 km (1.9 mi) northeast of the town of the same name, which is outside the park boundary. The springs was discovered many centuries ago by the Kootenay people, who, like today's visitors, came to enjoy the odorless mineral water that gushes out of the Redwall Fault at 44°C (111°F). Originally known as Sinclair Hot Springs after an early settler, the name was changed to Radium in 1915 for the high level of radioactivity in the water. With the declaration of Kootenay National Park in 1922, ownership reverted to the government.

Top to bottom: taking photos at the Vermilion River; Paint Pots; soaking in the Radium Hot Springs

Today the water is diverted from its natural course into commercial concrete pools, including one that is Canada's largest. Steep cliffs tower directly above the large hot pool (39°C/97°F), whose waters are colored a milky blue by dissolved salts, which include calcium bicarbonate and sulfates of calcium, magnesium, and sodium. The hot pool is particularly stimulating in winter, when it's edged by snow and covered in steam. Your head is almost cold in the chill air, but your submerged body melts into oblivion. The 25-meter swimming pool is cooler, and a surprise plunge pool changes temperature frequently from hot to frigid.

Towel and locker rentals are available, as are spa services. If you're camping at the park's Redstreak Campground, you can reach the complex on foot. The main parking lot, with spots for RVs, is across the highway, and a pedestrian underpass connects with the pool complex.

Scenic Drive

Parkway
The **Banff-Windemere Highway** (AB/BC 93, 94 km/58 mi) runs the length of Kootenay National Park. On the northeast end, it starts at **Castle Mountain Junction** on the Bow Valley Parkway northwest of Banff (29 km/18 mi) and southeast of Lake Louise (27 km/16.8 mi). On the southwest end of the park, the parkway ends at Radium Hot Springs. This drive takes 1.5 hours without stops.

From Castle Mountain Junction, the highway climbs steadily for 6 km (3.7 mi) to **Vermilion Pass** (1,680 m/5,510 ft), which is on the **Continental Divide.** At the divide, pull off on the south side of the highway where you can take a selfie in front of the old **Continental Divide sign.** You can also stand with one foot in Alberta and the other in British Columbia; flags on either side denote the province. The divide also marks the boundary between Banff and Kootenay

National Parks, plus the point at which water separates, flowing either to the Pacific or Atlantic Oceans.

The route drops into the long **Vermilion Valley,** roughly paralleling the **Vermillion River.** At **Vermilion Crossing,** you'll see the only commercialism in the heart of the park, but compared to neighboring Banff, the development is minuscule. Here you'll find the **Kootenay Park Lodge** complex, which includes cabin accommodations, a restaurant, and a general store (open mid-May-mid-Sept.).

The highway passes two signposted **mineral licks.** Check these for **bighorn sheep, mountain goats, elk,** and **moose.** You can also stop at picnic areas to see the **Kootenay River.**

At the south end of Kootenay Valley, stop at the **Kootenay Valley Viewpoint.** You'll take in the Mitchell and Kootenay mountain ranges, plus the valley. It's the perfect place to imagine the ancient ice that once filled the valley to nearly the mountain tops. From the viewpoint, the road climbs over **Sinclair Pass** (1,486 m/4,185 ft), followed by a steep descent into Radium Hot Springs.

Recreation

Hiking
The trails in Kootenay National Park range from short interpretive walks to challenging long treks through remote backcountry. However, only a few trails run for intermediate distances. All trails start from BC 93 on the valley floor, so you'll be facing a strenuous climb to reach the park's high alpine areas, especially those in the south. Prime hiking season is July to mid-September; many high-elevation trails can have avalanche hazards October through mid-June. The following hikes are listed from northeast to southwest.

★ Stanley Glacier
Distance: 8.4 km (5.2 mi) rt

Duration: 3 hours
Elevation gain: 350 meters (1,150 ft)
Effort: moderate
Trailhead: Stanley Glacier

Although this glacier is no more spectacular than those alongside the Icefields Parkway just an hour's drive away, the sense of achievement makes this trail well worth the effort. From the trailhead, a bridge crosses the upper reaches of the Vermilion River, then begins a steady climb through an area burned by devastating fires in 2003. Soon, the trail levels off and begins winding through a massive U-shaped glacial valley, crossing Stanley Creek at the 2.4-km (1.5-mi) mark. In open areas, fireweed, harebells, and yellow columbine carpet the ground. To the west, the sheer face of **Mount Stanley** towers above the forest.

The trail officially ends atop the crest of a moraine, with distant views to **Stanley Glacier.** It's possible (and worthwhile) to continue on the trail 1.3 km (0.8 mi) to the tree-topped **plateau** visible higher up the valley. After reaching the top of the first moraine beyond the official trail end, take the left fork, which switchbacks up and over another crest before making a steady ascent through slopes of loose scree to the plateau. Once on the plateau, you'll find a gurgling stream, a healthy population of marmots, and incredible views west to Stanley Glacier, where it spills from a hanging valley above cliffs. Be especially careful on the return trip; it's extremely easy to lose your footing on the loose rock.

Floe Lake

Distance: 20.8 km (13 mi) rt
Duration: 7 hours
Elevation gain: 730 meters (2,395 ft)
Effort: moderate-strenuous
Trailhead: Floe Lake

Of all the lakes in Kootenay National Park, this one is the most beautiful. Set in a high basin, **Floe Lake** tucks below an immense serrated ridge. Its western shore is rimmed with rubble and

Stanley Glacier

moraines from glaciers which are only remnants today. You can do the trail as a day hike, or as a backpacking trip (permit required). A forested wilderness campground sits adjacent to the lake, with picnic tables, food lockers, and tent sites. A warden cabin is also at the lake. If you spend one night, continue on the trail above the tree line to **Numa Pass** (5.4 km/3.4 mi) for exquisite wildflower meadows and bigger views before hiking out. The trail to Floe Lake also marks the southern end of the **Rockwall,** an immense, long limestone cliff.

From the trailhead, a bridge leads across the Vermilion River. The climb begins promptly when the trail turns up Floe Creek passing through a burned forest of lodgepole pine clinging to the steep canyon walls. After several long switchbacks to crest out of the canyon, the trail moderates to gentle terrain before the lake. Nestled in a glacial cirque, the gemlike lake's aquamarine waters reflect the Rockwall rising 1,000 m (3,280 ft) above

the far shore. In fall, stands of stunted larch around the lakeshore turn brilliant colors, adding to the incredible beauty.

Dog Lake

Distance: 5.2 km (3.2 mi) rt
Duration: 1.5 hours
Elevation gain: 40 meters (131 ft)
Effort: easy
Trailhead: McCloud Meadows Picnic Area

From the McCloud Meadows Picnic Area, two suspension bridges cross the Kootenay River to get you onto a forested trail. When you intersect with an old road, stay right to remain on the trail. At a junction just before the lake, turn right. The small green **Dog Lake** cowers below the immense **Mount Harkin** in the Mitchell Range.

Kindersley Summit

Distance: 20 km (12.4 mi) rt
Duration: 7-8 hours
Elevation gain: 1,050 meters (3,445 ft)
Effort: strenuous
Trailhead: Kindersley Pass

The elevation gain on this strenuous day hike will be a deterrent for many, but views from the summit will make up for the pain endured along the way. Due to the presence of grizzly bear, hikers are required to have at least four people in their group and to hike less than 3 meters (9 ft) apart.

The trail climbs through a valley before hitting switchbacks up across several avalanche paths. After cutting through more forest, the trail emerges at an alpine meadow on **Kindersley Pass.** The final 2-km (1.2-mi) slog gets you higher to **Kindersley Summit** (2,400 m/7,870 ft), a saddle between two slightly higher peaks. This is where the scenery makes the journey worthwhile. You'll enjoy views west to the Purcell Mountains, east to the Continental Divide, and, most spectacularly, north over the Kootenay River Valley.

An alternate return route to the valley floor follows **Sinclair Creek** down steep switchbacks from Kindersley Summit. This loop route shortens the overall distance by 2 km (1.2 mi) but also finishes at the Sinclair Creek Trailhead, about 1.1 km (0.7 mi) north of the Kindersley Pass Trailhead.

Juniper Loop-Sinclair Canyon

Distance: 6 km (3.7 mi) one way
Duration: 2.5-3 hours
Elevation gain: 320 meters (1,049 ft)
Effort: moderate
Trailhead: Radium Hot Springs pool complex

While this trail won't feel like wilderness, you can get some impressive scenery: a waterfall, a canyon, and a huge river valley. Watch for **bighorn sheep** that frequent the trail; in late fall, you may see rams displaying dominance rituals (give them plenty of distance). The trailhead is at the parking lot for the **Radium Hot Springs pools;** once you're done, you can go to the pools for a relaxing soak. Be ready for stairs and switchbacks that climb and descend several times.

From the parking lot, go through the tunnels to the pool complex to find the trailhead. Climb south uphill until the trail turns westward. It then crosses Radium Creek and passes along Sinclair Creek before climbing to the south rim of **Sinclair Canyon.** Here, there are spots where you can peer down into the canyon.

The trail then descends to the road, crosses it, and goes to an overlook of **Sinclair Falls.** Head southwest down the road to find the trailhead parking lot just inside the park entrance, which leads to the continuation of the loop trail. The trail switchbacks down, then climbs eastward along a ridge to a scenic overlook of the Columbia River Valley. Finally, continue east to drop back to the starting point.

You can also reach the trail from the north end of Redstreak Campground's H Loop. This spur connects with the loop trail near the west end of Sinclair Canyon, making a total hike distance of 6.6 km (4.1 mi).

Burgess Shale Fossil Beds Guided Hikes

The Burgess Shale Fossil Beds in Kootenay hold some of the world's best-preserved soft tissue imprints of 500-million-year-old marine invertebrates. The detailed fossils are left from a Cambrian sea, dating long before dinosaurs. They consist of sponges, brachiopods, and trilobites. See the **Burgess Shale Fossil Site** (10 km/6.3 mi rt, 8am-3:30pm, Fri.-Mon. June, Thurs.-Mon. July-Aug., adults C$55, seniors C$47, youth C$28) by hiking the **Stanley Glacier Trail** with a Parks Canada guide. You'll be able to pick up rocks containing the ancient fossils to examine their bones and other body parts; you can even take a selfie with one. The trail to the beds only goes to a certain point in the basin; from there you'll need to be able to walk off-trail across a rocky zone to get to the

fossil sites. **Reservations** (877/737-3783, reservation.pc.gc.ca) are required. You can make them starting in January to see this protected UNESCO World Heritage Site.

Backpacking
Permits and Campsites

For backpacking, **wilderness camping permits** (877/737-3783, reservation. pc.gc.ca, C$10 pp per night) are required. You can make **reservations** in advance, starting in January. For the Rockwall, make reservations as soon as the booking window opens. Reservations for July and August go fast. Campgrounds are equipped with food lockers, picnic tables, pit toilets, and tent sites.

TOP EXPERIENCE

★ The Rockwall
55 kilometers (34 miles)

One of the classic backpacking trails in the Canadian Rockies, the **Rockwall** is a 30-km-long (18.6-mi) east-facing escarpment that rises more than 1,000 meters (3,280 ft) from an alpine environment. In addition to the impressive long cliff, the trail also passes waterfalls, including the spectacular 365-m (1,200-ft) **Helmet Falls.** With viewpoints from many angles, the crevassed **Tumbling Glacier** spills into a multi-drop descent from the top of the Rockwall. Gorgeous **Floe Lake** cradles below the escarpment and remnant glaciers. En route, you'll also cross four passes (elevation gains range 280-830 m/920-2,720 ft). You can hike the route north to south, south to north, or do shortened loop segments. You'll want five days for the full route, to savor the experience and to add on side-trip explorations. Shorter loops need three days.

Four different trails provide access, each beginning along BC 93 and traversing a steep-sided valley to the Rockwall's base. Two of the routes start in the north at the Paint Pots, one leading up **Helmut Creek** (15 km/9.3 mi)

The Rockwall

for the northernmost entrance and the other heading up **Tumbling Creek** (10.5 km/6.5 mi) to reach the Rockwall Trail. A third entrance is at Numa Falls and follows **Numa Creek** (6.7 km/4.2 mi) up to the Rockwall Trail. A bridge gets you across the Vermilion River, but check ahead to ensure the trail is open (it was closed through 2021 for trail repairs). The fourth route launches from the Floe Lake Trailhead and goes to **Floe Lake** (10.4 km/6.5 mi), the southernmost entrance.

The **full route** (55 km/34 mi, 3-5 days) starts at Paint Pots and goes up Helmet Creek to the Rockwall Trail, ascending and descending between the Tumbling Creek and Numa Creek drainages to reach Floe Lake and exit via Floe Creek. You'll be about 13 km (8 mi) south of the Paint Pots, so you will need to set up a self-shuttle. One short loop that avoids the necessity of a shuttle starts and ends at the Paint Pots. It links **Helmet Creek-Tumbling Creek** (38 km/24 mi, 3 days); you can easily add on a day hike up to Tumbling Glacier before exiting.

Five backcountry campgrounds are located on the route: Helmet-Ochre Creek Junction, Helmet Falls, Tumbling Creek, Numa Creek, and Floe Lake. Many hikers skip the Helmet-Ochre Creek campground in favor of getting to Helmet Falls, but it's a good option if you get a late start on the trail.

Food, Accommodations, and Camping

Restaurants and accommodations within the park are limited. Plan on making lodging reservations 6-9 months in advance.

Restaurants and Lodges

The only lodging in the heart of the park along the highway is historic **Kootenay Park Lodge** (9500 BC 93 S., 250/434-9648, www.kootenayparklodge.com, mid-May-late Sept., C$244-300), a cabin complex at Vermilion Crossing. The 1923 lodge was one of many built by the Canadian Pacific Railway (CPR) throughout the Canadian Rockies. It consists of a main lodge with restaurant (5pm-8pm daily mid-May-mid Sept., C$14-22), 12 cabins, and a general store stocked with souvenirs and light snacks. The most basic cabins each have a bathroom, small fridge, and coffeemaker. The newer Vermilion Cabins have a separate bedroom and a fireplace. In the log dining room with a stone fireplace, dinner is served with fresh-made burgers, salads, and full-plated meals of chicken or pork. A couple vegan options are available. Note that this is the only dining facility inside the park.

The well-kept ★ **Cross River Wilderness Centre** (9272 Cross River Rd., 403/800-2564 or 877/659-7665, www.crossriver.ca, mid-May-early Oct., C$230-256, plus C$99-110/day/adult for meals) has a real sense of privacy and of being well away from the tourist path of Highway 93. That's because it is: The complex is tucked in a riverside setting 15 km (9.3 mi) down unpaved Settler's Road, which branches off the highway through Kootenay, 114 km (71 mi) from Banff and 32 km (20 mi) from Radium Hot Springs. The smart, spacious cabins are equipped with wood-burning fireplaces, toilets, sinks, and log beds draped in down duvets. Showers are located in the main building, along with the main lounge, cooking facilities, a dining area, and a deck. Specialty programs include guided hikes, yoga retreats, and nature-based arts, educational, and cultural programs.

★ **Nipika Mountain Resort** (9200 Settler's Rd., 250/342-6516 or 877/647-4525, nipika.com, May-Mar., C$185-507, two-night min.) has seven cabins with full bathrooms and kitchens with wood-burning stoves. The cabins sleep up to eight people (over 4 people additional C$70/adult/night). They are modern but were constructed in a very traditional manner: The logs were milled on-site, and the construction is dovetail notching. Guests bring their own food and spend their days hiking, mountain biking, fishing, and wildlife-watching. An extensive system of trails surrounds the resort, and they are groomed for cross-country skiing in winter. Offering loads of privacy, the resort is located along Settler's Road, which branches off the highway through Kootenay 114 km (71 mi) from Banff and 32 km (20 mi) from Radium Hot Springs.

Camping

Kootenay has three campgrounds. They all accept **reservations** (877/737-3783, www.pccamping.ca). Reservations usually open in January, and competition is high for July and August dates, plus weekends year-round. All campsites have picnic tables, fire pits, flush toilets, and dump stations. You can purchase **fire permits** (C$9) at the campground entrance or self-registration kiosk, and firewood is provided. Showers and hookups for RVs are only available at Redstreak. RVs and trailers should be 10.7 m (35 ft) or shorter; the majority of sites are intended for much smaller rigs.

Redstreak

The park's largest camping area is **Redstreak Campground** (232 sites, mid-May-mid-Oct., C$28-40), on a narrow plateau in the extreme southwest of the park. Options include full hookups (50 sites) and electrical-only hookups (38 sites), but most spots are unserviced (144 sites). In addition, the campground has 10 oTENTiks (C$123) or tent cabins. This campground has showers and a couple sites for longer RVs, as well as other amenities. In summer, park naturalists present free slideshows and talks several nights a week on topics like wolves, bears, and the park's human history. Trails lead

Top to bottom: Kootenay Park Lodge; general store at Kootenay Park Lodge; Redstreak Campground

◈ Side Trip: Nearby Provincial Parks

Three outstanding BC provincial parks flank the west side of Columbia River Valley. Contact the parks for trail conditions. Anglers will need to have a BC fishing license.

Whiteswan Lake Provincial Park

Popular with anglers and those seeking a refuge from the summer heat, **Whiteswan Lake Provincial Park** (250/422-3003, bcparks.ca, May-Sept.) is off the main tourist path but well worth seeking out. From Highway 93/95 south of Canal Flats, the rough access road climbs steadily, entering Lussier Gorge after 11 km (6.8 mi). Within the gorge, a steep trail leads down to **Lussier Hot Springs.** Two small pools have been constructed to contain the odorless hot water (43°C/110°F) as it bubbles out of the ground and flows into the Lussier River. One hour from the highway, the dirt road follows the southern shorelines of **Alces Lake** and the larger **Whiteswan Lake.** The lakes attract abundant birdlife like loons, grebes, and herons. They also attract anglers, who come for great rainbow trout fishing. Paddling and boating are also possible here. The park has five popular first-come, first-served **campgrounds** (114 sites, May-Sept., C$20-25).

Getting there: The access road to Whiteswan Lake Provincial Park branches off Highway 93/95. Find the junction 6 km (3.7 mi) south of Canal Flats. From this point, an unpaved road heads west for 20 km (12 mi) to the park boundary. The road can be rough after heavy rain, so allow at least 30 minutes from the highway.

Top of the World Provincial Park

The wild and remote **Top of the World Provincial Park** (no phone, bcparks.ca, open year-round) lies beyond Whiteswan Lake Provincial Park along an unpaved road. You can't drive into the park, but you can hike into picturesque **Fish Lake** (6 km/3.7 mi), the park's largest body of water. The trail climbs alongside the pretty Lussier River to the lake, which is encircled with Engelmann spruce and surrounded by high peaks. Trails from the lake lead to other alpine lakes and to a viewpoint that allows a good overall perspective on the high plateau for which the park is named. Fish Lake is productive for cutthroat and Dolly Varden trout.

This park has no services. For those who hike into Fish Lake, you can **camp** (C$5 pp) at four designated campsites. Or you can stay in the large 18-person **shared cabin** (C$15 pp, first come, first served) nestled in the trees.

Getting there: Top of the World Provincial Park is on the west side of the Continental

from the campground to the hot springs, town, and a couple of viewpoints. From Highway 93 in the town of Radium Hot Springs, drive up the Redstreak Road adjacent to the visitors center to reach the campground.

Marble Canyon

Across Highway 93 from the natural attraction of the same name, **Marble Canyon Campground** (61 sites, early July-early Sept., C$22) flanks a forested hillside accessed by a narrow, rough road.

While Marble Canyon busies with visitors during the day, the campground quiets down at night.

McLeod Meadows

Located on Highway 93 along the Kootenay River, **McLeod Meadows Campground** (88 sites, late July-early Sept., C$22) is 27 km (16.8 mi) north of Radium Hot Springs. A potholed road connects the campground's loops, which are tucked under the forest.

Divide, with the only access being a rough 52-km (32-mi) unpaved road that branches off Highway 93/95 just south of Canal Flats. From the road's end, you have to hike to Fish Lake to enter the park.

Height of the Rockies Provincial Park

The long and narrow **Height of the Rockies Provincial Park** (no phone, bcparks.ca, open year-round) protects a long section of the Canadian Rockies, bordering the Continental Divide. The park lies entirely in British Columbia, bordered by Elk Lakes and Peter Lougheed Provincial Parks to the east and Banff National Park at its narrow northern reaches. It is accessible only on foot and is not a destination for the casual day-tripper. Mountains dominate the landscape, with 26 peaks rising over the magical 3,050-meter (10,000-ft) mark. Mountain goats hang out on the massive, jagged peaks draped with hanging glaciers, and the lush remote valleys are home to high concentrations of elk and grizzly bears.

Accessed by trail, **primitive campgrounds** lie on the shores of **Connor** and **Queen Mary Lakes** (C$5 pp). Each lake also has a small **shared cabin** (C$15 pp, first come, first served).

Getting there: The park can be reached on foot from two directions. Neither is sign-posted, so before setting out for the park, pick up a good map of the area at a local information center or Forest Service office. Check on road and trail conditions.

Connor Lake is the most popular destination in the park's south. It is reached by driving through Whiteswan Lake Provincial Park, then continuing along a rough logging road that parallels the White River to its upper reaches. (The most important intersection to watch for is 11 km/6.8 mi from Whiteswan Lake; stay right, immediately crossing the river.) At the end of the road, a tortuous 72 km (45 mi) from Highway 93/95, is a small area for tents and horse corrals. From this trailhead, it's an easy walk up Maiyuk Creek and over a low ridge to Connor Lake.

Small **Queen Mary Lake** is generally the destination only for those on horseback or mountaineers continuing into the Royal Group. To get there, turn off Highway 93/95 at Canal Flats and follow a logging road up the Kootenay River for 48 km (30 mi). Then, it turns westward and climbs along the south side of the Palliser River 35 km (21.7 mi) farther to road's end and the trailhead. From this point, it's a 12-km (7.5-mi) hike up a forested valley, with numerous creek crossings, to the lake.

Transportation and Services

Emergency Services

For emergencies, go to the **Invermere and District Hospital** (850 10th Ave., Invermere, 250/342-9201, www.interiorhealth.ca), located 15 minutes south of Radium Hot Springs. You can also call **911.**

For emergencies along the Banff-Windemere Highway (BC 93) inside the park, you can find satellite phones at the Marble Canyon Day Use Area, Simpson River Trailhead, the Kootenay Crossing Warden Station (west side of Kootenay Crossing), and the Kootenay River Day Use Area. The phones connect automatically with emergency dispatch 24 hours a day year-round.

Gas

No gas is available inside the park. The closest fueling stations are outside the park at Radium Hot Springs and in Banff.

Cell Service

Cell reception is decent outside the park in the town of Radium Hot Springs and at Castle Mountain Junction on the park's east boundary. Inside the park, you will not have any cell service. The Radium Hot Springs complex has **pay phones.**

Radium Hot Springs

Radium Hot Springs is the gateway community for Kootenay National Park. It is located south of the park entrance around the junction of BC 93 and 95.

Sights
★ Bighorn Sheep
Radium is home year-round to bighorn sheep that wander through town and sometimes clog the roads. To distinguish bighorns from mountain goats, look for their brown horns, tawny fur, and white rumps. Male youngsters have shorter arced horns, but full-grown rams have huge curled horns that form a full circle. The sheep use those horns, smashing them together in dominance displays during the fall rut (Nov.-Dec.). In late spring and early summer, you'll see newborn lambs with the ewes, usually hanging in a separate group from the rams.

During the second week in May, the **Wings over the Rockies Nature Festival** (www.wingsovertherockies.org) presents educational, interactive programs on the local bighorn herd. On the first weekend in November, the town hosts the **Headbanger Festival,** which celebrates the annual rut, when rams often display dominance by butting heads.

Recreation
Golf
Radium Golf (800/667-6444, www.radiumgolf.ca, Apr.-Oct.) is a highlight of golfing in the Canadian Rockies, comprising two very different courses. One of them, the 6,818-yard, par 72 **Springs Course** (4714 Springs Dr., 250/347-6200, C$69-110), is generally regarded as one of British Columbia's top 10 resort courses. Immaculately groomed fairways following the land's natural contours,

near-perfect greens, and more than 70 bunkers filled with imported sand do little to take away from the surrounding mountainscape. Located south of town, the **Radium Course** (8100 Golf Course Rd., 250/347-6266, C$44-70) is much shorter but tighter and still challenging. Both courses have club and cart rentals; the Springs Course also has a driving range, chipping green, and restaurant.

Thrill Sports
Valley Zipline Adventures (8393 BC 93/95, 250/347-7627, valleyzip.com, daily Apr.-Oct., C$70-80) has seven ziplines that fly over Dry Gulch Valley. On this 1.5-hour guided tour, you'll have views of the Columbia River Valley Wetlands and Purcell Mountains across the valley. They also have a climbing wall and jump tower.

Food
International
Located in the Prestige Radium Hot Springs Resort, **Don Agave Cantina** (7493 Main St. W., 250/347-2340, www.prestigehotelsandresorts.com, Mon.-Sat. 5pm-9pm, C$13-20) serves a short menu of Mexican specialties: tacos, fajitas, and enchiladas. The margaritas go down easy.

Featuring the flavors of Austria, **Helna's Stube Restaurant** (7547 Main St. W., 250/347-0047, helnas.com, Wed.-Sun. 5pm-9pm, C$24-42) dishes up gourmet meals in a casual environment. It's the one place you can get tasty elk medallions and classic specialties like schnitzel. You can dine indoors or outdoors on the patio and deck.

Pubs
Horsethief Creek Pub and Eatery (7358 Main St. E., 250/347-6400, horsethiefpub.ca, 11:30am-10pm daily, C$14-27) serves up burgers and classic pub fare of ribs, poutine, and hot sandwiches, plus global flavors in rice and pasta dishes. Brews from regional breweries are on tap, and the bar whips up a full line of cocktails. In case you over-imbibe, you can reserve

the pub shuttle for a safe ride back to your hotel.

For a meal with a view, the **Springs Course restaurant** (4714 Springs Dr., 250/347-6200, www.radiumgolf.ca, noon-7pm daily Apr.-Oct., C$9-28) is at the golf course on the west side of the highway. The view from the patio, overlooking the Columbia River and Purcell Mountains, is nothing short of stunning. Sandwiches and burgers are the backbone of the menu, plus beer, wine, and cocktails.

Cafés and Quick Bites

The best coffee in town is poured at **Bighorn Cafe** (7527 Main St. W., 778/527-5055, www.bighorncafe.net, 6am-4:30pm daily, C$8-15), a friendly place serving espresso with all the options. They also offer fresh-baked quiche and pastries, breakfast burritos, sandwiches, and chili. Free wireless internet is available, too.

Along the main commercial strip near the visitors center is **Screamer's** (7518 Main St. E., 250/347-9335, www.screamersicecream.ca, noon-10pm daily summer), the place to hang out with an ice cream on a hot summer afternoon. You can also get hot dogs and subs.

Groceries

Mountainside Market (7546 Main St. E., 250/347-9600, 8am-9pm daily) has a decent choice of groceries, including fresh produce and baked goods. There's also an in-house deli and butcher.

Accommodations and Camping

Along the access road to Kootenay National Park, a string of motels come alive with color through summer as each tries to outdo the others with flashy floral landscaping. Make reservations for summer and holiday weekends six months in advance.

Hostels

Misty River Lodge (5036 BC 93, 250/347-9912, mistyriverlodge.ca, dorm beds from C$40, private rooms C$90-190) has hostel-style lodging. This converted motel has mixed dormitory rooms that sleep six and private rooms, some with kitchenettes. Amenities include a communal kitchen, lounge, and big deck with even bigger views to the distant Purcell Mountains.

Motels and Inns

Celadon Lodge (5000 BC 93, 778/527-5077, www.celadonlodge.com, from C$80) has motel-style rooms, each with a different combination of beds. Some have kitchenettes. **Apple Tree Inn** (4999 BC 93, 250/347-0011 or 800/350-1511, www.appletreeinnbc.com, Apr.-Oct., C$80-140) has family suites with one or two bedrooms and kitchenettes.

In the middle of the motel strip is the **Alpen Motel** (5022 BC 93, 250/347-9823 or 888/788-3891, www.alpenmotel.com, from C$80-140), which arguably has the best and brightest flowers out front. The air-conditioned rooms are the best along the strip. Under new ownership in 2020, **Gables Motel** (5028 BC 93, 250/347-9866 or 877/387-7007, www.gablesmotel.ca, C$80-145) has 17 smallish rooms, each of which has mountain views. Wheelchair-accessible rooms are available.

The **Radium Elk Park B & B** (4943 Saddle Wood Ln., 250/347-9522, www.radiumelkparkbnb.com, C$150-350, two-night min.) has three spacious rooms, including one condo-style suite, in a large home with a community great room. Several of the king beds can be split into twins. The self-serve breakfast can be continental or hot.

Resorts

Radium also has two resorts. On the west side of town, **Bighorn Meadows Resort** (10 Bighorn Blvd., 250/347-2323 or 877/344-2323, www.bighornmeadows.com, C$120-350) overlooks the Springs golf course and has an outdoor heated pool and two hot tubs. The units range from studios to two bedrooms, and each is spacious, modern, and fully equipped

◈ Side Trip: Columbia River Valley

A long lobe of ancient ice formed the Columbia River Valley bounded by the Purcell Mountains and Rocky Mountains. Today, the valley cradles the Columbia River, plus small towns and recreation communities mostly located on BC 93/95. Towns and resorts are listed here from north to south.

Invermere-on-the-Lake

West of the highway, **Invermere** is a small town on the northwest shore of **Lake Windermere,** filled with the warmest water in the region. As such, it's a popular summertime place to **swim, paddle,** and **boat.** A few downtown blocks offer **restaurants, shops,** and **art galleries.** From April to October, golfers flock to the area's nine **golf courses.** Accommodations in town see the highest rates in summer.

Panorama Mountain Resort

In the Purcell Mountains west of Invermere, **Panorama Mountain Resort** (250/342-6941 or 800/663-2929, www.panoramaresort.com) is a year-round self-contained resort with a base village and a residential subdivision connected by an open-air gondola to move visitors between the two. It also has a year-round water park and an extensive complex of hot springs pools. **Skiing** first put Panorama on the map, mainly because the resort boasts one of the highest vertical rises of North American ski resorts (1,200 meters (3,940 ft). In summer, there are **scenic chairlift rides, mountain biking, white-water rafting, tennis,** and a **golf course.** Accommodations in Panorama Mountain Village are all relatively new but vary greatly in size and amenities. Since summer is the off-season, you can get some great deals on lodging.

Fairmont Hot Springs Resort

Close to BC 93/95, **Fairmont Hot Springs Resort** (5225 Fairmont Resort Rd., 800/663-4979, www.fairmonthotsprings.com), about 35 km (22 mi) south of Radium Hot Springs, is a four-season resort sprawling around natural **hot spring pools,** a **spa,** and three **golf**

with a large kitchen. All rooms have balconies with outdoor furniture.

The **Prestige Radium Hot Springs Resort** (7493 Main St. W., 250/347-2300 or 877/737-8443, www.prestigehotels andresorts.com, C$135-280) sits at the town's main intersection. Its 87 rooms come with queen or king beds and kitchenettes, with a pet-friendly option. Facilities include a fitness room, indoor pool, hot tub, gift shop, spa services, and two restaurants. Complimentary bicycles are available.

Camping

Perfectly described by its name, **Dry Gulch Provincial Park** (27 sites, 250/422-3003, bcparks.ca, May-Sept., C$25) sits 4.5 km (2.8 mi) south of Radium Hot Springs. The campground has flush and pit toilets; each site has a picnic table and fire pit but no hookups. One campsite is accessible. You can make **reservations** (www.discovercamping.ca) up to four months in advance for 18 of the campsites for stays in mid-May to early September; the others are first come, first served.

For large RVs up to 13.7 meters (45 ft), **Canyon RV Resort** (5012 Sinclair Creek Rd., 250/347-9564, www.canyonrv.com, mid-Apr.-mid-Oct. C$47-65, no tents) has pull-through campsites, partial and full hookups, and patio sites. Grassy and landscaped sites tuck partially under shade trees. A path leads to the town of Radium, so you can walk to restaurants.

Information and Services
Emergency Services

For emergency medical treatment, go to

courses. For those staying at the resort, you can access several private outdoor pools with hot and cold-plunge pools, but there is also a public hot spring pool for day use. Other activities include **guided hikes, kayaking,** and **tennis.** In winter, a tiny old-school ski area at the top of the resort has **skiing, snowboarding,** and **tubing.** Accommodations include hotel rooms, lodge rooms, cabins, and cottages. A huge **RV campground** (235 sites) offers full hookups.

Kimberley

Tucked on the eastern edge of the Purcell Mountains, **Kimberley** has been reinvented from its old mining town roots to a **Bavarian village** with a downtown core of **shops** and **restaurants** around brick pedestrian-only streets. The heart of the summer action revolves around three **golf courses, hiking,** and **mountain biking.** You can even ride on the **Underground Mining Railway** (250/427-5070, kimberleysundergroundminingrailway.ca) through the old mine area. Winter has **cross-country skiing,** and **Kimberley Alpine Resort** (800/258-7669, skikimberley.com) cranks up the lifts for **downhill skiing** and **snowboarding.** Accommodations are available year-round in two locations: in town or at the ski resort. The resort is the newest with modern lodges, condos, and townhomes. On the St. Mary River, **Kimberley Riverside Campground** (140 sites, 877/999-2929, www.kimberleycampground.com) has hookups for RVs, and tents are welcome.

Cranbrook

As the largest town in the Columbia River Valley, **Cranbrook** is a commercial and cultural hub located on BC 3. The **Ktunaxa Interpretive Centre** (St. Eugene Resort, 777 Mission Rd., 250/417-4001, www.steugene.ca) focuses on the **art** and cultural heritage of Indigenous people. Nearby is the **Fort Steele Heritage Town** (9851 BC 93/95, 250/417-6000, www.fortsteele.ca), a restored **pioneer town** from the 1890s. Recreation includes **hiking, biking,** and five **golf courses.**

the **Invermere and District Hospital** (850 10th Ave., Invermere, 250/342-9201, www.interiorhealth.ca), located 15 minutes south of Radium Hot Springs. You can also call **911.**

Gas and Vehicle Charging Stations

Four gas stations surround the roundabout junction of BC 95 and 93. **Petro-Canada** (4929 BC 93) and **Radium Husky** (4918 BC 93) sit on opposite sides of BC 93 heading toward the national park entrance. Find an **electric vehicle charging station** at the **Radium Community Centre** (4863 Stanley St.).

Cell Service

You should be able to get good cell reception in Radium Hot Springs.

Tourist Information

Radium Hot Springs Visitor Information Centre (7556 Main St. E., 250/347-9331, 9am-5pm daily) contains services for Kootenay National Park and the Chamber of Commerce for Radium Hot Springs. You can get information on activities, events, recreation, restaurants, and lodging. The visitors center sponsors music, food vendors, and a farmers market (4pm-7pm Fri. July-Aug.) in summer.

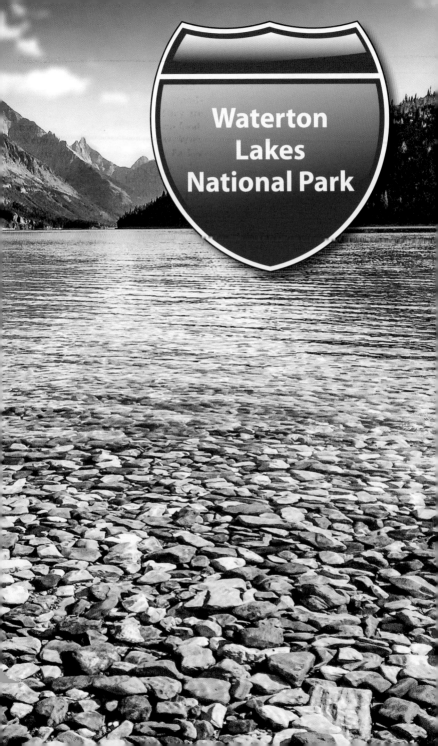

**Waterton
Lakes
National Park**

Highlights

★ **Cruise Waterton Lake:** Take a boat tour across this long, mountain-flanked lake that spans an international boundary (page 237).

★ **Gaze at Cameron Falls:** This waterfall cuts through various rocky ledges (page 237).

★ **Visit Prince of Wales Hotel:** This 1927 hotel maintains a British ambience with kilt-wearing bellhops and afternoon high tea. There's also an outstanding view (page 239).

★ **Wander through Red Rock Canyon:** This brilliant, colorful mosaic of layered sediments is evidence of the canyon's origins as an ancient inland sea (page 242).

★ **Climb up Bear's Hump:** Grunt up to this high knoll for a grand panoramic view of Waterton Townsite and Upper Waterton Lake (page 243).

★ **Hike to Crypt Lake:** Follow switchbacks up to seemingly impassable cliffs where a hidden tunnel curls into a hanging valley holding an idyllic lake (page 243).

★ **Paddle Cameron Lake:** This idyllic lake is tucked in a cirque. Look for grizzlies above the southern shore (page 251).

The tiniest of the parks in the Canadian Rockies, Waterton Lakes National Park packs in many wonders. On the Continental Divide's east side, mountains meet the prairie, which rage with wildflower blooms in early summer. With no transitional foothills, the eastern peaks plummet directly to grasslands. It's the perfect habitat for bears and other wildlife, plus its clear blue lakes harbor wild trout.

A long, glacier-gouged trough forms Upper Waterton Lake, the deepest lake in the Canadian Rockies and one that straddles the U.S.-Canadian border. Waterton's biggest claim to fame is its shared international boundary with Glacier National Park and their recognition together as the world's first International Peace Park, which itself is the world's first International Dark Sky Park.

Dominated by the Prince of Wales Hotel and Waterton Lake, the park serves as a destination itself as well as an entrance to Glacier National Park's remote north country. On any summer day, the Waterton Townsite bustles with shoppers, bicyclists, backpackers, boaters, and campers. It's a quintessential Canadian mountain town that embodies what Banff used to be before booming commercialism. The MV *International* shuttles hikers and sightseers across Waterton Lake and the international boundary to Goat Haunt, USA. Only two roads pierce the park's remarkable interior, both gateways to lakes, waterfalls, canyons, peaks, and wildlife.

Planning Your Time

You can explore **Waterton Lakes National Park** (403/859-5133, www.pc.gc.ca) in **one day** with an early start. You'll be able to take the **boat tour** on Upper Waterton Lake, drive the **Red Rock Parkway,** walk along the Townsite's lakeshore to **Cameron Falls,** explore shops in town, and dine at a restaurant. To see more of Waterton, plan a minimum of **three days** to hike **Crypt Lake,** sightsee on Red Rock and Akamina Parkways, and hike or take a boat tour over the international border to **Goat Haunt.**

Waterton is open 24 hours daily year-round. However, access and services vary seasonally. The biggest crowds show up in **July** and **August;** late spring and fall are less hectic times to visit. In winter, when some of the lakes freeze, you can nearly have the place to yourself.

The park's only public transportation are **hiker shuttles** to select locations; most visitors come by car.

Seasonal Driving Concerns

In summer, all roads in Waterton Lakes National Park are open. In winter, the main road into Waterton and the Townsite remains open and plowed during snowstorms. But the two scenic parkways that climb up higher into the mountains **close in winter,** from **mid-October to mid-May,** depending on weather. While **Red Rock Parkway** closes completely, **Akamina Parkway** is plowed to Little Prairie Day Use Area. (You can ski or snowshoe both closed roads in winter, but you may need avalanche gear in segments.)

Chief Mountain International Highway runs through a portion of Waterton Lakes National Park. It's open seasonally, from May to September. During those months, the Canadian and U.S. immigration and customs stations at the border close overnight. Border crossings are possible 9am-6pm daily in May and September and 7am-10pm from June to Labor Day.

Winter tires are required October-March. For road reports, check with **Drive BC** (800/550-4997, www.drivebc.ca) or **511 Alberta** (call 511, 511.alberta.ca).

Waterton Lakes National Park

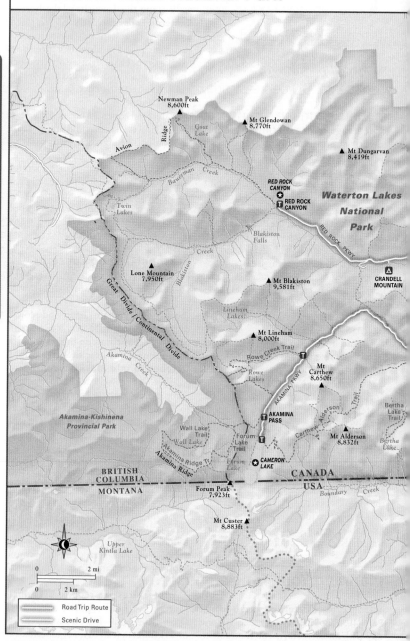

Newman Peak
8,600ft

Mt Glendowan
8,770ft

Mt Dungarvan
8,419ft

Avion Ridge

Goat Lake

Bauerman Creek

RED ROCK CANYON

RED ROCK CANYON

Waterton Lakes National Park

RED ROCK PKWY

Twin Lakes

Blakiston Falls

Blakiston Creek

Lone Mountain
7,950ft

Mt Blakiston
9,581ft

CRANDELL MOUNTAIN

Lineham Lakes

Mt Lineham
8,000ft

Akamina Creek

Rowe Creek Trail

Rowe Lakes

Great Divide / Continental Divide

Mt Carthew
8,650ft

AKAMINA PKWY

Akamina-Kishinena Provincial Park

Wall Lake Trail

Wall Lake

Akamina Ridge Tr

Akamina Ridge

Forum Lake Trail

Forum Lake

AKAMINA PASS

CAMERON LAKE

Carthew Alderson Trail

Mt Alderson
8,832ft

Bertha Lake Trail

Bertha Lake

BRITISH COLUMBIA

MONTANA

Forum Peak
7,923ft

CANADA

USA

Boundary Creek

Mt Custer
8,883ft

Upper Kintla Lake

0   2 mi

0   2 km

Road Trip Route

Scenic Drive

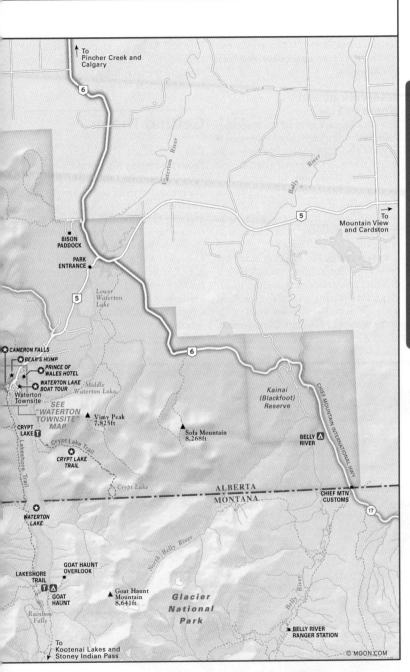

To Pincher Creek and Calgary

6

Waterton River

Belly River

5

To Mountain View and Cardston

BISON PADDOCK

PARK ENTRANCE

5

Lower Waterton Lake

6

Kainai (Blackfoot) Reserve

CHIEF MOUNTAIN INTERNATIONAL HWY

CAMERON FALLS

BEAR'S HUMP

PRINCE OF WALES HOTEL

WATERTON LAKE BOAT TOUR

Waterton Townsite

Middle Waterton Lake

SEE "WATERTON TOWNSITE" MAP

Vimy Peak 7,825ft

Sofa Mountain 8,268ft

BELLY RIVER

CRYPT LAKE

Crypt Lake Trail

CRYPT LAKE TRAIL

Lakeshore Trail

Crypt Lake

ALBERTA

MONTANA

CHIEF MTN CUSTOMS

17

WATERTON LAKE

North Belly River

GOAT HAUNT OVERLOOK

LAKESHORE TRAIL

GOAT HAUNT

Goat Haunt Mountain 8,641ft

Glacier National Park

Belly River

BELLY RIVER RANGER STATION

Rainbow Falls

To Kootenai Lakes and Stoney Indian Pass

© MOON.COM

Best Routes Through the Park

Waterton has minimal roads. The **main entrance road** goes to the Waterton Townsite. Branching off that are the two out-and-back **scenic parkways, Red Rock** and **Akamina.**

Reservations and Where to Stay

The park centers around the **Waterton Townsite,** a tiny year-round town that is home to about 100 people in winter with minimal services. Summer is a different story, when it balloons to nearly 2,000 residents. In this compact town, you can stay in lodges or camp; you can also leave your car parked in favor of walking to restaurants, shopping, boat rentals, boat tours, and a few trailheads.

Reservations for summer stays are imperative. For lodging, contact the individual properties **nine months** in advance for booking, especially for visits from July to mid-September. To get a site in the **Waterton Townsite Campground,** make reservations as soon as bookings are available for the year (usually in January). Tent and RV sites go fast for July and August, especially due to the convenience of the campground's location and the fact that it has the only RV hookups inside the park.

Getting There

Car
From Kootenay National Park

From **Kootenay National Park** to Waterton, the drive is 382 km (237 mi) and it takes a little more than four hours. Starting from **Radium Hot Springs** on the southeastern corner of Kootenay, the route descends south through the Columbia Valley on BC 93 to meet BC 3. Follow BC 3 east, passing Fernie and the Continental Divide, where the road becomes AB 93 in Alberta. At Pincher Creek, take AB 6 south to the park entrance.

Waterton Townsite

GETTING THERE

From Banff

From **Banff** to the Waterton Townsite is a 372-km (231-mi) drive that requires four hours. Take Trans-Canada Highway 1 east toward Calgary but turn south onto AB 22 before reaching the city. Follow AB 22 south to AB 3. Turn east (left) and drive AB 3 to Pincher Creek, where you pop south again on AB 6 to the park entrance road heading to the Townsite.

From Calgary

From **Calgary,** the drive to Waterton is 240 km (150 mi) and takes about 3.5 hours. Head south on AB 2 toward Fort Macleod. Turn west onto AB 3 to Pincher Creek. Turn south onto AB 6 to reach the park entrance for Waterton.

From Glacier National Park

From **Glacier National Park,** you can take two different routes to Waterton. But it depends on the season, as one closes in winter. Chief Mountain International Highway is the more scenic, shorter route that's open in summer. Both routes cross the international boundary between Canada and the United States.

The main, shorter route between neighboring Glacier and Waterton is via **Chief Mountain International Highway.** It's open seasonally, from May to September. During those months, the Canadian and U.S. immigration and customs stations at the border close overnight. Border crossings are possible 9am-6pm daily in May and September and 7am-10pm from June to Labor Day. From **St. Mary** on Glacier's east side to the main entrance of Waterton is 80 km (50 mi), which takes a little more than an hour. Take US 89 northeast through Babb to the signed entrance to Chief Mountain International Highway (MT 17) and turn left (north). You'll pass through open range where cows wander the road; drive slowly. Then, the road enters the northeastern corner of Glacier and passes through the international border into Waterton; neither park has an entrance station nor charges an entry fee on this road. After you've crossed into Canada, you're technically in Waterton Lakes National Park and the highway becomes AB 6. You'll drive out of and back into the eastern corner of Waterton, turn left onto AB 5, then turn left again onto the main entrance road into Waterton.

The longer route from St. Mary to Waterton goes through the **Piegan-Carway border station** (24 hours daily year-round); it's a 110-km (70-mi) drive that takes less than 1.5 hours. From **St. Mary,** drive US 89 north to the border. After crossing, the road becomes AB 2. Follow it north to Cardston, then cut west on AB 5 to reach Waterton's entrance road.

Air

Calgary International Airport (YYC, 403/735-1200 or 877/254-7427, www.yyc.com) is a major hub in Canada with domestic flights from all over as well as international flights. The airport is located

One Day in Waterton

Morning

Get an early start for driving **Red Rock Parkway** to get the best chances for wildlife-watching. Look for black bears, grizzly bears, bighorn sheep, and moose. At the road's terminus, walk around **Red Rock Canyon** and admire the namesake true-red rock. If you have time, you can also tack on **Blakiston Falls.**

Descend the road and drive to **Prince of Wales Hotel** for your first big view of **Waterton Lake.** Drop into the **Waterton Townsite** and stop at the **visitors center** before heading to lunch at the **Lakeside Chophouse** in the **Bayshore Inn.**

Afternoon

Work off your lunch by sauntering along Waterton Lake for the views to **Cameron Falls.** After returning, if you have time, rent a **surrey bike** from Pat's Gas Station to pedal about town. In the late afternoon, hop aboard the *International* for a **scenic boat tour** on Waterton Lake.

Evening

Cap off your day by dining in **Red Rock Trattoria.** Then, at dusk, take a drive along the park entrance road to watch for wildlife.

---

a bit north of the city of Calgary, so it's 282 km (175 mi) from Waterton, a drive of less than four hours. Car rentals and an on-demand shuttle that connects to area hotels are available at the airport.

It's possible to chop off part of the distance to Waterton by flying south to **Lethbridge Airport** (YQL, 417 Stubb Ross Rd., Lethbridge, www.lethbridgeairport. ca) in Alberta via **Air Canada** (888/247-2262, www.aircanada.com). Rent a car there to drive 140 km (87 mi) to Waterton, a 1.5-hour drive.

Visiting the Park

Entrances and Fees

The only park entrance station is on the **main park entrance road,** located at the junction of AB 5 and AB 6. The **entrance gate** is **open 24 hours daily year-round,** but it's only staffed early May-early October. There are no entrance stations on the two small portions of Chief Mountain International Highway that pass through Waterton.

One-day passes (C$20 family/vehicle, C$10 adults, C$9 seniors, kids 17 and younger free) are valid until 4pm the day following purchase, but you can add on as many days that you need. If you are touring all of the Canadian Rockies national parks, a **Discovery Pass** (C$140 family/vehicle, C$70 adults, C$60 seniors) may be a more economical option. It is valid for entry into all Canadian national parks for one year from purchase. Both types of passes are available from the entrance station; the Discovery Pass can also be purchased in advance online.

No entrance fees are charged to enter Waterton from Glacier National Park by foot or tour boat. The tour boat, however, charges a fee.

Visitors Centers

The **Waterton Lakes National Park Visitor Information Centre** (Windflower Ave., 403/859-5133, 9am-5pm daily year-round) features a theater and interpretive displays on the Blackfoot Confederacy of First Nations people, biodiversity, and park flora and fauna, as well as some hands-on activities. It also provides information on the park and road conditions, wilderness-use permits, fishing licenses, and maps. Outside the building is a natural-features playground. The visitors center is within a block or two from most lodges and the Townsite campground.

Sights

★ Waterton Lake

Set in a north-south trough gouged by Pleistocene glaciers, **Waterton Lake** is the deepest lake in the Canadian Rockies at 149 meters (487 ft) deep. (It's actually Upper Waterton Lake, which feeds Middle and Lower Waterton Lakes, but no one calls it that.) The water holds giant lake trout (23 kg/50 lbs) and tiny opossum shrimp, which are relics of the ice age. Spanning the international boundary, the narrow lake, resembling a fjord, is more than 11 km (7 mi) long. Visitors travel over its waters in the 1927 wooden *International* tour boat. Be ready for big, whitecap-inducing winds on this lake.

Waterton Shoreline Cruises (at the marina at the junction of Mount View Rd. and Waterton Ave., 403/859-2362, www.watertoncruise.com, 10am, 1pm, 4pm, and 7pm daily July-Aug., 10am and 1pm daily May-June and Sept.-early Oct., adults C$55 round-trip, kids C$27) operates the historic *International* on Upper Waterton Lake. During the two-hour tour on the wooden 200-passenger boat, which has been cruising here since 1927, knowledgeable guides punctuate their patter with humor. For the best views, go for a sunny seat on the boat's top deck. If the weather is brisk, just bundle up. June-late September, the boat usually docks for 30 minutes at Goat Haunt, allowing enough time to walk to the ranger station pavilion to see the full length of the lake. Shoulder season launches, which are often on the *Miss Waterton* instead, do not stop at Goat Haunt. Buy tickets at least one hour in advance; to guarantee space, buy them a day in advance.

International Peace Park Plaza

Together, Waterton and Glacier became the first International Peace Park in the world. An outdoor interpretive site celebrates this recognition, plus the honoring of the pair as a World Heritage Site and International Biosphere Reserve. In the Townsite, tour the plaza and paved walkway between the Bayshore Inn and the marina. The walkway loops around the pier with interpretive signs, providing views of Prince of Wales Hotel and the expanse of Upper Waterton Lake southward into Glacier. Benches and chairs offer places to sit to absorb the views.

★ Cameron Falls

Picturesque **Cameron Falls** is on the edge of Waterton Townsite on Evergreen Avenue. In June, water roars through its slots, but the flow drops substantially by August. Cameron Creek has eroded a massive fold of the Waterton Formation, a 600-million-year-old rock layer, which makes the water plunge in multiple directions. Sit on a bench at the base, or climb the short, steep, north-side switchback trail to reach overlooks.

Cameron Lake

Tucked in a glacial cirque at the terminus of Akamina Parkway, **Cameron Lake** reflects the steep slopes of Mount Custer. Across the glacially fed lake sit the remnants of Herbst Glacier in Montana, where avalanches catapult down the slopes into good bear habitat. Tour interpretive exhibits, rent a rowboat or canoe to paddle around the lake's shoreline, or saunter the trail along the west shore, watching for moose, shorebirds, and bears. From here, hikers also climb the Carthew Summit and Alderson Lake Trail to trek to the Townsite.

Goat Haunt, USA

A tiny seasonal enclave housing rangers, **Goat Haunt, USA,** is at Waterton Lake's southern end in Glacier National Park. Accessed only by boat or on foot,

WATERTON LAKES NATIONAL PARK

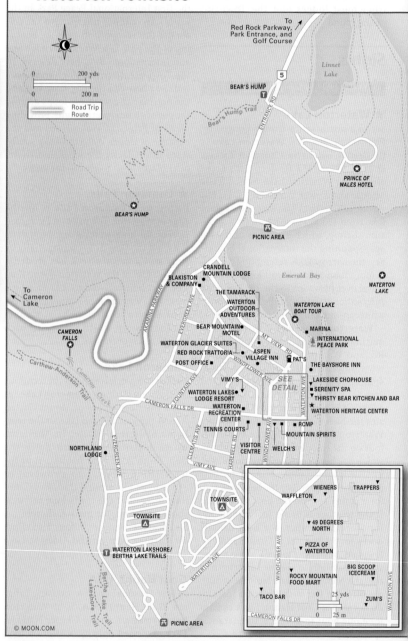

Waterton Townsite

To Red Rock Parkway, Park Entrance, and Golf Course

Linnet Lake

5

BEAR'S HUMP

Bear's Hump Trail

PRINCE OF WALES HOTEL

ENTRANCE RD

0   200 yds
0   200 m

Road Trip Route

BEAR'S HUMP

PICNIC AREA

CRANDELL MOUNTAIN LODGE

Emerald Bay

WATERTON LAKE

BLAKISTON & COMPANY

To Cameron Lake

THE TAMARACK

WATERTON OUTDOOR ADVENTURES

WATERTON LAKE BOAT TOUR

AKAMINA PARKWAY

EVERGREEN AVE

BEAR MOUNTAIN MOTEL

MT. VIEW RD

MARINA

INTERNATIONAL PEACE PARK

CAMERON FALLS

WATERTON GLACIER SUITES

RED ROCK TRATTORIA

ASPEN VILLAGE INN

POST OFFICE

PAT'S

Carthew-Anderson Trail

Cameron Creek

WINDFLOWER AVE

THE BAYSHORE INN

VIMY'S

SEE DETAIL

LAKESIDE CHOPHOUSE

SERENITY SPA

THIRSTY BEAR KITCHEN AND BAR

WATERTON HERITAGE CENTER

FOUNTAIN AVE

WATERTON LAKES LODGE RESORT

WATERTON AVE

CAMERON FALLS DR

WATERTON RECREATION CENTER

CLEMATIS AVE

TENNIS COURTS

HARPELL RD

RCMP

MOUNTAIN SPIRITS

NORTHLAND LODGE

EVERGREEN AVE

VISITOR CENTRE

WINDFLOWER AVE

WELCH'S

VIMY AVE

TOWNSITE

TOWNSITE

WATERTON LAKESHORE/ BERTHA LAKE TRAILS

WATERTON AVE

Bertha Lake Trail

Lakeshore Trail

PICNIC AREA

© MOON.COM

SEE DETAIL

WIENERS

TRAPPERS

WAFFLETON

49 DEGREES NORTH

PIZZA OF WATERTON

WINDFLOWER AVE

BIG SCOOP ICECREAM

ROCKY MOUNTAIN FOOD MART

WATERTON AVE

TACO BAR

ZUM'S

0   25 yds
0   25 m

CAMERON FALLS DR

Wildfire and Wildflowers

Much of the landscape in Waterton Lakes National Park shows evidence of the aggressive **Kenow Fire,** which swept through the park in fall 2017. It started from lightning in neighboring Akamina-Kishinena Provincial Park but moved quickly into Waterton. It gobbled up 70 percent of the park's forest and 80 percent of the trails. While the fire spared the Townsite's hotels, restaurants, shops, and campground, it burned Crandell Mountain Campground, the visitors center, and the park's two scenic parkways, all of which have since been repaired.

fireweed

The remains of burned aspen groves and conifers line the entrance road, Red Rock Parkway, and Akamina Parkway as well as nearby trails. But it's not all bad news: Moose, elk, bighorn sheep, and bears have returned to the affected areas, and bird counts are back to near normal. The fire also revealed some 7,000-year-old Blackfoot trails and camps that are now protected archaeological sites.

Perhaps best of all, the fire was a boon for Waterton's famed wildflower displays. Ash from the fire put nitrogen back into the soil; the wildflower blooms since then have been even more spectacular. You can see fields of wildflowers along roadways, particularly the entrance road and Red Rock Parkway. Blooms usually start in mid-June along lower elevations and continue throughout July. Look for fields of tall pink fireweed in burned zones and large yellow arrowleaf balsamroots, members of the sunflower family, on sunny slopes. Bear grass, a showy white clump of blossoms on a tall stalk, appears in July. The annual **Waterton Wildflower Festival** (mywaterton.ca) is held for 10 days in mid-June with workshops, guided hikes, and flower walks.

Goat Haunt sees hundreds of visitors per day in midsummer. Most arrive via the *International* tour boat. Buy tickets at least one hour in advance; to guarantee space, buy them a day in advance. At Goat Haunt, you can check out interpretive signs telling the story of the International Peace Park or hike to Goat Haunt Overlook, Kootenai Lakes, Rainbow Falls, and beyond. Hikers can reach Goat Haunt from Waterton via the Waterton Lakeshore Trail.

Bison Paddock

Once roaming the plains in vast numbers, wild bison, which are called *linii* by the Blackfoot people, have all but vanished from North America. Waterton's

Bison Paddock contains a small herd. Bison weigh close to 2,000 pounds and look like shaggy cows. But don't be lured into thinking they're docile: They are extremely unpredictable and aggressive. You can see the bison from a **viewing area** (2 km/1.2 mi west of the park entrance road on AB 6) or via a narrow, potholed road (4 km/2.5 mi long, no trailers) that's at the north end of the viewing area; it loops through the paddock.

★ Prince of Wales Hotel

Designated a National Historic Site, the seven-story, 90-room **Prince of Wales Hotel** (844/868-7474 or 403/859-2231, www.glacierparkcollection.com, daily early June-mid-Sept.) took more than a

SIGHTS

Wildlife-Watching

Wildlife can be easy to spot in Waterton, especially along the prairies and mountains. Look for **grizzly bears, black bears,** and **moose** along the park entrance road and Red Rock Parkway. You can also spot **bighorn sheep** and **deer** grazing on lawns in the Townsite. Animals tend to be more active around dawn and dusk. Maintain a safe distance from wildlife: Stay about three bus lengths away from elk, deer, bighorn sheep, and moose, and maintain 100 yards (100 m) from bears and wolves.

Watching wildlife can be easy from the car but aim to use **pullouts** rather than stopping in the roadway. Bring **binoculars** for better viewing. If you don't have a pair, you can rent one from **Pat's Gas Station** (224 Mount View Rd., 403/859-2266, www.patswaterton.com, C$15).

year to build. Constructed by the Great Northern Railway, the hotel opened its doors in 1927. Even if you are not staying here, drop in to see its massive lobby with floor-to-ceiling windows looking down Waterton Lake or take high tea in the afternoon. Walk out on the bluff for the best photographic views of Waterton Lake. Beware the howling winds that can rip off hats.

Scenic Drives

Akamina Parkway

The **Akamina Parkway** (16 km/10 mi, open May-Oct.) underwent major reconstruction after the 2017 Kenow Fire. West of the Prince of Wales Hotel, the signed road climbs steeply from Waterton Townsite as it curves above Cameron Creek Gorge. It passes trailheads to multiple destinations and several picnic areas. The route climbs along the base of **Mount Crandell,** squeezing between hulking mountains, to **Cameron Lake,** where you can tour interpretive exhibits. For the return descent to the Townsite, shift into second gear; you can always smell the hot brake pads of those who don't. This drive takes about 25 minutes each way.

Red Rock Parkway

Red Rock Parkway (15 km/9.3 mi, open May-Oct.) travels through the 2017 Kenow Fire zone to terminate at Red Rock Canyon. Locate the signed turn-off midway on the park entrance road. The narrow road climbs through grasslands, winds through a canyon, and opens up into meadows along **Blakiston Creek.** Early July often brings on a wildflower show. Bring binoculars for watching bears and bighorn sheep. The road is quite narrow but passable for trailers and RVs. It passes Crandell Mountain Campground about midway and several picnic areas. The parkway ends at two parking areas, which have restrooms. A self-guided trail leads around **Red Rock Canyon.** Give yourself about 25 minutes each way for this drive.

Chief Mountain International Highway

The **Chief Mountain International Highway** (48 km/30 mi) provides a connection between Waterton Lakes National Park and Glacier National Park. It crosses the international border at Chief Mountain Customs. The Canadian and U.S. immigration and customs stations at the border are open seasonally (7am-10pm daily June-Labor Day, 9am-6pm daily May and Sept.). The border is closed overnight.

From the park entrance road, turn right onto AB 5 and right again onto Chief Mountain International Highway. The route starts with a long sweeping climb up to an overlook of the Waterton Valley. Stop here to read the interpretive signs and survey the valley. You can even spot the Prince of Wales Hotel perched on its knoll in the distance below the mountains. Continuing east, you'll notice fresh growth after the 1998 Sofa Mountain Fire on both sides of the road. The route exits the park briefly to cross the Blood Indian Reserve for the Kainai, park of the Blackfoot Confederacy, before crossing the **Belly River** back into the park. After passing the entrance to Belly River Campground, the road climbs to the international border. From there, the road enters **Glacier National Park** (no entrance station) and undulates over rolling aspen hills and past beaver ponds to curve around **Chief Mountain,** imposing and alone on Glacier's northeast corner. You'll also get views of the Mother and Papoose, two small peaks on a ridge west of Chief Mountain. A few unmarked pullouts offer good photo ops. Drive this open range carefully, for cows wander the road. As St. Mary Valley comes into view, the road descends to reach US 89. This drive takes about an hour each way.

Recreation

Hiking

Almost all trails except for Crypt Lake and the south end of the Waterton Lakeshore Trail burned in the 2017 Kenow Fire, so shade is minimal. Lower-elevation trails (Bear's Hump, Waterton Lakeshore) usually become snow-free in May. Snow melts off other trails in June, but can linger on high-elevation trails (Avion Ridge, Carthew Summit, Bertha Lake) into early July. Use ice axes for crossing steep snowfields. For current trail conditions, look on the Parks Canada website (www.pc.gc.ca) or stop by the visitors center. The **Waterton Lakes National Park Gem Trek map**

Top to bottom: Prince of Wales Hotel; Red Rock Canyon; overlook on Chief Mountain International Highway

(877/921-6277, www.gemtrek.com) has trails inside the park, plus Akamina-Kishinena Provincial Park and Goat Haunt in Glacier.

Shuttles by water and land aid trailhead access. **Waterton Shoreline Cruises** (403/859-2362, www.watertoncruise.com) operates the Crypt Lake and Goat Haunt boats. **Waterton Outdoor Adventures** (The Tamarack, 214 Mount View Rd., 403/859-2378, www.hikewaterton.com) operates bus shuttles. **Pat's Gas Station** (224 Mount View Rd., 403/859-2266, www.patswaterton.com, C$7-15/day) rents bear spray and hiking poles.

Hikers going to Goat Haunt trails on foot or by boat must have **passports;** register the morning of your departure with the **CBP ROAM** via a smartphone app you can download before arrival. Look online (www.nps.gov/glac) for updated status reports for trails in Glacier National Park.

Red Rock Parkway
★ Red Rock Canyon
Distance: 1 km (0.6 mi) loop
Duration: 30 minutes
Elevation gain: 40 meters (130 ft)
Effort: easy
Trail surface: narrow, rough pavement; dirt with roots and rocks
Trailhead: end of Red Rock Parkway

From the bridge over Red Rock Canyon, walk down and up either side of the loop. Water chiseled the canyon, exposing the lustrous red mudstone. Iron-rich argillite sediments are layered on top of each other, some turning red from oxidation, others remaining green. Evidence of the ancient Belt Sea appears in mud cracks and ripple marks. These are some of the region's oldest exposed sedimentary rock, created 1.5 billion years ago. At the top of the loop, you'll stare down a dizzying drop to the creek, a distance that took up to 10,000 years to carve.

Blakiston Falls
Distance: 2 km (1.2 mi) rt
Duration: 45 minutes
Elevation gain: 30.5 meters (100 ft)
Effort: easy
Trail surface: narrow dirt path with roots, rocks, and stair steps
Trailhead: end of Red Rock Parkway

Just after you cross the main bridge at the trailhead over Red Rock Canyon, turn left to descend along the creek until it joins **Bauerman Creek**. After a jog to the right, you'll cross a second bridge over that creek. Follow the trail as it climbs through the burned forest until you see **Blakiston Creek.** At **Blakiston Falls,** stair steps and several platforms overlook the roaring falls with Mount Blakiston looming above.

Goat Lake and Avion Ridge
Distance: 12.6-22.5 km (7.8-14 mi) rt
Duration: 4-8 hours
Elevation gain: 500-930 meters (1,640-3,050 ft)
Effort: moderate-strenuous
Trail surface: narrow dirt path with roots and loose rocks
Trailhead: end of Red Rock Parkway

The two routes of this hike begin and end on the Snowshoe Trail, an old dirt roadway that permits bicycles.

The route to **Goat Lake** and back is 12.6 km (7.8 mi). At 4 km (2.5 mi) up the Snowshoe Trail, you'll reach the Goat Lake junction. Turn right for Goat Lake and abruptly climb a relentless uphill into the hanging valley above. Just before Goat Lake, the trail moderates in pitch. Anglers fish here for rainbow trout. Retrace your steps to return.

The **Avion Ridge Loop** is 22.5 km (14 mi) in total. Most hikers tackle it **clockwise** as the climb is more gradual (but some prefer the vertical ascent via Goat Lake in favor of a less-steep descent). Continue up the Snowshoe Trail from the Goat Lake junction. At 8.2 km (5.1 mi), you'll reach the Snowshoe campsites and another junction. Go right to head north, passing above Lost Lake and climbing to **Avion Ridge**. From here, an unmaintained trail (8 km/5 mi) ascends along a barren, windswept ridge.

The trail arcs above a cirque right on the boundary of Waterton Lakes National Park (you'll see signs). Endless peaks parade in all directions. As the trail swings north, it descends to a saddle, traverses a steep sidehill, and reaches a pass above Goat Lake. A knee-pounding descent through wildflower meadows plummets to the lake and then to the Snowshoe Trail junction. Turn left to return to the trailhead.

Waterton Townsite
★ Bear's Hump

Distance: 2.8 km (1.7 mi) rt
Duration: 1.25 hours
Elevation gain: 168 meters (550 ft)
Effort: strenuous
Trail surface: narrow dirt path with rocks and stair steps
Trailhead: Bear's Hump

This short grunt up to an overlook yields exceptional views, but prepare for heat due to the Kenow Fire stripping away shady vegetation. For cooler temperatures, go in early morning or evening after the hump shades the east-facing slope.

The rebuilt route promptly climbs upward, gaining elevation rapidly, some in steep steps. As the trail switchbacks up to pop out on the **Bear's Hump,** a rocky outcropping on Mount Crandell's ridge, it offers one of the best views of the Waterton Townsite, the Prince of Wales Hotel, the prairie, and Middle and Lower Waterton Lakes. On top, views extend down Upper Waterton Lake into Glacier National Park.

★ Crypt Lake

Distance: 17 km (10.6 mi) rt
Duration: 5.5-7 hours
Elevation gain: 701 meters (2,300 ft)
Effort: moderate-strenuous
Trail surface: narrow dirt path with roots and loose rocks; metal stairs

Top to bottom: hiking Avion Ridge; Parks Canada interpretive guide with a family on the Bertha Lake trail; Crypt Lake Trail

Trailhead: Crypt Landing, accessible by boat from Waterton Townsite

From the marina in the Waterton Townsite, catch the water taxi operated by **Waterton Shoreline Cruises** (403/859-2362, www.watertoncruise.com, daily late May–early Oct., C$28 round-trip) to cross Upper Waterton Lake to Crypt Landing. July–early September, it departs the marina at 8:30am, 9am, and 10am and Crypt Landing at 4pm and 5:30pm. Spring and fall boats go only at 10am and 5:30pm. Buy tickets the day before or at least one hour in advance.

From Crypt Landing, the climb bolts up 19 switchbacks through a wooded hillside along **Hellroaring Creek.** At the sixth switchback, an alternate, steeper route drops and climbs the edge of Hellroaring Creek to see its waterfalls; you can take one route up and the other down. Soon the trail passes **Twin Falls,** and lodgepole pines give way to open meadows and boulder fields at **Burnt Rock Falls,** where the trail shoots up another 18 switchbacks. This exposed climb can be a scorcher, but it yields a full view of the tall **Crypt Falls** spilling from the hanging valley.

The trail appears to dead-end in the headwall, but a hidden route leads to a narrow, 3-meter (10-ft) steel ladder that climbs up to a tunnel. The low-clearance tunnel demands an awkward walk or crawl. It emerges onto a cliff with a steel cable to hold onto when crossing. Then the trail breaks into a tight cirque housing **Crypt Lake,** which drains from an underwater channel. The **international boundary** crosses the lake's southern end.

To catch the return boat, hikers speed down the trail en masse. Take the earliest and latest boats to have the maximum time for hiking, especially if you want to add on the loop around the lake (1.8 km/1.1 mi). For wildflowers, the trail is best in early July.

Bertha Lake
Distance: 11.4 km (7 mi) rt

Duration: 4 hours
Elevation gain: 451 meters (1,480 ft)
Effort: strenuous
Trail surface: narrow dirt path with roots and rocks
Trailhead: Bertha Lake

From the parking lot, the trail starts with a gradual climb along the western shore of Waterton Lake. Just before the junction, an overlook with a bench takes in the view south to Mount Cleveland, the highest peak in Glacier National Park. Taking the right fork at the junction, head across a steep hillside to **Lower Bertha Falls,** where pounding waters crash through bedrock. You can turn around here for a 6.4-km (4-mi) round-trip hike.

To continue to Bertha Lake, cross the bridge below the falls and climb incessant switchbacks up through the burned forest hillside beside **Upper Bertha Falls,** a larger sister of the lower falls. Soon the trail crests a knoll high above narrow **Bertha Lake.** To reach the shore, descend 160 meters (525 ft) to the campground near its outlet. To return, climb back up to the overlook of the lake and retrace your path back to town.

Waterton Lakeshore Trail to Goat Haunt
Distance: 13 km (8 mi) one-way
Duration: 4 hours
Elevation gain: minimal
Effort: easy-moderate
Trail surface: narrow dirt path with roots and rocks
Trailhead: Bertha Lake

Bordering the west lakeshore of Waterton Lake, the trail begins at the Bertha Lake Trailhead. After 1.5 km (1 mi), a junction divides the trail to Bertha Lake and the Waterton Lakeshore Trail. Turn left, dropping in a quick, steep descent to Bertha Bay Campground on the lake. The trail climbs up and down with intermittent lake views until the **international boundary** at 6.1 km (3.8 mi). The dock at **Boundary Bay** makes an idyllic lunch spot.

After the trail crosses the border, it becomes more level until entering the well-signed maze of trails at the end of Waterton Lake. Follow signs to Goat Haunt and catch the boat back to the Townsite. Before you leave in the morning, buy your return ticket with Waterton Shoreline Cruises. Bring your passport and file your trip with the CBP ROAM app before departing in the morning. You can also hike this route in reverse, by taking the boat first to Goat Haunt and then hiking back to Waterton Townsite.

Goat Haunt

To access the Goat Haunt trails in Glacier National Park, you must first take the **boat shuttle** (Waterton Shoreline Cruises, 403/859-2362, www.watertoncruise.com, daily June-late Sept., adults C$55 round-trip, kids C$27) from the marina in the Waterton Townsite. Day hikers bound for Goat Haunt trails need round-trip tickets: one for the 10am boat and a reserved spot on a return boat. Hikers using the boat need to bring **passports** and file trip plans with the **CBP ROAM** smartphone app the morning of their scheduled hike.

Goat Haunt Overlook
Distance: 3.2 km (1.9 mi) rt
Duration: 2 hours
Elevation gain: 257 meters (844 ft)
Effort: very strenuous
Trail surface: narrow dirt path with roots and rocks
Trailhead: behind the ranger station at Goat Haunt in Glacier National Park

This is a short but steep hike from the boat dock at Goat Haunt on Waterton Lake. Follow the paved trail past the first right-hand turn to a dirt trail and hike south toward Fifty Mountain on the Continental Divide Trail. At the signed junction, turn left. The trail climbs gently for a short distance before it turns straight up a steep uphill. It's a grunt, but the view is well worth the climb. At the **Goat Haunt Overlook,** you can gander down-lake to the Waterton Townsite and the Prince of Wales Hotel.

Rainbow Falls
Distance: 2.3 km (1.4 mi) rt
Duration: 1 hour
Elevation gain: minimal
Effort: easy
Trail surface: uneven dirt path with roots and rocks
Trailhead: behind the ranger station at Goat Haunt in Glacier National Park

Follow the paved trail to the first junction, taking the right fork onto dirt. The trail wanders through thick forests, filled with mosquitoes in early summer. Just before reaching the Waterton River, take a left turn at the signed junction, heading up the east bank toward **Rainbow Falls.** The falls is actually a series of cascades cutting troughs in the bedrock, but it's a great place to sit.

Kootenai Lakes
Distance: 9 km (5.6 mi) rt
Duration: 3-3.5 hours
Elevation gain: minimal
Effort: easy
Trail surface: uneven dirt path with roots and rocks
Trailhead: behind the ranger station at Goat Haunt in Glacier National Park

Kootenai Lakes attracts hikers thanks to frequent moose sightings and occasional sightings of nesting trumpeter swans. At Goat Haunt, follow the paved trail past the first right-hand turn to a dirt trail and hike on the Continental Divide Trail, heading south toward Fifty Mountain. The trail wanders through old-growth forest. At the signed junction, turn right toward the campground. When you reach the lakes, they look more like a widening of the river, with brushy clumps of willows in the middle. These are the attraction for the moose. Enjoy the view from the rocky beach or grassy bank. If you eat lunch here, do so on the beach or in the cooking area to protect the cleanliness of the tenting sites for those sleeping in bear country.

Akamina Parkway
Rowe Lakes and Lineham Ridge
Distance: 8.4-17.2 km (5.2-10.6 mi) rt

Duration: 2.5-6 hours

Elevation gain: 575-945 meters (1,886-3,100 ft)

Effort: moderate-strenuous

Trail surface: narrow dirt path with roots and loose rocks

Trailhead: Rowe Tamarack

This trail allows for three different destinations of varying lengths: Lower Rowe Lake, Upper Rowe Lakes, and Lineham Ridge. In July the route bursts with wildflowers: yellow arnica, paintbrush, and purple lupine. The climb starts through thin burned forest that cuts through avalanche paths, following Rowe Creek. At 3.9 km (2.4 mi), a spur trail splits off to **Lower Rowe Lake** (8.4 km/5.2 mi rt). For those wanting the shortest trek, turn around here.

Continuing on from the junction, the trail ascends into a broad meadow at the base of a giant cirque. After you cross the creek, the left fork climbs steep switchbacks to **Upper Rowe Lakes** (12.8 km/7.9 mi rt). This pair of scenic shallow lakes is fringed with wildflowers.

For Lineham Ridge, the right fork after the creek crossing swings around the cirque to climb from subalpine wildflower meadows into alpine tundra. Red argillite colors the mountainside. From the ridge, **Lineham Lakes** appear below. At the saddle below Mount Lineham, you can opt to climb off-trail east to the peak or continue on the rugged trail west up **Lineham Ridge** (17.2 km/10.6 mi rt). At the top, you can look down Blakiston Creek before retracing your route to the trailhead.

Carthew Summit and Alderson Lake

Distance: 20 km (12.5 mi) one-way from Akamina Parkway

Duration: 6-7 hours

Elevation gain: 439 meters (1,440 ft)

Effort: strenuous

Trail surface: narrow dirt path with roots and rocks

Trailhead: Cameron Lake

Preferred for its point-to-point route, this trail climbs to **Carthew Summit,** where alpine tundra stretches along a windswept ridge. Be prepared for strong winds, even on a sunny summer day. Some winds may even force you to crawl over the pass. From the summit, views span deep into Glacier National Park's interior.

From Cameron Lake, the trail switchbacks above the east side of the lake to a plateau containing **Summit Lake.** The path then arcs around a large basin gaining elevation until cresting Carthew Summit for expansive views. That's where the plunge begins, dropping steeply down a small ridge into a little hanging valley and along a pair of tarns rimmed with wildflowers in late July. As the trail crests the hanging valley, it drops steeply again to **Alderson Lake.** Once you depart the lake, avalanche chutes cut through the burned timbers en route to Cameron Falls at Waterton Townsite.

To do this hike as a point-to-point route ending at the Townsite, catch the **Cameron Express hiker shuttle** (403/859-2379, www.hikewaterton.com,

mid-June-Sept., reservations required) to Cameron Lake or set up your own shuttle. You can also skip the shuttle and hike out and back from the Townsite (19.3 km/12 mi rt, 1,023 m/3,356 ft elevation gain), but it demands much more climbing to reach the summit. The trail grunts up to Alderson Lake before climbing along a cliff wall to reach the pair of tarns. The final ascent to Carthew Summit creeps into alpine tundra inhabited only by tiny wildflowers. Enjoy the view and return via the same route.

Akamina Ridge, Forum Lake, and Wall Lake

Distance: 8.8-18.3 km (5.4-11.4 mi) rt
Duration: 3-7 hours
Elevation gain: 110-905 meters (361-2,970 ft)
Effort: moderate-strenuous
Trail surface: narrow dirt path with roots and rocks
Trailhead: Akamina Pass

This hike starts and ends in Waterton Lakes National Park, but crosses over the Continental Divide and into **Akamina-Kishinena Provincial Park.** Hikers looking for shorter adventures can choose either Wall Lake or Forum Lake as a destination, but the longer and more challenging Akamina Ridge Loop offers the best views. All three routes launch from the same trailhead and climb to **Akamina Pass** (3 km/1.9 mi rt) through the 2017 Kenow Fire zone. After a short distance, you'll come to a junction.

To hike to **Forum Lake** (8.8 km/5.4 mi rt), turn left. The trail climbs moderately up to the snowmelt-fed lake, surrounded by steep talus slopes. You'll see grizzly bear diggings in meadows around the basin and perhaps see the bears themselves. Give them a wide berth.

For **Wall Lake** (10.4 km/6.5 mi rt), turn right at the junction. The relatively level trail passes a backcountry campground and crosses streams before ascending to Wall Lake, which is set in a dramatic cirque tucked against abrupt limestone walls. A primitive trail arcs around the lake, where you can find beaches to enjoy.

hiking in the alpine tundra of Carthew Summit

The strenuous **Akamina Ridge Loop** (18.3 km/11.4 mi rt) combines both lakes with a spectacular ridge walk between them. From Forum Lake, follow the rough unmaintained trail that ascends the western ridge up through a rock band where you'll need to use your hands for climbing. Once above the band, the walking is easier as you work up to the ridge. At the ridge, the route rolls over peaks and knolls through alpine tundra rampant with miniature plants like pink moss campion struggling to survive. To the south, Glacier's remote Kintla Peak stands with Agassiz Glacier while a sea of peaks stretches in all directions. At the end of the ridge, the trail drops steeply back down to Wall Lake. From Wall Lake, hike back to the junction for the two lakes and return over Akamina Pass to the trailhead.

Backpacking

Backpackers in Waterton have two destination options: Waterton Lakes National Park or Glacier National Park accessed through Waterton (most routes start at Goat Haunt). Both destinations require permits that backpackers can get at the Waterton visitors center. For Glacier's trails, the visitors center can only issue permits for trips launching from Chief Mountain or Goat Haunt trailheads; payment must be by credit card.

For backcountry **camping** in Waterton, **wilderness use permits** (adults C$10 pp per night, ages 16 and younger free, C$12 reservation fee) can be picked up at the Waterton Lakes Visitor Centre 24 hours or less before your trip. Make **advance reservations** up to 90 days prior to your trip, starting April 1, by calling the visitors center (403/859-5133). For kids, the easiest trip is the Waterton Lakeshore

traversing Akamina Ridge

Trail; camp at Bertha Bay or Boundary Creek.

Tamarack Trail
39 kilometers (24 miles)
A few lakes tuck under the Continental Divide on the western boundary of Waterton. Launch from the Red Rock Canyon trailhead, hiking west along Bauerman Creek to Twin Lakes for the first night. Then go south to Lone Lake for the second night. The final day climbs over the knife-edged Lineham Ridge to round through a glacier-scoured cirque before descending Rowe Creek to the exit at the Rowe Lakes trailhead. Set up shuttles for the three-day trip through **Waterton Outdoor Adventures** (403/859-2379, www.hikewaterton.com).

Stoney Indian Pass
47 kilometers (29 miles)
Hiking the Waterton Lakeshore Trail launches this backpacking trip (4-6 days) over Stoney Indian Pass in

Glacier National Park. Lop off walking down Waterton Lake to Goat Haunt by hopping the boat run by **Waterton Shoreline Cruises** (403/859-2362, www.watertoncruise.com). Pick up a permit in Waterton, file trip plans with CBP ROAM, and take your passport. Spend the first night at Kootenai Lakes (KOO) watching moose. Then climb to Stoney Indian Pass (STO) for the second night, tucked below the Stoney Indian parapets. Split your remaining nights in campsites at lakes in the Mokowanis Valley: Mokowanis Lake (MOL), Glenns Lake Head (GLH) or Foot (GLF), Cosley Lake (COS), and Gable (GAB). Exit at Chief Mountain Customs. Make reservations for the shuttle from **Waterton Outdoor Adventures** (403/859-2379, www.hikewaterton.com) to return to Waterton.

Biking
All roadways in Waterton offer good cycling, but be ready to ride with cars at your elbows on narrow-cornered roads with minimal shoulders, especially Red Rock Parkway and Akamina Parkway. Be prepared to encounter bears on both roads. **Red Rock Parkway** (15 km/9.3 mi) offers a unique cycling opportunity in spring and fall, when the road is closed to vehicles. The paved **Kootenai Brown Trail** (7 km/4.3 mi) connects the park entrance with Waterton Townsite, offering the best family-friendly bicycling option with big scenery. For campers traveling by bicycle, campgrounds have bear-resistant storage containers.

Parks Canada levies heavy fines for riding on sidewalks, grass, or trails designated for hiking only. Alberta law requires children under age 18 to wear a helmet while bicycling. Given the narrow roads and the fact that most drivers are gaping at the scenery or looking for bears, and that winds can gust riders off bikes, it's a wise idea for riders of all ages to wear helmets.

Mountain Bike Trails

Four rough, unpaved trails in Waterton permit mountain biking. For current trail conditions, check with the visitors center. Get a complete list of all mountain biking trails at the visitors center. Here are two of the best:

Near the end of Akamina Parkway, **Akamina Pass Trail** (3 km/1.9 mi rt) climbs a stiff, steep slope to the Continental Divide, which is the boundary between Waterton Lakes National Park and Akamina-Kishinena Provincial Park, plus Alberta and British Columbia. From there, the trail winds to **Wall Lake** (10.4 km/6.4 mi rt) in the provincial park.

At the end of Red Rock Parkway, the **Snowshoe Trail** (16.4 km/10.2 mi rt) follows Bauerman Creek to the Snowshoe backcountry campground. An abandoned fire road with a fairly wide berth, the trail has some steep sections and creek fords for spice.

Rentals

Pat's Gas Station (224 Mount View Rd., 403/859-2266, www.patswaterton.com, C$20-30/hr) rents mountain bikes, tandem bikes, and e-bikes. Pat's also rents its famous two-person four-wheel surrey bikes for tootling around the Townsite; they're fun for a spin on the flat roads, but hills are difficult with only one gear. **Blakiston and Company** (102 Mount View Rd., 800/456-0772, www.blakistonandcompany.com, 9am-8pm daily mid-May-mid-Sept., shorter hours in shoulder seasons, C$35/hr) rents e-bikes.

Water Sports

Waterton Lakes National Park bans all motorized boats (except for those that are sealed and quarantined for 90 days). Parks Canada instituted the ban to protect the lakes and downstream waterways

Top to bottom: cycling the Kootenai Brown Trail; surrey rentals from Pat's Gas Station; windsurfing on Upper Waterton Lake

from aquatic invasive species. Hand-launched, human- or wind-powered watercraft are still allowed with a free required permit after a self-inspection; you can pick one up at the visitors center.

Waterton Lakes

Winds are frequently high on **Upper Waterton Lake;** you may want to hug the shoreline when the wind kicks up or paddle only when waters are calm. Be aware that whitecaps are common, with an average wind speed of 32 kph (20 mph). Novice paddlers will find calmer, more sheltered water on **Emerald Bay,** a great spot for launching that is just one block from the Blakiston rental shop. Strong paddlers can **overnight at backcountry camps** at Bertha Bay and Boundary Creek in Waterton, and Goat Haunt in Glacier. Get required wilderness camping permits and advanced reservations at the **Waterton Lakes Visitor Centre** (403/859-5133) for Bertha Bay and Boundary Creek (adults C$10 pp per night, ages 16 and under free, C$12 reservation fee) and for Goat Haunt (adults C$7 pp per night, C$40 advance reservation). All three campsites have docks, but you'll need to completely beach and secure boats at night due to high winds.

Because winds on Upper Waterton Lake often rage, expert sailboarders, kite surfers, and windsurfers launch from **Windsurfer Beach** on Waterton Avenue. No rentals are available, so bring your own gear including wet suits or dry suits, as the glacier-fed lake is freezing cold. You should know how to water-start and self-rescue; it's not a place for beginners.

Middle Waterton Lake, Lower Waterton Lake, and the **Dardanelles** (the waterway connecting the two lakes) have exceptional wildlife-watching, birding, and less-hefty gales. Hay Barn and Marquis Picnic Areas offer good put-ins for paddling these sections.

Rent canoes, single and tandem kayaks, and paddleboards from **Blakiston and Company** (102 Mount View Rd., 800/456-0772, www.blakiston andcompany.com, 9am-8pm daily mid May-mid-Sept., shorter hours in shoulder seasons, C$30-60/hr). The company also rents 6- and 10-person floats (C$60-85/hr). **Pat's Gas Station** (224 Mount View Rd., 403/859-2266, www.patswaterton. com, C$25/hr) rents single-person kayaks and paddleboards.

★ Cameron Lake

Cameron Lake is the ideal spot for paddling your own rig or a rental boat. Winds are often less cantankerous than on the larger lakes, and the views are tantalizing, especially with glassy water reflecting the mountains on the border of Canada and the United States. Avoid beaching at the southern half of the lake to protect the prime grizzly bear habitat there. **Cameron Lake Boat Rentals** (403/627-6643, www.cameronlakeboatrentals.com, 8am-6:30pm daily July-Aug., 9am-5pm daily June and Sept., C$30-45/hr) rents canoes, kayaks, paddleboards, paddleboats, and rowboats. Rates include life jackets and paddles.

Horseback Riding

Waterton's open grassland prairies flanking the mountains mean that you get big views on trail rides with **Alpine Stables** (off the park entrance road opposite the golf course, 403/859-2462 summer, 403/653-2089 winter, www.alpinestables. com, 9am-5pm daily May-Sept., C$50-200). The stables have small saddles and can accommodate kids as young as five years old. Reservations are highly recommended. Wear long pants and sturdy shoes or boots. One-hour rides depart on the hour for meadow and lakeshore tours, with 1.5- and 2-hour versions offered less frequently. Longer rides tour trails for 3-8 hours.

Golf

Focusing on your putting can be difficult with such huge scenery. And not only are sand traps a hazard, but sometimes

RECREATION

grizzly bears are, too. Located 3 km (1.8 mi) north of the Townsite, the 18-hole **Waterton Golf Course** (403/859-2114, golfwaterton.com, dawn-dusk daily May-Oct., C$75-90 with cart, C$50-55 without cart) is an original Stanley Thompson design like the Banff Springs and Jasper courses. The pro shop rents clubs, and a licensed clubhouse keeps guests fed and watered on its patio, which has outstanding views. Many of Waterton's hotels offer golf packages in May and after mid-September.

Food

In this remote resort oasis in a national park, food prices can be high. If you're camping or backpacking, consider bringing supplies with you, as groceries are limited. In late summer, blackflies descend for several weeks on the Townsite, even in restaurants. Just think of them as small wildlife. No dressing up is required

for dining; casual clothes, including hiking attire, are acceptable.

With a few exceptions, restaurants in the Townsite cluster along Waterton and Windflower Avenues. The two streets have a European feel with patio and sidewalk dining. Only Vimy's and Red Rock Trattoria stay open year-round; all other restaurants are open daily May-September. In spring and fall, some restaurants often shorten their hours or days. Many restaurants sell hiker lunches at C$16-20, perfect for taking on the trail.

Lodges

In the Bayshore Inn, the ★ **Lakeside Chophouse** (111 Waterton Ave., 403/859-2211, www.bayshoreinn.com, 7am-10pm daily) packages up scenery with fine dining. It is the only restaurant with outdoor patio seating on Waterton Lake. The dining room serves breakfast, lunch, dinner, light meals, international wines, and cocktails. Breakfast (C$10-22) brings on egg dishes and a daily buffet

trail ride with Alpine Stables

mid-summer. Lunch and dinner (C$13-50) feature burgers, sandwiches, salads, and an eclectic global cuisine. The after-5pm menu also adds on grilled aged AAA Alberta beef and bison steaks. Be sure to save room for wild Saskatoon berry pie. Reservations are recommended. The adjoining **Fireside Lounge** (noon-1am daily) also serves pizza, burgers, sandwiches, salads, and pastas.

At Waterton Lakes Lodge Resort, **Vimy's Lounge and Grill** (101 Clematis Ave., 403/627-9815 or 403/859-2150, www.watertonlakeslodge.com, 7am-10pm daily, shorter hours in winter) offers four dining options in summer: a lounge downstairs, an outside patio, upstairs dining with a view of Mount Cleveland, and outside upper deck dining. Breakfast (C$10-18) includes multiple variations on eggs Benedict. Lunch and dinner (C$19-40) have burgers, sandwiches, and salads, plus, in the evening, Alberta steaks and dinner entrées that rotate seasonally. It's also one place you can usually get the Canadian classic appetizer of poutine: homemade french fries drowning in cheese curds and gravy.

The historic **Prince of Wales Hotel** (844/868-7474, front desk 403/859-2231, www.glacierparkcollection.com, daily early June-mid-Sept.) puts on a regal view of Waterton Lake from massive floor-to-ceiling windows in the **Royal Stewart Dining Room.** Breakfast (6:30am-10am, C$12-20) specializes in eggs Benedict and omelets, while the lunch (11:30am-2pm, C$12-20) and dinner (5pm-9:30pm, C$18-38) menus introduce classics from Great Britain such as bangers and mash and Canadian prime rib. Reservations are recommended in midsummer. The British atmosphere goes into full swing with **afternoon tea** (noon-4pm daily, adults C$33, kids C$18) in the hotel lobby overlooking Waterton Lake. Make reservations for this full meal of finger sandwiches and a sugar-fest of desserts: pastries, fruits, and berries. Pour your tea from signature porcelain servers. It's a unique experience, but mostly about the atmosphere. You can also enjoy the hotel views down-lake with a lighter meal and cocktail from the **Windsor Lounge** (11:30am-10pm).

Italian

In Waterton Glacier Suites the contemporary ★ **Red Rock Trattoria** (107 Windflower Ave., 403/859-2004, www.redrockcafe.ca, 5pm-9pm daily, C$18-42) serves up classic Italian appetizers, pastas, and entrées built with fresh and sometimes local ingredients. Order a bottle of fine Italian wine to accompany your multicourse meal and top it off with tiramisu. Make reservations as seating is limited.

Two pizza restaurants, which sit next to each other on Windflower Avenue, offer seating indoors or outdoors. They also make to-go pizzas for your motel, beach, or campsite. ★ **49 Degrees North** (303 Windflower Ave., 403/859-3000, www.49degreesnorthpizza.com, noon-10pm daily, C$12-30) makes pizza and calzone doughs fresh daily, including gluten-free, and bakes in a stone-deck-fired oven. It also serves soup, salads, and appetizers. Next door, the longtime Waterton staple **Pizza of Waterton** (305 Windflower Ave., 403/859-2660, www. pizzaofwaterton.com, 7am-9pm daily, C$12-30) serves handcrafted pizzas, sandwiches, wraps, hiker lunches, beer, wine, and cocktails out of Pearl's Café. Breakfast (until 11am) has waffles, eggs, and sandwiches.

Mexican

The graffiti-walled **Taco Bar** (310 Windflower Ave., 403/915-2294, watertontacos.wixsite.com/thetacobar, 11:30am-9:30pm daily summer, shorter hours spring and fall, cash only) brings the flavors of Mexico to Canada with burritos, tacos, and bowls filled with meat or veggies, beans, and cheese. They also serve gluten-free and kid-sized options. The crisp citrus slaw and fresh-made salsas add zing.

Pubs

With indoor or patio seating, the **Thirsty Bear Kitchen & Bar** (111 Waterton Ave., 403/859-2211, www.thirstybearwaterton. com, 11am-1am Sun.-Thurs., 11am-2am Fri.-Sat., C$16-22) serves pub fare such as burgers, wraps, fish tacos, and yam fries, accompanied by Alberta craft beers and Caesars (similar to a Bloody Mary). It doubles as the town's only nightclub, with live music and dancing usually on weekends.

Family-Friendly

Two family restaurants anchor opposite ends of the same block. Their appeal comes from large, diverse menus with broad Canadian choices for breakfast, lunch, and dinner plus indoor or shaded outdoor sidewalk dining, and beer, wine, and cocktails. To decide between them, browse their outdoor menus and assess waiting lines. Both serve up omelets,

sandwiches, salads, burgers, kids' meals, gluten-free and vegetarian options, and lighter or heavier meals. **Zum's Eatery** (116 Waterton Ave., 403/859-2388, zums. ca, 8am-9:30pm daily, C$12-26) specializes in crispy fried chicken, pub-style fish-and-chips, and baby back ribs in its house Guinness barbecue sauce. The signature dessert is a tasty Saskatoon berry pie. In addition to lighter meals, **Trappers Mountain Grill** (106 Waterton Ave., 403/859-2445, 8am-8pm daily, C$12-45) serves up barbecue with a smokehouse process that finishes with broiling.

Cafés and Quick Bites

Waterton is full of tiny eateries (C$5-15) where you can enjoy varied flavors for dining in or grabbing portable food to go for the road or trail. A local favorite with outdoor picnic tables for seating, ★ **Wieners of Waterton** (301 Windflower Ave., 403/859-0007, www. wienersofwaterton.com, 7am-9pm daily) knows how to pile large, high-end sausages with choose-your-own fresh toppings on homemade buns. Hot dogs come from local butchers, and sweet potato fries are served with tasty homemade sauces.

With the scent of sweet waffles wafting out into the street, **Waffleton** (301 Windflower Ave., 403/339-2131, 7:30am-2:30pm daily) tops fresh-baked buttermilk and Belgian liege waffles with fruits, whipped cream, ice cream, frozen Greek yogurt, Nutella, or multiple other toppings.

Accommodations and Camping

In Waterton, all hotels sit within walking distance in the compact town. No matter where you stay, you can walk to restaurants, shopping, boat tours, or hiking. (Staying at Prince of Wales Hotel requires a 15-minute walk to town; all others are within a block or two of restaurants.)

All hotels have wireless internet access. Six hotels (except Prince of Wales and Northland Lodge) outfit rooms with televisions, but channels are limited to just a handful. Reservations are absolutely mandatory for midsummer. Only two hotels have views of Waterton Lake: Prince of Wales and Bayshore Inn. Only Waterton Lakes Lodge and Waterton Glacier Suites are open year-round; all others are summer only.

Rates are highest in July and August. If you're in search of a budget option, drive 35 minutes north to Pincher Creek for less-expensive chain motels. Many of Waterton's hotels offer golf and activity packages. During the off-season (May-early June, late Sept.-Oct., and winter), most properties drop their rates substantially, making travel cheaper at a crowd-free time.

Lodges and Bed-and-Breakfasts

Located on a bluff above Waterton Lake, historic ★ **Prince of Wales Hotel** (7.6 km/4.7 mi south of the park entrance station, 403/859-2231 or 844/868-7474, www.glacierparkcollection.com, late May-late Sept., C$250-350, suite C$600-800) is a seven-story wonder named for the prince who later became King Edward VIII. Kilted bellhops greet visitors, and high tea is served in the afternoon. Its lobby, with floor-to-ceiling windows, swings with a huge rustic chandelier. Lakeview rooms allow you to shower while looking into Glacier National Park, and mountain-view guest rooms let you spy on bighorn sheep. But despite its grand facade, the building is old, creaky, and thin-walled, and the upper stories seem to sway in high winds. Be prepared for tiny sinks and small baths, many installed in what were once closets. The guest rooms have phones but no other amenities. A cantankerous elevator

Top to bottom: Lakeside Chophouse; Red Rock Trattoria; Prince of Wales Hotel

accesses upper floors but requires a bell-hop to run, rendering it unavailable at all hours. Top-floor lodgers get a work-out climbing the stairs. A restaurant, a gift shop selling English bone china and Waterford crystal, and a lounge sur-round the lobby. You can reach town via a 5 minute drive or a 15-minute walk down a trail.

With mountain views from many of the rooms, the **Waterton Lakes Lodge Resort** (101 Clematis Ave., 403/859-2150 or 888/985-6343, www. watertonlakeslodge.com, C$170-360 summer, C$120-270 winter) has 80 modern, air-conditioned guest rooms. Some include kitchenettes, suites, fire-places, jet tubs, or are pet-friendly. The pleasant accommodations are in 11 two-story chalets. For 2nd-floor units, you'll need to climb the stairs, but some upstairs rooms include skylights and vaulted ceilings. Guests get free use of the on-site Waterton Health Club and Recreation Centre pool, hot tub, and workout room. The resort also has a res-taurant and bar.

The 17-room **Crandell Mountain Lodge** (102 Mount View Rd., 403/859-2288 or 866/859-2288, www.crandell mountainlodge.com, mid-Apr.-mid-Oct., C$110-350) is tucked beneath its name-sake peak. The two-story circa-1940 inn has a variety of country-themed guest rooms, from standard rooms up to three-room suites with full kitchens and fire-places. In a private garden area, a huge deck with a barbecue and lounge chairs begs for afternoon relaxation.

For park-history buffs, the quiet **Northland Lodge** (408 Evergreen Ave., 403/859-2353, www.northlandlodge.ca, mid-May-early Oct., C$150-275, two-night min. in summer) holds appeal. Louis Hill, builder of the Prince of Wales Hotel and many of Glacier National Park's historic hotels, constructed the Swiss-style lodge as his private residence circa 1948, although he never lived here. Two of the lodge's nine guest rooms share

a bath, and the rest have private baths; guest rooms are split among three lev-els. A large balcony is great for soaking up the views with coffee and homemade muffins with Saskatoon berry jam in the morning. A 10-minute walk leads to shopping and restaurants.

Motels

One of only two hotels on Waterton Lake, ★ **The Bayshore Inn** (111 Waterton Ave., summer 403/859-2211 or 888/527-9555, www.bayshoreinn.com, May-early Oct., C$160-460) offers lakefront guest rooms with prime views from private balconies. Family rooms, deluxe suites, and pet-friendly rooms are available, along with less-pricey guest rooms with mountain views. The complex has a lounge, a sa-loon, restaurants, a hot tub, a gift shop, satellite internet access, an ice cream shop, and the Serenity Spa. Located adjacent to the marina, it sits on the Townsite's main block that houses most of the shopping. Lakeside rooms overlook lawn, trees, and the lake.

With mountain views and large rooms, ★ **Waterton Glacier Suites** (107 Windflower Ave., 403/859-2004 or 866/621-3330, www.watertonsuites.com, C$175-380 summer, C$130-200 winter) has 26 units with private balconies for enjoying the mountain scenery. Room amenities include fridges, microwaves, air-conditioning, and whirlpool tubs. Some guest rooms have gas fireplaces, and 2nd-floor units require walking stairs.

Sporting red metal roofs (you won't get lost looking for these), the aging **Aspen Village Inn** (111 Windflower Ave., 403/859-2255 or 888/859-8669, www.aspenvillageinn.com, May-early Oct., C$120-350) combines a two-story motel with 16 cottages that accommo-date 2-8 people. Some are pet-friendly or come with kitchens. The units sur-round mowed lawns, a playground, and an outdoor barbecue picnic area. Complimentary access to the Waterton

Health Club and Recreation Centre is included.

The ★ **Bear Mountain Motel** (208 Mount View Rd., 403/859-2366, bearmountainmotel.com, mid-May-Sept., C$115-260), a 1960s wood-and-masonry motel, has 36 small one- and two-bedroom units, several of which have tiny kitchenettes and living rooms with hide-a-beds. Expect clean, basic guest rooms with no frills and a pay phone near the office; these are the most affordable rooms in town. A shared patio has a microwave, grills, and picnic tables.

Campgrounds
Inside the Park

Waterton Lakes National Park campgrounds have flush toilets, drinking water, kitchen shelters, and bear-resistant food storage lockers. With the exception of the Townsite campground, most campground sites have fire rings, and firewood is supplied, which costs C$9 per site for a burn permit. Check online (www.pc.gc.ca) for campground details.

With the entrance on Evergreen Avenue, the ★ **Waterton Townsite Campground** (Apr.-Oct., unserviced sites C$23-28, electrical or full hookups C$33-40) is citified with a mowed lawn, but it sits on prime real estate with gorgeous views and within walking distance to restaurants in town. The huge campground borders the beach and a trail leading to the Townsite. A few trees shade some sites, but most are open, offering little privacy. Go for spots nearest the lake in the G loop but be prepared for winds. For more sheltered scenery, go for the Cameron Creek E loop sites. Fires are only permitted in the kitchen shelters, but the campground includes hot showers, dishwashing stations, a dump station, and several restroom buildings. In midsummer, the campground fills by late morning. Make

Top to bottom: Waterton Glacier Suites; The Bayshore Inn; Waterton Townsite Campground

◈ Side Trips from Waterton

Akamina-Kishinena Provincial Park

Where Waterton Lakes National Park meets the Continental Divide, **Akamina-Kishinena Provincial Park** (205/489-8540, www.gov.bc.ca/bcparks) begins. The small park flanks the international boundary of Montana's Glacier National Park and runs westward to the North Fork of the Flathead River. It's part of the same slice of the Rockies that provides corridors for grizzly bears and wolves. Geologic wonders display themselves in **Forum Peak**'s 1.3-billion-year-old sedimentary rocks, and rare plants like the pygmy poppy grow here.

This remote park is accessible only on foot from Akamina Parkway in Waterton Lakes National Park. From Waterton, hikers can access the park via a circa-1920 trail that starts at **Akamina Pass.** The **Akamina Creek backcountry campground** (10 sites, discovercamping.ca, year-round, C$5 pp per night) has tent pads, an outhouse, and food storage. From the Akamina Pass Trailhead, hike 2.4 km (1.5 mi). The signed campground spur trail leads to the campground. From the campground, you can hike to Forum Lake, Wall Lake, or do the strenuous Akamina Ridge Loop.

Island Lake Lodge in Fernie

Fernie

Located on BC 3 west of the Continental Divide and Waterton, this mountain town tucks below the jagged Lizard Range. Locals crowd into **The Curry Bowl** (931 7th Ave., 250/423-

reservations (877/737-3783, 519/826-5391 outside North America, reservation.pc.gc.ca, C$12 per reservation) starting in January.

On the opposite side of Mount Crandell from the Townsite, **Crandell Mountain Campground** (mid-May-early Sept., C$23-28) is located 6.8 km (4.2 mi) up the Red Rock Parkway. It nestles along Blaikiston Creek with mountain views. Due to significant damage from the 2017 Kenow Fire, the campground is under construction with the aim of re-opening in 2022. Check online for the status of this campground including RV limits, updated facilities, and reserveable sites.

On Chief Mountain Highway, the first-come, first-served **Belly River Campground** (mid-May-early Sept., C$16) has 24 pleasant sites for small RVs and tents in aspen groves with hand-pumped well water and both pit and flush toilets. Some sites are shaded, and some are in meadows. It is a good location for watching wildlife and birding, and it is the closest campground to the Chief Mountain border crossing for those who want to scamper across the boundary first thing in the morning. The campground is 26 km (16 mi) from the Waterton Townsite.

In winter, when all other campsites have closed, sites are available at the first-come, first-served **Pass Creek Winter Campground** (Nov.-Apr., free). Located along the park entrance road, the eight sites offer primitive camping with only a

2695, www.currybowlfernie.com) for fresh southeast Asian food. Just outside of town you'll find skiing, hiking, and mountain biking fun.

Fernie Alpine Resort (5339 Ski Hill Rd., 800/258-7669, skifernie.com) runs lifts in winter for skiing and snowboarding. In summer, the lift riders are mountain bikers and hikers. From the summit, the **Timber Ridge Loop Trail** (5 km/3 mi rt, 3-4 hrs) trots along the top of the Lizard Range, following orange markers and navigating a steep cliff with a cable handhold. Broad views take in mountains and the town of Fernie far below.

On a back road out of Fernie, the upscale **Island Lake Lodge** (250/423-3700 or 888/422-8754, www.islandlakelodge.com) has quiet lodge rooms and dining on Island Lake. In winter, guided snowcat-skiing adventures let you glide through powder in the Lizards. Summer has outstanding trail hiking opportunities.

Frank Slide

In 1903, part of Turtle Mountain fell away in an immense landslide that buried part of Frank, a mining town. Today, AB 3 drives right through the site of the landslide, with giant rocks from the slide on either side of the road. West of Waterton, **Frank Slide Interpretive Centre** (Crowsnest Pass, 403/562-7388, frankslide.ca, 10am-5pm daily year-round) has exhibits and shows movies about the event. Outside, interpretive trails tour parts of the boulder field.

Head-Smashed-In Buffalo Jump

For those coming from Calgary, **Head-Smashed-In Buffalo Jump** (275068 Hwy. 785, Fort Macleod, 403/553-2731, headsmashedin.ca), northeast of Waterton, is one of the best stops you can make. The UNESCO World Heritage Site shares the early life of Indigenous people, namely the Blackfoot, who depended on bison for survival. Buffalo jumps were used to harvest bison. The interpretive center's interior is laid out so you can follow the entire process of bison harvesting. Outside, trails go to archaeological cliff jump sites. Interpretive programs are held daily in summer. The site is 18 km (11 mi) northwest of Fort Macleod.

---

pit toilet and a woodstove (firewood provided) in the unlighted kitchen shelter. Water from the creek may be boiled or purified for use. Pass Creek is 5 km (3.1 mi) from the Townsite.

Outside the Park

Often windy, **Crooked Creek Campground** (AB 5, 6 km/3.7 mi east of the park entrance, 403/653-1100, crooked creekcampground.ca, mid-Apr.-early Oct., C$25 tents, C$28-45 RVs) has 80 close-knit sites adjacent to the highway in a grassy setting. Amenities include flush toilets, showers, Wi-Fi, a dump station, a cook shack, laundry, ice, fire rings, and firewood. Reservations start mid-January.

Transportation and Services

Emergency Services

For emergencies, dial 911 or contact the **Royal Canadian Mounted Police** (RCMP, 202 Waterton Ave., 403/859-2244 or 403/627-2113) during summer months or **Parks Canada Wardens** (215 Mount View Rd., 403/859-2224) year-round. The nearest hospitals are 50 km (31 mi) away: **Pincher Creek Health Centre** (1222 Bev McLachlin Dr., Pincher Creek, 403/627-1234) and **Cardston Health Centre** (144 2nd St. W., Cardston, 403/653-5234). To contact the park's emergency ambulance, call 403/859-2636.

Gas and Vehicle Charging Stations

Pat's Gas Station (224 Mount View Rd., 403/859-2266, www.patswaterton. com) is much more than a place to gas up or buy propane for the RV. Pat can perform minor car repairs, but go to Pincher Creek for serious vehicle repairs. The parking lot at the marina (224 Mount View Rd.) has an **electric vehicle charging station.**

Currency

Due to Waterton's proximity to the international border, most businesses, including restaurants, shops, and lodges, will accept U.S. currency; however, return change will be given in Canadian currency. For conversions, most businesses use the bank exchange rate, but some have their own policies. Use a credit card as much as possible to get the bank exchange rate. Waterton has **no banks;** the nearest banking services are in Cardston and Pincher Creek.

Cell Service and Internet Access

Cell phones can get reception in the Townsite, but not on the internal parkway roads or at Goat Haunt. **Waterton Wi-Fi** services restaurants, motels, and the campground with two options. The **free service** offers limited speeds and intermittently cuts out, but it's enough to get a few emails and look up the weather; the **fee service** has faster speeds and is more dependable.

Tours

Waterton Shoreline Cruises (at the marina at the junction of Mount View Rd. and Waterton Ave., 403/859-2362, www. watertoncruise.com, 10am, 1pm, 4pm, and 7pm daily July-Aug., 10am and 1pm daily May-June and Sept.-early Oct., adults C$55 round-trip, kids C$27) operates the historic *International* on Upper Waterton Lake. During the two-hour tour on the wooden 200-passenger boat, which has been cruising here since 1927, knowledgeable guides punctuate their patter with humor. For the best views, go for a sunny seat on the boat's top deck. If the weather is brisk, just bundle up. **June-late September,** the boat usually docks for 30 minutes at Goat Haunt, allowing enough time to walk to the ranger station pavilion to see the full length of the lake. Shoulder season launches, which are often on the *Miss Waterton* instead, do not stop at Goat Haunt. Buy tickets at least one hour in advance; to guarantee space, buy them a day in advance.

Getting Around
Driving and Parking

In Waterton Townsite, find **public parking lots** at the marina, visitors center, picnic areas, trailheads, and Cameron Falls. Large public lots sit at **Cameron Lake** at the end of Akamina Parkway and **Red Rock Canyon** at the end of Red Rock Parkway.

Shuttles
Overland Shuttles

Waterton Outdoor Adventures (214 Mount View Rd., 403/859-2378, www. hikewaterton.com, daily June-Sept., C$30-50 pp) runs scheduled and custom **hiker shuttles** from their location in town. Make reservations online to be guaranteed a seat. They also run shuttles to the Tamarack Trail for point-to-point hikes. Shuttle riders returning to Waterton must pay their own park entry fees. The **Cameron Express Shuttle** (departs 7:30am and 9am daily late May-mid-Sept., $18) goes to the Carthew Summit Trailhead at Cameron Lake. Mountain bikers can take this shuttle to ride the Akamina Pass trails and then ride the road downhill back to town.

Water Shuttles

Waterton Shoreline Cruises (403/859-2362, www.watertoncruise.com) operates two boat services that serve as hiker shuttles to trailheads. The **Crypt Lake**

Water Shuttle (daily late May-early Oct., C$28) departs from the marina for a 15-minute ride across Upper Waterton Lake to Crypt Landing, where the Crypt Lake trail begins. Shuttles depart the marina at 10am; earlier departures are added to the schedule June-early September at 8:30am and 9am. Return boats leave Crypt Landing at 5:30pm, with a 4pm boat added in summer. Purchase tickets a day in advance or at least one hour before departure.

The tour boat to **Goat Haunt** (daily June-late Sept., adults C$55 round-trip kids C$27) also functions as a hiker shuttle. It accesses trailheads in northern Glacier and provides transportation back to Waterton after hiking the Lakeshore Trail to Goat Haunt. Buy your return ticket in the morning before hiking down the lake. Day hikers bound for Goat Haunt trails need round-trip tickets: one for the 10am boat and a reserved spot for a selected return boat. Hikers using the boat need to bring passports and file trip plans with the CBP ROAM smartphone app the morning of their scheduled hike.

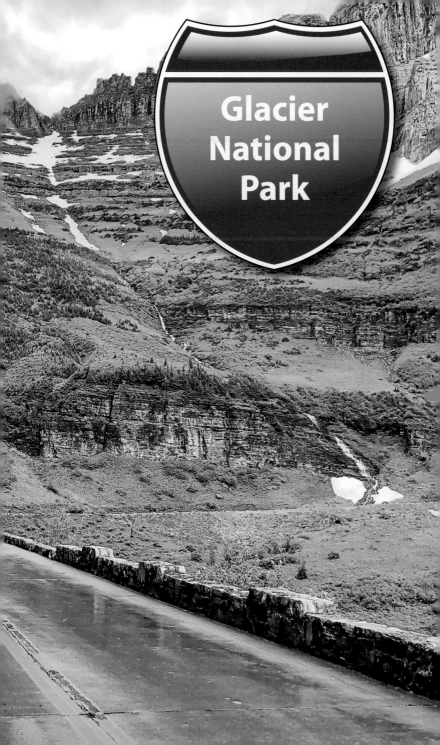

Glacier
National
Park

Highlights

★ **Leap into Lake McDonald:** Take a refreshing swim in the park's largest lake, paddle its clear waters, or tour on a historic wooden boat below its peaks (page 273).

★ **Visit Lake McDonald Lodge:** Sit in a rocker on the back porch of this historic lodge with a hunting motif in the lobby that harkens back to an earlier era (page 273).

★ **Touch the Continental Divide at Logan Pass:** At the highest point on Going-to-the-Sun Road, waters stream toward both the Pacific and Atlantic Oceans (page 273).

★ **Stay at Many Glacier Hotel:** Overnight at the park's grandest lodge set on the shore of Swiftcurrent Lake at the hub of multiple valleys with trails (page 276).

★ **Take a Boat Tour in Many Glacier:** Hop on a boat tour that crosses two lakes with unbeatable views. Sometimes moose or bears can be seen along the shore (page 277).

★ **Cruise Going-to-the-Sun Road:** Tour this stunning road as it cuts through immense cliffs and glacier-carved mountains dripping with waterfalls (page 278).

★ **Hike Highline Trail:** Traverse this high-elevation path along the Continental Divide to historic **Granite Park Chalet** (page 282).

★ **Trek to Hidden Lake Overlook:** Follow the trail to look down at Hidden Lake, perhaps spotting baby mountain goats en route (page 283).

★ **Plunge into Iceberg Lake:** Swim with icebergs, if you dare, in this utterly frigid lake that gleams with ice floating in blue waters (page 285).

★ **See Grinnell Glacier:** Hike to the park's most-visited glacier before it melts completely (page 287).

Glacier National Park is the undisputed "Crown of the Continent." It's a place where the earth's forces have left their imprints on the landscape with jagged arêtes, red pinnacles,

and glacier-carved basins. Acres of lush green parkland plunge from jagged summits. Waterfalls roar, ice cracks, and rockfall echoes in scenery still under the paintbrush of change.

In this rugged national park, grizzly bears and wolves top the food chain. Mountain goats prance on precarious ledges. Wolverines romp in high glacial cirques. Bighorn sheep graze in alpine meadows while pikas shriek nearby.

The Continental Divide splits Glacier into the west side and the east side. Thick evergreen forests dominate the west, the historical lands of the Kootenai, Pend Oreille, and Flathead peoples. Wildflower meadows are interspersed between aspen parklands on the east side, which was the original land of the Blackfeet Nation.

Slicing through the park's heart, the historic Going-to-the-Sun Road twists and turns on a narrow climb. Tunnels, arches, and bridges lead sightseers to precipices where seemingly no road could go, allowing anyone to experience Glacier's alpine splendor. Hiking trails cross beneath frigid waterfalls and over high passes with blue-green lakes strung like pearls along glaciated valleys. After dark the Milky Way sprawls above in this dark sky park. You can absorb the dramatic scenery through tours on historic boats or iconic red buses, or simply watch wildlife from the deck of idyllic Many Glacier Hotel.

Planning Your Time

In **Glacier National Park** (406/888-7800, www.nps.gov/glac), you can sightsee the entire Going-to-the-Sun Road over and back in **one day.** But you'll only have time for a short hike or two (if you can find parking). Most visitors to Glacier plan to stay **3-7 days,** splitting time between the park's east and west sides. Different segments of the park offer varied experiences with scads of hiking trails. Aim to split your time between the east side and west side of the park, with at least a day to get into more remote parts.

Without stopping for sightseeing, you'll need **two hours** to drive the Sun Road **one way** from Apgar to St. Mary. Packing a lunch alleviates waiting in restaurant lines (and there are no food services in the alpine section, from Avalanche to Rising Sun). Because the Logan Pass parking lot fills to capacity from 6am to 6pm in summer, consider taking a **tour bus** rather than driving yourself. You can absorb the scenery better, and your bus is guaranteed parking at Logan Pass and other stops. Be aware: On busy summer days, Going-to-the-Sun Road draws far more than double the amount of cars than parking spaces. Bring your patience and plan accordingly for sightseeing or hiking.

In the **lower elevations** of the park, campgrounds, lodging, and restaurants are generally open **June through September.** July and August are the busiest months, with September close behind. Since higher elevation trails usually are buried by snow until mid-July (and sometimes the Sun Road doesn't open until July), crowds can be bigger in June in low-elevation valleys. Once the road is open, expect big crowds all along it.

Driving in Glacier National Park is not easy. Narrow roads built for cars in

Glacier National Park

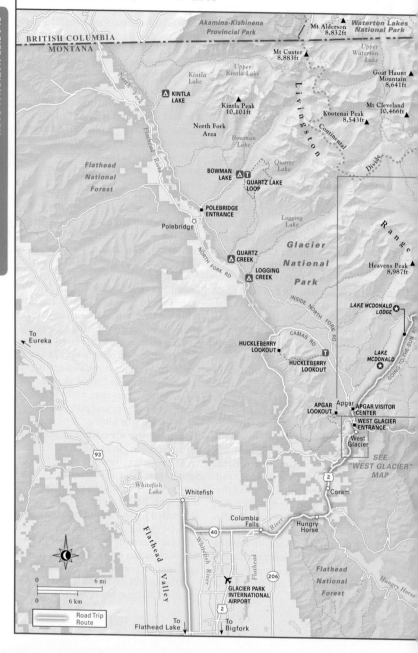

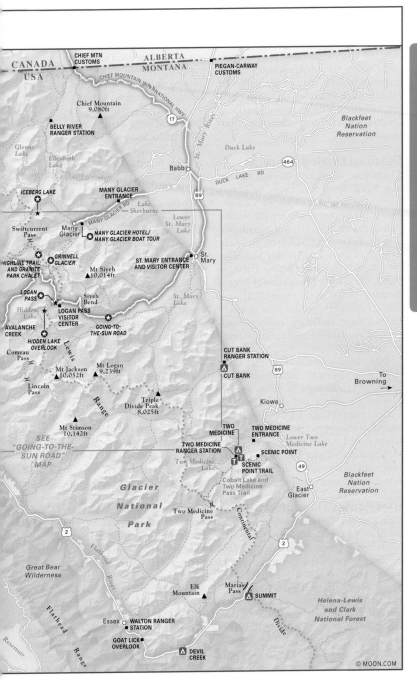

CANADA
USA

CHIEF MTN
CUSTOMS

ALBERTA
MONTANA

PIEGAN-CARWAY
CUSTOMS

CHIEF MOUNTAIN INTERNATIONAL HWY

Chief Mountain
9,080ft

17

St. Mary River

Blackfeet
Nation
Reservation

Glenns
Lake

BELLY RIVER
RANGER STATION

Elizabeth
Lake

Duck Lake

464

Babb

DUCK LAKE RD

89

ICEBERG LAKE

MANY GLACIER
ENTRANCE

Lake
Sherburne

Swiftcurrent
Pass

MANY GLACIER RD

Many
Glacier

MANY GLACIER HOTEL/
MANY GLACIER BOAT TOUR

Lower
St. Mary
Lake

GRINNELL
GLACIER

HIGHLINE TRAIL
AND GRANITE
PARK CHALET

ST. MARY ENTRANCE
AND VISITOR CENTER

St.
Mary

Mt Siyeh
10,014ft

LOGAN
PASS

Siyeh
Bend

St. Mary
Lake

Hidden
Lake

LOGAN PASS
VISITOR
CENTER

GOING-TO-
THE-SUN ROAD

AVALANCHE
CREEK

Lewis

HIDDEN LAKE
OVERLOOK

Comeau
Pass

Mt Jackson
10,052ft

Mt Logan
9,239ft

CUT BANK
RANGER STATION

Lincoln
Pass

Range

Triple
Divide Peak
8,025ft

CUT BANK

89

To
Browning

Kiowa

Mt Stimson
10,142ft

SEE
"GOING-TO-THE-
SUN ROAD"
MAP

TWO
MEDICINE

TWO MEDICINE
ENTRANCE

Lower Two
Medicine Lake

TWO MEDICINE
RANGER STATION

SCENIC POINT

Two Medicine
Lake

SCENIC
POINT TRAIL

49

Glacier

Cobalt Lake and
Two Medicine
Pass Trail

East
Glacier

Blackfeet
Nation
Reservation

National

Two Medicine
Pass

Park

2

Continental

2

Flathead River

Great Bear
Wilderness

Marias
Pass

SUMMIT

Helena-Lewis
and Clark
National Forest

Elk
Mountain

Flathead

Divide

Reservoir

Range

Essex

WALTON RANGER
STATION

GOAT LICK
OVERLOOK

DEVIL
CREEK

© MOON.COM

the 1930s barely fit today's SUVs, much less RVs and trailers. With no shoulders and sharp curves, roads require reduced speeds and shifting into second gear on extended descents to avoid burning brakes. Many visitors prefer taking **park shuttles** to avoid driving and the hassle of finding parking. Shuttles are also convenient for point-to-point hikes.

Seasonal Driving Concerns

The alpine segment of **Going-to-the-Sun Road,** from Avalanche to Rising Sun, including Logan Pass, opens when plows clear the road, repair winter damage, and reinstall log guardrails, sometime from mid-June to mid-July. The road closes again for the winter in mid-October. Before driving, check the park's **Recreational Access Display** (www.nps.gov/applications/glac/dashboard) for real-time status of the Sun Road, including weather, campground availability, and major parking lot availability.

Snow, avalanches, and weather make driving on Going-to-the-Sun Road unpredictable, although its western tail is plowed all winter to Lake McDonald Lodge. Even though US 2 is open year-round, it's snowy in winter and sometimes closed due to avalanches. Chains may be required over Marias Pass on the route; studded tires are an acceptable alternative but aren't required.

Best Routes Through the Park

Going-to-the-Sun Road bisects the park from east to west. **US 2** hugs Glacier's southern border. Both are two-lane roads; however, the seasonal Going-to-the-Sun Road (mid-June-mid-Oct.) is the more difficult drive than year-round US 2. The Sun Road does not permit RVs or vehicles with trailers over 21 feet (6.4 m) long or 10 feet (3 m) tall. This is due to the narrow roadway, tights curves, cliff walls, and rock overhangs. To cross between the east and west sides of Glacier, large RVs must use US 2.

Bicyclists are restricted on the west side of the Sun Road in July and August from 11am to 4pm. This includes both directions along Lake McDonald and uphill only from Avalanche to Logan Pass.

Reservations and Where to Stay

In 2021, Glacier began requiring tickets for entry to **Going-to-the-Sun Road** during peak hours to help ease overcrowding. Find current ticketing policies on the park's website. **Reservations** (www.recreation.gov, $2/vehicle) are available 60 days in advance, but they go fast. (Some tickets are held in reserve and released two days ahead.) You'll need to pay the park entry fee even with a reservation. If you have activity or lodging reservations on the Sun Road, you won't need an entry ticket.

Glacier has **seven lodges** and **13 campgrounds** within its boundaries. Anchoring Going-to-the-Sun Road on either end, **West Glacier** and **St. Mary** are gateway towns outside the park. Both have lodges, restaurants, and campgrounds that only operate over the summer. West Glacier is where most guide companies are based. St. Mary is on the Blackfeet Nation's reservation. **East Glacier** is an eat-and-sleep place on the Blackfeet Nation's reservation that most people use as a base camp for exploring Two Medicine.

Advance reservations for all in-park lodgings are **imperative,** especially for July and August. Contact **Xanterra** (855/733-4522, www.glaciernationalparklodges.com) **13 months** in advance for Many Glacier Hotel, Lake McDonald Lodge, Rising Sun Motor Inn, Swiftcurrent Motor Inn, and Apgar Village Inn. Make reservations **13-16 months** ahead with **Pursuit Glacier Park Collection** (844/868-7474, www.glacierparkcollection.com) for Apgar Village Lodge and Motel Lake McDonald.

One Day in Glacier National Park

Glacier's biggest attraction is the 50-mile (81-km) **Going-to-the-Sun Road.** From West Glacier or St. Mary, the drive on the historic road over Logan Pass yields a taste of the park's grandeur, with waterfalls, immense glacier-carved valleys, and serrated peaks. To beat the crowds at Logan Pass, go there first thing, and then tour the west and east sides of the road. Pack a lunch to spend your time in the scenery, and plan to drive over and back for the full experience.

Morning

Depart early (by 6-6:30am) to drive directly to **Logan Pass,** since the parking lot often fills by 7am. At the pass, nab a photo of the Continental Divide sign, tour the small visitors center, and walk the paved self-guided interpretive trails. Climb the boardwalk and trail to **Hidden Lake Overlook** for views of Hidden Lake.

If you want to avoid the stress of getting a parking spot at Logan Pass, take a **red bus tour** (www.glaciernationalparklodges.com) or the Blackfeet-led **Sun Tour bus** (www.glaciersuntours.com). You can soak up the scenery rather than focusing on driving the narrow, cliffy road. Plus, tour buses get **guaranteed parking** at Logan Pass.

Afternoon

After departing the pass, pull over at **Oberlin Bend Overlook** to take in the views of the road's west side. Stop at **Big Bend** to see waterfalls and **The Loop** to photograph **Heavens Peak.** Drop through the **West Side Tunnel** and follow **McDonald Creek** downstream to **Lake McDonald.**

If you head east from Logan Pass, enjoy the views around the **East Side Tunnel** before stopping at **Jackson Glacier Overlook** to spy a glacier through binoculars. Then pull into **Sun Point** to walk out on the bluff for views of **St. Mary Lake.**

Evening

At Lake McDonald, plan to dine at **Russell's Fireside Dining Room** and stay overnight at **Lake McDonald Lodge.** At St. Mary Lake, overnight at **Rising Sun Motor Inn** with dinner at **Two Dog Flats Grill.**

Most of Glacier's 13 campgrounds are **first-come, first-served.** Reservations (877/444-6777, www.recreation.gov) are accepted for **Fish Creek, St. Mary,** and **Many Glacier** starting **six months** in advance. Reserve group campsites **12 months** in advance for **St. Mary** and **Apgar.**

For **backpacking,** secure an advance reservation ($40) for a **backcountry permit** ($7 pp per day) starting in mid-March. For **Granite Park Chalet** and **Sperry Chalet,** which are reached only by trail, make reservations in early January through **Belton Chalets** (406/387-5654 or 888/345-2649, www.graniteparkchalet.com, www.sperrychalet.com).

Getting There

Car
Crossing the Border

To drive to Glacier from Waterton requires going through the **Chief Mountain border crossing** (7am-10pm daily June-Labor Day, 9am-6pm daily May and Sept.) on Chief Mountain International Highway. If you're coming from other destinations in Canada, you can go through the **Piegan-Carway border crossing** (24 hours daily year-round). Passports and/or international travel IDs are required.

From Waterton Lakes National Park

From **Waterton Lakes National Park,** two

routes cross the international boundary between Alberta and Montana. The shorter and more scenic route arcs across **Chief Mountain International Highway** and is 50 miles (81 km) and takes a little more than an hour. However, the operating status of the highway is linked to the Canadian and U.S. immigration and customs stations at the **Chief Mountain border** (7am-10pm daily June-Labor Day, 9am-6pm daily May and Sept.). From **Waterton,** drive AB 5 across the Waterton River to the signed entrance to Chief Mountain Highway. Turn right and follow it to the international boundary; after crossing into the United States, the road descends as MT 17. You'll pass through open range where cows wander the road; drive slowly. The road crosses in and out of Waterton and Glacier, but there are no entrance stations to collect fees. Turn right onto US 89 to reach the entrance to Glacier at St. Mary.

The longer route is 70 miles (110 km) and takes just under 1.5 hours. It goes through the **Piegan-Carway border station** (24 hours daily year-round). From **Waterton,** drive east on AB 5 to Cardston and then south on AB 2 to the border. After crossing into the United States, the road becomes US 89, which drops into St. Mary.

From Kootenay National Park

From Kootenay National Park to West Glacier, Montana, is 225 miles (360 km) and takes a little more than four hours to drive. Starting from **Radium Hot Springs** on the southeastern corner of Kootenay, the route descends south through the Columbia Valley on BC 93 to meet BC 3. Follow BC 3/93 east toward Elko, and then turn south on BC 93 to Roosville on the Canadian-U.S. border (24 hours daily year-round). After crossing, continue south on US 93 through Eureka to Whitefish. Drive with caution: Deer frequent the road between Eureka and Whitefish, earning it the nickname "Deer Alley." In downtown Whitefish,

US 93 turns south again at the third stoplight. Drive 2 miles (3.2 km) to the junction with MT 40, with signs for Glacier. Turn left onto MT 40, which joins US 2 just before Columbia Falls, goes through several small burgs, and reaches West Glacier and the west entrance of Glacier.

From Banff

From **Banff,** the quickest route to Glacier goes to St. Mary, Montana, on the east end of Going-to-the-Sun Road. It's 255 miles (410 km) and takes less than five hours. Follow Trans-Canada Highway 1 east toward Calgary, then go south on AB 2 toward Fort Macleod. Continue south through Cardston to the **Piegan-Carway border crossing** (24 hours daily year-round). After crossing the Canadian-U.S. border, the road becomes US 89. Follow it southwest to St. Mary at Going-to-the-Sun Road's east entrance.

From Calgary

From **Calgary** to St. Mary, Montana, is 175 miles (280 km) and takes about 3.5 hours. Head south on AB 2 toward Fort Macleod and continue south through Cardston to the **Piegan-Carway border crossing** (7am-11pm daily year-round). After crossing the Canadian-U.S. border onto US 89, drive southwest to St. Mary at Going-to-the-Sun Road's east entrance.

From Flathead Valley

From **Kalispell,** follow US 2 northeast through Columbia Falls and Hungry Horse to West Glacier. This route is 33 miles (53 km) and takes about 40 minutes to drive. From **Whitefish,** the drive to West Glacier is 26 miles (42 km) and takes about 30 minutes via MT 40 and US 2.

From Yellowstone National Park

To get from **Yellowstone** to Glacier National Park takes **six hours** of driving. The three main routes are each about 360 miles (580 km).

From Gardiner, Montana

From Yellowstone's north entrance at **Gardiner,** two routes of almost equal distance go to East Glacier.

The first route from Gardiner goes via **Great Falls** and is 365 miles (585 km). Head north on US 89, then east on I-90. Take exit 340 to go north on US 89 again to Great Falls. From here, go north on I-15 to exit 348 and then head west on MT 44, also called the Valier Highway. After reaching US 89 once again, turn north. At US 2, go west through Browning to East Glacier.

The second route goes via **Bozeman** and **Helena** and is 360 miles (580 km). Follow US 89 north to I-90. Head west on I-90 past Bozeman to Three Forks. Take exit 274, heading north on US 287 to Helena. Then drive north on I-15. Just past Wolf Creek, take exit 228 to drive north on US 287 along the Rocky Mountain Front. In Choteau, the route joins US 89, continuing north. At US 2, head west through Browning to East Glacier.

From West Yellowstone, Montana

From Yellowstone's west entrance to East Glacier goes through **Helena** and is 360 miles (580 km). From **West Yellowstone,** drive north on US 191. Turn west onto US 287 to arc around Hebgen Lake, pass through the Quake Lake landslide zone, and follow the Madison River north through the Madison Valley. Just north of Harrison, turn left onto MT 359 to Cardwell. Pass under I-90, following MT 2 west to reach MT 69 heading north again to Boulder. Merge onto I-15 north through Helena. Just past Wolf Creek, take exit 228 to go north on US 287 along the Rocky Mountain Front. In Choteau, the route joins US 89, continuing north. At US 2, head west through Browning to East Glacier.

Air

The closest place to fly in to reach the park is **Glacier Park International Airport** (FCA, 4170 US 2, 406/257-5994, www. iflyglacier.com) in Kalispell, Montana, on the west side. With most flights, you can arrive and get into the park on the same day. It's about 25 miles (40 km) to West Glacier and Apgar from the airport. To reach the eastern part of the park, you'll drive through Glacier via Going-to-the-Sun Road.

Located 10 minutes outside Great Falls, east of Glacier, the **Great Falls International Airport** (GTF, 406/727-3404, www.gtfairport.com) is the next closest airport to the park. From the airport to East Glacier is 140 miles (225 km), which takes about 2.5 hours. To reach St. Mary, it's a 155-mile (250-km) drive that takes three hours.

Another option is **Calgary International Airport** (YYC, 403/735-1200 or 877/254-7427, www.yyc.com). To reach the east side of Glacier at St. Mary, the drive is about 185 miles (300 km) and takes under four hours. You can chop off part of the distance by flying south to **Lethbridge Airport** (YQL, 417 Stubb Ross Rd., Lethbridge, www.lethbridgeairport. ca) via **Air Canada** (888/247-2262, www. aircanada.com). Rent a car there to drive 78 miles (125 km) to St. Mary, a two-hour drive. Flying into either of these airports means crossing the international border to reach Glacier.

Train

Glacier is one of the rare U.S. national parks serviced by train. In fact, much of the park's development came from the Great Northern Railway, and Amtrak offers an updated way to reach the park on a historic rail line.

The daily Empire Builder run by **Amtrak** (800/872-7245, www.amtrak. com) stops at several locations at Glacier National Park. High summer travel volumes make reservations imperative. Heavy freight traffic, spring flooding, and winter avalanches can cause delays of several hours or more. Three stops are year-round in the Glacier environs:

Essex, West Glacier, and Whitefish. East Glacier is a summer-only stop. Check with Amtrak for schedules.

The westbound route originates in Chicago, stopping at Milwaukee, St. Paul-Minneapolis, and Fargo plus smaller towns on its way to Glacier. The ride from Chicago to East Glacier takes about 30 hours or more.

Eastbound trains starting in Seattle and Portland join in Spokane and stop in Whitefish before reaching West Glacier in a little more than 15 hours. From West Glacier, the train skirts the southern edge of Glacier, stopping in Essex and East Glacier.

Bus

Greyhound (800/231-2222, www.greyhound.com) has one bus daily to **Whitefish,** originating in Missoula (1660 W. Broadway). In Whitefish, the bus drops passengers curbside at the O'Shaughnessy Arts Center (1 Central Ave.). No bus service connects to Glacier, but you can hop the Amtrak train a block away to reach West Glacier or East Glacier.

Visiting the Park

Entrances and Fees

There are three entrances on Glacier's west side. **West Glacier** (year-round) is at the junction of US 2 and Going-to-the-Sun Road. The **Camas Road entrance** (mid-May-Oct.) is accessed from the Outside North Fork Road north of Columbia Falls. But you won't reach the entrance station until the east end near Fish Creek Road.

There are four entrances on Glacier's east side. The entrance at **St. Mary** (May-Oct.) is on the east end of Going-to-the-Sun Road. The **Many Glacier entrance** (mid-May-early Nov.) is partway up Many Glacier Road. The **Two Medicine entrance** (late May-Oct.) is on Two Medicine Road, accessible from MT 49.

The **Cut Bank entrance** (June-Sept.) is on Cut Bank Creek Road, accessible from US 89.

Entrance passes are valid for seven days. Vehicle entrance costs $35 ($25 winter), motorcyclists pay $30 ($20 winter), and hikers and bicyclists pay $20 ($15 winter). When entrance stations are not staffed, you can buy passes at nearby kiosks. **Annual passes** ($70) can be purchased in advance online (www.recreation.gov).

Visitors Centers

Glacier National Park has three tiny visitors centers, all on Going-to-the-Sun Road. Each has Junior Ranger Program booklets, information on ranger-led walks and talks, evening amphitheater schedules, brochures, trail and road conditions, and weather reports. Inside each center is a **Glacier National Park Conservancy bookstore** (406/892-3250, http://glacier.org). All three centers are shuttle stops and have water bottle refill stations and restrooms.

Apgar Visitor Center

Anchoring the west entrance of Going-to-the-Sun Road, the small **Apgar Visitor Center** (406/888-7800, 8am-6pm daily mid-June-Aug., shorter hours fall-spring) is the place to find fishing and boating information. Interpretive signage highlights information for all major park regions. Paved biking and walking trails lead from the visitors center to Apgar Village, Lake McDonald, and Apgar Campground. The parking lot accommodates big RVs, and you can leave your car all day to use shuttles or take guided tours.

The **Apgar Backcountry Permit Office** (406/888-7859 May-Oct., 406/888-7800 Nov.-Apr., 7am-4:30pm daily May-Sept., 8am-4pm daily Oct.) is opposite the old red schoolhouse in Apgar. This is the main office for acquiring permits for overnight backpacking or paddling trips. The office gets swarmed for the first 2-3 hours of each morning in July and August; lines begin forming at 6am.

Logan Pass Visitor Center

Logan Pass Visitor Center (406/888-7800, 9am-7pm daily mid-June-Aug., shorter hours Labor Day-mid-Sept.) perches at the apex of Going-to-the-Sun Road. This is a seasonal outpost with an information desk, a few displays, a small fireplace, and minimal seating. Due to the elevation, expect harsher weather including wind, rain, and snow even in August.

St. Mary Visitor Center

Located at the east entrance to Going-to-the-Sun Road, the **St. Mary Visitor Center** (406/888-7800, 8am-5pm daily late May and mid-Aug.-early Oct., 8am-6pm daily June-mid-Aug.) is the largest in the park, with displays on Indigenous cultural history. The theater hosts slide presentations, evening naturalist programs, the acclaimed Native America Speaks program, and the popular Two Medicine Lake Singers and Dancers. The backcountry desk issues **backcountry permits** (7am-4:30pm daily late May-late Sept.). Astronomy programs take place outdoors, where you can see the night sky from the St. Mary Observatory telescope on two high-resolution screens. Walk to the visitors center via a trail and wooden bridge from St. Mary Campground or on the paved pathway from St. Mary; drive through the park entrance to reach the parking lot, where you can park all day for free to catch the shuttle up the Sun Road.

Sights

Going-to-the-Sun Road

Apgar

Perched at the outlet of Lake McDonald on the lower west side of the Sun Road, this seasonal village comes alive in summer with lodging, dining, a few shops, and a campground. You can rent canoes, kayaks, paddleboards, and small motorboats for enjoying the lake, and bicycles for pedaling the paved Apgar Bike Trail. You'll also find the Apgar Visitor Center, shuttle stops, and the Apgar Nature Center for kids.

★ Lake McDonald

As the largest lake in the park, **Lake McDonald** (10 mi/16.1 km long) flanks one-third of the Sun Road's west side. It fills a valley scooped out by a glacier. Lining the trough, **Howe** and **Snyder Ridges** are lateral moraines left from that ancient ice-age relic. The road has frequent **pullouts;** the best are midway between Apgar and Sprague Creek Campgrounds. If glassy waters reflect Stanton Peak, snag a photo. One of the best ways to experience the lake is via the **tour boat** from Lake McDonald Lodge.

★ Lake McDonald Lodge

At Lake McDonald's east end, the historic **Lake McDonald Lodge** was designed to resemble a hunting lodge. The tall, stately cedar-log lobby cluttered with stuffed mountain goats and mounted heads of bighorn sheep, deer, elk, and moose is a taxidermist's delight (or an animal lover's nightmare). Look for the woodland caribou still represented among the furry creatures here, even though it no longer exists in the park. Because this National Historic Landmark was built prior to the road, the front door actually opens lakeside, facing the original boat approach.

★ Logan Pass

At the highest point on the Sun Road, **Logan Pass** sits atop the **Continental Divide** (6,646 ft/2,026 m), shedding water to both the Pacific and Atlantic Oceans. With its altitude and location between mountainous hulks, weather can be windy and chilly even in midsummer. For evidence, look at the gnarled trees, growing low in krummholz or thick mats for protection against the elements. Explore the visitors center, take a selfie in

Going-to-the-Sun Road

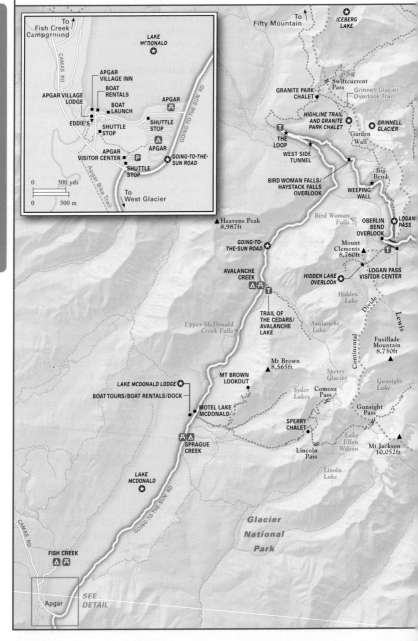

Inset map (Apgar detail):

To Fish Creek Campground
CAMAS RD
LAKE McDONALD
APGAR VILLAGE INN
BOAT RENTALS
BOAT LAUNCH
APGAR VILLAGE LODGE
EDDIE'S
APGAR
SHUTTLE STOP
SHUTTLE STOP
APGAR
GOING-TO-THE-SUN ROAD
SHUTTLE STOP
APGAR VISITOR CENTER
Apgar Bike Trail
To West Glacier
0   500 yds
0   500 m

Main map labels:

To Fifty Mountain
ICEBERG LAKE
Swiftcurrent Pass
GRANITE PARK CHALET
Grinnell Glacier Overlook Trail
HIGHLINE TRAIL AND GRANITE PARK CHALET
GRINNELL GLACIER
Garden Wall
THE LOOP
WEST SIDE TUNNEL
Big Bend
BIRD WOMAN FALLS/ HAYSTACK FALLS OVERLOOK
WEEPING WALL
LOGAN PASS
▲ Heavens Peak 8,987ft
Bird Woman Falls
OBERLIN BEND OVERLOOK
GOING-TO-THE-SUN ROAD
Mount Clements ▲ 8,760ft
LOGAN PASS VISITOR CENTER
AVALANCHE CREEK
HIDDEN LAKE OVERLOOK
TRAIL OF THE CEDARS/ AVALANCHE LAKE
Hidden Lake
Upper McDonald Creek Falls
Avalanche Lake
Continental
Divide
Lewis
Fusillade Mountain 8,750ft
Mt Brown ▲ 8,565ft
Sperry Glacier
Gunsight Lake
MT BROWN LOOKOUT
LAKE McDONALD LODGE
BOAT TOURS/BOAT RENTALS/DOCK
MOTEL LAKE McDONALD
Syder Lakes
Comeau Pass
Gunsight Pass
SPERRY CHALET
Lake Ellen Wilson
Mt Jackson 10,052ft ▲
Lincoln Pass
SPRAGUE CREEK
LAKE McDONALD
Linoln Lake
CAMAS RD
FISH CREEK
GOING-TO-THE-SUN RD
Glacier National Park
Apgar
SEE DETAIL

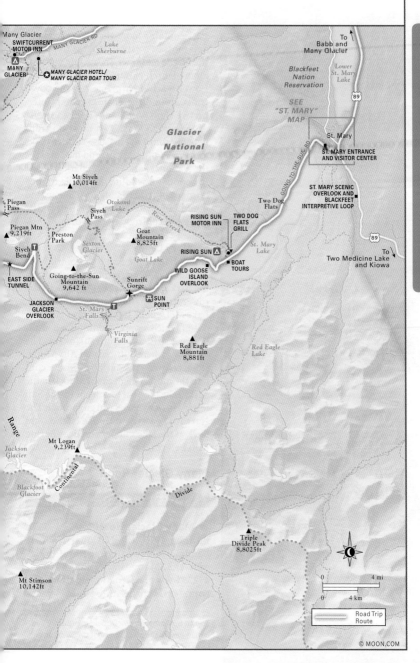

Many Glacier
SWIFTCURRENT
MOTOR INN

MANY GLACIER RD

Lake
Sherburne

MANY
GLACIER

MANY GLACIER HOTEL/
MANY GLACIER BOAT TOUR

To
Babb and
Many Glacier

Blackfeet
Nation
Reservation

Lower
St. Mary
Lake

89

Glacier
National
Park

SEE
"ST. MARY"
MAP

St. Mary

ST. MARY ENTRANCE
AND VISITOR CENTER

Mt Siyeh
10,014ft

GOING-TO-THE-SUN RD

Piegan
Pass

Otokomi
Lake

Siyeh
Pass

Rose Creek

Two Dog
Flats

ST. MARY SCENIC
OVERLOOK AND
BLACKFEET
INTERPRETIVE LOOP

Piegan Mtn
9,219ft

Preston
Park

Goat
Mountain
8,825ft

RISING SUN
MOTOR INN

TWO DOG
FLATS
GRILL

Siyeh
Bend

Sexton
Glacier

Goat Lake

RISING SUN

St. Mary
Lake

89

To
Two Medicine Lake
and Kiowa

EAST SIDE
TUNNEL

Going-to-the-Sun
Mountain
9,642 ft

Sunrift
Gorge

BOAT
TOURS

WILD GOOSE
ISLAND
OVERLOOK

JACKSON
GLACIER
OVERLOOK

St. Mary
Falls

SUN
POINT

Virginia
Falls

Red Eagle
Mountain
8,881ft

Red Eagle
Lake

Range

Mt Logan
9,239ft

Jackson
Glacier

Continental

Blackfoot
Glacier

Divide

Triple
Divide Peak
8,8025ft

Mt Stimson
10,142ft

0   4 mi

0   4 km

Road Trip
Route

© MOON.COM

front of the Continental Divide sign, and scan surrounding slopes for mountain goats, bighorn sheep, and bears. Logan Pass contains more than 30 rare plants and mosses, so stick to paths to protect the fragile meadows. In late July, the pink alpine laurel, paintbrush, and monkey-flower reach their prime. On the paved trails around the visitors center, interpretive signs with hand-cranked speakers appeal to kids. Two must-do trails depart from Logan Pass: Hidden Lake and the Highline Trail. You may also see the National Park Service "Bark Ranger" in action; for wildlife safety, the trained border collie herds bighorn sheep and mountain goats away from high traffic areas and confrontations with humans.

St. Mary Lake

About half of the Sun Road on the east side follows along second-largest lake in the park. **St. Mary Lake** fills a much narrower valley than its larger counterpart, Lake McDonald. It forms a blue platform out of which several stunning red argillite peaks rise. Its width shrinks in The Narrows, where buff-colored Altyn limestone resisted erosion. These strata contain the most ancient exposed rock in the park. Take the boat tour from Rising Sun to get a better view as you go through The Narrows, pass **Wild Goose Island,** and dock at the lake's upper end near Baring Falls before returning.

Many Glacier Road

TOP EXPERIENCE

★ Many Glacier Hotel

Built in 1915, the National Historic Landmark **Many Glacier Hotel** (milepost 11.5, Many Glacier Rd., 855/733-4522, www.glaciernationalparklodges.com, early June-mid-Sept.) graces

Top to bottom: Lake McDonald in autumn; Logan Pass meadows; tour boat on Swiftcurrent Lake

Swiftcurrent Lake's shore. The five-story, 211-room hotel is owned by the National Park Service and is operated by Xanterra. A $30 million restoration straightened the leaning structure, restored the dining room to its historic look, revamped the lobby, rebuilt the historic helical stairway to the lower level, and replaced windows, doors, the roof, siding, and decks. Warm up on a cold day around the huge fireplace in the massive lobby, or lounge on its large deck overlooking Swiftcurrent Lake and a mountainous panorama while scanning slopes with binoculars for bears. Join park naturalists for a tour of the historic hotel. Check the park newspaper for the current schedule.

★ Many Glacier Boat Tour

In Many Glacier, jump on a pair of historic wooden boats for a tour of two lakes with **Glacier Park Boat Company** (406/257-2426, glacierparkboats.com, daily mid-June-mid-Sept., round-trip adults $34, children $17). Catch the 1961-vintage *Chief Two Guns* at **Swiftcurrent Lake**'s boat dock behind Many Glacier Hotel. In 75 minutes, you'll cruise across the lake, hike over a hill, hop aboard the 1945 *Morning Eagle* for a cruise on **Lake Josephine,** and return. Don't forget your camera, although you may have difficulty cramming the view into the lens. Tours depart at 9am, 11am, 2pm, and 4:30pm, with additional launches at 1pm and 3pm from July 1, and 8:30am from mid-July. Two of the launches offer guided round-trip walks to Grinnell Lake (2 mi/3.2 km), and the earliest boat has a ranger-led hike to Grinnell Glacier. Tours sell out, but you can make reservations by phone or in person at the dock at least one day in advance.

Two Medicine Road
Two Medicine Lake

At the terminus of Two Medicine Road, **Two Medicine Lake** is the highest road-accessible lake in Glacier. Peaks surround its blue waters. The lakes are all that remain of the giant ice field that filled the valley and flowed out onto the prairie past Browning. To explore Two Medicine Lake, jump on the historic *Sinopah* tour boat, or if the waters are calm, paddle its shoreline, swim in its chilly clear waters, or fish for brook trout.

Inside North Fork Road

Head to the remote North Fork on Glacier's west side for real rusticity. The Outside North Fork Road goes to **Polebridge,** the most remote park entrance. Polebridge is a tiny collection of cabins, a restaurant, and a store and the hub of the North Fork Valley. It's a rustic off-the-grid (no electricity) locale where you won't have cell service and most restrooms consist of pit toilets.

Crossing the North Fork of the Flathead River, you'll reach the Polebridge entrance station followed by the bumpy dirt **Inside Road.** It's a potholed, bouncing ride to scenic lakes. The road has **vehicle length restrictions** (21 ft/6.4 m maximum; no trailers) and can be closed when parking is full at the lakes. Check before driving up to Polebridge by stopping at the Apgar Visitor Center or using the **Recreational Access Display** (www.nps.gov/applications/glac/dashboard).

Bowman Lake

A channel of clear blue water, **Bowman Lake** (7 mi/11.3 km northeast of the Polebridge entrance station) sits in a narrow, glacier-scoured trough stretching toward chiseled Thunderbird Peak. Its narrow, fjord-like shape squeezes in between the hulks of Numa and Rainbow Peaks, the latter rising straight up from the south shore. Lake waters offer paddling and fishing, trails lead to high vistas, and you can soak up evening quiet in the campground. In winter, the icy expanse and snow-laden crags call to cross-country skiers, who ski on the road pockmarked with wolf and elk tracks.

Kintla Lake

It can take an hour or more to drive the road to **Kintla Lake** (15 mi/24 km north of the Polebridge entrance station). Kintla's tiny campground tucked deep in the trees offers a quiet place to decompress. Set between Starvation and Parke Ridges, the narrow lake curves up-valley as a prelude to Upper Kintla Lake. Haul a canoe or kayak to Kintla Lake for secluded, serene (motors are banned) paddling or fishing.

US 2

Goat Lick

As US 2 slices through the southern tip of Glacier, it passes the **Goat Lick** (milepost 182.6), a huge mass of gray rock that is actually an exposed fault containing salts like calcium, magnesium, and potassium. This is where mountain goats congregate when winter is over and they're craving minerals. Goats hop sure-footedly along the steep cliff faces to slurp at the minerals. The well-marked overlook has a couple of viewing areas: one at the interpretive sign and the other at the end of a short, wheelchair-accessible walkway. Bring your binoculars for better viewing. You can also catch sight of the goats on the slopes above the Goat Lick bridge on the highway.

Scenic Drives

TOP EXPERIENCE

★ Going-to-the-Sun Road

Of all the scenic roads in the national parks, **Going-to-the-Sun Road** (50 mi/81 km, 2-4 hrs) stands in a class by itself. For some, the tight curves that hug cliff walls mean white-knuckle driving. But for most, the route's beauty, diversity, color, flora, fauna, and raw wildness will leave an impression like no other. The road is an engineering wonder, cutting through cliffs and using local stone for masonry. Many park visitors drive it more than once during their stay.

For big waterfall shows, drive it in late June or early July. For alpine wildflowers, go in late July or early August. For fewer crowds, go mid-September to mid-October. To avoid the hassles of parking, crowded overlooks, and congested traffic, take a bus tour with one of two companies that are guaranteed parking at Logan Pass: **Sun Tours** (406/732-9220 or 800/786-9220, www.glaciersuntours. com) or the **red buses** (855/733-4522, www.glaciernationalparklodges.com).

From St. Mary on the east side, the route snakes along turquoise **St. Mary Lake.** Explore **Logan Pass**, if parking is available. Descending the west side yields big views. Walk the **Trail of the Cedars** at Avalanche to enjoy the giant trees. At **Lake McDonald,** tour historic **Lake McDonald Lodge** and stop at several of the pullouts along the lake to skip rocks from the shore before reaching Apgar and West Glacier.

Planning Tips

In 2021, Glacier began requiring **entry tickets** to Going-to-the-Sun Road during **peak hours.** Find current ticketing policies on the park's website. **Reservations** (www.recreation.gov) are available online 60 days in advance and cost $2 per vehicle. If you have activity or lodging reservations on the Sun Road, you won't need an entry ticket.

Going-to-the-Sun Road is open 24 hours daily mid-June through mid-October...usually. Weather, construction, fires, and snow can affect its status. Weather, plowing, and sometimes construction will dictate the spring opening, which has no set date. In years with heavy snow and stormy springs, Logan Pass tends to open mid-June or later. During summer the road may close temporarily for snowstorms, washouts, accidents, or fires. The park regularly updates **road status reports** (406/888-7800, www.nps. gov/glac).

In fall, the road usually closes in mid-October, but heavy snowfall can mean an earlier closure. In winter, the road is closed from Lake McDonald Lodge to St. Mary. In spring, the closed portion spans Avalanche to Rising Sun until the Logan Pass section opens.

From July through August, expect crowds. To avoid the hordes, drive in early morning or early evening, when lighting is better for photography and wildlife is more active. **In midsummer, the Logan Pass parking lot fills by 6am.** The park service controls the entrance, admitting a car only when one departs. If the parking lot is full, skip Logan Pass for the time being and return later in the day; parking usually opens up again around 6pm.

Vehicle Restrictions
Large vehicles are restricted on Going-to-the-Sun Road **between Avalanche Campground and Rising Sun.** Because the road is narrow and has overhangs, **vehicles must be less than 21 feet (6.4 m) in length, 10 feet (3 m) high, and 8 feet (2.4 m) wide.** These dimensions include side mirrors, bumpers, and bike racks. Remember to retract side extension mirrors; you'll see broken ones in the gutter claimed by cliff walls. Even though smaller truck-camper units may be allowed, drivers will feel pinched on the skinny road.

Recreation

Hiking
The hiking season in Glacier is based on snow. Lower elevation trails along Lake McDonald, St. Mary Lake, and Many Glacier are often snow-free late May to mid-October. High-elevation trails often retain snow on steep slopes until mid-July; this includes the Highline, Piegan and Siyeh Passes, Grinnell Glacier,

Top to bottom: waterfall on Going-to-the-Sun Road; Wild Goose Island in St. Mary Lake; Huckleberry Lookout

Ptarmigan Tunnel, Cobalt Lake, and Dawson-Pitamakin Loop. Snow can return to these trails in September.

Trail junctions are well signed, but maps are helpful to navigate the maze of trails in some areas. Visitors centers and ranger stations at Many Glacier and Two Medicine have free non-topographic maps of hiking trails; these maps are also on the park's website.

Apgar
Rocky Point
Distance: 1.4-1.6 miles (2.3-2.6 km) rt
Duration: 1 hour
Elevation gain: none
Effort: easy
Trail surface: dirt with roots and rocks
Trailhead: Fish Creek Campground Loop D or the start of the Inside North Fork Rd.

Rocky Point is a short interpretive romp along Lake McDonald's north shore through the 2003 Robert Fire and up a rock promontory. Places of heavy burn with slow regrowth alternate with lighter burn now clogged with lush greenery. Don't forget your camera: The view from **Rocky Point** looks up the lake toward the Continental Divide and includes grand Mount Jackson and Mount Edwards to the south. From the promontory, loop back on the Lake McDonald Trail.

Apgar Lookout
Distance: 7 miles (11.3 km) rt
Duration: 4 hours
Elevation gain: 1,868 feet (569 m)
Effort: moderate
Trail surface: narrow, dirt with roots and rocks
Trailhead: end of Glacier Institute Rd.
Directions: Take the first left after the west entrance station at the Glacier Institute sign. At the first fork, follow the sign to the horse barn and veer left, crossing over Quarter Circle Bridge. Drive to the road's terminus at the trailhead.

Beginning with a gentle walk, the trail soon climbs steeply uphill toward the first of three long switchbacks (hike in the morning on hot days). As the trail ascends, some large burned sentinels stand as relics from the 2003 Robert Fire amid the thick growth of new lodgepoles pressing in on the trail. Snippets of views look down on the Middle Fork, Rubideau Basin, and West Glacier. Following the third switchback, the trail traverses the ridge to **Apgar Lookout** and a cluster of radio antennas. From this aerie, tall trees allow only partial views of the park's southern sector, Lake McDonald, and peaks of the Livingston Range.

Huckleberry Lookout
Distance: 12 miles (19.3 km) rt
Duration: 6 hours
Elevation gain: 2,725 feet (831 m)
Effort: strenuous
Trail surface: narrow, dirt with roots and rocks
Trailhead: 6 miles (9.7 km) up Camas Rd. from Apgar, just past McGee Meadows

Huckleberry Lookout Trail is aptly named, for huckleberries do abound in this area. Due to a heavy concentration of the berries attracting a significant bruin

population in fall, check with the park service about potential trail closures.

The trail begins with a gentle walk through lodgepole forest before steadily gaining elevation among larches. The trail steepens around high-angled meadows to reach a saddle. In a reprieve from the climb, the trail traverses two bowls until it crests the Apgar Range for the final scenery-laden ascent to **Huckleberry Lookout** (which is staffed in the summer). A spectacular view of the North Fork Valley and the Livingston Range unfolds. Glacier's six highest peaks are visible.

Going-to-the-Sun Road

Hikes off Going-to-the-Sun Road are top-notch. Around Lake McDonald, trails all begin in the forest, but climb to incredible heights. At Logan Pass and eastward, most trails provide quicker access to alpine meadows and spectacular scenery. Shorter trails are ultra-crowded in midsummer; you may feel like you're walking in a parade to Avalanche Lake or Hidden Lake Overlook. Longer hikes such as Siyeh Pass get away from the masses. The season for Going-to-the-Sun Road hiking is limited by the road's opening and closing.

Trail of the Cedars and Avalanche Lake

Distance: 0.9-4.7 miles (1.4-7.6 km) rt

Duration: 0.5-3 hours

Elevation gain: 0-477 feet (145 m)

Effort: easy-moderate

Trail surface: accessible boardwalk and hard surface on Trail of the Cedars; dirt, roots, and rocks for Avalanche Lake

Trailhead: across from Avalanche Picnic Area and shuttle stop

With interpretive signs, the **Trail of the Cedars** boardwalk guides visitors on a loop that crosses two footbridges over Avalanche Creek. The route tours the lush rainforest, where fallen trees become nurse logs, fertile habitat for hemlocks and tiny foamflowers. Immense black cottonwoods furrowed with deep-cut

Avalanche Gorge on Trail of the Cedars

bark and huge 500-year-old western red cedars dominate the forest. At **Avalanche Gorge,** the creek slices through red rocks. To finish the 0.9-mile (1.4-km) loop, continue on the hard-surface walkway past large burled cedars to return to the trailhead.

The trail to **Avalanche Lake** exits from Trail of the Cedars just past Avalanche Gorge. Turn uphill for the short grunt to the top of the water-carved gorge. Be extremely careful: Too many fatal accidents have occurred from slipping. From there, the trail climbs steadily through woods littered with glacial erratics, large boulders left from the receding glacier (some still retain scratch marks left from the ice). At Avalanche Lake, a cirque with steep cliffs and tumbling waterfalls provides the backdrop. An additional 0.7-mile (1.1-km) path goes to the lake's less-crowded head, where anglers find better fishing. If you hike this trail earlier or later in the day, make noise to ward off bears.

Granite Park Chalet via The Loop Trail
Distance: 8 miles (12.9 km) rt
Duration: 4 hours
Elevation gain: 2,402 feet (732 m)
Effort: moderate-strenuous
Trail surface: narrow dirt path with roots and rocks
Trailhead: The Loop Trailhead and shuttle stop

The Loop Trail is mostly used by hikers exiting the Highline Trail, but when the Highline Trail has too much snow, this trail makes a worthy hike with **Granite Park Chalet** as a scenic destination. Since the 2003 Trapper Fire, views have improved, but the lack of shade means there is little relief from the sun's blazing heat.

The trail crosses a tumbling creek before joining up with the Packer's Roost trail. Note this junction: You do not want to miss it when hiking back down. From there, the trail climbs two long switchbacks before it crests into the upper basin to the chalet. In June or by late September, snow can cover the last mile or so. The chalet (late June-early Sept.)

has no running water but does sell candy bars and bottled water (cash only).

★ Highline Trail and Granite Park Chalet
Distance: 11.4 miles (18.3 km) one-way
Duration: 5-6 hours
Elevation gain: 975 feet (297 m) up; 3,395 feet (1,035 m) down
Effort: strenuous
Trail surface: narrow, dirt and rocks
Trailhead: across from Logan Pass parking lot and shuttle stop

Many first-time hikers stop every 10 feet to take photos on this hike. Severe acrophobes are intimidated by its exposed drop-offs. The trail starts through a cliff walk above the Sun Road before crossing a meadow of wildflowers that gave the Garden Wall arête its name. The trail then ascends Haystack Saddle. From there, it climbs to its high point before dropping and swinging through several large bowls. After passing Bear Valley, it pops up to **Granite Park Chalet** atop a

knoll with 360-degree views, at 7.4 miles (11.9 km). Most day hikers head down The Loop Trail (4 mi/6.4 km) to catch the shuttle.

To exit the area, some hikers opt to hike out over Swiftcurrent Pass to Many Glacier (7.6 mi/12.2 km one-way) and catch a shuttle. You can also hike to the chalet and back to Logan Pass (14.8 mi/24 km rt).

Carry more water than usual due to altitude, wind, and sun, or filter water from the stream below the chalet. The chalet (late June-early Sept.) does not have running water, but does sell bottled water, sodas, and snacks (cash only).

Due to steep, snow-filled avalanche paths, the Highline Trail usually stays closed into July. Check online or at a visitors center before hiking the Highline to get current information on possible capacity limits or flow-of-traffic restrictions.

Be aware: Changes may impact the first section of the Highline by making the trail one-way only from Logan Pass, adding an exit trail to Big Bend, or using a timed permit entry.

★ Hidden Lake Overlook

Distance: 2.6-5 miles (4.2-8 km) rt
Duration: 2-4 hours
Elevation gain: 482-1,258 feet (147-383 m)
Effort: moderate
Trail surface: wide boardwalk with stairs and rocky dirt
Trailhead: behind Logan Pass Visitor Center and shuttle stop

Regardless of crowds, Hidden Lake Overlook is a spectacular hike. Avoid long lines of hikers by going shortly after sunrise or in the evening. The trail is often buried under feet of snow until mid-July or later, but tall poles mark the route. Once the trail melts out, a boardwalk climbs the first half through alpine meadows where fragile shooting stars and alpine laurel dot the landscape with pink. The trail ascends through mud-cracked and ripple-marked rocks from

Highline Trail

the ancient Belt Sea. The trail climbs past moraines, waterfalls, mountain goats, and bighorn sheep. At Hidden Pass on the Continental Divide, an **interpretive platform** (2.6 mi/4.2 km rt, 482 ft/147 m) overlooks the lake's blue waters.

For ambitious hikers or anglers, the trail continues down steeply to **Hidden Lake** (5 mi/8 km rt, 1,258 ft/383 m). Just remember: What drops must come back up. After late September, bring ice cleats for walking the trail.

Piegan Pass

Distance: 8.8 miles (14.2 km) rt or 11.5 miles (18.5 km) one-way
Duration: 4-6 hours
Elevation gain: 1,739 feet (530 m)
Effort: moderate
Trail surface: dirt path with roots and rocks
Trailhead: Piegan Pass, Siyeh Bend shuttle stop

Piegan Pass, named for the Pikuni or Piegan people of the Blackfeet Nation, sneaks a close look at the Continental Divide. After climbing through subalpine forest and turning north at the first trail junction, the trail breaks out into **Preston Park,** bursting with purple fleabane, blue gentians, white valerian, and fuchsia paintbrush. During the climb, spy four glaciers: **Piegan, Jackson, Blackfoot,** and **Sperry.** A signed trail junction splits the Piegan Pass Trail from the Siyeh Pass Trail. The trail is often snowbound until early July.

Shortly after the junction, the Piegan Pass Trail heads into the seemingly barren alpine zone as it crosses the base of Siyeh Peak. But miniature flowers bloom and serve as food for pikas. The trail sweeps around a large bowl, where two steep snowfields often linger until mid-July, to **Piegan Pass.** Return to **Siyeh Bend** (8.8 mi/14.2 km rt) or drop down to see the waterfalls of Piegan Valley before reaching **Many Glacier Hotel** (11.5 mi/18.5 km one-way), then return via shuttle.

Siyeh Pass

Distance: 10 miles (16.1 km) one-way
Duration: 6 hours
Elevation gain: 2,278 feet (694 m)
Effort: strenuous
Trail surface: dirt path with roots and rocks
Trailhead: Piegan Pass, Siyeh Bend shuttle stop

Siyeh Pass Trail crosses through such different ecosystems that the entire trail nearly captures the park's diversity. It usually holds big deep snowfields until at least early July. The trail begins with a climb through subalpine forest broken by meadows, where it passes two well-signed junctions; go left at the first, right at the second. As the trail leads through **Preston Park,** one of the best flower meadows, with purple fleabane and fuchsia paintbrush, **Piegan Glacier** and the massive south face of **Siyeh Peak** come into view. Switchbacks ascend above the tree line, providing a look at the hanging valley below.

The switchbacks appear to lead to a saddle, which is **Siyeh Pass.** But eight more turns climb above the pass before swinging through a cliff to the divide between Boulder and Baring Creeks. Be wary of your lunch; there are aggressive golden-mantled ground squirrels here. Due to the elevation, snow can bury the steep switchbacks south of the divide until mid-July. You'll get views of **Sexton Glacier** clinging to the side of Going-to-the-Sun Mountain and St. Mary Lake far below. The trail descends 3,446 feet (1,050 m) past goats, bighorn sheep, and a multicolored cliff band before traversing the flanks of Goat Mountain and dropping a couple hot miles through the 2015 Reynolds Creek Fire to end at the Sunrift Gorge on Going-to-the-Sun Road, where there's a shuttle stop.

St. Mary and Virginia Falls

Distance: 2-3.4 miles (3.2-5.5 km) rt
Duration: 1-2 hours
Elevation gain: 216 feet (66 m)
Effort: easy

Trail surface: dirt path with roots and rocks
Trailhead: St. Mary Falls

In midsummer, this short, two-waterfall trail sees a constant stream of people. On Going-to-the-Sun Road, two trailheads descend to the St. Mary Fall Trail, one from the shuttle stop and the other from the vehicle parking lot. Note the sign at the junction and be sure to take the correct spur trail on the return.

The trail drops through several well-signed junctions in the regrowing forest from the 2015 Reynolds Creek Fire. At **St. Mary Fall,** a multi-drop waterfall cuts through a small gorge into blue-green pools. A bridge crosses the river, affording an excellent vantage point. Then the trail switchbacks up to **Virginia Falls,** a broad veil-type waterfall spewing mist. A short spur climbs to the base of Virginia Falls. Be wary of slippery rocks and strong currents at both falls. Nesting near both waterfalls, water ouzels (American dippers) are dark gray birds easily recognized by their dipping action, up to 40 bends per minute.

Many Glacier

Trails are crowded in this part of the park. Most trailheads depart from Many Glacier Hotel, Swiftcurrent parking lot, or the picnic area. The Many Glacier tour boat also serves as a hiking shuttle so you can whittle down miles on the Grinnell Lake and Grinnell Glacier trails. Reservations for boats going up the lake are advised; to take the return trip, you can pay when boarding at the head of Lake Josephine (cash only) for a one-way trip back to Many Glacier Hotel.

★ Iceberg Lake

Distance: 10.4 miles (16.7 km) rt
Duration: 5 hours
Elevation gain: 1,193 feet (364 m)
Effort: moderate
Trail surface: narrow dirt path with roots and rocks

Top to bottom: Siyeh Pass Trail; wildflowers on Piegan Pass; St. Mary Fall

Trailhead: behind Swiftcurrent Motor Inn cabins

The trail to Iceberg Lake begins with a short, steep jaunt straight uphill, with no time to warm up your muscles gradually. Within 0.4 mile (0.6 km) you reach a junction. Take note of the directional sign here, and watch for it when you come down. On the return, some hikers zombie-walk right on past it.

From the junction, the trail maintains an easy railroad grade to the lake. Make noise on this trail, known for frequent bear sightings. Wildflowers line the trail in July: bear grass, bog orchids, penstemon, and thimbleberry. Red argillite outcroppings offer places to survey the valley and peaks. As the trail swings north, it enters a pine and fir forest and crosses **Ptarmigan Falls,** a good break spot (don't feed the aggressive ground squirrels here). Continue straight, passing the Ptarmigan Tunnel Trail, and swing west through multiple avalanche paths. After crossing a creek, the trail climbs the final bluff, where a view of stark icebergs against blue water unfolds. Brave hikers dive into **Iceberg Lake** but be prepared to have the frigid water suck the air from your lungs.

Ptarmigan Tunnel

Distance: 11.4 miles (18.3 km) rt
Duration: 5 hours
Elevation gain: 2,304 feet (702 m)
Effort: moderate-strenuous
Trail surface: narrow dirt path with roots and rocks
Trailhead: behind Swiftcurrent Motor Inn cabins

Depending on snowpack, the tunnel doors are usually open mid-July to late September; check to confirm the status. Traversing the same trail as Iceberg Lake, the route begins with a steep uphill climb before leveling out into a gentle ascent around Mount Henkel. Just past **Ptarmigan Falls,** the Ptarmigan Tunnel route cuts to the right off the Iceberg Trail. The climb goes aggressively uphill before assuming an easier grade through meadows to **Ptarmigan Lake.**

From the lake, the route to the tunnel leads up two switchbacks on a scree slope. Tiny, fragile alpine plants struggle to survive on this barren slope; protect them by staying on the trail. The 183-foot (56-m) **Ptarmigan Tunnel,** 6 feet (1.8 m) wide and 9 feet (2.7 m) tall, cuts through Ptarmigan Wall. Walk through for the burst of red rock color on the other side. Admire the trail engineering along the north side's cliff wall and drop down 0.25 mile (0.4 km) to see **Old Sun Glacier** on Mount Merritt.

Lake Josephine and Grinnell Lake

Distance: 2.2-7.8 miles (3.5-12.6 km) rt
Duration: 1-4 hours
Elevation gain: 75 feet (23 m)
Effort: easy
Trail surface: dirt and rocks
Trailhead: on the south side of Many Glacier Hotel, at Swiftcurrent Picnic Area, and via the tour boat from Many Glacier Hotel

For the shortest walk (2.2 mi/3.5 km rt), catch the **tour boat** across Swiftcurrent Lake and Lake Josephine to hike to Grinnell Lake. From the upper boat dock on Lake Josephine, a level trail goes to a suspension bridge over Cataract Creek before climbing up a short hill to a trail junction. Continue straight to drop down to the milky turquoise waters of Grinnell Lake and the giant multitiered waterfall across the lake. Return to the same dock.

For a longer hike, begin from **Many Glacier Hotel,** following the south trail winding around Swiftcurrent Lake to the boat dock opposite the hotel. A third starting point begins at **Swiftcurrent Picnic Area,** where the trail follows Swiftcurrent Lake to that same boat dock opposite the hotel. Pop over the hill to Lake Josephine, where the trail hugs the north shore. At junctions, stay left on the lower trail to wrap around Josephine's west end to reach the Grinnell Lake junction near the upper Josephine boat dock. Then follow the same route as the shorter walk. Return via your original route (7.8 mi/12.6 km rt) or shorten the length by hopping the tour boat back to Many Glacier Hotel (5 mi/8 km rt).

★ Grinnell Glacier

Distance: 11 miles (17.7 km) rt
Duration: 6 hours
Elevation gain: 1,619 feet (493 m)
Effort: moderate-strenuous
Trail surface: narrow and rocky dirt path; rock steps
Trailheads: on the south side of Many Glacier Hotel, at Swiftcurrent Picnic Area, or via the tour boat from Many Glacier Hotel

In early summer, a large steep snowdrift frequently bars the path into the upper basin into July; check on status before hiking. The most accessible glacier in the park, **Grinnell Glacier** still requires stamina as most of its elevation gain is within a short distance. To hike the entire route from the picnic area, follow Swiftcurrent Lake's west shore to the upper boat dock. From Many Glacier Hotel, round the southern shore to meet up with the same dock. Bop over the hill and hike around Lake Josephine's north shore.

At the first junction toward Lake Josephine's west end, the Grinnell Glacier Trail diverges uphill. As the trail climbs through multicolored rock strata, Grinnell Lake's milky turquoise waters come into view below. Above, you'll spot Gem Glacier and Salamander Glacier, both shrunken to static snowfields, long before Grinnell Glacier appears. The trail ascends on a cliff stairway where a waterfall douses hikers before passing a rest stop with outhouses. A steep grunt up the moraine leads to the **overlook** of the glacier and **Upper Grinnell Lake.** You can explore the maze of paths crossing the bedrock to Upper Grinnell Lake's shore and the glacier's edge, but do not walk out on the ice, as it harbors deadly hidden crevasses. To return, you can hike back to

Top to bottom: Iceberg Lake; Grinnell Glacier; Scenic Point Trail at Two Medicine

your starting trailhead or trim off mileage by catching a return boat from the upper Josephine dock (8.5 mi/13.7 km rt) to Many Glacier Hotel. Many hikers take the boat shuttle both ways (7.8 mi/12.6 km rt).

Swiftcurrent Valley and Lookout
Distance: 3.6-16.2 miles (5.8-26 km) rt
Duration: 2-8 hours
Elevation gain: 100-3,496 feet (30.5-1,066 m)
Effort: easy-strenuous
Trail surface: narrow dirt path with roots and rocks
Trailhead: Swiftcurrent parking lot

This scenic trail with various turn-around points satisfies hikers of all abilities with stunning lakes, waterfalls, wildlife, and wildflowers. Additionally, both Swiftcurrent Pass and Lookout sit smack on top of the Continental Divide. The trail winds through pine trees and aspen groves, reaching a junction for **Fishercap Lake** (0.7 mi/1.1 km rt). This short spur trail is well worth taking for the chance to see moose. Back on the main trail, the path rolls gently up to **Red Rock Lake and Falls** (3.6 mi/5.8 km rt). Enjoy the lake scenery, scan the slopes for bears, and take the quick spur trail that drops to the base of the frothy falls. The trail continues through meadows rampant with Sitka valerian as well as intermittent forests, and crosses a swinging bridge to **Bullhead Lake** (7.8 mi/12.6 km rt) at the head of the valley, where you may spot bighorn sheep on the scree slopes above.

From the lake, the trail switchbacks uphill and cuts around a cliff face with impressive views of waterfalls, lakes in the valley below, and red mountainsides. The trail climbs through stunted firs and meadows to reach **Swiftcurrent Pass** (13.2 mi/21.2 km rt), where a giant cairn and bell tower (but no bell) remains. Just west of the pass is a junction. Go left and downhill for **Granite Park Chalet** (0.9 mi/1.4 km one-way) and stunning views of Heavens Peak. Go right and uphill to climb so many switchbacks that you'll lose count to reach **Swiftcurrent Lookout** (16.2 mi/26 km rt), the highest trail destination in the park. The lookout surveys glaciers, peaks, wild panoramas, and the plains. Many Glacier Hotel looks minuscule. Enjoy the one-of-a-kind view from the outhouse.

Two Medicine

Trails in Two Medicine are less crowded than those along Going-to-the-Sun Road. You can trim mileage off some hikes by taking the Two Medicine Lake tour boat as a shuttle. Make reservations if you are traveling on it up the lake; for the return trip, show up at the upper dock and pay cash when you board.

Scenic Point
Distance: 7.4 miles (11.9 km) rt
Duration: 4 hours
Elevation gain: 2,124 feet (647 m)
Effort: moderate-strenuous
Trail surface: narrow dirt path with roots and rocks
Trailhead: milepost 6.9 up Two Medicine Rd.

Scenic Point is one short climb with big scenery. The trail launches up through a thick subalpine fir forest. A short side jaunt en route allows a peek at **Appistoki Falls.** As switchbacks line up like dominoes, stunted firs give way to silvery dead and twisted limber pines. Broaching the ridge, the trail enters seemingly barren alpine tundra. Only alpine bluebells and pink mats of several-hundred-year-old moss campion cower in crags.

On the ridge, the trail traverses a north-facing slope; avoid the early-summer steep snowfield by climbing a worn path that goes above it before descending to **Scenic Point.** To reach the actual Scenic Point above the trail, cut off at the sign, stepping on rocks to avoid crushing fragile alpine plants. At the top, views plunge several thousand feet straight down to Lower Two Medicine Lake and across the plains. Retrace your steps for outstanding views of Two Medicine Lake on the return.

Rockwell Falls, Cobalt Lake, and Two Medicine Pass

Distance: 6.8-15.8 miles (10.9-25.4 km) rt
Duration: 4-8 hours
Elevation gain: minimal-2,518 feet (767 m)
Effort: easy-strenuous
Trail surface: narrow dirt path with roots and rocks
Trailhead: adjacent to Two Medicine boat dock

Follow the gentle South Shore Trail along Two Medicine Lake past beaver ponds and bear-scratched trees to Paradise Creek, crossing on a swinging bridge. At the signed junction, turn left to wander through avalanche paths with uprooted trees shredded like toothpicks. Cross the creek below **Rockwell Falls** (6.8 mi/10.9 km rt) on a log bridge; spur trails explore the falls on both sides.

Continuing on to **Cobalt Lake** (11.2 mi/18 km rt), the trail climbs up several switchbacks into an upper basin, where views open up and wildflowers abound. The ascent climbs at a moderate pitch until a short steep grunt right before the lake. Surrounded by rockfall that houses pikas, the dark blue lake sits below cliffs that harbor mountain goats.

The climb to **Two Medicine Pass** (15.8 mi/25.4 km rt) gets above the tree line. The path cuts up through alpine tundra along the windblown pass. From the high point atop Chief Lodgepole Mountain, you'll stare straight down a dizzying drop to Cobalt Lake with Two Medicine Lake in the distance.

Dawson-Pitamakin Loop

Distance: 17.9-mile (29-km) loop
Duration: 7-9 hours
Elevation gain: 2,909 feet (887 m)
Effort: strenuous
Trail surface: narrow dirt path with roots and loose rocks
Trailhead: Pray Lake Bridge in Two Medicine Campground

This trail takes one monster loop around Rising Wolf Mountain, crossing three passes: Pitamakin, Cut Bank, and Dawson. The latter two passes have strong winds that can knock you off-balance. Between the passes, the route crosses bighorn sheep summering terrain, offering opportunities to see newborns. Although this loop can be done from either direction, approaching **Dawson Pass** first is much steeper than **Pitamakin Pass.** So pick your route based on your preference or aversion to uphill grunts and knee-pounding descents. Taking the Two Medicine boat one direction shortens the route (15.3 mi/24.6 km rt).

After crossing the Pray Lake Bridge at Two Medicine Campground, the trail promptly splits. Go right to climb Pitamakin Pass first. The trail ascends the southeast flank of Rising Wolf and drops to cross Dry Fork Creek before climbing to **Old Man Lake.** From the lake junction, climb switchbacks to **Pitamakin Pass** to cross the narrow arête perched above Pitamakin Lake. The climb continues through alpine tundra overlooking **Lake of the Seven Winds** to reach the high point above **Cut Bank Pass.** The top-of-the-world traverse then heads south to **Dawson Pass.** Those with a fear of heights will be uncomfortable, but it's the best part of the trail. From Dawson Pass, the trail plunges to the North Shore Trail. Go left along Two Medicine Lake to complete the loop or go right, and then left at all junctions, to reach the boat dock. This loop can also be done as a backpacking trip.

North Fork

Hiking in the North Fork leads to stunning vistas, but be prepared to earn your views by tromping through thick, mosquito-ridden forests. The Inside Road limits vehicle length (21 ft/6.4 m maximum; no trailers).

Numa Lookout

Distance: 10.2 miles (16.4 km) rt
Duration: 5.5 hours
Elevation gain: 2,927 feet (892 m)
Effort: moderately strenuous
Trail surface: narrow dirt path with roots and rocks
Trailhead: Bowman Lake

Although the bulk of the trail crawls through deep forest, the view from Numa Lookout is well worth the climb. Following the northwest shore of Bowman Lake, the trail winds through damp cedars to a junction. Take the left fork to climb steadily uphill past a small, boggy mosquito pond and ascend switchbacks. After coming within view of the lookout, the treed slope breaks into dry, open meadows. **Numa Lookout,** which is staffed during fire season, has views across Bowman Lake at the steep massif of Square, Rainbow, and Carter Peaks.

Backpacking
Continental Divide Trail
117 miles (188 km)

On the **Continental Divide National Scenic Trail** (CDT, 3,100 mi/4,990 km), the northernmost route is in Glacier National Park (117 mi/188 km). Strong backpackers can cover Glacier's CDT in a week, but most prefer at least **10 days.** Weaving together backcountry campsites (by permit) and shared hiker campsites in front-country campgrounds, you can launch a CDT trek from Marias Pass Trailhead and finish by hiking across the border on the Waterton Lakeshore Trail into Canada. En route, the trail crosses high vistas usually snow-free after mid-July: Scenic Point, Pitamakin Pass, Triple Divide Pass, Piegan Pass, Swiftcurrent Pass, and Northern Highline. Because the route uses popular backcountry campsites, apply for an advance reservation permit in mid-March.

From Marias Pass, embark on the Autumn Creek Trail/CDT, heading to East Glacier to spend the first night in a hostel. Then, climb over Scenic Point (Blackfeet Tribal Conservation Permit required, $10) to overnight at Two Medicine Campground in a shared hiker campsite. Augment food supplies at the camp store. Continuing north, camp at Old Man Lake (OLD), Morning Star Lake (MOR) or Atlantic Creek (ATL), Red

Eagle Lake Head (REH) or Foot (REF), and Reynolds Creek (REY). After climbing over Piegan Pass to Many Glacier, camp in a shared hiker campsite at Many Glacier Campground, take a break from trail food by dining at 'Nell's in the Swiftcurrent Motor Inn, and resupply at the camp store. After departing Many Glacier, overnight at Granite Park (GRN), Fifty Mountain (FIF), and Kootenai Lakes (KOO). Finish the route by hiking the Waterton Lakeshore Trail across the boundary to the Waterton Townsite in Canada. Passports are required.

Northern Circle
52 miles (84 km)

Hike the **Northern Circle** for **5-7 days** in either direction to take in prime fishing lakes and high passes. To complete the loop, start and finish at one of five trailheads: Swiftcurrent, Iceberg-Ptarmigan Tunnel, Poia Lake, Chief Mountain Customs, or Goat Haunt.

The classic route launches in Many

Glacier from the Iceberg-Ptarmigan Tunnel Trailhead to drop into the Belly River drainage. Then connect Elizabeth, Cosley, and Glenns Lakes (fording the outlet river at Cosley) to ascend the Mokowanis River drainage. The route pitches up to Stoney Indian Pass and quickly plunges to Stoney Indian Lake, where the campground's wall-less pit toilet takes in surrounding peaks. After descending into Waterton Valley, the trail climbs to the immense meadows at Fifty Mountain. A long day traipses up and down through multiple high-elevation basins along the Continental Divide to the Granite Park Chalet before crossing over Swiftcurrent Pass to return to Many Glacier, exiting at the Swiftcurrent Trailhead.

Of the 12 backcountry campsites on or near the route, the best are Elizabeth Lake Foot (ELF), Cosley Lake (COS), Stoney Indian Lake (STO), Fifty Mountain (FIF), and Granite Park (GRN). Ptarmigan Tunnel usually opens mid-July, and the park service usually opens steep snowfields between Fifty Mountain and Granite Park by late July. Get walk-in permits for July, but advance reservations for Fifty Mountain and Stoney Indian Lake are only available starting August 1. Prepare for high-elevation snow in September.

Gunsight Pass
28 miles (45 km)

This four-day trek is best hiked from Jackson Glacier Overlook west over **Gunsight Pass** to finish at Lake McDonald Lodge, but you can do it in reverse or shorten it to three days. Spend the first night at **Gunsight Lake** (GUN). Then, climbing over Gunsight Pass, often crossing a steep snowfield or two in July and encountering mountain goats, descend to the boulder camp at **Lake Ellen Wilson** (ELL) for the second night. For the third night, a short ascent pops over Lincoln Pass to **Sperry Campground** (SPE), which was burned in the 2017

backpacking on Gunsight Pass Trail above Lake Ellen Wilson

Sprague Fire. Set up camp, hang your food, and hike up through Comeau Pass to Sperry Glacier. On the final day, descend to Lake McDonald Lodge.

Dawson-Pitamakin Loop
18.4 miles (29.6 km)
Although this route can be done as a day hike, you can also make a **three-day** backpacking trip of it. The **Dawson-Pitamakin Loop** takes a top-of-the-world Continental Divide traverse between high passes through bighorn sheep summering habitat and alpine tundra. Hike this loop in either direction, starting from the trailhead at Two Medicine Campground. Camp one night each at Old Man Lake (OLD) and No Name Lake (NON). The route is snow-free some summers by early July, but advance reservations are not available until July 15.

To extend this hike up the historic **Inside Route** (32 mi/52 km, 4-5 days), head north from Pitamakin Pass to Morning Star Lake (MOR), Triple Divide Pass, and Red Eagle Lake (REH or REF) to reach St. Mary, where a shuttle aids in returning to your vehicle.

Rental Gear and Guides
Backpacking rental gear is available through **Glacier Outfitters** (196 Apgar Loop Rd., Apgar, 406/219-7466, www.goglacieroutfitters.com) and **Glacier Guides** (11970 US 2 E., West Glacier, 406/387-5555, glacierguides.com). For guided backpacking, Glacier Guides leads group trips that depart weekly for three, four, or six days, as well as custom trips, which are the best option for families with kids.

Permits
Permits ($7 pp per night) are required. Starting mid-March, the park service accepts online requests for **advance reservations** ($40 extra). You'll still need to pick up the physical permit the day before your trip and pay the per-person fees. If you don't have an advance reservation, you can still nab a permit in person 24 hours prior to a trip. Current availability is updated frequently on the park's website. If you have your heart set on a **specific route in July-August,** be in line by 5:30am at the **Apgar Backcountry Permit Office** (406/888-7859 May-Oct., 406/888-7800 Nov.-Apr., 7am-4:30pm daily May-Sept., 8am-4pm daily Oct.) or **St. Mary Visitor Center** (406/888-7800, daily late May-early Oct., backcountry permit desk 7am-4:30pm)). You can also get permits in person at **Many Glacier Ranger Station, Two Medicine Ranger Station,** and **Polebridge Ranger Station.** During winter, permits are available at park headquarters by appointment (406/888-7800, Nov.-Apr.).

Biking
Going-to-the-Sun Road
Going-to-the-Sun Road is an unforgettable bicycle trip. While the 3,500-foot (1,067-m) climb up the west side seems intimidating, it's not steep, just a constant uphill grind amid stunning scenery.

Locals relish **spring riding** when the Sun Road is closed to cars. Cycling begins in early April as soon as snowplows free the pavement while the west-side road remains closed to vehicles from Lake McDonald Lodge or Avalanche, and the east side remains closed from Rising Sun. Riders climb up as far as plowing operations permit. Consult the park website to check on access, as construction or spring plowing limits cycling some days. Avalanche conditions may exist in the upper elevations.

In **summer,** when the Sun Road opens to vehicles, strong riders who are comfortable being pinched between cliffs and cars head for Logan Pass. Some riders return the way they came; others continue on to the other side. But due to heavy midday traffic, bicycles are not permitted 11am-4pm daily June 15-Labor Day in two sections on the west side: along Lake McDonald between the Apgar Road junction and Sprague Creek, and climbing

Sky-Gazing in Glacier

TOP EXPERIENCE

Recognized as an International Dark Sky Park, Glacier is a wonderful place to stay up after dark. Due to minimal light pollution, stars light up the sky on moonless nights, and you can see the Milky Way.

Logan Pass Star Parties

stars over Logan Pass

Logan Pass is one of the best places to view the night sky. The Big Sky Astronomy Club collaborates with the park service to host **Logan Pass Star Parties** (dates vary, 9:30pm-midnight, late July-early Sept.) with constellation tours and telescope viewing of planets, star clusters, and nebulae. The events usually take place about four nights per summer. For admittance, each vehicle must have a ticket; they are free from Apgar or St. Mary Visitor Centers. Tickets go fast, so plan to be at the visitors center by 8am on the day before the event to get them. For dates, consult the park newspaper or check on the park's website.

Star-Gazing Programs

Astronomy programs take place at the **St. Mary Observatory** (dates vary, 10pm-midnight, summer) when weather and dark skies permit. The observatory is in the St. Mary Visitor Center parking lot, where the telescope transfers real-time images onto two high-definition outdoor screens for viewing.

In the parking lot at **Apgar Visitor Center** (dates vary, 10pm-midnight, summer), rangers set up powerful **telescopes** for viewing stars and planets when weather and dark skies permit.

Self-Guided Stargazing

With Going-to-the-Sun Road open 24 hours daily, you can drive up to **Logan Pass** on your own for stargazing. Choose a moonless night, turn off all white lights, and use red flashlights to help your eyes adapt to the darkness, which will take about 30 minutes. Even with the naked eye, you can spot the International Space Station passing overhead. When the sky gets really dark, the Milky Way appears.

Solar Viewing

Rangers set up special **solar viewing telescopes** (dates vary, afternoons, July-Aug.) on sunny, clear days. Check the park newspaper or on the park's website for times. In Apgar, the telescopes are usually set up at Apgar Village Green across from Apgar Village Inn. In St. Mary, solar telescopes are set up outside the St. Mary Visitor Center.

uphill between Avalanche Campground and Logan Pass. From the west side, head out from Lake McDonald by 6:30am for adequate time to pedal to Logan Pass. In early summer, long daylight hours allow for riding after 4pm, when traffic lessens.

The east side has no restrictions, but it's still easier to ride early or late in the day with fewer cars on the road. Some shuttle buses are equipped with bicycle racks. Catch the shuttles only at official stops.

Because the Sun Road is so narrow, it

is not the place for a family ride, except when the road is closed to cars.

Apgar Bike Trail

The paved **Apgar Bike Trail** (4 mi/6.4 km rt) links Apgar with West Glacier. The gentle trail provides the best route for family bicycling, with ice cream rewards on either end.

Inside Road

Mountain bikers can ride the sections of the **Inside Road** that are closed to cars to Anaconda Creek, where multiple creeks have washed out the road. The section from Logging Creek Ranger Station south to Anaconda Creek (9 mi/14 km rt) tours along Sullivan Meadows, ponderosas, and aspens. The segment from Camas Creek north to Anaconda Creek (13 mi/21 km rt) climbs and drops hills until reaching the steep descent down Anaconda Hill to Anaconda Creek. Check with the Apgar Visitor Center for conditions, especially downed trees.

Rentals, Guides, and Shuttles

Glacier Outfitters (196 Apgar Loop Rd., Apgar, 406/219-7466, www. goglacieroutfitters.com, mid-May-mid-Sept.) rents bicycles for adults and kids, e-bikes, tagalongs, trailers, and car racks. **Polebridge Outfitters** (265 Polebridge Loop, Polebridge, 406/888-5229, www. polebridgemerc.com, May-Oct.) rents mountain bikes and e-bikes.

In spring, when Going-to-the-Sun Road is closed to vehicles, **Glacier Guides** (11970 US 2 E., West Glacier, 406/387-5555, glacierguides.com) leads bicycle tours on the west side and has bicycle and e-bike rentals. A **shuttle with a bike trailer** (starts mid-May, 9am-5pm weekends only, free) runs from Apgar Visitor Center to Lake McDonald Lodge and Avalanche.

Top to bottom: cycling Going-to-the-Sun Road; horseback trail ride; paddling Lake McDonald

Horseback Riding

Swan Mountain Outfitters (406/387-4405 or 877/888-5557, www.swanmountainglacier.com, daily late May-early Sept., $55-200) operates three corral locations: in Apgar, at Lake McDonald Lodge, and in Many Glacier. One- and two-hour trail rides depart several times daily. You'll be in a line of as many as 15 horses during your ride, but the scenery is well worth it. Reservations are strongly advised. Be sure to wear long pants; you'll be a lot less sore afterward. For safety, wear sturdy shoes or hiking boots, not sandals.

Located on Glacier Institute Road just inside the West Glacier entrance station, the **Apgar Corral** (1-3 hrs or half day) uses forested trails that flank Lower McDonald Creek. The half-day ride to Apgar Lookout requires a minimum of four people.

Located across Going-to-the-Sun Road from the Lake McDonald Lodge complex, the **Lake McDonald Lodge Corral** (1-2.5 hrs or all day) leads trail rides through the valley for views of McDonald Creek, lichen-laden cedars, and peaks. Full-day rides go to Trout Lake or Sperry Chalet.

Adjacent to the Many Glacier Hotel parking lot, the **Many Glacier Corral** (1-2 hrs, half day, or all day) guides trail rides to Swiftcurrent Lake, Lake Josephine, and Cracker Flats. Half-day rides go up into the Piegan Valley or Sherburne Overlook. All-day rides go on varied trails.

Paddling and Boating

Glacier National Park has strict boating and paddling guidelines in order to protect its pristine waters from invasive aquatic species. All watercraft coming into the area must stop at inspection stations. The lakes are only open in summer and only available by **permit** to boaters and paddlers who have passed an inspection. Jet Skis are banned on all lakes. For most short-term visitors, the procedure alone for getting a permit prohibits trailering a powerboat from home,

as all **gas-powered boats** and their trailers must be inspected, sealed, and quarantined for 30 days to completely dry out before a permit is issued. **Electric-powered** and **hand-propelled watercraft** can get a same-day inspection and permit to launch immediately without quarantining. Get inspections at **St. Mary Visitor Center** (7am-4:30pm daily June-Sept.) or in Apgar for **Lake McDonald** (7am-9pm daily mid-May-Oct., shorter hours May and late Sept.-Oct.). Inspections and permits are available at the **Many Glacier Ranger Station** (7am-4:30pm daily).

Lake McDonald

Lake McDonald has only one boat ramp in Apgar, but hand-carried craft can launch from Sprague Creek Picnic Area or several pullouts along the lake. When the lake is placid, these locations make for prime morning and evening paddling. The lake is **open mid-May to October.**

Find two boat rental companies in **Apgar**. Rentals include life jackets, paddles, and fuel. From the Apgar boat rental dock near Apgar Village Inn, **Glacier Park Boat Company** (406/257-2426, glacierparkboats.com, 10am-6pm daily late May-June, 9am-7pm daily July-early Sept., $15-30/hr) rents paddleboards, canoes, single and double kayaks, rowboats, and small motorboats. From the lake in Apgar, **Glacier Outfitters** (196 Apgar Loop Rd., 406/219-7466, www.goglacieroutfitters.com, 9am-5pm daily May-Sept., $24-40 for 2 hrs) rents paddleboards, kayaks, and canoes. They also have a 24-hour rental option, so you can take your boat to other lakes in Glacier.

St. Mary, Many Glacier, and Two Medicine

Glacier's east-side lakes offer outstanding paddling, but the larger lakes are subject to big winds. Be aware of changing conditions for safety. The park's east-side lakes are **open June to September.**

St. Mary Lake has gusty winds that can

Rafting in Glacier

Two Wild and Scenic Rivers provide the boundary for Glacier on the west and south-west sides, converging at West Glacier, the rafting capital for Glacier. All trips are outside the park but right on the boundary where they offer scenery, wilderness, flat-water float sections, and white water. Half-day and full-day trips run the **Middle Fork of the Flathead,** which has scenic float sections interrupted by raging white water. White-water trips provide splashy fun, good for families and youths; kids 6 and under usually need to stick to scenic floats. Overnights are best on the **North Fork of the Flathead,** which has a more wilderness feel. Rafting season runs **May to September,** with high water usually peaking in late May. By late August, both rivers run at their lowest levels with plenty of exposed, dry gravel bars.

Guides

Four rafting companies in West Glacier lead white-water trips, overnights, and scenic, dinner, barbecue, and evening floats. Expect to pay about $60-95 for half-day trips or $100-130 for full day; kids run $10-25 less.

♦ **Glacier Raft Company:** 106 Going-to-the-Sun Rd., 406/888-5454 or 800/235-6781, glacierraftco.com

♦ **Great Northern Whitewater:** 12127 US 2 E., 406/387-5340 or 800/735-7897, greatnorthernresort.com

♦ **Montana Raft Company:** 11970 US 2 E., 406/387-5555, glacierguides.com

♦ **Wild River Adventures:** 11900 US 2 E., 406/387-9453 or 800/700-7056, www.riverwild.com

Rentals and Shuttles

♦ **Polebridge Outfitters** (265 Polebridge Loop, Polebridge, 406/888-5229, www.polebridgemerc.com, $60-80) rents inflatable kayaks for one or two people.

♦ **Glacier Guides** (11970 US 2 E., West Glacier, 406/387-5555, glacierguides.com) rents rafts, inflatable kayaks, and overnight gear, plus it runs shuttles for rafters on the North Fork of the Flathead River.

challenge novice boaters but that skilled windsurfers enjoy. Keep alert to conditions. The lake allows only non-trailered electric-powered motorboats and hand-propelled watercraft; no trailers are allowed to enter the water. The boat launch is at Rising Sun. From there, you can cross up-lake to **Silver Dollar Beach** below Red Eagle Mountain. No rentals are available.

Many Glacier has smaller lakes that are more protected from big winds, surrounded by stunning scenery and sometimes moose. Only nonmotorized boats are permitted: sailboats, kayaks, rowboats, paddleboards, and canoes. Kayakers can cross **Swiftcurrent Lake** and paddle the connecting slow-moving **Cataract Creek** upstream to **Lake Josephine,** where a shoreline loop makes a scenic tour. The public boat ramp on Swiftcurrent Lake sits east of the picnic area. Rent rowboats and single or double kayaks from **Glacier Park Boat Company** (boat dock at Many Glacier Hotel, 406/257-2426, glacierparkboats.com, 8am-7pm daily July-early Sept., shorter hours June and Sept., $18-22/hr) for use only on Swiftcurrent Lake. Paddles and life jackets are included.

On calm days, kayaks, canoes, and paddleboards tour the shoreline of **Two Medicine Lake.** But it's one of the windiest lakes in the park, so boaters need to keep an eye on waves; if whitecaps pop up, get off the lake. Some paddlers prefer the tiny **Pray Lake** in Two Medicine Campground for its more protected water. Two Medicine Road terminates at the public boat ramp, so it's easy to find. Hand-propelled watercraft and non-trailered electric-powered boats are allowed. Located at the Two Medicine boat dock, **Glacier Park Boat Company** (406/257-2426, glacierparkboats.com, 8am-6:30pm daily July-mid-Sept., shorter hours June, $18-28/hr) rents canoes, single and double kayaks, rowboats, and small motorboats. Life jackets, paddles, and fuel are included.

North Fork

The remote **Kintla Lake** and **Bowman Lake** (June-Sept.) have prime paddling for kayaks, canoes, and paddleboards. Kintla allows only hand-propelled watercraft, while Bowman allows non-trailered electric motors of 10 horsepower or less. These are quiet waters that appeal to paddlers. While both lakes have stellar paddling on calm days, their waters can kick up with gusty winds in minutes. Wildlife closures are marked with orange buoys at the head of each lake, where bald eagles nest.

All boaters and paddlers must pick up **permits** after an inspection at the station across from the Apgar boat ramp (7am-9pm daily June-Sept.) **before driving up the North Fork.** With a backcountry permit, paddlers can camp overnight in campgrounds at the heads of Kintla and Bowman Lakes. Be aware: The roads to both lakes limit vehicle length (21 ft/6.4 m maximum; no trailers).

In Polebridge, **Polebridge Outfitters** (265 Polebridge Loop, 406/888-5229, www.polebridgemerc.com, $40-80)

rents paddleboards and inflatable kayaks. Make reservations online.

Fishing

Glacier provides a stunning backdrop for fishing. No fishing licenses are required, but check current fishing regulations at visitors centers or on the park's website.

The camp stores at Lake McDonald Lodge and Rising Sun sell a few tackle items. **Glacier Outfitters** (196 Apgar Loop Rd., Apgar, 406/219-7466, www. goglacieroutfitters.com, 9am-5pm daily mid-May-late Sept., shorter hours in shoulder seasons) rents fishing gear.

Lake McDonald is a haven for kokanee, lake trout, whitefish, and cutthroat. Hike to the chilly inlet streams on the south end of **Avalanche Lake** for westslope cutthroat that have been kept genetically pure by the gorge's falls. The **Hidden Lake Trail** goes to Hidden Lake, which holds good-size Yellowstone cutthroat trout, but it is closed until July 31 due to bears feeding on spawning trout.

Accessible in the **North Fork** via the rugged Inside Road from the Polebridge entrance, quiet **Kintla** and **Bowman Lakes** attract anglers. For hikers, the three **Quartz Lakes** hop with native trout and whitefish. The most popular North Fork fishing is on the **North Fork of the Flathead River,** where licenses are required from the west shore outside the park, but not the east shore inside the park. Purchase licenses at **Glacier Outdoor Center** (12400 US 2 E., West Glacier, 406/888-5454 or 800/235-6781, glacierraftco.com) before driving up the North Fork.

In **St. Mary,** hike to **Red Eagle Lake** for the best fishing for native westslope cutthroat. **Many Glacier** offers lots of fishing holes at Grinnell, Josephine, Swiftcurrent, Red Rock, Bullhead, and Ptarmigan Lakes. **Cataract Creek** between Lake Josephine and Swiftcurrent Lake contains brook trout.

In the **Two Medicine Valley,** brook

trout populate the lakes. For **Two Medicine Lake,** anglers have more success casting from a boat rather than the heavily timbered and brushy shore. Flanking Two Medicine Campground, **Pray Lake** is a great place to take kids to fish.

Food

The majority of restaurants and convenience stores in Glacier are run by **Xanterra** (855/733-4522, www.glacier nationalparklodges.com). Although small, menus focus on local ingredients and offer options for vegetarians, vegans, kids, and travelers on a budget.

Inside the Park
Going-to-the-Sun Road

There are limited restaurants on the Sun Road, and only at lower elevations. Pack a picnic lunch to take advantage of the scenery. Restaurants offer lunches to go, and convenience stores sell picnic foods.

Picnic areas line lower elevations on or near the road. They have flush or vault toilets and picnic tables. Some have firepits with grills; bring your own firewood. Around Lake McDonald, you can picnic at **Fish Creek, Apgar,** and **Sprague Creek,** all near the shore. The picnic area at **Avalanche Creek** sits at the confluence with larger McDonald Creek. On the east side, find picnic areas at windy **Sun Point** and **Rising Sun,** both with short trails.

At **Lake McDonald Lodge** (288 Lake McDonald Lodge Loop, 855/733-4522, daily mid-May-late Sept.), the headliner dining room is ★ **Russell's Fireside Dining Room,** full of historical ambience and decorated with chandeliers painted in Indigenous patterns. The north windows have a peekaboo lake view, but during dinner the blinds usually need to be pulled down as the hot sun blazes in. Breakfast (6:30am-10am, $9-18) is a choice of continental buffet, full buffet, or menu entrées. Lunch (11:30am-2pm, $10-18) serves small plates, burgers,

sandwiches, salads, and pasta. Dinner (5pm-9:30pm, $17-30) can go casual with burgers, salads, and pasta or full-on dining with charcuterie, shared appetizers, and plated entrées of fish or meats.

Also inside the lodge, the cozy **Lucke's Lounge** (11:30am-10pm, $10-19) serves a more limited menu of appetizers, sandwiches, burgers, and salads. The bar also stocks plenty of local microbrews along with wine and craft cocktails. The best option for families is the cafeteria-style **Jammer Joe's Grill and Pizzeria** (11am-9pm, closes early Sept., $11-22), located across from the lodge. It has a broad menu that includes wraps and salads plus foods with kid appeal, like pizza and burgers.

As the only restaurant in Apgar, **Eddie's Café & Mercantile** (236 Apgar Loop Rd., 406/888-5361, www.eddiescafe gifts.com, 8am-10pm daily May-mid-Sept.) has lines in midsummer. It serves breakfasts and lunches ($9-16), including hiker lunches to go. Dinner ($13-26) has burgers, sandwiches, trout, buffalo meatloaf, and steak. Montana microbrews or wine can accompany dinner. Dine inside or outside on the streetside deck. An outdoor stand serves ice cream cones and basic espresso drinks, and you can also buy convenience foods, drinks, camping supplies, ice, and firewood at Eddie's Mercantile next door.

Located at Rising Sun across from the motor inn, **Two Dog Flats Grill** (406/732-5523, daily mid-June-mid-Sept.) is the only restaurant on the east side of Going-to-the-Sun Road. It serves breakfast 6:30am-10am ($6-11). Lunch and dinner are served 11am-10pm ($10-26), with full plated dinners starting at 5pm. The casual American fare includes sandwiches, burgers, pasta, salads, and home-style grill dinners. Beer and wine are available, too. Ask for a south window table to see Red Eagle Peak. When crowded with bus tours midsummer, you may have to wait for a table. If the line is really long, go 6 miles (9.7 km) east to St. Mary for more dining options; the evening return drive offers good wildlife-watching along Two Dog Flats.

Many Glacier

In **Many Glacier Hotel** (milepost 11.5, Many Glacier Rd., 855/733-4522, daily early June-mid-Sept.), the ★ **Ptarmigan Dining Room** has massive windows that look out on Swiftcurrent Lake, Grinnell Point, and Mount Wilbur. The views provide strong competition for the renovated interior, mimicking the dining room's original look in 1915. For breakfast (6:30am-10am, $12-18), choose between a continental buffet or hot entrée buffet. Lunch (11:30am-2:30pm, $10-22) serves pasta, salads, sandwiches, and burgers. Dinner (5pm-9:30pm, $12-44) has prime rib, Wagyu steak, duck, fish, and more casual burgers, pasta, and salads. For small plates, sandwiches, salads, and pasta, go to the adjacent **Swiss Room bar** (11:30am-10pm, $8-21).

At the Swiftcurrent Motor Inn, **'Nell's** (2 Many Glacier Rd., 406/732-5531, 6:30am-10pm daily, $6-16) has tables with maps for discussing trails. The café crowds at mealtimes due to its location adjacent to the campground, cabins, and motel. Breakfast can go light or traditional. Appetizers, sandwiches, pasta, pizza, and salads frame the diner-style lunch and dinner menu.

The **Many Glacier Picnic Area** has picnic tables, firepits with grills, and toilets. Best of all, it has views of Mount Altyn, where you can spot bears, bighorn sheep, and mountain goats.

Two Medicine

On the shore of Two Medicine Lake, **Two Medicine Campstore** (end of Two Medicine Rd., 8:30am-6pm daily summer) operates in what used to be the historic dining hall for Two Medicine Chalets. A tiny café in the back of the store sells espresso, soft-serve ice cream, cold drinks, muffins, cinnamon rolls, breakfast burritos, soup, bison chili, and several types of pasties.

The **Two Medicine Picnic Area** is on a loop along Two Medicine Lake with views of Rising Wolf Mountain. On windy days, select a site with some trees for wind breaks. It has picnic tables, fire rings with grills, and toilets.

Outside the Park
St. Mary

At the lodge at **St. Mary Village** (junction of Going-to-the-Sun Road and US 89, 406/892-2525, front desk 406/732-4431, www.glacierparkcollection.com, daily early June-late Sept.), the **Snowgoose Grille** looks up at striking Singleshot Mountain. The dining room serves up breakfast (6:30am-10am, $9-15), lunch (11:30am-2:30pm, $12-16), and dinner (5pm-9:30pm, $14-31). No reservations are taken. For an alternative, order sandwiches and appetizers in the adjacent **Mountain Bar** (11:30am-10pm daily), or on warm days sit on the deck overlooking Divide Creek.

St. Mary is home to two family-run cafés, where reservations are not taken and no alcohol is served. The Hilton family runs the **Park Café** (3147 US 89, 406/732-9979, parkcafeandgrocery. com, 7am-9pm daily early June-mid-Sept., shorter hours early and late season, $10-22). Homemade berry pies are baked every morning, and they serve breakfast, lunch, and dinner with a few Tex-Mex options. For a throwback experience, **Johnson's World Famous Historic Restaurant** (21 Red Eagle Rd., 406/732-5565, johnsonsofstmary.squarespace. com, 7am-9pm daily mid-May-late Sept., $9-27) serves up most of its daily specials family style with home-baked bread. The small, old-fashioned restaurant serves its eggs, bacon, and hash browns all on one big platter for the entire table. The soup lunch shows up in a large tureen. Dinner features country foods, served individually or family style.

East Glacier

In the historic Glacier Park Lodge, the

St. Mary

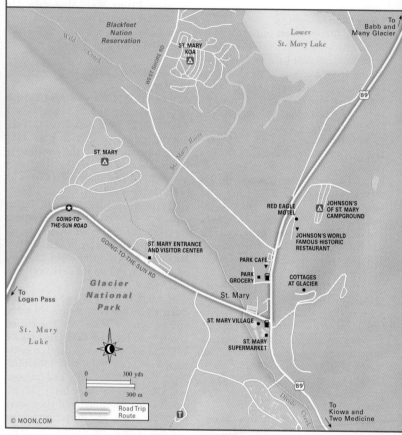

Blackfeet
Nation
Reservation

Wild Creek

WEST SHORE RD

ST. MARY
KOA

Lower
St. Mary Lake

To
Babb and
Many Glacier

89

St. Mary River

ST. MARY

RED EAGLE
MOTEL

JOHNSON'S
OF ST. MARY
CAMPGROUND

GOING-TO-
THE-SUN ROAD

GOING-TO-THE-SUN RD

ST. MARY ENTRANCE
AND VISITOR CENTER

JOHNSON'S WORLD
FAMOUS HISTORIC
RESTAURANT

PARK CAFÉ

PARK
GROCERY

COTTAGES
AT GLACIER

To
Logan Pass

Glacier
National
Park

St. Mary

ST. MARY VILLAGE

St. Mary
Lake

ST. MARY
SUPERMARKET

0   300 yds

0   300 m

Road Trip
Route

© MOON.COM

89

Divide Creek

To
Kiowa and
Two Medicine

Great Northern Dining Room (1 Midvale Rd., 406/892-2525, front desk 406/226-5600, www.glacierparkcollection.com, daily early June-late Sept.) has the best mountain views of any restaurant in town. The view and the historical ambience draw diners to the restaurant, which doesn't take reservations. Breakfast (6:30am-10am, $10-17) is frequently a huge buffet or à la carte breakfast dishes. Dinner (5pm-9:30pm, $18-35) has steak, fish, and vegetarian dishes. Order bag lunches one day in advance.

The line of people on the front porch of ★ **Serrano's Mexican Restaurant** (29 Dawson Ave., 406/226-9392, www.serranosmexican.com, 5pm-10pm daily May-Sept., $10-21) attests to its tasty food. The made-from-scratch Veggie Delight and Enchilada Especial top the choices of house specialties and pacify hungry hikers. Eat inside the cozy dining room with wooden booths or sit on the deck out back. Either way, the margaritas go down easy.

Opposite the train station, **Two Medicine Grill** (314 US 2, 406/226-9227, www.seeglacier.com, 6:30am-9pm daily spring-fall, shorter hours in winter, $6-15) is a local hangout for diner-type meals, espresso drinks, gooey homemade cinnamon rolls, wild huckleberry shakes, bison burgers, and pies made with a butter crust. You can sit on one of the eight stools at the bar or eat in the tiny dining room.

North of the railroad tracks, the **Whistle Stop Restaurant** (1024 MT 49, 406/226-9292, 7am-9pm daily June-Sept., $7-28) serves up the breakfast specialties of huckleberry-stuffed French toast and baked oatmeal. Lunch and dinner bring on barbecue platters, plus burgers including bison. Top it off with huckleberry pie.

West Glacier

At the historic **Belton Chalet** (12575 US 2 E., 844/868-7474, www.glacier parkcollection.com, mid-May-early Oct., $8-38), you can dine in the intimate **Belton Grill** (5pm-10pm daily), by the fireplace in the **Taproom** (3pm-midnight daily), or on the **deck** for views of Apgar Mountain. The chalet serves shared plates, salads made with local ingredients, and entrées that include bison meatloaf, Montana Wagyu beef, and fish.

Two restaurants serve café fare. Menus are geared toward a variety of tastes, and adults can sip beer and wine. The **West Glacier Restaurant** (200 Going-to-the-Sun Rd., 406/888-5359, www.glacierparkcollection.com, 7am-9pm daily mid-May-late Sept., $10-33) caters to hungry hikers with sandwiches and burgers of all kinds: beef, elk, and lentil. The beer crowd heads to the adjacent bar, locally known as **Freda's,** to order saloon food. With a large menu, the family-owned **Glacier Highland** (12555 US 2 E., 406/888-5427, glacierhighland.com, 7:30am-10pm daily mid-Apr.-mid-Oct., $10-33) bakes huckleberry pancakes for breakfast and serves fresh huckleberry pie for dessert. Dinner specialties include buffalo meatloaf, steak, and rainbow trout.

From an orange food truck surrounded by festive picnic tables, the **Wandering Gringo** (12135 US 2 E., 11:30am-7:30pm Wed.-Mon. late May-early Sept., $3-12) wraps up fresh tacos and burritos. Prepare for outside dining only and mosquitoes in early summer at this locals' hangout. In the Crown of the Continent Discovery Center, **La Casita** (12000 US 2 E., 406/471-2570, noon-7:30pm Mon.-Sat. May-Sept., $5-20) dishes up authentic chimichangas, quesadillas, tacos, and mole with ample portions from family recipes. The salsas, guacamole, and tortillas are made fresh daily.

Polebridge

The red-planked ★ **Polebridge Mercantile** (265 Polebridge Loop, 406/888-5105, polebridgemerc.com, 7am-9pm daily summer, shorter hours Apr.-June and Sept.-Oct.), or "Merc," is a place to pick up forgotten camping items and a couple groceries. But most of the Merc's fans go for the fresh-from-the-propane-oven pastries, cookies, breads, huckleberry bear claws, and cinnamon rolls, all based on recipes passed down through successive owners. Other treats include espresso, ice cream, and deli sandwiches for the road or trail.

A rustic solar-powered restaurant in a tiny, funky old log cabin, the **Northern Lights Saloon** (255 Polebridge Loop, 406/888-9963, www.thenorthernlightssaloon.com, 11am-9pm daily late May-mid-Sept., $10-30) is where hikers stop to celebrate with a beer, a glass of wine, or a cocktail, and then linger over a meal. Expect to relax over your meal rather than gobble and go; this is not a fast-food joint. The limited menu has vegetarian options, plus elk burgers and rainbow trout. Saturday night usually serves prime rib. The unique backwoods ambience is the draw. Outdoor seating makes for great people-watching, and live music happens frequently in summer.

West Glacier

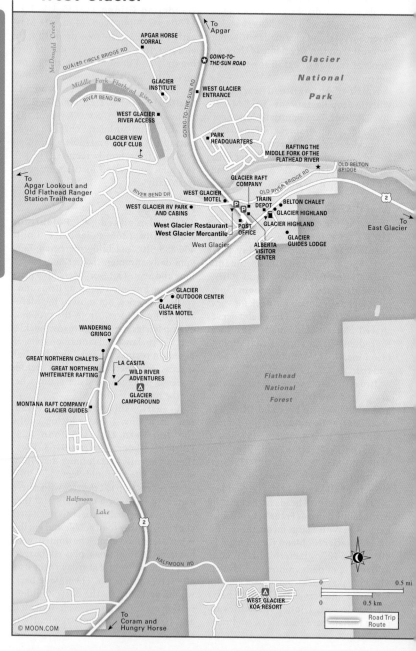

To Apgar

GOING-TO-THE-SUN ROAD

APGAR HORSE CORRAL

QUARTER CIRCLE BRIDGE RD

McDonald Creek

Middle Fork Flathead River

RIVER BEND DR

GLACIER INSTITUTE

WEST GLACIER ENTRANCE

WEST GLACIER RIVER ACCESS

GOING-TO-THE-SUN RD

PARK HEADQUARTERS

Glacier National Park

GLACIER VIEW GOLF CLUB

To Apgar Lookout and Old Flathead Ranger Station Trailheads

RIVER BEND DR

WEST GLACIER MOTEL

RAFTING THE MIDDLE FORK OF THE FLATHEAD RIVER

OLD BELTON BRIDGE

OLD RIVER BRIDGE RD

GLACIER RAFT COMPANY

WEST GLACIER RV PARK AND CABINS

TRAIN DEPOT

BELTON CHALET

GLACIER HIGHLAND

GLACIER HIGHLAND

To East Glacier

West Glacier Restaurant
West Glacier Mercantile

POST OFFICE

West Glacier

ALBERTA VISITOR CENTER

GLACIER GUIDES LODGE

GLACIER OUTDOOR CENTER

GLACIER VISTA MOTEL

WANDERING GRINGO

GREAT NORTHERN CHALETS

LA CASITA

GREAT NORTHERN WHITEWATER RAFTING

WILD RIVER ADVENTURES

GLACIER CAMPGROUND

MONTANA RAFT COMPANY/ GLACIER GUIDES

Flathead National Forest

Halfmoon Lake

HALFMOON RD

WEST GLACIER KOA RESORT

To Coram and Hungry Horse

© MOON.COM

0   0.5 mi

0   0.5 km

Road Trip Route

Accommodations and Camping

Inside the Park

Accommodations in Glacier are old, lacking air-conditioning, in-room TVs, internet, phones, and elevators. Although the lodges are busy during the day, they quiet down at night. Reservations are a must inside the park. Most lodges are operated by **Xanterra** (855/733-4522, www.glaciernationalparklodges.com), which takes bookings 13 months in advance. These go fast.

Cell reception is only available at the Apgar lodges, although Wi-Fi and pay phones are often available in lobbies. All properties have restaurants and convenience stores either on-site or nearby.

Going-to-the-Sun Road
Lodges
All lodges on the Sun Road have shuttle stops, so you can ditch the car and let someone else do the driving.

On Lake McDonald's beach, every one of the 36 guest rooms in the two-story ★ **Apgar Village Inn** (62 Apgar Loop Rd., late May-mid-Sept., $185-320) has an unobstructed million-dollar lake view. Although the nondescript guest rooms were redecorated in 2015, not much else has changed since it was built in 1956. Some guest rooms include kitchenettes, and family units can sleep up to six.

A National Historic Landmark, ★ **Lake McDonald Lodge** (288 Lake McDonald Lodge Loop, mid-May-late Sept., $118-515) graces the southeast lake shore. Centered around a massive stone fireplace and hunting lodge-themed lobby full of trophy specimens, the complex has four types of accommodations: main lodge rooms, cabin rooms, Cobb House suites, and Snyder Hall. Dial back your expectations to the mid-1900s, and you'll be delighted with the location and historical ambience. Some lakeside rooms

have views. Most rooms are small with bathrooms converted from original closets. Snyder Hall has shared bathrooms. Cobb House has two-room suites with televisions.

Pursuit (844/868-7474, www.glacierparkcollection.com) operates two Lake McDonald properties and accepts reservations 13-16 months in advance. In Apgar, under huge old-growth cedars along McDonald Creek, **Apgar Village Lodge and Cabins** (33 Apgar Loop Rd., late May-late Sept., $120-335) offers 20 small motel rooms and 28 rustic cabins, some with kitchens, within a few steps of Lake McDonald. The creek cabins (6, 7, and 8) are particularly serene, with chances to see wildlife and the sound of the stream. In the Lake McDonald Lodge complex, the 1950s-style two-story **Motel Lake McDonald** (3 Lake McDonald Lodge Loop, mid-June-mid-Sept., $180-200) has spartan rooms set deep in the cedars with no lake views.

Rising Sun Motor Inn (2 Going-to-the-Sun Rd., mid-June-mid-Sept., $182-200) is a funky 1940s motor inn with board-and-batten construction. The rooms were revamped in 2016 and have diminutive private baths. A trail to Otokomi Lake begins near the store, and access to St. Mary Lake is across the street, along with the boat tour dock. It's hard to beat this location; it's the closest lodging to Logan Pass.

Backcountry Chalets
Glacier has two backcountry chalets that remain from its early days, when Great Northern Railway erected chalets throughout the park and guests traveled between them via horseback. Despite their rustic amenities and **hiking or horseback as the only access,** these are ultra-popular. **Reservations** open in January and sell out promptly. Take a flashlight to find the composting vault toilets at night (no flush toilets). Pack along earplugs, as snores resound through thin walls.

Set at the same elevation as Logan Pass, ★ **Granite Park Chalet** (406/387-5654 or 888/345-2649, www.graniteparkchalet. com, late June-early Sept.) sits atop a knoll with a 360-degree view. The main chalet contains the kitchen, dining room, and guest rooms. More rooms are in another building. Twelve guest rooms sleep 2-6 people each ($120 first person in room, $82 per added person). This chalet functions somewhat like a hostel. Bring your own sleeping bag. Meals are not supplied; haul your own food to cook in the kitchen. Pots and pans are available for cooking on the 12-burner propane stove with an oven, but you'll need to bring your own mugs, plates, bowls, eating utensils, and water filter. With **no running water,** guests haul water for cooking and washing from 0.2 mile (0.3 km) away. For hikers looking to lighten their load, purchase linen service ($25 for sheets, a pillow, and blankets), preorder freeze-dried food ($2-15/item), and purchase environmentally friendly disposable plates and utensils. Stay for two nights to allow time for hiking to Grinnell Overlook, Swiftcurrent Lookout, or Ahern Pass. Most hikers reach the chalet from **Logan Pass** (7.6 mi/12 km) or climb up from **The Loop** (4 mi/6.4 km); use Going-to-the-Sun Road shuttles to connect with trailheads at Logan Pass and The Loop. Another access is via the uphill climb over **Swiftcurrent Pass** (7.6 mi/12 km); using shuttles to return to Swiftcurrent, you can exit via a different trail.

The Sprague Fire burned **Sperry Chalet** (406/387-5654 or 888/345-2649, www. sperrychalet.com, mid-July-mid-Sept.) in 2017, but it has since been rebuilt. It offers hikers and horseback riders three meals and a warm bed, which means hauling only a day pack with some extra clothing. Set in a timbered cirque, the chalet has a dining hall and sleeping lodge with private rooms that sleep 2-6 people each ($240 for first person in room, $160 per additional person in room) in bunks or

Lake McDonald Lodge

beds with bedding included. Faucets put out cold water only. Country roasts rotate for nightly dinners, but the menu has maintained culinary sensibilities from the 1950s, with canned fruits and vegetables. Trail lunches packed for you are plain, with a meat sandwich (no lettuce or tomato), candy bars, and fruit leather. However, outstanding bakery goods use decades-old recipes for cookies, freshly baked breads, and pies. Stay for two nights to hike to Sperry Glacier on your middle day. To reach Sperry, make the big climb from **Lake McDonald** (6.2 mi/10 km) or hike a strenuous ascent over two passes from **Jackson Glacier Overlook** (14 mi/23 km). You can use shuttles between the trailheads.

Many Glacier

Lodges

★ **Many Glacier Hotel** (milepost 11.5, Many Glacier Rd., early June-mid-Sept., $220-590) is the largest of the park's historic lodges and the most popular due to

its stunning location. Set on Swiftcurrent Lake, the immense National Historic Landmark cowers below surrounding peaks. The lodge centers around its massive four-story lobby with a huge fireplace. Some guest rooms and suites (some with decks) face the lake, while eastside guest rooms get the sunrise, with a unique morning wake-up call as the horses jangle to the corral. A Swiss theme pervades the hotel, with gingerbread cutout deck railings and bellhops dressed in lederhosen. Activities include paddling, trail riding, red bus and boat tours, and hiking. What the hotel lacks in amenities it makes up for in historical ambience, dramatic scenery, bear-watching, and convenience to many trailheads.

Motels and Cabins

At Many Glacier Road's terminus, **Swiftcurrent Motor Inn** (2 Many Glacier Rd., mid-June-mid-Sept., $120-200) has cabins and simple motel rooms. Heated cabins come with or without bathrooms. For austere units without baths, a central comfort station and shower house with lukewarm water awaits. Historical charm isn't the lure but rather the price and utter convenience to trailheads such as Red Rock and Bullhead Lakes, Granite Park Chalet, Swiftcurrent Pass and Lookout, Iceberg Lake, and Ptarmigan Tunnel.

Campgrounds

Glacier has 13 campgrounds (406/888-7800, www.nps.gov/glac). All campsites have picnic tables, fire rings with grills, firewood for sale, picnic tables, and flush or vault toilets. No hookups for RVs are available. Shared sites ($5-8 pp) for hikers and bikers have bear-resistant food storage. For first-come, first-served campgrounds, historic and current fill times are posted online. Use the previous few days to gauge when to arrive to claim a site. You can also find out the campground status on the **Recreational Access Display** (www.nps.gov/applications/glac/dashboard). **Reservations** (877/444-6777, www.recreation.gov) are taken up to six months in advance for Many Glacier, St. Mary, and Fish Creek Campgrounds; sites go fast as soon as they open for booking. All other campgrounds are first come, first served.

Going-to-the-Sun Road

On Going-to-the-Sun Road, six campgrounds offer coveted locations, but none are at Logan Pass. Amenities include shuttle stops, flush toilets, and potable water.

Apgar Campground (Apgar Loop Rd., 0.4 mi/0.6 km from Going-to-the-Sun Rd., 194 sites, Apr.-Nov., RV limit 40 ft/12.2 m, $20) is within a short walk of Apgar Village and Lake McDonald. A paved trail connects with the main shuttle stop, the visitors center, and the Apgar Bike Trail. A separate walking path leads to Apgar Village's restaurant, gift shops, and boat dock. Ten group campsites (9-24 people, 4-5 cars, minimal room for RVs, $65) may be reserved 12 months in advance. **Primitive camping** (Apr. and mid-Oct.-Nov., $10) has pit toilets available but no running water. In winter, you can camp free at the plowed **Apgar Picnic Area,** which has a vault toilet.

Fish Creek Campground (end of Fish Creek Rd., 178 sites, June-early Sept., RV limit 35 ft/10.7 m, $23) is one of three campgrounds in the park that can be reserved. Tucked under cedars, lodgepole pines, and larches, Loops C and D have the best sites, adjacent to Lake McDonald, although Loop B has some larger, more level sites. A few lukewarm token-operated showers are available. Fish Creek is northeast of Apgar.

The small **Sprague Creek Campground** (0.9 mi/1.4 km southwest of Lake McDonald Lodge, 25 sites, mid-May-mid-Sept., RV limit 21 ft/6.4 m, $20) is a prize, sitting right on Lake McDonald's shore in a timbered setting with shaded sites. A few sites have prime waterfront locations. Unfortunately, several sites also abut Going-to-the-Sun Road, with a view of cars driving by. After dark, the road noise plummets. Kayakers and canoers have lakefront access, and the beach sunsets are spectacular.

Set in a cedar-hemlock and fern rainforest, **Avalanche Campground** (6 mi/9.7 km northwest of Lake McDonald Lodge, 87 sites, mid-June-early Sept., RV limit 26 ft/7.9 m, $20) makes the closest westside base for exploring Logan Pass. The trail to Avalanche Lake departs from the campground's rear. The rainforest, with its dark, overgrown forest canopy, allows little sunlight, and the moist area sprouts thick patches of thimbleberries and sometimes a good collection of mosquitoes.

Rising Sun Campground (6 mi/9.7 km west of St. Mary, 83 sites, late May-mid-Sept., RV limit 25 ft/7.6 m, $20) is on the lower hillside of Otokomi Mountain by St. Mary Lake. The sun drops down early behind Goat Mountain, creating a long twilight. While the 2015 Reynolds Creek Fire bypassed the larger trees in the lower campground, it left burnt trees on the hillside above the upper campsites. Adjacent to the campground is a restaurant, camp store, hot showers, and a trailhead to Otokomi Lake. Beach access is across Going-to-the-Sun Road, with a picnic area, boat ramp, and boat tours.

St. Mary Campground (north of visitors center, 183 sites, mid-May-mid-Sept., RV limit 35 ft/10.7 m, $23) campsites in open meadows or tucked among aspens with best views in the C loop sites. Token-operated showers with lukewarm water are available. A trail crosses the St. Mary River on a wooden bridge to connect with the visitors center, St. Mary's restaurants, shuttles, and shops, but it has no access to St. Mary Lake. Two group campsites (9-24 people, 4 cars, minimal room for RVs, $65) may be reserved 12 months in advance. This campground has shoulder-season **primitive camping** (late Apr.-mid-May and late Sept.-Nov., $10) and **winter camping** (free) with pit toilets and no water. This is one of the three campgrounds in the park that accepts reservations.

Many Glacier

★ **Many Glacier Campground** (end of Many Glacier Rd., 110 sites, late May-mid-Sept., RV limit 35 ft/10.7 m, $23) packs treed sites at the base of Grinnell Point. As the most coveted campground in the park, **reservations** are essential; half of the sites can be reserved in advance, but for first-come, first-served campsites, plan to arrive by 7am. Nearby trails depart for Red Rock, Bullhead, and Iceberg Lakes as well as Ptarmigan Tunnel and Swiftcurrent Pass. From the picnic area, a five-minute walk down the road, trails depart to Lake Josephine and Grinnell Lake, Grinnell Glacier, and Piegan Pass. Across the parking lot, Swiftcurrent Motor Inn has a restaurant, laundry, hot showers, and a camp store. If bears frequent the campground, tent camping may be restricted, with only hard-sided vehicles allowed. In fall (mid-Sept.-Oct.), after the campground water is turned off for the season, **primitive camping** (vault toilets only, no water, $10) is allowed.

Two Medicine

Two Medicine Campground (end of Two Medicine Rd., 99 sites, late May-late Sept., RV limit 32 ft/9.7 m, $20) yields views of bears foraging on Rising Wolf Mountain, especially from the A and C Loops. The campground surrounds the small Pray Lake, a good place for paddling, fishing, or chilly swimming, and sites 95, 99, and 100 are along the outlet river. Tenters should choose sheltered sites due to abrupt high winds. The North Shore Trail departs right from the campground, leading in both directions around Rising Wolf Mountain. A seven-minute walk connects with the boat tour and rental dock. **Primitive camping** (late Sept.-Oct., $10) has pit toilets and no water.

Off US 89 between Two Medicine and St. Mary, **Cut Bank Campground** (end of Cut Bank Rd., 14 sites, June-mid-Sept., $10) has ultraquiet campsites under tall firs on Atlantic Creek, a great place to escape crowds. This primitive campground has pit toilets and no running water. It can only fit very small RVs, and trailers are not recommended. A nearby trailhead departs to Medicine Grizzly Lake and Triple Divide Pass.

North Fork

Glacier's seasonal **North Fork campgrounds** are only accessible via the rough dirt Inside Road from the Polebridge entrance station. Vehicle lengths are limited (21 ft/6.4 m maximum, no trailers) due to the narrow lane. The attraction is the quiet and smaller campgrounds. These are mosquito-filled in summer, serene in September, and closed in winter when the roads are buried in snow. Early September to October, Bowman and Kintla Campgrounds permit **primitive camping** ($10); bring water or haul it from lakes.

At the foot of Kintla Lake, **Kintla Lake Campground** (13 sites, June-mid-Sept., $15) is a one-hour drive north of Polebridge. Tucked under large trees, the campground has hand-pumped water and small sites that are close together. Lake paddling is outstanding.

At the foot of Bowman Lake, **Bowman Lake Campground** (48 sites, late May-early Sept., $15) is 30 minutes from Polebridge. Under a mixed conifer forest, the campground has running water, and a five-minute walk leads to the lakeshore and the boat ramp for paddling. Trails connect to Quartz Lakes and Numa Lookout.

Two tiny campgrounds best for tent campers flank the Inside Road south of Polebridge. No running water is available, so bring your own or plan to purify stream water. **Quartz Creek Campground** (7 sites, July-Nov., $10) sits 8 miles (13 km) southeast of Polebridge adjacent to Quartz Creek, about a 30-minute drive. **Logging Creek Campground** (7 sites,

July-Sept., $10), near Logging Creek Ranger Station, is popular for anglers heading to Logging Lake; it's located 10.5 miles (17 km) southeast of Polebridge, about a 45-minute drive.

Outside the Park
St. Mary
St. Mary Village

At the entrance to Going-to-the-Sun Road, **St. Mary Village** (junction of US 89 and Going-to-the-Sun Rd., 844/868-7474, www.glacierparkcollection.com, early June-late Sept., $109-390) sprawls across a large complex with hotel rooms, cabins, and motel rooms as well as shopping, restaurants, a bar, a coffee shop, and a grocery. You can walk five minutes to the park entrance, shuttles, and St. Mary Visitor Center.

At the high end, the three-story **Great Bear Lodge** contains modern hotel comforts in chic lodge style with satellite TV (limited channels), air-conditioning, wet bars, mini-fridges, and the only elevator in the immediate area. Some rooms include fireplaces and jetted tubs. Third-floor rooms have large panoramic mountain views.

Less-pricey guest rooms are clustered in older lodges and small cabins. Great for small families, the **Glacier Cabins** line up along Divide Creek. The cozy, modern one-bedroom cabins include kitchenettes and porch picnic tables for enjoying the creek ambience. The older **main lodge** has tiny cedar-walled guest rooms with small baths. Upgraded guest rooms in the **West Lodge** include satellite TV and air-conditioning. Older **East Motel** guest rooms allow pets, but don't offer satellite TV or air-conditioning. The newest options are **tiny homes** that sleep four people and have kitchenettes and detached nearby bathhouses.

Cabins and Motels

High on a bluff with spectacular views of Glacier, the seven upscale **Cottages at Glacier** (300 Going-to-the-Sun Rd. E., 406/309-4231, www.thecottagesatglacier. com, mid-May-mid-Oct., $275-725, 2-night min.) offer big picture windows with the most dramatic scenery in St. Mary. The spacious two-bedroom cabins can sleep 6-9 and have large decks facing the mountains, gas barbecues, fully equipped kitchens, rock fireplaces, air-conditioning, satellite TV, and broadband internet.

The **St. Mary KOA** (106 West Shore Dr., 406/732-4122 or 800/562-1504, www. goglacier.com, mid-May-Sept., $90-400) has a variety of cabins. Budget cabins have no baths or kitchens and require you to bring sleeping bags and use the communal showers and toilets. Higher-end cabins come with baths, kitchens, and bedding. Amenities at the KOA include barbecues, outdoor pool, hot tub, splash park, summer breakfasts, and wireless internet. The KOA also offers full hookups for RVs and tent campsites.

Sitting above St. Mary and with views of Napi Point, **Johnson's of St. Mary** (21 Red Eagle Rd., 406/732-4207, johnsonsofstmary.squarespace.com, mid-May-late Sept., $75-187) rents a few cabins and runs an older campground with RV hookups, mountain views, and tent sites. Next door, the **Red Eagle Motel** (23 Red Eagle Rd., 406/732-4453, www. redeaglemotelrvpark.com, mid-Apr.-Oct., $110-140) has 23 plain guest rooms that have small bathrooms with showers. Its sister campground is the **Heart of Glacier RV Park** (406/450-0035, $45-50) with 22 full hookup sites but no bathroom or shower facilities.

East Glacier
Hostels

For budget travelers, East Glacier has two hostels, both open May-September. Located one block from the train depot, **Backpacker's Inn** (29 Dawson Ave., 406/226-9392, www.serranosmexican. com) has three dorms ($20 pp, bring sleeping bags), plus two cabins ($50) located in the backyard of Serrano's

Mexican Restaurant. Six blocks from the train station, **Brownie's Hostel** (1020 MT 49, 406/226-4426, brownieshostel.com) is in a renovated old two-story building with a fully equipped communal kitchen, mixed gender dorms ($25 pp), private bedrooms ($49-74), and a deli, bakery, and convenience store. Brownie's also has internet access.

Lodges and Cabins

Historic **Glacier Park Lodge** (1 Midvale Rd., 844/868-7474, www.glacierpark collection.com, early June-late Sept., $150-450) is right across from the train depot. It's the only historic lodge with an outdoor swimming pool (heated, but still chilly), golf course, and pitch-and-putt. The best rooms face the mountains. Lodge rooms, suites, and family rooms are available, along with a chalet. Expect tiny baths (converted from original closets), thin walls, slanted floors, cantankerous hot water, and no TV, air-conditioning, or elevators. A restaurant, lounge, snack shop, and gift shop surround the lobby, which has Wi-Fi. Red bus tours depart from the hotel. Make reservations a year in advance.

On the east edge of town amid aspen trees, ★ **Travelers Rest Lodge** (20987 US 2 E., 406/226-9143 summer, 406/378-2414 winter, www.travelersrestlodge.net, May-mid-Oct., $130-180) has roomy log cabins with gas fireplaces and fully equipped kitchenettes. Each is positioned so that its covered deck has privacy and mountain views. The nicely decorated cabins sleep 2-4 in log-hewn beds.

Motels

Several summer-only older motels line MT 49 north of Glacier Park Lodge. Rates are lowest in spring and fall. The **Mountain Pine Motel** (909 MT 49, 406/226-4403, www.mtnpine.com,

Top to bottom: cabin at St. Mary Village; Glacier Park Lodge in East Glacier; Belton Chalet in West Glacier

May-late Sept., $82-142) offers 25 tidy guest rooms surrounding a lawn tucked under tall, shady trees; some are adjoining rooms for families. Two small cabin complexes have older facilities, some with kitchenettes: **East Glacier Motel and Cabins** (1107 MT 49, 406/226-5593, www.eastglaciermotelandcabins.com, May-mid-Oct., $120-349) and **Jacobson's Cottages** (1204 MT 49, 406/226-4422, http://jacobsonscottages.com, May-Sept., $140-200).

A few year-round motels are in "downtown" East Glacier, south of the tracks. Rates are highest in summer and lowest in winter. The **Whistling Swan Motel** (512 US 2, 406/226-4412 or 406/226-9227, www.seeglacier.com, $65-160) is run by the same family that owns the Two Medicine Grill. Its 10 pine-walled guest rooms offer various bed configurations, and you can get loads of advice from the owners, who are avid hikers. The **Dancing Bears Inn** (40 Montana Ave., 406/226-4402, dancingbearsinn. com, $84-230) has 16 guest rooms with continental breakfast and Wi-Fi; some guest rooms have kitchenettes. The **Circle R Motel** (406 US 2, 406/226-9331, www. circlermotel.net, $94-222) has newer rooms, older rooms, and nearby cabins.

Campgrounds

The small **Y Lazy R RV Park** (junction of Lindhe Ave. and Meade St., 406/226-5505, mid-May-Sept., tents $25, hookups $30) sits on an open, rough grass-and-dirt area overlooking Midvale Creek and big views of surrounding mountains. Amenities include flush toilets, picnic tables, coin-op showers, a dump station, a large laundry, and hookups for electricity, water, and sewer.

West Glacier

Pursuit Accommodations

Pursuit operates several properties in West Glacier under the **Glacier Park Collection** (844/868-7474, www. glacierparkcollection.com). Usually rates

are lower in spring and fall. All of their properties except the Belton Chalet are between the Middle Fork River, the railroad tracks, and West Glacier Village, and they are linked to the village by walking and biking trails.

Located across from Belton Train Depot, the historic **Belton Chalet** (12575 US 2 E., mid-May-early Oct., $145-225) has a cozy lobby with a large fireplace. Simple guest rooms are a slice of history, boasting original wainscoting and wood floors, push-button lights, twig tables, and historical photos, but no phones, TVs, air-conditioning, or alarm clocks. Original closets were converted into in-room baths with showers.

Opened in 2019, **West Glacier RV Park and Cabins** (River Bend Dr., May-Sept., $75-300, no tents) is the newest campground. Campsites accommodate RVs and trailers up to 80 feet (24 m) in pull-through and back-in sites that have grass but no shade trees. Cabins have one queen bed and a double futon, plus a small kitchen and gas grill outside.

The small, older, no-frills guest rooms at **West Glacier Village Motel** (200 Going-to-the-Sun Rd., late May-mid-Sept., $120-250) meet the needs of budget travelers.

Lodges and Cabins

Several raft companies offer lodges and cabins that have Wi-Fi, TVs, and air-conditioning. **Glacier Guides Lodge** (120 Highline Blvd., 406/387-5555, glacier-guides.com, May-mid-Oct., $170-235) is an ecofriendly lodge with 12 guest rooms for two people each. Amenities include mini-fridges, continental breakfast, and two lounge areas for relaxing outside the guest rooms. Its location tucked back in the woods under mossy cliffs makes it one of the quietest places around. **Glacier Outdoor Center** (12400 US 2 E., 406/888-5454 or 800/235-6781, glacierraftco.com, mid-Apr.-Oct., $160-1,100) has log cabins that sleep 6-14 people. Set back from the highway amid birch trees surrounding a trout pond, the cabins include log furniture, decks, full kitchens, and gas fireplaces. **Great Northern Chalets** (12127 US 2 E., 406/387-5340 or 800/735-7897, greatnorthernresort.com, May-mid-Oct., $155-425) rents log chalets that can sleep 2-10 people. Set around a landscaped garden pond but in view of the highway, the cozy two-story, Glacier-themed structures have kitchens, and several have sweeping views of the peaks.

Ten minutes outside the town center, **The Great Bear Inn** (5672 Blankenship Rd., 406/250-4220 or 406/212-3501, www.thegreatbearinn.com, late May-Sept, $235-340) offers seclusion in the woods and the most upscale lodging in West Glacier. Large lodge rooms come in several styles, with the high-end guest rooms including king beds, rock fireplaces, and balconies. All rooms have mini-fridges, televisions, and wine glasses. Two cabins with lofts and kitchens offer more privacy.

Set in the forest and back from the highway, the **West Glacier KOA** (355 Half Moon Flats Rd., 406/387-5341 or 800/562-3313, www.koa.com, May-Sept., $100-350) has 19 deluxe cabins that each sleep 2-8 people. They come with kitchens or kitchenettes, linens, and bathrooms. Some have lofts, balconies or decks, gas grills, and outdoor firepits. For those on a budget, 28 bare-bones cabins have no kitchens, no bed linens (bring sleeping bags), and share communal campground bathrooms. Cabin guests have access to a heated swimming pool, hot tubs, evening programs, an ice cream shop, Wi-Fi, and summertime breakfasts and dinners. The KOA also has RV hookups and tent sites ($40-105).

Campgrounds
Glacier Campground (12070 US 2 E., 406/387-5689 or 888/387-5689, www.glaciercampground.com, May-Sept., $30-50) sits in lush undergrowth that surrounds private sites separated by birch and fir trees. RV hookups are for water and electricity only, but the campground has a mobile pump-out service ($25). Several cabins ($50-70) share a covered outdoor cooking area with gas burners and a barbecue. RVs are limited to 32 feet (9.6 m).

Polebridge
The **North Fork Hostel** (80 Beaver Dr., 406/888-5241, nfhostel.com, late May-early Sept., $25-80) offers mixed dorm bunks, private guest rooms, tepees, cabins, a trailer, and campsites. Reservations are strongly advised. The hostel is off the electric grid, but you won't be roughing it. A huge storage battery powers phone, fax, and Wi-Fi; propane powers the lights, cooking stove, and refrigerator; and wood heats up the cedar hot tub. The hostel has a shared living room, fully equipped kitchen, outhouses, and baths with hot showers. Bring food, towels, and sleeping bags, or rent linens ($5). The hostel also rents out the equally rustic wood-heated **Square Peg Ranch Cabin** ($100-160, 3-night min.) nearby, which can sleep six people.

Located 4 miles (6.4 km) south of Polebridge, **North Fork Cabins** (8954 North Fork Rd., 406/871-7717, polebridgecabins.com, May-Aug., $95-185) are upscale by North Fork standards. They have propane heat, generator electricity, private baths with flush toilets and showers, and outdoor firepits. The larger cabins sleep five and have kitchenettes and porches with outstanding views. Smaller cabins sleep three and lack kitchens.

Polebridge Mercantile (265 Polebridge Loop, 406/888-5105, polebridgemerc.com, May-Oct., $90-125) has four tiny, bare-bones cabins that have stoves, coolers, and outhouses. Fill water bottles at the Merc.

◆ Side Trip: Blackfeet Reservation

dancing in regalia at North American Indian Days

Located on the east side of Glacier, the **Blackfeet Reservation** extends across rolling plains from the Canadian border to south of East Glacier. An artificially straight line forms the boundary between the park and the reservation. Today, the reservation is home to nearly two-thirds of the 17,000-plus members of the Blackfeet Nation, who refer to themselves as Niitsitapi (nee-itsee-TAH-peh), which translates to "the real people."

The 1800s brought devastating misery to the Blackfeet with a smallpox epidemic, decimation of buffalo herds, starvation, and the slaughter of a peaceful band by the U.S. government. By the middle of the century, the first treaty with the United States defined Blackfeet territory as two-thirds of eastern Montana, starting at the Continental Divide. By the century's end, Blackfeet leaders, desperate to help their destitute people, negotiated with the U.S. government for their survival by selling off portions of the reservation in trade for tools, equipment, and cattle. Glacier, from the Continental Divide to the eastern boundary, was one of these trades, purchased for a mere $1.5 million in 1896.

Today, the Blackfeet economy is based mostly on cattle ranching and agriculture. In 2016, the Blackfeet began reintroducing bison, so you may get a glimpse of the herds, especially on US 2. In 2020, after a 30-year struggle, the Blackfeet finally gained protection for the sacred Badger-Two Medicine area with the cancellation of illegal oil and gas leases. Still in dispute today are Indigenous hunting and fishing rights in Glacier. These were retained in the original sale but the government attempted to revoke them when Glacier became a national park in 1910.

Experience Blackfeet Culture

INSIDE GLACIER

◆ **Sun Tours** (406/732-9220 or 800/786-9220, www.glaciersuntours.com): Blackfeet guides with this Blackfeet-owned company lead tours over Going-to-the-Sun Road with interpretation steeped in their people's cultural history and park lore.

Transportation and Services

Emergency Services

For emergencies inside or outside the park, call **911**. On Glacier's west side, the nearest hospitals are the two Logan Health facilities (www.logan.org). The larger one is in Kalispell (310 Sunny View Ln., 406/752-5111) and the smaller one is in Whitefish (1600 Hospital Way, 406/863-3500). Both are 35 minutes from West Glacier and can be up to 90 minutes from Logan Pass, depending on traffic. On Glacier's east side, **Blackfeet Community Hospital** (760 Blackweasel Rd., Browning, 406/338-6100) is 20 minutes from East Glacier and one hour from St. Mary.

- **Running Eagle Falls** (Two Medicine Rd.): This interpretive site and nature trail (0.6 mi/1 km rt) to a waterfall honors Running Eagle, a female warrior named Pitamakin who had her vision quest here.

- **Native America Speaks** (park lodges, St. Mary Visitor Center, and campground amphitheaters, free): For more than three decades, this acclaimed program has featured members of the Blackfeet, Salish, and Kootenai people who share their culture and heritage with attendees. For some of these programs, **Jack Gladstone,** a Grammy-nominated Blackfeet musician, presents *Triple Divide: Heritage and Legacy* (www.jackgladstone.com), which blends storytelling and music into a walk through Glacier's history from the Blackfeet perspective. Check the park newspaper for schedules.

- **Two Medicine Lake Singers and Dancers** (St. Mary Visitor Center, ticketed event): These performances, demonstrating Blackfeet dances in full traditional regalia, draw standing-room-only crowds.

ON THE BLACKFEET RESERVATION

- **St. Mary Scenic Overlook and Blackfeet Interpretive Loop** (2 mi/3.2 km south of St. Mary on US 89): This paved, wheelchair-accessible overlook yields an impressive panoramic view of Glacier, made even more striking by two metal tepee sculptures.

- **Museum of the Plains Indian** (junction of US 2 and US 89, Browning, 406/338-2230, www.doi.gov/iacb/museum-plains-indian): Exhibits display phenomenal beadwork, leather, tools, and clothing to tell the story of the Northern Plains Indians. The museum also exhibits the work of contemporary artists and craftspeople, and periodically hosts Native America Speaks programs.

- **North American Indian Days** (powwow grounds behind Museum of the Plains Indian, Browning, 406/338-7521, blackfeetcountry.com): Over four days in early July, this annual family-friendly festival celebrates Indigenous cultures in vibrant, stunning color with dancing, drumming, singing, games, rodeos, horse racing, sporting events, food, crafts, and traditional regalia. All people are welcome to attend.

- **Lodgepole Gallery and Tipi Village** (US 89, 2.5 mi/4 km west of Browning, 406/338-2787, www.blackfeetculturecamp.com): You can spend the night in a traditional double-walled canvas tepee, visit an art gallery featuring Blackfeet artists, or go on Blackfeet-guided tours of the reservation.

Gas and Repairs

Fuel up before you go as no gas stations are inside the park. Find gas in West Glacier, East Glacier, and St. Mary. For vehicle repairs, you'll need to go to Browning or towns in Flathead Valley.

Cell Service and Internet Access

Cell service and internet connectivity in Glacier is extremely limited, thanks to high mountains that block reception. In general, plan to be out of reach while you travel inside the park on most roads, trails, campgrounds, picnic areas, and lodges. Internet is equally limited.

Cell reception is available in St. Mary, East Glacier, West Glacier, and Apgar. The visitor centers at Apgar and St. Mary have limited Wi-Fi. Plan to download all necessary items **before you arrive in the park.**

Tours
Bus Tours

Two bus-tour companies operate in Glacier, both traveling the scenic Going-to-the-Sun Road. You'll get the inside story on the park from both companies' guides. Neither include park entrance fees, meals, or guide gratuities.

Departing from East Glacier, Browning, St. Mary, and West Glacier, the Blackfeet-owned and -guided **Sun Tours** (406/732-9220 or 800/786-9220, www.glaciersuntours.com, daily mid-June-mid-Sept.) drives air-conditioned buses with huge windows. Interpretation is steeped in Blackfeet cultural history and park lore.

The historic **red jammer buses** with rollback canvas tops are operated by **Xanterra** (855/733-4522, www.glaciernationalparklodges.com, daily late May-Sept.). Tours depart from all the park's lodges for Going-to-the-Sun Road and other destinations.

Boat Tours

Scenic boat tours take place in five different lakes with multiple departures daily. It's best to buy tickets in advance online, but some walk-up tickets may be available at the docks. **Glacier Park Boat Company** (406/257-2426, glacierparkboats.com, daily June-Sept.) operates the boat tours on **Lake McDonald, Two Medicine Lake, St. Mary Lake,** and in Many Glacier on **Swiftcurrent Lake** and **Lake Josephine.**

Getting Around
Driving
US 2 and Marias Pass

It's no Going-to-the-Sun Road, but this two-lane highway still has gorgeous scenery of Glacier and a few miles actually go through the park (no entrance station, no fee). The drive from East Glacier to West Glacier along US 2 is 56 miles (90 km) and takes 70 minutes. Large RVs and trailers must use this route, as they are banned from driving over Going-to-the-Sun Road. The route follows a fairly long, gentle descent from Marias Pass to West Glacier. In winter, plows clear and sand the road frequently to keep it passable for travel.

Outside North Fork Road

The mostly dirt, two-lane **Outside North Fork Road** (open year-round), also called the "North Fork," is the access road to Polebridge and the Polebridge entrance station to the park. Be prepared for washboards, potholes, ruts, dust in summer, slush or mud in fall and spring, and ice in winter. It is intermittently plowed in winter as far as the Canadian border, but do not attempt it without good snow tires; carry chains and emergency supplies in the car.

From Apgar, drive the paved Camas Road to the North Fork Road; turn right to drive north to Polebridge, where another right goes to the Polebridge Mercantile, and a left turn to cross the North Fork of the Flathead River to the Polebridge entrance (25 mi/40 km, 1 hr). From Columbia Falls, the first portion of the North Fork is paved as it exits town, but soon turns to dirt (32 mi/52 km, 1 hr).

Inside North Fork Road

Not for everyone, the primitive gravel **Inside North Fork Road** (mid-May-Oct., no RVs over 21 ft/6.4 m; no trailers) contains precipitous narrow drops, curves, and climbs. Monster potholes, ruts, and washboards are commonplace; spaces wide enough for two vehicles to pass are rare. Speeds top out at 20 mph (32 kph). High-clearance vehicles are best. Check the **Recreational Access Display** (www.nps.gov/applications/glac/dashboard) or with Apgar Visitor Center or Polebridge Ranger Station for current conditions before embarking. When cars pack out parking lots and campgrounds at Bowman and Kintla Lakes, the park restricts uphill traffic to the lakes until space opens. To avoid the lineup, plan to enter the park and head up to the lakes before 9am.

Since 2014, flood damage has closed a portion of the road between Logging Creek and Camas Creek (11 mi/17.7 km). Due to the closure, vehicles can no longer complete the whole road in one shot and must enter via two access points. From the south, enter from **Fish Creek,** then continue to the Camas Creek closure (6.5 mi/10.5 km).

The northern access to the road is via the **Polebridge entrance station.** From here, you can go north or south on the Inside Road. A mile north of the Polebridge Ranger Station, the curvy **Bowman Lake Road** (6 mi/10 km, 0.5 hr) turns off toward Bowman Lake. If you continue northward, the Inside Road terminates at **Kintla Lake** (14 mi/23 km, 1 hr). From the entrance station, travel south to reach the Logging Ranger Station, Logging Creek trailhead, and two small, remote campgrounds: **Quartz Creek** (8 mi/13 km, 0.5 hr) and **Logging Creek** (10.5 mi/17 km, 0.75 hr). The road is closed at Logging Creek.

Hiker Shuttles

Free shuttles service **Going-to-the-Sun Road** (daily July-Labor Day, limited in Sept.). These are not guided tours. Between Apgar and St. Mary, shuttles stop at lodges, trailheads, campgrounds, and Logan Pass. Get on or off at any of the stops denoted by interpretive signs. No tickets are needed, and no reservations are taken. Departing every 15-30 minutes, these extremely popular shuttles enable point-to-point hiking on some of Glacier's most spectacular trails. Check schedules and routes on the park's website.

Two companies operate fee-based shuttles on Glacier's east side. For hikers and backpackers, these aid in doing point-to-point trails, and for travelers without vehicles, they help connect with the Sun Road shuttles. Find schedules and rates online. **Pursuit Glacier Park Collection** (844/868-7474, www.glacierparkcollection.com, daily early June-late Sept.) runs van service north-south between East Glacier, Two Medicine, and St. Mary. **Xanterra** (855/733-4522, www.glaciernationalparklodges.com, daily July-Labor Day) operates shuttles between Many Glacier and St. Mary.

Hikers and backpackers also use **tour boats** as shuttles to reduce foot miles. **Glacier Park Boat Company** (406/257-2426, https://glacierparkboats.com, daily June-Sept.) carts hikers across **Two Medicine Lake** and in Many Glacier across **Swiftcurrent Lake** and **Lake Josephine.** Both add early morning Hiker Express shuttles in July-August. If you want to take a round-trip ride, you can make an advance reservation. No reservations are necessary to catch a return boat; pay cash upon boarding. Return shuttles run until all hikers are accommodated.

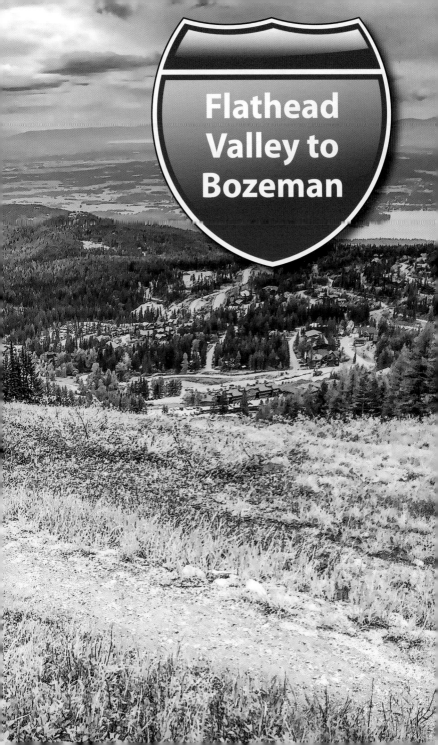

Flathead Valley to Bozeman

Highlights

★ **Find year-round fun at Whitefish Mountain Resort:** Ski or snowboard this winter wonderland, or find summer adventures like mountain biking, zipline tours, an aerial park, an alpine slide, and scenic chairlift rides (page 327).

★ **Climb Mount Aeneas:** Hike the short trail up the highest peak in Jewel Basin. From the summit are seemingly infinite views (page 339).

★ **Admire Flathead Lake from land or water:** Boat or paddle the clear blue waters or drive around the perimeter of the largest freshwater lake west of the Mississippi (page 344).

★ **Take a scenic drive through the Bison Range:** Admire bison roaming on the Flathead Indian Reservation along with elk and birds, among spring wildflowers (page 348).

★ **See the origins of a mighty river at Missouri Headwaters State Park:** This park marks the confluence of the Madison, Jefferson, and Gallatin Rivers, the launching point of the Missouri River (page 352).

★ **Hike to Hyalite Creek and Lake:** Walk this trail to admire 11 different waterfalls (page 353).

★ **Go underground at Lewis and Clark Caverns State Park:** Tour through limestone caverns to see dripstones, stalactites, and cave popcorn in the third largest cave system in the country (page 354).

★ **Ski or snowboard at Big Sky Resort:** Strap on your gear and enjoy one of the largest ski areas in North America (page 363).

Flathead Valley to Bozeman

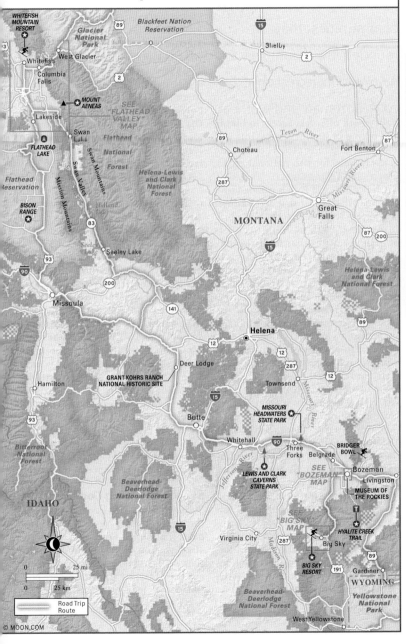

WHITEFISH MOUNTAIN RESORT

Glacier National Park

Blackfeet Nation Reservation

89

15

Shelby

2

West Glacier

Whitefish

Columbia Falls

2

MOUNT AENEAS

SEE FLATHEAD VALLEY MAP

Teton River

Lakeside

Choteau

Fort Benton

87

Swan Lake

Flathead

89

FLATHEAD LAKE

Flathead National Forest

287

Great Falls

Missouri River

Flathead Reservation

Swan Mountains

Helena-Lewis and Clark National Forest

BISON RANGE

Mission Mountains

Swan Valley

Holland

MONTANA

83

Seeley Lake

Seeley Lake

87 200

90

93

200

141

15

Helena-Lewis and Clark Forest

Missoula

Helena

89

12

12

Deer Lodge

287

GRANT-KOHRS RANCH NATIONAL HISTORIC SITE

Townsend

12

Hamilton

15

Missouri River

Butte

93

Whitehall

MISSOURI HEADWATERS STATE PARK

90

BRIDGER BOWL

Bitterroot National Forest

Three Forks

Belgrade

SEE BOZEMAN MAP

Bozeman

Livingston

LEWIS AND CLARK CAVERNS STATE PARK

Jefferson River

MUSEUM OF THE ROCKIES

Beaverhead-Deerlodge National Forest

IDAHO

SEE BIG SKY MAP

HYALITE CREEK TRAIL

15

Virginia City

287

Madison River

Big Sky

89

0   25 mi

0   25 km

BIG SKY RESORT

191

Gardiner

WYOMING

Road Trip Route

Beaverhead-Deerlodge National Forest

Yellowstone National Park

West Yellowstone

© MOON.COM

This fun route across Montana connects two communities that are surrounded by mountains and have outdoor recreation at their core. Bozeman and Flathead Valley both offer fast access to hiking and biking in summer and skiing and snowboarding in winter. They also are gateway hubs for two national parks, Glacier and Yellowstone.

Glacier National Park is rimmed with seasonal villages that shut down almost completely between October and April. In contrast, Flathead Valley consists of three towns that bustle year-round. Kalispell is the largest town and sits at the center of the valley; Columbia Falls, in the northeast, is closer to Glacier. On the north end, Whitefish is a resort town, with Whitefish Lake and Whitefish Mountain Resort offering a plethora of summer and winter recreation.

Bozeman is a college town about the same size as Kalispell. Home to Montana State University, the town swells with 15,000 students during the academic year. But when many students return home for summer, visitors show up, using the town as a gateway to reach nearby Yellowstone. Outside of Bozeman down the Gallatin Valley is Big Sky, a wealthy unincorporated resort town that sports a ski and summer resort.

Between the two locales are small towns and rural communities. A few state parks and historic sites are worthwhile stops. For campers, endless choices of state parks and national forest campgrounds yield plenty of options in the Rocky Mountain ranges between Flathead Valley and Bozeman.

Planning Your Time

On the west side of **Glacier National Park,** Flathead Valley has four major towns. You can make a base camp in one town and still visit the others, as they are just 15-40 minutes apart by car. **Whitefish** is a year-round resort town. **Bigfork** is a summer resort town on Flathead Lake. **Columbia Falls** is the closest town to Glacier Park; it and **Kalispell** are working towns. With a minimum of **three days** in Flathead Valley you can have lake, hiking, and mountain biking adventures.

On the opposite side of the Rocky Mountains, **Bozeman** is a college town that doubles as a gateway to **Yellowstone.** As a recreation mecca, it has access to hiking, mountain biking, rafting, and skiing. Posh **Big Sky Resort,** one of the largest ski resorts in the country, is nearby. While you can certainly buzz through in **one day,** you'll enjoy the area more with **at least three days.**

Driving across Montana, between Glacier and Yellowstone, takes one full day, or around 5-7 hours without stops; exact drive times depend on your origin and destination points. You may have time for one or two short sightseeing stops. But if you can extend the trip by a day or two, plenty of **state parks** and **historic sites** along the way are worth exploring. For those with even more time, the **Swan Valley** and **Flathead Lake** are two locales between Flathead Valley and Bozeman that justify another **three days.**

Seasonal Driving Concerns

Between Flathead Valley and Bozeman, the route crosses several **mountain passes,** although none are exceptionally high. You can expect to encounter snow on them any time between October and early May, but snowstorms are possible any time of year. **Tire chains** may be required in winter conditions, and **studded tires** are allowed (Oct. 1-May 31) instead of chains.

To check highway conditions for Montana, call **511** or go to the state's **travel information site** (https://mdt. mt.gov/travinfo). Many highway and interstate rest areas close during winter; you can check their services and status on the same website.

Best Routes

Several routes go between Glacier and Yellowstone, generally traveling from Flathead Valley via **US 93 and I-90** to Bozeman. The easiest route is 325 miles (520 km) and takes a little over five hours. Most of the route has two- and four-lane roads with wide shoulders and rest areas. Follow US 93 south from Kalispell and along the **west side of Flathead Lake** to reach **Missoula.** From Missoula, drive east on I-90 through **Butte** to **Bozeman.**

An alternative scenic route tours the narrow curvy roads that are a bit slower going on the **east side of Flathead Lake.** Take US 93 south from Kalispell, turn left (east) onto MT 82, turn right (south) onto MT 35 through **Bigfork,** and pass Flathead Lake's cherry orchards to meet up with US 93 in **Polson.** Continue south to Missoula and then on to Bozeman. This route's distance is 320 miles (515 km) and it takes a little over five hours.

For a gorgeous drive lined with lakes and mountains through Flathead and Lolo National Forests, connect to I-90 via the **Swan Valley.** This route has more curves and narrower roads, but it also offers loads of campgrounds. From Kalispell, take US 93 south, turn left (east) onto MT 82 and follow it to MT 35. Turn right, then immediately left at the stoplight onto MT 83 without going into Bigfork. The road turns south down the Swan Valley between the Swan and Mission mountain ranges, passing Swan Lake and Seeley Lake. Stay alert: This route sees copious deer along the road. At **Clearwater Junction,** turn left onto

MT 200 and drive for 24 miles (39 km). Then turn right on MT 141 and continue for 33 miles (53 km). Turn right again on US 12 and continue for 9 miles (15 km). At Beck Hill Road, turn left and continue for 3.5 miles (6 km) to reach the entrance to I-90 East. Merge on to I-90 and head east until you reach Bozeman. This route is 310 miles (500 km) and takes about six hours.

Reservations and Where to Stay

Of the four towns in Flathead Valley, **Whitefish** is the year-round town with summer and winter recreation, plus Whitefish Lake is nearby, making it the most ideal place to base yourself outside of Glacier. Make reservations **6-9 months** in advance for lodging from June to September and winter holidays. In summer when lodging packs out, you can often find last-minute rooms at adjacent **Whitefish Mountain Resort** or in **Kalispell.**

Bozeman is home to Montana State University; motels fill up in fall when the school hosts football games, so you may need to book a few months ahead if your trip overlaps with a game. Otherwise, you can usually get reservations a day or two in advance, except for winter holidays. For winter holidays at **Big Sky Resort** book a **year** in advance; otherwise, **6-9 months** will suffice.

Getting There

Car
From Banff and Kootenay National Parks

The route to Flathead Valley from **Banff National Park** is 300 miles (480 km) and takes about 5.5 hours. From **Banff Townsite,** take Trans-Canada Highway 1 west, then take BC 93 heading south through Radium Hot Springs and the Columbia River Valley. Cross the international border at Roosville. Once in Montana, the highway becomes US 93. Continue south on US 93 through Whitefish to Kalispell.

If you're starting from **Radium Hot Springs** outside of **Kootenay National Park,** the drive is 215 miles (345 km) and takes about four hours. Head south on BC 93 and cross the border at Roosville. Once in Montana, the highway becomes US 93. Continue south on US 93 through Whitefish to Kalispell.

Air

To fly into Flathead Valley, go through **Glacier Park International Airport** (FCA, 4170 US 2, 406/257-5994, www. iflyglacier.com), which is somewhat centrally located between the four towns. Rental cars are available. From the airport, it's 12 miles (19 km) and 15-20 minutes northwest to Whitefish and 10 miles (16 km) and 15-20 minutes southwest to Kalispell. It's 9 miles (14 km) and 15 minutes northeast to Columbia Falls and 25 miles (40 km) and 35 minutes southeast to Bigfork.

Bozeman Yellowstone International Airport (BZN, 850 Gallatin Field Rd., Belgrade, 406/388-8321, www.bozemanairport.com) has more flights than the Glacier airport. Rental cars are available. Bozeman is located 10 miles (16 km) and 15 minutes east of the airport on I-90. Big Sky is 45 miles (72 km) south via US 191, a one-hour drive.

Missoula International Airport (MSO, 5225 US 10 W., Missoula, 406/728-4381, flymissoula.com) has six airlines with nonstop service to about a dozen major cities. The airport is 6 miles (10 km) northwest of the city.

In Butte, **Bert Mooney Airport** (BTM, 101 Airport Rd., Butte, 406/494-3771, www.butteairport.com) connects only with Salt Lake City via Delta. The airport is 5 miles (8 km) south of the city.

Train

The Empire Builder train, run by **Amtrak** (800/872-7245, www.amtrak.com), stops at the **Whitefish station** (500 Depot St., Whitefish) twice daily. Reservations are a must in summer. The westbound route originates in Chicago, stopping at Milwaukee, St. Paul-Minneapolis, and Fargo, then continues to East Glacier (summer only), Essex, and West Glacier along Glacier's southern boundary on its way to Whitefish. The ride from Chicago to Whitefish takes more than 30 hours. Eastbound trains starting in Seattle and Portland join in Spokane to reach Whitefish in a little more than 15 hours.

Bus

Greyhound (800/231-2222, www. greyhound.com) services Whitefish, Kalispell, Missoula, Butte, and Bozeman. Connections to larger cities are via Billings and Spokane, Washington. Whitefish and Kalispell are on a separate route, running once daily to Missoula, where a transfer is required to reach Bozeman.

Columbia Falls

Sprawling along the highway, Columbia Falls is the closest town to Glacier National Park and Glacier Park International Airport. It's a bedroom community for workers in Glacier and the neighboring resort town of Whitefish. In summer, the town has a public outdoor swimming pool, water park, and a Thursday-night farmers market with music, food, and family fun.

Getting There

Whitefish is 10 miles (16 km) and 15 minutes to the west, and **Kalispell** is 17 miles (27 km) and 30 minutes south.

From **West Glacier** on the southwest corner of Glacier National Park, drive west on US 2 for 17 miles (27 km) and 20 minutes to reach Columbia Falls. From **East Glacier,** take US 2 west for 72 miles (116 km), a drive of just under 1.5 hours.

Flathead Valley

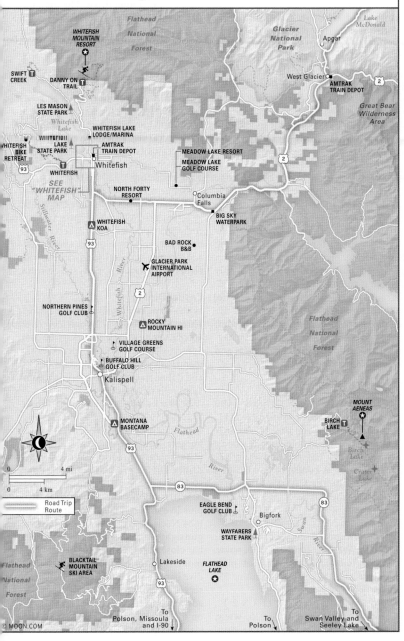

Lake McDonald

Glacier National Park

Apgar

Flathead National Forest

WHITEFISH MOUNTAIN RESORT

West Glacier

AMTRAK TRAIN DEPOT

Great Bear Wilderness Area

SWIFT CREEK

DANNY ON TRAIL

LES MASON STATE PARK

Whitefish Lake

WHITEFISH LAKE LODGE/MARINA

WHITEFISH LAKE STATE PARK

WHITEFISH BIKE RETREAT

AMTRAK TRAIN DEPOT

Whitefish

MEADOW LAKE RESORT

MEADOW LAKE GOLF COURSE

SEE "WHITEFISH" MAP

NORTH FORTY RESORT

Columbia Falls

Stillwater River

WHITEFISH KOA

BIG SKY WATERPARK

River

BAD ROCK B&B

Whitefish River

GLACIER PARK INTERNATIONAL AIRPORT

NORTHERN PINES GOLF CLUB

ROCKY MOUNTAIN HI

VILLAGE GREENS GOLF COURSE

BUFFALO HILL GOLF CLUB

Kalispell

Flathead National Forest

MONTANA BASECAMP

Flathead

MOUNT AENEAS

BIRCH LAKE

Birch Lake

Crater Lake

0   4 mi

0   4 km

Road Trip Route

83

EAGLE BEND GOLF CLUB

Bigfork

Swan River

WAYFARERS STATE PARK

BLACKTAIL MOUNTAIN SKI AREA

Lakeside

FLATHEAD LAKE

Flathead National Forest

93

To Polson, Missoula and I-90

To Polson

To Swan Valley and Seeley Lake

© MOON.COM

Recreation
River Sports

The **Flathead River,** a giant waterway, runs right through Columbia Falls with a few small rapids here and there. River access points offer places to paddle, float, or fish. Because of dam control and cold glacial water, do not expect blue-ribbon trout fishing; however, the river does carry many native and nonnative species. You can launch rubber rafts, kayaks, and canoes from two sites on US 2: one near the House of Mystery at **Bad Rock Canyon's west end** and the other east of downtown at **Teakettle,** before crossing the bridge over the river. The next site downriver is **Kokanee Bend,** about 5 miles (8 km) south of town.

Ambling portions of the river flow slowly enough for flat-water paddling and rafting, plus adept paddleboarders. However, currents can be strong, so only go out if you have the skills. Located adjacent to the Teakettle river access site, **Cloud 9 River Rentals** (350 US 2 E., 406/871-8001, cloud9riverrentals.com) rents river rafts, fishing pontoons, kayaks, and paddleboards. Life jackets and paddles are included in the rates.

Golf

Meadow Lake Golf Course (490 St. Andrews Dr., 406/892-2111, meadowlakegolf.com, greens fees $62-75, carts $20) has 18 holes among woods, with some tight fairways and lots of adjacent houses. A couple of ponds and a creek separate the fairways, and some trees shade the course.

Swimming

The **Pinewood Family Aquatic Center** (925 4th Ave. W., 406/892-3500, www.cityofcolumbiafalls.org, Mon.-Sat. mid-June-late Aug., $2 pp) has a bromine 25-meter pool and kids' play pool.

Big Sky Waterpark (7211 US 2 E., Columbia Falls, 406/892-5025, www.bigskywp.com, 11am-6pm Tues.-Sun.

mid-June-Labor Day, $18-28) is a great place to take the kids to unwind after a hot day and a long drive. The park has 10 big and little slides along with a wading pool, hot pool, mini golf, and bumper cars. After 3pm, rates drop.

Food
Cafés

Uptown Hearth Bakery (619 Nucleus Ave., 406/897-5555, www.uptownhearth.com, 7am-3pm Wed.-Sun., $4-13) bakes fresh crusty breads, French pastries, and savory delights. The bakery serves breakfast, lunch, and espresso with indoor and outdoor seating.

Frequently crowded, **Montana Coffee Traders' Columbia Falls Cafe** (30 9th St. W., 406/892-7696, www.coffeetraders.com, 7am-2pm daily, $7-12) serves huge breakfast omelets, muffins, scones, salads, wraps, and deli sandwiches, with plenty of vegetarian options and espresso.

Casual Dining

With attention to atmosphere and flavors, **Three Forks Grille** (729 Nucleus Ave., 406/892-2900, www.threeforksgrille.com, 5pm-close daily, $10-31) sprinkles the menu with burgers, bowls, salads, steaks, and Italian flavors. Sunday brunch (9am-1pm) rolls out eggs Benedict.

★ **Backslope Brewing** (1107 9th St. W., 406/897-2850, backslopebrewing.com, 11am-8pm daily, $10-15) serves burgers, bowls, fresh salads, and small plates made with locally sourced ingredients. On tap are four craft beers plus seasonal options.

With indoor and outdoor seating plus live music, **Gunsight Bar and Grill** (624 Nucleus Ave., 406/897-2820, www.gunsightbar.com, 11:30am-close daily, bar closes later, $8-16) is a place with a modern-historical vibe; it used to be a dive bar. The family-friendly restaurant serves big burgers and sandwiches, salads, and appetizers. The bar has 20 beers on tap, mostly from Montana, plus specialty cocktails.

Accommodations and Camping

Summer rates are highest, but you can find lower rates and deals during the rest of the year.

Accommodations

Owned by Xanterra, which runs the Glacier National Park lodges, **Cedar Creek Lodge** (930 2nd Ave. W., 303/265-7010 or 855/733-4522, www.glaciernationalparklodges.com, $90-410) tips its hat to Glacier with cedars and park themed artwork in the lobby. Over three floors, it has rooms with king- and queen-size mattresses, as well as family suites, plus an indoor pool and fitness center. Rates include a hot breakfast and free shuttles to West Glacier (summer) and Whitefish Mountain Resort (winter).

North Forty Resort (3765 MT 40 W., 406/862-7740 or 800/775-1740, northfortyresort.com, $120-340) has 23 log cabins and one glamping tent clustered under tall evergreens with community hot tubs and saunas. The cabins, which sleep 5-10 people, have log furnishings, kitchens, barbecues, and picnic tables.

In a quiet area 10 minutes from town, **Bad Rock Bed and Breakfast** (480 Bad Rock Dr., 406/892-2829, www.badrock.com, June-mid-Sept., $210-270) has nine rooms, some in log cabins and others in a river-rock and log-frame house. All have private baths. Breakfast is a large Montana-style affair, sometimes featuring Belgian waffles heaped with fruit.

Outside Columbia Falls and set among big trees, the quiet **Meadow Lake Resort** (100 St. Andrews Dr., 406/892-8700 or 800/321-4653, meadowlake.com) is on an 18-hole golf course, with indoor and outdoor swimming pools, a spa, and tennis courts. The resort has hotel rooms ($90-260) and vacation rentals, including full homes and condos with 1-3 bedrooms.

Top to bottom: Flathead River in Columbia Falls; Backslope Brewing; Alpine Slide at Whitefish Mountain Resort

One Day in Flathead Valley

With one day in Flathead Valley, focus on Whitefish for the plethora of recreation and resort town amenities.

Morning
Start by heading up to **Whitefish Mountain Resort.** Hop on the scenic lift to get whisked to the summit of Big Mountain for panoramic views of Glacier National Park. After you've taken it all in, hike down the **Danny On Trail** to the base lodge, where you can eat lunch on the patio.

Afternoon
Drive to **Whitefish Lake** and rent a kayak or paddleboard from the **Whitefish Lake Lodge Marina.** After you've paddled to your heart's content, settle into a brew or cocktail at the lodge's tiki bar patio or the upstairs lounge deck to enjoy the views. Then head to downtown Whitefish to stroll through the shops.

Evening
Finish out your day with dinner at **Tupelo Grille** downtown.

Campgrounds

Right in town in a manicured grass setting surrounded by trees, **Columbia Falls RV Park** (103 US 2 E., 406/892-1122 or 888/401-7268, columbiafallsrvpark.com, early Apr.-early Oct., from $28 tents, from $49 RVs) has hookups for electricity, sewer, and water and can accommodate big rigs with slideouts. Amenities include flush toilets, hot showers, dump stations, wireless internet, cable TV, and laundry.

Transportation and Services
Emergency Services

For medical, fire, or police emergencies in Flathead Valley, call 911. For medical emergencies in Columbia Falls, **Logan Health** (1600 Hospital Way, Whitefish, 406/863-3500, www.logan.org) is closest.

Gas

Two gas stations in town are located on the north side of US 2: **Mike's Conoco** (1645 9th St. W.) and **Town Pump** (502 9th St. W.).

Cell Service

Cell service is generally very good in Columbia Falls; there's a Verizon tower in town.

Getting Around

The **Mountain Climber bus** (406/758-5728, flathead.mt.gov/eagle, $1-3, cash only) runs weekday routes in Columbia Falls. Pay the fare as you board.

Many hotels have **shuttles** that will meet you at the airport. Flathead Valley taxis include **Glacier Taxi** (406/250-3603, glaciertaxi.com) and **Arrow Shuttle** (406/300-2301, arrowshuttletaxi.com).

Whitefish

The year-round recreation capital of Flathead Valley, downtown Whitefish fits compactly into several blocks next to the Amtrak station. A railroad town transformed into a resort town, Whitefish boasts boutiques, restaurants, bars, art galleries, and theaters. Loaded with varied accommodations, it is where most visitors to Flathead Valley opt to stay. In the summer, downtown streets crowd with shopping tourists, especially during the Tuesday-evening farmers market. In winter, its ski town heritage is celebrated at the Winter Carnival in early February.

Whitefish flanks Whitefish Lake and sprawls below Big Mountain, where

Whitefish Mountain Resort operates winter skiing and summer activities.

Getting There

Whitefish is 10 miles (16 km) and 15 minutes from **Columbia Falls.** It's 26 miles (42 km) and 35 minutes from **West Glacier.** From either Columbia Falls or West Glacier, hop on US 2 and drive west to the junction with MT 40. At the stoplight, US 2 turns left (south), but the road going straight becomes MT 40. Continue on MT 40 until it reaches US 93 and turn right to reach Whitefish.

The town is 17 miles (27 km) and 20 minutes north of **Kalispell** on US 93.

Sights

★ Whitefish Mountain Resort

Whitefish Mountain Resort (end of Big Mountain Rd., 406/862-2900, www. skiwhitefish.com) is a two-season recreational resort with accommodations, restaurants, rentals, events, and day lodges at the summit and base area. In winter (daily early Dec.-early Apr.), skiers and snowboarders whoosh down from Big Mountain's summit, where snow ghosts, or ice-encrusted bent firs, compete with the view of Glacier National Park.

During summer (10am-5:30pm daily mid-June-Labor Day, 10am-5:30pm Fri.-Sun. Labor Day-late Sept.) the resort's **scenic lift rides** ($12-20) whisk riders via gondolas or open chairs to the summit of Big Mountain for views of Flathead Valley and Glacier National Park. You can eat lunch in the Summit House and visit the **US Forest Service Summit Nature Center** (10am-5pm daily mid-June-Labor Day, free) for hands-on exhibits. Kids can do a Junior Ranger program, and you can join a guided walk (twice daily Thurs.-Mon.). The **Danny On hiking trail** also connects with the summit; you can ride the lift one direction ($12) and hike the other. The lifts also access downhill and cross-country **mountain bike trails** ($27-32 for 2 hrs, $33-44 for full day) with

rentals available on site, including bikes, full face helmets, and pads.

Other summer activities take place out of the base lodge at the resort. **Zipline tours** ($60-96) let you sail through the air high above the ground on a six-line route. The **Alpine Slide** ($10/ride) offers speed thrills sledding down two different tracks. Even little kids can ride, with an adult accompanying. For a physical challenge, tackle the **Aerial Adventure Park** ($32-50) to traverse bridges, cables, and ziplines suspended above the ground (while you're clipped into a safety harness) in courses of graduated difficulty. Several activities target younger kids ($10-12): **summer tubing, Spider Monkey Mountain,** and the **Strider Bike Park.** Adventure packages include multiple activities at discounted rates.

Whitefish Lake

Just west of town, **Whitefish Lake** buzzes in summer. Anglers hit the lake in early morning and evening, while midday is a frenzy of water-skiers, Jet Skiers, party barges, kayakers, and canoers. Swimmers cool off at Whitefish Lake State Park, City Beach, and Les Mason State Park. In winter, when ice covers the lake, hockey players make their own rinks, and anglers ice fish.

City Beach is always a good place to go to watch the sunset or on calm days to see the reflection of Big Mountain in the water. It's on the south end of the lake, on Lakeside Boulevard.

Recreation

Danny On Trail

Distance: 4 miles (6.4 km) one-way
Duration: 2 hours
Elevation gain: 2,400 feet (732 m)
Effort: moderate
Trailhead: Whitefish Mountain Resort
Directions: Drive 7 miles (11.3 km) north of Whitefish on Wisconsin Ave. and Big Mountain Rd., following signs.

The **Danny On Trail** is heavily trafficked in summer. One reason is the

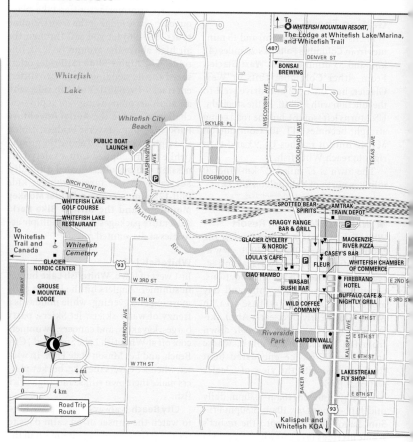

Whitefish

To ↑ ✪ WHITEFISH MOUNTAIN RESORT,
The Lodge at Whitefish Lake/Marina,
and Whitefish Trail

(487) DENVER ST

▼ BONSAI
BREWING

*Whitefish
Lake*

*Whitefish City
Beach*

SKYLES PL

WISCONSIN AVE

COLORADO AVE

TEXAS AVE

**PUBLIC BOAT
LAUNCH** ■

WASHINGTON AVE

EDGEWOOD PL

BIRCH POINT DR

Whitefish

SPOTTED BEAR
SPIRITS

AMTRAK
TRAIN DEPOT

**WHITEFISH LAKE
GOLF COURSE**

**WHITEFISH LAKE
RESTAURANT**

CRAGGY RANGE
BAR & GRILL

MACKENZIE
RIVER PIZZA

To
Whitefish
Trail and
Canada

*Whitefish
Cemetery*

River

GLACIER CYCLERY
& NORDIC

CASEY'S BAR

FAIRWAY DR

(93)

LOULA'S CAFE

FLEUR

WHITEFISH CHAMBER
OF COMMERCE

**GLACIER
NORDIC CENTER**

W 3RD ST

CIAO MAMBO

WASABI
SUSHI BAR

■ FIREBRAND
HOTEL

E 2ND S

**GROUSE
● MOUNTAIN
LODGE**

W 4TH ST

KARROW AVE

WILD COFFEE
COMPANY

BUFFALO CAFE &
NIGHTLY GRILL

E 3RD ST

E 4TH ST

KALISPELL AVE

*Riverside
Park*

GARDEN WALL
INN

E 5TH ST

E 6TH ST

W 7TH ST

BAKER AVE

LAKESTREAM
FLY SHOP

E 8TH ST

0 ___ 4 mi

0 ___ 4 km

Road Trip
Route

To
Kalispell and
Whitefish KOA ↓

(93)

---

outstanding views. The other is because of the **chairlift** (daily mid-June-Labor Day, Fri.-Sun. to late Sept., $12), which you can take in either direction to do a one-way hike. While you can hike with a leashed pooch, dogs may not ride the chairlift. Even without the chair ride, you can hike this trail through October.

After beginning in Whitefish Mountain Resort Village, the hiker-only trail switchbacks up through a forested slope and crosses ski runs as it sweeps eastward around the mountain. You'll get views of Flathead Valley below as

you go. Snow hangs in the upper back slopes through June; valerian and penstemon bloom in July; huckleberries scent the air in August. Junctions are marked: Stay left to go directly to the top. You can also loop through **Flower Point** for a longer hike (5.6 mi/9 km one-way total).

At the East Rim junction, turn left for a gentle, scenic loop before the final steep ascent to the summit. Panoramas at the top span Glacier National Park to Flathead Lake, and you can reward yourself with snacks from the Summit House.

Whitefish Trail

With year-round hiking access (use snowshoes or spikes in winter), the **Whitefish Trail** (www.whitefishlegacy.org) has 43 miles (69 km) of paths and 14 different trailheads. The multiuse trails welcome hikers, mountain bikers, equestrians, snowshoers, and skiers. Download maps and get directions to trailheads online.

Lion Mountain Trail

Distance: 3 miles (4.8 km) rt
Duration: 1.5 hours
Elevation gain: 260 feet (79 m)
Effort: easy-moderate
Trailhead: Lion Mountain, Whitefish Trail
Directions: Take US 93 north from downtown Whitefish for 2.2 miles (3.5 km) and turn right on Lion Mountain Loop Rd. to reach the trailhead on the left.

This short, logged forest loop ambles up gentle grades. The route starts with an ultrashort loop perfect for families with small kids. From the top of the family loop, continue straight ahead for the ascent up through several basins to a signed four-way junction at the top. Turn right for the short loop to the summit of **Lion Mountain,** which overlooks Skyles Lake, and return to the junction. From the junction, the trail heading south drops for the return loop on an old road to the family loop. The Whitefish Trail also continues northwest from the junction to several other trailheads.

Swift Creek Trail

Distance: 1-5 miles (1.6-8 km) rt
Duration: 1-3 hours
Elevation gain: 260 feet (79 m)
Effort: easy-moderate
Trailhead: Swift Creek, Whitefish Trail
Directions: From Whitefish, drive Wisconsin Ave. and East Lakeshore Dr. for 8.3 miles (13.4 km) around the north side of Whitefish Lake to the trailhead on the right.

Top to bottom: Danny On Trail; mountain biking at Whitefish Mountain Resort; chairlift at Whitefish Mountain Resort

From the trailhead, walk a short distance to a three-way junction. From this point, a hard-packed, wheelchair-accessible trail goes left through a beautiful old-growth forest to a scenic overlook of **Swift Creek.** Just before the overlook is a second three-way junction. Those wanting to stay on the accessible trail should return the way they came. Or you can turn north onto a dirt trail that continues through the forest to another three-way junction. Turn left for a short descent to a junction where a left turn goes to another view of Swift Creek. Continuing on, the trail descends before climbing to a plateau and circling through to cross a gravel road. From here the trail climbs steeply up several switchbacks where you'll start to see the downed trees from a winter windstorm in 2020. At the top, the trail undulates up and down across ridges with views southward to the hills on the other side of Whitefish Lake. After the trail drops to an overlook of **Smith Lake,** it cruises around the south side above the lake to the Smith Lake Trailhead. Return the way you came, and veer left at both three-way junctions to complete a loop.

Biking

Around Whitefish, the **Whitefish Trail** (www.whitefishlegacy.org) provides 43 miles (69 km) of curvy, multiuse dirt single-track trails with fun terrain for mountain bikers. Current maps to the system's 14 developed trailheads can be found online. Most routes are cross-country trails; find the downhill thrills at **Spencer Mountain Trailhead.**

For single-track, lift-served mountain biking, **Whitefish Mountain Resort** (end of Big Mountain Rd., 406/862-2900, www.skiwhitefish.com, 10am-5:30pm daily mid-June-Labor Day, 10am-5:30pm Fri.-Sun. Labor Day-late Sept., $27-32 for 2 hrs, $33-44 for full day) hauls bikes and riders up two chairlifts. Twenty-two downhill routes descend the mountain in three zones for different abilities. Lower-mountain trails allow for skill building, while the Kashmir Flow Trail and cross-country trails work for intermediates. Steep, hair-raising downhill descents with natural obstacles cater to advanced riders. The resort rents bikes ($38-54 for 2 hrs, $68-87 for full day) and downhill protective gear ($18-35). Learn to downhill in beginner programs (11am and 2pm daily, $114, including rental gear).

Whitefish Shuttle (406/212-0800, www.whitefishshuttle.com) runs **bike shuttles** to the Whitefish Trail trailheads, hotels, and up to Lake McDonald Lodge or Avalanche during spring biking season on Going-to-the-Sun Road in Glacier. They also guide bike tours.

Mountain Bike Center

Tucked in the woods north of Whitefish, the **Whitefish Bike Retreat** (855 Beaver Lake Rd., 406/260-0274, www.whitefishbikeretreat.com, year-round, day pass $10) is a trailside biker haven. Day passes allow access to the skills park, flow and berm trails, pump track, and two bike-washing stations. Trails connect to the Whitefish Trail system near the Beaver Lake Trailhead. The camp store rents bikes ($35-55). Lodging is in a large bunkhouse with repurposed bicycle parts serving as fixtures and railings. Choose from private rooms ($120-175) or shared bunkrooms ($55 pp). Campsites ($50) have picnic tables, bear-resistant food storage, a dishwashing station, flush toilets, and showers.

Rentals and Repairs

Glacier Cyclery (326 E. 2nd St., 406/862-6446, www.glaciercyclery.com, $45-90) rents touring bikes, roadies, hybrids, mountain bikes, fat bikes, and e-bikes, plus car racks, utility trailers, and Burleys. They also have an assembly service, so you can ship your bike to them ahead of your arrival. The shop also describes popular routes online and maintains a ride board with recent trail updates.

Golf

The city-owned **Whitefish Lake Golf Course** (1200 US 93 N., 406/862-4000, golfwhitefish.com, late May-Oct., greens fees $40-65) is Montana's only 36-hole course. The north course and south course both have mountain views. Courses are open dawn to dusk. Amenities include rental clubs and carts, a pro shop, instruction, a driving range, and restaurants.

Water Sports
Paddling and Boating

Whitefish Lake has two public launch sites with boat ramps at **Whitefish Lake State Park** and **City Beach**. Before launching private boats, boats must pass inspections for aquatic invasive species. Whitefish also has a decontamination station, if you need to clean your boat before an inspection.

The lake has only one marina, and it does not have a boat launch. **Whitefish Lake Lodge Marina** (The Lodge at Whitefish Lake, 1390 Wisconsin Ave., 406/863-4020, lodgeatwhitefishlake. com, mid-May-Sept.) has rentals, mooring, and fuel service. Rentals include ski boats, pontoon boats, and personal watercraft ($95-200/hr) and kayaks, canoes, and paddleboards ($35-40/hr). Paddling lessons and tours, including a twilight tour, are available.

Other shops in town also rent paddlecraft for $30-50. **Sportsman** (6475 US 93 S., 406/862-3111, www.sportsmans kihaus.com) rents canoes, kayaks, and paddleboards. **Paddlefish Sports** (105 Wisconsin Ave., 406/260-7733, www. whitefishpaddleboards.com) rents paddleboards. You can also rent paddling watercraft at Whitefish Lake State Park and Les Mason State Park.

Fishing

Whitefish Lake draws anglers for its lake trout and whitefish. During winter, some anglers ice fish. Northern pike, lake trout, and kokanee are common, and it is regularly stocked with westslope cutthroat trout. You can get locally made, hand-tied flies plus tackle and gear at **Lakestream Fly Shop** (669 Spokane Ave., 406/862-1298, www.lakestream.com). They also guide fishing trips on lakes and the Flathead River ($400 half day, $500 full day).

Swimming

Find beaches with buoyed swimming zones (no lifeguards) at three locations on **Whitefish Lake.** Located closest to downtown, **City Beach** (406/863-2473, free) is a kid favorite due to its sandy beach. **Montana State Parks** (stateparks. mt.gov, Montana residents free, $8/vehicle) manages beach areas on opposite sides of the lake. **Les Mason State Park** (2650 E. Lakeshore Dr., Apr.-Nov.) has summer rentals of paddleboards, kayaks, and canoes and is a day-use area, while **Whitefish Lake State Park** (1615 W. Lakeshore Dr., year-round) has a campground and boat launch.

Winter Sports
Downhill Skiing and Snowboarding

Located 7 miles (11 km) north of Whitefish, **Whitefish Mountain Resort** (end of Big Mountain Rd., 406/862-2900, www.skiwhitefish.com, early Dec.-early Apr., $43-85) lives up to its former name of Big Mountain with 12 lifts and four terrain parks. Big bowls, glades, and long cruisers head off the summit in every direction, and views from the summit on sunny days yield the entire panorama of Glacier's peaks. You can even find good tree skiing in the mountain's famous fog. The resort's village contains restaurants, shops, rental gear, a ski school, childcare, and lodging options, from economy to upscale.

Cross-Country Skiing

Glacier Nordic Center (1200 US 93, 406/862-9498, www.glaciernordicclub. com, 9:30am-5:30pm daily Dec.-Mar.) grooms trails on **Whitefish Lake Golf**

Course (7.5 mi/12 km, late Dec.-Feb., $6-12) and at the **Big Mountain trailhead** (14.3 mi/23 km, mid-Dec.-Mar.). They also rent ski packages ($10-25) and teach lessons ($50). The club's website has grooming updates and information on other nearby ski trails, such as Round Meadows. Additional ski rental shops in town include **Sportsman** (6475 US 93 S., 406/862-3111, www.sportsmanskihaus. com) and **Glacier Cyclery and Nordic** (326 E. 2nd St., 406/862-6446, www. glaciercyclery.com).

Food and Drink

As a resort town, Whitefish is overloaded with outstanding restaurants. Because of the crowds, make reservations to avoid long waits in summer or winter. In spring and fall, a few restaurants alter their hours.

International

Ciao Mambo (234 E. 2nd St., 406/863-9600, www.ciaomambo.com, 4pm-9pm Sun.-Thurs., 4pm-10pm Fri.-Sat., $12-32) transports diners to Italy in a cramped, noisy dining room with an open kitchen and Italian wines. Start with the Tootsie Roll appetizers (ricotta-stuffed phyllo dough on marinara), choose from multiple homemade pastas for entrées, and finish with tiramisu or cannoli.

Wasabi Sushi Bar and Ginger Grill (419 2nd St., 406/863-9283, www.wasabimt. com, 5pm-10pm daily, $8-22) is a long-time favorite for locals. Fusion rolls, *nigiri*, sashimi, sake, and grilled Asian specialties are served in a relaxed, bright atmosphere surrounded by wasabi-green walls.

Southern

At ★ **Tupelo Grille** (17 Central Ave., 406/862-6136, www.tupelogrille.com, 5pm-10pm daily, $14-42), the flavors come from New Orleans, with gumbo, andouille sausage, and shrimp and grits. The Zydeco Combo is a crawfish-shrimp cake, fried catfish, crawfish étouffée, and jambalaya. The eatery also serves grilled steaks, and nightly specials usually include fish. Top off dinner with their yummy bread pudding.

Fine Dining

At Whitefish Lake Golf Course, **Whitefish Lake Restaurant** (1200 US 93 N., 406/862-5285, www.whitefishlakerestaurant.com, 11am-5pm and 5:30pm-10pm daily, $31-48) offers historical ambience in a renovated 1937 log building. Lunch is served on the deck or in the clubhouse. Dinner is served in the dining room. The New Zealand mussels appetizer can lead into roast duckling, steaks, or prime rib. Smaller-portioned plates are available, too.

Only one restaurant overlooks Whitefish Lake. Settle in for the romance of watching the sunset across the water at ★ **The Lodge at Whitefish Lake Boat Club** (1380 Wisconsin Ave., 406/863-4000, www.lodgeatwhitefishlake.com, 7am-11am and 5pm-10pm daily, $27-70). Meals are served in the dining room or on the deck with specialties of fish, elk, and steaks that take on seasonal flavors. An adjacent lounge with an outdoor deck serves lunch and dinner (11am-9pm daily, $10-22).

Cafés and Quick Bites

With the appeal of a classic patisserie, **Fleur** (103 Central Ave., 406/730-8486, www.fleurbakeshop.com, 7am-4pm Mon.-Fri., 7am-2pm Sat.-Sun.) serves espresso with fresh breads, French pastries, desserts, and small plates.

Loula's Café (300 2nd St. E., 406/862-5614, www.whitefishrestaurant.com, 7am-3pm daily, $6-13) starts the day with lemon-stuffed French toast followed by fresh salads and sandwiches. Top your meal with one of Mary Lou and Laura's trademark fresh-baked fruit pies, or buy one to go.

Wild Coffee Company (309 Central Ave., 406/730-2833, www.wildcoffee companymt.com, 7am-2pm daily, $7-11) serves topped toasts, stuffed biscuits, and sandwich melts.

Great for families, **MacKenzie River Pizza** (9 Central Ave., 406/862-6601, www.mackenzieriverpizza.com, 11am-10pm daily, $10-22) serves up traditional and eclectic pizzas with sourdough, natural-grain, or gluten-free crusts. Local microbrews are on tap.

Pubs and Bars

Over multiple stories, **Casey's Bar** (101 Central Ave., 406/862-8150, www.caseyswhitefish.com, noon-close daily) mixes together a restaurant, bar, casino, dance hall, and summer rooftop dining for the best view in downtown Whitefish. With outside seating in summer, **The Craggy Range Bar & Grill** (10 Central Ave., 406/862-7550, www.thecraggyrange.com, 11am-10pm daily) has live music. The classy **Spotted Bear Spirits** (503 Railway St., 406/730-2436, www.spottedbearspirits.com, 4pm-8pm daily) inhabits a downtown location perfect for enjoying the artsy seasonal cocktails made with fresh, organic ingredients.

In an old house with a dog-friendly outdoor space, **Bonsai Brewing Project** (549 Wisconsin Ave., 406/730-1717, bonsaibrew.com, noon-8pm Tues.-Sun.) has five regular and five rotating beers on tap, and a grill serving sandwiches, burgers, dogs, and bowls.

Accommodations and Camping

Whitefish is the only Flathead Valley town that offers luxury lodging, but it also has a myriad of less-pricey options, including chains and independent hotels. Several offer packages, including golfing and skiing. Locate vacation homes and cabins to rent through **Lakeshore Rentals** (406/863-9337 or 877/817-3012, www.lakeshorerentals.us).

Lodging reservations are mandatory in summer, but when options in town book up, rooms are usually still available at Whitefish Mountain Resort. In town,

summer has the highest rates; Whitefish Mountain Resort has its highest rates in winter. Find off-season deals in spring and fall.

Hotels

With a two-story lobby draped with a giant wrought-iron chandelier and a river-rock fireplace, ★ **The Lodge at Whitefish Lake** (1380 Wisconsin Ave., 406/863-4000 or 877/887-4026, lodgeatwhitefishlake.com, $550-730) is the only hotel on Whitefish Lake. Upscale rooms overlook the water, facing the sunset; other guest rooms have mountain views. Viking Lodge rooms are across the street, accessed via an enclosed bridge. Spacious multi-bedroom suites and condos ($900-1,300) have balconies and fireplaces. The lodge has an indoor hot pool fed by a waterfall, indoor hot tub, summer outdoor pool and year-round outdoor hot tub, full-service marina, boat rentals, day spa, restaurants, and a lounge.

The **Firebrand Hotel** (650 E. 3rd St., 406/863-1900 or 844/863-1900, firebrandhotel.com, $120-450) has 81 rooms and five suites, spa and concierge services, and a fitness center. Rooms have accents from burnished steel, reclaimed wood, and tile. For families, some rooms adjoin. The two-story lobby has a restaurant, and the rooftop patio has a hot tub.

Grouse Mountain Lodge (2 Fairway Dr., 844/868-7474, www.glacierparkcollection.com, $115-300) sits on the golf course, which turns into a groomed Nordic ski center in winter. It has an indoor pool, outdoor hot tubs, and restaurant. Guest rooms come in six configurations, including basic hotel rooms and upscale suites with rain showers.

Bed-and-Breakfasts

Just north of downtown, the spacious **Good Medicine Lodge** (537 Wisconsin Ave., 406/862-5488, goodmedicinelodge.com, $135-395) provides rooms and suites with private baths. The gourmet breakfast consists of three or four courses, including a hot entrée, often made with local ingredients. Light hors d'oeuvres and wine are served in the evening. Amenities include an outdoor hot tub, ski storage room, and several restful common areas.

With modern log architecture, **Hidden Moose Lodge** (1735 E. Lakeshore Dr., 406/862-6516 or 888/733-6667, hiddenmooselodge.com, $120-330) centers around a spacious great room and an outdoor sitting deck overlooking gardens and woods. Both have river-rock fireplaces. Montana-themed rooms and suites have a queen or king bed and large bathrooms, some with Jacuzzi tubs. Amenities include breakfasts, complimentary evening drinks, and an outdoor hot tub.

Within two blocks of downtown Whitefish, the circa-1920 **Garden Wall Inn** (504 Spokane Ave., 406/862-3440 or 888/530-1700, gardenwallinn.com, $225-450) is furnished with antiques, historical photos of Glacier, and warmth from a real log-burning fireplace in the living room. Guest rooms, which include a two-bedroom suite, have private baths.

Resorts

Whitefish Mountain Resort (end of Big Mountain Rd., 406/862-2900 or 877/754-3474, www.skiwhitefish.com, $125-680) has a variety of lodging options, ranging from budget to luxury, motel rooms to condos, as well as vacation homes ($230-1,400). The resort has its highest room rates during the winter ski season. July through August runs a close second. Fall and spring are very inexpensive, but lodging options are limited, and no lifts, shops, or restaurants are open.

Guest Ranches

Adjacent to a small lake and Spencer Mountain, **Bar W Guest Ranch** (2875 US 93 W., 406/863-9099 or 866/828-2900, www.thebarw.com, packages from $2,166) houses guests in a western lodge, cabin suites, and glamping in upscale

pools at The Lodge at Whitefish Lake

canvas tents. Ranch activities pile on trail rides, fishing, rodeo, canoeing, archery, and campfires. Three- and six-night packages include meals, lodging, and ranch activities.

Campgrounds

Set in the woods right on Whitefish Lake, **Whitefish Lake State Park** (1615 W. Lakeshore Dr., 406/862-3991 summer, 406/751-4590 winter, stateparks.mt.gov, year-round, RV limit 40 ft/12.2 m, $18-28) has 25 sites and is perfect for swimming and launching boats but not for sleeping, as trains frequently rumble on the tracks crossing the park. With a good set of earplugs, you can survive the night. Amenities include flush toilets, showers, picnic tables, fire rings with grills, firewood, running water, bear-resistant storage lockers, and a shared biker-hiker site ($8 pp). Water is only on from May to September.

Whitefish KOA (5121 US 93 S., 406/862-4242 or 800/562-8734, www.

glacierparkkoa.com, mid-Apr.-mid-Oct., tents $50-72, RV hookups $72-95, $6-10 pp for more than two campers) sits shielded from the highway by thick forest. The outdoor pool attracts kids, while oldsters gravitate to the adults-only hot tub. Amenities include flush toilets, showers, picnic tables, fire rings, hookups, laundry, a dump station, a camp store, wireless internet access, free mini golf, and a restaurant.

Transportation and Services
Emergency Services

For emergencies, call **911**. **Logan Health** (1600 Hospital Way, 406/863-3500, www.logan.org) is the hospital in Whitefish.

Gas

Find gas in Whitefish at **Town Pump** (US 93 and MT 40), **Safeway** (13th Ave. and Baker Ave.), and **Alpine Village Market** (721 Wisconsin Ave.).

Cell Service

Cell service in Whitefish is reliable, including at Whitefish Mountain Resort.

Getting Around

The **Mountain Climber bus** (406/758-5728, flathead.mt.gov/eagle, $1-3, cash only) runs weekday routes between Kalispell and Whitefish. Pay the fare as you board.

The free **SNOW Bus** (bigmtncommerial.org) goes multiple times daily from Whitefish to Whitefish Mountain Resort July to early September and early December to early April.

Many hotels have **shuttles** that will meet you at the airport. Flathead Valley taxis are **Glacier Taxi** (406/250-3603, glaciertaxi.com) and **Arrow Shuttle** (406/300-2301, arrowshuttletaxi.com).

Kalispell

The nucleus of Flathead Valley, with three golf courses, restaurants, and shopping, is also its largest town. In historic downtown Kalispell, you can tour a unique art museum. In August, catch the Northwest Montana Fair and Rodeo. The blocks around US 93 and US 2 comprise the business district, with downtown extending south; north on US 93 are the big box stores.

Getting There

Kalispell is 15 miles (24 km) and 25 minutes south of **Whitefish** on US 93. From **West Glacier,** Kalispell is 33 miles (50 km) and 45 minutes southwest via US 2. The same route passes through Columbia Falls and by Glacier Park International Airport.

Sights
Hockaday Art Museum

The **Hockaday Museum of Art** (302 2nd Ave. E., 406/755-5268, www.hockadaymuseum.org, 10am-5pm Tues.-Sat., $2-5 adults, kids free) features Montana pottery, jewelry, and paintings.

Both permanent and special exhibits feature works by regional Indigenous and Glacier National Park artists.

Recreation
Biking

The **Great Northern Historical Trail** (railstotrailsofnwmt.com) runs a paved **bike rail trail** (12 mi/19.3 km) from Meridian Road to Smith Lake in Kila. Another segment goes south to Somers for those who want to enjoy Flathead Lake as a destination (12 mi/19.3km). Find trailhead parking for both at Meridian Road and Derns Road. Maps are online.

Rentals and Repairs

Kalispell has multiple bike shops that rent, sell, and repair bikes. Bike rentals usually run $30-70 per day, including helmets. Closest to the rail trails, **Sportsman** (145 Hutton Ranch Rd., 406/755-6484, www.sportsmanskihaus.com) rents mountain and road bikes.

Hockaday Art Museum in Kalispell

Golf

Kalispell's golf courses are open dawn to dusk; in June, this means you have 16 hours of daylight to choose from. Most courses ($30-75) are open April to October. All have rentals, pro shops, instruction, driving ranges, restaurants, and lounges.

Northern Pines Golf Club (2 US 93 N., 406/751-1950, northernpinesgolfclub.com) is a Scottish links-style course. With few trees, views open up to Big Mountain and Glacier National Park, and the Stillwater River runs adjacent to the back nine. **Buffalo Hill** (1176 N. Main St., 406/756-4530 or 888/342-6319, www.golfbuffalohill.com) has the older Cameron Nine that abuts the highway. The newer 18-hole course is moderately difficult with a varied terrain. **Village Greens** (135 Palmer Dr., 406/752-4666, montanagolf.com) surrounds its bent-grass greens with a few trees, ponds, and houses on an easier 18-hole course.

Food and Drink

Kalispell has national chain restaurants along US 93, but not in the few blocks of the downtown area.

Cafés

Bonelli's Bistro (38 1st Ave. E., 406/257-8669, www.bonellisbistro.com, 8am-3pm Mon.-Sat., $7-16) dishes up Mediterranean breakfasts, lunches, espresso, and homemade desserts with fresh local ingredients, many organic. Many menu items come gluten-free, dairy-free, egg-free, or low-calorie, and the kitchen will accommodate allergies. Stop by **Ceres Bakery** (318 S. Main St., 406/755-8552, www.ceresbakerymt.com, 7am-3pm Mon.-Sat.) for an espresso with a sticky sweet potato roll, croissant, or savory treat. **Montana Coffee Traders' Kalispell Cafe** (111 Main St., 406/756-2326, www.coffeetraders.com, 7am-2pm Mon.-Sat., 8am-2pm Sun., $8-13) serves breakfast scrambles and wraps, lunch sandwiches and salads, pastries, and espresso.

Classic American

In an old forge, ★ **DeSoto Grill** (227 1st St. W., 406/314-6095, www.desotogrill.com, 11am-9pm Tues.-Sat., $12-35) barbecues brisket, pork, ribs, chicken, salmon, and elk sausage in sandwiches or platters. À la carte sides include house-made cornbread, pork belly collard greens, baked beans, potato salad, and slaw. Several mac-and-cheese bakes are on the menu, too.

Hops Downtown Grill (121 S. Main St., 406/755-7687, www.hopsmontana.com, 5pm-9pm Tues.-Sat., $12-30) is the place to go for upscale burgers (beef, elk, and yak) and griddle meatloaf with gravy. Try the duck wings appetizer. Pair the meal with wine or Montana craft beers.

Breweries and Pubs

SunRift Beer Company (55 1st Ave. W. N., 406/314-6355, sunriftbeer.com, brewery noon-8pm daily, restaurant noon-11pm

Mon.-Sat., $10-21) rolls out craft beers accompanied by smoked meats and beer biscuits.

Two breweries in town just serve beer, no food. **Kalispell Brewing Company** (412 Main St., 406/756-2739, www.kalispellbrewing.com, noon-8pm Mon.-Sat.) serves up German-style lagers and ales in a building that once served as a car dealership. It has a rooftop deck for outside seating. **Bias Brewing** (409 1st Ave. E., 406/730-3020, www.biasbrewing.com, noon-8pm daily) has a small selection of craft beers.

Accommodations and Camping

Kalispell has several chain hotels sprawled on the outskirts of downtown, including around the strip mall areas. The pickings are otherwise slim. Rates will be highest in summer.

Hostels

Downtown above Wheaton's Cycle, the **Kalispell Hostel** (214 1st Ave. W., 406/270-1653, www.kalispellhostel.com, Apr.-Sept., $50-85) has a historical ambience. Three private bedrooms sleep two people each. Shared amenities include a kitchen and bathroom with shower.

Hotels

Right in downtown Kalispell's shopping district, the historic **Kalispell Grand Hotel** (100 Main St., 406/755-8100 or 800/858-7422, kalispellgrand.com, Apr.-Sept., $75-185) feels like it's set a century back in time. The lobby still has a tin ceiling, an ornate pump organ, and the original wide oak-banister stairway. Renovated guest rooms have smaller baths with showers.

Campgrounds

Commercial campgrounds are scattered

Top to bottom: biking on the Great Northern Historical Trail; mountain goat on summit of Mount Aeneas; kayaker on the Wild Mile of the Swan River around Kalispell. Standard amenities include hookups, flush toilets, hot showers, dump stations, laundries, playgrounds, cable TV, Wi-Fi, fire rings, and picnic tables.

The nearest Kalispell campground to Glacier, **Rocky Mountain "Hi" RV Park and Campground** (825 Helena Flats, 406/755-9573 or 800/968-5637, www.glaciercamping.com, year-round, RV hookups $37-51, tents $27) has grassy sites tucked between large fir trees. The setback from the highway reduces road noise. With swimming, fishing, and canoeing in a wide spring-fed creek, it's a good campground for kids.

Opened in 2020, **Montana Basecamp** (1000 Basecamp Dr., 406/756-9999, montanabasecamp.com, late Apr.-Oct., $80-130) has all paved back-in sites with big views and lawns and can accommodate the largest RVs. It is adjacent to the paved Great Northern Historical Trail for bicycling and walking.

Transportation and Services
Emergency Services
Logan Health (310 Sunny View Ln., 406/752-5111, www.logan.org) is the town's hospital.

Gas
Find gas at **Town Pump** (US 93 and Reserve St.), two **Conoco stations** (196 3rd Ave. N. E. and 1319 US 93 S.), and **Costco** (2330 US 93 N.).

Cell Service
Kalispell has good cell phone reception.

Getting Around
The **Mountain Climber bus** (406/758-5728, flathead.mt.gov/eagle, $1-3, cash only) runs weekday routes in Kalispell and to Whitefish. Pay the fare as you board. Seasonal buses go to Whitefish Mountain Resort (Sat. mid-Dec.-early Apr.) or Glacier National Park (daily summer, $3-5).

Many hotels have **shuttles** that will meet you at the airport. Two regional taxi companies are **Glacier Taxi** (406/250-3603, glaciertaxi.com) and **Arrow Shuttle** (406/300-2301, arrowshuttletaxi.com).

Bigfork

A summer resort town, Bigfork is a small yet charming cultural and recreation hub. Quaint gift shops and art galleries fill its several-block-long village, and its historic one-lane steel bridge crosses the Swan River. Recreation opportunities abound in the Swan Mountains and Flathead Lake. In early June, the town hops with the Bigfork Whitewater Festival, when kayakers shoot the Swan's Wild Mile.

Getting There
Bigfork is 15 miles (24 km) and a little over 20 minutes from **Kalispell.** The quickest route goes south on US 93 and east (left) on MT 82, then south (right) on MT 35. From **West Glacier,** it's a 41-mile (66-km), 45-minute drive to Bigfork. Head west on US 2 to MT 206. Turn left (south) onto MT 206 to reach MT 35, where a left turn takes you to Bigfork.

Recreation
Hiking
In the Swan Mountains above Bigfork, **Jewel Basin** is a hiking-only area loaded with trails. Accessible late June with snow lingering on some routes into July, trails are snow-free into October. "The Jewel" is so named for the 27 alpine fishing lakes that sparkle in its basins. Weekends crowd with cars at the Camp Misery Trailhead. Trail signage is scanty, so take a map from the trailhead kiosk.

★ **Mount Aeneas**

Distance: 5.9 mile (9.5 km) loop
Duration: 3-4 hours
Elevation gain: 1,779 feet (542 m)
Effort: moderate-strenuous
Trailhead: Camp Misery Trailhead in Jewel Basin
Directions: From Bigfork, follow MT 35 north and

turn east onto MT 83. Turn north onto Echo Lake Rd. and drive for 3 miles (5 km) to Jewel Basin Rd. (Forest Service Rd. 5392). Drive 7 miles (11 km) of steep, bumpy, narrow dirt and gravel road to Camp Misery. Mount Aeneas is the highest peak in the Jewel and offers big views for little work, but don't expect solitude at the summit. From the top, you'll see Flathead Lake, Glacier National Park, the Bob Marshall Wilderness Complex, and the Swan Mountains.

Combined with Picnic Lakes, the trail loops on a ridge and through a lake basin. Begin hiking up Trail 717, a wide road-bed. When the trail reaches a four-way junction, stay on 717, heading uphill. After a few switchbacks, you'll pass a microwave tower before waltzing with the mountain goats along an arête to the summit of **Mount Aeneas.** From the summit, drop down through the **Picnic Lakes Basin.** At the lakes, take Trail 392, then turn right onto Trail 68 and left onto Trail 8 back to the trailhead. From Camp Misery, **Picnic Lakes** (1.7 mi/2.7 km) also makes a good little-kid destination; just reverse the route by taking Trails 8, 68, and 392.

Birch Lake

Distance: 6 miles (9.7 km) rt
Duration: 3 hours
Elevation gain: 800 feet (244 m)
Effort: moderate
Trailhead: Camp Misery Trailhead in Jewel Basin
Directions: From Bigfork, follow MT 35 north and turn east onto MT 83. Turn north onto Echo Lake Rd. and drive for 3 miles (5 km) to Jewel Basin Rd. (Forest Service Rd. 5392). Drive 7 miles (11 km) of steep, bumpy, narrow dirt and gravel road to Camp Misery.

A short hop over a ridge along with a skip down a trail puts hikers on the shore of Birch Lake, a great destination for kids. Swim in the lake's west end, but don't expect balmy waters. This clear snowmelt pond retains its chill even in August.

Begin hiking up the broad roadway of Trail 717 to the four-way junction. Take the right fork onto Trail 7. The trail curves around the lower flanks of Mount Aeneas as it descends to the lake; you'll have to hike up this on the way out. A trail circles **Birch Lake,** but the best place to stop is on its clearly visible peninsula. For those with more stamina, another 2.5 miles (4 km) puts you on the boulder shoreline of Crater Lake.

Water Sports

The **Swan River** runs through Bigfork after dropping over a small dam. Skilled paddlers launch onto the river at the bridge above the dam and work through the slow current upstream and float back down with views of the Swan Mountains. Below the dam, white-water kayakers wearing dry suits gravitate to the freezing cold water released into a frothy series of cascades. These Class IV-V rapids are called the **Wild Mile,** a short 1.25-mile (2-km) stretch that drops 100 feet (30.5 m). The best water is from May to July, especially Wednesday nights, when the dam releases.

If you want to go out on Flathead Lake, rent a boat from **Bigfork Outdoor Rentals** (110 Swan River Rd., 406/837-2498, www.bigforkoutdoorrentals.com), **Bigfork Pontoons** (131 Sunrise Terrace, 406/471-7003, bigforkpontoonrentals), or **Narrow Path Adventures** (29120 Six Point Dr., 406/300-3047, narrowpathmt.com). For canoes, kayaks, or stand-up paddle-boards, visit **Base Camp Bigfork** (8525 MT 35, 406/871-9733, basecampbigfork. com). Bigfork Outdoor Rentals also has paddlecraft available for rent.

Bigfork Anglers (405 Bridge St., 406/837-3675, bigforkanglers.com) is a fly shop, gear shop, and guide service. Go here to find out what flies to use to fish the Swan River or Flathead River. They guide drift boat fishing trips on the Flathead River for 1-2 anglers ($400 half day, $500 full day). Fishing licenses are not included in rates.

Golf

With the highest greens fees in Flathead Valley, **Eagle Bend Golf Course** (279

Eagle Bend Dr., 406/837-7310 or 844/780-9945, eaglebendgolfclub.com, greens fees $90) is ranked among the top 50 public courses in the country. The challenging 27-hole course is a Jack Nicklaus design with big variety in its fairway layouts. From different tees, you can see Flathead Lake, the Swan Mountains, and Glacier National Park. Facilities include a driving range, restaurant, and pro shop with club and cart rentals.

Food and Drink
Sushi
Located upstairs in Twin Birch Square, **SakeTome Sushi** (459 Electric Ave., 406/837-1128, saketomesushi.com, 5pm-9pm Mon.-Sat., $7-25) garners a loyal following. The restaurant includes a bar, indoor seating, and deck seating. Find sashimi, *nigiri,* and fun specialty rolls made with sustainably caught fish.

Cafés
In downtown Bigfork, the **Pocketstone Café** (444 Electric Ave., 406/837-7223, www.pocketstonecafe.com, 7am-2:30pm daily, $7-16) serves espresso and inventive twists on café staples from home-baked goods to omelets and sandwiches. The huckleberry jalapeño burger is a house specialty, and the Reuben tops the charts with its house-made sauerkraut, rye bread, corned beef, and sauce.

Locals heading to Jewel Basin for hiking always fuel up at the family-run **Echo Lake Café** (1195 MT 83, 406/837-4252, www.echolakecafe.com, 6:30am-2:30pm daily, $9-16), where breakfast and lunch are served all day.

Breweries and Bars
Flathead Lake Brewing Co. Pubhouse (116 Holt Dr., 406/837-2004, https://flatheadlakebrewing.com, 11am-10pm daily, $10-22) brews a full lineup of IPAs, porters, and fruity flavors. With a deck overlooking Flathead Lake, upstairs dining, and downstairs Chicago pizza cellar, it serves a humungous menu of pub specialties, burgers, sandwiches, and salads.

The **Garden Bar and Grill** (451 Electric Ave., 406/837-9914, 11am-2am daily, $7-14, cash only) is the local watering hole with 20 microbrews on tap. You can eat burgers inside or out back in the funky garden, with live music on summer weekend evenings.

Accommodations
The town's most economical lodging is **Timbers Motel** (8540 MT 35 S., 406/837-6200, timbersmotel.com, mid-May-Oct., $105-150), a Wyndham Travelodge located within a five-minute drive of Eagle Bend Golf Course. It has a heated pool, hot tub, and sauna.

In downtown Bigfork adjacent to the historic steel bridge over the Swan River, **Bridge Street Cottages** (309 Bridge St., 406/837-2785 or 888/264-4974, bridgestreetcottages.com, $125-445) offers upscale lodging. Four of the units overlook the Swan River. Surrounded by small perennial gardens, these well-furnished one-bedroom cottages come with fully equipped kitchens and fireplaces. Suites are smaller, with just a fridge and a microwave. You can walk to restaurants.

Averill's Flathead Lake Lodge (150 Flathead Lake Lodge Rd., 406/837-4391, www.flatheadlakelodge.com, mid-June-Aug.) is a family-owned working dude ranch. Lodging, meals, and activities are all included in one price for a week: Rates start at $4,123 for adults. Rates for children are lower. With horseback riding, fishing, swimming, waterskiing, tennis, and sailing, the ranch centers around the classy log lodge and cabins. You can park the car and dive into vacation mode, as the ranch coordinates all the activities.

Transportation and Services
Emergency Services
For emergencies, call **911. Logan Health** (310 Sunny View Ln., Kalispell,

406/752-5111, www.logan.org) is the closest emergency medical facility.

Gas
Find gas at **Cenex** (junction of MT 35 and MT 83) and **Conoco** (8263 MT 35).

Cell Service
Cell service is somewhat marginal in Bigfork, depending on your carrier and location. Verizon has the best service. Portions of trails in Jewel Basin have no service.

⚑ Side Trip: Swan Valley and Seeley Lake

Swan Valley presents an alternate route from Flathead Valley to I-90, via MT 83. East of Bigfork and running north-south, this route has more curves and narrower roads, but for campers, the rewards are many, with campgrounds sprinkled along almost the entire route. If you have the time, it's worth staying for three days to hike and enjoy the lakes.

Driving MT 83 south from Bigfork through Swan Valley to Clearwater Junction is 90 miles (145 km) and takes a little more than 1.5 hours. The route passes through Flathead and Lolo National Forests and is lined with mountains and valley lakes, all the while following the Swan River upstream. Cutting between the Swan and Mission mountain ranges, the road arcs around **Swan Lake,** passing the tiny village of the same name. After a long, forested section, the road passes a series of lakes: Rainy, Alva, Inez, and Seeley. Between Rainy Lake and Lake Alva, the road crests a low forested pass into the Clearwater River drainage. The town of **Seeley Lake,** anchoring the south end, is on its namesake lake. Continuing south to pass Salmon Lake, the road follows the Clearwater River downstream

to Clearwater Junction. Stay alert: This route sees copious deer along the road.

Getting There
From **West Glacier** to **Swan Lake** in the northern part of Swan Valley is 60 miles (94 km) and takes a little over an hour. Head west on US 2 to MT 206; drive south until MT 206 terminates at MT 35. Continue south as the road jogs through Creston to the junction with MT 83 north of Bigfork. Follow MT 83 east and south into the Swan Valley. The drive to **Seeley Lake** at the southern end of Swan Valley is 115 miles (185 km) and takes a little more than two hours.

From **Whitefish** to **Swan Lake** is 52 miles (84 km), a one-hour drive. From **Kalispell,** the drive is 35 miles (56 km) and takes about 45 minutes. From either town, take US 93 south, turn left (east) onto MT 82, and follow it to MT 35. Turn right, then immediately left at the stoplight onto MT 83 without going into Bigfork. Continue on MT 83 into the Swan Valley. From Whitefish to **Seeley Lake** the drive is 110 miles (175 km) and takes two hours. The drive from Kalispell to Seeley Lake is 95 miles (155 km) and takes just under two hours.

From **Bigfork** to **Swan Lake** is 17 miles (27 km), a 25-minute drive. Go north on MT 35 to the junction with MT 83 and turn right to head into the Swan Valley. The drive to **Seeley Lake** is 75 miles (120 km) and takes just under 1.5 hours.

Recreation
Holland Lake
Set back from the highway, **Holland Lake** in Flathead National Forest is the prize destination in the Swan Valley. Below Holland Peak, the scenic lake lures paddlers and boaters for waterskiing and fishing. Hiking trails depart from here, hugging the lake to reach roaring **Holland Falls** (3.2 mi/5 km rt). A steep trail climbs to **Holland Lookout** (7 mi/11.2 km rt) for dramatic views into the wilderness area,

and a stunning **loop trail** (12 mi/19 km rt) ties together **Upper Holland Lake** and the smaller **Sapphire Lake** in an alpine bowl of wildflowers and huckleberry bushes in the Bob Marshall Wilderness.

Mission Mountains Wilderness

One of the best hikes in Swan Valley goes to three gorgeous lakes. In the **Mission Mountains Wilderness** (www.fs.usda.gov), the shortest trail leads through the forest to **Glacier Lake** (3 mi/4.8 km rt), which is fed by a waterfall at the head of the lake. A side trail climbs further to a junction that splits to serene **Heart Lake** (8.6 mi/13.8 km rt) or **Turquoise Lake** (12 mi/19 km rt), a more strenuous trail to waters tinted with its namesake color. To reach the trailhead from MT 83, turn west onto Kraft Creek Road (Forest Rd. 561) and drive for 11.5 miles (18.5 km) to the end of the road.

Lolo National Forest

In **Lolo National Forest** (406/677-2233, www.fs.usda.gov/lolo), near Seeley Lake, the **Morrell Falls National Recreation Trail** (5.4 mi/8.7 km rt) goes to Morrell Lake and Morrell Falls, a gorgeous double tumble of frothing water and mist. Find the trailhead at the end of Morrell Falls Road 4364.

Water Sports

North of Seeley Lake, the **Clearwater Canoe Trail** (3.5 mi/5.6 km one-way, 2 hrs) offers a slow-moving scenic waterway for paddlers from the launch point (Forest Rd. 17597) to Seeley Lake and the take-out at Seeley Lake Ranger Station (3583 MT 83, Seeley Lake). From there, a walking trail (1 mi/1.6 km one-way) leads back to the launch point to easily retrieve your vehicle.

Many lakes in the Swan Valley have boat launches, mostly at campgrounds. Find them on Swan Lake, Lake Alva, Lake Inez (undeveloped boat launch), Seeley Lake, and Salmon Lake.

Food, Accommodations, and Camping

The historic **Holland Lake Lodge** (end of Holland Lake Rd., 406/754-2282, www.hollandlakelodge.com) sits right on its namesake lake. It has nine lodge rooms ($300), six lakefront cabins ($340), and a restaurant (8:30am-9:45am, noon-2pm, and 5:45pm-8:45pm daily, $32-39) that's open to the public. Three meals a day are included in the lodging rates.

Campgrounds abound on this route, either right on MT 83 or nearby on side roads. These are mostly primitive **Forest Service campgrounds** (www.fs.usda.gov). Open May to September, they have vault toilets, picnic tables, and fire pits. Most cost $10-20 per site.

In **Flathead National Forest** (www.fs.usda.gov/flathead), campgrounds are located at **Swan Lake, Holland Lake,** and **Lindbergh Lake. Reservations** (877/444-6777, www.recreation.gov) are available six months in advance for Swan and Holland Lakes.

In **Lolo National Forest** (www.fs.usda.gov/lolo), campgrounds are located at **Lake Alva, Lake Inez** (free camping), **Seeley Lake** (at Lakeside, Big Larch, River Point, and Seeley Lake campgrounds), and **Salmon Lake.** Sites at Lakeside and River Point are reservable (www.recreation.gov) six months in advance.

Transportation and Services

Emergency Services

The closest hospitals are **Logan Health** (310 Sunny View Ln., Kalispell, 406/752-5111, www.logan.org) in Kalispell and **St. Patrick Hospital** (500 W. Broadway, Missoula, 406/543-7271, www.providence.org) and **Community Medical Center** (2827 Fort Missoula Rd., Missoula, 406/728-4100, communitymed.org) in Missoula.

Gas

Seeley Lake has two gas stations: **Sinclair** (3072 MT 83) and **Conoco** (3182 MT 83).

There are several other gas stations in the Swan Valley area.

Cell Service

Cell service is not available in most of the Swan Valley. However, Seeley Lake does have service, thanks to a cell tower.

Polson and Flathead Lake

The clear blue Flathead Lake sits below the Mission Mountains. Rimmed with small towns, the lake is long, with the north end in Flathead Valley and the south half on the Flathead Reservation. The east side harbors famous cherry orchards; some are U-pick and others have stands on the road. On the western shore, Lakeside anchors the north end while Polson flanks the south end. Bigfork sits at the northeast end of the lake.

Getting There

The drive from **Kalispell** to **Polson** is 50 miles (81 km), a one-hour drive down US 93 along the west shore of Flathead Lake. From **Bigfork,** Polson is 35 miles (56 km) south on the curvy MT 35, along the east shore of Flathead Lake. This drive takes about 45 minutes.

★ Flathead Lake

Stretching 28 miles (45 km) long and 15 miles (24 km) wide, **Flathead Lake** is the largest freshwater lake west of the Mississippi. Its 188 square miles (487 sq km), six state parks, islands, deep fishing waters, and wildlife refuges make it a summer play land. Highways circle the lake with public access at 13 different points. Between Lakeside and Polson, paddlers and boaters can explore **Wild Horse Island State Park,** home to wild horses, bighorn sheep, and big views of Flathead Lake. The southern half of the lake is in the Flathead Indian Reservation.

Flathead Lake

Tours

From Lakeside, **Far West Boat Tours** (7135 US 93 S., 406/844-2628, www.flatheadlakeboattour.com, 1pm and 7pm Sun.-Wed., 1pm Thurs.-Sat. late June-early Sept., $10-22) launches a cabin cruiser. Sit upstairs in the sun for bigger views. From Polson, **Shadow Cruises** (Kwataqnuk Resort and Casino, 49708 US 93, 800/882-6363, www.kwataqnuk.com, noon Thurs.-Sat., $20) has 1.5-hour tours around the south end of Flathead Lake. On select days, they also offer sunset, dinner, brunch, and other specialty cruises.

Boating

Flathead Lake has several launch sites with boat ramps. Most sites are open May to October and charge $5-10 for launching private boats. The lake has 13 public access points, six of which are in state parks maintained by **Montana Fish, Wildlife, & Parks** (https://fwp.mt.gov). On the north end of the lake, easy-to-reach launch sites are at Somers and Lakeside. Near Bigfork, Wayfarers State Park has a launch site. On the south end of the lake, Big Arm State Park, Polson, and Blue Bay are easiest to reach.

Rental boats are available around the lake. Expect to pay $90 per hour for Jet Skis and $125-250 per hour for water-ski boats, pontoon fishing boats, and party barges. In addition to your rental fee, you'll need to pay for the gas you use. Rental companies in the towns surrounding Flathead Lake include **Wild Wave Rentals** (130 Bills Rd., Lakeside, 406/844-2400, wildwaverentals.com), **Riverside Recreation** (412 2nd St. W., Polson, 406/883-2300, www.boatflathead.com) and **Flathead Boat Company** (50230 US 93 S., Polson, 406/883-0999, www.flatheadboatcompany.com). Bigfork also has a few spots for renting boats.

Paddling

Flathead Lake provides flat water in its bays, although winds can kick up big waves. The most popular Flathead Lake paddling destination is **Wild Horse Island State Park,** with a launch at the public beach in Dayton. Other lake launch locations are at nearby state parks and in Somers, Lakeside, Bigfork, and Polson. Canoes, kayaks, and paddleboards rent for $25-40 per hour. Rental companies in the towns surrounding Flathead Lake include **Paddle Board Outfitters** (5327 US 93, Somers, 406/212-2300, www.paddleboardoutfitters.org), **Sea Me Paddle** (7220 US 93, Lakeside, 406/249-1153, www.seamepaddle.com), and **Flathead Raft Company** (50362 US 93, Polson, 406/883-5838, www.flatheadraftco.com). There are a couple places to rent paddlecraft in Bigfork as well.

Fishing

Flathead Lake teems with cutthroat, giant trophy lake trout, mountain and lake whitefish, largemouth bass, bull trout, and yellow perch. It's good for all types of

fishing: bait, lure, fly-fishing, and trolling. Montana fishing licenses are only valid on the north half of the lake. For fishing on the south end, you need a license from the Flathead Reservation. You can get both at **Sliter's Ace Hardware** (108 Stoner Loop, Lakeside) and **Wal-Mart** (36318 Memory Ln., Polson).

Fishing Charters

Fishing charters are located mostly on the north end of the lake. Options include **Flathead Lake Charters** (Bigfork, 406/837-3632 or 406/270-8833, www.flatheadlakecharters.com), **Howe's Fishing** (Bigfork and Lakeside, 406/257-5214, www.howesfishing.com), **Captain Mike's Fish-N-Fun** (Somers, 406/250-6246, flatheadlakefishing.com), **Flathead Lake Fishing Charters** (Lakeside, 406/407-0881, flatheadfishingcharters.com), and **Flathead Lake Monster Charters** (Woods Bay, 406/314-8304, www.flatheadlakemonstercharters.com).

Campgrounds

Five **Montana state park campgrounds** (stateparks.mt.gov, $4-34) rim Flathead Lake. They all offer access to the waterfront for fishing, swimming, paddling, and boating. **Reservations** (montanastateparks.reserveamerica.com) are taken for summer. The campgrounds have picnic areas, boat ramps, sites for RVs with electrical hookups, some tent sites (some of which are walk-ins), and shared bicycle sites. Most are open April to October, although often water is only available May to September. The west side of Flathead Lake has two campgrounds, accessed via US 93: **West Shore State Park,** south of Lakeside, and **Big Arm State Park,** north of Polson. On the lake's east side, MT 35 connects with **Wayfarers State Park** near Bigfork, **Yellow Bay State Park** (tents only),

Top to bottom: paddling Flathead Lake; Tamarack Brewing Company; Big Arm State Park campground

midway between Bigfork and Polson, and **Finley Point State Park** in the southeast corner.

Lakeside

Located on the northwest side of Flathead Lake, Lakeside serves as a tiny summer resort town and a base for skiers in winter.

Recreation

Sitting above Lakeside and Flathead Lake, **Blacktail Mountain** (13990 Blacktail Rd., 406/844-0999, blacktailmountain.com, Wed.-Sun. mid-Dec.-early Apr., $22-45, discounts for half day) attracts families for skiing and snowboarding with four lifts and family-friendly pricing. They have rentals, lessons, and a day lodge with cafeteria and restaurant/bar.

For cross-country skiers, **North Shore Nordic** (www.northshorenordic.org, Dec.-Mar., donations accepted) grooms trails daily for classic and skate skiing on Blacktail Road below Blacktail Mountain. Two trailheads are located 8 miles (13 km) and 9.5 miles (15 km) up Blacktail Road from US 93.

Food and Drink

Tamarack Brewing Company (105 Blacktail Rd., 406/844-0244, www. tamarackbrewing.com, 11am-10pm daily, $9-25) puts out about a dozen beers, including the light golden Bear Bottom Blonde, a robust amber Yard Sale Ale (named after ski lingo for someone who crashes hard, littering the hill with skis and poles), and a smooth Switchback Stout. Pair with a big menu of pub food, including pizza. Inside seating can be noisy; outside patio seating abuts the creek. Tamarack also has a location in Missoula.

Accommodations and Camping

Edgewater RV Resort (7140 US 93, 406/844-3644, www.edgewaterrv.com, May-Sept.) divides its resort complex on both sides of the highway to encompass lakefront amenities. At the lake are a dock and swimming area. Accommodations include RV sites with full hookups that can fit big rigs ($60), cabins with kitchens ($180), and condos ($165-200).

Polson

Located on the south end of Flathead Lake, Polson enjoys a slightly warmer climate than Flathead Valley to the north. Its arid prairie landscape on the western side attests to that with different vegetation.

Food

Cherries BBQ Pit (105 2nd St. E., 406/571-2227, 11am-7pm Mon.-Fri., $8-25) serves local, fresh, and homemade food, smoking meats over cherry wood from nearby orchards. The menu has sandwiches, ribs, chicken, and sides, plus seven different sauces.

Finley Point Grill (35427 MT 35, 406/887-2020, www.finleypointgrill.com, 4pm-10pm Tues.-Sat., $16-36) serves fish and steak with an emphasis on locally sourced ingredients.

Accommodations and Camping

Owned and operated by the Confederated Salish and Kootenai Tribes, **Kwataqnuk Resort and Casino** (49708 US 93, 800/882-6363, www.kwataqnuk.com, from $102) has a prime location on the shore of Flathead Lake with views of the Mission Mountains. The resort has 107 rooms and suites, an indoor pool, patio bar, restaurant, and casino.

The **Polson/Flathead Lake KOA** (200 Irvine Flats Rd., 406/883-2151, www. koa.com, mid-Apr.-mid-Oct., tents $48-63, RVs $62-90) has tent sites, RV sites with full hookups, and cabins (from $98) with or without private baths. It also has a heated pool (summer only).

Transportation and Services

Emergency Services

St. Joseph Medical Center (6 13th Ave. E., Polson, 406/883-8433, www.providence.

★ Side Trip: Bison Range

On the Flathead Indian Reservation, the **Bison Range** (58355 Bison Range Rd., Moeise, 406/644-2211, bisonrange.org, 6am-8pm daily) preserves herds of bison on rare intermountain grasslands. In late 2020, the restoration of the range was passed from U.S. federal possession to the Confederated Salish and Kootenai Tribes, to be held in federal trust. This land has long been home to the Qlispé, Sélis, and Ksanka people, who call it the "Fenced-In Place where Buffalo Live."

bison

For visitors, **bison herds** are the highlight, but the range also offers outstanding bird-watching and sightings of **elk, bighorn sheep,** and **pronghorn antelope** as well as other wildlife. Mid-May to mid-June is the best time to see **bison calves.**

The entrance fee is $10 per vehicle, payable at the **visitors center** (9am-5pm daily mid-May-early Oct.). The center has exhibits on wildlife and natural history, as well as information on the importance of the bison to the local Indigenous people. You can also pick up maps for the refuge's scenic drives and get information on a few short walking trails. The rangers can also tell you where wildlife is currently hanging out. Trailers are not permitted on the two longer scenic drives; you can leave them in the visitors center parking lot.

org) is an emergency medical facility in Polson.

Gas

Gas is available along US 93 or MT 35 in Bigfork, Lakeside, and Polson.

Cell Service

Cell service can be spotty to nonexistent around Flathead Lake; some service is available in the towns of Bigfork, Lakeside, and Polson.

Missoula

Located right on I-90, Missoula flanks the Clark Fork River. Home to the University of Montana (hence the "M" on the mountainside above it), Missoula is a town that celebrates both football and music. The outdoor **Kettlehouse Amphitheater** (605 Cold Smoke Ln.,

Bonner) brings in big-name musicians during summer, and the historic **Wilma Theater** (125 Bank St.) and the intimate **Top Hat** (134 W. Front St.) in downtown have long been music staples. All three venues are run by event promoter **Logjam Presents** (406/830-4640, https://logjam-presents.com).

Getting There

From **West Glacier** to Missoula is 155 miles (250 km), which takes three hours via US 2 and US 93. From Kalispell, Missoula is 120 miles (195 km) south on US 93, a drive of a little over two hours. From Polson, the route is also via US 93, for a 70-mile (113-km) drive that takes a little over one hour.

Recreation

The **Clark Fork River**, which runs right through town, is a kayaking and rafting river from May to September. Kayakers

Scenic Drives

The refuge's scenic drives are gravel roads with interpretive sites en route. The three gravel drives are open as weather conditions permit. Prairie Drive and Red Sleep Mountain Drive do not allow RVs or trailers longer than 30 feet (9 m). Bring binoculars to aid with watching wildlife, and stay 75 feet (23 m) away from bison, which often appear docile but can cause serious injuries. Late May to June is the best time for prolific wildflowers, especially yellow arrowleaf balsamroot.

♦ **West Loop Road:** This loop (1 mi/1.6 km, 6am-8pm daily year-round) usually has bison hanging out near the road. It is the only road that allows trailers and large RVs. Plan for 15-20 minutes or more depending on the visible wildlife.

♦ **Prairie Drive:** This auto tour (14 mi/23 km, 6am-8pm daily year-round) goes along Mission Creek, where you are likely to see pronghorn and deer in addition to bison. The drive takes about 35-45 minutes or more, depending on wildlife sightings.

♦ **Red Sleep Mountain Drive:** This longer, more rugged, and one-way route (19 mi/31 km, 7am-6pm daily mid-May-early Oct.) has switchbacks and steep grades. Allow two hours for this drive, where you're likely to see bison, bighorns, and other wildlife. The loop joins up with Prairie Drive.

Getting There

From **Polson**, the refuge is 35 miles (56 km) south via US 93 and MT 212. The drive takes just under an hour. From **Missoula**, the refuge is 50 miles (81 km) north via I-90, US 93, and MT 212, for an hour-long drive.

and accomplished paddleboarders gravitate to **Brennan's Wave** near Caras Park downtown to surf on it and refine techniques. White-water rafting on the river happens west of Missoula on the **Alberton Gorge.** A tributary of the Clark Fork, the **Blackfoot River,** east of Missoula, is the best place for scenic floats.

The **Trail Head** (221 E. Front St., 406/543-6966, www.trailheadmontana. net) has the biggest selection of rentals, with canoes, kayaks, paddleboards, rafts, camping gear, and clothing from their store downtown.

Most river guiding companies offer half-day ($55-70) and full-day ($70-85) white-water and scenic trips. Some companies add on river kayaking, paddleboarding adventures, and trips with meals. Missoula's rafting companies include **10,000 Waves Raft and Kayak Adventures** (190 Sawmill Gulch Rd., Alberton, 406/549-6670,

10000-waves.com), **Zoo Town Surfers** (1001 S. 4th St. W., 406/546-0370, www. zootownsurfers.com), and **Lewis and Clark Trail Adventures** (912 E. Broadway St., 406/728-7609, trailadventures.com).

Hiking
Mount Sentinel M Trail

Distance: 1.5 miles (2.4 km) rt
Duration: 1.5 hours
Elevation gain: 620 feet (189 m)
Effort: strenuous
Trailhead: University of Montana campus parking lot, east side of Campus Dr.

You can see the large "M" for the University of Montana from many locations around Missoula, including the freeway. Its perch on the open hillside of Mount Sentinel gives it the perfect point from which to survey the town, valley, and surrounding mountains. The trail climbs relentlessly up 11 exposed switchbacks, some with benches for resting, to reach the M. Return down the same switchbacks.

Food and Drink

One of many Missoula brewpubs, **Tamarack Brewing Company** (231 W. Front St., 406/830-3113, www. tamarackbrewing.com, 11am-10pm daily, $9-25) is a sports bar downstairs and a casual eatery upstairs serving pizza and other typical pub grub. Brunch (10am-1pm) is served on Saturdays and Sundays. Tamarack also has a location in Lakeside, on the west shore of Flathead Lake.

Bob Marshall Biga Pizza (241 W. Main St., 406/728-2579, www.bigapizza.com, 11am-8pm daily, $10-21) serves up sandwiches, calzones, and pizza—even one made with a Flathead cherry chutney. A downright decadent choice is the pizza topped with caramelized sweet potatoes, bacon, and maple chipotle. Vegan, vegetarian, and gluten-free options are available.

Accommodations and Camping

Missoula has scads of chain motels that are easily accessible off I-90. Otherwise, there are several options for camping. Right in town, **Missoula KOA** (3450 Tina Ave., 406/549-0881 or 800/562-5366, missoulakoa.com, year-round) is an urban campground offering RV sites with full hookups ($46-75), tent sites ($35-50), camping cabins ($67-82), and typical KOA amenities, including a summer-only outdoor pool and two hot tubs.

Two campgrounds line US 93 north of I-90. **Jellystone Park** (9900 Jellystone Ave., 406/543-9400 or 800/318-9644, www.campjellystonemt.com, May-mid-Oct., $36-52) has full hookup sites for RVs, tent sites, camping cabins, and a summer-only outdoor heated swimming pool.

East of Missoula by 25 minutes, **Beavertail Hill State Park** (29895 Bonita Station Rd., Clinton, 406/825-2207, stateparks.mt.gov/beavertail-hill, May-Oct.,

$9-34) sits on the Clark Fork River. It has campsites for RVs with electrical hookups, tent sites, and tepee rentals ($50). Make reservations online (montanastateparks. reserveamerica.com).

Transportation and Services

Emergency Services

Emergency rooms are at **St. Patrick Hospital** (500 W. Broadway St., 406/543-7271, www.providence.org) and **Community Medical Center** (2827 Fort Missoula Rd., 406/728-4100, community med.org).

Gas

Several large gas stations flank all sides of the junction of US 93 with I-90.

Cell Service

Cell service is reliable in Missoula.

Getting Around

With the Clark Fork River bisecting Missoula, many paved **walking** and **bike paths** parallel and cross the river.

Missoula's bus service is **Mountain Line** (mountainline.com, free). Maps and schedules are available online.

Public parking is available at four parking structures: Bank Street (next to Higgins Street Bridge), Central Park (128 W. Main St.), Park Place (201 E. Front St.), and Roam (305 E. Front St.). Most offer free parking for the first hour and $1 per hour after that.

Butte

Most travelers bypass Butte, save for wanting to see the famed Berkeley Pit, one of the largest open-pit mines (and a Superfund site). The mine is so huge you can see it from I-90. If you want a closer look, you can visit the viewing platform above it. In mid-July, music fans gather in Butte for the annual three-day Montana Folk Festival.

Getting There

From **West Glacier,** the most direct route to Butte is via MT 83 and the Swan Valley, a 250-mile (400-km) drive of four hours. From **Seeley Lake,** it's 130 miles (210 km) and a little over two hours to Butte via MT 200, MT 141, MT 12, and I-90. From **Missoula,** the 120-mile (190-km) drive south to Butte on I-90 takes a little under two hours.

Sights

Butte National Historic Landmark District

In the 19th century, Butte was one of the biggest mining towns in the West. Its National Historic Landmark District includes the Copper King Mansion, several Chinatown buildings, and the Berkeley Pit.

The narrated **Trolley Tour** (1000 George St, 406/723-3177, www.buttechambersite. org, 2 hrs, $18-20 adults, $8-15 youths) drives by the highlights of this district on the Old Number One. Reservations are recommended.

You can get a feel for the life of the Copper Barons by touring the 34 rooms at the **Copper King Mansion** (219 Granite St., 406/782-7580, thecopperkingmansion.com, 10am and noon daily May-Sept., $10 adults, $5 children). You'll learn about the family that built it, its operation, and the antiques in it.

Mai Wah Museum (17 W. Mercury St., 406/723-3231, www.maiwah.org, 10am-4pm Tues.-Sat. June-Sept., $5-8) preserves artifacts and buildings from Butte's Chinatown. The large immigrant community started shops and restaurants when Chinese people were forced out of mining in the 1880s.

You can explore the **World Museum of Mining** (155 Museum Way, 406/723-7111, miningmuseum.org, 10am-5pm Tues.-Sat. Apr.-Oct., $5-9) on a self-guided outside tour around 50 buildings and 66 mine yard exhibits. Or you can don a hard hat to go on a guided tour down

to the muddy underground of the mine ($18-21 adults, $14 youths).

Food, Accommodations, and Camping

Sparky's Garage (222 E. Park St., 406/782-2301, www.sparkysrestaurant. com, 11am-9pm daily, $10-18) gives you lots to look at while you wolf down pub-style offerings that include burgers, sandwiches, and barbecue. There are Montana microbrews on tap or order a signature cocktail, like the Big Sky Tea (a take on a Long Island iced tea). The restaurant is filled with classic car memorabilia, and you can actually dine in the bed of an old Chevy truck.

Loads of national chain motels populate Butte. But for a more immersive experience of the historic town, overnight in the **Copper King Mansion Bed-and-Breakfast** (219 Granite St., 406/782-7580, thecopperkingmansion.com, $105-150). Five rooms, decorated in 19th-century antiques, have private or shared bathrooms.

Butte KOA Journey (1601 Kaw Ave., 406/782-8080, www.koa.com, mid-Apr-mid-Oct.) has campsites for tents ($35-40) and RVs with hookups ($46-75) plus camping cabins without bathrooms ($71). It also has an outdoor pool in summer.

Transportation and Services

Emergency Services

St. James Healthcare (400 S. Clark St., 406/723-2500, www.sclhealth.org) has an emergency room.

Gas

Conoco (19 S. Montana St.) and **Cenex** (2801 Harrison St.) are near I-90.

Cell Service

Butte has good cell reception.

Getting Around

Butte-Silver Bow Transit operates **The Butte Bus** (buttebus.org, 6:45am-6:15pm

Mon.-Fri., 8:45am-4:45pm Sat., free), with service throughout the city. Maps and schedules are online.

Three Forks

This tiny town is one of the best places to grab a bite to eat on I-90. **Wheat Montana Farms Bakery and Deli** (Exit 274, 10778 US 287, 406/582-4572, www. wheatmontana.com, 6am-6pm daily) has gooey cinnamon rolls, fresh breads, deli sandwiches, and non-GMO wheat flours and cereals to take home.

★ Missouri Headwaters State Park

The area is also home to **Missouri Headwaters State Park** (Exit 278, 1585 Trident Rd., 406/285-3610, fwp.mt.gov, daily year-round, Montana residents free, nonresidents $8/vehicle), a National Historic Landmark where the confluence of the Madison, Jefferson, and Gallatin Rivers launches the beginning of the mighty Missouri River's 2,565-mile journey. The park has multiple interpretive sites about the headwaters, Indigenous culture, the Lewis and Clark expedition (which camped here in 1805), and wildlife, including moose and American pelicans.

Just past the park's campground, the **Confluence of the Jefferson and Madison Rivers** create the Missouri River. Benches at the site allow you to enjoy the views, which are especially good at sunset. Farther north, on the opposite side of the road, the **Gallatin Confluence** has a paved trail that climbs past sod-roofed interpretive kiosks to an overlook of the Gallatin River. A wide dirt trail goes higher, to a point with 360-degree views of the Missouri River to the west and the Gallatin cruising to meet it.

The park's popular **campground** (17 sites, year-round, $18) takes reservations (montanastateparks.reserveamerica.com, $12) up to six months in advance for dates

Museum of the Rockies in Bozeman

from May through September. The rest of the year, the sites are first come, first served.

Bozeman

Home of Montana State University, Bozeman is a cow town turned college town and recreational hub. It's also a gateway to Yellowstone National Park, with the north entrance at Gardiner a little over an hour to the southeast and the west entrance two hours south.

Getting There

From **West Glacier,** it's a 360-mile (580-km), six-hour drive to Bozeman via US 2, US 93, and I-90. This is the easier route, with straighter roads and wide shoulders. While the 330-mile (530-km) route from West Glacier to Bozeman through the **Swan Valley** is technically shorter, it may end up taking the same amount of time due to the narrow roads with

no shoulders and lots of curves. A third route, which is 340 miles (550 km) and six hours from West Glacier to Bozeman, follows US 2 east to Browning before heading south along the **Rocky Mountain Front** on US 89, US 287, and I-15 and then exiting onto US 287 to I-90. The segment along the Rocky Mountain Front can be slower going due to strong winds and narrow, shoulderless roads.

From **Butte,** it's an 85-mile (140-km), 1.5-hour drive over Homestake Pass on the Continental Divide via I-90 to reach Bozeman.

Sights
Museum of the Rockies

The renowned **Museum of the Rockies** (600 W. Kagy Blvd., 406/994-2251, museumoftherockies.org, 9am-4pm daily, $14.50 adults, $9.50 children 5-17) attracts dinosaur fans. It is home to one of the largest dinosaur fossil collections in the world, and even boasts a full T. rex skeleton. Other permanent exhibits cover regional culture, history, and art. It also has a planetarium that shows a few different space-themed programs.

Recreation
Hiking
★ Hyalite Creek and Lake

Distance: 2.4-11 miles (3.8-18 km) rt
Duration: 1.5-5.5 hours
Elevation change: 1,880 feet (573 m)
Effort: easy-moderate
Trailhead: Hyalite Creek Trailhead #427 in Custer Gallatin National Forest
Directions: From Main St. in Bozeman, drive 19th Ave. south to Hyalite Canyon Rd. Turn left, climbing past Hyalite Reservoir to the trailhead.

For waterfall fans, this trail packs in 11 waterfalls that gush fully in early summer. The shared-use trail attracts so many users that the Forest Service regulates days for horseback and bike riding, but hikers can go any day.

The route begins with a wheelchair-accessible trail to **Grotto Falls** (2.4 mi/3.8 km rt). Drop off the main trail onto spurs

★ Side Trip: Lewis and Clark Caverns State Park

Lewis and Clark Caverns (25 Lewis and Clark Caverns Rd., Whitehall, 406/287-3541, fwp.mt.gov) are the third largest subterranean caves in the United States, behind Carlsbad and Mammoth. The caves are accessible only via guided tour, where you'll be able to see rooms of fantastical stalactites, ribbons, dripstones, columns, cave popcorn, and flowstones. Here, over time, water carried calcite through the living limestone cave, creating dramatic formations like Grandma's Kitchen, Snow White's Coffin, the Sumo Wrestler, and Bridal Veil Falls. On the tour, you'll scoot through Beaver Slide, feel calcite building up on handrails, and experience total darkness as your guide tells the story of a CCC worker lost for three days in the caverns. The park also has hiking and mountain biking trails, plus it offers evening programs including stargazing.

cave formations inside Lewis and Clark Caverns

Trailers are not allowed on the steep road that climbs up to the visitors center and caverns, but parking is available near the park entrance. The visitors center is in a mountain saddle and is open year-round. It has a few exhibits and sells tickets for the cave tours.

Cave Tours
Guided cave tours happen in summer (May-Sept., $15 adults, $10 children). To reach the cave entrance, you must walk about 1.3 miles (2 km) uphill. Since the cave is 48°F (9°C) year-round, wear a warm layer. In addition to the tour fee, you'll pay a day-use fee (MT

to reach the other waterfalls en route; some may thin to trickles by fall. Small **Hyalite Lake,** named for the hyalite opal found here, is tucked in a bowl at the base of Hyalite Peak. Tumbling from the Gallatin Crest, **Hyalite Creek** plunges from Hyalite Lake through a glacial valley canyon pinched by cliffs.

Biking
Mountain biking abounds around Bozeman, especially on trails in **Custer Gallatin National Forest** (www.fs.usda.gov/custergallatin). One of the most strenuous intermediate rides, highly lauded in the biking community, is the **Bangtail Divide** (24 mi/39 km rt, elevation change 5,100 ft/1,554 m), a single-track loop in the Bangtail Mountains

north of town. **Crosscut Mountain Sports Center** (16621 Bridger Canyon Rd., 406/586-9690, www.crosscutmt.org) has 14 miles (23 km) of mountain biking trails with graduated levels of difficulty. **Owenhouse Cycling** (35 S. Black Ave., 406/587-5404, www.owenhousecycling.com) rents mountain bikes, road bikes, and e-bikes.

Paddling
Hyalite Reservoir (end of Hyalite Canyon Rd., Gallatin National Forest) offers a good place for novice paddlers to try out canoeing, kayaking, or paddleboarding. Park and launch near the pavilion on the south side of the reservoir. You can rent kayaks and paddleboards with life jackets and paddles at **Big Boys Toys** (25 New

residents free, nonresidents $8/vehicle) when you enter the park. Tickets for the Classic and Paradise Tours can only be purchased on-site on the day of the tour (but call ahead to confirm availability).

♦ **Classic Tour** (2 hrs): This tour explores about 0.7 mile (1.1 km) of the cave system. You'll descend 600 steps, slide down a ramp, waddle a bit, and experience utter darkness when the guide flips off the lights.

♦ **Paradise Tour** (1.5 hrs): This tour is available for people with mobility issues, young children, and those who may not want to be in tight spaces. It requires about 1 mile (1.6 km) of walking to tour the largest and most lavish cave of the system. Plan to arrive early to get tickets, as this tour often sells out.

♦ **Wild Cave Tour** (3 hrs): This challenging tour requires physical agility to climb, crawl, scramble, and wriggle your way through the cavern. Helmets, kneepads, gloves, and headlamps are provided. This tour requires advance reservations.

Camping
Located near the Jefferson River at the park entrance, the **campground** (40 sites, year-round, $18-24) has sites for tents and RVs. Amenities include potable water (May-Sept. only), showers, flush toilets, one accessible site, 12 electrical sites, and a dump station. The campground also has three accessible cabins ($54) and a tepee ($30). Make **reservations** (montanastateparks.reserveamerica.com, $12 fee) up to six months in advance for May to September. Otherwise, sites are first come, first served.

Getting There
Lewis and Clark Caverns is about halfway between Butte and Bozeman. From **Butte,** the park is 40 miles (64 km) east on I-90 and MT 2, a 45-minute drive. From **Bozeman,** the park is 50 miles (81 km) west on I-90, US 287, and MT 2, a 50-minute drive.

Ventures Dr., 406/587-4747, bigboystoysrentals.com, $35-50/day).

Golf
Cottonwood Hills (8955 River Rd., 406/587-1118, www.cottonwoodhills.com, greens fees $52/18 holes, $28/9 holes) has an 18-hole championship course and a 9-hole course, plus club and push-cart rentals. **Bridger Creek Golf Course** (2710 McIlhattan Rd., 406/586-2333, bridgercreek.com, greens fees $45) takes in a backdrop of the Bridger Mountains on its 18 holes. The clubhouse rents clubs and power carts.

Winter Sports
Less than 30 minutes from downtown,

Bridger Bowl (15795 Bridger Canyon Rd., 406/587-2111, bridgerbowl.com, Dec.-early Apr., $63 adults, $25-40 youths) is Bozeman's ski area with fun runs, terrain parks, and four day lodges with restaurants. Its ridged terrain attracts expert skiers who need avalanche transceivers to access its challenging slopes via the Schlasman's chairlift.

Crosscut Mountain Sports Center (16621 Bridger Canyon Rd., 406/586-9690, www.crosscutmt.org, 9am-6pm daily Dec.-Mar., $15-25) has groomed trails for cross-country skiing. Select trails are designated for snowshoeing and winter fat biking. The area rents skate and classic skis plus snowshoes and teaches ski lessons.

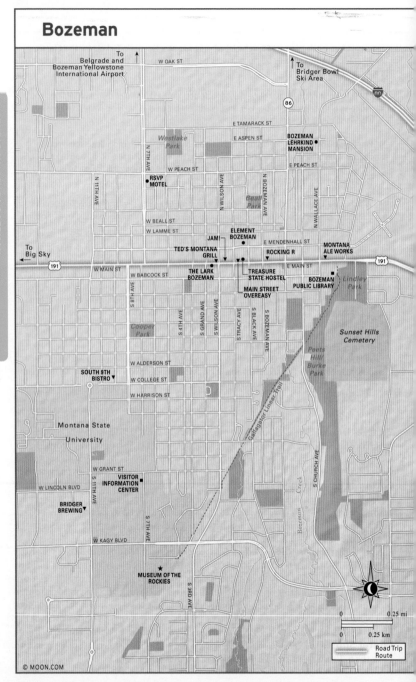

Bozeman

To
Belgrade and
Bozeman Yellowstone
International Airport

To
Bridger Bowl
Ski Area

W OAK ST

86

E TAMARACK ST

Westlake
Park

E ASPEN ST

BOZEMAN
LEHRKIND
MANSION

N 7TH AVE

W PEACH ST

E PEACH ST

N 11TH AVE

RSVP
MOTEL

N WILSON AVE

N BOZEMAN AVE

Bear
Park

N WALLACE AVE

W BEALL ST

W LAMME ST

JAM!

ELEMENT
BOZEMAN

E MENDENHALL ST

MONTANA
ALE WORKS

To
Big Sky

TED'S MONTANA
GRILL

ROCKING R

191

W MAIN ST

W BABCOCK ST

THE LARK
BOZEMAN

TREASURE
STATE HOSTEL

E MAIN ST

191

S 8TH AVE

MAIN STREET
OVEREASY

BOZEMAN
PUBLIC LIBRARY

Lindley
Park

S 4TH AVE

S GRAND AVE

S WILSON AVE

S TRACY AVE

S BLACK AVE

S BOZEMAN AVE

Sunset Hills
Cemetery

Cooper
Park

Poets
Hill/
Burke
Park

W ALDERSON ST

SOUTH 9TH
BISTRO

W COLLEGE ST

W HARRISON ST

Gallagator Linear Trail

Montana State
University

W GRANT ST

S 11TH AVE

VISITOR
INFORMATION
CENTER

S CHURCH AVE

W LINCOLN BLVD

S 7TH AVE

BRIDGER
BREWING

W KAGY BLVD

Bozeman Creek

MUSEUM OF THE
ROCKIES

S 3RD AVE

0   0.25 mi

0   0.25 km

Road Trip
Route

© MOON.COM

Food and Drink
Bistros
Reservations are in order for **South 9th Bistro** (721 S. 9th Ave., 406/404-1244, www.south9thbistro.com, 5pm-close Tues.-Sat. $12-44). Its French-inspired menu delivers ratatouille and beef bourguignon, among other options. Seating is indoors on two floors or on the patio in summer.

On its rotating menu, **Feast Raw Bar & Bistro** (270 W. Kagy Blvd., Ste. C, 406/577-2377, www.feastbozeman.com, 5pm-9pm daily, $15-40) features seasonal organic foods that have been sustainably sourced. Entrées can include cioppino, duck pad Thai, or bison tenderloin. For a lighter meal, you can get shared plates or order from the raw bar, which serves oysters, shellfish, ceviche, and bison carpaccio.

Steakhouse
Founded by media mogul Ted Turner, who has a bison ranch in the area, **Ted's Montana Grill** (105 W. Main St., Ste. B, 406/587-6000, www.tedsmontanagrill. com, 11am-10pm daily, $12-50) is an American steakhouse that specializes in bison: burgers, meatloaf, brisket, and ribs.

Cafés
Main Street Overeasy (9 E. Main St., 406/587-3205, 7am-2pm daily, $7-16) is the place to go for breakfast, including pancakes, eggs Benedict, and huevos rancheros. Lunch has sandwiches and burritos. There are gluten-free options, too.

At **Jam!** (25 W. Main St., 406/585-1761, jamonmain.com, 7am-3:30pm daily, $7-14), you can get breakfast all day with crepes, pancakes, Benedicts, and omelets or smaller bites, like mini cinnamon rolls or avocado on toast. Lunch has salad, sandwiches, burgers, and fish tacos. Beverages include espresso, kombucha, beer, and wine (still and bubbly).

Breweries and Pubs
In an old railroad freight house, **Montana Ale Works** (611 E. Main St., 406/587-7700, www.montanaaleworks.com, 4pm-9pm daily, $11-30) carries 40 beers on tap, many of them regional craft brews, and they serve cocktails and wine to accompany locally sourced beef and bison burgers, steaks, sandwiches, small plates, and salads. You can even get a gluten-free beer and meal.

Bridger Brewing (1609 S. 11th Ave., 406/587-2124, www.bridgerbrewing. com, 11am-9pm daily, $12-26) uses locally grown hops and wheat to make their beers. They specialize in unique pizzas, including a dairy-free option with yam and bacon, fig and chicken, and pesto and lamb. They also have variations on the classics, made with bison and andouille sausage.

Accommodations and Camping
Bozeman has loads of chain hotels, open year-round, with the highest rates in summer and around college football games. Winter sees the lowest rates. You can also find vacation homes and cabins through **Bozeman Cottage Vacation Rentals** (bozemancottage.com) or **Mountain Home** (www.mountain-home. com).

Hostels
Treasure State Hostel (27 E. Main St., 406/624-6244, treasurestatehostel.com, from $28-34) has small dorm rooms with 2-5 twin/bunk combos and private rooms ($42-68). Rates include linens, Wi-Fi, and breakfast. Its downtown location has restaurants and bars nearby.

Hotels and B&Bs
In downtown Bozeman, **The Lark Bozeman** (122 W. Main St., 406/624-3070 or 866/464-1000, www.larkbozeman.com, $110-380) has modern rooms crafted of leather, metal, and wood and spiffed up with local art. Each room is different, with various bed configurations.

One block from downtown's main street, **Element Bozeman** (25 E. Mendenhall St., 406/582-4972 or 888/236-2427, www.marriot.com, $130-360) is a stylish urban hotel with studios and suites. Rooms have full kitchens, and the hotel has a fitness room, indoor pool, and a complimentary grab-and-go breakfast bar.

Bozeman Lehrkind Mansion (719 N. Wallace Ave., 406/585-6932, www.bozemanbedandbreakfast.com, $170-350) has nine B&B rooms in a colorful 1897 Queen Anne-style Victorian mansion listed on the National Register of Historic Places. Hot breakfasts include organic egg dishes, homemade muffins, and fresh fruits. The mansion is within walking distance of downtown.

The boutique **RSVP Motel** (510 N. 7th Ave., 406/404-7999, rsvphotel.com, $100-290) has chic rooms with various bed combinations. It has an outdoor pool that is open in summer, and an on-site restaurant.

Lodges

Located 20 minutes outside downtown with views of the Spanish Peaks, **Gallatin River Lodge** (9105 Thorpe Rd., 406/388-0148 or 888/387-0148, www.grlodge.com, $170-950) is a luxury ranch with suites and rooms that have jet tubs, fireplaces, Tiffany lamps, and custom wood furnishings. The on-site Gallatin River Grill features fine dining, and you can go fly-fishing on the Gallatin River.

Campgrounds

Camping in town is at **Bozeman Hot Springs Campground and RV Park** (81123 Gallatin Rd., 406/587-3030 or 888/651-5802, bozemancampground.com, year-round, $43-90). The campground has RV sites with full hookups, tent sites, and cabins (bring your own bedding). Summer swimming at neighboring Bozeman Hot Springs and breakfast are included in rates. Water is only available late spring to October.

Custer Gallatin National Forest (Bozeman Ranger District, Hyalite Canyon Rd., 406/522-2520, www.fs.usda.gov/custergallatin, mid-May-mid-Sept.) has campgrounds south and north of town. Due to their location in the mountains, they are often cooler on summer nights than in town. **Reservations** (877/444-6777, www.recreation.gov) are accepted six months in advance. Amenities include picnic tables, firepits, and vault toilets.

- South of Bozeman up Hyalite Canyon are three ultra-popular campgrounds that take reservations and have potable water. **Langohr Campground** (19 sites, RV limit 32 ft/9.7 m, $20) sits on Hyalite Creek surrounded by early summer wildflowers. The prized **Hood Creek Campground** (25 sites, $20) flanks Hyalite Reservoir with water views from several sites, and it has two accessible campsites. The small **Chisolm Campground** (10 sites, $20) sits on a forested loop near Hyalite Reservoir.

- North of Bozeman in the Bridger Mountains are two first-come, first-served campgrounds. **Battle Ridge** (13 sites, RV limit 30 ft/9 m, free), off MT 86, has no potable water. Farther up the steep gravel Fairy Lake Road off MT 86, **Fairy Lake** (9 sites, RV limit 32 ft/9.7 m, free) has potable water and delays opening until July due to snow.

Transportation and Services
Emergency Services

An emergency room is at **Bozeman Health Deaconess Hospital** (915 Highland Blvd., 406/414-5000, www.bozemanhealth.org).

Gas

Find gas at **Casey's Corner** (1420 N. 7th Ave.) and **Costco** (2505 Catron St.), both near I-90.

Cell Service

Cell service is reliable in Bozeman, but not in the mountains surrounding town.

Getting Around

Streamline Bus (streamlinebus.com, 6:30am-7:15pm Mon.-Wed., 6:30am-7:15pm and 8pm-2:30am Thurs.-Fri., 7:30am-6:15pm and 8pm-2:30am Sat.) is a free bus service in Bozeman. Check route maps and schedules online.

Karst Stage (406/556-3540 or 800/287-4759, www.karststage.com) operates shuttles and buses from Bozeman Yellowstone International Airport daily year-round to Big Sky. The **Skyline Bus** (406/995-6287, www.skylinebus.com) links Bozeman with Big Sky multiple times daily in summer and winter, but weekdays only in fall and spring.

Taxi services include **AAA Yellow Cab** (406/220-3111), **Greater Valley Taxi** (406/388-9999, greatervalleytaxi.com), and **Black Bird Limousine** (406/624-8600, bozemanlimoservice.com).

Big Sky

Big Sky is a bustling, sprawling upscale resort below Lone Peak. Summer and winter bring on the crowds, rocketing the population from 2,500 to 10,000 in the unincorporated community. Due to the proximity to Yellowstone, some visitors prefer staying at Big Sky rather than the closer West Yellowstone simply because of the ambience, luxury accommodations, and breathing room. Big Sky draws the rich and famous with lodges, vacation homes, and shopping hubs sprawled across several miles.

Getting There

Three routes go from **West Glacier** to Big Sky, all taking over six hours. The easiest route is 390 miles (630 km) and takes about 6.5 hours. Take US 2 west to US 93, following it south to I-90 and through Butte, then south on US 191.

The other two routes, though shorter in mileage, have curvier, narrower roads, so driving is slower going. The route through the **Swan Valley** is 365 miles (585 km) and takes a little over six hours in ideal conditions. Traffic can slow your time considerably. From MT 83 (Swan Valley), take MT 200, then MT 141 to US 12 into Helena. From there, take US 287 south to I-90, then take US 191 south to reach Big Sky. The route through Browning and the **Rocky Mountain Front** is 370 miles (595 km) and technically only takes a little over six hours, but windy conditions can mean a slower drive. Take US 2 east to Browning, then take US 89 and US 207 south. Next, take I-15 south to Helena, then US 287 to I-90 and US 191 to get to Big Sky.

From **Bozeman** to Big Sky is 45 miles (72 km) and takes one hour. Follow US 191 west and then south.

Karst Stage (406/556-3540 or 800/287-4759, www.karststage.com) operates shuttles and buses from Bozeman Yellowstone International Airport daily year-round to Big Sky.

Sights
Lone Mountain

For Montana, **Lone Mountain** (11,166 ft/3,403 m) isn't one of the highest peaks, but it is prominent, rising high above the Big Sky valley. From several sides, you can see the alpine zone sweep up rugged, cliff-ridden ridges to its pointed summit. Skiers and snowboarders at Big Sky Resort take the tram to the summit to ski three sides. In summer, golfers see it while teeing off, mountain bikers ride on it, hikers tour its trails, photographers try to catch its sunrise light, and sightseers ride lifts to the summit.

For adventurous sightseers, the half-day **Lone Peak Expedition** (Big Sky Resort, 800/548-4486, bigskyresort. com, daily mid-June-late Sept., from $80 adults, $60 kids) goes to the summit of Lone Mountain. The guided expedition goes by chairlift, safari vehicle, and tram to reach the summit, where views take in three states and two national parks. You can also view the peak from **scenic chairlift rides** (10am-5pm daily

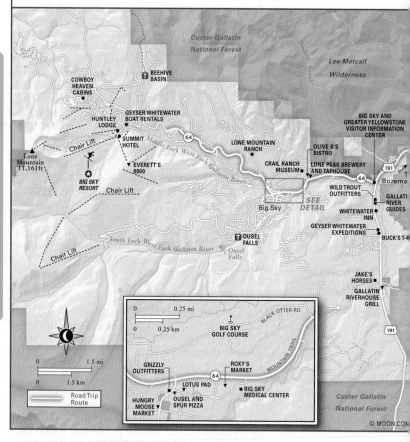

Big Sky

mid-June-late Sept., $18-30 adults, $15-20 kids and seniors) on two lifts.

Crail Ranch Museum

Big Sky is home to historic ranches. The **Crail Ranch Museum** (2110 Spotted Elk Rd., 406/993-2112, bscomt.org) is a group of log buildings from the 1902 homestead. A small museum contains photos, documents, and artifacts that will give a taste of the early ranchers in Big Sky. Visitors can take a self-guided tour (daylight hours) or volunteer-guided tour (noon-3pm Sat.-Sun. July-Aug., free).

Recreation
Hiking
Ousel Falls

Distance: 1.6 miles (2.6 km) rt
Duration: 1 hour
Elevation change: 450 feet (135 m)
Effort: easy
Trailhead: Ousel Falls in Custer Gallatin National Forest
Directions: From Big Sky Town Center, take Ousel Falls Rd. 1.6 miles (2.6 km) southwest to the trailhead parking lot.

This heavily traveled, short walk goes to a waterfall on the **South Fork of the**

One Day in Big Sky

With one summer day in Big Sky, you can experience the best of the outdoors.

Morning
Start with a short hike to **Ousel Falls** to enjoy the froth. Afterwards, head to **Olive B's Big Sky Bistro** for an early lunch.

Afternoon
Drive up to **Big Sky Resort.** Take the **Lone Peak Expedition** to stand on the towering summit of Lone Mountain for the huge views. After returning, take the **scenic chairlift ride** to enjoy the view of Lone Peak, where you just were.

Evening
Celebrate your day by dining at the **Horn and Cantle** at Lone Mountain Ranch or **Lone Peak Brewery & Taphouse.**

West Fork of the Gallatin River. The route is lined with wildflowers in July as the trail drops to a bridge across the river and then climbs along the south side of the river to **Ousel Falls.** At the falls, picnic tables offer places to sit. The falls, named for the American dipper, tumble down stair steps, which toss up a cool mist. Pick up an interpretive trail guide at the trailhead.

Beehive Basin
Distance: 6.6 miles (10.6 km) rt
Duration: 3-4 hours
Elevation change: 1,625 feet (495 m)
Effort: moderate
Trailhead: Beehive Basin in Custer Gallatin National Forest
Directions: From Lone Mountain Trail 1.4 miles (2.3 km) north of the Big Sky Resort turnoff, turn right onto Beehive Basin Rd. and drive 1.7 miles (2.7 km) to the trailhead parking lot on the left.

Trail #40 goes to scenic Beehive Basin, a bit of a grunt after the deceptively easy start. But the scenery more than makes up for it. In early June, you may encounter snow on the trail and ankle-deep streams to cross. But by July, wildflowers cover the meadows in rampant color. Later in summer, the meadow grasses turn gold.

From the trailhead, cross the creek and ascend north through meadows with intermittent trees. After climbing several switchbacks, the trail enters the upper **Beehive Basin** and works north to **Beehive Lake,** a small, narrow, shallow lake surrounded by meadows. It tucks at the base of rugged **Beehive Peak** in the Spanish Peaks.

Specimen Creek and Shelf Lake
Distance: 15.4 miles (24.8 km) rt
Duration: 8 hours
Elevation change: 2,300 feet (700 m)
Effort: strenuous
Trailhead: Specimen Creek on US 191 in Yellowstone National Park

Big Sky has quick access to this remote trail in Yellowstone National Park. It goes through a grizzly bear management area, so it's important to hike with a minimum of four people. You'll see plenty of trees that have been clawed by grizzlies. You can also backpack this trail, but you'll need a permit, available in West Yellowstone.

This level, mostly forested trail follows Specimen Creek up valley to a small alpine lake surrounded by meadows. After 2 miles (3.2 km; 1 hr), the trail enters the 2007 Owl Creek Fire burn and reaches a **fork.** (Hikers out just to enjoy the creek with meadows of early summer wildflowers can turn around at this junction.) To continue on, take the left fork up the

Specimen Creek Trail following the **North Fork.** At 4.1 miles (6.6 km; 2 hrs), the trail reaches a meadow where hikers must ford **Specimen Creek.** At 5.9 miles (9.5 km; 3 hrs), the trail reaches a second **junction.** Take the left fork up the steep switchback climb to the **Sky Rim Trail** and **Shelf Lake.** Sheep and Bighorn Peaks become visible as the trail breaks out of the trees.

Biking

Big Sky has scads of mountain biking trails. An easy gravel trail tours **Crail Ranch Meadow** (2.6 mi/4.2 km). Off Aspen Leaf Drive, the dirt single-track **Hummock Trail** (3 mi/4.8 km) rolls a triple loop over hummocks made by ice-age landslides; it's suitable for intermediate riders. A paved trail parallels **Lone Mountain Trail** (MT 64, 6 mi/9.7 km rt) between Town Center and US 191. **Grizzly Outfitters** (11 Lone Peak Dr., 406/995-2939 or 406/551-9470, www.grizzlyoutfitters.com) rents mountain, town, road, and kids' bikes.

Big Sky Resort (800/548-4486, bigskyresort.com, 9am-4pm daily summer) has lift-accessed downhill trails, including an intermediate flow trail. Cross-country single- and double-track trails for beginners and intermediate riders lead from Big Sky Village on loops across Andesite Mountain and through Moonlight Basin north of Lone Peak. **Different Spokes Bike Shop** (50 Big Sky Resort Rd., 406/995-5841, bigskyresort.com, 8:30am-5pm daily early June-late Sept.) rents cross-country and downhill bikes (helmets and full pads included). Tours, lessons, and coaching are available.

Water Sports
Boating

Tiny **Lake Levinsky** at Big Sky Resort offers a tame place for boating. **Geyser Whitewater Expeditions** (46651 Gallatin

Top to bottom: Lone Mountain; mountain biking in Big Sky; tram at Big Sky Resort

Rd., 406/995-4989, www.raftmontana.com, 10am-6pm daily summer, $15/hr) rents pedal boats, canoes, kayaks, and paddleboards from the shore. Day passes and Family Adventure Cards offer more economical rates.

Rafting

The **Gallatin River** meanders and crashes through the Gallatin Canyon, creating prime white-water rafting. Through the canyon, the river goes from slow swirly pools to thundering wave trains of almost continuous Class II-IV rapids. Most of the rafting is north of Big Sky in the 13 miles between Greek Creek and Spanish Creek.

Two companies guide half-day ($55-90) and full-day ($81-120) trips on scenic float sections, Class II-III white water, or Class II-IV white water for the wildest ride. Boats depart multiple times daily. **Geyser Whitewater Expeditions** (46651 Gallatin Rd., 406/995-4989, www.raftmontana.com) is based in Big Sky. **Montana Whitewater Raft Company** (63960 Gallatin Rd., 406/763-4465, www.montanawhitewater.com) is based in Gallatin Gateway, about 16 miles (26 km) north of Big Sky.

Fishing

The **Gallatin River** ranks as one of the prime rivers to fly-fish for trout in Montana. The waters hold brown and rainbow trout. Anglers are not permitted to float much of it, making wading the way to fish.

Fishing guide services operate out of Big Sky: **Grizzly Outfitters** (11 Lone Peak Dr., 406/554-9470 or 406/995-2939, www.grizzlyoutfitters.com), **Gallatin River Guides** (47430 Gallatin Rd., 406/995-2290, montanaflyfishing.com), and **Wild Trout Outfitters** (47520 Gallatin Rd., 406/995-2975 or 800/423-4742, wildtroutoutfitters.com). All offer a variety of trips, gear rentals, and instruction. Rates run $300-500 for a half day and $400-600 for a full day for two people.

Golf

Golfing at Big Sky can be a challenge, between the views of Lone Mountain and the wildlife that saunters out on the course. **Big Sky Golf Course** (2100 Black Otter Rd., 406/995-5780, bigskyresort.com, dawn-dusk daily May-Sept., greens fees and carts $54-100) is an 18-hole links-style par 72 Arnold Palmer course. The clubhouse offers rentals and instruction and has a restaurant.

Thrill Sports

In summer, **Big Sky Resort** (800/548-4486, bigskyresort.com, 9am-4pm daily mid-June-mid-Sept., rates vary, combo pass available) brings on the thrill sports. You can fly through the air on ziplines, feel the rush of a giant swing, monkey around on a climbing wall, or fling around on the bungee trampoline. Reservations are advised for ziplines.

Winter Sports

★ Downhill Skiing and Snowboarding

Big Sky Resort (50 Big Sky Resort Rd., 800/548-4486, bigskyresort.com, 9am-4pm daily late Nov.-mid-Apr.), with neighboring Moonlight Basin and Spanish Peaks, is one of the biggest ski areas in North America, with runs across four mountains. With its summit on Lone Mountain Peak, the ski area has one of the taller vertical drops in the country containing broad groomers, gladed tree runs, challenging steeps, and seven terrain parks. Access is via 36 lifts, including an eight-passenger chairlift with bubble covers for inclement weather. Lift ticket rates change throughout the season ($75-195 adults). Lower rates are available for advance purchase, multiday options, seniors, kids 7-14 (kids under 7 free), and in lodging packages.

Cross-Country Skiing

With one of the largest Nordic ski trail systems, **Lone Mountain Ranch** (750 Lone Mountain Ranch Rd., 406/995-4644, www.lonemountainranch.com, dawn-dusk daily late Nov.-mid-Apr., $30-35) grooms 85 km (53 mi) of trails for skate and classic skiing. Even though the trail system spans 2,200 feet (670 m) in elevation, routes are designed on different loops for beginners, experts, and skill levels in between. The outdoor ski shop (8am-5pm daily) offers lessons, rentals, repairs, and guided cross-country ski trips into Yellowstone.

Food
Restaurants
Big Sky is an upscale resort community where you can expect dining prices to be higher than elsewhere. In summer and winter, make reservations for dinner or you may have a long wait.

Fine Dining
At Lone Mountain Ranch, the ★ **Horn and Cantle** (800 Lone Mountain Ranch Rd., 406/995-4644, www.hornandcantle.com, 7am-10am, 11am-2pm, and 5pm-9:30pm daily mid-May-mid-Oct. and early Dec.-early Apr., $20-110) elevates dining with artistic plates of farm-to-table meals with fresh, lively flavors. Bison, lamb, rib-eye, and trout are regionally sourced. Appetizers are a must, and the desserts are exquisite. The **saloon** (11am-10pm) is the place to experience old Montana, with cocktails and homemade infusions, as well as lighter dining.

On US 191, **Buck's T-4** (46625 Gallatin Rd./US 191, 406/995-4111 or 800/822-4484, www.buckst4.com, 5:30pm-9pm daily late May-mid-Oct. and late Nov.-mid-Apr., $16-50) specializes in pheasant, deer, bison, lamb, wild game meatloaf, and hand-cut steaks. Duck bacon adds a flair to several dishes.

International
Olive B's Big Sky Bistro (151 Center Ln., 406/995-3355, www.olivebsbigsky.com, 11am-9pm Mon.-Fri., 4pm-9pm Sat. late May-mid-Oct. and early Dec.-mid-Apr., $27-39) serves classic French bistro fare including a lobster mac and cheese,

steaks, seafood, and elk, as well as huckleberry martinis.

The **Lotus Pad** (47 Town Center Ave., 406/995-2728, lotuspad.net, 5pm-close daily year-round, $14-30) serves organic Asian meals with local veggies. The menu specializes in curries, stir-fries, noodle dishes, and seafood, plus specialty cocktails and sake.

Classic American
Lone Peak Brewery & Taphouse (Meadow Village, 48 Marketplace Dr., 406/995-3939, www.lonepeakbrewery.com, 11am-10pm daily winter, 11:30am-9pm Wed.-Sun. spring-fall, $10-20) pours craft beers from 14 taps. Pub-style sandwiches, burgers, rice bowls, bison quesadillas, and salads can sate the appetites of meat lovers and vegetarians alike.

Ousel and Spur Pizza Company (Big Sky Town Center, 50 Ousel Falls Rd., 406/995-7175, www.ouselandspurpizza.com, 5pm-close daily year-round, $17-30) specializes in elk sausage pizza, but you can also get versions with the classic toppings, as well as Italian pastas with local ingredients. There are gluten-free and vegetarian options, too.

Gallatin Riverhouse Grill (45130 Gallatin Rd., 406/995-7427, riverhousebbq.com, 3pm-close daily year-round, $12-28) fires up the barbecue for burgers, chicken, sandwiches, brisket, sausage, and ribs. Platters serve families and pile on the traditional sides.

Big Sky Resort
Restaurants at **Big Sky Resort** (50 Big Sky Resort, bigskyresort.com, daily early June-Sept. and early Dec.-mid-Apr.) are open seasonally. For Tuscan specialties, antipasti, paninis, pasta, Italian wine, and drool-worthy desserts that look more like artistry than food, dine at **Andiamo Italian Grille** (406/995-8041, 11am-10pm daily, $19-35). For spectacular mountain views while dining, take the lift up to **Everett's 8800** (406/995-8800, winter, lift ticket additional; 10am-3pm Sun.-Tues.,

10am-3pm and 5:30pm-8:30pm Wed.-Sat., $31-60) for upscale meals.

Dining Experiences

Reservations are required for cookouts. Most do not serve alcohol; some permit BYOB (call ahead to ask).

At Big Sky Resort, diners venture as a group on a snowcat to the **Montana Dinner Yurt** (1 Lone Mountain Trl., 406/995-3880, www.bigskyyurt.com, 6:30pm-10pm daily late Nov.-mid-Apr., $175 adults, $145 kids). After arriving at the woodstove-heated yurt, guests can sled outside or drink cocoa around the fire before a three-course dinner featuring peppercorn filet mignon is served and finished with chocolate fondue. Musical entertainment is part of the gig.

From **Lone Mountain Ranch** (750 Lone Mountain Ranch Rd., 406/995-2782, www.lonemountainranch.com, 6:30pm-10pm daily mid-Dec.-Mar., $145-190), a horse-drawn sleigh slides through the snowy woods to the cozy North Fork Cabin for dinner. Dress for the cold with hat and gloves; wranglers will also supply blankets for the 20-minute ride. A woodstove heats the cabin, which glows by the light of oil lanterns. Prime rib with all the trimmings and sides is served family-style; live music and storytelling provide the entertainment.

Accommodations and Camping

The upscale resort community of Big Sky offers more than 3,000 rooms, condos, townhomes, and vacation homes with modern conveniences. It has accommodations across the spectrum, from family hotels to ultra-pricey luxury vacation homes, but lacks chain hotels. Several property management companies rent condos, townhomes, and vacation homes, including **Big Sky Luxury Rentals** (406/668-3956, vacationbigsky.com) and **Big Sky Vacation Rentals** (888/915-2787, www.bookbigsky.com). Rates are highest in winter and next highest in summer; spring and fall are off-season.

Motels

Two motels are located roadside on US 191, just south of the turnoff to the ski resort. A longtime Big Sky staple, **Buck's T-4 Lodging** (46625 Gallatin Rd./US 191, 800/822-4484, www.buckst4.com, late May-mid-Oct. and late Nov.-mid-Apr., $145-320) has rooms remodeled in 2019 with two queens or one king bed. Stays include a hot breakfast.

Owned by Big Sky Resort, **Whitewater Inn** (47214 Gallatin Rd./US 191, 800/548-4486, bigskyresort.com, year-round, $120-230) has rooms with 2-3 queen beds or one king, as well as pet-friendly rooms, a fitness room, a hot tub, and an indoor swimming pool with a 90-foot (27-m) slide. A continental breakfast is included.

Guest Ranches

Secluded in a side canyon with a wilderness feel, ★ **Lone Mountain Ranch** (750 Lone Mountain Ranch Rd., 406/995-4644, lonemountainranch.com, mid-May-mid-Oct. and early Dec.-early Apr., $595-800 pp per night summer with 5-night minimum, $425 pp per night winter with 4-night minimum, reduced rates for kids) has packages that include lodging, activities, and meals. Lodging is in quaint log cabins with no televisions, air-conditioning, or phones. Woodstoves make them cozy. In winter, Nordic ski trails wind between the cabins, which scatter on both sides of the burbling creek, and sleigh-ride dinners head to a cozy remote cabin. Ranch programs include horseback riding, fishing, hiking, kids' programs, Yellowstone tours, and skiing (seasonal). The dining room serves outstanding meals.

Located 12 miles (19.5 km) south of Big Sky, the historic **320 Guest Ranch** (205 Buffalo Horn Creek Rd., 406/995-4283, www.320ranch.com, year-round, $140-515) flanks the Gallatin River. Lodging is in 29 small one-room duplex cabins, 12 two-bedroom cabins with efficiency kitchens, and seven three-bedroom luxury log homes. Summer has horseback riding and fly-fishing; winter offers sleigh rides. The restaurant is open in summer only.

Big Sky Resort

For extensive hotels, condos, cabins, townhomes, vacation homes, and especially slopeside options for winter and summer, check **Big Sky Resort** (50 Big Sky Resort Rd., 800/548-4486, bigskyresort.com, early June-Sept. and early Dec.-mid-Apr.). The resort offers lodging and activity packages. Rates are highest in winter during the ski season and lower in summer. Book holiday lodging one year in advance. Resort fees will add about 19 percent to rates.

The three-story **Village Center** ($230-1,220) has luxury suites and condos to sleep 2-10 people with plush designer mountain decor. Studios and one-, two-, and three-bedroom condos have 2-3 full bathrooms. The center has an outdoor pool, hot tub, and fitness room. The high-rise luxury **Summit Hotel** ($240-4,200) has studios with queen beds, hotel rooms with two queens or a king, condos, and penthouses. Rates usually include breakfast. Condo suites have 1-3 bedrooms, plus kitchens and 1-3 bathrooms. Penthouses, which have 2-4 bedrooms, have housed political notables such as the Obamas and Bidens. **Huntley Lodge** ($155-680) was an early mainstay but has seen several upgrades. Dining, shopping, a spa, an outdoor swimming pool and hot tubs, fitness center, sauna, and tennis courts are in the complex. Huntley Lodge rooms have 2-3 queen beds with mountain views or lofts as options. **Cowboy Heaven Cabins** ($255-800, 3-5 nights minimum) are modern two-bedroom log cabins with full kitchens, fireplaces, two small bathrooms, living and dining area, and private outdoor hot tubs.

Campgrounds

In **Custer Gallatin National Forest** (Bozeman Ranger District, 3710 Fallon St., Bozeman, 406/522-2520, www.

fs.usda.gov, mid-May-late Sept., $16-20), several campgrounds for tents and RVs line the Gallatin Canyon along US 191. They are popular with locals as quick getaways from Bozeman for fishing, river rafting and kayaking, and hiking. Make **reservations** (877/444-6777, www.recreation.gov) six months in advance. Facilities include picnic tables, fire rings with grills, vault toilets, drinking water, bear boxes, garbage service, firewood for sale, and wheelchair-accessible toilets and campsites.

The three most popular campgrounds sit right on the highway and the Gallatin River, the first two located just north of Big Sky. **Greek Creek Campground** (14 sites) sits on a sunny loop. **Moose Creek Flat Campground** (13 sites), the closest campground to Big Sky, lines up along the Gallatin River. South of Big Sky in the Upper Gallatin Canyon, **Red Cliff Campground** (65 sites) is the closest to Yellowstone. It's tucked in a young Douglas fir forest with electrical hookups ($28) at half the sites.

Two quieter campgrounds are tucked up side canyons north of Big Sky. **Spire Rock Campground** (19 sites, no potable water) huddles below Storm Castle Mountain, surrounded by lush undergrowth of thimbleberries, wild roses, and vine maples. **Swan Creek Campground** (14 sites, RV limit 45 ft/14 m) is in the steep-walled Swan Creek Canyon in grassy meadows and forest.

Transportation and Services
Emergency Services

The **Big Sky Medical Center** (334 Towne Center Ave., 406/995-6995, www.bigskymedicalcenter.com) has 24/7 emergency care. The nearest hospital is **Bozeman Health Deaconess Hospital** (915 Highland Blvd., Bozeman, 406/414-5000, www.bozemanhealth.org), 45 miles (72 km) away in Bozeman.

Gas

Big Sky has two gas stations on US 191:

Exxon (47650 Gallatin Rd.) and **Conoco** (90 Lone Mountain Trl.).

Cell Service

Cell service is fairly reliable in Big Sky but nonexistent in the Gallatin Canyon.

Getting Around

The **Skyline Bus** (406/995-6287, www. skylinebus.com, hours vary seasonally year-round, free) connects the various base areas of Big Sky Resort with businesses on the highway, including motels. It makes about 15 stops around the Big Sky area. A bus also runs between Bozeman and Big Sky ($5, cash only, purchase tickets at Big Sky Resort). Buses run daily in summer and winter but only Monday-Friday in fall and spring.

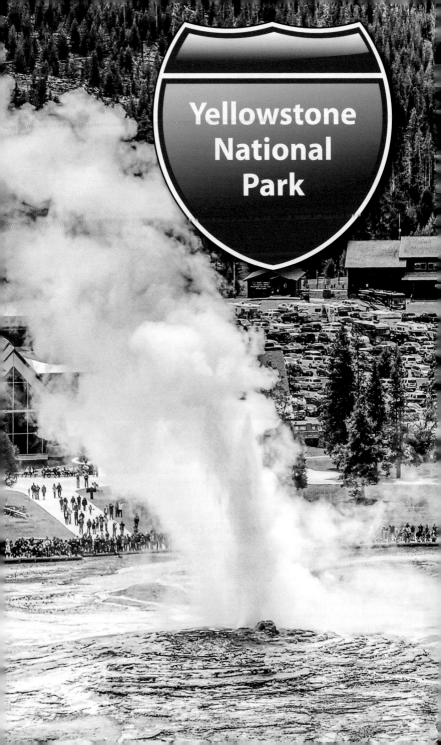

Yellowstone
National
Park

Highlights

★ **Stroll along the Mammoth Hot Springs Terraces:** Walk among the lower formations of these otherworldly travertine terraces (page 378).

★ **See Wildlife:** Huge bison herds, elk, pronghorn antelope, bears, wolves, bighorn sheep, and raptors range across **Lamar Valley** (page 380). The vast **Hayden Valley** (page 388) is also home to bison and elk, as well as waterfowl.

★ **Walk through Norris Geyser Basin:** It's the hottest and most changeable geothermal basin in the park (page 380).

★ **Admire the Colors at Grand Prismatic Spring:** The largest hot springs in the United States has vivid blue water surrounded by radiating browns and oranges (page 383).

★ **Set Your Watch at Old Faithful Geyser:** This geyser spews hot water into the air about every 90 minutes (page 383).

★ **Appreciate "Parkitecture":** The log lobby of the 1904 **Old Faithful Inn** holds a massive stone fireplace (page 387).

★ **Stare Down into Grand Canyon of the Yellowstone:** From 10 overlooks, view the thunderous Upper or Lower Falls and the colorful canyon (page 387).

★ **Ride in a Snowcoach:** Experience the volcanic landscape of the park in winter for a steaming clash of heat and ice (page 425).

Earth's tremendous forces gave Yellowstone its volatile landscape. This supervolcano makes its presence known, spitting, oozing, and bubbling constantly. Steam roils out of vivid-colored pools, muddy cauldrons burp smelly gases, and blasts of hot water shoot high into the air. In Yellowstone, there's always something happening.

This park packs in the iconic attractions. Old Faithful erupts frequently, drawing huge crowds that "ahhh" in unison, and the blue Grand Prismatic Spring radiates outward with orange arms, creating the largest hot spring in the United States. One of the longest free-flowing rivers in the country plunges over precipices via roaring waterfalls and squeezes through the Grand Canyon of the Yellowstone. Yellowstone Lake is one of the United States' largest high-elevation lakes.

Wildlife, too, can be found in abundance here. The high sagebrush prairies make animals easy to spot. Pronghorns, wolves, and grizzly bears enchant visitors, and bison frequently cause traffic jams when they walk between cars on the roads. In fall, bull elk bugle during the rut.

As the first national park in the United States, Yellowstone preserves some of the best experiences in the entire country. Bring your binoculars, camera, and walking shoes, and plan to give yourself plenty of time here.

Planning Your Time

It's possible to tour **Yellowstone National Park** (307/344-7381, www.nps.gov/yell) by driving the **Grand Loop Road** in one day, but you'll find your visit more enjoyable if you give yourself **at least four days.** Pack picnic lunches so you won't be pressed by hunger to forego sightseeing. Schedule your visits to areas with **geysers** around their **eruption times.** Stop at visitors centers or use the NPS app to **check eruption schedules.** Before arriving, check online or on the NPS app for park updates and information on road construction, conditions, permit requirements and availability, and closures.

Both the **wildlife** and the **geothermal features** in Yellowstone are active **year-round. High season** is **July-August,** when crowds are at their highest. June and September are still busy, but with fewer people overall. Spring, late fall, and winter are the least crowded times to visit the park. At the **geyser basins,** crowds thicken **midday,** but lessen early or late in the day.

Yellowstone does not have a shuttle or bus system. You'll need a private vehicle to get around the park. The only alternative is taking a private tour.

Seasonal Driving Concerns

The northern road through Yellowstone, between Gardiner and Cooke City, stays open year-round, except for temporary closures when there's heavy snow in winter. **Snow tires** are recommended on the northern road in winter. All other **park roads close** in **winter,** from **November-mid-April,** when only snowmobiles and snowcoaches are permitted. Starting the third week in **April,** roads open between Mammoth Hot Springs, Norris Geyser Basin, West Yellowstone, Old Faithful, and Grand Canyon of the Yellowstone. In **early May,** the East and South Entrance roads open to connect with Canyon Village and Yellowstone Lake. Dunraven Pass and Craig Pass open in **late May,** with heavy snow causing later openings in some years.

Throughout spring and fall, expect periodic **snow squalls** and **temporary road closures** for weather. During **bison**

Yellowstone National Park

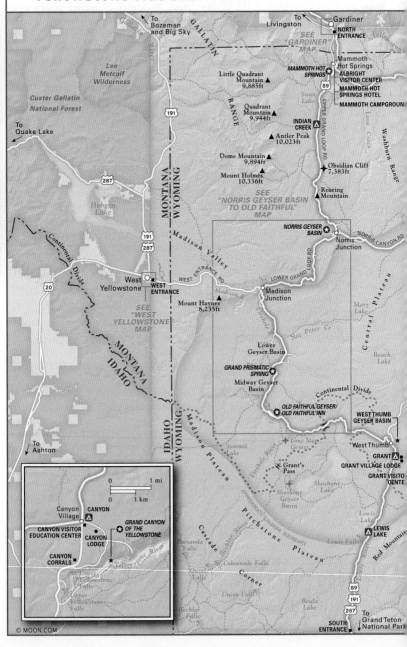

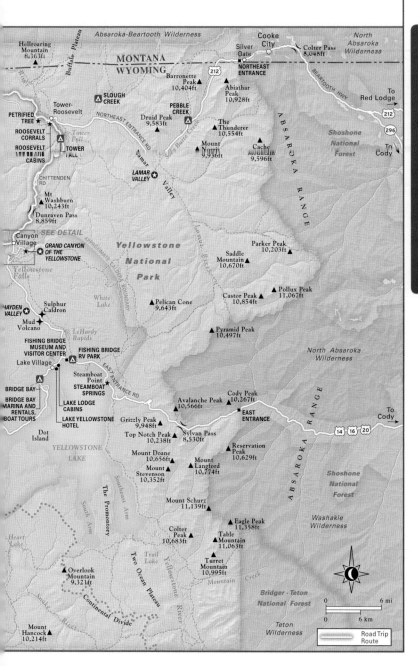

Hellroaring Mountain 8,363ft

Absaroka-Beartooth Wilderness

MONTANA
WYOMING

Buffalo Plateau

Cooke City

Silver Gate

212

NORTHEAST ENTRANCE

Colter Pass 8,048ft

North Absaroka Wilderness

To Red Lodge

212

Barronette Peak 10,404ft

PEBBLE CREEK

Abiathar Peak 10,928ft

BEARTOOTH HWY

Shoshone National Forest

296

To Cody

SLOUGH CREEK

Tower-Roosevelt

PETRIFIED TREE

ROOSEVELT CORRALS

ROOSEVELT CABINS

NORTHEAST ENTRANCE RD

Druid Peak 9,583ft

The Thunderer 10,554ft

A
B
S
A
R
O
K
A

R
A
N
G
E

Mount Norris 9,936ft

Cache Mountain 9,596ft

Tower Fall

TOWER FALL

CHITTENDEN RD

Mt Washburn 10,243ft

Dunraven Pass 8,859ft

SEE DETAIL

Canyon Village

GRAND CANYON OF THE YELLOWSTONE

Yellowstone Falls

LAMAR VALLEY

Lamar Valley

Soda Butte Creek

Lamar River

Yellowstone National Park

Parker Peak 10,203ft

Saddle Mountain 10,670ft

GRAND LOOP RD NORTH

Pelican Cone 9,643ft

Castor Peak 10,854ft

Pollux Peak 11,067ft

White Lake

HAYDEN VALLEY

Sulphur Caldron

Mud Volcano

LeHardy Rapids

Pyramid Peak 10,497ft

North Absaroka Wilderness

FISHING BRIDGE MUSEUM AND VISITOR CENTER

Lake Village

FISHING BRIDGE RV PARK

EAST ENTRANCE RD

Steamboat Point

STEAMBOAT SPRINGS

BRIDGE BAY

BRIDGE BAY MARINA AND RENTALS, BOAT TOURS

LAKE LODGE CABINS

LAKE YELLOWSTONE HOTEL

Dot Island

YELLOWSTONE LAKE

Southeast Arm

Avalanche Peak 10,566ft

Cody Peak 10,267ft

EAST ENTRANCE

Grizzly Peak 9,948ft

Top Notch Peak 10,238ft

Sylvan Pass 8,530ft

Mount Doane 10,656ft

Mount Stevenson 10,352ft

Mount Langford 10,774ft

Reservation Peak 10,629ft

A
B
S
A
R
O
K
A

R
A
N
G
E

To Cody

14 16 20

Shoshone National Forest

The Promontory

South Arm

Mount Schurz 11,139ft

Colter Peak 10,683ft

Table Mountain 11,063ft

Eagle Peak 11,358ft

Washakie Wilderness

Heart Lake

Two Ocean Plateau

Trail Lake

Yellowstone River

Turret Mountain 10,995ft

Overlook Mountain 9,321ft

Continental Divide

Snake River

Mount Hancock 10,214ft

Mountain Creek

Bridger - Teton National Forest

Teton Wilderness

0   6 mi
0   6 km

Road Trip Route

migrations (Apr.-June and Oct.-Nov.), you may get stuck in a long line of cars in the Gibbon and Firehole Canyons.

Best Route Through the Park

Yellowstone's main road is one big loop: **Grand Loop Road** connects Mammoth Hot Springs, Norris Geyser Basin, Madison Junction, Old Faithful, West Thumb Geyser Basin, Yellowstone Lake, Fishing Bridge, Hayden Valley, Canyon Village, and Tower Junction. All park entrance roads connect with Grand Loop Road. Only one road cuts through the middle of the loop: **Norris Canyon Road** runs from Canyon Village on the east side to Norris on the west side. From the southeast corner of the loop, the South Entrance Road connects to Grand Teton National Park.

Reservations and Where to Stay

Inside Yellowstone, lodges and campgrounds are open **May-October** (some have slightly shorter seasons). Reservations open **May 1** for the following year. Book in advance with **Xanterra** (307/344-7311 or 866/439-7375, www. yellowstonenationalparklodges.com). Only two park lodges are open in winter: You can drive to **Mammoth Hot Springs Hotel,** but the Snow Lodge is only accessible by snowcoach. Winter reservations open mid-March for the year ahead.

Bordering the North Entrance, **Gardiner** is the rafting capital of Yellowstone: The town flanks both sides of the Yellowstone River. The town packs out in summer with visitors basing themselves here. It's about a 15-minute drive south to Mammoth Hot Springs.

West Yellowstone is packed with restaurants and lodges serving summer visitors that enter the park through its busiest entrance station. In winter, it's the launch point for snowmobile and snowcoach tours to Old Faithful.

Just outside the Northeast Entrance, the tiny villages of **Silver Gate** and **Cooke City** are throwbacks to another era. In winter, the Northeast Entrance Road from Yellowstone dead-ends here, but in summer (late May-Oct.) these villages are the western portal for the Beartooth Highway. Technology has not made major inroads here; **no cell service** is available, and **internet is limited.**

For lodging in **Gardiner, Silver Gate, Cooke City,** and **West Yellowstone,** book **12 months** in advance for summer and **6 months** in advance for the rest of the year.

Getting There

Car
From Flathead Valley

The drive to **West Yellowstone** (the park's western entrance) from **Kalispell** in Flathead Valley is 380 miles (610 km) and takes six hours. Take US 93 south to Missoula and then go east on I-90 to Cardwell. Then take MT 359, US 287, and US 191 to West Yellowstone.

To reach **Gardiner** (the park's northern entrance) from Kalispell, the drive is 395 miles (635 km) and takes a little over six hours. Follow US 93 to I-90. Continue east on I-90 through Bozeman. Turn south onto US 89 at Livingston to reach Gardiner.

From Bozeman

From **Bozeman** to **West Yellowstone** is a 90-mile (145-km) drive that takes at least two hours; it's the **most popular route** into Yellowstone and thus gets clogged with traffic. Go south on US 191 to reach West Yellowstone and the park's West Entrance.

It's 53 miles (85 km) from Bozeman to **Gardiner,** a one-hour drive. Take I-90 east to Livingston, then go south on US 89 to reach Gardiner and the park's North Entrance.

From Grand Teton National Park

The drive to Yellowstone's **South**

One Day in Yellowstone

Make the most of your day by packing a **picnic lunch** for touring Lower Grand Loop Road (96 mi/155 km). Get an early start to beat the crowds.

Morning
Head straight for the **Old Faithful Visitor Education Center** to learn about geysers and other geothermal features. Find out when **Old Faithful** is scheduled to erupt and organize your time accordingly. Watch the geyser erupt, and walk portions of the **Upper Geyser Basin,** especially **Geyser Hill.** Take a few minutes to wander through historic **Old Faithful Inn.**

Head east on Lower Grand Loop Road to West Thumb Junction and turn north to cruise along **Yellowstone Lake.** When you get hungry, stop at one of the picnic areas along the lake or Yellowstone River.

Afternoon
With binoculars in hand, head to **Hayden Valley** for **wildlife-watching.** You'll probably run into a bison jam, but you may also see elk, bears, wolves, coyotes, deer, and waterfowl. Be sure to use the pullouts when you spot animals.

Continue north to the **Grand Canyon of the Yellowstone.** Take the South Rim Road to go to **Artist Point** for the classic view of the Lower Fall and canyon. Then, stop at Uncle Tom's parking lot to walk to the overlook of the Upper Fall.

Evening
Dine in **Canyon Village.** If you've made reservations, you can eat at the **M66 Bar & Grill.** Otherwise, go to the **Canyon Lodge Eatery.** Spend the night at **Canyon Lodge and Cabins.**

Entrance from **Jackson,** Wyoming, is 57 miles (92 km) and takes about 1.5 hours. Go north on US 26/89/189/191 to Moran, then continue north on US 89/189/191 to reach the park's South Entrance.

Note: This entrance is closed from November to early May. It's a 290-mile (470-km) drive of about six hours to get to Yellowstone from Jackson by taking WY 22, 33, and 32, then US 20 and 191 to reach the North Entrance at **Gardiner.**

From Glacier National Park
The drive to West Yellowstone from East Glacier is 360 miles (580 km) and takes about six hours. Take US 2 east and then go south on US 89, US 287, and I-15. At Boulder, Montana, go south on MT 69 and then head east on I-90 for just one exit, when you'll take MT 359 south. Next, take US 287 southeast to US 191 to reach West Yellowstone.

From East Glacier, the drive to Gardiner is also 360 miles (580 km) and takes about six hours. Take US 2 east and then go south on US 89, US 287, and I-15. At Boulder, Montana, go south on MT 69 and then head east on I-90. At Livingston, go south on US 89 to Gardiner.

Air
There are a handful of airports that are relatively close to Yellowstone. **Bozeman Yellowstone International Airport** (BZN, 406/388-8321, 850 Gallatin Field Rd, Belgrade, MT, www.bozemanairport. com) is the closest and largest airport for reaching Yellowstone's West and North Entrances. The airport is 90 miles (145 km; 1.75 hrs) north of West Yellowstone and 87 miles (140 km; 1.5 hrs) north of Gardiner. Winter travelers basing themselves out of Mammoth, Gardiner, Big Sky, or West Yellowstone should fly into Bozeman. Most visitors heading straight to Old Faithful use this airport.

While **Billings Logan International Airport** (BIL, 1901 Terminal Cir., Billings, MT, 406/247-8609, www.flybillings.com) is open year-round, it's best used as a summer-only hub due to winter road closures on the Beartooth Highway (late May-mid-Oct.). From the airport to the Northeast Entrance near Cooke City is 130 miles (210 km; 2.75 hrs).

Yellowstone Regional Airport (COD, 2101 Roger Sedam Dr., Cody, WY, 307/587-5096, http://flyyra.com), in Cody, Wyoming, is convenient for reaching the East or Northeast Entrances to Yellowstone—but only from May to October, when roads are open for the season. This airport is not a winter option. COD is 83 miles (134 km; 2 hrs) to the Northeast Entrance near Cooke City and 55 miles (89 km; 1.25 hrs) to the East Entrance.

Yellowstone Airport (WYS, 721 Airport Rd., West Yellowstone, MT, 406/646-7631, www.yellowstoneairport.org, early May-mid Oct.) operates less than 5 miles (8 km) outside of West Yellowstone.

Jackson Hole Airport (JAC, 1250 E. Airport Rd, Jackson, WY, 307/733-7682, www.jacksonholeairport.com) is a 50-mile (80-km), 90-minute drive to Yellowstone's South Entrance. Flights to Jackson Hole are usually more expensive than to other area airports.

Bus and Shuttle

Karst Stage (800/287-4759, www.karststage.com) provides shuttle services from the Bozeman airport to Gardiner, Mammoth Hot Springs, and West Yellowstone.

Based in West Yellowstone, **Yellowstone Road Runner** (406/640-0631, yellowstoneroadrunner.com) operates a year-round taxi and van service to local airports (West Yellowstone, Bozeman, Jackson Hole), as well as Yellowstone campgrounds and trailheads. Their vehicles have bike racks.

Visiting the Park

Entrances and Fees

The **entrance fee** is **$35** per vehicle ($30 motorcycles, $20 pedestrians and cyclists) and is good for seven days. An **annual pass** to the park costs $70.

Yellowstone has five entrance stations:

- **North Entrance** (US 89, near Gardiner) is open **year-round** and provides the closest access to Mammoth Hot Springs.

- **Northeast Entrance** (US 212, west of Cooke City) provides access to Lamar Valley and Grand Loop Road at Tower Junction. Winter snow may temporarily close this entrance, and all roads east of Cooke City close in winter.

- **West Entrance** (US 20, West Yellowstone), the park's busiest entrance, is open mid-April to early November. In winter, only

snowcoaches and snowmobiles can use this entrance.

- **East Entrance** (US 20), located between Fishing Bridge and Cody, Wyoming, is open mid-May to early November.
- **South Entrance** (US 89/191/287), located on the border between Yellowstone and Grand Teton National Park, is open mid-May to early November.

Visitors Centers

Yellowstone's five major visitors centers have park maps, trail information, brochures, and road updates. Kids can pick up Junior Ranger booklets ($3) at any of the visitors centers. Each location also houses **Yellowstone Forever bookstores** (406/848-2400, www.yellowstone.org), which sell hiking maps, books, and souvenirs.

Albright Visitor Center

In Mammoth Hot Springs, **Albright Visitor Center** (307/344-7381, 8am-6pm daily summer, 9am-5pm daily fall-spring) has exhibits covering cultural history, wildlife, and the northern area of the park. It also has a **backcountry office** (8am-4:30pm daily June-Aug.) with permits for backcountry camping, boating, and fishing.

Old Faithful Visitor Education Center

In front of Old Faithful Geyser, the **Old Faithful Visitor Education Center** (307/344-2751, 8am-8pm daily late Apr.-early Nov., 9am-5pm daily mid-Dec.-Feb.) is the place to learn about geysers, hot springs, mud pots, and fumaroles. Several naturalist-led tours depart from here. The center also shows a rotating lineup of films about the park. The daily film schedule is posted outside the theater. A special kids' room takes a hands-on approach for young scientists. Geyser eruption predictions are also available via

Mammoth Hot Springs

phone (304/344-2751), on social media (Twitter.com/GeyserNPS), or via the NPS app.

Canyon Visitor Education Center

In Canyon Village, **Canyon Visitor Education Center** (307/344-7381, 8am-6pm daily May-early Nov.) features films, murals, photos, and interactive exhibits that explore the powerful geologic forces of fire and ice that created Yellowstone's supervolcano. Highlights include a huge relief model of the park that traces its geologic history, a 9,000-pound rotating kugel ball that shows volcanic hot spots around the globe, and one of the world's largest lava lamps to show how magma works. You can even check the strength of the current earthquakes resounding underground. The visitors center also contains a **backcountry office** (8am-4:30pm daily June-Aug.).

Fishing Bridge Museum and Visitor Center

On the north end of Yellowstone Lake, the log-and-stone **Fishing Bridge Museum and Visitor Center** (307/344-7381, 8am-7pm daily late May-early Sept.) is tucked into the trees on the East Entrance Road, less than a mile from the historic Fishing Bridge. Built in 1931, the small museum is now a National Historic Landmark and contains bird and waterfowl specimens plus other wildlife. The outdoor amphitheater hosts naturalist presentations.

Grant Visitor Center

In Grant Village, **Grant Visitor Center** (307/344-7381, 8am-7pm daily late May-early Oct.) has exhibits and a movie that details the story of the fierce burn season of 1988. For backpacking, boating, or fishing permits, the **backcountry office** (8am-4:30pm daily June-Aug.) is adjacent to the visitors center.

Sights

North Yellowstone
★ Mammoth Hot Springs

Open year-round, Mammoth Village is home to the Albright Visitor Center, Mammoth Hot Springs Hotel, historic Fort Yellowstone, a campground, a picnic area, and other services. But the main attractions are the stately elk that often lounge on lawns and the fantastical sculptures of the hot springs' travertine terraces. Mammoth is not a spa, nor does it have developed hot springs for soaking.

Lower Terrace

Raised boardwalks and stairways loop through the lower terrace of **Mammoth Hot Springs,** where limestone creates travertine terraces. The boardwalks offer an opportunity to view the changing calcium carbonate sculptures, and sulfur fills the air.

Follow the northwest boardwalk to see **Liberty Cap,** a 37-foot-tall (11-m) dormant hot springs cone. Across from Liberty Cap is **Opal Spring,** which amasses a new foot of travertine every year. Past Liberty Cap, a spur on the right leads to the colorful **Palette Spring,** where thermophiles (organisms that proliferate in hot water) create orange and brown colors. Continue on the main boardwalk to circle the loop around **Minerva Terrace,** known for its striking travertine sculptures that alternate between watery and dry. **Cleopatra, Mound,** and **Jupiter Terraces** flank the stairs that climb to the overlook at the Upper Terrace Drive parking lot. A spur boardwalk with steps heads left to the remarkable orange and brilliant white sinter **Canary Spring.**

Access the boardwalk at one of three lower parking lots on the park road south of Mammoth Village or walk there from the Albright Visitor Center. From the

Wildlife-Watching Hot Spots

♦ **Swan Lake Flat:** South of Mammoth, Swan Lake Flat yields frequent sightings of bears, birds, elk, bison, and wolves.

♦ **Lamar Valley:** Driving into Lamar Valley catapults you back to the days of the park's earliest visitors, with a seemingly endless herd of bison. Pronghorn antelope feed nearby, and wolves cruise through looking for the old or infirm. You can also spot bighorn sheep and mountain goats near cliffs on the surrounding mountains.

pronghorn antelope in Lamar Valley

♦ **Madison River:** In fall, watch bugling bull elk round up harems of cows. Bison often block traffic on the road. Deer munch grass on the fringes of the meadows, and trumpeter swans float in slow-moving eddies.

♦ **Hayden Valley:** Spot larger animals as well as trumpeter swans in Hayden Valley. Bison feed next to the Yellowstone River, and grizzly bears and moose use the area, too. Look for harlequin ducks in early summer at LeHardy Rapids.

♦ **Tower-Roosevelt:** Bighorn sheep cluster for safety from predators in the cliffs around the Tower Fall area.

♦ **Mammoth Hot Springs:** In the village of Mammoth, elk hang out on the lawns.

♦ **Fishing Bridge:** During spawning season in June and July on the Yellowstone River, stand on the historic Fishing Bridge to see wild cutthroat trout, plus bald eagles and grizzly bears as they fish.

♦ **Pelican Creek:** In spring, Pelican Creek turns into a prime bear feeding area. Look also for bald eagles and moose.

parking lot, be ready to climb multiple stairways to reach the Upper Terrace. The NPS app has a guide to the Lower Terrace.

Upper Terrace
Above Mammoth Hot Springs, the one-way, single-lane **Upper Terrace Drive** (0.75 mi/1.2 km, mid-May-early Nov., no trailers or RVs over 25 ft/7.6 m) snakes through unique limestone features created from once-active hydrothermals. Several overlooks offer views of the Gallatin Mountains, the village below, the lower terraces, and **Canary Spring.** The road passes by the striking **Orange Spring Mound.**

Locate the entrance to the Upper Terrace about 2 miles (3.2 km) south of Mammoth Village on the road toward Norris. The area is groomed for cross-country skiing in winter.

Swan Lake Flat
On the Grand Loop Road about 10 minutes south of Mammoth, the sagebrush

prairie of **Swan Lake Flat** offers a great chance to see gray wolves, grizzly bears, and elk. Tiny **Swan Lake,** which once filled the entire flat, often houses trumpeter swans in summer, along with other waterfowl. Look for a small parking lot on the west side. Bring binoculars, cameras, and telephoto lenses.

TOP EXPERIENCE

★ Lamar Valley

Park guides often refer to the massive **Lamar Valley** as America's Serengeti due to its hefty amount of wildlife. The Lamar River flows through the sagebrush valley where immense herds of **bison** feed. Between herds, look for **pronghorn, bighorn sheep, elk, bears, coyotes, wolves,** and **sandhill cranes.** In late fall, listen for bighorn sheep butting horns or elk bugling as displays of dominance.

From Tower Junction, follow the Northeast Entrance Road east past the turnoff for Slough Creek. Multiple pullouts along the road allow for observation. Wildlife is most active at **dawn and dusk;** bring spotting scopes, cameras, and binoculars.

Geyser Basins
★ Norris Geyser Basin

At the entrance to Norris Geyser Basin, the **Norris Geyser Basin Museum & Information Station** (307/344-7381, 9am-6pm daily mid-May-mid Oct.) houses exhibits on geothermal features. Rangers lead several programs, including walks into the geyser basin. Completed in 1930, the log-and-stone building is a National Historic Landmark. A **Yellowstone Forever bookstore** (406/848-2400, www.yellowstone.org) is housed in an adjacent building.

Of Yellowstone's thermal basins, **Norris Geyser Basin** is the hottest, measuring

Top to bottom: Porcelain Basin at Norris Geyser Basin; Silex Spring at Fountain Paint Pots; Grand Prismatic Spring in Midway Geyser Basin

459°F (237°C) at 1,087 feet (331 m) below the surface. With features 115,000 years old, it is also the oldest geothermal basin. The most vigorous of the park's geyser basins, Norris has some features that change daily, many due to earthquakes. It also contains rare acidic geysers; you'll smell the rotten egg stench.

Interpretive boardwalks and paths tour two hydrothermal basins: **Back Basin** and **Porcelain Basin.** The *Norris Geyser Basin Trail Guide* ($1, available at visitors centers) or the NPS app can aid in touring the site. Explore the boardwalks and trails in three ways: self-guided, with a ranger-led walk, or from an access trail (1 mi/1.6 km) from Norris Campground. Due to the changing nature of the basin, boardwalks may be closed for reconstruction.

Back Basin

The thinly forested **Back Basin** double-loop (1.5 mi/2.1 km) houses two geysers that each hold world records: the tallest geyser and the largest acidic geyser. Heading south from the museum, the boardwalk first reaches **Emerald Spring** with its striking blue color created from the yellow sulfur minerals, near-boiling water, and colorful thermophiles. Continue south to unpredictable **Steamboat Geyser,** which shoots small bursts of water up to 40 feet (12 m) in the air. (Its world-record eruptions of 300-400 ft/91-122 m happen infrequently.) The geyser set recent records for the number of eruptions, with 32 in 2018 and 48 in 2019. The geyser links underground to the blue-green **Cistern Spring,** which puts out so much sinter that pipes often clog and force water to the surface in new pools.

Turn left to stay on this outer loop as it winds past the red-orange rimmed pool of **Echinus Geyser.** With unpredictable eruptions, it's the world's largest acidic geyser—on par with vinegar. After passing several fumaroles, geysers, hot springs, and mud pots, **Porkchop Geyser**

roils turquoise water but is more like a hot spring (it hasn't erupted since 1989).

The outer loop completes at the junction near **Palpitator Spring.** Continue north through the Back Basin, past **Minute** and **Monarch Geysers,** to return to the museum junction and connect with the Porcelain Basin.

Porcelain Basin

The wide-open **Porcelain Basin** is named for its color. Two boardwalk loops (0.5 mi/0.8 km) circle the acidic basin that contains the park's highest concentration of silica; thermophiles add brilliant splashes of green or red. From the museum junction, turn left past turquoise **Crackling Lake,** a hot pool that bubbles along the edges of the basin. The loop brings you to the defunct **Pinwheel Geyser** and active **Whirligig Geyser,** which spills into a runoff stream full of orange iron oxide and green thermophiles. A smaller boardwalk loop heads left past roaring **Hurricane Vent** and colorful **Porcelain Springs,** a hot pool that's sometimes dry. Complete the loop and return to the museum by heading south.

Artists Paintpots

South of Norris Junction, **Artists Paintpots** gets its name from its bubbling gray mud pots. A sunny gravel, dirt, boardwalk, and stair-step trail (1 mi/1.6 km) starts by cutting through lodgepoles still recovering from the 1988 fire. The path tours past small geysers, fumaroles, light blue pools, and red crusts. Thermophiles add the bright colors. Stinky hydrogen sulfide gas leaks from underground, and the mud pots burp and spurt.

At the junction, turn in either direction; the remainder of the trail loops around the side of **Paintpot Hill.** The base of the hill holds bubbling hot springs, clear hot pools, and streams with thermophiles. Geothermal features at the bottom of the loop have more water, while the famous paint pots at the top are formed of thicker clay; they emit gasses that scent the air. By late summer, the mud pots thicken or dry up when less water feeds them.

Lower Geyser Basin
Fountain Paint Pots

Between Madison Junction and Old Faithful, **Fountain Paint Pots** is an interpretive boardwalk loop (0.5 mi/0.8 km) that includes all four hydrothermal features in the park: geysers, mud pots, hot springs, and fumaroles.

At the boardwalk junction, look left into the blue **Celestine Pool** or right for the colorful bacterial mats of thermophiles formed in the runoff from the silica-rich, turquoise **Silex Spring** straight ahead. The trail then divides around pink and gray **Fountain Paint Pot**, bubbling more in the liquid clay of early summer but thicker by fall. (Its clay was used to paint the former hotel across the road.) The trail splits to circle **Red Spouter,** named for the red clay that acts like a mud pot, hot springs, or steam vent based on changing water amounts throughout the year. As the boardwalk continues west downhill, several geysers spurt and fume. When **Fountain Geyser** erupts, it can shoot water in the air for longer than 20 minutes. The smaller neighboring **Clepsydra Geyser,** which sputters nonstop from several vents, may pause when Fountain erupts.

Pick up the *Fountain Paint Pot Trail Guide* ($1) at visitors centers or use the audio tour on the NPS app.

Great Fountain Geyser

On the one-way Firehole Lake Drive between Madison Junction and Old Faithful, **Great Fountain Geyser** shoots 75-220 feet (23-67 m) high every 10-14 hours. Unlike Old Faithful's short durations, Great Fountain's eruptions last about an hour, with short bursts of water interspersed between quiet periods. The geyser ushers in a long, dramatic prelude to erupting. Water floods the vent, and

bubbles appear about 30 minutes later. As the water boils into giant bubbles followed by one big burp, the eruption begins.

Midway Geyser Basin

Midway Geyser Basin is between Madison Junction and Old Faithful. The basin only has four thermal features, but they are huge. Two are the largest hot springs in Yellowstone.

From the parking area (on the west side of the Grand Loop Road), head south to walk over the bridge across the Firehole River. Start the 0.7-mile (1.1-km) loop, admiring the thermophile colors in the stream pouring into the river. After climbing up a boardwalk switchback, go south along the dormant **Excelsior Geyser.** Excelsior is now a stunning turquoise hot pool spilling water into the Firehole River. Beyond the Excelsior crater, steam pours from the larger **Grand Prismatic Spring,** which commands the high point of the loop. Turn north to

finish the loop, passing the clear blue pools of smaller **Turquoise** and **Indigo Springs.**

★ Grand Prismatic Spring

At 370 feet (113 m) across and 121 feet (37 m) deep, **Grand Prismatic Spring** is the largest hot spring in Yellowstone and the third largest in the world. Enjoy the glorious hues: fiery arms of orange, gold, and brown thermophiles that radiate in a full circle from the yellow-rimmed, blue hot pool. Hot water discharges in all directions across the mound. See it from the Midway Geyser Basin boardwalk or the overlook loop on the Fairy Falls Trail.

Upper Geyser Basin

The Upper Geyser Basin is the most popular hydrothermal basin, drawing thousands of visitors each day in summer but few in winter. It contains a maze of four miles of boardwalk, dirt, and paved interpretive loops through the largest concentration of geysers in the world. Walkers, bikers, and wheelchairs share the paved portion; in winter, the snow-covered pavement is groomed for cross-country skiing. Often, herds of buffalo or elk feed in the meadows in between geothermal features. Signs at trail junctions have maps to assist with route-finding. The Old Faithful Visitor Education Center and the NPS app predict eruption times for six geysers: Old Faithful, Castle, Grand, Great Fountain, Daisy, and Riverside. Pick up the interpretative *Old Faithful Trail Guide* ($1) at the visitors center or use the audio tour on the NPS app.

★ Old Faithful Geyser

Old Faithful Geyser anchors the Upper Geyser Basin. When Old Faithful erupts, it shoots hot water as high as 185 feet (56 m). It's not the tallest geyser in the park,

Old Faithful Geyser

but it is one of the most regular, erupting about every 90 minutes for 1.5-5 minutes. Often, the geyser sputters for 20 minutes before erupting, spewing water that percolated into its huge underground chamber 250-500 years ago. The eruption occurs when water is forced upwards through its fist-sized constriction. Expect massive crowds of people in summer; benches surrounding the geyser fill 30 minutes in advance of eruptions. Winter eruptions see only a handful of people. Old Faithful is behind the Old Faithful Visitor Education Center, which posts eruption times. A 0.7-mile (1.1-km) rubberized, boardwalk, and pavement loop circles the famous geyser.

Geyser Hill Loop

From the Old Faithful viewing area, head east across the Firehole River to climb the boardwalk and stairs that ring **Geyser Hill,** which is sprinkled with several active geysers. Geyser Hill is a 1.3-mile (2-km) walk from the visitors center, and a boardwalk connects it with the Firehole River Loops.

On the south section of this loop, turn left to view **Beehive Geyser,** which can shoot up 200 feet (61 m) but has an irregular schedule. The smaller nearby **Anemone** and **Plume Geysers** erupt regularly, the first about every 10 minutes and the second hourly. Continue north past Beehive to find the clear blue **Heart Spring** near the cones of the interconnected **Lion Group,** a family of geysers called Little Cub, Big Cub, Lioness, and Lion, the last of which heralds eruptions with a roar. Turn right to access the upper part of this loop. Admire the radiant color and ledges of **Doublet Pool.** From here, a spur trail heads north to **Solitary Geyser,** which surges with short bursts every 4-8 minutes.

Top to bottom: Giant Geyser at the Firehole River; the cone of Grotto Geyser; Biscuit Basin

Norris Geyser Basin to Old Faithful

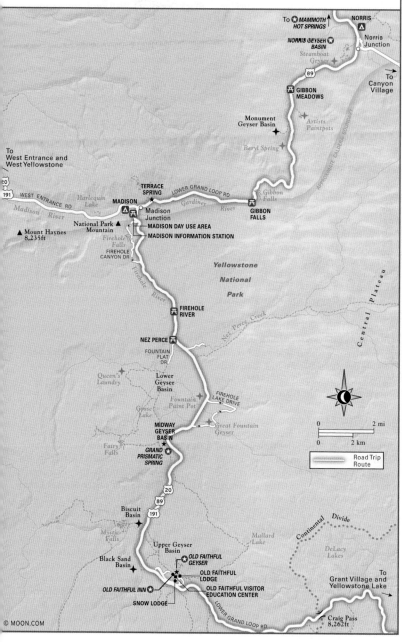

To MAMMOTH HOT SPRINGS

NORRIS

Norris Junction

NORRIS GEYSER BASIN

Steamboat Geyser

89

To Canyon Village

GIBBON MEADOWS

Monument Geyser Basin

Artists Paintpots

Beryl Spring

To West Entrance and West Yellowstone

20 191

WEST ENTRANCE RD

Harlequin Lake

Madison River

TERRACE SPRING

MADISON

LOWER GRAND LOOP RD

Gibbon Falls

GIBBON FALLS

Gardiner River

Madison Junction

National Park ▲ Mountain

▲ Mount Haynes 8,235ft

Firehole Falls

FIREHOLE CANYON DR

MADISON DAY USE AREA

MADISON INFORMATION STATION

Yellowstone

National

Park

Firehole River

FIREHOLE RIVER

Nez Perce Creek

NEZ PERCE

FOUNTAIN FLAT DR

Queen's Laundry

Lower Geyser Basin

Goose Lake

Fountain Paint Pot

FIREHOLE LAKE DRIVE

Great Fountain Geyser

MIDWAY GEYSER BASIN

Fairy Falls

GRAND PRISMATIC SPRING

Central Plateau

0   2 mi

0   2 km

Road Trip Route

20 89

Biscuit Basin

191

Mystic Falls

Upper Geyser Basin

Black Sand Basin

OLD FAITHFUL GEYSER

OLD FAITHFUL LODGE

Mullard Lake

Continental Divide

DeLacy Lakes

OLD FAITHFUL INN

OLD FAITHFUL VISITOR EDUCATION CENTER

SNOW LODGE

To Grant Village and Yellowstone Lake

LOWER GRAND LOOP RD

Craig Pass 8,262ft

© MOON.COM

Firehole River Loop

Northwest of Geyser Hill, the bigger Firehole River Loop crosses two bridges to take in the famous hot pools of the Upper Geyser Basin, plus more geysers, fumaroles, and springs.

At the southern start of this loop is **Castle Geyser,** a cone geyser built into the largest sinter formation in the world. About every 14 hours, Castle Geyser erupts for 20 minutes and then pumps out copious steam. Continue north and turn right to cross the Firehole River and reach **Grand Geyser,** a predictable fountain geyser that throws water 200 feet (61 m) skyward in several short bursts. To the north sit a pair of interconnected hot springs, **Beauty Pool** and **Chromatic Pool.** When the water level rises in one, it drops in the other.

As the boardwalk crosses the river again, you might get to see the erratic **Giant Geyser** throw water up 300 feet (91 m). At the junction with the paved trail, **Grotto Geyser** squirts water from its odd-shaped cone for sometimes up to 24 hours. Continue north on the paved trail to **Riverside Geyser,** which shoots an arc of water at six-hour intervals over the Firehole for about 20 minutes. The striking green, orange, and yellow **Morning Glory Pool** marks the turnaround point.

Daisy Geyser Basin Loop

From the paved trail on the west side of the Firehole River, the **Daisy Geyser Basin** loops through smaller, but unique features. **Daisy Geyser** erupts every 2-3 hours with water spewing outward. Further west, **Punch Bowl** boils in its raised sinter bowl that is 10 feet (3 m) in diameter.

Biscuit Basin

One of several hydrothermal basins in Upper Geyser Basin, **Biscuit Basin** holds a collection of smaller volcanically heated features, accessed by a boardwalk (0.7 mi/1.1 km) that ascends into the basin to circle hot pools, geysers, and fumaroles.

After crossing the Firehole River on a footbridge, the boardwalk tours past **Black Opal Pool, Wall Pool,** and **Sapphire Pool.** The latter is the most commanding feature, a hot pool of crystal-clear blue water that once used to be a geyser. At the junction, go either way to circle the basin. Highlights on the upper loop include the yellow **Mustard Spring** and **Jewel Geyser,** which shoots water in the air about every 10 minutes. Use the audio tour on the NPS app for more information about the basin.

Biscuit Basin is on the park road, 2 miles (3 km) north of the Old Faithful turnoff and south of the Midway Geyser Basin. From the Old Faithful Visitor Education Center, it is a 5.9-mile (9.5-km) round-trip hike or bike to the basin. From the paved trail, take the Daisy Geyser Loop junction and turn west. At the next junction, turn north to reach Grand Loop Road. A trail continues on the opposite side to reach the back of the geyser basin. (Bikes must turn right onto the road to reach the parking lot.)

Black Sand Basin

In the Upper Geyser Basin, **Black Sand Basin** has a 0.6-mile (1-km) boardwalk across Iron Spring Creek with two short spurs that tour past small geysers and colorful hot pools. The basin acquired its name from the bits of obsidian that speckle the area. On the creek's edge, **Cliff Geyser** blows water from a small crater. Eruptions last 0.5-3 hours, with copious steam spewing out. At the boardwalk junction, turn right to see **Sunset Lake,** named for its yellow-orange rim, and left to see **Emerald Pool,** colored from its algae. Before hopping back in the car, walk a tiny spur off the north corner of the parking lot to see **Opalescent Pool,** fed by the almost constantly erupting **Spouter Geyser,** which flooded an area of lodgepoles. The dead trees are now known as **Bobby sox trees** due to the white socks around their silica-soaked trunk bases.

Reach Black Sand Basin by driving 0.5 mile (0.8 km) northwest of Old Faithful. It's also possible to hike there (4.4 mi/7 km round-trip) from Old Faithful Visitor Education Center. From the paved trail, turn left to take the Daisy Geyser Loop cutoff. After touring past the basin geysers and pools, cross Grand Loop Road to reach Black Sand Basin.

★ Old Faithful Inn
Built in 1903-1904 from surrounding logs, tree limbs, and rhyolite stone, Old Faithful Inn wows visitors. With a steep-pitched roof and gabled dormers, the lobby vaults five stories high and is centered around a stone fireplace with a handcrafted clock built from wood, copper, and iron. Today, this National Historic Landmark houses 327 guest rooms in two wings. Walk around the lobby balcony to take in all the historical intricacies, and watch Old Faithful Geyser erupt from the deck. The distinctive inn is reputed to be the largest log building in the world. Daily **tours** (hours vary, early May-early Oct., free) are available.

Canyon and Lake Country
★ Grand Canyon of the Yellowstone
South of Canyon Village are three entrances to **Grand Canyon of the Yellowstone**, the iconic, 20-mile-long (32-km) canyon cut through lava rhyolite. The **Yellowstone River** chewed a colorful swath 1,000 feet (305 m) deep through the landscape. The river plunges over the **Upper Falls** before thundering down the **Lower Falls,** the tallest and most famous falls in the park. Roads and trails with multiple overlooks flank the North and South Rims. If you have only a few minutes, stop at **Artist Point** on the South Rim or **Lookout Point** on the North Rim.

Some overlooks have short, easy paved routes, while others have descents that require strenuous climbs back up. The high elevation may cause labored breathing for those coming from sea level. Prepare for crowds in summer: tour buses disgorge swarms of visitors, parking lots are congested, and restrooms have long lines. Visit in early morning or evening for fewer people. Pick up a trail guide ($1) at visitors centers.

North Rim
The one-way **North Rim Drive** (east side of Lower Grand Loop Rd., south of Canyon Junction) visits four signed overlooks of the canyon, Yellowstone River, and the 308-foot (94-m) Lower Falls. The first stop is **Brink of the Lower Falls,** where a paved walkway with stairs leads to an overlook for views. Reaching the actual brink requires a steep drop in elevation through multiple switchbacks to the platform, where underfoot you can feel the thundering water as it plummets over the lip. The second stop accesses **Lookout Point** via a quick paved ascent to an overlook of the Lower Falls and canyon. Just before the overlook, a 0.4-mile (0.6-km) switchback-and-boardwalk stairway trail plunges elevation to **Red Rock Point**, a perch closer to the Lower Falls.

The third stop on North Rim Drive is **Grand View,** a paved descent to the overlook. Near the end of North Rim Drive, turn right onto the two-lane road to reach the rebuilt **Inspiration Point** for the fourth and more distant view up the canyon. While the Lower Falls is not visible, the four newly rebuilt Inspiration Point rock-and-steel walkway platforms (three are wheelchair-accessible) offer spiraling views of the canyon and river.

At another turnoff south of North Rim, turn east at the signed road to **Brink of the Upper Falls.** Walk a few minutes upstream to a left turn for the short descent to the platform at the brink. The falls mesmerize with its roaring plunge.

South Rim
Farther south of the turnoff to Brink of the Upper Falls, turn onto **South Rim Drive** and cross the Chittenden Bridge to

reach two main signed parking areas that have viewpoints of the canyon. At **Uncle Tom's Point** (west side of the drive), park and follow the easy paved walkway to the **Upper Falls** viewpoint that faces the waterfall. North of the parking lot, a steep short trail follows switchbacks and steel stairways to drop 500 feet (152 m) in elevation to **Uncle Tom's Overlook,** a small steel platform yielding the closest view of the **Lower Falls.** Most visitors count the stairs as they slog back up. South Rim Drive terminates at the parking lot for **Artist Point.** An easy, paved walkway leads to the classic view of the canyon and Lower Falls.

★ Hayden Valley

Occupying immense forest-rimmed meadows between Canyon and Fishing Bridge, **Hayden Valley** once held an arm of Yellowstone Lake. Today, it's a top spot for wildlife-watching, as **bison** jams are common here. Also look for **coyote, moose, bison, elk, raptors, grizzly bears, trumpeter swans, wolves,** and hordes of **Canada geese.** The **Yellowstone River** meanders through the sagebrush and grass valley, giving it a bucolic feel.

No off-trail travel is allowed, and most waterways are closed to fishing in order to protect the sensitive area. Bring binoculars, spotting scopes, and cameras. Drive slowly and use the multiple pullovers to watch wildlife.

Mud Volcano

Before you see **Mud Volcano,** you'll smell the rotten-egg scent of hydrogen sulfide gas billowing from the earth. A 0.7-mile (1.1-km) boardwalk and trail tours several thermal features; the two most prominent ones are on the lower and shorter boardwalk loop. Mud Volcano is a burbling pot of watery clay that especially amuses kids when they can stand the stench. Nearby, hot steam from 170°F (77°C) water belches from **Dragon's Mouth Spring.** At the high end of the longer paved and stair-step boardwalk loop,

Lower Falls in Grand Canyon of the Yellowstone

Black Dragon's Cauldron gapes from a large cave, bubbling up from a crack with the dark color created from iron sulfides. Pick up a trail guide ($1) at visitors centers or use the NPS app for an audio tour.

At a pullout across the road to the north is one of the park's most acidic hot springs. On par with battery acid, **Sulphur Cauldron** boils with yellow color created from sulfur and bacteria.

Yellowstone Lake

The natural **Yellowstone Lake** is the largest water body in Yellowstone National Park and one of the largest high-elevation freshwater lakes in North America. With the exception of thermal areas, the lake freezes over with ice in winter and often doesn't melt out until late May or early June, which means chilly water for swimming. Snowmelt causes the water to rise to its highest level in early June, flooding some south-end beaches and closing Gull Point Drive. Boating and paddling usually starts in mid-June. During summer and fall, afternoon winds frequently whip the lake into whitecaps.

Located partly inside the Yellowstone Caldera, the northern section of the lake has its origins in volcanic activity and lava flows, while the southern arms formed from glaciers. The lake's thermal activity includes geysers, fumaroles, and hot springs. **West Thumb Geyser Basin** is the most accessible of these; the largest is a huge vent at the lake bottom that bulges up 100 feet (31 m).

The lake's six islands and shoreline attract wildlife. Look for trumpeter swans, pelicans, ducks, eagles, herons, and other shorebirds. A *Lake Queen* boat tour offers the easiest way to get on the lake and around **Stevenson Island.**

West Thumb Geyser Basin

On West Thumb Bay in Yellowstone Lake, the **West Thumb Geyser Basin** (northeast of West Thumb Junction) is a smaller caldera within the larger Yellowstone Caldera. The geyser basin dumps more than thousands of gallons of hot water daily into the lake and contains three geysers and 11 hot springs, plus fumaroles and mud pots. Two loops (0.8 mi/1.3 km) guide visitors around the thermal features. **West Thumb Information Center** (307/344-7381, 9am-5pm daily late May-early Oct.) is a small, log building with exhibits on West Thumb Geyser Basin. This is where you can ask about the vent on the floor of Yellowstone Lake, and pick up a trail guide ($1) or use the NPS app for an audio tour.

The larger boardwalk loop cruises the lakeshore where early park visitors once cooked fish in **Fishing Cone.** The striking turquoise and emerald **Abyss Pool** may be one of the deepest in the park. **Twin Geyser** has two vents that shoot water. Many of the colorful hot pools derive their hues from heat-happy thermophiles.

Scenic Drives

Grand Loop Road

You can drive the entire **Grand Loop Road** (142 mi/229 km) in a day. It takes about five hours without stops. But driving the full loop requires stamina and you'll have time for only a few sights on the way. Many visitors split the Upper Loop from the Lower Loop for more sightseeing time.

Upper Grand Loop Road

Upper Grand Loop Road (70 mi/113 km, late May-early Nov.) links Mammoth Hot Springs, Norris Geyser Basin, Canyon Village, and Tower Junction, creating a loop by cutting across the Norris-Canyon Road. The segment from **Mammoth to Tower Junction** is open year-round; all other segments of the Upper Grand Loop Road are closed in winter. You can drive the entire loop in three hours without stops.

From **Mammoth Hot Springs** to Norris Junction, the road climbs south through the hoodoos and along the cliffs of **Golden Gate** (a lichen-covered rhyolite formation of rock) before topping out at **Swan Lake Flat.** Continuing south, you'll pass **Obsidian Cliff**, an archaeological site resulting from a 180,000-year-old rhyolite lava flow that crystallized with bits of shiny black volcanic glass (the site is closed to visitors; you can only gaze from afar). Early Indigenous people quarried the sharp obsidian for making knives, arrowheads, and other tools.

The next stop is **Roaring Mountain,** a toxic mountainside billowing with tree-killing heat, gases, and steam. Get out of the car at the interpretive site to hear the fumaroles hissing. Shortly after, you'll reach **Norris Geyser Basin.**

From Norris Junction, go east to **Canyon Junction** at **Canyon Village.** Continue the loop north from Canyon Village to climb over **Dunraven Pass,** the highest car-accessible point in

bison jam on Grand Loop Road

Yellowstone, where you may feel short of breath stepping from the car. Descend to **Tower Fall** to see the ribbon of water plunge in a freefall from its brink between rhyolite spires. At **Calcite Springs,** follow the boardwalks to overlooks above the **Narrows of the Yellowstone River** to see basalt columns made from lava and the white and yellow springs at the edge of the **Yellowstone River.** Then, drop to **Tower Junction.**

From Tower Junction, head west, taking a side spur to see **Petrified Tree,** once a giant redwood from a wetter climate that was preserved in the supervolcano eruption. Then, stop at **Undine Falls,** where **Lava Creek** tumbles down three tiers. Back in the car, complete the loop by driving west to Mammoth Hot Springs.

Lower Grand Loop Road

Lower Grand Loop Road (96 mi/155 km, late May-early Nov.) links Norris Junction, Madison Junction, Old Faithful, West Thumb Junction, Yellowstone Lake, Fishing Bridge, Hayden Valley, and Grand Canyon of the Yellowstone. The loop route uses the Norris-Canyon Road. Driving the entire loop without stops will take four hours.

From **Norris Geyser Basin** to Madison Junction, the road drops south past bison grazing in **Gibbon Meadows** and **Artists Paintpots.** You'll descend into the supervolcano's caldera, passing **Beryl Spring,** a steaming pool. As the narrow canyon squeezes in, it forms **Gibbon Falls,** a cascade-type waterfall frothing from every rock ledge that's visible from multiple interpretive viewpoints.

From Madison Junction to **Old Faithful,** the route passes through the **Lower, Middle,** and **Upper Geyser Basins.** Three short side detours (no RVs or trailers) in this section offer sights and wildlife-watching:

- Near Madison Junction, one-way **Firehole Canyon Drive** (2 mi/3.2 km, 15 min.) is a steep and narrow road that goes to a scenic overlook of **Firehole Falls.**

- At the Nez Perce Picnic Area, the two-way **Fountain Flat Drive** (1 mi/1.6 km, 10 min.) is a good place for **wildlife-watching,** particularly for elk and bison.

- The one-way **Firehole Lake Drive** (3.3 mi/5.3 km, 30 min.) passes eight thermal features, including **Great Fountain Geyser, White Dome Geyser** (erupts at 15-30 min. intervals), and the brown **Firehole Lake.**

From Old Faithful to **West Thumb,** the route bounces twice over the **Continental Divide.** Water from **Isa Lake,** located at **Craig Pass,** has the unique status of flowing toward both the Pacific Ocean and the Gulf of Mexico.

From West Thumb to **Canyon Village,** the road curves around the west shores of **Yellowstone Lake.** South of Bridge Bay, the conifer-lined **Gull Point Drive** (2.1

mi/3.4 km, 10 min., often closes late May-June due to flooding) leads to **Gull Point Picnic Area,** where a long sandbar extends out into the lake at **Gull Point**—a good place for fishing and beachcombing. The road passes **Bridge Bay** and **Lake Village** before following the **Yellowstone River** north to **Mud Volcano, Hayden Valley,** and the entrances of **Grand Canyon of the Yellowstone.**

North Entrance Road

Open year-round, the two-lane **North Entrance Road** (5 mi/8 km) starts as US 89 in Gardiner, Montana. Drive under the stone-and-mortar **Roosevelt Arch,** one of the best human-built park entrances in the country. Its cornerstone was laid in 1903. A signed shortcut road directs large RVs to bypass the narrow entrance, but cars can still drive through it, and pedestrians can walk through the open pedestrian doorways. Beyond the arch, the road climbs south through ancient mudflows, crossing the **45th Parallel** at the bridge over the Gardner River, then hitting the Montana/Wyoming state line, before reaching **Mammoth Hot Springs** in about 15 minutes.

Northeast Entrance Road

The **Northeast Entrance Road** (29 mi/47 km) is open year-round and takes about an hour to drive. The road originates inside the park at Tower Junction. It crosses the **Yellowstone River,** a 692-mile (1,114-km) river that is the park's longest and the last major free-flowing river in the Lower 48. From there, it climbs into **Lamar Valley** and swings northeast along **Soda Butte Creek** into the **Absaroka Mountains** (pronounced Ab-zor-ka). After Pebble Creek, the road climbs into narrow **Ice Box Canyon,** flanked by frozen waterfalls in winter and spring before ascending further into a narrow, forested valley tucked below **Barronette Peak,** which spouts with waterfalls in May and harbors **mountain goats** in its cliffs. At the **Northeast Entrance,** the road exits

Yellowstone and enters the tiny villages of **Silver Gate** and **Cooke City.** In winter (Nov.-May), the route dead-ends at Cooke City due to snowbound roads, but in summer, you can connect with the **Beartooth Highway** (late May-Oct.).

West Entrance Road

For an evening wildlife-watching drive, take the **West Entrance Road** (14 mi/23 km, late Apr.-early Nov.), which connects **West Yellowstone** to **Madison Junction.** The road parallels the **Madison River,** with sprawling meadows that fill with **bison** in summer and **elk** herds in fall. Pullouts provide places to watch, but don't become so enamored by the megafauna that you miss **eagles** in the trees or **bobcats** hunting along the river. This drive takes about 30 minutes.

East Entrance Road

The **East Entrance Road** (27 mi/43 km, late-May-early Nov.) connects the East Entrance Station with **Yellowstone Lake** and takes about an hour to drive. From the entrance station, the road climbs steeply through cliffs overlooking **Middle Creek.** A pullout affords views down into the glacier-carved terrain. Amid howling winds, 8,524-foot (2,598-m) **Sylvan Pass** cuts through a rocky slot in the **Absaroka Mountains.** In a small parking lot at the summit, scan the hillsides for **bighorn sheep** and gaze at long, thin waterfalls.

Continue down to **Sylvan** and **Eleanor Lakes,** where small pullouts allow photo ops. For a giant view, take the paved side spur of **Lake Butte Road** (1 mi/1.6 km, no RVs or trailers) to **Lake Butte Overlook** for views out over **Yellowstone Lake.** After reaching the north shore of the lake, the road curves around **Steamboat Point,** a collection of puffing, noisy fumaroles, and **Mary Bay,** a volcanic caldera. It terminates at the original log **Fishing Bridge,** which is worth a walk across and back to admire the **Yellowstone River** and perhaps see spawning trout mid-June to early July.

South Entrance Road

The forested **South Entrance Road** (22 mi/35 km, 45 min., mid-May-early Nov.) connects the South Entrance of Yellowstone (at the border with Grand Teton National Park) with **Grant Village** and **West Thumb.** The road passes **Lewis Lake,** Yellowstone's third-largest lake. It empties into the **Lewis River,** which tumbles over **Lewis Falls,** gushing with high water in June and joining into the **Snake River.** This drive takes about 45 minutes.

Recreation

Hiking

Yellowstone's naturalist rangers lead **free interpretive hikes** daily in the summer. These guided walks tour the Upper Geyser Basin, Norris Geyser Basin, the South Rim of Grand Canyon of the Yellowstone, and other trails. Consult the park newspaper for current offerings. Reservations are required for some hikes; call 307/344-2750 or register in person at visitors centers.

Expert-led educational hikes are also available through **Yellowstone Forever Institute** (406/848-2400, www.yellowstone.org, year-round; rates vary), ranging from day hikes to multiday backpacking trips. Some of the hiking programs operate out of the institute's cabin complex in Lamar Valley.

Yellowstone Hiking Guides (406/848-1144, www.yellowstonehikingguides.com, from $150 pp) leads hikes in Lamar Valley, Grand Canyon of the Yellowstone, and the Upper Geyser Basin. Rates include the services of a licensed guide, lunch, and snacks. Groups meet at the trailhead.

North Yellowstone
Bunsen Peak and Osprey Falls
Distance: 4.2-10.8 miles (6.6-17 km) rt
Duration: 3-7 hours
Elevation change: 1,278 feet (389 m)
Effort: strenuous

Trailhead: Old Bunsen Peak Rd.

Bunsen Peak, a volcanic cone named for Robert Bunsen, who invented the Bunsen burner, contains a summit weather station; the building and connecting power lines pose a minor disruption to the wilderness feel. In summer, go early to nab a parking spot at this popular trailhead.

Starting in a sagebrush meadow, the trail climbs through steep forests to the summit. Shortly after starting the climb, spot the Golden Gate from above along with Glen Creek Canyon hoodoos. The trail winds back and forth around the mountain, passing **Cathedral Rock,** where views plunge to Mammoth Hot Springs. Steep switchbacks then lead across talus slopes to the summit of **Bunsen Peak** (4.2 mi/6.6 km total). The reward is the view of Electric Peak in the Gallatin Range and the scenic landscape of Gardners Hole. For the shortest distance, retrace your route back down.

Strong hikers can lengthen the loop to see **Osprey Falls** (10.8 mi/17 km total) on the Gardner River. From Bunsen Peak, descend eastward to the **Old Bunsen Peak Road** and turn left to find the **Osprey Falls Trailhead.** The route traverses the edge of **Sheepeater Canyon;** the basalt-columned **Sheepeater Cliffs** are visible on the opposite side. Drop down steep, narrow, sunny switchbacks into the ravine to admire **Osprey Falls.** After climbing back up (780 ft/238 m in elevation), follow the old road north around Bunsen Peak to return to your vehicle. Those wanting to avoid the Bunsen Peak climb can hike out and back on the old road to see Osprey Falls for a total distance of 8.8 miles (14.2 km).

Wraith Falls
Distance: 0.8 mile (1.3 km) rt
Duration: 45 minutes
Elevation change: 74 feet (23 m)
Effort: easy
Trailhead: pullout on the south side of Grand Loop Rd., 0.5 mile (0.8 km) east of Lava Creek Picnic Area

Launch onto this trail by walking through

a sagebrush-scented meadow blooming with columbine and buckwheat in early summer. An intermittent **boardwalk** crosses small streams and marshes. The route tucks itself between coniferous tree islands, crosses **Lupine Creek,** and climbs one switchback to reach the viewing platform. **Wraith Falls** cascades down a wide-angled rock face that's squeezed into a canyon. In June, the water fills the full width, but by September, the water thins to appear like two parallel falls.

Lost Lake Loop

Distance: 4 miles (6.4 km) rt
Duration: 2.5 hours
Elevation change: 608 feet (185 m)
Effort: moderate
Trailhead: behind Roosevelt Lodge

This trail has plenty of things to see: a waterfall, a small lake, Petrified Tree, and views of the Absaroka Mountains. The trail is also used by horses; step to the downhill side of the trail when horses approach unless the horse's wrangler instructs otherwise. Remain still until they have passed.

From behind Roosevelt Lodge, take the left spur to the **Lost Creek Falls Trail** that climbs up a pine-shaded ravine to **Lost Creek Falls.** Return to the junction to continue up the **Lost Lake Trail.** Switchbacks head up the steep hill to reach the small bridge at the outlet of **Lost Lake.** The trail rims the lake until it heads west through another ravine to **Petrified Tree.** From the Petrified Tree parking lot, the trail mounts a hill east to a sagebrush meadow before dropping to swing behind **Tower Ranger Station** and then around to Roosevelt Lodge. It's also possible to start from the Petrified Tree trailhead.

Garnet Hill

Distance: 8 miles (12.8 km) rt
Duration: 4 hours
Elevation change: 580 feet (177 km)
Effort: moderate
Trailhead: 0.3 mile (0.5 km) northeast of Tower Junction on the Northeast Entrance Rd.

Often frequented by pronghorn, bison, and elk, this trail loops through sagebrush and glacial erratics. The north end of the loop passes through cooler forests flanking the Yellowstone River and Elk Creek before gaining elevation on the return. There's little shade for much of the route, so plan to hike early on hot days.

From the trailhead, hike to a junction where you can go either direction to circle the forested bluff of **Garnet Hill.** Starting on the eastern side of the loop, the trail soon meets up with the **Yellowstone River** to follow the water downstream, eventually entering a steep-sloped canyon. After crossing **Elk Creek,** the route meets a junction with the Hellroaring Trail; turn left to follow Elk Creek upstream. In **Pleasant Valley,** after crossing back over Elk Creek, several horse and stagecoach routes connect with the trail. You'll also pass **Yancy's,** where Roosevelt Lodge hosts outdoor barbecues. Stay left at all of these intersections to return to your first junction and retrace your steps back to the trailhead.

Minimal parking is available across the road from the trailhead. Alternate parking is at Tower Junction on the service road south of Upper Grand Loop Road, between the gas station and Roosevelt Lodge entrance road. For those parking at Tower Junction, walk across the road and take the stagecoach trail to Yancy's to connect with the loop. You can also walk the road to reach the main trailhead.

Narrows of the Yellowstone River

Distance: 4 miles (6.4 km) rt
Duration: 2.5 hours
Elevation change: 393 feet (120 m)
Effort: easy
Trailhead: Yellowstone River Picnic Area

A steep grunt uphill through sagebrush meadows with pink sticky geranium and arrowleaf balsamroot leads to the east rim of the **Narrows of the Yellowstone River.** The trail saunters along the rim above the deep canyon with several viewpoints. In one mile, the trail overlooks **Calcite Springs.** As it traverses a ridge above the Yellowstone River, the route affords spectacular views of the narrows, sculpted minarets, and columnar basalt. It's also a good place to spot **bighorn sheep, osprey,** and **peregrine falcons.** Pronghorn cross the ridge, and marmots live in the rocks. In two miles, you'll reach a **four-way trail junction,** which is where most hikers turn around. Those with gumption drop to the Yellowstone River and head back on the spur trail that plunges steeply to the historic **Bannock Indian Ford** (adds 0.8 mi/1.3 km rt).

Trout Lake
Distance: 1.2 miles (2 km) rt
Duration: 1 hour
Elevation change: 220 feet (67 m)
Effort: easy
Trailhead: small pullout with limited parking on the Northeast Entrance Rd., between Soda Butte Trailhead and Pebble Creek Campground

An idyllic little pool, **Trout Lake** is actually the largest of three small lakes tucked near the Northeast Entrance Road in the **Absaroka Mountains.** From the trailhead, the path catapults vertically through a Douglas fir forest to the lake. At the top, the **route splits** to circle the lake. Go either way. The trail rims the shoreline, which is semi-forested on the east shore and has open meadows on the west shore. In early summer, phlox blankets the hillsides, cutthroat trout spawn in the inlet stream, and **osprey** hang around to fish. Short unmaintained trails connect with Shrimp and Buck Lakes.

Geyser Basins
Harlequin Lake
Distance: 1.5 miles (2.4 km) rt
Duration: 1 hour
Elevation change: 102 feet (31 m)
Effort: easy
Trailhead: West Entrance Rd., 1.9 miles (3 km) west of Madison Junction
Directions: Park in the pullout on the south side of the road opposite the trailhead.

This easy walk is popular with families and campers staying at **Madison Campground.** Potential **wildlife sightings** include elk (in June and fall), beaver, and waterfowl. A short ascent through a lodgepole corridor climbs up a hill to swing west and reach the south shore of **Harlequin Lake.** Copious yellow pond lilies, water rushes, and cattails rim the shallow, small, fishless lake by late summer. Look for beaver-chewed trees and a beaver lodge across the lake.

Sentinel Meadows and Queen's Laundry
Distance: 3.8 miles (6.1 km) rt
Duration: 2 hours
Elevation change: 45 feet (14 m)
Effort: easy-moderate
Trailhead: Fountain Flat Dr. parking lot

From the trailhead, walk south on the old road to the bridge over the **Firehole River,** where the riverside **Ojo Caliente** hot spring pours water down yellow sulfur channels. Cross the bridge to find the trail junction on the right. Turn west to walk through grasslands, crossing Fairy and Sentinel Creeks. In wet seeps, the trail can disappear.

At **Sentinel Meadows,** thermal features come into view; the first is **Mound Spring,** the largest. Several smaller cones spread around the meadows. (Use caution in exploring the basin, as thermal features can be dangerous.) Follow the trail south between the forest and the multiple smaller cones. The next major thermal is **Queen's Laundry Geyser.** On top of the sinter mound is an old, roofless log structure that was built in 1881 to serve as the bathhouse for soaking in the hot spring (soaking is no longer allowed).

Fairy Falls and Grand Prismatic Overlook
Distance: 6.8 miles (10.9 km) rt
Duration: 3.5 hours
Elevation change: 129 feet (39 m)
Effort: easy-moderate
Trailheads: Fairy Falls parking area
Directions: Find the trailhead on the west side of the road between Biscuit Basin and Midway Geyser Basin.

At 197 feet (60 m), Fairy Falls is the park's fourth-highest waterfall, and it provides a scenic year-round destination for hikers, bikers, and skiers. A spur loop en route adds an overlook of Grand Prismatic Spring with its cobalt hot spring and fiery arms of thermophiles. Bears close this trail in spring until **late May.**

From **Fairy Falls Trailhead,** cross the Firehole River and hike the abandoned road. To climb to the overlook of **Grand Prismatic Spring** (1.7 mi/2.7 km rt), take the signed spur to ascend to the platform.

From there, descend westward to reach another junction on the old road. Continue west to the signed junction **Fairy Falls.** Hike through a young lodgepole forest to the base of the falls. In summer, the falls plunge ribbon-like into a pool; in winter, it's an ice sculpture. (Cross-country skiers can catch a snowcoach shuttle from Old Faithful to ski from the parking area.) To hike from Old Faithful, allow five hours (9 mi/14.5 km rt).

Mystic Falls and Biscuit Basin Overlook
Distance: 2.4-3.9 miles (3.8-6.3 km) rt
Duration: 1-3 hours
Elevation change: 135-545 feet (41-166 m)
Effort: moderate
Trailhead: Biscuit Basin parking area

At Biscuit Basin, a short boardwalk loop provides hiking access to Mystic Falls and the overlook trail. Bears close the trail in spring until **late May.** The route can be hot in summer with sparse shade.

From the Biscuit Basin parking area, follow the **boardwalk trail** through the basin to the trailhead for Mystic Falls. Turn right and hike through young lodgepoles and meadows to a junction. Take the left fork and ascend into the canyon along the **Little Firehole River** to **Mystic Falls** (2.4 mi/3.8 km rt), a waterfall that feeds a series of cascades.

Top to bottom: Trout Lake Trail; Dunraven Pass Trail up Mount Washburn; Brink of the Lower Falls at Grand Canyon of the Yellowstone

To continue to the overlook for Biscuit Basin, climb upward from the falls. South-facing switchbacks go to another junction at the forested ridgetop. Turn right to reach **Biscuit Basin Overlook.** As the trail crosses the ridge and descends, you'll get multiple views of Biscuit Basin, the Firehole River, and steam rising across the Upper Geyser Basin. At the junction, take the left fork to return to Biscuit Basin.

From Old Faithful, you can follow the trail system through the Upper Geyser Basin to go to Biscuit Basin, Mystic Falls, and Biscuit Basin Overlook (8 mi/12.9 km rt).

Observation Point

Distance: 2.1 miles (3.4 km) rt
Duration: 1 hour
Elevation change: 237 feet (72 m)
Effort: moderate
Trailhead: Old Faithful Visitor Education Center

Most hikers coordinate the walk up to Observation Point with an eruption of **Old Faithful Geyser.** From the overlook, you can look down on the masses of people surrounding the geyser and watch it blow, but the steam plume sometimes occludes the water spouting, depending on wind direction. In winter, when the ground is snow-covered, wear snowshoes or cleats.

From the Old Faithful Visitor Education Center, circle the east side of Old Faithful Geyser, heading toward **Geyser Hill,** and cross the Firehole River. After crossing the bridge, turn right at the sign for **Observation Point.** The trail switchbacks uphill, making a small loop at the top. At the point, claim your spot in the trees to watch Old Faithful erupt. In winter, you may be the only one there, but in summer, you'll join a crowd. To descend, walk down the loop then continue westward on the trail through the forest to **Solitary Geyser.** From the geyser, a dirt trail connects south with the boardwalk on Geyser Hill near **Aurum Geyser.** Go east on the boardwalk to retrace your route across the Firehole River and back to Old Faithful.

Mallard Lake

Distance: 7-8.4 miles (11.3-13.5 km) rt
Duration: 4-5 hours
Elevation change: 867-945 feet (264-288 m)
Effort: moderate
Trailhead: Behind the employee cabins of Old Faithful Lodge or 3.8 miles (6.1 km) north of Old Faithful at Mallard Creek Trailhead

Tiny Mallard Lake, set in the forest on the edge of the Central Plateau, is one of the few places to get away from the crowds around the geyser basins. Anglers won't find fish in its sterile waters, but wildlife sightings can include bison, elk, and bears. While lupine, harebells, and paintbrush line the trail in early summer, the air also fills with copious mosquitoes. In winter, the route serves as a cross-country ski trail.

The easier route starts at **Old Faithful** (7 mi/11.3 km rt). From Old Faithful, cross the **Firehole River** to hike through long green corridors of lodgepole regrowth from the 1988 fire and a rocky ravine with lichen-covered volcanic boulders. High points offer peek-a-boo views of the Upper Geyser Basin before reaching **Mallard Lake.**

The slightly harder route starts from **Mallard Creek Trailhead** (8.4 mi/13.5 rt). From the trailhead, the route traverses through lodgepole forest to reach a junction with the trail from Old Faithful shortly before the lake.

Lone Star Geyser

Distance: 4.8 miles (7.7 km) rt
Duration: 3 hours
Elevation change: 65 feet (20 m)
Effort: easy
Trailhead: Lone Star Geyser Trailhead or the adjacent Kepler Cascades parking area

From the Lone Star Geyser Trailhead, walk south along the old **asphalt service road** through conifers along the meandering Firehole River. The route passes a large meadow (look for wildlife) before ascending a gentle hill to the geyser basin. **Lone Star Geyser,** a 12-foot-tall (3.6-m) pink and gray sinter cone, sits tucked away, hidden from the hubbub of the Upper Geyser Basin. The geyser erupts about every **three hours** with spurts lasting 30 minutes. If you see the geyser go off, add the date and time to the logbook in the old interpretive stand. (There's usually a pen there.)

To hike from **Old Faithful** (8.2 mi/13.2 km rt) head to the Old Faithful cabin complex and hop onto the **Mallard Lake Trail.** After crossing the Firehole River, turn right to follow the signage to **Kepler Cascades.** The trail climbs through forest and meadows until it parallels Grand Loop Road and crosses to the Kepler Cascades parking lot, adjacent to the Lone Star Geyser Trailhead.

Canyon and Lake Country
Mount Washburn
Distance: 5.4-6.4 miles (8.7-10.3 km) rt
Duration: 4-5 hours
Elevation change: 1,400-1,483 feet (427-452 m)
Effort: strenuous (due to elevation)
Trailhead: Dunraven Pass, on the east side of Grand Loop Rd., north of Canyon Village; or Chittenden Rd., north of Dunraven Pass

At 10,243 feet (3,122 m), the Mount Washburn Lookout yields a 360-degree panorama. On a clear day, hikers can see the Grand Canyon of the Yellowstone, Yellowstone Lake, and even the Tetons. There are two routes that reach the lookout: The Chittenden Trail is steeper and has a bit more elevation gain than the Dunraven Pass Trail, but both high-elevation trails climb up switchbacks in a steady plod on former roads.

The **Dunraven Pass Trail** (6.4 mi/10.3 km, hikers only) traverses a southern slope before swinging north. It then follows four switchbacks up a west slope to crest a long ridge for a scenic walk that finishes with a long circle up to Mount Washburn Lookout. In upper elevation cliffs and meadows, look for **bighorn sheep.**

The steeper **Chittenden Trail** (5.4 mi/8.7 km, bicycles allowed) ascends just below a ridge with a few switchbacks thrown in. On the final ridge, the trail swings east and then switchbacks west for the last steps to the summit of Mount Washburn.

At the summit, **Mount Washburn Lookout** is an ugly three-story cement block covered in radio equipment. Visitors can access only two levels. An **observation room** with windows on three sides has interpretive displays and a viewing scope. A windy **deck** offers views. Restrooms are available.

Slopes may be **snow-covered in June** but burst with alpine wildflowers by July. Plan to **descend before early afternoon** to avoid thunderstorms. Even though the treeless trail looks hot, **bring warm clothing;** the summit is often windy and cold. Due to the trail's popularity, you'll have company at the lookout.

Cascade Lake and Observation Peak
Distance: 4.4-9.6 miles (7.1-15.5 km) rt
Duration: 2.5-5 hours
Elevation change: 60-1,389 feet (18-423 m)
Effort: easy-strenuous
Trailhead: Cascade Picnic Area on Grand Loop Rd., north of Canyon Junction

June and July usually bring on bluebells, prairie smoke, and elephant's head louse-wort in the meadows en route to **Cascade Lake** (4.4 mi/7.1 km rt), the easternmost lake in the Chain of Lakes. Pack insect repellent through September to ward off copious mosquitoes. Spring snowmelt can make the lower elevations of this trail muddy in marshy areas.

From the trailhead, a relatively flat route crosses through large meadows made marshy by myriad streams, especially near the lake. (Some streams have footbridges.) Just before Cascade Lake, the trail reaches the junction. Go left to the lake. Cradled in a basin surrounded by meadows, the lake is covered by lily pads on its southwest end. Look for **trumpeter swans.**

Since snow can still cover **Observation Peak** (9.6 mi/15.5 km rt) in June, many hikers wait until July to hike this trail. To reach the rocky 9,415-foot (2,870-m) summit, turn north at the signed junction before Cascade Lake. Climbing at a steady clip, the trail crosses a broad ridge for a long ascent through the 1988 burn area. Views stretch out for miles. From the summit, where an old wood-and-stone fire lookout perches, you can see Grebe Lake below and Hayden Valley stretching to the south. Return the way you came.

Grebe Lake

Distance: 6.6 miles (10.6 km) rt
Duration: 3-4 hours
Elevation change: 350 feet (107 m)
Effort: easy
Trailhead: Grebe Lake Trailhead on Grand Loop Rd., west of Canyon Junction

Grebe Lake, the largest of the Chain of Lakes, holds rainbow trout and arctic grayling that lure anglers. Prepare for swarms of mosquitoes throughout summer.

From the trailhead, hike northward through a lodgepole forest that is regrowing from the 1988 fires. Portions of the trail are dusty, hot, and open, with downed timber. After arcing over a gentle hump, the trail reaches the southeast corner of **Grebe Lake** to arc north partially around the lake. Meadows and marshes surround the scenic lake. When high water abates after June, beaches appear on the north shore.

An alternate route to Grebe Lake comes from **Cascade Lake,** starting at Cascade Picnic Area (8 mi/12.9 km rt). By setting up a shuttle, you can also hike point-to-point to Cascade and Grebe Lake, starting at **Cascade Picnic Area** north of Canyon Junction and exiting at the **Grebe Lake Trailhead** (7.5 mi/12 km total).

North Rim of Grand Canyon of the Yellowstone

Distance: 3.8-6.6 miles (6.1-10.6 km) one-way
Duration: 3-4 hours
Elevation change: 250-1,500 feet (76-457 m)
Effort: easy-strenuous
Trailhead: Wapiti Lake Trailhead on South Rim Dr.
Directions: Park at Wapiti Picnic Area on the east side of South Rim Dr. Walk back across the Chittenden Bridge to find the trailhead heading north.

This trail is not about backcountry solitude, but rather tremendous views of the Grand Canyon of the Yellowstone. A combination of paved and dirt trails link multiple overlooks; the route includes steel stairways and boardwalks down to overlook platforms. You can start at either the north or south end to hike the entire trail or shorten the distance by driving some segments. (In several places, the trail crosses parking lots on North Rim Drive.) Spur trails also drop down via switchbacks and steep stairways to viewing platforms; all require climbing back up.

To start at the **south end** of the North Rim Trail, cross **Chittenden Bridge** to follow the **Yellowstone River** downstream (heading north). Quickly, the trail reaches the first viewpoint at **Brink of the Upper Falls.** A spur trail drops to an overlook of the **Upper Falls.** Continue north, passing the parking lot for Brink of the Upper Falls, to the ribbon-like **Crystal Falls** as it spews from a slot in the North Rim cliffs.

Next, the larger **Lower Falls** comes into view; follow the trail to a junction where a spur plummets 600 feet (183 m) down switchbacks and stairs to the **Brink of the Lower Falls.** Climb back up and continue further to **Lookout Point Trailhead,** where a short trail pops up to **Lookout Point** and a longer trail plunges 500 feet (152 m) down switchbacks and steep stairs to **Red Rock Point.**

Returning to the North Rim Trail, continue north to **Grand View Point,** where a short, paved trail drops to the viewpoint. The trail then curls northeast to the **Inspiration Point** parking lot, where you can take in canyon views from four viewpoints.

To hike the trail in reverse, start at the **north end** by parking at Inspiration Point parking lot. For a hike with the smallest amount of elevation gain, skip all the side trips to viewpoints. This will total 3.8 miles (6.1 km).

South Rim Trail to Point Sublime

Distance: 5.1 mi (8.2 km) rt
Duration: 3 hours
Elevation change: 250 feet (76 m)
Effort: easy-strenuous
Trailhead: Wapiti Picnic Area on South Rim Dr.

The South Rim Trail has multiple overlooks of the Grand Canyon of the Yellowstone. From the **Wapiti Picnic Area,** a forested walk heads north following the **Yellowstone River** to the first viewpoint at the **Upper Falls,** where a spur trail drops to the viewpoint. After circling north on the bluff for snippets of views, the strenuous **Uncle Tom's Trail** plunges 500 feet (152 m) down paved switchbacks and 328 metal stair steps (that you have to climb back up) to an overlook. Skip this if you want an easy walk.

Past Uncle Tom's Trail, the route continues east through the forest with several viewpoints along the canyon rim. Walk northeast through the Artist Point parking lot to reach the trail to **Artist Point** and continue on to **Point Sublime.** On this section, exposed overlooks (with no railings) require caution. Take in the depth of the canyon; its walls and hoodoos become far more colorful with smears of reds and pinks above the frothy blue water. The trail dead-ends at Point Sublime at a log railing where the forest claims the canyon. Return the way you came.

Clear Lake and Ribbon Lake

Distance: 2.2-7.3 miles (3.5-11.7 km) rt
Duration: 1.5-4 hours
Elevation change: 950 feet (290 m)
Effort: easy
Trailhead: Wapiti Picnic Area on South Rim Dr.

This trail climbs gently to tour three small lakes, each one strikingly different.

From the south end of the Wapiti Picnic Area parking lot, head east to ascend the hillside trail. The open meadows afford expansive views of Mount Washburn and Hayden Valley. At the fork, turn left.

The **Ribbon Lake Trail** ascends east through the forest to **Clear Lake** (2.2 mi/3.5 km rt), a shallow lake fed by runoff from Forest Hot Springs. After passing through the thermal zone, the trail reaches a junction. Turn north for the short jaunt to narrow **Lily Pad Lake** (3.6 mi/5.8 km rt), where lily pads can grow so thick the water is barely visible. Return to the main trail and continue east to **Ribbon Lake.** This third lake sits amid scenic meadows and forest. Follow the trail farther north to see the lake, then backtrack to the trail junction. To complete the loop (7.3 mi/11.7 km rt), follow the trail south from Ribbon Lake to the junction with the **Wapiti Lake Trail** and turn right. This trail wanders through thermal areas, so stay on the path for safety. After the trail breaks out of the forest onto the hillside, descend to the original fork to return to the parking lot.

Avalanche Peak

Distance: 5 miles (8 km) rt
Duration: 4 hours
Elevation change: 2,094 feet (638 m)
Effort: strenuous
Trailhead: East Entrance Rd., 17 miles (27 km) east of the Fishing Bridge Junction
Directions: Park on the south side of the road at the west end of Eleanor Lake and find the trailhead across the road.

Get an early start on this trail to avoid regular afternoon lightning and rain squalls, and prepare for strong winds at the summit by packing warm layers. This trail often remains covered in snow until **July;** avoid hiking in September and October due to bear activity.

Cross the East Entrance Road to find the trail catapulting straight up the mountain with minimal switchbacks. Launching in thick forest, the path climbs steeply until breaking out of the trees across a scree slope to a **false summit.** Trails diverge around the false summit, created by hikers trying to shortcut or walk around snowfields.

The route crawls left onto an open, narrow ridge where the in-your-face views of the surrounding Absaroka peaks are the lure to continue onward. The ridge traverse leads to a stunning conclusion at the 10,566-foot (3,220-m) summit of **Avalanche Peak.** From the summit, you'll have an impressive panorama to soak up: In the foreground is Yellowstone Lake, then the backbone of the Absaroka-Beartooth Wilderness; beyond are the distant Tetons. On the descent, be cautious on scree; the small rocks feel like walking on marbles.

Backpacking

Backpackers must obtain **permits** ($3 pp, children 8 and younger free) for assigned backcountry campsites. Permits are available in person 48 hours in advance from the backcountry offices. Make **advance reservations** (www.nps. gov/yell/planyourvisit, $25 fee) starting January 1 for the year ahead.

Mount Holmes
21.2 miles (34 km)
The Gallatin Mountains have the best backpacking in the northern part of the park. Until **July,** snow can clog the upper elevations of the route to 10,336-foot (3,160-m) **Mount Holmes.** After that, the route is usually accessible. On this three-day trip, you'll camp for **two nights** at **Winter Creek** (campsite 1C4 or 1C5), near the junction for Trilobite Lake. The next day, climb to the summit for immense views (lightning burned down the lookout in 2019). Due to bear concentration, the park service recommends having four people in your party.

Bechler River Trail
30 miles (48 km)
The king of Yellowstone backpacking trips gets you farther away from day hiker crowds. The **Bechler River Trail** descends into Bechler River Canyon and the land of waterfalls. While you can backpack the trail in **3-5 days** point-to-point from the Lone Star Geyser Trailhead to the Bechler Ranger Station, you'll need to add **eight hours** for the shuttle back. To avoid the shuttle, you can hike to Colonnade Falls in the canyon and back in **5-6 days** (40 mi/64 km rt). Set your daily mileage to allow you to reach the core canyon campsites (9B4-9B9), especially Ouzel, Colonnade, and Albright Falls. Due to snow and water levels, **permit reservations** are only available from **July 15** onward. While elevation gain is minimal (980 ft/298 m), crossing the Continental Divide twice, fording multiple streams and the river adds difficulty.

Heart Lake
21 miles (34 km)
Competition for permits is keen for Heart Lake, which is closed until **July 1** due to its prime grizzly habitat. On this three-day trip, you'll spend **two nights** at **Heart Lake** and climb the steep 2,700-foot (823-m) vertical trail up **Mount Sheridan** on the middle day. Campsite 8H1 is the most secluded; campsites 8H5 and 8H6 are closest to the trail. Heart Lake is the fourth-largest lake in the park, a place where anglers go after cutthroat trout.

Part of the Continental Divide Trail, Heart Lake Trail passes through thick stands of lodgepoles and small wetland meadows to climb over the Continental Divide and descend to the lake on the way in (remember you must climb back up on the return trip). From the trailhead, hike southeast where the landscape opens up with views, thermal areas with hot springs along **Witch Creek,** and Mount Sheridan rising from the west shore of the lake. The lake has a seasonal **backcountry ranger station,** which may not be staffed. The north shore of the lake offers pebbly beaches for scenic lunch spots, lake enjoyment, and

Soak in Hot Springs

Yellowstone's natural hot springs are deadly hot; that's why it's illegal to soak in them. But here are three places you can enjoy a hot soak:

♦ Inside Yellowstone, the natural **Boiling River Hot Springs** (dawn-dusk daily midsummer-late spring, free, swimsuits required) spills into the **Gardner River.** Soak in the river where the cooler water tempers the sizzling hot spring. Use caution due to temperature extremes, slippery rocks, and strong currents. Changing facilities are not available. High water closes the location late spring-early summer. Find the unmarked parking lot for the Boiling River Trailhead on the east side of US 89 between Gardiner and Mammoth Hot Springs. You'll need to walk 0.5 mile (0.8 km) to two stair-step entrances that lead to the soaking areas.

♦ For a more cultivated setting outside the park, soak at **Yellowstone Hot Springs** (24 E. Gate Rd., Corwin Springs, 833/977-7464, www.yellowstonehotsprings.com, 1pm-9pm Tues.-Sun., $5-18, $4 towels). The mineral hot springs feed three outdoor pools. The main pool is kept at 102°F (39°C), while two smaller pools provide a 104°F (40°C) hot soak or a 70°F (21°C) cool plunge. Drive 10 minutes north of Gardiner on US 89 to reach Gate Road for the hot springs.

♦ A historic Montana retreat located 33 miles (53 km) north of Gardiner, **Chico Hot Springs** (163 Chico Rd., Pray, MT, 406/333-4933, 8am-11pm daily year-round, $9 adults, $4 seniors and kids under 6) has two outdoor pools. The large pool is kept around 96°F (36°C) while the small pool is hotter, at 103°F (39°C).

watching **Rustic Geyser,** plus 10 backcountry campsites.

Biking

Biking is not permitted on trails inside the park but **paved and dirt roads** offer places to ride. From **late March to mid-April,** roads open to bicyclists, but remain closed to vehicles. These roads include Mammoth to Norris, Tower Junction to Tower Fall, South Entrance Road to West Thumb, and East Entrance Road to Sylvan Pass. Confirm current road status on the park's website. Riders need to be aware of narrow shoulders and curvy roads with large RVs on them.

It's best to bring your own bike, but there is one rental option in the park. In Old Faithful, the **Snow Lodge** (307/344-7311, www.yellowstonenationalparklodges.com, daily late May-early Sept.) rents bikes and helmets (from $8 for 1 hr) for adults and children. Add on kiddie trailers or bike trains for $5-20.

Bikes are only permitted on **three** **shared hiker-biker routes** in the Old Faithful area. These wide level remnants of old asphalt roadbeds are perfect places for family biking. **Fountain Flats Road** (4 mi/6.4 km one-way, late May-early Nov.) links the Fountain Flat Drive parking lot with the Fairy Falls Trailhead. The bike route passes Goose Lake and the Grand Prismatic Spring overlook, neither of which allow bikes. Park your bike at the rack at Fairy Falls, then walk over.

A round-trip ride connects **Old Faithful Inn** with **Biscuit Basin** (5 mi/8 km). Start at Hamilton's Store (1 Old Faithful Rd.) to ride the paved path along the south side of the Firehole River. Turn left onto the second Daisy Geyser Loop entrance, then turn right onto a single-track trail that leads to Grand Loop Road near Biscuit Basin.

The **Lone Star Geyser Trail** (4.8 mi/7.7 km rt) offers a pleasant forest ride along the Firehole River to Lone Star Geyser. Park at Lone Star Geyser Trailhead or Kepler Cascades.

Mountain bikers can ride several old dirt roads in the park:

- For 1,500 feet (457 m) of climbing, the **Old Gardiner Road** (5 mi/8 km one-way, late Apr.-early Nov.) connects Gardiner with Mammoth Hot Springs. While cars can only go downhill from Mammoth, bikers can go both directions. Road access is behind Mammoth Hot Springs Hotel or at the North Park Entrance Station.

- South of Mammoth, **Bunsen Peak Loop** (6 mi/9.6 km one-way, May-early Nov.) starts from Bunsen Peak Trailhead to circle Bunsen Peak's east side. The trail drops through employee housing before joining the Grand Loop Road between the Upper and Lower Terraces.

- On the Grand Loop Road east of Mammoth, **Blacktail Plateau Drive** (6 mi/9.6 km one-way, mid-July-early Nov.) rolls through higher-elevation terrain with wildlife. Vehicles can only go eastbound, but bicyclists can travel in both directions.

- The most challenging mountain bike ride goes to **Mount Washburn Lookout.** From the Chittenden Road parking lot, bikers grunt 2.7 miles (4.3 km) up to the lookout. The difficulty is compounded by the 10,243-foot (3,122-m) summit elevation, but the return trip sails downhill. (The Dunraven Pass route is not open to bikers.)

Horseback Riding

Two **corrals** (307/344-7311, www.yellowstonenationalparklodges.com) in Yellowstone offer **horseback rides** ($55-75). From the **Roosevelt Corrals** (daily early June-early Sept.), wranglers lead one-hour rides departing between noon-1:30pm to go around sagebrush flats, while the two-hour ride at 9:15am travels to Lost Lake. From the **Canyon Corrals** (daily late June-early Sept.), wranglers lead one-hour rides 8-9 times daily through meadows and pine forests along Cascade Creek. Two-hour rides, departing at 8:45am, go to the rim of Cascade Canyon.

Yellowstone Wilderness Outfitters (406/223-3300, www.yellowstone.ws, June-Sept., from $1,400) guides overnight pack trips to many destinations. A four-day trip goes to Heart Lake, and a six-day trip rides the Thorofare Trail to the Yellowstone River headwaters. Guides with degrees in wildlife biology can expand your understanding of fishing, photography, wildlife-watching, and bear safety.

Wear long pants, sturdy shoes (no sandals), and a hat for sun protection. Children must be 5-8 years old (exact minimum age varies by trip). Make reservations in advance and tip your wrangler 15 percent for day trips, 20 percent for overnights.

Water Sports
Boating and Fishing

Motorized boats are only allowed on Yellowstone Lake and Lewis Lake. Jet Skiing, parasailing, wakeboarding, waterskiing, and boats longer than 40 feet (12 m) are banned. Complete boating regulations, along with permit requirements, licenses, and hazard maps are available on the park's website; be aware of seasonal closures for wildlife and birds.

Permits are required for all boats, fishing, and backcountry boat camping. All boats must pass an Aquatic Invasive Species (AIS) inspection before a **boating permit** (motorized: $10/7 days, $20/season; nonmotorized: $5/7 days, $10/season) can be issued. Clean and decontaminate your boat before bringing it to Yellowstone; be sure it is drained and dry. **Fishing permits** (adults from $18/3 days, under 16 years free) are required for anglers. **Overnight permits** ($3 pp, children under 8 free) are required for all overnight anchoring locations and on-land campsites, available 48 hours in advance from a backcountry office. **Advance reservations** (www.nps.gov/yell/

planyourvisit, $25 fee) can be submitted starting January 1 for the year ahead. You can pick up all permits at the **South Entrance Station** (US 89/191/287), **Grant Village Backcountry Office** (307/344-2160, June-Sept.), or **Bridge Bay Ranger Station** (307/344-7381, mid-May-Sept.).

Fishing Rivers

No boating or paddling is allowed on Yellowstone's rivers, only fishing. In fact, native trout inhabit some of Yellowstone's rivers, making them prime for fly-fishing. Most of the rivers begin to clear of runoff sediments by early July, when the real fishing begins. Most anglers wade in, but you can fish from shore. Consult with fly shops in West Yellowstone and Gardiner for the best flies to use for the season.

The western region of Yellowstone serves as headwaters for Montana's blue-ribbon trout streams. Inside the park, the **Firehole, Madison,** and lower **Gibbon Rivers** offer prime fly-fishing for rainbow and brown trout. Riffles and slow ambling stretches alternate with deep pools. Only fly-fishing is permitted on these rivers. If you don't have a fly rod, just attach a fly on a casting rod.

In the northern region of the park, multiple rivers harbor wild native trout on the **Gardner River, Slough Creek, Soda Butte Creek,** and **Lamar River.** The deeper, wider, and bigger **Yellowstone River** adds more pools for casting. Hiking anglers can also find fishing with less pressure on **Blacktail Deer Creek** and **Hellroaring Creek.** Runoff usually clears from streams in early July.

For kids, smaller creeks work best for fishing. Take them to the picnic areas at the Gardner River or Lava Creek, or near the campgrounds of Slough, Indian, or Pebble Creeks. Near Norris, the **Gibbon River** at Virginia Meadows and **Solfatara Creek** offer good places to gain fishing skills. Near Madison Junction, take the kids to the large meadows that flank the **Madison River.**

trail ride from Roosevelt Corrals

Yellowstone Lake

With 141 miles (226 km) of shoreline and six islands, Yellowstone Lake offers expansive water for boating, angling, island touring, and overnighting. Touring the east shore of the lake is best in the morning, as afternoon winds can push heavy onto the shore. Docks allow places to tie up for island explorations.

Two **marinas** operated by Xanterra (307/344-7311, www.yellowstonenationalparklodges.com) are tucked into sheltered bays. Located on West Thumb, **Grant Village Marina** (mid-June-Oct.) has a boat launch with a cement ramp, docks, and boat slips but no services. **Bridge Bay Marina** (June-Oct. for boat launch, daily mid-June-early Sept. for rentals and charters) has a boat launch with cement ramp, docks, moorage, rentals, a store, and gas. The marina rents 18-foot (5.5-m) boats with 40-horsepower outboard motors ($60/hr). To avoid paddling the long distance across open water, make advance reservations for a **shuttle** from Bridge Bay Marina (reservations 307/344-7311, summer shuttle office 307/242-3893, www.yellowstonenationalparklodges.com, mid-June-mid-Sept., starts at $214), which can take up to six people with gear and a few canoes or kayaks.

Lewis Lake

Lewis Lake is prized for its beauty, quiet ambience, and fishing for brown trout. Though it is smaller than Yellowstone Lake, afternoon winds still churn up waves. Most winds come from the west or southwest, so you'll find more sheltered boating along the west shore. The lake connects with the larger Shoshone Lake via the **Lewis Channel;** however, motorized boats are not permitted up the channel beyond the signed closure. If you have an outboard motor, you can detach the motor and chain it up with a lock onshore at the sign to row upstream.

A **boat launch** with a cement ramp and dock is located adjacent to the Lewis Lake Campground, accessed from a well-signed turnoff on the South Entrance Road. Parking areas are designated for day-use and overnight boaters.

Shoshone Lake

Shoshone Lake is on every serious paddler's bucket list: It has seclusion, wildlife, a geyser basin, an access via a river channel (after paddling across Lewis Lake), and no road or motorized boat access. Lewis Channel is about 3 miles (5 km) long as the crow flies, but river convolutions make the route longer.

Shoshone Lake is divided into two sections by **the Narrows,** a pinch in the shoreline squeezing the lake to a half-mile. The Narrows provides the best place to cross open water, if you must do so. Otherwise, the southeast shore is the safest travel route; winds hammer the east shore with waves up to three feet. To visit **Shoshone Geyser Basin,** with 80 active geysers, beach boats at the landing area denoted with an orange marker. Find

the area in a small bay in the northwest corner of the lake where a trail connects to the geyser basin. You can overnight at one of 16 boating **campsites** on the north or south shore.

Guided Tours

Based out of Jackson, **Geyser Kayak** (307/413-6177, www.geyserkayak.com) leads day or overnight paddle trips in sea kayaks. On Yellowstone Lake, the day trips and a shorter sunset tour paddle West Thumb, including thermal features (daily late May-Sept., from $200). Multiday trips (from $1,600 for up to 3 people) go out late June-September: Four- or six-day trips go into the Southeast Arm of Yellowstone Lake; three- or four-day trips paddle on Lewis and Shoshone Lakes. Rates include kayaks, life jackets, meals, and guides. Plan to tip 15 percent for day trips and 20 percent for overnights.

On Yellowstone Lake, **Bridge Bay Marina** (307/344-7311, www.yellowstone nationalparklodges.com, daily mid-June-early Sept.) has charters by reservation for fishing or sightseeing ($103/hr). Boats can hold up to six people; only three can fish at a time. Rates include fishing rods and tackle. Tip your guides 15 percent (20 percent if you catch lots of fish).

Swimming

Geothermal features can scald, thus swimming is not permitted in the hot pools in geyser basins. A swimming hole opens on the **Firehole River** once high water abates in early July. On Firehole Canyon Drive (one-way), park near the outhouses and descend wooden stairs to the river. There is no lifeguard; swim at your own risk. Outside the park at Hebgen Lake, you can swim at **Rainbow Point Campground.**

You can swim in Yellowstone's lakes; however, it is illegal to swim near thermal features where the water is warmest. There are no designated swimming areas or lifeguards; swim at your own

risk. In Yellowstone Lake, the water is a bone-chilling 35°F (1.7°C) in June. In August, temperatures in some areas may reach the low 60s (15.5-20.5°C). About six miles north of West Thumb Junction, a sand bar cuts the waves and lets the water get a few degrees warmer. Watch for signs of hypothermia in kids, offshore winds, sudden whitecaps, and thunderstorms.

Winter Sports
Cross-Country Skiing and Snowshoeing

Winter transforms Yellowstone into a prime cross-country ski and snowshoe locale. With the exception of the plowed road between Gardiner, Mammoth, and Cooke City, all other roads closed to wheeled vehicles are open for skiing. Some have snowcoach and snowmobile traffic. All hiking trails turn into ungroomed winter ski and snowshoe trails, including Biscuit Basin, Fairy Falls, Spring Creek, and trails around the geyser basins (boardwalks can get icy). Winter trail maps are located on the park website and at Albright Visitor Center.

Around Mammoth Hot Springs, **Upper Terrace Loop, Bunsen Peak Trail,** and **Blacktail Plateau Trail** are groomed for cross-country skiing. Other trails for skiers are the **Snow Pass, Sheepeater,** and **Indian Creek-Bighorn Loop** trails. **Warming huts** sit at the Indian Creek and Upper Terrace Trailheads. Parking to access all trails is at Upper Terrace Loop and the lower Bunsen Peak Trailhead. The **Old Gardiner Road Trail,** located behind the hotel, and **Upper Terrace Loop** provide good snowshoeing.

At **Old Faithful,** the park service grooms several roads for skate and classic skiing or snowshoeing. One groomed ski trail ascends a gentle grade to **Lone Star Geyser,** while a less-traveled loop tours through the cabins of **Old Faithful Lodge** with views of the Firehole River. The park service also grooms a trail from **Old Faithful Inn** to **Morning Glory Pool,** but geothermal hot spots cause melt-outs;

Rafting the Yellowstone River

The **Yellowstone River** (Class I-IV) flows through **Gardiner** and Yankee Jim Canyon, where wave trains throw up a rolling kick for white-water rafting. Below the canyon, the river settles into a calmer pace, better for scenic floats.

Guided trips go **May to September,** including white-water, scenic floats, and inflatable kayaks, and trips range from half days ($52) to full days ($85-99). You can also opt for a paddle-saddle combo or a fly-fishing trip. Reservations are recommended. Tip your river guide 15 percent. Outfitters include:

♦ **Flying Pig Adventure Company** (511 Scott St. W., 888/792-9193, www. flyingpigrafting.com)

♦ **Montana Whitewater** (603 Scott St., 406/848-7398, www.montanawhitewater. com)

♦ **Wild West Rafting** (220 W. Park St., 406/848-2252, www.wildwestrafting.com)

♦ **Yellowstone Raft Company** (111 2nd St., 406/848-7777 or 800/858-7781, www. yellowstoneraft.com)

you may have to remove skis in order to walk across the bare pavement.

Rentals, Shuttles, and Guides

In Mammoth Hot Springs and Old Faithful's Snow Lodge, the **Bear's Den Ski Shop** (Xanterra, 307/344-7311, www. yellowstonenationalparklodges.com, 7:30am-5pm daily mid-Dec.-Feb.) rents gear (including snowshoes, gaiters, cross-country skis, poles, ski boots, and cleats) for a half or full day for $3-15 per item. A full-day ski package costs $27. The shop also offers repairs, waxing, lessons, and guided tours.

Ski shuttles ($24 each way, kids half price) go from **Mammoth to Indian Creek** or from **Old Faithful to Fairy Falls Trailhead** and other locales. **Snowcoaches** also go to Grand Canyon of the Yellowstone for sightseeing, ski touring, or snowshoe touring (from $230). Make reservations for shuttles and snowcoaches with Xanterra when booking your lodging.

Park naturalists guide free two-hour **snowshoe tours** (2pm Wed. and Fri.-Sun. late Dec.-Feb.) around Upper Terrace

Drive in winter. Bring snowshoes, winter layers, and a day pack to meet at Upper Terrace Drive parking lot.

Yellowstone Expeditions (536 Firehole Ave., West Yellowstone, 406/646-9333 or 800/728-9333, http:// yellowstoneexpeditions.com, late Dec.-early Mar., from $1,260 pp) leads bucket list-worthy cross-country ski and snowshoe tours from their yurt camp. Located near Grand Canyon of the Yellowstone, the camp is the only overnight winter facility on the park's east side. Two large yurts serve as the dining room and kitchen, which rolls out yummy meals. A sauna soothes muscles after skiing, and a heated restroom building has a hot shower and large pit toilet rooms. Visitors sleep in two-person heated huts. Guides lead daily ski tours from camp or after a short shuttle ride. Multiday packages include snowcoach transportation from West Yellowstone and on daily ski treks, lodging, sleeping bags with flannel sheets, meals, and guide service. Rental skis or snowshoes are available. January rates are lowest, when daylight hours are shortest. Tip 20 percent.

Snowmobiling

Yellowstone's roads are open to snowmobiles **mid-December to mid-March.** You can go with commercial concessionaires or self-guided via the **annual lottery for limited permits** (apply in Sept.). Guided snowmobile tours travel inside Yellowstone on quieter, less stinky machines (which are required by the park).

Guided snowmobile tours ($270-280 per machine) launch from West Yellowstone into the national park to either **Old Faithful** (65 mi/105 km rt, 8 hrs) or **Grand Canyon of the Yellowstone** (90 mi/145 km rt, 9 hrs). Because the roads are groomed daily, you don't need previous experience, although it definitely helps. Rates do not include park entrance fees, meals, taxes, or 15 percent guide gratuity. Insulated snowsuits, gloves, boots, and helmets are available to rent for $15-30. Avalanche gear (beacons, probes, shovels, and airbags, $50) may be required. Make reservations through **Yellowstone Vacations** (415 Yellowstone Ave., 800/426-7669, www.yellowstonevacations.com) or **See Yellowstone Tours** (217 Yellowstone Ave., 800/221-1151, www.seeyellowstone.com). **Backcountry Adventures** (224 N. Electric St., 406/646-9317 or 800/924-7669, www.backcountry-adventures.com) also guides tours ($220) in the park and Gallatin National Forest. All three companies also rent snowmobiles ($150-260).

Food

Inside the Park

Xanterra (307/344-7311, www.yellowstonenationalparklodges.com) operates the park restaurants, grills, and cookouts. Most restaurants are first come, first seated; **reservations** are mandatory in winter for dinner at **Mammoth Hotel Dining Room** and **Snow Lodge** and in summer for the **Old West Dinner Cookout.** Reservations are also required for dining at **Old Faithful Inn, Canyon Lodge M66 Bar & Grill, Lake Yellowstone Hotel,** and **Grant Village Dining Room.** Make all dining reservations when you book your lodging; if you are not staying in a lodge that requires dinner reservations but would like to eat at one, you can book dinner reservations 60 days in advance. In all park restaurants, casual dress is common; no dresses, heels, or ties needed.

Regional specialties include elk, bison, and local farm-raised meats. You can find healthy, vegan, vegetarian, and gluten-free options alongside multi-course, meat-heavy meals. All restaurants serve beer, wine, and cocktails, plus children's menus. You can order lunches to-go in advance. Some restaurant hours and meal services lessen after mid-September.

Preorder to-go lunches, purchase convenience foods from Yellowstone General Stores, or pack your own cooler goodies to have a picnic lunch (and avoid the lines at restaurants). Yellowstone has scads of **picnic areas around Grand Loop Road.** Use the map you received at the entrance station to locate the picnic area that will suit your itinerary for the day. Most picnic areas are equipped with tables and accessible restroom facilities that are sometimes vault toilets. Pack out your trash. The only picnic areas that permit fires are Nez Perce, Whiskey Flat, Spring Creek, and Norris Meadows.

Mammoth Hot Springs

Located across from the Mammoth Hot Springs Hotel, the ★ **Mammoth Hotel Dining Room** (6:30am-10am, 11:30am-2:30pm, and 5pm-10pm daily late Apr.-early Nov. and mid-Dec.-early Mar.; shorter dinner hours mid-Sept.-early Nov. and mid-Dec.-early Mar., $12-32) overlooks the parade grounds where wildlife often adds entertainment. This certified-green restaurant changes menus between winter and summer, offering farm-to-table fare year-round. In summer, breakfast also includes an all-you-can-eat buffet ($15 adults, $8 kids).

Lunches feature salad, sandwiches, and burgers; dinner adds meat, fish, and pasta entrées. Reservations are required for dinner in winter. Appetizers are also served in the adjacent **Terrace Lounge. Mammoth Terrace Grill** (7am-9pm daily late Apr.-mid-Oct., hours vary seasonally, $3-10) serves breakfast, burgers, sandwiches, and snacks.

Roosevelt Lodge

Lauded by many locals as the best food in the park, ★ **Roosevelt Lodge Dining Room** (7am-10am and 11:30am-9:30pm daily June-Sept., $8-30) offers western-style dining and a varied menu. Breakfast skillets, Tex-Mex dishes, bison, and smoked barbecue ribs are house specialties.

The **Old West Dinner Cookout** (dusk daily early June-mid-Sept., $66-102 adults, $53-92 children ages 8-11) is adventure dining. Guests saddle up or ride a wagon from the Roosevelt Corrals to **Yancy's Hole.** At the cookout, wranglers grill up steaks to order and serve up traditional cookout sides along with coffee cooked on a fire. (With advance notice, vegetarian options can replace the steak.) Check-in times at the Roosevelt Corral range between 2:30pm-4:45pm (hours vary seasonally). Horseback rides take 1-2 hours to reach the site; the wagon ride takes 30-45 minutes. All return rides take 30 minutes. Reservations are required.

Old Faithful

In the historic Old Faithful Inn, the ★ **Old Faithful Inn Dining Room** (daily early May-mid-Oct.) is an experience of ambience. The log dining room, with its immense fireplace and woven twig chairs, harkens back to another era. **Breakfast** (6:30am-10am, $6-15) serves up traditional egg and griddle dishes. **Lunch** (11:30am-2:30pm, $10-18) has burgers, sandwiches, and salads. Breakfast and lunch are first come, first served. **Dinner** (4:30pm-10pm, $15-35) mixes lighter options with specialties

such as pork osso bucco, pasta, fish, and quail. Dinner reservations are required. For faster service, **buffets** (breakfast and lunch $14-18 adults, $7-9 kids; dinner $33 adults, $12 kids) are offered at all meals. Lunch has a western buffet with trout, pulled pork, and barbecue-style sides. Dinner rolls out the prime rib. The inn has two alternatives for lighter meals, snacks, and to-go items for travel: the **Bear Pit Lounge** (11:30am-11pm) and the **Bear Paw Deli** (6am-6pm).

In the Snow Lodge, the modern **Obsidian Dining Room** (daily late Apr.-late Oct., hours shorten mid-Dec.-Feb.) is a contemporary lodge with gas fireplaces and trendy western chandeliers. In summer, the restaurant serves only breakfast and dinner; in winter, it also serves lunch. For **breakfast** (6:30am-10:30am, $6-15), the smoked salmon eggs Benedict is a specialty. A faster alternative, the breakfast buffet ($15 adults, $8 kids) is offered in summer and winter but only when the lodge reaches a certain capacity. **Lunch** (11:30am-3pm winter only, $10-17) has salads, burgers, sandwiches, and chili. For **dinner** (5pm-10:30pm, $10-38), salads and burgers provide lighter options; larger entrées include trout, prime rib, duck, and pork osso bucco. Reservations are required for dinner in winter. The **Geyser Grill** (10:30am-9pm late Apr.-early Nov., closes 3:30pm winter, $4-10) has burgers, sandwiches, soups and chili, fries, beer, and wine.

With a cafeteria and deck overlooking its namesake geyser, the **Old Faithful Lodge** (daily mid-May-Sept.) is the place to go for light, quick meals, especially if you are waiting for Old Faithful to blow. You can even grab to-go sandwiches and claim your seat on the benches surrounding the geyser. The **cafeteria** (11am-9pm, $7-15) serves ice cream, grain and noodle bowls, gyros, chili, barbecue plates, and full dinners of bison meatloaf, trout, turkey, or chicken. The **Bake Shop** (6:30am-9pm, closes noon in Sept.) serves baked goods, beverages, wraps, sandwiches, salads, breakfast burritos, oatmeal, and ice cream.

Canyon Village

The huge **Mission 66 dining facility** (daily mid-May-mid-Oct.) at Canyon Lodge flaunts its original 1960s color schemes and appearance. The **M66 Bar & Grill** serves breakfast (6:30am-10:30am, $7-12) of egg dishes and griddle plates. For dinner (5pm-10pm, $11-30), reservations are required. Dine on seasonal entrées of grilled trout, bison burgers, bison and elk bratwurst, prime rib, or pasta. Two stations at **Canyon Lodge Eatery** serve up wok-fried Asian dishes with choices of sauces, as well as stews, braises, and rotisserie chicken, plus veggies, greens, potatoes, or pasta. The eatery offers breakfast (6:30am-10am, $6-11), lunch, and dinner (11:30am-3pm and 4:30pm-10pm, $10-17) with cafeteria-style seating. Stop by **Canyon Lodge Falls Café** (6am-9pm daily mid-May-early Sept., $4-12) for grab-and-go foods.

Lake Village

The ★ **Lake Yellowstone Hotel Dining Room** (daily mid-May-early Oct.) in the Lake Yellowstone Hotel is the headliner place to dine. Surrounded on three sides by large windows with peekaboo views of the lake, the dining room clusters tables around white columns that echo the exterior architecture of the colonial building. Order **breakfast** (6:30am-10am, $7-17) off the menu; if you're in a hurry, go for the buffet. Specialties include eggs Benedict on crab cakes and huckleberry cream cheese-stuffed French toast. **Lunch** (11:30am-2:30pm, $10-18) features burgers, sandwiches, salads, noodle bowls, and trout. **Dinner** (5pm-10pm, $17-40) offers multiple courses with appetizers, soups, and salads followed by entrées of fresh fish, bison, elk, lamb, salads, or burgers. Advance reservations are required

for dinner. The **Deli** (7am-8pm, $4-12) serves breakfast croissants and quiche, soups, salads, sandwiches, espresso, and desserts.

At Lake Lodge, **Wylie's Canteen** (6:30am-10:30am, 11:30am-3pm, and 4:30pm-9:30pm daily early June-early Sept., $6-16) has breakfast sandwiches and à la carte items. Lunch and dinner include sandwiches, burgers, and fried chicken.

Grant Village

Tucked in the forest, the ★ **Grant Village Dining Room** (daily late May-Sept.) is a vaulted room with a wood ceiling and large-paned windows looking out on the lake through trees. **Breakfast** (6:30am-10am, $5-15) can be ordered from the menu; for a quicker meal, choose the breakfast buffet. **Lunch** (11:30am-2:30pm, $10-15) includes salads, burgers, sandwiches, and fish entrées. **Dinner** (5pm-10pm, $16-33) adds on specialties of trout, prime rib, and bison meatloaf. Dinner reservations are required.

Sitting on the lake at the marina on West Thumb Bay, **Grant Village Lake House Restaurant** (daily late May-late Sept.) has prime window views for relishing sunrise or sunset colors glowing on the lake. Breakfast (6:30am-10:30am, $15) is a basic buffet, while dinner (5pm-9pm, $11-30) includes prime rib, elk and bison bratwurst, pasta, trout, and flatbreads.

Other Dining

Yellowstone General Stores (406/586-7593, www.visityellowstonepark.com) sell convenience foods and several have diners inside. Stores are located at **Mammoth Hot Springs, Tower Fall, Canyon Village, Fishing Bridge, Lake Village,** and **Grant Village. Old Faithful** has two stores. Most of the stores have a food service counter; at Canyon Village, Lake Village, and Old Faithful, you can get sit-down service for breakfast, ice cream, soda fountain treats, burgers, and sandwiches.

Gardiner

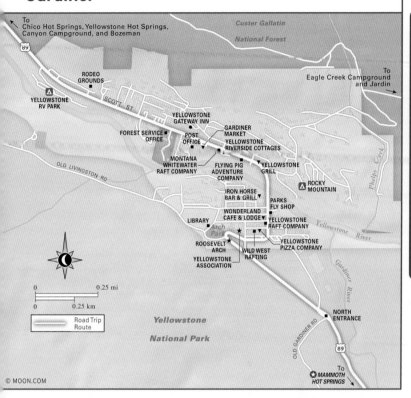

To Chico Hot Springs, Yellowstone Hot Springs, Canyon Campground, and Bozeman

Custer Gallatin National Forest

To Eagle Creek Campground and Jardin

RODEO GROUNDS

YELLOWSTONE RV PARK

SCOTT ST.

YELLOWSTONE GATEWAY INN

FOREST SERVICE OFFICE

POST OFFICE

GARDINER MARKET

YELLOWSTONE RIVERSIDE COTTAGES

OLD LIVINGSTON RD.

MONTANA WHITEWATER RAFT COMPANY

FLYING PIG ADVENTURE COMPANY

YELLOWSTONE GRILL

ROCKY MOUNTAIN

Phelps Creek

IRON HORSE BAR & GRILL

PARKS FLY SHOP

LIBRARY

WONDERLAND CAFE & LODGE

Arch Park

YELLOWSTONE RAFT COMPANY

Yellowstone River

ROOSEVELT ARCH

WILD WEST RAFTING

YELLOWSTONE PIZZA COMPANY

YELLOWSTONE ASSOCIATION

Gardiner River

0   0.25 mi
0   0.25 km

Road Trip Route

Yellowstone National Park

NORTH ENTRANCE

OLD GARDINER RD.

To MAMMOTH HOT SPRINGS

© MOON.COM

Outside the Park

Gardiner

A small café, **Yellowstone Grill** (404 Scott St., 406/848-9433, 7am-2pm Tues.-Sun. summer, 8am-2pm Tues.-Fri., 8am-noon Sat.-Sun., $11-15) is a combination bakery, grill, and Mexican restaurant that serves fresh breakfast and lunch dishes. Go with a burrito, quesadilla, or tacos, or choose from omelets, blueberry pancakes, soups, salads, wraps, and burgers. They also serve espresso drinks. The bakery's specialty is caramel cinnamon rolls.

Yellowstone Pizza Company (210 Park St., 406/848-9991, http://yellowstonepizzacompany.com, 11am-10pm daily May-Oct., shorter hours in winter, $10-30) dishes up 12-inch pizzas

cooked in a brick oven with regular or gluten-free crust. Elk or bison pizza is the house specialty. You can also get salads or the pasta of the day. In summer, outdoor dining on the upstairs deck yields views of the Roosevelt Arch.

With a fireplace indoors and patio seating, **Wonderland Café** (206 Main St., 406/223-1914, wonderlandcafeandlodge.com, 7am-9pm daily, $12-45) is a place to drop in for espresso drinks and tasty bakery treats, or stop for a bigger meal at breakfast, lunch, or dinner. Their menu includes locally sourced ingredients, vegetarian, vegan, gluten-free, and organic options, plus a full bar of Montana beers, wine, and cocktails. Food selections alter seasonally, but often include elk and

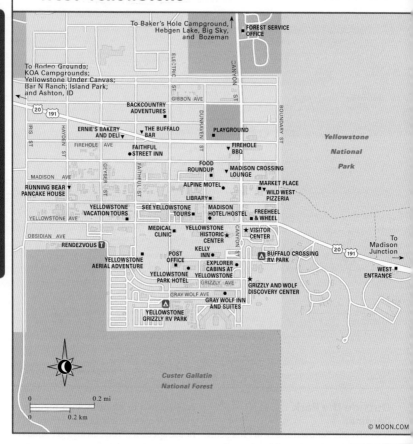

West Yellowstone

To Baker's Hole Campground, Hebgen Lake, Big Sky, and Bozeman

FOREST SERVICE OFFICE

To Rodeo Grounds; KOA Campgrounds; Yellowstone Under Canvas; Bar N Ranch; Island Park; and Ashton, ID

ELECTRIC ST

CANYON ST

GIBBON AVE

BACKCOUNTRY ADVENTURES

DUNRAVEN ST

BOUNDARY ST

ERNIE'S BAKERY AND DELI

THE BUFFALO BAR

PLAYGROUND

FIREHOLE AVE

FAITHFUL STREET INN

ST

FIREHOLE BBQ

Yellowstone

National

Park

FOOD ROUNDUP

MADISON CROSSING LOUNGE

MADISON AVE

GEYSER ST

FAITHFUL ST

ALPINE MOTEL

MARKET PLACE

RUNNING BEAR PANCAKE HOUSE

LIBRARY

WILD WEST PIZZERIA

YELLOWSTONE VACATION TOURS

SEE YELLOWSTONE TOURS

MADISON HOTEL/HOSTEL

FREEHEEL & WHEEL

YELLOWSTONE AVE

OBSIDIAN AVE

MEDICAL CLINIC

YELLOWSTONE HISTORIC CENTER

CANYON ST

VISITOR CENTER

To Madison Junction

RENDEZVOUS

POST OFFICE

KELLY INN

BUFFALO CROSSING RV PARK

YELLOWSTONE AERIAL ADVENTURE

EXPLORER CABINS AT YELLOWSTONE

WEST ENTRANCE

YELLOWSTONE PARK HOTEL

GRIZZLY AVE

GRAY WOLF AVE

GRIZZLY AND WOLF DISCOVERY CENTER

GRAY WOLF INN AND SUITES

YELLOWSTONE GRIZZLY RV PARK

Custer Gallatin National Forest

0   0.2 mi

0   0.2 km

© MOON.COM

bison. Dinner entrées feature burgers, ribeye, fish, and pasta.

In summer, you can eat outdoors on a deck overlooking the Yellowstone River at the **Iron Horse Bar & Grille** (212 Spring St., 406/848-7888, noon-9:30pm daily May-Sept., $10-28). Specialties include elk tacos, elk meatloaf, bison burgers, house-smoked pulled pork and ribs, local microbrews, and huckleberry margaritas.

For camping meals or picnic lunches, the small **Gardiner Market** (701 Scott St., 406/848-7524, www.gardinermarket.

com, 7am-11pm daily summer, 7am-8pm daily winter) sells fresh produce and meat, baked goods, convenience foods, deli items, and beer, wine, and liquor.

West Yellowstone

For breakfast, lunch, and espresso, **Ernie's Bakery and Deli** (406 US 20, 406/646-9467, erniesbakery.com, 7am-2pm daily, $6-19) churns out baked goods, bagels, omelets, eggs Benedicts, and breakfast sandwiches until 11am. For lunch, they offer deli sandwiches, salads, and wraps. You can order boxed lunches online by

7pm the evening before for morning pickup or call at 6:30am the day of.

A second-generation, family-run restaurant, **Running Bear Pancake House** (538 Madison Ave., 406/646-7703, www.runningbearph.com, 6am-2pm daily year-round, $8-16) keeps the griddle hot with pancakes, omelets, and specialty French toast made from apple-pecan and other sweet breads. Order lunch (11am-2pm) to eat in the restaurant or boxed lunches to go.

Casual dining options are plentiful in West Yellowstone. **Firehole Bar-B-Que Co.** (120 Firehole Ave., 406/641-0020, www.fireholebbqco.com, 11am-10pm daily May-Sept., $9-17) may have a short menu, but its Texas-style barbecue brisket, pulled pork, and turkey can be accompanied with classic sides for a quick meal. A long-time town staple, the **Buffalo Bar** (335 US 20, 406/646-1176, www.thebuffalobar.com, 8am-2am daily year-round, $10-40) has a broad menu that dishes up bison in many forms: nachos, burritos, meatballs, chili, and ribeye. The **Wild West Pizzeria & Saloon** (14 Madison Ave., 406/646-4400, wildwestpizza.com, 11am-11pm, $12-27) makes a hand-tossed crust for their specialty pizzas. You'll choose from red, pesto, or white sauce. You can also design your own pie and get hot sandwiches or pasta.

Located in the 1918 West Yellowstone school building, the **Madison Crossing Lounge** (121 Madison Ave., 406/646-7621, www.madisoncrossinglounge.com, 5pm-10pm daily May-Oct. and mid-Dec.-mid-Mar., $13-40) serves steaks, fish, burgers, chicken, and pasta. Regional microbrews, worldwide wines, whiskey, and specialty cocktails add to the fine-dining ambience.

West Yellowstone has two year-round grocery stores open 7am-10pm daily; prices may be a bit higher than at your local big-city market. The **Market Place** (22 Madison Ave., 406/646-9600) has takeout foods, deli, produce, meats, gluten-free, organic, and a liquor store.

The **Food Roundup Supermarket** (107 Dunraven St., 406/646-7501) is smaller.

Cooke City and Silver Gate

In Cooke City, stop in at the **Bearclaw Bakery** (309 E. Main St., Cooke City, 406/838-2040, 5am-11am Tues.-Sun. late May-Sept., shorter hours in winter, $4-15) for gluten-free and vegan baked goods or the house specialty French toast in this tiny café that also serves as the front room for an auto and snowmobile shop.

In a 1940s log cabin, the **Beartooth Café** (207 E. Main St., Cooke City, 406/838-2475, beartooth-cafe.edan.io, 11am-9:30pm daily late May-late Sept., $9-30) is run by a fourth-generation family with meals made from scratch, including appetizers and desserts.

Combining Montanan and Malaysian foods, the family-run **MontAsia** (102 E. Main St., Cooke City, 406/838-2382, www.montasia.ninja, mid-May-mid-Sept., $9-18) serves up steak and fries, potstickers, curry, and noodles.

The **Cooke City Store** (101 Main St., Cooke City, 406/698-8353, https://cookecitystore.com, 8am-8pm daily mid-May-Sept.) has limited groceries.

In Silver Gate, the **Log Cabin Café** (106 US 212, Silver Gate, 406/838-2367, www.thelogcabincafe.com, 5:30am-10pm daily May-Oct. $9-30) serves up organic, home-baked, and fresh ingredients. Try the grilled pumpkin bread with Montana honey for breakfast.

The **Silver Gate General Store** (109 US 212, 406/838-2371, www.pineedgecabins.com, 8am-9pm daily May-Oct., shorter hours in fall) has some groceries and rents spotting scopes for wildlife-watching.

Accommodations and Camping

Inside the Park
Lodges and Cabins
Xanterra (866/439-7375 or 307/344-7311,

www.yellowstonenationalparklodges.com) operates nine summer lodges and two winter lodges on Grand Loop Road inside Yellowstone. Competition for in-park lodging is fierce: **Book in advance starting May 1** for the following year. You may be able to pick up last-minute reservations due to cancellations, but choices for room types will be limited. The highest rates are mid-June through early September; spring and fall have lower rates.

In keeping with the historical ambience, many of the rooms and cabins lack televisions, radios, telephones, and air-conditioning. Most rooms have double or queen beds; specify your needs when making reservations. If you are a light sleeper, bring earplugs; if you are traveling during midsummer heat, you may want to bring a small fan with an extension cord (very few are available from the front desks). ADA-compliant rooms are available. Some of the cabins permit pets for an added fee of $25. Free internet access (which can be very slow) is usually available in public spaces of lodges.

Mammoth Hot Springs

In a busy tourist center, the circa 1911 ★ **Mammoth Hot Springs Hotel** (1 Grand Loop Rd., May-early Nov. and mid-Dec.-Feb., $118-330 rooms and cabins, $503-602 suites) is a large complex with 79 hotel rooms, 125 cabins, and two restaurants. The hotel saw a $30 million renovation completed in 2019 that added bathrooms to all hotel rooms. Two high-end suites have a bedroom and a sitting room with a couch, chairs, and trundle bed. Cabin options include rustic cabins with no bathrooms, cabins with baths, and ones that feature hot tubs. In winter, Mammoth is the only hotel in the park accessible by private vehicles on plowed roads.

Tower Junction

Roosevelt Lodge and Cabins (Grand Loop Rd. at Northeast Entrance Rd.,

Old Faithful Inn

June early Sept., $110-170) has backwoods authenticity with no cell service or internet. The location of the 1920s lodge is perfect for dawn and dusk wildlife-watching drives up Lamar Valley. The lodge has a dining room and a line of cane rockers on the front porch that overlooks the dusty parking lot. Two types of small uninsulated cabins surround the lodge. The spartan **Roughrider cabins** contain beds and wood-burning stoves for heat but require walking to the nearby community toilet-and-shower house. **Frontier cabins** come with bathrooms and beds. Walk to the neighboring corral for trail rides, wagon rides, and Old West Dinner Cookouts.

Old Faithful

Old Faithful has three lodging options, with about 600 rooms total, all within a five-minute walk from the visitors center and Old Faithful Geyser. Only Snow Lodge has wireless internet. Bathrooms come in four types: tub-shower combo, shower only (shower stalls are small), shared baths down the hall, or communal toilets and showers in a separate cabin. Specify your needs when reserving a room; a few ADA-compliant rooms and cabins are available.

The most-requested lodge in the park, ★ **Old Faithful Inn** (May-early Oct., $145-522 rooms, $563-1,070 suites) is a National Historic Landmark. The Old House, or the main log lodge, was built in 1903-1904, with the east wing added in 1913-1914 and west wing in 1927-1928. As such, room styles, sizes, and ambience are a throwback to the last century. The Old House contains the immense lobby, dining room, lounge, snack bar, and a deck over the portico for watching Old Faithful Geyser erupt. The 327-room inn has 11 styles of rooms, some overlooking Upper Geyser Basin and Old Faithful Geyser. Historic rooms in the Old House (no elevator) have fixtures with minimal outlets for charging electronics and either private baths with clawfoot tubs or shared marble-and-tile baths with showers down the hall. The two more modern (but still dated) wings have elevators and hotel rooms with private baths. Upper-end suites have sitting rooms, bedrooms, and private baths.

Old Faithful Lodge (mid-May-Sept., $110-185) is close to Old Faithful Geyser, but removed from the hubbub of the visitors center. You can sit on the lodge deck or in the lobby to watch the geyser blow. Inside, the huge stone-and-log lodge has a snack shop and a food court cafeteria. Between the lodge and the Firehole River, 96 simple small bare-bones motel-style rooms are in rustic duplex or four-plex cabins with tiny windows and no porches. From cabins 112-116 and 200-203, you can step right out the door to watch Old Faithful. Cabins 22-25 and 31-35 overlook the Firehole River. Some have private baths; others require walking to a nearby communal bathroom and shower cabin.

Built in 1989-1999 with modern

Side Trip: Cody, Wyoming

On the east side of Yellowstone, Cody serves as a gateway to the park half of the year. During winter, access to the park is only by snowmobile. Cody relishes its cowboy heritage. Founder Buffalo Bill Cody figures prominently in the town's legacy, and in summer, nightly rodeos and staged gunfights erupt in a celebration of Cody's Wild West roots.

Sights and Entertainment

In the center of town, the **Buffalo Bill Center of the West** (720 Sheridan Ave., 307/587-4771, htttp://centerofthewest.org, 8am-6pm daily May-mid-Sept., shorter hours mid-Sept.-May, $19-20 adults, $14 kids) is a collection of five museums that include exhibits on western art, Indigenous heritage, firearms, natural history, and Buffalo Bill. Outside the center are several wildlife sculptures and *The Scout* (between Sheridan Ave. and Monument St.), a bronze statue of Buffalo Bill Cody. Cody also has a **historic village** and **walking trail.**

The **Cody gunfight** (in front of Irma Hotel, 1192 Sheridan Ave., 6pm Mon.-Sat. June-mid-Sept., free) bursts out in summer. Actors take to the street in front of the historic Irma with a 30-minute shoot-'em-up performance. Crowds pack the curbs with standing room only, so you'll want to nab your spot around 5:45pm.

The **Cody Rodeo** (519 W. Yellowstone Ave., 307/587-5155, www.codystampederodeo.com, 8pm-10pm daily June-Aug., gates open at 7pm, $21 adults, $11 kids 7-12) whoops it up with bronc and bull riding, barrel racing, and a kids' calf scramble. Late June usually has one night of extreme bull riding, featuring top riders and top kicking bulls. The stands are covered, but if the weather looks foreboding, bring layers—the rodeo goes on even in rain. The week of July 4 ups the rider caliber to PRCA heavyweights (start times vary, reserved seats for July 4 finals cost $25). **Tickets** are available in advance online (www.codystampederodeo.com) or at the ticket office (1031 12th St.).

Food and Accommodations

The Local (1134 13th St., 307/586-4262, http://thelocalcody.com, 9am-2pm and 5pm-9pm Tues.-Sat., $10-38) serves breakfast, lunch, and dinner, relying on local, sustainable, and organic ingredients. The imaginative, upscale menu changes seasonally but includes gluten-free, vegan, and vegetarian options. Sandwiches, bowls, and entrées are designed around fish, bison, pheasant, and beef.

Cody is full of history, and its hotels are part of that. **Chamberlin Inn** (1032 12th St., 888/587-0202, www.chamberlininn.com, $135-375) once served as the courthouse. Today it's an elegant boutique hotel with fresh flowers, chocolates, and luxury linens in the rooms. The two-story redbrick building has 21 guest rooms; all are different and some have kitchenettes. Specialty rooms at higher rates include the garden cottage and historic courthouse residence.

Getting There

The routes between Cody and Yellowstone are only open mid-May to early November, due to snow-buried roads in winter. The East Entrance of Yellowstone connects with Cody via the **Buffalo Bill Scenic Byway** (US 14/16/20, 52 mi/84 km, 1 hr), loaded with campgrounds and a few guest ranches. The Northeast Entrance of Yellowstone goes to Cody via **Chief Joseph Scenic Byway** (WY 296, 82 mi/132 km, 2 hrs).

western architecture, ★ **Snow Lodge** (May-late Oct. and mid-Dec.-Feb., $130-400) sits behind the visitors center with no views of the geyser basin and partially surrounded by parking lots. The 134 rooms are larger and have modern-style bathrooms and furnishings. Cabins are located a short walk from the lodge. The lodge has a restaurant, grill café, lounge, gift shop, and winter ice rink and ski shop. Hotel-style rooms with one king or two queen beds and log furnishings are in the three-story main lodge, accessed by elevator. Cabins contain motel-style rooms clustered in plain duplex or quad buildings. In winter, **snowcoaches** ($130 adults one-way, kids half-price) take you from Mammoth to the Snow Lodge. They go twice daily in each direction for the four-hour trip. You can also get a snowcoach from Flagg Ranch or West Yellowstone through other companies.

Canyon Village

With more than 500 rooms in a huge complex that includes several restaurants, ★ **Canyon Lodge and Cabins** (mid-May-mid-Oct., $214-450 lodge and cabin rooms, $594-851 suites) has hotel rooms in multistory lodges and motel-style rooms in four- or six-unit cabins. It is the largest facility in the park and has the newest accommodations with elevator access. Five three-story, stone-and-wood lodge buildings built in 2016 have recycled glass counters and electric car charging stations. Two other lodges, Cascade (no elevator) and Dunraven, were built in the 1990s. Two-bedroom suites have a king room, queen room, and sofa-sleeper in a sitting room. Some rooms have refrigerators. The lobby has wireless internet.

Lake Village

Lake Yellowstone Hotel is a historical experience—not a luxury resort. Built in 1891, ★ **Lake Yellowstone Hotel and Cabins** (mid-May-Sept., $220-590 cabins and rooms, $601-800 suites) is a striking colonial building with tall Ionic columns, a bright yellow exterior, and an entrance facing the lake. A National Historic Landmark, it is the oldest operating hotel in Yellowstone. Amenities include a sunroom, dining room, bar, deli, and internet in the renovated hotel rooms. Behind the hotel, more economical options with no lake views include the basic two-story **Sandpiper Lodge** and the small yellow 1920s duplex cabins. Make dinner reservations when you book lodging, as the dining room packs out with lines.

Across a large meadow from Yellowstone Lake, **Lake Lodge Cabins** (early June-late Sept., $170-270) is a complex of rustic buildings. The single-floor, log lodge has a large porch with old-style cane-and-wood rockers and its classic log-raftered interior houses a lobby with two stonework fireplaces, cafeteria with wireless internet, and a bar. Behind the lodge, 186 heated cabins accessed by paved roads come in three styles, all with private baths. Set in wild grasses and conifers on paved loops, the **Western Cabins** have 4-6 large, modern motel rooms. Built in the 1920s, there are small duplex **Frontier Cabins** and the tiny **Pioneer Cabins.** Take a flashlight for walking after dark to and from the lodge.

Grant Village

Located at Grant Village at the southern end of West Thumb on Yellowstone Lake, **Grant Village Lodge** (late May-Sept., $295) is a collection of six buildings with hotel rooms. Built in 1984, each two-story building contains 50 rooms that come in two styles with private baths and wireless internet. Premium rooms have a refrigerator; standard rooms do not. Lodgepoles have grown up around the buildings, cutting off lake views. The complex includes two restaurants, a bar, and Yellowstone General Stores. A short walk drops to the beach and mostly empty marina, or to the restaurants, the visitors center, the lake, and the outdoor amphitheater for evening ranger talks.

⬥ Side Trip: More Volcanic Wonders

If volcanoes are your thing, you'll enjoy these three locales that are part of the volcanic activity connected with the Yellowstone supervolcano. Access them from West Yellowstone.

Quake Lake

In 1959, the Hebgen Lake Earthquake shook Yellowstone strong enough to cause a mountain to landslide which dammed up the Madison River to form Quake Lake. It also killed 28 people. The site is about 25 miles (40 km) northwest of West Yellowstone via US 287, a half-hour drive.

Learn about the event at **Earthquake Lake Visitor Center** (US 287, 206/682-7620, http://fs.usda.gov, 10am-6pm daily late May-mid-Sept., free), part of the Custer Gallatin National Forest. Walk the outdoor path to Memorial Boulder for views of the rubble.

Drive along **Quake Lake** to see the interpretive sites, flooded tree trunks, and the landslide at the north end.

Island Park

On US 20, about 30 miles (48 km; 30-min. drive) southwest of West Yellowstone in Idaho, the **Island Park caldera** is what's left from a volcanic eruption 2.1 million years ago. The huge caldera sits partly inside Yellowstone. The smaller **Henrys Fork caldera** formed inside the Island Park caldera 1.3 million years ago; the two share a western rim. The residual heat produces warm springs that make for a rich habitat for wildlife and aquatic animals.

Highlights include roaring **Mesa Falls,** a wide plunge on the Henrys Fork River, and **Big Springs,** an idyllic natural pool that stays 52°F (11°C) year-round. The historic **Mesa Falls Visitor Center** (Upper Mesa Falls Rd., ranger district 208/558-7301, http://fs.usda.gov,

Campgrounds

Campground amenities include potable water, picnic tables, accessible campsites, bear boxes for food storage, fire rings with grills, and flush or vault toilets, but no showers at most. Many of these campgrounds have smaller sites; visitors with larger RVs should go for the reservation campgrounds. In summer, first-come, first-served campgrounds can fill before 8am. Once you get a campsite, it's best to make that your base camp and drive to various park locations from there rather than trying to find a new campsite every few days.

Of the 12 campgrounds in Yellowstone, the largest five accept **reservations** (Xanterra, 307/344-7311, www.yellowstonenationalparklodges.com, $27-32 except Fishing Bridge) **12-18 months** in advance:

• **Madison** (278 sites, May-mid-Oct.) located at Madison Junction. The campground is frequented by bison and elk.

• **Canyon** (270 sites, late May-mid-Sept., showers) in Canyon Village. Sites are tucked around tight loops on the forested hillside above Canyon Village.

• **Fishing Bridge RV Park** (310 sites, early May- Sept., full hookups and showers, $80) in Fishing Bridge. Hard-sided units are required; tents and pop-up tent trailers are not allowed. Yellowstone Lake is nearby plus the Fishing Bridge store.

• **Bridge Bay** (432 sites, late May-early Sept.) near Lake Village. Some sites have views of Yellowstone Lake. Boat rentals are nearby.

• **Grant Village** (430 sites, mid-June-mid-Sept.) on the West Thumb of Lake Yellowstone. Grant Village is nearby.

Three other campgrounds in the park's north section allow reservations

9:30am-5:30pm daily summer, $5/vehicle), part of the Caribou-Targhee National Forest, has exhibits on history, geology, plants, and wildlife.

Float the **Warm River** on a tube at **Warm River Campground** (Warm River Rd., off the Mesa Falls Scenic Byway) or wet a line fly-fishing on the Henrys Fork in **Harriman State Park** (3489 Green Canyon Rd., Island Park, 208/558-7368, http://parksandrecreation.idaho.gov, year-round, $5/vehicle).

Stay at one of 11 **campgrounds** (877/444-6777, www.recreation.gov, late May-Sept., $13-35). Several campgrounds have electrical hookups and accept reservations.

Craters of the Moon

Craters of the Moon National Monument and Preserve (Arco, ID, 208/527-1335, www.nps.gov/crmo, $10 per car), located 100 miles (305 km) and three hours southwest of West Yellowstone, contains 25 cones and 60 lava flows from eight major volcanic eruptions. These created a rough, blackened landscape. Tour the **visitors center** (1266 Craters Loop Rd., 208/527-1335, 9am-6pm daily May-Nov., 9am-4:30pm daily Dec.-Apr.), then hike trails that tour the moon-like landscape.

The 3.5-mile (5.6-km) **North Crater Flow Trail** departs from the campground to cross one of the youngest lava flows and climb through the crater. You can explore caves formed in the lava, including the 800-foot-long (244-m) **Indian Tunnel** (free permit required, pick up from visitors center).

For a scenic drive or bicycle ride, the paved 7-mile (11-km) **Loop Road** tours the lava field. Interpretive overlooks allow you to see volcanic features.

At **Lava Flow Campground** (May-Nov., $8-15, no reservations), mounds of hardened black lava separate sites for tents and RVs into private nooks.

(877/444-6777, www.recreation.gov) six months in advance: **Mammoth** (85 sites, year-round, reservations May-mid-Oct., $25), **Slough Creek** (23 sites, mid-June-early Oct., $20), and **Pebble Creek** (27 sites, mid-June-late Sept., $20).

Campers without reservations should head to the park's **first-come, first-served campgrounds** ($15-20): **Indian Creek** (70 sites, mid-June-mid-Sept.), **Norris** (100 sites, late May-late Sept.), **Tower Fall** (31 sites, late May-late Sept.), and **Lewis Lake** (85 sites, mid-June-early Nov.) in the early morning to try and nab a spot.

Outside the Park
Gardiner
Lodges and Motels
Most of Gardiner's lodging properties, including several national chain motels, rim the highway through town on the north side of the bridge crossing the Yellowstone River. Rates are highest June-September. Make reservations **6-12 months** in advance.

Yellowstone Gateway Inn (103 Bigelow Ln., 406/848-7100, https://yellowstonegatewayinn.com, year-round, $100-390) has 16 suites with full kitchens, 1-2 bedrooms, a living room, framed wildlife photographs, and access to communal barbecue grills. Each unit sleeps 2-8 people. The master bedroom has a king bed, while the second bedroom has a queen. One or two sofa beds are in the living room. The ground-level suites include a few steps up to the door, and each unit has a tiny outdoor patio with seating; some have views of Electric Peak.

On the Yellowstone River, **Yellowstone Riverside Cottages** (521 Scott St. W., 406/848-7719 or 877/774-2836, www.yellowstoneriversidecottages.com, year-round, $100-400) has a hot tub and a large wooden deck with seating that overlooks the river; a wooden stairway drops to the shoreline. Cottages and balcony suites have full kitchens. Balcony suites are newer. Some of the tiny older cabins have thin walls.

Ten minutes north of Gardiner, **Dreamcatcher Tipi Hotel** (20 Maiden Basin Dr., 406/848-9447 or 844/313-7684, www.dreamcatchertipihotel.com, mid-May-Sept., $320) appeals to those wanting to sleep in a tepee but with modern glamping comforts of high-end furnishings, electric fireplaces, and private bathhouses with heated floors. Nearby in a quiet spot on the river, the **North Yellowstone Lodge and Hostel** (1083 US 89 S., 406/823-9683, www. northyellowstonehostel.com, mid-May-Sept., $49 dorms) has shared dorm rooms with bunk beds and shared bath facilities down the hall, plus a communal kitchen, dining room, living room, and recreation room.

Campgrounds

Gardiner has two RV campgrounds. **Rocky Mountain Campground & Cabins** (14 Jardine Rd., 406/848-7251, www. rockymountainrvpark.com, May-Sept., $80-90) perches on a tightly packed bluff above town, within walking distance to restaurants. **Yellowstone RV Park** (121 US 89 S., 406/848-7496, www. rvparkyellowstone.com, May-Oct., $69-76 hookups, $40 tents) overlooks the Yellowstone River from grassy sites between the river and highway.

Near Gardiner, **Custer Gallatin National Forest** (Gardiner Ranger District, 805 Scott St., 406/848-7375, www.fs.usda.gov, first-come first-served, year-round, $7 for one vehicle, $3 each additional vehicle) operates two campgrounds without drinking water, so bring your own. Closest to town on Jardine Road, **Eagle Creek Campground** (16 sites) has commanding views across the valley into Yellowstone. About 20 minutes north of Gardiner on US 89, **Canyon Campground** (17 sites) separates some campsites between huge boulders and

junipers, making them best for tents and small RVs. Watch for rattlesnakes.

West Yellowstone
Motels and Lodges

West Yellowstone sees huge crowds in summer, so make reservations **6-12 months** in advance. Summer sees the highest prices, with rates $100-200 higher than winter, spring, and fall.

Built in 1912, the **Madison Hotel Motel and Hostel** (139 Yellowstone Ave., 406/646-7745 or 800/838-7745, www. madisonhotelmotel.com, mid-May-early Oct., $67 dorms) has small, gender-separated second-floor dorm rooms with single beds and shared bathroom-shower facilities down the hall.

West Yellowstone abounds with relic motels from the 1950s or earlier. These are the places where you can get less expensive lodging. The **Alpine Motel** (120 Madison Ave., 406/646-7544, www. alpinemotelwestyellowstone.com, mid-May-mid-Oct., $81-208) has small rooms with small bathrooms and thin walls but is super clean.

Perfect for large families or small groups, **Faithful Street Inn** (120 N. Faithful St., 406/646-1010, www. faithfulstreetinn.com, $150-750) has nine cabins, townhomes, and houses with 2-8 bedrooms and full kitchens.

DNC Parks and Resorts (877/600-4308, www.visityellowstonepark.com) runs several properties, with seasonal packages that bundle up activities in Yellowstone with their lodging. Two of their hotels come with pools and hot tubs: **Gray Wolf Inn and Suites** (250 S. Canyon St., mid-Dec.-mid-Mar., mid-Apr.-early Nov., $99-539), which has family suites with kitchens, and the **Yellowstone Park Hotel** (201 Grizzly Ave., May-mid-Oct. $211-571) that has boutique-style rooms, some with whirlpool tubs and fireplaces. Their **Explorer Cabins at Yellowstone** (250 S. Canyon St., year-round, $175-700) has 50 modern cabins with kitchenettes, and community fire pits provide places to roast the s'mores supplied at check-in.

The **Kelly Inn** (104 S. Canyon St., 800/2594672, www.yellowstonekellyinn. com, year-round, $110-330) has carved bears climbing up outside railings to stare in windows. Large rooms have king or queen beds; the new Grizzly building includes rooms with queen beds and singles or bunks to accommodate families with kids. The inn has a free continental breakfast, indoor pool, hot tub, sauna, outdoor patio with gas fire pit, laundry, pet walk, and play areas.

Outside of town, the **Bar N Ranch** (890 Buttermilk Creek Rd., 406/646-0300, www.bar-n-ranch.com, mid-May-mid-Oct., mid-Dec.-early Mar., $170-700) has high-end accommodations in the large main log lodge or in cabins. On-site amenities include an outdoor heated pool, hot tub, and restaurant.

Campgrounds

In West Yellowstone, the large **Yellowstone Grizzly RV Park** (210 S. Electric St., 406/646-4466, www. grizzlyrv.com, May-mid-Oct., RVs $56-110) has landscaped gardens and lawns with aspens and lodgepole pines providing partial shade. Sites are roomy enough for slide-outs and awnings. The smaller **Buffalo Crossing RV Park** (101B S. Canyon St., 406/646-4300, www.buffalocrossingrvpark.com, June-late Aug., $50-75) is tucked behind the Yellowstone Giant Screen Theater in a large gravel parking lot. Railroad ties divide the sites from each other.

About 10 minutes outside West Yellowstone are two large adjacent **KOA campgrounds** (800/562-7591 reservations, https://koa.com, mid-May-Sept., RVs $50-110, tents $40-70) set in shady pine forests and around sunny mowed lawns. **Yellowstone Park West Gate KOA** (3305 Targhee Pass Hwy., 406/646-7606) has an indoor pool and hot tub. **Yellowstone Park Mountainside KOA**

(1545 Targhee Pass Hwy., 406/646-7662) has fewer amenities.

In a broad field on the Bar N Ranch, **Yellowstone Under Canvas** (890 Buttermilk Creek Rd., 888/496-1148, www.mtundercanvas.com, late May-early Sept., $230-1,175) has luxury camping in safari and cabin-style canvas tents and suites. These luxury tents include beds, furniture, and heat. Baths with hot water, showers, and flush toilets are in separate private facilities.

Two **Custer-Gallatin National Forest campgrounds** (Hebgen Lake Ranger District, 406/823-6961, www.fs.usda. gov, mid-May-Sept., $20-28, $8 extra vehicle) are near West Yellowstone. Flanking the Madison River, **Baker's Hole Campground** (73 sites, 33 electrical hookups, no reservations) is closest to the park, where the trout-fishing river slows to a crawl in convoluted oxbows through willow wetlands that provide habitat for moose and birds. Further afield under a lodgepole pine forest, **Rainbow Point Campground** (85 sites, 2 loops have electrical hookups; reservations 877/444-6777, www.recreation.gov) sits on an east arm of Hebgen Lake with a boat launch, docks, fishing, and swimming.

Cooke City and Silver Gate

Because the towns sit at 7,500 feet (2,286 m) in elevation, the altitude may bother some people, causing labored breathing or fitful sleeping. Make reservations for July-August and winter holidays.

In Cooke City, **High Country Motel and Cabins** (113 W. Main St., Cooke City, 406/838-2272, www. highcountrymotelandcabins.com, year-round, $90-190) has 11 motel rooms and four log cabins. Some rooms have kitchens. The family-run **Elk Horn Lodge** (103 Main St., Cooke City, 406/838-2332, www.elkhornlodgemt.com, year-round, $90-190, 4-night min. in summer) has six large rooms and two cabins with kitchenettes.

◈ Side Trip: Beartooth Highway

Beartooth Highway

The **Beartooth Highway** (68 mi/109 km, www.beartoothhighway.com, late May-mid-Oct.) climbs over Beartooth Pass at 10,947 feet (3,337 m), the most dramatic road to reach Yellowstone. Above tree line, the alpine tundra dominates the terrain. Flanked by deep snowbanks in early summer and wildflowers in late August, the route yields 360-degree views of more than 20 gray granite peaks that top 12,000 feet (3,658 m). The road can close during summer for snowstorms, and afternoon thundershowers are frequent.

In Silver Gate, **Silver Gate Lodging** (109 US 212, Silver Gate, 406/838-2371, silvergatelodging.com, mid-May-Oct., $150-330) is a collection of cabin and motel complexes. Older, spartan cabins lack kitchenettes; others are newer, nicer, and have kitchenettes; all have bathrooms with showers.

Campgrounds
Along US 212, east of Cooke City, **Custer Gallatin National Forest** (Gardiner Ranger District, 406/848-7375, www.fs.usda.gov, $8-9 first vehicle, $3 additional car) has two campgrounds. Due to the prevalence of bears, the campgrounds permit **hard-sided RVs only** (no tents or pop-up tent trailers). The **Soda Butte Campground** (27 sites, July-Sept.) overlooks Soda Butte Creek. Nearby **Colter Campground** (18 sites, mid-July-Sept.) has views of the Absaroka Mountains. Both campgrounds are first come, first served.

Transportation and Services

Emergency Services
Medical conditions can be treated at the **Mammoth Clinic** (Mammoth Village, 307/344-7965, hours vary, open year-round), **Lake Clinic** (307/242-7241, hours vary, open mid-May-mid-Sept.) in Lake Village, and **Old Faithful Clinic** (Old Faithful Ranger Station, 307/545-7325, hours vary, open mid-May-Sept.). In an emergency, call 911 to be directed to the nearest open medical facility.

Outside the park, the nearest hospitals and clinics are **Livingston HealthCare Hospital** (320 Alpenglow Ln., Livingston, MT, 406/222-3541, www.livingstonhealthcare.org), **Livingston HealthCare Urgent Care** (104 Centennial Dr., Ste. 103, Livingston, MT, 406/222-0030), **West Park Hospital**

Red Lodge, Montana, a small town with two-story historic facades in its downtown, serves as the northeast anchor of the highway. From there, the road squeezes through **Rock Creek Canyon** to climb slowly. As the canyon widens, its walls heighten. From a meadow at a cluster of campgrounds, the road switchbacks up to **Rock Creek Vista Point,** an interpretive stop with an overlook that allows you to peer thousands of feet down Rock Creek Canyon and across to high-elevation alpine plateaus.

From there, the highway switchbacks higher onto the **Beartooth Plateau,** skirting the rim with views into the **Absaroka-Beartooth Wilderness.** After crossing from Montana into Wyoming and rounding above **Twin Lakes,** the **Beartooth Basin Summer Ski Area** on the Twin Lakes Headwall appears.

Scenic overlooks en route to **Beartooth Pass** are worthy stops; at the pass, you can spot the **Beartooth Peak** looking like a narrow cuspid. From the pass, the road descends through alpine meadows and bogs to pass **Island Lake** and **Beartooth Lakes.** Between them sits **Top of the World** (2823 US 212, 307/587-5368, www.topoftheworldresort.com, 8am-7pm Mon.-Sat., 8am-6pm Sun. late May-mid-Oct., shorter hours in early and late season), a funky little seasonal store.

A dirt spur road goes to **Clay Butte Lookout** (Shoshone National Forest Rd. 142, open when staffed by volunteers, 10am-5pm Wed.-Sun. mid-July-early Sept.). Built in 1942 by the Civilian Conservation Corps, the lookout has interpretive information on the history of firefighting, the 1988 fires, geology, Beartooth Plateau wildlife, and local flora.

After dropping down via a couple switchbacks, the highway reaches the **Clarks Fork of the Yellowstone** and climbs again to **Cooke City** and the **Northeast Entrance** to Yellowstone, the route's southwestern terminus. Allow about four hours to do this drive with sightseeing stops. It's about two hours with no stops.

(707 Sheridan Ave., Cody, WY, 307/527-7501, www.westparkhospital.org), **West Yellowstone Clinic** (11 Electric St., 406/646-9441, chphealthmt.org), **Bozeman Deaconess Hospital** (915 Highland Blvd., Bozeman, MT, 406/414-5000, www.bozemandeaconess.org), and **St. John's Medical Center** (625 E. Broadway, Jackson, WY, 307/733-3636, www.stjohns.health).

Gas and Vehicle Charging Stations

Find gas at Mammoth Hot Springs, Tower Junction, Canyon Village, Fishing Bridge, Grant Village, and Old Faithful. For major repairs, head to West Yellowstone or Gardiner.

Electric vehicle charging stations are at Mammoth Hot Springs, Canyon Village, Old Faithful, and Fishing Bridge. Outside the park, charging stations are in Gardiner and West Yellowstone.

Cell Service and Internet Access

Cell service is available in Mammoth Hot Springs, Old Faithful, Lake Village, Fishing Bridge, Grant Village, and Canyon Village. Otherwise, it is not available in most places in Yellowstone. Most of the park lodges have internet available for guests. Visitors centers do not have public internet.

Visitor Information

The **Gardiner Chamber of Commerce** (216 Park St., Gardiner, 406/848-7971, www.visitgardinermt.com) maintains an information center. Get information on Gardiner, Custer Gallatin National Forest, and Absaroka-Beartooth Wilderness, as well as recreation, lodging, and dining. The **Custer Gallatin National Forest** (805 Scott St., Gardiner, 406/848-7375, www.fs.usda.gov) has a district office in Gardiner with maps and forest, camping, and trail information.

The **West Yellowstone Visitor Information Center** (30 Yellowstone Ave., West Yellowstone, 307/344-7381, www.nps.gov/yell, 8am-8pm daily May-Sept., 8am-4pm Mon.-Fri. mid-Dec.-late Apr.) is located in West Yellowstone (outside the park) at the corner of Canyon Street and the park entrance road. Inside the building is the **West Yellowstone Chamber of Commerce** (406/646-7701, www.destinationyellowstone.com) and a National Park Service desk. In addition to information, the park service desk issues **backcountry permits** (8am-4:30pm daily June-Aug.). Restrooms are also available.

The **Cooke City Chamber of Commerce** (206 W. Main St., Cooke City, 406/838-2495, www.cookecitychamber.org) runs a tiny visitors center with current conditions on the Beartooth Highway, local outfitters and guides, and information on the Custer Gallatin and Shoshone National Forests. It also has Wi-Fi for visitors.

Tours

Yellowstone Forever Institute (406/848-2400, www.yellowstone.org) offers expert-led educational tours year-round. Naturalist guides take you to various locations aboard buses to watch wildlife. While some programs are high energy, others are more like tours. Private tours, one-day, and multiday programs are available with varied locations and rates. Multi-day programs are based out of park hotels, Lamar Buffalo Ranch Field Campus, or the Yellowstone Overlook Field Campus in Gardiner.

For a taste of early western travel, take a **stagecoach tour** with the **Stagecoach Adventure** (Xanterra, 307/344-7311, www.yellowstonenationalparklodges. com, daily June-early Sept., $16 adults, $9 children 3-11). From the Roosevelt Corrals, the half-hour ride in a replica stagecoach gives a glimpse into the park's history, and authenticity comes from the dust. The brave can ride up top.

Bus Tours

Departing from most of the park lodges, **Xanterra tours** (307/344-7311, www. yellowstonenationalparklodges.com, May-Sept., $61-135) offer options that include circling Yellowstone in a day, visiting geyser basins, touring at sunset, wildlife-watching, and photo safaris.

Departing from Gardiner, **Yellowstone Vacations** (905 Scott St. W., Gardiner, 406/848-5171, www. yellowstonevacations.com, 8am-5pm daily) guides full-day bus tours to Lamar Valley year-round and Lower Grand Loop Road or Upper Grand Loop Road late May-early November. In winter, snowcoach trips go to Old Faithful or Grand Canyon of the Yellowstone.

From West Yellowstone, several companies run **sightseeing tours** (from $75). Interpretive guides drive buses or vans, stopping for geyser basins, scenery, and wildlife. From May-early November, most tours circle Lower Grand Loop Road to take in Old Faithful, Yellowstone Lake, Grand Canyon of the Yellowstone, wildlife, and several geyser basins. Upper Grand Loop tours go to Mammoth Hot Springs, Tower Fall, Dunraven Pass, and Grand Canyon of the Yellowstone. In winter, **snowcoach tours** ($135-170) go to Old Faithful or Grand Canyon of the Yellowstone. Most tours are full day.

- **Yellowstone Vacation Tours** (415 Yellowstone Ave., West Yellowstone, 800/426-7669, www. yellowstonevacations.com) guides full-day tours in yellow mini- or big buses, both with large windows. Tours circle Lower Grand Loop Road and Upper Grand Loop Road. In winter, 30-passenger sightseeing coaches with big windows go to Old Faithful and Grand Canyon of the Yellowstone.

- **See Yellowstone Tours** (211 Yellowstone Ave., West Yellowstone,

800/221-1151, www.seeyellowstone. com) drives sightseeing vans with large windows on morning, evening, or full-day tours around the Lower Grand Loop and Upper Grand Loop. Picnic lunches are included. Winter snowcoaches are oversized vans with large windows that go to Old Faithful and Grand Canyon of the Yellowstone.

Boat Tours

To get out on Yellowstone Lake, take the **Yellowstone Lake Scenic Cruise** (1 hr, departs 5-7 times daily mid-June-early Sept., $20 adults, $12 children). From Bridge Bay Marina, the *Lake Queen* circles Stevenson Island, home to osprey, eagles, ducks, herons, and other shorebirds. The interpretive tour fills you in on the lake's history, geology, and natural history while the enclosed boat shelters passengers from strong afternoon lake winds. Reservations are highly recommended midsummer. Plan to arrive at the marina 15 minutes prior to launch.

★ Winter Snowcoach Tours

From mid-December through early March, visitors can tour the snow-buried roads of Yellowstone in heated snowcoaches, which are converted vans or buses with huge tires or tracks. Snowcoach tours **require reservations;** book tours **6-9 months** in advance or at the same time you make your lodging reservations. Rates for trips do not include entrance fees into the park, lunch, or tips for drivers (15 percent).

From Mammoth Hot Springs Hotel, **Xanterra** (307/344-7311, www.yellowstone nationalparklodges.com) operates snowcoach tours ($60-280) that go to Norris Geyser Basin or Old Faithful. For lodgers at Old Faithful, shorter daily tours (2-4.5 hours) go wildlife-watching, evening sightseeing, and geyser exploring; full-day tours visit Grand Canyon of the Yellowstone or go on a photo safari.

Backcountry Adventures (224 N. Electric St., West Yellowstone, 406/646-9317 or 800/924-7669, www. backcountry-adventures.com) guides winter snowcoach tours to Old Faithful or Grand Canyon of the Yellowstone.

Getting Around

Driving around the park is easy, but you must have your own vehicle; no shuttles are available. RVs can easily get around the park roads, although some are narrow with no shoulders. With the exception of the northern road, which is open year-round, all of the park roads open for the summer between mid-April and late May, then close in early November. In winter (early Nov.-mid-Apr.), the park roads are closed to private vehicles; snowcoaches and snowmobiles are the only way to access most of the park.

Parking lots pack out from June to September, usually from 9am to 5pm each day. Plan to see sights outside of these times to avoid parking hassles and traffic. Always park in designated areas, never on roadside grass or meadows. Find RV parking at Old Faithful, Norris Geyser Basin, Canyon Village, and Mammoth Hot Springs. Many lots at the smaller geyser basins do not allow trailers or RVs.

Grand Teton and Jackson Hole

Highlights

★ **Get hands-on at the Laurance S. Rockefeller Preserve Center:** Enjoy sensory-based exhibits at this **visitors center** (page 434), then venture outside to hike to **Phelps Lake** (page 444).

★ **Cruise or paddle Jackson Lake:** Experience the largest lake in the park by boat tour (page 435) or paddle its islands from Colter Bay (page 450).

★ **Tour Jackson Lake Lodge:** This National Historic Landmark commands a prime spot to take in the full view of the Tetons (page 436).

★ **Gaze at Grand Teton:** The Grand tops all other peaks in the Tetons. Climb it (page 446), hike below it at **Bradley Lake** (page 442), or just admire it from Teton Park Road (page 436).

★ **Enjoy Jenny Lake:** Circle this placid gem at the base of the Tetons via a shoreline trail (page 436).

★ **Take a Scenic Drive:** The **Teton Park Road** curls right under the mountains, offering chances to see the alpine peaks and the glaciers that perch upon them (page 438).

★ **Hike to Hidden Falls and Inspiration Point:** Boat across Jenny Lake to hike to a waterfall and a rocky viewpoint (page 444).

★ **Go Backpacking on Teton Crest Trail:** This high-elevation trek is one of the best in the Rockies (page 445).

★ **Bike the Multi-Use Pathway:** Enjoy the thrill of riding right under the Tetons (page 447).

The jagged peaks of Grand Teton National Park dominate the scenery, commanding attention from almost every location in the park. They rise, a series of teeth that culminate in the Grand Teton, luring mountain climbers, hikers, photographers, and artists.

Visitors have two options for experiencing the Tetons: See them from the floor of Jackson Hole or hike into the mountains. Hiking up glacier-carved canyons into the Tetons requires stamina, and for backpackers, the Teton Crest Trail is peppered with high passes and giant rock-slab ledges that lead up vertical spires. But at much lower elevations, where the valley meets the mountains, easy trails lead to idyllic lakes that filled in behind glacial moraines. You can drive to Jenny Lake, the most scenic. Some lakes you can reach by paddle.

For sightseers, scenic drives and boat tours get you a different view of the awe-inspiring peaks. Bicyclists can also take a leisurely pedal on a paved pathway to enjoy gazing up at the Tetons.

Across Jackson Hole, the Snake River cuts through sagebrush meadows, a perfect spot for families to relax on rubber rafts and for anglers to fly-fish for trout. The river is also home to abundant wildlife: It lures moose, eagles, otters, and pelicans to its winding convolutions, while the meadows are home to bison, pronghorn, and elk. Grizzly and black bears visit both habitats.

This is a place where every experience will leave an indelible memory. Grant Teton is a true bucket-list park.

Planning Your Time

For all its high peaks, **Grand Teton National Park** (307/739-3399, www.nps.gov/grte) is actually a small park, easy to see in **one day.** From Yellowstone, you can drive south to Jackson Lake Junction and then continue down Teton Park Road to Moose to see the big sights. Hikers will want **3-4 days** to explore several of the park's trails. Before arriving, check online or on the NPS app for park updates and information on road construction, conditions, permit requirements and availability, and closures.

In **summer,** all visitors centers, campgrounds, lodges, marinas, and services are open. **July** and **August** see the biggest crowds in Grand Teton. Parking gets tight, campers must claim sites early, boat tours book out, and low-elevation trails crowd with hikers. But as you climb up canyons into the mountains, the number of hikers thins.

Spring and **fall** offer quieter times to visit, but not all in-park services are open. While US 26/89/191 is open **year-round** from Jackson to Flagg Ranch, most of the other roads open in **May.** Spring brings the chance to see bison and pronghorn newborns, and during fall, the air fills with the sound of elk bugling.

Most in-park facilities are **closed November-April.** Lower-elevation trails are snow-free by late May. Higher-elevation trails may not melt out until mid-July and can see snow again in September. **Jackson Lake** is at its best in summer, with the ice melting out early May-early June. By August, lake levels drop, making beaches bigger and water temperatures less frigid. **June** is the park's wettest month; **July** is the driest.

Grand Teton National Park

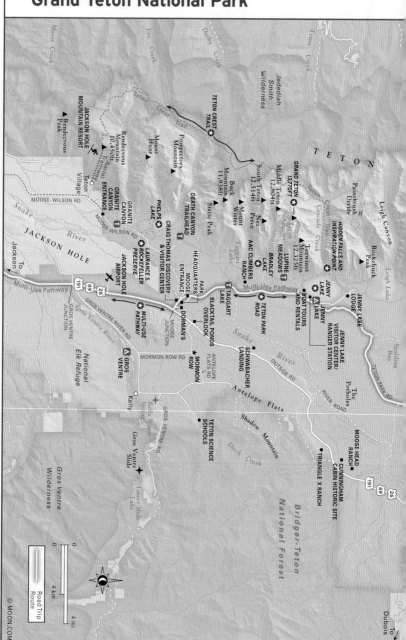

© MOON.COM

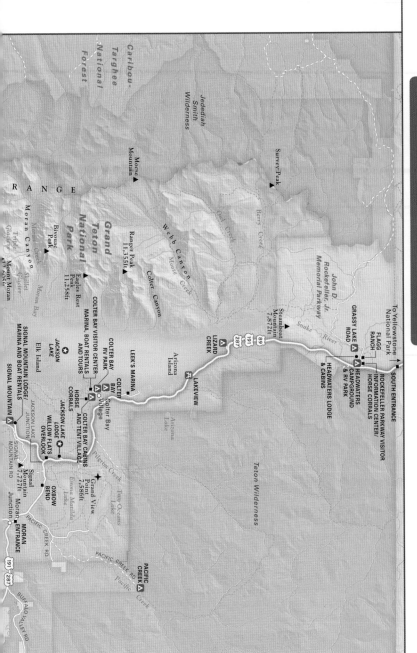

One Day in Grand Teton

Morning
Take an early morning drive on the Moose-Wilson Road to **Laurance S. Rockefeller Preserve Center.** Hike to **Phelps Lake** and tour the **visitors center.**

Afternoon
Drive to Moose for lunch at **Dornan's,** where you can dine outside with views of the Tetons. Afterwards, drive north on **Teton Park Road,** stopping at **Teton Glacier Turnout** for a view of **Grand Teton.**

Stop at **Jenny Lake** to walk to the overlooks at the lake. Head to the **Mount Moran Turnout** to view the black dike and glaciers. Continue north, driving up **Signal Mountain** to take in the huge view of the park, including the peaks and **Jackson Lake.** After turning north at Jackson Lake Junction, pull into **Willow Flats Overlook** to scan the meadows for elk.

Evening
At **Jackson Lake Lodge,** take in the views outside. Celebrate your day by dining in the **Mural Room** with panoramic vistas. At dusk, drive to **Oxbow Bend** for evening wildlife-watching and to see the sun set behind **Mount Moran** before returning to Jackson Lake Lodge for the night.

No public shuttles are available. You will need a vehicle to see the park. Grand Teton National Park consists of two-lane roads. Speed limits vary 25-55 mph (40-90 kph), with nighttime speed limits dropping to 45 mph (70 kph) in order to protect wildlife. US 26/89/191/287 has been the "local speedway," often making the road a wildlife slaughterhouse. Wildlife crossing areas are rarely signed, and lighting at dusk and dawn makes spotting animals more difficult. Drive slowly at night.

Seasonal Driving Concerns
From November through April, **Teton Park Road** closes from Signal Mountain Lodge to Taggart Lake Trailhead (but that section is groomed for cross-country skiing and snowshoeing). The **Moose-Wilson Road** also closes November-May. In winter, even plowed roads may close temporarily for heavy snow. Snow tires are recommended in winter; chains are a good idea, too.

Best Route Through the Park
The best route through the park makes a loop, combining **Teton Park Road** with **US 26/89/191.** Also called Inside Road, Teton Park Road yields up-close views of the Teton Mountains. The highway, also known as the Outside Road, allows for broader views of the entire range.

Reservations and Where to Stay
Four of the park lodges take reservations 366 days in advance with **Grand Teton Lodging Company** (307/543-3100, www.gtlc.com). Independent lodges take reservations **12-16 months** in advance. All campgrounds, including two that have RV hookups, take reservations six months ahead through **Recreation.gov** (877/444-6777, www.recreation.gov).

Additional lodging is nearby at **Teton Village,** a mile outside the Granite Canyon Entrance, and **Jackson,** which is 13 miles (21 km) south of the visitors center at Moose.

Getting There

Car
From Yellowstone National Park
It's just an 8-mile (13-km) drive to Grand Teton from the **South Entrance of Yellowstone.** Exit Yellowstone via the South Entrance Road and enter John D. Rockefeller Jr. Memorial Parkway. You'll know you're in Grand Teton when you reach the entrance sign (no entrance station).

From Salt Lake City
The fastest route from **Salt Lake City** to Grand Teton is 290 miles (465 km) and takes five hours. Head north on I-15 to exit at Brigham City. Then follow US 89 north to Alpine Junction. Turn right onto US 26/89 to Hoback Junction to continue north on US 26/89/189/191 to Jackson, Wyoming. Turn north on US 26/89/189/191 to reach the park.

From Denver and Rocky Mountain National Park
The drive from **Grand Lake,** Colorado, on the east side of Rocky Mountain National Park, to Grand Teton is 465 miles (750 km) and takes eight hours. Go south on US 34 to Granby and northwest on US 40. Go north on CO 125 through Walden and into Wyoming, where the highway becomes WY 230 to Riverside and continues north as WY 130 through Saratoga. Continue to I-80, then head west to Rock Springs. From Rock Springs, take US 191 north to Pinedale. After Pinedale, US 191 becomes US 189/191. At Hoback Junction, turn north on US 26/89/189/191 to reach Jackson. Turn north on US 26/89/189/191 to reach the park.

The drive to Grand Teton from **Denver** is 510 miles (820 km) and takes 8.5 hours. Head north on I-25. Take Exit 296B onto CO 14, heading westward to Fort Collins, to connect with US 287 north to Laramie. At Laramie, go west on I-80 to Rock Springs. Then take US 191 north to Pinedale. US 191 then becomes US 189/191. At Hoback Junction, turn north on US 26/89/189/191 to reach Jackson. Turn north on US 26/89/189/191 to reach the park.

Air
Jackson Hole Airport (JAC, 1250 E. Airport Rd, Jackson, 307/733-7682, www.jacksonholeairport.com) is actually inside Grand Teton National Park, just north of Jackson. Major cities across the country have direct flights to Jackson Hole, but some flights run seasonally in winter or summer. Flights to Jackson Hole are usually more expensive than to other area airports.

A two-hour drive west of Grand Teton National Park, **Idaho Falls Regional Airport** (IDA, 2140 N. Skyline Dr., Idaho Falls, ID, 208/612-8221, www.idahofallsidaho.gov) often has cheaper flights than flying into Jackson Hole. Some flights are daily, while others are weekly or summer only.

Bus and Shuttle
Mountain States Express (307/733-4629, www.mountainstatesexpress.com) runs daily shuttles to and from the airport in Salt Lake City, Utah, to Jackson. (Visitors will then need a car or bike or to join a tour to get to the park.) **Salt Lake Express** (877/714-6104, www.saltlakeexpress.com) shuttles go between Salt Lake City Airport or Idaho Falls Airport and Jackson.

Visiting the Park

Entrances and Fees
Entrance into Grand Teton National Park costs **$35** per vehicle ($30 motorcycles, $20 pedestrians and cyclists) for seven days. An **annual pass** to the park costs $70.

The **north entrance** to Grand Teton National Park has no pay station. A portion of the park along US 26/89/191/287 also has no entrance stations. Three entrance stations are open year-round:

- **Moran Entrance** is west of Moran Junction on US 26/89/191/287, 30 miles (48 km) north of Jackson.

- **Moose Entrance** is on Teton Park Road on the west side of the Snake River and Moose. It's 14 miles (23 km) north of Jackson.

- **Granite Canyon Entrance** is north of Teton Village on the Moose-Wilson Road. In winter, the road is only open for cars for about a half-mile beyond the entrance station for ski and snowshoe trailhead access. No RVs or trailers are permitted on the Moose-Wilson Road and therefore not permitted through this entrance station.

Visitors Centers

All visitors centers have information on trail and road conditions, maps, weather, Junior Ranger Programs, and ranger-led walks and talks. Visitors centers also have **Grand Teton Association stores** (307/739-3606, www.grandtetonassociation.org) that sell maps and books on wildlife, wildflowers, hiking, history, geology, and natural history.

Rockefeller Parkway Visitor Information Center

At Flagg Ranch on John D. Rockefeller, Jr. Memorial Parkway, **Rockefeller Parkway Visitor Information Center** (Grassy Lake Rd., 307/739-3399, 9am-4pm daily early June-early Sept.) is a one-room log cabin with a small exhibit on John D. Rockefeller, Jr., who donated the land for the parkway.

Colter Bay Visitor Center

In Colter Bay Village at the marina, the **Colter Bay Visitor Center** (307/739-3399, 8am-7pm daily early June-early Sept., 8am-5pm daily early May-early June and early Sept.-early Oct.) has boating and backcountry permits. An auditorium shows documentaries on the park.

You can participate in interpretive programs, see craft demonstrations, and go on tours of the tiny **Indian Arts Museum,** which features intricate beadwork, clothing, jewelry, tools, and weapons.

Jenny Lake Visitor Center

The small **Jenny Lake Visitor Center** (307/739-3399, 8am-7pm daily mid-May-late Sept., shorter hours spring and fall) is at South Jenny Lake. The center has a relief map of the park and a few geology exhibits. Also in the complex is the **Jenny Lake Ranger Station** (307/739-3343, 8am-5pm daily early June-early Sept.), which is where to get backcountry camping and boating permits, and information on mountain climbing routes and conditions.

Craig Thomas Discovery & Visitor Center

The **Craig Thomas Discovery & Visitor Center** (307/739-3399, 8am-7pm daily Apr.-Oct., shorter hours spring and fall), sometimes called the Moose Visitor Center, has large windows that take in the Teton Mountains. It has exhibits on the natural history of the park and mountaineering, large bronze wildlife sculptures, a climbing wall, kid-friendly exhibits, and a topographic map that shows wildlife migration and glacier progression. The theater here shows a documentary on the park, and Native Americans crafts are displayed on select days. The information desk has permits for backcountry camping and boating.

★ Laurance S. Rockefeller Preserve Center

The **Laurance S. Rockefeller Preserve Center** (307/739-3399, 9am-5pm daily early June-late Sept.) is on a large preserve that was once a ranch owned by the Rockefeller family. This visitors center contains visual, tactile, and auditory exhibits that appeal to the senses. Watch high-definition nature videos, view an ultra-large Phelps Lake mosaic photograph made from tiny nature photos, and listen to natural soundscapes. Rangers lead daily talks and hikes. Kids can check out a backpack and journal to use while hiking the preserve's trails. The parking lot is limited to 50 cars and is usually full 10am-4pm; plan your visit early in the morning or late in the afternoon and add time for stops on the Moose-Wilson Road (no RVs or trailers).

Sights

Jackson Lake Area
★ **Jackson Lake**

Jackson Lake is huge. It's fed by the Snake River in the north and lake water exits its southwest side via the Jackson Lake Dam into the Snake River. The dam has deepened the lake from its natural glacial origins. Fifteen islands inhabit the lake, including **Elk Island,** the largest. Overlooks at the head of the lake, Signal Mountain, and Jackson Lake Dam offer good viewpoints.

From the Colter Bay Marina, catch a **Jackson Lake boat tour** (307/543-2811, www.gtlc.com, daily late May-late Sept., $40-72 adults, $20-44 kids) to get out on the water and soak up the lustrous views of Mount Moran. Cruises (90 min., 10:15am, 1:15pm, and 3:15pm daily) motor out through the islands on Jackson Lake. June through early September, cruises also go to Elk Island for breakfast, lunch, or dinner around a campfire. Reservations are required.

You can explore the lake on a cruise and paddle its islands. **Three marinas** offer boat launch sites; two rent boats. Kayaking and canoeing are best in the protected islands surrounding Colter Bay or below Signal Mountain. Short hikes follow the shoreline at Colter Bay, and swimmers can float in the buoy-marked

Top to bottom: Jackson Lake; Grand Teton; tour boat on Jenny Lake

picnic area. Anglers can fish year-round or ice fish in winter.

For lakeview dining, eat at Signal Mountain Lodge or go alfresco at one of several picnic areas. Campers can pitch a tent at **Lizard Creek, Colter Bay,** and **Signal Mountain Campgrounds,** which have multiple beach access points. Boaters and paddlers can find solitude at 15 primitive **backcountry campsites** that rim the lake.

★ Jackson Lake Lodge

With views of Mount Moran and Jackson Lake, **Jackson Lake Lodge** (101 Jackson Lake Lodge Rd., 307/543-3100, www.gtlc. com, mid-May-early Oct.) is a National Historic Landmark. Windows in the Mural Dining Room restaurant frame the Teton Mountains, competing for attention with the *Rendezvous Murals* by Carl Roters, a late-20th-century American artist. John D. Rockefeller Jr. hand-selected the lodge's location on Lunch Tree Hill for its unobstructed mountain views. Commissioned by Rockefeller and built in 1955, the three-story lodge uses the modern international architecture of its era. It houses a small collection of Indigenous artifacts including pottery, baskets, beadwork, weavings, and arrowheads from people of the Northern Rockies.

Teton Park Road
★ Grand Teton

Like the Matterhorn, the **Grand Teton** spirals up into a pinnacle. You can spot its pointy 13,770-foot (4,200-m) summit from almost anywhere in Jackson Hole. Carved by erosion from ice, water, and wind, the spire commands the highest point in the Tetons. A lure for climbers, the Grand Teton serves as a notch in the belts of mountaineers who summit its vertical cliffs. For hikers, the best ways to enjoy the peak are via the **Paintbrush Canyon-Cascade Canyon Loop** or **Bradley Lake.** Photographers can catch the sunrise glow from **Mormon Row,** and **Teton Glacier Turnout** (Teton Park Rd.) offers the closest drive-up viewpoint.

★ Jenny Lake

Created behind a moraine in a glacial depression, **Jenny Lake** is a placid place of beauty. The lake beckons photographers and artists to capture mountain reflections in the morning before afternoon winds crop up. Visitors can lodge or camp and spend days hiking, biking, boating, paddling, fishing, swimming, climbing, backpacking, and wildlife-watching. South Jenny Lake houses a small visitors center, ranger station, store, and campground, and has scenic boat tours.

Jenny Lake Historic District contains a homestead cabin that serves as the ranger station. To enjoy the lake, take the 0.5-mile (0.8-km) paved, wheelchair-accessible **Discovery Trail** from the plaza outside the visitors center. It goes to interpretive stops, three boulder-rimmed overlooks with seating to absorb views, and several stairways to the beach for wading or swimming. The trail also goes to the boat dock for tours, shuttles, and paddling rentals, and links with the Jenny Lake Trail around the lake.

Signal Mountain

Formed in part from ash falling from the Yellowstone supervolcano and a glacier leaving it as moraine, **Signal Mountain** rises alone above the valley of Jackson Hole, resulting in big views. Drive or bike the 5-mile (8-km) paved road (May-Oct.) that leads to the summit. There you'll find two overlooks: **Jackson Point Overlook,** on the south, with majestic Teton Mountain views, and the **summit overlook** at the top. Tiny parking areas don't have room or turnaround space for large RVs and trailers, but you can leave trailers in the parking lot at the base. When driving up, be cautious of bikers zooming down from the top.

Wildlife-Watching in Grand Teton

Wildlife-watching is best around dawn or dusk. But you may also see animals midday. Bring binoculars or spotting scopes to aid in viewing from safe distances. Be cautious when driving roads, as some wildlife use them as travel corridors. For wildlife photography, bring telephoto lenses; do not approach animals to get selfies. Here are some of the best spots in the park to watch for wildlife—and they're not bad settings for photos, either:

moose in Sawmill Ponds

SIGHTS

♦ **Willow Flats Overlook:** On US 89/191/287 between the turnoffs to Jackson Lake Lodge and Teton Park Road is the large Willow Flats Overlook. Often, you can spot elk or moose from here. Morning also lights up Jackson Lake beyond the willow meadows with a backdrop of the Teton Mountains.

♦ **Oxbow Bend:** Slow-moving convolutions of water yield wildlife habitat and outstanding landscapes for photographers. One mile east of Jackson Lake Junction, Oxbow Bend is one of the best places for bird-watching and spotting river otters, beavers, or muskrats in the water, or moose foraging on willows. Squawking and grunting American pelicans add to the cacophony from songbirds, and osprey and bald eagles hunt for fish.

♦ **Schwabachers Landing:** The beaver ponds and slough provide outstanding birding and moose habitat; photographers frequently shoot sunrise reflection photos of the Teton Mountains. The short paved and potholed gravel Schwabacher Road accesses the landing from US 26/89/191 between Glacier View and Teton Point Turnouts.

♦ **Blacktail Ponds Overlook:** Moose often feed in the ponds, and the habitat is good for osprey, waterfowl, and songbirds. Active beavers maintain the dams, which keep the ponds in water. The overlook is 1.3 miles (2 km) north of Moose Junction.

♦ **Antelope Flats:** Drive or bike Antelope Flats Road to see bison, pronghorn, moose, coyote, and raptors such as northern harriers or American kestrels. Elk migrate through in spring and fall. It's also a good area in spring to spot bison and pronghorn newborns.

♦ **Moose-Wilson Road:** Bears sometimes feed on berries along the road, and moose frequent Sawmill Ponds.

Antelope Flats
Mormon Row

In the southeast corner of the park, **Mormon Row** (off Antelope Flats Rd.) is a treat for history buffs, photographers, and wildlife fans. The tract was originally a Mormon ranch settlement that started in the 1890s and grew to 27 homesteads. Today, it retains six clusters of buildings, one ruin, and the famous **Moulton barn** that appears in the foreground of so many photos of the Grand Teton. In morning light, even amateur photographers can capture impressive images. Pick up a self-guided tour brochure near the pink house or use the free audio tour on the NPS app.

Scenic Drives

TOP EXPERIENCE

★ Teton Park Road

From Moose at the south end to Jackson Lake Junction at the north end, **Teton Park Road** (Inside Road, 20 mi/32 km, May-Oct.) gives up-close views of the Teton Mountains. The road **closes in winter** from Signal Mountain Lodge to Taggart Lake Trailhead.

From Moose, start by driving north on Teton Park Road. Just past the Moose Entrance Station, turn right to explore **Menor's Ferry Historic District,** with a self-guided tour (free audio tours on NPS app) of the buildings from the 1890s and the replica ferry. Continuing north, stop at **Teton Glacier Turnout.** While binoculars will get you a closer view, you can still get a good look with your naked eye by staring up at the small glacier and its crevasses, visible by midsummer, perched in a pocket below the north face of **Grand Teton.**

Stop at **South Jenny Lake** to walk from the visitors center to the lake

Top to bottom: Moulton barn on Mormon Row; Mount Moran; Colter Bay Lakeshore Trail

overlooks on the Discovery Trail. To add on a side tour of **Jenny Lake Road** (4 mi/6 km, 15 min., May-Oct.), return to Teton Park Road and turn west at North Jenny Lake. Stop at the **Cathedral Group Turnout** for views of the Grand Teton, Owen, and Teewinot. After String Lake Junction, Jenny Lake Road becomes **one-way** as it passes **Jenny Lake Lodge** and **Jenny Lake Overlook,** where you can nab one more look at the lake and peaks.

Continuing north on Teton Park Road, stop at the **Mount Moran Turnout** to examine the black dike and two small glaciers in its upper cliffs. You can see two tiny glaciers, **Falling Ice** and **Skillet,** plus the narrow sandstone cap on the summit.

You can add on a side trip up **Signal Mountain** by driving up **Signal Mountain Road** (5 mi/8 km, May-Oct.) to Jackson Lake Overlook for spectacular views. After returning to Teton Park Road, continue north across the dam to reach US 89/191/287. Teton Park Road takes about 45 minutes to drive straight through. With stops and side trips, it takes 2.5-3 hours.

Moran Junction to Moose Junction

From Moran Junction to Jackson the north-south **Outside Road** (US 26/89/191, 18 mi/29 km, year-round) has changing views of the Teton Mountains through the eastern portion of the park. Watch for bison, elk, moose, and pronghorn, especially when driving at dusk. (To protect wildlife, speed limits reduce to 45 mph/70 kph sunset-sunrise.) South of Moran Junction, turn right to see the **Cunningham Cabin Historic Site,** an original Jackson Hole homestead built in 1888. The log cabin with a sod roof served as a home, smithy, and barn for the small Cunningham ranch.

Next, stop at **Snake River Overlook** to see the riffles of the 13th largest river in the country and walk along the bluff to snap photos with the Teton backdrop.

The **Snake River** headwaters come from Yellowstone.

Stop at **Teton Point Turnout** for panoramic mountain views and **Blacktail Ponds Overlook** for wildlife-watching. You can also add on a side trip to **Mormon Row** (2 mi/3 km east on Antelope Flats Rd.) just before reaching Moose Junction. You'll need about 40 minutes to do this drive.

Moran Junction to Yellowstone

US 89/191/287 (29 mi/47 km, year-round) runs from Moran Junction to the South Entrance to Yellowstone. This section takes one hour to drive straight through. Stop at **Oxbow Bend Turnout,** a good place for watching birds and wildlife before reaching Jackson Lake Junction. Continue north to **Willow Flats Overlook** for another spot to see elk in the marshy willows before stopping at **Jackson Lake Lodge.** Of the two marinas on this road, **Colter Bay** offers the better sightseeing because of the views from the picnic area.

Continuing north, you'll crest the head of **Jackson Lake,** where a long pullover affords dramatic views southward of the Tetons. Then the road enters the forest and **John D. Rockefeller Jr. Memorial Parkway,** an area that burned in the 2016 Berry Fire. After crossing the **Snake River,** you'll pass **Flagg Ranch** before reaching Yellowstone.

Moose-Wilson Road

Moose-Wilson Road (8 mi/13 km, mid-May-Oct. no vehicles over 23 ft/7 m or trailers) snuggles into prime wildlife habitat along the southern base of the Tetons between the Granite Canyon and Moose Entrance Stations. Spot moose and birds at **Sawmill Ponds Pullout** and visit the **Laurance S. Rockefeller Preserve.**

The skinny, shoulder-less paved and gravel road has bumps, potholes, and curves; it shrinks to one lane in many places and requires slow speeds. On busy days, the road clogs with about 1,000 vehicles. The park has plans to pave it all, add designated pullouts, and change the north entrance location, so expect construction impacts and closures. Go early in the day or late in the evening to avoid crowds. You'll need about half an hour to do this drive.

Inside-Outside Loop

The **Inside and Outside Roads** combine three roads for a loop route totaling 42 miles (68 km), which takes 1.5 hours to drive without stops. **Teton Park Road** (Inside Road) goes from Moose Junction to Jackson Lake Junction, **US 89/191/287** goes from Jackson Lake Junction to Moran Junction, and **US 26/89/191** (Outside Road) goes from Moran Junction to Moose to complete the circle.

Recreation

Hiking

Most lower-elevation trails along the base of the Tetons are snow-free by **late May,** but trails that crest high passes may be buried in snow until **late July,** making ice axes necessary for safe travel on steep inclines. Weather conditions for high-elevation hikes are usually best from mid-July to August, but expect afternoon thundershowers and lightning. In September, snow returns to the high passes.

In summer, **naturalist rangers** guide short hikes (2-3 hrs, daily, free). These hikes are loaded with interpretive stops and are great for families. Check the park newspaper for current offerings and schedules. To buy last minute hiking, backpacking, or climbing necessities, go to **Moosely Mountaineering** (12170 Dornan Rd., Moose, 307/739-1801, www.skinnyskis.com, May-Sept.).

Colter Bay

Colter Bay has a maze of trails with loads of junctions. Find non-topographical maps of the **Colter Bay-Hermitage Point** trails at visitors centers.

Colter Bay Lakeshore Trail

Distance: 2 mile (3 km) loop
Duration: 1.5 hours
Elevation change: 100 feet (30 m)
Effort: easy
Trailhead: Colter Bay Visitor Center

The Colter Bay Lakeshore Trail is a double loop that follows the shoreline of small Colter Bay. Begin on the paved trail that rims the north shore of the **marina** to tour a breakwater spit. After walking the spit, head west on the trail toward a tiny **isthmus** of rocks that connects two parts of the peninsula. Once across the isthmus, go either way to make the loop. Side trails reach beaches that yield views across Jackson Lake to the Teton Mountains. Upon returning to the causeway, follow your original tracks back to the visitors center, or take the other **spur trail** northeast toward the swimming beach and then return to the visitors center on a trail paralleling the road.

Heron Pond and Swan Lake

Distance: 2.6 miles (4.1 km) rt
Duration: 1.5 hours
Elevation change: 200 feet (60 m)
Effort: easy
Trailhead: Swan, Heron, and Hermitage Point

A series of ponds named for birds flanks the hillside east of Colter Bay Village. The ponds have significant growths of yellow pond lilies, leaving little visible water, but they make prime habitat for a variety of wildlife: sandhill cranes, trumpeter swans, osprey, muskrats, river otters, and great blue herons.

The trail starts on an **old service road** that curves around the south edge of Colter Bay. After leaving the bay, climb over a loosely forested hill to **Heron Pond,** where the trail follows the northeastern shore to several ultra-scenic viewpoints of Mount Moran and Rockchuck Peak. At the southeast corner of the pond, turn left at the trail junction to reach **Swan Lake.** After following the shore northward, the trail returns to a junction where going straight will curve around **Jackson Lake Overlook** back to the trailhead.

Jackson Lake Area
Grand View Point
Distance: 2.2 miles (3.5 km) rt
Duration: 2-3 hours
Elevation change: 550 feet (170 m)
Effort: moderate
Trailhead: Grand View Point
Directions: Drive 0.9 mile (1.5 km) north of Jackson Lake Lodge on US 89/191/287. Take the unmarked, rough, narrow dirt road east, veering right at 0.1 mile (160 m) and climbing 0.7 mile (1.1 km) farther to the trailhead.

Grand View Point is an aptly named 7,286-foot (2,221-m) summit with panoramic views of Jackson Lake and the Tetons. The route goes from the Grand View Point parking area to the overlook. From the trailhead, hike up a steep 0.2-mi (0.3-km) connector trail to reach the **Grand View Point Trail.** The trail ascends steeply through meadows and forest. From the signed **Grand View summit,** you overlook Two Ocean and Emma Matilda Lakes. West of the summit, a large rocky bluff takes in the jagged peaks of Mount Moran and the Cathedral Group of Grand Teton, Mount Owen, and Teewinot Mountain.

Two Ocean Lake
Distance: 6.4 miles (10.3 km) rt
Duration: 3 hours
Elevation change: 395 feet (120 m)
Effort: easy
Trailhead: Two Ocean Lake
Directions: Take the paved Pacific Creek Rd. 2 miles (3.2 km) to a junction with Two Ocean Rd. Turn left and drive 2.4 miles (3.9 km) on dirt road to the trailhead.

This flat trail loops around Two Ocean Lake, a trough gouged from the Pacific Creek glacial lobe. The trail travels through forests and meadows, with more open meadows on the north shore

Top to bottom: Grand View Point; Taggart Lake Trail; Amphitheater Lake

and denser forest on the south shore. In June, yellow arrowleaf balsamroot dominates the meadows, while in fall, golden aspens light up the hillside. Distant views of the Tetons line the horizon. The lake is home to trumpeter swans, waterfowl, and moose. Bears enjoy cow parsnip in early summer and patches of huckleberries and thimbleberries in midsummer.

From the trailhead, start on the **north-shore trail** for the bigger views first. The meadow-lined trail goes 3.4 miles (5.5 km) with a short climb and descent to a **junction** at the head of the lake. From the junction, a steep trail grunts up to **Grand View Point.** If you tack on the point up and back, it will add 2.2 miles (3.5 km) to your total. To continue around the lake from the junction, turn left to return 3 miles (4.8 km) along the forested south side to the trailhead.

Many hikers opt to combine Two Ocean Lake with **Emma Matilda Lake** and **Grand View Point.** The distance ranges 9.3-13.2 miles (15-21.3 km), depending on the routes chosen around the lakes.

Emma Matilda Lake
Distance: 9.9-10.7 miles (15.9-17.2 km) rt
Duration: 5-6 hours
Elevation change: 1,050 feet (320 m)
Effort: moderate
Trailhead: Emma Matilda or Two Ocean Lake
Directions: Take the paved Pacific Creek Rd. 1.5 miles (2.4 km) to the Emma Matilda Trailhead for the shorter loop. For the longer loop, drive 0.5 mile (0.8 km) farther to Two Ocean Rd. Turn left and drive 2.4 miles (3.9 km) on dirt road to the trailhead at Two Ocean Lake.

The Emma Matilda and Two Ocean Lake Trailheads both access Emma Matilda Lake. From the **Emma Matilda Trailhead,** hike 0.6 mile (1 km) to the lake. From **Two Ocean Lake Trailhead**, hike 1 mile (1.6 km) to the lake. Once there, the route loops 8.7 miles (14 km) around the lake. Circling the lake will take you through two fire zones from burns in 1994 and 1998, where new growth is changing the flora.

On the north shore of the lake, the trail climbs about 400 feet (120 m) up a ridge that yields views of the lake backed by the Teton Mountains. A loose Douglas fir forest covers the ridge, and you can see Jackson Lake Lodge in the distance. Near the trail junction that goes to Jackson Lake Lodge, a **spur trail** cuts to **Lookout Rock** for views of the lake. From the junction, bear left to circle the south shore of the lake, where the trail travels through a dense forest of spruce and fir.

Many hikers opt to combine Emma Matilda Lake with **Two Ocean Lake** and **Grand View Point.** From the Two Ocean Lake Trailhead, the distance ranges 9.3-13.2 miles (15-21.3 km), depending on the routes chosen around the lakes.

Teton Park Road
★ Taggart and Bradley Lakes
Distance: 3-5.9 miles (4.8-9.4 km) rt
Duration: 2-4 hours
Elevation change: 400-900 feet (122-274 m)
Effort: easy-moderate
Trailhead: Taggart Lake

Two lower-elevation lakes sit at the base of Avalanche and Garnet Canyons. For a shorter hike, go to Taggart Lake and back. The longer loop adds on Bradley Lake, where you can stare straight up at **Grand Teton.** When the lake is glassy, the Grand Teton reflects like a mirror. Get an early start in order to claim a parking spot at this popular trailhead. Anglers fish both lakes, and on hot days, both lakes make good swimming holes.

From the trailhead, the trail curves north to cross a tumbling stream before ascending through conifers and meadows growing on glacial moraines to a **signed junction.** If you are planning to hike both lakes, you will loop back to this junction. Turn left to hike to **Taggart Lake** (3 mi/4.8 km rt). Explore the small peninsula to the south for a place to enjoy the water and views.

To continue the loop to **Bradley Lake** (5.9 mi/9.4 km rt), circle north around the shore of Taggart Lake to climb two switchbacks that crest a forested glacial moraine. After dropping to a **signed junction,** turn left to visit Bradley Lake. Beaches flank the east shore, while the north side contains a **footbridge** crossing the outlet. This is also where you'll have the best views of soaring **Grand Teton.** After the lake, retrace your steps back to the last junction and take the fork heading left to climb over the moraine again and complete the loop to the first junction to return to the trailhead.

Surprise and Amphitheater Lakes

Distance: 10.1 miles (16.2 km) rt
Duration: 6 hours
Elevation change: 2,966 feet (904 m)
Effort: strenuous
Trailhead: Lupine Meadows

Surprise and Amphitheater Lakes cluster together in a high, narrow subalpine basin on an eastern ridge extending from Grand Teton. Since this out-and-back trail provides access for many technical climbing routes, you may see people loaded with ropes, helmets, and gear. Start early, as the sun-soaked climb can be hot midday.

Begin by hiking a trail that ascends a moraine ridge to the junction with the **Taggart Lake Trail.** At the junction, continue uphill to follow switchbacks that climb steeply on the open, east-facing slope. Views of Jackson Hole get bigger the higher you go; Bradley Lake is below to the south.

Follow the switchbacks as they climb through a broken forest of whitebark pines and whortleberry. Nearing the lake basin, look up for views of the **Grand Teton.** At **Surprise Lake,** descend to the shore and enjoy the lake, or circle the lake's east shore to its outlet to overlook Jackson Hole. The main trail passes above the north side of Surprise Lake to climb into the small hanging valley housing **Amphitheater Lake,** tucked at the base of Disappointment Peak. After the lake, a rough trail climbs north to a saddle for a partial view of the Grand, glacial moraine, and immense cliffs.

Jenny Lake Area

For hikes in the Jenny Lake area, you can trim mileage with a **boat shuttle** (307/734-9227, www.jennylakeboating.com, 7am-7pm daily mid-May-Sept., shorter hours in shoulder seasons, $18 adults, $10 kids round-trip; $10 adults, $8 kids one-way). Reservations are not required; just show up at the east- or west-side dock. Shuttles run every 10-15 minutes.

Jenny Lake Loop

Distance: 7.3 mile (11.7 km) loop
Duration: 3.5 hours
Elevation change: 380 feet (116 m)
Effort: moderate
Trailhead: Jenny Lake Visitor Center or String Lake

This undulating trail loops completely around Jenny Lake; part of the path is paved near the visitors center, but most of the trail is dirt. Unless you hike in early morning or late evening, expect to meet crowds in midsummer (and a full parking lot). All trail junctions are well signed.

From the **Jenny Lake Visitor Center,** follow the Jenny Lake Overlooks Trail to the stairway at the end. Ascend the stairs and continue on the path northward in a counterclockwise direction around the lake. You'll pass **Rock Beach,** a short **spur trail** (leading to Jenny Lake Campground), and **Jenny Lake Overlook** as the trail crosses between the lake and North Jenny Lake Drive.

When the trail reaches **String Lake Trailhead,** head west, crossing a bridge over the String Lake outlet stream. At the junction, head left above the north shore of Jenny Lake through the remains of the 1999 Alder Fire. You'll pass large boulders (glacial erratics) before reaching multiple trail junctions. Continue straight as trails head up to **Cascade Canyon,** down to the west boat shuttle dock, and up to **Hidden Falls** and **Inspiration Point.** After crossing Cascade Creek on a **wooden bridge,** you'll reach another junction. Continue straight south along the shore of Jenny Lake and in the forest passing several junctions. Stay left at all of them. Pass the Jenny Lake boat launch to reach the **bridge** crossing the Jenny Lake outlet at the east tour boat dock to return to the visitors center.

★ Hidden Falls and Inspiration Point
Distance: 2 miles (3.2 km) rt
Duration: 2 hours
Elevation change: 443 feet (135 km)
Effort: moderate
Trailhead: Jenny Lake Visitor Center

Hidden Falls is a 200-foot (61-m) tumbler in Cascade Canyon, and Inspiration Point is a rocky knoll perched between Mount Teewinot and Mount St. John. Given the point's perch, the scope of views from the summit lives up to its name. You'll look straight down on the blue waters of Jenny Lake, up to the peaks on both sides, and across Jackson Hole to the Gros Ventre Mountains. Hikers clog this trail. The trail reaches Lower Inspiration Point but no longer connects to Upper Inspiration Point and Cascade Canyon due to a landslide. Plan on adding an extra hour or more to your total trip time due to long lines for the boat shuttle (fee). For the **ranger-led hike**, pick up tokens first thing in the morning at Jenny Lake Visitor Center to join the guided hike (meet 8:30am, daily June-early Sept., limit of 25 people, boat shuttle fee).

From the **west boat shuttle dock,** head up the trail to the signed junction. Turn left and the uphill climb starts promptly. Follow the signs for Hidden Falls as the trail climbs along the north side of frothing Cascade Creek. At a junction for **Hidden Falls,** turn left to ascend Cascade Creek to the bridge crossing to the south side of the creek. Continue to the junction with the **Hidden Falls Overlook** spur.

To continue to **Inspiration Point,** cross the two upper **bridges** over Cascade Creek, then climb a sweeping traverse into the rock of **Lower Inspiration Point.** The slope can get hot in mid-summer; mornings are best for hiking to the point. Enjoy the view before retracing your steps back to the west boat shuttle dock.

String and Leigh Lakes
Distance: 3.7 miles (6 km)
Duration: 2 hours
Elevation change: 325 feet (99 m)
Effort: easy
Trailhead: String Lake

This trail circles String Lake and takes in the southern tip of Leigh Lake; it's less crowded than Jenny Lake. Hike counter-clockwise to get the big views down the western side of the loop.

Start from the **String Lake Trailhead** and hike north along the forested eastern shore of String Lake. Stop frequently along the shallow sand-bottomed lake to look for moose and waterfowl. To the north, Mount Moran rises into view while Teewinot Mountain pokes above the trees southward. At the south end of Leigh Lake, a trail junction splits right and continues up the east side of Leigh Lake to Bearpaw Lake. Stay straight instead to follow a **short spur** to the edge of the deeper **Leigh Lake** for the views.

Return to the junction and head west to cross the **bridge** at the rocky outlet of Leigh Lake. Enjoy the view of Boulder Island from the bridge, then continue westward as the trail climbs through a lodgepole forest to a second **junction.** Turn left to break out of the woods and onto the open slopes of **Rockchuck Peak** and Mount St. John with views of Teewinot Mountain. The trail gradually descends to the foot of String Lake where it meets the **Jenny Lake Trail.** Turn left and cross the **bridge** at the outlet of String Lake to return to the String Lake Trailhead.

Moose-Wilson Road
★ Phelps Lake
Distance: 3.1-6.6 miles (5-10.6 km) rt

Duration: 2-4 hours
Elevation change: 350-400 feet (107-122 m)
Effort: easy-moderate
Trailhead: Laurance S. Rockefeller Preserve Center

A maze of trails surrounds the low-elevation Phelps Lake in the Laurance S. Rockefeller Preserve. Trails circle the lake, which sits at the bottom of Open and Death Canyons. From various viewpoints around the lake, hikers are rewarded with stunning views of the Teton Mountains. The lake is a year-round destination, although you'll need skis or snowshoes in winter. Reservations are required for the **ranger-led hike** (307/739-3654, 9:30am daily early June-Sept.) to Phelps Lake.

Most hikers opt to park at the **Laurance S. Rockefeller Preserve Center.** Arrive before 9am to claim a parking spot in the small lot. If it's full, you'll need to hike in via the Death Canyon Trailhead. From the center, you can design your own route through the maze of trails. Junctions are well signed to help in selecting routes. The shortest and easiest route to Phelps Lake is the **Lake Creek-Woodland Trail Loop** (3.1 mi/5 km rt). The loop tours forests and meadows on both sides of a creek, offering opportunities to watch moose. At the lake, enjoy contemplation from several different constructed rock-slab overlooks.

The **Aspen Ridge-Boulder Ridge Loop** (5.8 mi/9.3 km rt) climbs through large talus fields and aspens that shimmer gold in fall to reach Phelps Lake. The longest hike, the **Phelps Lake Loop** (6.6 mi/10.6 km rt), climbs via Lake Creek to reach the lake and then loops around the lake for a changing perspective of the Teton Mountains.

Backpacking

In the popular backpacking areas of the Tetons, some campsites are assigned. Otherwise, camping is dispersed throughout a backcountry zone. All backpackers are required to carry food in a **bear canister** (permit offices have loaners) and have a backcountry camping

permit. Apply online (www.recreation. gov, apply early Jan.-mid-May, $45 fee) to guarantee your permit in advance. **First-come, first-served permits** ($35 fee) are available in person 24 hours before departure. Competition for walk-in permits is high in July and August; a line usually forms at the Jenny Lake Ranger Station or Craig Thomas Discovery & Visitor Center one hour before the 8am opening. For more details, see the backcountry camping brochure on the park's website.

Paintbrush Canyon-Cascade Canyon
19 miles (31 km)

The **Paintbrush Canyon-Cascade Canyon loop** is a stunning **three-day** backpacking trip. Outstanding scenery, including the high Paintbrush Divide, Lake Solitude, and the Grand Teton highlight the route. Camp one night each at Holly Lake (use Upper Paintbrush zone as alternate) and North Fork Cascade zone.

TOP EXPERIENCE

★ Teton Crest Trail
38-58 miles (61-93 km)

The king of backpacking trips is the **Teton Crest Trail,** a high-altitude romp with major elevation gains and descents. The route crosses Fox Creek Pass, Death Canyon Shelf, Mount Meek Pass, Alaska Basin, Hurricane Pass, and Paintbrush Divide. Traversing the trail northward, the central Tetons dominate the scenery. The 38-mile (61-km) point-to-point route requires a shuttle between trailheads (Granite Canyon and String Lake) and a minimum of **four days** to complete. Many crest hikers chop off the huge climb up Granite Canyon by taking the aerial tram (9am-5pm daily mid-May-early Oct., $47 adults, kids 5 and under free) at Jackson Hole Mountain Resort to join the Teton Crest Trail from Rendezvous Mountain. (Taking the tram reduces total distance to 34 mi/55 km.)

For the 58-mile (93-km) loop trip,

plan to camp at Marian Lake (use Upper Granite as alternate), Death Canyon Shelf, South Fork Cascade, and Upper Paintbrush. The Valley Trail helps start and end your trip at Jenny Lake. The longer route requires **five days.**

Climbing

Technical climbing skills are required to reach eight of the Teton summits. If you do not possess the skills, do not attempt to summit peaks; hire a guide service instead. Climbing permits are not required, but you will need a **backcountry camping permit** to camp overnight. Most of the prominent peaks seen from Jackson Hole can be climbed in one extremely long day. Due to rockfall year-round, climbers must wear **helmets.** Until late July, **ice axes** (and the skill to use them correctly) may be necessary on steep snowfields to access routes.

Spring is rainy, accompanied by thawing ice and snow that produce copious rockfall and wet slab avalanches. **Mid-July to August** offers the most temperate weather, but afternoons frequently see sporadic rains, cold, wind, and lightning. By **September,** snow usually appears at high elevations, followed by heavy winter snow, frigid temperatures, high winds, and avalanches.

Jenny Lake Ranger Station (307/739-3343, 8am-5pm daily June-early Sept.) has current climbing conditions, information, and a climbing register. The rangers are climbers who know the area, risks, difficulties, routes, and what type of experience you need for different climbs. They also update conditions and mountaineering scene information online at www.tetonclimbing.blogspot.com.

★ Grand Teton

Climbing Grand Teton requires **14 miles (23 km)** of hiking and **6,545 feet (1,995 m)** of ascent and descent. Most climbers take an ultra-long day from the valley floor. More than 35 technical climbing routes lead to the summit with countless variations, and climbers pioneer new routes almost every year. The most popular route for climbing the Grand is the exposed **Upper Exum Ridge,** a classic in mountaineering.

Guides and Schools

Two companies guide climbs and ski mountaineering trips year-round in Grand Teton National Park. Most climbing camps, schools, and guided climbs happen in **summer.** Ski mountaineering trips happen in winter. Private guides can go one-on-one with you to the summit of the Grand, or you can go with a group (after successfully passing prerequisites). In most cases, the companies will supply all the technical climbing gear. **Exum Mountain Guides** (307/733-2297, exumguides.com) is at South Jenny Lake. **Jackson Hole Mountain Guides** (307/733-4979, themountainguides.com) is based in Jackson.

Biking

Summer offers the best cycling weather, despite some afternoon thundershowers and strong winds. Cyclists can ride all park roads, but shoulders are narrow and giant RVs will zoom by. Cyclists can camp in **shared biker and hiker campsites** ($12-13/person) at Headwaters, Lizard Creek, Colter Bay, and Signal Mountain Campgrounds.

Jenny Lake Scenic Drive (3 mi/4.8 km) offers a family-friendly ride with a designated bike lane; though the road is one-way for vehicles, bicyclists can ride in both directions.

Mountain bikes are not permitted on trails but can ride paved paths or dirt roads. **Antelope Flats Road** offers biking with sagebrush and scenery, but prepare for high winds due to the wide-open plain. Extend the ride by touring the historic Mormon Row.

★ Multi-Use Pathway

The bike ride with the best views is the **Multi-Use Pathway** (29 mi/47 km, dawn-dusk, snow-covered in winter), a paved cycling and walking path that parallels the roads between Jenny Lake, Moose, Antelope Flats Road, and Jackson. The mostly level path is perfect for cyclists who don't want to contend with RV traffic and for families with kids. Use caution: Wildlife (including bison) also walk on the trail, and pathways intersect with road crossings. The southern section, from Jackson to Gros Ventre Junction, closes November-April for migrating elk. For the most scenic segment, the Moose-Jenny Lake Pathway (7.7 mi/12.4 km) saunters just below the Tetons.

Guides and Rentals

Located on the Multi-Use Pathway, Dornan's **Adventure Sports** (12170 Dornan Rd., Moose, 307/733-2415, dornans.com, 9am-6pm daily early May-late Sept.) rents road bikes and mountain bikes ($30-75 adults, $22-40 kids) by the hour or for full days. They also carry

biking the Multi-Use Pathway between Moose and Jenny Lake

e-bikes, tag-alongs, and Burleys for towing kids, or bike racks for hauling gear to ride elsewhere. Helmets and flat-repair kits are included.

Horseback Riding

Grand Teton Lodging Company (307/543-3100 reservations, 307/543-2811, www.gtlc.com) operates three corrals and offers trail rides ($50-80). Kids age 7 and younger can ride ponies ($5). Make advance reservations, and wear long pants and sturdy shoes.

Colter Bay Village corrals (daily early June-early Sept.) offers one-hour trail rides (1pm and 1:30pm) to Jackson Lake Overlook and Heron Pond; two-hour rides add on Swan Lake (8:30am and 9am). Trail rides departing from **Jackson Lake Lodge corrals** (daily late May-early Oct.) go to Emma Matilda Lake (2 hrs, 9am and 9:30am). Shorter excursions wow with Teton views (1 hr, 1:45pm and 2:15pm). **Flagg Ranch corrals** (John D. Rockefeller Pkwy., 307/543-2861 reservations, daily June-Aug.) runs one-hour trail rides (9:45am, 12:30pm, and 3pm) through forests.

Water Sports
Permits

You'll need multiple permits for boating, floating, and paddling. First, pick up a State of Wyoming **Aquatic Invasive Species (AIS) sticker** (Wyoming Game and Fish, 307/777-4600, wgfd.wyo.gov, motorized $10-30; nonmotorized $5-15) after passing an inspection at the Moran or Moose boat inspection stations or elsewhere in Wyoming.

Next, buy a Grand Teton National Park permit at **Colter Bay Visitor Center** or **Craig Thomas Discovery and Visitor Center. Motorized boat permits** ($40) include boats with any type of motor. **Nonmotorized boat permits** ($12) cover canoes, kayaks, rowboats, paddleboards, sailboards, rafts, packrafts, drift boats, inflatables, and dories.

If you want to boat or paddle camp overnight, pick up a **backcountry camping permit** ($35 fee, 3-night limit) for specific primitive shoreline campsites that have fire rings and bear boxes. Permits are available first come, first served within 24 hours of departure. During July and August, competition for overnight camping permits on **Jackson Lake** has boaters lining up an hour before the backcountry office opens at 8am at Colter Bay. You can also get advance **reservations** (877/444-6777, www.recreation.gov, apply early Jan.-mid-May, $45 fee).

Boating
Jackson Lake

Filling a trough scooped out by an ice-age glacier, **Jackson Lake** is so big that it takes multiple days to explore all of its nooks and crannies. Fifteen islands, several peninsulas, and numerous bays provide places to get away from crowds. To enjoy the solitude of your own beach, go to the west shore between Steamboat

Mountain and Mount Moran. By August, the lake level drops, which enlarges beaches. Jackson Lake has 15 lake-accessed **campsites** (permit required) for overnighting, some located on islands.

Motorboats, nonmotorized boats, sailboats, sailboarding, and waterskiing are allowed on Jackson Lake; Jet Skis and motorized personal watercraft are not. While the image of cutting lazy turns in glassy water below the sun-drenched Teton Mountains sounds idyllic, the reality is quite different. Due to chilly water, most water-skiers wear wetsuits or drysuits, and afternoon winds often cause big waves.

Jenny Lake

Boating on **Jenny Lake** is a quiet, tranquil experience, as only motorboats with 10 horsepower or less are permitted, plus any hand-propelled boats. Sailboats, sailboards, waterskiing, and Jet Skis are not allowed. The boat launch is located on **Lupine Meadows Road.** After crossing the bridge over Cottonwood Creek, turn right to reach the dirt ramp and small loop for trailer parking.

Boat Launches, Marinas, and Rentals

If you have a small hand-carried watercraft, you can launch from any beach where you can haul it. Otherwise, Jackson Lake has three developed boat launches with cement ramps, docks, and trailer parking for day-use, overnight, and long-term. Each has restaurants, boat services, boat gas, buoy rentals, and some boating supplies. All boat rentals are first come, first served and include life jackets.

- **Leek's Marina** (307/543-2831, www. signalmountainlodge.com, daily late May-late Sept.) does not have rentals.

- **Colter Bay Marina** (307/543-2811, www. gtlc.com, daily late May-late Sept.) rents 16-foot (4.9-m) aluminum motorboats ($48/hr, 2-hr min.).

- **Signal Mountain Lodge Marina** (307/543-2831, www.signalmountain

rental boats at Colter Bay Marina

lodge.com, daily mid-May-mid-Sept., $42-145/hr) rents deck cruisers and pontoon boats that hold 8-10 people. Smaller runabouts and fishing boats can fit five people.

Paddling
★ Jackson Lake

Paddlers can find fun cubbyholes to explore on **Jackson Lake,** with islands and protected bays the best places for touring. Due to big winds that can arise on Jackson Lake, avoid open-water paddles. Take shoreline routes for safety. The most sheltered paddles are from **Signal Mountain Marina** or **Colter Bay Marina,** where islands offer wind protection.

Two Ocean Lake

Paddlers relish **Two Ocean Lake,** since it doesn't permit motorboats. It offers a quiet venue for shoreline paddles, wildlife-watching, and distant scenery of the Teton Mountains. Trumpeter swans inhabit the waters, and autumn paddles yield spectacular gold hillsides of aspens.

Jenny Lake and Vicinity

Despite the presence of shuttle boats, **Jenny Lake** makes for excellent paddling. For the Jenny Lake boat launch, head to Lupine Meadows Road, just south of Jenny Lake. Turn right immediately after the bridge over Cottonwood Creek.

North of Jenny Lake, **String Lake** connects via a rocky shallow stream portage to **Leigh Lake.** String Lake has a canoe and kayak launch site, located in the second parking lot on the left on the String Lake Picnic Area road off North Jenny Lake Road. Paddlers can overnight (permit required) at **Leigh Lake** in solitude at eight prime **campsites.**

Rentals

First-come, first-served rentals of canoes, single kayaks, and tandem kayaks run $22-40 per hour with life jackets and paddles included. You can rent them at **Colter Bay Marina** (307/543-2811, www.

gtlc.com, daily late May-late Sept.), **Signal Mountain Lodge Marina** (1 Inner Park Rd., 307/543-2831, www. signalmountainlodge.com, daily mid-June-mid-Sept.), and **Jenny Lake** (Jenny Lake boathouse, 307/734-9227, www. jennylakeboating.com, daily mid-June-mid-Sept., shorter hours in fall). You can also rent kayaks, canoes, and paddleboards at Dornan's **Adventure Sports** (12170 Dornan Rd., Moose, 307/733-3307, https://dornans.com, daily early May-late Sept.).

River Rafting and Kayaking

In rafts, dories, canoes, or river kayaks, paddlers can float the **Wild and Scenic Snake River** (April-mid-Dec.). It has Class II moving water from Jackson Lake Dam to Moose, but paddlers need river savvy for maneuvering around snags and debris, strong currents, braided channels, and logjams. Afternoon winds seem to unleash upriver gales, and spring water is cold, fast, and unforgiving. This river is not for discount store blowup rafts (inner tubes and air mattresses are not allowed). Pick up a river map from a visitors center or on the park website for information on launch locations, river distances, and take-outs.

Guides

Daily **float trips** (mid-May-Sept., $80-85 adults, $50-65 kids) head down the Snake River where the guide does all the maneuvering; you sit back to absorb views of the peaks and wildlife. From Moose, transportation is via bus or van to Deadman's Bar for launching; trips end back in Moose. The total trip takes 3-4 hours, with 2 hours on a raft that holds 10-12 people. Reservations are required; some companies offer discounts for booking in advance online. Plan to tip your guide 15 percent.

Lodges inside the national park book float trips for guests. Otherwise, go with **Barker-Ewing Scenic Float Trips** (307/733-1800 or 800/365-1800, www.barkerewing.

com), **Solitude Float Trips** (307/733-2871, www.grand-teton-scenic-floats.com), or **Triangle X-National Park Float Trips** (307/733-5500, nationalparkfloattrips.com).

Fishing

Grand Teton National Park is one of those places that combines stunning scenery with exceptional fishing. While spin-casting works, especially on **Jackson Lake**, fly-fishing is the iconic method for the **Snake River** or small lakes. Waters swim with native cutthroat and introduced brown, rainbow, and lake trout. Fishing regulations for closures, creel limits, and lure and bait requirements are available on the park website.

To fish inside the park requires a **Wyoming state fishing license** ($6-14 daily, $56/5 days), sold at Dornan's in Moose, Colter Bay Marina, and Signal Mountain Lodge Marina.

Guides

For **guided fishing** on **Jackson Lake** ($115/hr for 1-2 people) make reservations through two marinas: **Colter Bay Marina** (307/543-2811, www.gtlc.com, daily late May-late Sept.) or **Signal Mountain Lodge Marina** (307/543-2831, www.signalmountainlodge.com, daily mid-May-mid-Sept.), which also offers a four-hour trip ($370 for 1-2 people).

On the **Snake River,** each raft, drift boat, or dory can take 1-2 anglers, plus the guide ($500-625 for 1-2 people). Reservations are required. Make them through **Grand Teton Lodging Company** (307/543-2811, www.gtlc.com, daily May-Sept.), **Snake River Angler** (307/733-3699, www.snakeriverangler.com), **Grand Teton Fly Fishing** (307/690-0910, www.grandtetonflyfishing.com), or **Grand Fishing** (307/734-9684, grandfishing.com).

Swimming

Jackson Lake has plenty of beaches for swimming, but there are no lifeguards and the water is frigid. Even in August, the chilly water may not hit 60°F (15.5°C). While you can swim anywhere in Jackson Lake except for marinas, **Colter Bay swimming beach** (Colter Bay Picnic Area) has a buoy-marked swimming zone. **String Lake** is shallow, so water tends to heat up a little warmer there than elsewhere. Swimming access is from the picnic area.

Winter Sports
Cross-Country Skiing and Snowshoeing

When snow settles on Grand Teton National Park, snow-buried roads and trails turn into cross-country ski and snowshoe routes. Trails are not marked in winter, so you're on your own for route-finding—don't assume the previous ski tracks go where you want to go. Bring a map, GPS, or compass, and know how to navigate. Pick up a brochure at a visitors center that shows popular ski and snowshoe routes, where to park vehicles, and winter wildlife closure zones. Check conditions at **Jackson Hole Avalanche Forecast** (307/733-2664, jhavalanche.org) if you are going into the mountains.

From the Taggart Lake Trailhead to Signal Mountain Lodge, **Teton Park Road** (14 mi/23 km, mid-Dec.-mid-Mar.) is groomed twice a week for skate and classic skiing. Follow protocol on the groomed trail: Snowshoers should walk on the smooth grooming, not the tracks cut for skiing.

Guides and Rentals

In winter, rangers guide interpretive **snowshoe walks** (307/739-3399, late Dec.-mid-Mar., free). The two-hour tours meet at the Taggart Lake Trailhead to look for tracks, study snow science, and examine the ecology of winter. Reservations are required; snowshoes are available.

For winter tours, **Hole Hiking Experience** (307/690-4453, www.holehike.com) offers cross-country ski and snowshoe trips. **Teton Backcountry**

Guides (307/353-2900, tetonbackcountryguides.com) leads backcountry skiing, cross-country skiing, or snowshoe tours.

You can rent backcountry skis, cross-country skis, and snowshoes for adults and kids in Jackson and Teton Village.

Food

Most restaurants inside the park are first come, first served, with the exception of the Mural Room and Poolside Barbecue at Jackson Lake Lodge, Jenny Lake Lodge, and the Colter Bay cookouts. Expect to wait in line for seating, especially during the peak summer season. Dress is casual; however, diners in Jackson Lake Lodge's Mural Room and Signal Mountain Lodge's Peaks Restaurant tend to spiff up for meals, and Jenny Lake Lodge has a dress code. All restaurants have kids' menus.

The two best picnic areas are lakeside with fire rings and grills (bring your own wood). **Colter Bay** is on Jackson Lake with a buoyed swimming area. **String Lake,** accessed via North Jenny Lake, has trailheads and slightly warmer water.

Flagg Ranch

In Headwaters Lodge, **Sheffields Restaurant & Bar** (100 Grassy Lake Rd., 307/543-2861, www.gtlc.com, daily mid-June-Sept.) serves breakfast (7am-10am, $7-16) from the menu or a buffet, lunch (11:30am-2pm, $9-21), and dinner (5:00pm-9:30pm, $13-32) of prime rib, salmon, burgers, and quick plates. The western-style **bar** (6:30am-11pm) serves coffee in the morning and light meals from a limited menu.

Leek's Marina

With indoor and outdoor picnic tables, **Leek's Pizzeria** (Leek's Marina, 307/543-2831, www.signalmountainlodge.com, 11am-10pm daily late May-early Sept., $10-26) has partial views of Jackson Lake and the Teton Mountains from its deck.

It serves pizza, including gluten-free options, and by the slice, plus pasta, salads, and Italian sandwiches.

Colter Bay

Colter Bay Village has two adjacent restaurants, both run by **Grand Teton Lodging Company** (307/543-2811, www.gtlc.com). Neither one takes reservations. The **Café Court Pizzeria** (11am-10pm daily late May-early Sept., $4-25) has pizza by the slice or full pizzas, either house specialties or customized. You can also get appetizers, subs, salads, beer, wine, and pizza to go. At ★ **Ranch House** (daily late May-early Oct.), dine in rustic booths or in the bar from a smaller menu. The restaurant serves local bison (from outside the national park), all-natural beef, sustainable seafood, and some locally sourced produce plus beer, wine, and cocktails. Breakfast (6:30am-10:30am, $6-18) is off the menu or a buffet. Lunch (11:30am-1:30pm, $8-17) and dinner (5:30pm-9pm, $11-26) have lighter

soups, chili, and salads, or barbecue-style steaks, brisket, and ribs.

The western-style Colter Bay cookouts are a fun way to dine, set around a campfire with a scenic backdrop of Jackson Lake and the Tetons. The **Cookout boat cruises** (307/543-2811, June-mid-Sept., $50-72 adults, $25-42 kids) go to Elk Island for a hot breakfast (7:15am Fri.-Wed. summer, 8am Fri.-Wed. fall), picnic lunch (12:15pm Mon., Wed., and Fri.-Sat.), or steak and trout dinner (5:15pm Fri.-Wed.). Reservations are required.

Jackson Lake Lodge

Jackson Lake Lodge (101 Jackson Lake Lodge Rd., 307/543-2811, www.gtlc.com, daily mid-May-early Oct.) has distinctly different dining. All facilities have kids' menus and healthy, sustainable foods that are locally sourced, plus vegetarian, gluten-free, and low-fat options. Make **reservations** (307/543-3463, accepted starting late May) for dinner in the Mural Room and Poolside Barbecue.

Dining in the ★ **Mural Room** is an experience for the panoramic views of the Grand Tetons outside and the western murals inside. Dinner reservations are imperative. For breakfast (7am-9:30am daily, $10-20), partake of the buffet or order from the menu. Lunch (11:30am-1:30pm daily, $12-22) serves elk chili, organic greens, sandwiches, and fish entrées. For dinner (5:30pm-9:30pm daily, $18-48), entrées include prime rib, elk ribeye, bison, trout, and salmon.

With big windows and a patio for gazing at the Tetons, the **Blue Heron Lounge** (11am-midnight, $11-26) has burgers, sandwiches, soups, salads, small plates, and a few entrées. Regional beers, wine, and signature cocktails are served until midnight.

Revamped to its original 1950s diner decor, the **Pioneer Grill** serves classic American meals. Breakfast (6am-10:30am, $4-15) can be continental or full entrées. Lunch and dinner menus (11am-10pm, $8-26) have soups,

Mural Room at Jackson Lake Lodge

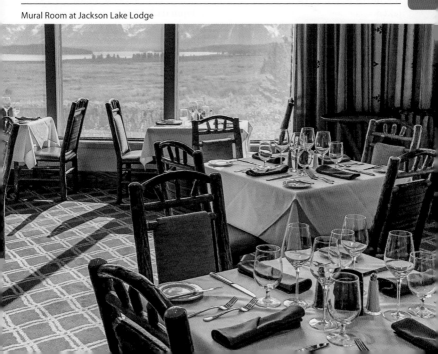

salads, sandwiches, wraps, burgers, wings, steaks, and trout. The soda fountain serves homemade ice-cream milkshakes, including huckleberry.

Early June to late August, the **Poolside Cantina** (11am-4pm, $5-10) serves salads, tacos, burritos, and ice cream bars. In the evening, it becomes the **Poolside Barbecue** (5:30pm-8pm, $29 adults, $15 kids, reservations required), serving beef brisket, pulled pork, ribs, and chicken, with a baked potato bar and traditional sides. You can also roast s'mores over the fire and listen to live music.

Signal Mountain Lodge

At **Signal Mountain Lodge** (1 Inner Park Rd., 307/543-2831, www.signalmountain lodge.com, daily mid-May-early Oct., hours shorten in fall), two adjacent restaurants serve meals that emphasize local sources, sustainable dining, and organic ingredients. Both have kids' menus, gluten-free and vegetarian options, and outstanding views of Jackson Lake and the north Tetons. No reservations are taken.

Relax in the lodge-style atmosphere of the **Peaks Restaurant** (5:30pm-10pm, $14-43) with upscale dinners of small plates, multiple courses, and generous western entrées of trout, beef, bison, and fish. Blackberries and huckleberries doctor up the signature cocktails. Finish with their famous blackberry pie.

With indoor dining or outdoor deck seating, ★ **Trapper Grill** (7am-10pm) has a large menu with choices for families and hungry hikers. Breakfast (7am-11am, $10-15) serves egg dishes. Lunch and dinner menus ($10-20) have soups, salads, sandwiches, burgers, and Tex-Mex entrées such as trout tacos. The giant nachos are a post-hiking favorite.

Jenny Lake

The dining room at ★ **Jenny Lake Lodge** (400 Jenny Lake Loop, 307/543-2811, www.gtlc.com, daily June-early Oct.) is an experience in itself. The log lodge has an intimate restaurant with views of the peaks for a romantic setting. Local food sources are used, and the wine list spans the world. Vegetarian, gluten-free, vegan, organic, all-natural, and low-fat options are available. Breakfast (7:30am-10am, $34) is a gourmet prix fixe menu; you select your starter, egg dish, and sweets. Lunch (11:30am-1:30pm, $12-18) features sandwiches, burgers, salads, and trout and grits. Dinner (6pm-9pm, $98) is a five-course prix fixe affair with menus rotating on a five-night schedule. **Reservations** are recommended for breakfast and lunch and are required for dinner. Lodge guests can make dinner reservations when they book their lodging; non-guests can make reservations beginning March 1. Diners are expected to wear dressy attire (like dresses or jackets and slacks) for dinner.

Moose

Dornan's (307/733-2415, dornans.com) has two restaurants in their complex, plus a deli. **Pizza Pasta Company** (11:30am-9:30pm daily year-round, shorter hours in winter, $9-25) serves pasta, pizza, hot sandwiches, sauté bowls, soups, and salads. Rooftop seating (adults only) and patio dining have outstanding views of the Tetons. Indoor seating is sometimes crowded and noisy, but there's a fireplace for cold days. Order in line at the food counter and wait for the staff to deliver food to your table. Beer, wine, and cocktails are ordered separately from the **Spur Bar.**

Summers bring on the old-time ★ **Chuckwagon** (daily early June-early Sept.) for cowboy fare in a covered outdoor pavilion with picnic tables and mountain views. You can even eat in a tepee. Breakfast (7am-11am, $8-10) includes traditional cowpoke entrées plus all-you-can-eat pancakes. Lunch (noon-3pm, $8-14) has barbecue sandwiches and burgers. Dinner (5pm-9pm, $14-35) is a western barbecue with choice of entrée: New York strip steak, baby back pork ribs, beef brisket, or blackened Idaho red trout. On Sundays, prime rib is added. Beer and wine are served. Mondays feature hootenannies, while Tuesday-Saturday nights have live music.

The small **Moose Trading Post & Deli** (9am-5pm daily winter, 8am-8pm daily summer $8-9) makes deli sandwiches. Dine at one of a few indoor tables or take your meal to-go for hikes. The store also sells groceries, freeze-dried meals, trail mix, cheeses, and baked goods. A wine shop is on-site, and espresso and ice cream are sold June-August.

Groceries

Located in Colter Bay Village, **Colter Bay General Store** (7am-9:30pm daily late May-late Sept.) is a small grocery with a deli, fresh fruits and veggies, free-range meat and poultry, fresh-baked pastries, and camping supplies. At South Jenny Lake, the **general store** (8am-7pm daily mid-May-mid-Sept.) carries a few convenience foods and minimal camping supplies. **Headwaters Lodge at Flagg Ranch** and **Signal Mountain Lodge** carry convenience-type items with a few limited groceries.

Accommodations and Camping

All of the park lodges are seasonal, open late spring into fall. Expect rusticity without televisions, radios, or air-conditioning; only a few units at Signal Mountain Lodge offer air-conditioning. Rates are for double occupancy; add on $6-20 per additional person. Taxes run about 9 percent.

Lodges
Grand Teton Lodging Company
Grand Teton Lodging Company (307/543-3100, www.gtlc.com) operates four lodging complexes. Make **reservations 366 days** in advance.

Headwaters Lodge & Cabins (100 Grassy Lake Rd., June-late Sept., $240-330) sits at Flagg Ranch, in an area with no cell service or Wi-Fi. The river-rock-and-log lodge houses the front desk, restaurant, bar, gift shop, and convenience store. The lodge's cabins are actually a row of motel rooms. Paved walkways lead to the cabins; carts are provided for moving your bags. Standard, deluxe, and premium rooms have two queens or one king, en suite baths, and shared front porches with rocking chairs. In the adjacent campground, tiny budget-friendly **camper cabins** ($78) have no electricity, but they include bunk beds with thin mattress pads (bring your own bedding) and outside picnic tables and firepits. Walk to communal bathrooms and showers.

Colter Bay Village has two lodging options: log cabins and canvas tent cabins. Wi-Fi is not available in either. These are the most popular cabins in the park due to their location, where you can park the car for several days while you paddle, swim, boat, and hike. **Colter Bay Cabins** (late May-late Sept., $200-275) are small, rustic cabins a five-minute walk from the lake. Cabin options range in size and privacy; the private one- and two-room cabins have their own bathrooms, but you'll share facilities if you're in one of the semi-private cabins. For an experience reminiscent of summer camp, **Colter Bay Tent Village** (late May-early Sept., $80) has tent cabins that are part log and canvas with wood floors. Each can sleep four people on pull-down bunks with thin mattresses. Heat comes from stoking a fire in an old-fashioned potbelly stove. Outside covered patios have a picnic table, fire pit with grill, and bear box. Bring your own sleeping bags or rent bedding. Communal bathrooms are a short walk away.

Popular due to its views, ★ **Jackson Lake Lodge** (101 Jackson Lake Lodge Rd., mid-May-early Oct., $346-480 rooms and cottages, $771-875 suites) is a National Historic Landmark. Built in 1955, with a dining room, lounge, and patio, the lodge commands a panoramic view of the Tetons from its tall lobby windows. The lodge doesn't actually sit on the shore of Jackson Lake; it overlooks Willow Flats. The property includes several restaurants, gift shops, horse corrals, and a heated, outdoor swimming pool (late May-Aug.). The lodge has 385 rooms; all have private baths and Wi-Fi. Rooms are in three locations: on the third floor of the main lodge, separate two-story lodges, or cottages that are actually motel rooms in single-story buildings.

Secluded in the woods at North Jenny Lake, ★ **Jenny Lake Lodge** (400 Jenny Lake Loop, 307/543-3100, www.gtlc.com, June-early Oct., $555-1,230) offers a slice of old-style rustic luxury. The 37 log cabins, built in 1920, have been revamped with modern amenities but still have old-fashioned rockers on each porch for soaking up views. The complex includes a dining room that specializes in gourmet and multi-course meals. Guests can use cruiser-style bicycles and go horseback riding. Lodging is in **three types of log cabins:** freestanding cabins, duplex cabins that share a common porch, and cabin suites. All the cabins have western furnishings, private bathrooms, wireless internet, handmade quilts, and down comforters.

Independent Lodges

★ **Signal Mountain Lodge** (1 Inner Park Rd., 307/543-2831, www.signalmountain lodge.com, mid-May-mid-Oct., $230-445) has million-dollar views of Jackson Lake, Mount Moran, and the Teton Mountains. Make **reservations 16 months** out. The complex has two restaurants, a bar, marina, motorboat rentals, canoe and kayak rentals, laundry and showers, gift shops, campground, camp store, and wireless internet. The lodge has a variety of different room options with or without views. Some of the units have extra amenities such as gas fireplaces, jetted tubs, microwaves, mini-fridges, and sitting areas. Older rustic log cabins can sleep 2-6 people. Motel-style rooms can sleep 2-4 people. Premier Western Rooms have wood furnishings and air-conditioning. Lakefront units have kitchenettes plus balconies or shared patios.

On Teton Park Road, the American Alpine Club operates the **American Alpine Club Climber's Ranch** (307/733-7271 summer, 303/384-0110 fall-spring, americanalpineclub.org, early June-mid-Sept., $22 ACC members, $33 nonmembers). Small shared dorm-style log cabins sleep 4-6 people each on wooden bunks (bring your own sleeping gear). Bathrooms and shower houses are gender-separated. The outdoor cook shelter has dishwashing sinks, picnic tables, bear boxes, and coolers.

On the Snake River in Moose is the family-owned **Dornan's Spur Ranch Cabins** (307/733-2522, dornans.com, May-Oct. and Dec.-Mar., 3-night min. in summer, $125-380). The 12 cabins sleep 4-6 people each, with handcrafted furniture, down comforters on beds, and full kitchens. Some are duplexes, and most have covered decks with barbecue grills and views of the Tetons.

Guest Ranches

Several guest ranches line US 26/89/191 between Moose and Moran Junction. From these ranches, the views of the Teton Mountains provide an exquisite backdrop for horseback riding—one of the main reasons to stay at a guest ranch. Rates are all-inclusive with meals, activities, and lodging in cabins with private bathrooms.

★ **Triangle X Ranch** (2 Triangle X Ranch Rd., 307/733-2183, trianglex. com, mid-May-mid-Oct. and late Dec.-mid-Mar.) has been operated for five generations by the Turner family. Early June-late August is peak season, requiring seven-night stays ($1,996-2,850 pp weekly). Lodging is in one-, two-, or three-bedroom log cabins with private bathrooms.

Moose Head Ranch (21255 N. US 89, 307/733-3141, www.mooseheadranch. com, early June-mid-Aug., $450-800 pp per night) is a 1925 family-run homestead and dude ranch. Log cabins for guests surround the main lodge, where gourmet breakfasts and lunches are served buffet-style. Sunday nights have cookouts.

Campgrounds

All developed campgrounds in the park can be reserved (877/444-6777, www. recreation.gov) six months in advance. Except for Colter Bay RV Park, sites have picnic tables, fire rings, drinking water, flush toilets, and bear boxes for food storage. Some campgrounds have shared hiker-biker sites ($12-13 pp) and ADA-compliant campsites and toilets.

Headwaters Campground & RV (101 Grassy Lake Rd., reservations 307/543-2861, 175 sites, mid-May-Sept., $42 tents, $85 RVs) is at Flagg Ranch. It has full hookups for RVs, which are limited to 45 feet (14 m). The forested campground's sites vary from fully shaded under large spruces and firs to partly sunny with a lack of understory, yielding little privacy. The eastern loops sit closest to the highway, but traffic dwindles at night. RV campsites have gravel pull-throughs wide enough for slide-outs and awnings. **Colter Bay RV Park** (Colter Bay Village, 307/543-3100, 103 sites, early May-early Oct., $86-91) has full hookups with no RV length limits. No tents or fires are permitted in the RV park, but you can use your own gas or charcoal grill.

The remaining park campgrounds are first come, first served, with most filling in morning in summer. The ultra-scenic **Lizard Creek** (43 drive-in sites, 17 walk-in tent sites, early June-early Sept., $34) sits on the north end of Jackson Lake. RVs are limited to 30 feet (9 m).

Colter Bay Campground (350 sites without hookups, 9 walk-in tent sites, 11 group sites, and 13 ADA-compliant campsites with electricity, late May-Sept., $36-64) is in a lodgepole forest. Some

loops are generator-free zones. Sites are assigned at the staffed check-in station. If you arrive after the station closes, a whiteboard lists available sites.

★ **Signal Mountain Campground** (1 Inner Park Rd., 81 sites, 4 tent-only campsites, 1 ADA-compliant site with electricity, mid-May-mid-Oct., $36-58) overlooks Jackson Lake with million-dollar views from some sites. A mix of fir and spruce trees provides some shade, but most small campsites are sunny midday. Low brush and trees create partial privacy. RVs are limited to 30 feet (9 m). Due to its popularity, this campground can fill by 8am.

In a hilly, loose pine forest with big boulders, **Jenny Lake Campground** (49 tent sites, 3 ADA-compliant sites, early May-late Sept., $32) has front-row seating with exceptional scenery right below the Teton Mountains. Each site allows a maximum of two tents, one vehicle or two motorcycles, and six people. Bathroom facilities are vault toilets. No RVs are allowed, and vehicles must be shorter than 14 feet long (4.3 m). This ultra-popular campground fills by 9am, but you may need to start trolling for a site around 7am.

Gros Ventre Campground (350 sites, 10 ADA-compliant sites with electricity, early May-early Oct., $33-64) sits opposite the National Elk Refuge just south of Kelly. Amenities include flush toilets, a dump station, and an amphitheater for evening interpretive programs. Seven huge loops circle the flat, sagebrush plateau under large cottonwood trees that lack understory for privacy but provide shade. Each campsite can fit two vehicles, two tents, and six people. The campground is a haven for moose. Gros Ventre is often the last campground to fill in the park, usually by 4pm.

The gravel **Grassy Lake Road** (Ashton-Flagg Ranch Rd.) has first-come, first-served primitive campsites (14 sites, June-Sept., free). They have vault toilets and picnic tables but no water. Find the sites in the first 10 miles (16 km) west of Flagg Ranch.

Transportation and Services

Emergency Services

In an emergency, **ranger stations** are at Colter Bay Village, Moran Entrance Station, Jenny Lake, and Flagg Ranch. At Jackson Lake Lodge, **Grand Teton Medical Clinic** (307/543-2514, grandtetonmedicalclinic.com, 9am-5pm daily mid-May-early Oct.) can take care of most situations except severe emergencies. The closest hospital, **St. John's Medical Center** (625 E. Broadway, Jackson, 307/733-3636, www.stjohns.health), is about 30 miles (48 km) south of Moran Junction.

Gas

In summer, **gas stations** operate at Flagg Ranch, Colter Bay Village, Jackson Lake Lodge, and Signal Mountain Lodge. Moran and Moose have gas stations open year-round.

Cell Service and Internet Access

Most developed areas of Grand Teton National Park have **cell phone service,** including Colter Bay, Jackson Lake Lodge, Signal Mountain Lodge, Jenny Lake, Moose, and Moran. Cell service is generally sketchy or non-existent in the mountains and outside of developed areas.

Wi-Fi is available at Jackson Lake Lodge, Signal Mountain Lodge, and the Craig Thomas Discovery & Visitor Center. Colter Bay Village has Wi-Fi available in public locations such as restaurants, launderettes, and lodge lobbies.

Tours

Bus Tours

Departing at 8:30am from Jackson Lake Lodge, **scenic bus tours** (307/543-2811, www.gtlc.com, late May-early Oct.) offer guided narration to the sights in Grand Teton (4 hrs, Mon., Wed., and Fri., $92 adults, $52 kids). Reservations are required.

Boat Tours

From the Colter Bay Marina, catch a **Jackson Lake boat tour** (307/543-2811, www.gtlc.com, daily late May-late Sept., $40-72 adults, $20-44 kids) to get out on the water and soak up the lustrous views of Mount Moran. Cruises (90 min., 10:15am, 1:15pm, and 3:15pm daily) motor out through the islands on Jackson Lake. June through early September, cruises also go to Elk Island for breakfast, lunch, or dinner around a campfire. Reservations are required.

Cruise around Jenny Lake to see the Teton Mountains from a different perspective. From the dock at South Jenny Lake, **Jenny Lake Boating** (307/734-9227, www.jennylakeboating.com, 11am, 2pm, and 5pm daily mid-May-Sept., $25 adults, $20 seniors, $15 kids) guides one-hour interpretive tours on open boats. Spring and fall tours depart each day at noon and 2pm. Reservations are recommended.

Wildlife Tours

Grand Teton is full of wildlife to spot. Tours can take you to the hot spots. Guides usually supply binoculars for all participants and spotting scopes. Tours rates do not include park entrance fees or gratuities for guides (15 percent). Reservations are required.

The **Teton Science School** (700 Coyote Canyon Rd., Jackson, 307/733-1313, www.tetonscience.org, daily year-round) leads half-day and full-day wildlife expeditions. They are taught by biologists and naturalists. Guests ride in Sprinter vans with roof hatches that allow standing to view animals. The tours start at $750 for 1-3 people, plus $100 per person additional.

Other tour companies include **Buffalo Roam Tours** (307/413-0954, buffaloroamtours.com), **BrushBuck Tours** (307/699-2999, www.brushbucktours.

com), **Eco Tour Adventures** (307/690-9533, www.jhecotouradventures.com), and **Jackson Hole Wildlife Safaris** (307/690-6402, jacksonholewildlifesafaris.com).

Getting Around
Shuttles and Taxis
Shuttles in Grand Teton are minimal, but for guests of **Grand Teton Lodging Company** (www.gtlc.com), complimentary shuttles run between Jackson Lake Lodge, Colter Bay Village, South Jenny Lake, and the town of Jackson. From Jackson Hole Airport, you can reserve a ride with **Snake River Taxi** (307/413-9009, www.snakerivertaxi.com) to reach lodges in Grand Teton National Park.

Jenny Lake Boating (307/734-9227, www.jennylakeboating.com, 7am-7pm daily early June-early Sept., 10am-4pm daily spring and fall; $10-18 adults, $8-10 kids) helps chop down hiking mileage with their shuttles across Jenny Lake. They run every 10-15 minutes throughout the day. Reservations are not required.

Jackson Hole

At Jackson Hole's south end, the town of Jackson anchors the southern portal for exploring Grand Teton and Yellowstone National Parks. From its antler arches in the Jackson Town Square to the iconic Million Dollar Cowboy Bar, the town melds the Old West with modern places to stay and dine. Local breweries, galleries, shops, music, theater, and coffee shops let you explore the culture, while a trip to the National Elk Refuge in winter lets you count up hundreds of elk.

On the west side of Jackson Hole, Teton Village snuggles just outside Grand Teton National Park. The village is home to upscale hotels and restaurants that cluster at the base of Jackson Hole Mountain Resort. In winter, the resort's steep runs lure skiers and snowboarders.

In summer, the tram whisks sightseers and hikers to the summit of Rendezvous Mountain for stunning views of Jackson Hole and the Tetons.

Contrary to Grand Teton National Park, Jackson Hole works as a year-round destination. Swarms of visitors descend on Jackson Hole in summer when the national park is in full swing. The second busiest season is winter.

The **Jackson Hole and Greater Yellowstone Visitor Center** (532 N. Cache St., 307/733-3316, www.jacksonholechamber.com, 8am-7pm daily summer, 9am-5pm daily winter) has interpretive displays, educational programs, information, and Junior Ranger activity booklets. The interagency center also represents the National Elk Refuge, Grand Teton National Park, Bridger-Teton National Forest, and Jackson. The center also rents bear canisters and panniers, and an on-site **Grand Teton Association shop** (307/739-3606, grandtetonassociation.org) sells field guides, maps, and hiking books.

Sights
Jackson Town Square
In downtown Jackson, the **Town Square** is a year-round attraction. Four antler arches, each made from 2,000 tightly intertwined elk antlers, serve as entrances at the square's four corners. In summer, authentic horse-drawn **stagecoaches** (9am-9pm daily, $4-6) give 10-minute rides, and a **gunfight reenactment** (6pm Mon.-Sat., free) is put on by the Jackson Hole Playhouse at the northeast corner of the park. In winter, you can ice skate for free (rentals $12).

Snow King Mountain
In summer, **Snow King Mountain** (402 E. Snow King Ave., 307/201-5464, snowkingmountain.com, 10am-9pm daily summer, hours shorten spring and fall, from $20 adults, $5 kids 6 and under) offers **scenic gondola rides** that zip riders to the summit of Snow King Mountain. With

Jackson

To
National Museum of Wildlife Art,
Airport, Grand Teton and
Yellowstone National Parks

26
89
191

CREEKSIDE MARKET
AND DELI

Murie
Family
Park

National

Elk Refuge

JACKSON HOLE AND
GREATER YELLOWSTONE
VISITOR CENTER

WYOMING GAME AND
FISH DEPARTMENT

GLENWOOD ST

SADDLE BUTTE DR

Multi-Use Path

LEWIS AND CLARK
EXPEDITIONS

BRIDGER-TETON
NATIONAL FOREST
OFFICE

MERCILL AVE

CACHE DRIVE

INN ON
THE CREEK

Flat Creek

MILLWARD ST

JACKSON HOLE
HISTORICAL SOCIETY
AND MUSEUM

P
PUBLIC
RESTROOMS

TETON COUNTY
RECREATION
CENTER

GILL AVE

GILL AVE

RUSTY
PARROT
LODGE

Miller
Park

THE BLUE
LION

TETON
MOUNTAINEERING

SNAKE RIVER
ANGLER

LIBERTY BURGERS

THE MERRY
PIGLETS

HOTEL
JACKSON

HAND FIRE
PIZZA

THE
CLOUDVEIL

P
PUBLIC
RESTROOM

To
National Elk
Refuge

PUBLIC
RESTROOMS

JACKSON HOLE
PLAYHOUSE

SKINNY
SKIS

MADE

JACKSON
TOWN
SQUARE

CENTER ST

DELONEY AVE

HUFF
HOUSE

P
DAVE HANSEN
WHITEWATER

THE WORT
HOTEL

SILVER DOLLAR
BAR

LOCAL

CAFE
GENEVIEVE

PERSEPHONE
CAFE

26 89 191

W BROADWAY

TERRA OF
JACKSON HOLE

E BROADWAY

To
Hoback Sports,
Jackson Hole Mountain Resort
and Teton Village

BIN 22

MILLION DOLLAR
COWBOY BAR

PEARL STREET
MARKET

STIO

THE SNAKE
RIVER GRILL

VALLEY
BOOKSTORE

CLISSOLD ST

JACKSON ST

PEARL ST

ROADHOUSE
BREWING
COMPANY

PEARL ST

WILLOW ST

POST
OFFICE

SIMPSON AVE

SIMPSON AVE

JACKSON HOLE
CENTER FOR THE ARTS

GLENWOOD ST

CACHE DRIVE

0   200 yds

0   200 m

COWBOY
VILLAGE
RESORT

SNAKE RIVER
BREWING

MILLWARD ST

KING ST

Road Trip
Route

To
Jackson Hole Rodeo

To
Snow King Mountain

© MOON.COM

360-degree views, the summit is the best place to gaze down on the town below and across Jackson Hole to the Teton Mountains.

National Museum of Wildlife Art

Five minutes north of Jackson, the **National Museum of Wildlife Art** (2820 Rungius Rd., 307/733-5771, www.wildlifeart.org, 9am-5pm daily May-Oct., 9am-5pm Tues.-Sat., 11am-5pm Sun. Nov.-Apr., $13-15) fuses its stone architecture into the landscape; walk the perimeter trails to view 30 outdoor sculptures of elk, bison, eagles, fish, and moose. Inside, 14 galleries hold paintings, drawings, and sculptures of wildlife from North America and Europe. Use the audio wands or mobile apps to access interpretive info. Highlights include the largest collection of Carl Rungius works in the United States, artifacts from ancient Indigenous groups, and Ken Bunn's *Silent Pursuit,* a mountain lion sculpture. A kids' room has hands-on activities.

National Elk Refuge

Bordering the town of Jackson, the **National Elk Refuge** (www.fws.gov) has wildlife-watching year-round. The refuge was established to preserve the Jackson elk herd. In early spring, **migratory birds** arrive and **elk calving** happens, and **bull elk** shed their antlers; many migrate from the refuge to summer at higher elevations before retuning in late fall. Around 7,000 elk winter at the refuge, and you can also spot **bison, pronghorn, bighorn sheep**, **wolves, trumpeter swans,** and **mule deer.** In winter, **horse-drawn sleigh rides** (307/733-0277, www.nersleighrides.com, $27 adults, $15 kids, reservations available) go wildlife-watching. Pick up tickets and catch the shuttle at the Jackson Hole visitors center.

From Jackson, US 26/89/191 parallels the western boundary of the refuge with pullovers for wildlife-watching. From the east end of Broadway Street, you can drive the dirt **Refuge Road** (3.5 mi/5.6 km), where pullouts allow for wildlife-watching and photography.

Jackson Hole Mountain Resort

Jackson Hole Mountain Resort (3275 W. Village Dr., 307/733-2292 or 888/333-7766, www.jacksonhole.com) is a ski and snowboard resort that offers sightseeing, mountain biking, hiking, and thrill sports in the summer. The **Aerial Tram** (9am-5pm daily mid-May-early Oct., $47 adults) is the easiest way to get on top of a mountain in the Tetons. The tram whisks riders up to the 10,450-foot (3,185-m) summit of **Rendezvous Mountain,** overlooking Grand Teton National Park. At the summit, you'll stare down at Jackson Hole and across the Teton summits to the Grand Teton itself. You can take photos, walk to viewpoints, eat waffles at tiny **Corbet's Cabin,** or hike trails. Some people may feel sluggish or lightheaded from the elevation upon reaching the summit.

While the tram goes to the top of the mountain, the **Bridger Gondola** (9am-5pm daily mid-May-early Oct., adults $40-45) goes to the **Rendezvous Lodge** located below the Casper Ridge Cliffs at the intersection of several trails. On the ride up, you'll be privy to excellent views over the valley floor.

Scenic Drives
Teton Pass

Driving **Teton Pass** (46 mi/74 km) across the Teton Mountains is one of the steepest climbs in the country, ascending at a 10 percent grade in places. From Jackson, the curvy route to the summit ascends 11 miles (18 km) west along WY 22, with a few pullouts offering views of Jackson Hole, the **Snake River,** and the **Gros Ventre Mountains.** Then the road drops on ID 33 for about 12 miles (19 km) through a canyon of **Caribou-Targhee National Forest** to Victor, Idaho. While the road is open year-round, it frequently closes in winter for avalanche control work. It takes about one hour to do this drive.

Recreation
Hiking
Hole Hiking Experience (307/690-4453, www.holehike.com, Jackson, year-round) guides day hikes, mixed programs of hiking with rafting or other activities, and customized multiday backpacking trips. Hikes in Bridger-Teton and Caribou-Targhee National Forests are led by seasoned naturalists.

In Jackson, rent hiking and backpacking gear from **Teton Mountaineering** (170 N. Cache St., 307/733-3595, www.tetonmtn.com), **Skinny Skis** (65 W. Deloney Ave., 307/733-6094, www.skinnyskis.com), or **Teton Backcountry Rentals** (565 N. Cache St., 307/828-1885, tetonbcrentals.com). Teton Backcountry also rents bear spray at Jackson Hole Airport.

Snow King Mountain
Distance: 3.6 miles (5.8 km) rt
Duration: 3 hours
Elevation change: 1,571 feet (479 m)

Effort: strenuous
Trailhead: corner of Snow King Ave. and Cache St.
Snow King Mountain in Bridger-Teton National Forest yields a 360-degree view of the Tetons, National Elk Refuge, Gros Ventre Mountains, and the town of Jackson. Prepare for a grunt as the route climbs up a combination of trail and service roads that switchback up the slope. To avoid the knee-pounding descent, take the gondola down from **Snow King Mountain** (402 E. Snow King Ave., 307/201-5464, snowkingmountain.com, 10am-9pm daily summer, shorter hours spring and fall, from $20 adults, $5 kids 6 and under).

From the base area, find the **Snow King Summit Trail** above the ticket office at the chairlift and gondola. Climb up three switchbacks, passing the Sink or Swim Trail, to a signed junction with a mountain road. Turn west and traverse the slope to the end of a switchback, where the steep work begins. Climb up three more switchbacks on the dirt road.

columbine in the Teton Mountains

The route crests out on the ridge, where a dirt road reaches the summit and the top of the gondola.

Rendezvous Mountain

Distance: 15 miles (24 km) rt
Duration: 8-9 hours
Elevation change: 4,139 feet (1,262 m)
Effort: extremely strenuous
Trailhead: Jackson Hole Mountain Resort

It's one long ascent to climb 10,450-foot (3,185-m) Rendezvous Mountain at Jackson Hole Mountain Resort. To chop the mileage in half, most people hike to the summit and take the **Aerial Tram** (3275 W. Village Dr., 307/733-2292 or 888/333-7766, www.jacksonhole.com, 9am-5pm daily mid-May-early Oct., $47 adults) in one direction. You can also hire a hiking guide via advance reservation.

Take the **Wildflower Trail** (4.2 mi/6.8 km) to switchback up ski slopes through mostly open meadows. Views get bigger the higher you go. The trail crosses the Summit Trail service road several times. At the top of the Bridger Gondola (9am-5pm daily mid-May-early Oct., adults $40-42, those who want to bail on the ascent here can take the lift back down. To go on, the **Summit Trail** (3.3 mi/5.3 km) mostly follows service roads with less steep grades to reach the top of **Rendezvous Mountain** and the Aerial Tram. From the 360-degree summit, views east take in Jackson Hole, the Snake River, and Gros Ventre Mountains. To the north, the peaks of Grand Teton National Park line up, including Grand Teton.

Top of the World Trail

Distance: 0.5 mile (0.8 km) loop
Duration: 20-30 minutes
Elevation change: 175 feet (53 m)
Effort: easy
Trailhead: top of the Aerial Tram at Jackson Hole Mountain Resort

This short roadbed loop around the **summit of Rendezvous Mountain** may be easy going down, but the altitude will make the uphill return more difficult. Panoramic views take in Grand Teton and Granite Canyon in the national park. Take your time to soak up the scenery.

Cirque Trail

Distance: 1.8 miles (2.9 km) one-way
Duration: 1.5 hours
Elevation change: 1,323 feet (403 m)
Effort: moderate down, strenuous up
Trailhead: top of the Aerial Tram at Jackson Hole Mountain Resort

The **Cirque Trail** connects the top of the Aerial Tram with Bridger Gondola. Most hikers take the tram up and hike down to the gondola before riding back down to Teton Village, but reversing the route works if you want more of a challenge.

From below Corbet's Cabin at the summit, follow the trail in a steep descent of a ridge, plummeting in short switchbacks on a boulder spine with rough block steps. The trail swings north into the cirque to drop through steep wildflower meadows and under dramatic cliffs to the

top of the gondola. Views sweep across Jackson Hole on the entire route.

Biking

In Jackson, rental bikes and gear are available at **Hoback Sports** (520 W. Broadway Ave., 307/733-5335, hobacksports.com) and **Snow King Mountain Sports** (402 E. Snow King Ave., 307/201-5096, snowkingmountain.com). Both generally carry mountain bikes, pathway bikes, and kids' bikes, plus trailers for tots. Rentals come with helmets and sometimes bike locks.

Road Biking

Although **Teton Pass** (WY 22) has no bike lane for ascending, it's the prime ride for cyclists who like climbing. Start early to beat traffic. From Jackson, the road to Teton Pass is 13 miles (21 km).

Paved pathways for biking parallel the park's roads. About 56 miles (90 km) of the multi-use **Jackson Hole Pathway** (www.friendsofpathways.org) connects Jackson with Teton Village, the National Elk Refuge, Moose, and Jenny Lake; maps are available online. The pathway along the elk refuge is usually closed in winter for wildlife protection, and only a few sections are plowed in winter.

Mountain Biking

Single-track trails abound in Bridger-Teton National Forest surrounding Jackson Hole. The closest riding complex is the **Snow King Trails** (Snow King Mountain, 402 E. Snow King Ave., 307/201-5464, snowkingmountain.com), where mountain bikers can ride to the summit of Snow King or loop the **Skyline Trail** and **Cache-Game Trails.** A downloadable map that includes the Cache-Game Trails is online.

West of Jackson, the **Teton Pass Trail Network** (www.friendsofpathways.org) has several mountain biking routes, including **Old Pass Road** (3.9 mi/6.3 km one-way), for those who want to climb to or descend from the pass. Some trails

are for downhill mountain biking only, while others are multiuse. The website has maps that specify which trails are open to specific user groups.

Jackson Hole Mountain Resort (Teton Village, 307/733-2292, www.jacksonhole.com, 10am-5pm late May-early Sept., $50) has lift-accessed mountain biking via the Teewinot Lift and Sweetwater Gondola, a bike park, rentals, and tours. The bike park trails have jump tracks, banked corners, and skills features for beginners through advanced riders.

Horseback Riding

Spring Creek Ranch (1600 N. East Butte Rd., 307/732-8104, www.springcreekranch.com, June-mid-Oct., $60-80) guides trail rides on East Gros Ventre Butte with big views of Jackson Hole and the Tetons. Wear long pants, sturdy shoes, and a sun hat. Make reservations and tip your wrangler 15 percent.

Water Sports

Boaters need to have current **registration** and an Aquatic Invasive Species (AIS) sticker, available after passing an inspection (Wyoming Game and Fish, https://wgfd.wyo.gov, $10-30 motorized, $5-15 nonmotorized). Forest Service permits are not needed for rafting day trips (unless you have a large group), but you will need a Wyoming AIS sticker.

River Rafting

From Jackson, **white-water rafting trips** (daily June-mid-Sept., 3.5 hrs, $85-90 adults, $65-75 kids) run Class III+ rapids through **Snake River Canyon.** It's one of the classic day trips for white water, but don't expect wilderness; its popularity can mean lots of boats, and parking areas are crowded at access sites. From the put-in at West Table southwest of Hoback Junction, the white-water section runs 7.4 miles (11.9 km) to the Sheep Gulch takeout. You'll hit rapids such as Double D, Haircut Rock, Blind Canyon, and Big Kahuna. Spring high water can increase the difficulty; the river is usually runnable May-September. Easier float sections are upriver from West Table.

Smaller rafts (6-8 people, higher rates) give more splash, while large rafts can fit 10-16 people; either way, you paddle. Forest Service fees may not be included in the rates; inquire when booking. Plan to tip 15 percent. Most companies have 4-5 departures daily for white-water trips. Make reservations with **Mad River Boat Trips** (1255 S. US 89, 800/458-7238, www.mad-river.com), **Dave Hansen Whitewater** (225 W. Broadway, 307/733-6295, www.davehansenwhitewater. com), **Jackson Hole Whitewater** (945 W. Broadway, 888/700-7238, www.jhww. com), or **Lewis and Clark Expeditions** (335 N. Cache St., 800/824-5375, www. lewisandclarkriverrafting.com).

Paddling

The **Snake River** is a prime waterway for kayaking. The stretch from Grand Teton Park to Hoback Junction (25 mi/40 km south of Jackson) provides meandering Class I-II floating with river accesses at Moose, Wilson Bridge, and South Park Bridge. South of Jackson, a trail for kayakers accesses **King's Wave** for surfing.

For paddling lakes in Grand Teton National Park or for those skilled enough to tackle rivers, **Rendezvous River Sports** (945 W. Broadway, 307/733-2471, www. jacksonholekayak.com) rents canoes, stand-up paddleboards, rafts, and touring, river, inflatable, and tandem kayaks, including accessories. They also offer lessons and guided tours.

Fishing

Fly-fishing anglers gravitate to Jackson Hole, especially for fine-spotted cutthroat trout in the **Snake River,** south of Grand Teton National Park. You'll need a Wyoming state **fishing license** ($6-14 daily, $56 for 5 days), sold at fly shops in Jackson.

Fishing **guides** (daily May-Oct., starts at $480 half day or $580 full day for 2 people) abound for wade-fishing or float-fishing. Book a guide with **Snake River Angler** (185 Center St., 307/733-3699, snakeriverangler.com), **Jackson Hole Anglers** (888/458-7688, jacksonhole-anglers.com), or **Fish the Fly** (307/690-1139, fishthefly.com). For beginners, **Jackson Hole Fly Fishing School** (802 Powderhorn Ln., 307/699-3440, www. jhflyfishingschool.com) teaches the basics in the Introduction to Fly Fishing class ($70 adults, $50 kids).

Winter Sports
Skiing and Snowboarding

Snow King Mountain (402 E. Snow King Ave., Jackson, 307/734-3194, http:// snowkingmountain.com, Dec.-late Mar., from $50) is a small family-friendly ski hill with three lifts, night skiing, half-day afternoon rates, and a terrain park.

With a big vertical (4,139 ft/1,262 m), steep chutes, and a reputation as an experts-only ski area, **Jackson Hole Mountain Resort** (3275 W. Village Dr., 307/739-2654, www.jacksonhole.com, late Nov.-early Apr., $100-170 adults) in reality has only half of its terrain devoted to advanced runs. The rest is rolling groomers for beginners and intermediates. The resort has 12 lifts, including the Aerial Tram that goes to the summit of Rendezvous Mountain. There are also several terrain parks, restaurants, and rental shops at the resort.

Backcountry and Heli-Skiing

The Tetons are a backcountry ski paradise if you're versed in avalanche safety. Teton Pass and Jackson Hole Mountain Resort side country are the most popular places to go. Check on **avalanche conditions** (307/733-2664, http:// jhavalanche.org) before departing.

Guides from **Jackson Hole Mountain Resort** (307/733-2292, www.jacksonhole. com) lead trips that go beyond the resort. **High Mountain Heli-Skiing**

(307/733-3274, www.heliskijackson.com, mid-Dec.-Mar., $1,450 pp) has access to five mountain ranges surrounding Jackson Hole.

In Jackson, rent gear at **Teton Mountaineering** (170 N. Cache St., 307/733-3595, tetonmtn.com), **Skinny Skis** (65 W. Deloney Ave., 307/733-6094, www.skinnyskis.com), or **Teton Backcountry Rentals** (565 N. Cache St., 307/828-1885, tetonbcrentals.com).

Cross-Country Skiing and Snowshoeing
Teton Pines Nordic Center (3450 N. Clubhouse Dr., Wilson, 307/733-1005, www.tetonpinesnordiccenter.com, daily mid-Nov.-early Mar., $10-18) grooms 16 km (10 mi) of golf course trails daily for skate and classic skiing, plus offers rentals and lessons. **Jackson Hole Nordic** (jh-nordic.com) provides information on local trails and grooming reports for skiing or snowshoeing.

Skinny Skis (65 W. Deloney Ave., 307/733-6094, www.skinnyskis.com, $15-30/day) rents snowshoes and offers packages for ski touring, metal-edge touring, and skate-skiing. **Hole Hiking Experience** (866/733-4453, www.holehike.com) guides cross-country ski trips and snowshoe tours.

Snow Tubing
King Tubes (Snow King Mountain Resort, 402 E. Snow King Ave., 307/201-5667, snowkingmountain.com, 1pm-8pm daily mid-Dec.-Mar., $20 pp 1 hr, $10 each additional hr) requires no skill on the snow to have some fun sliding. Ride the Magic Carpet uphill, then sail down one of three lanes.

Thrill Sports
In summer, **Snow King Mountain** (402 E. Snow King Ave., 307/733-5200, snowkingmountain.com, hours vary by activity, daily late May-early Sept.) turns into a

Top to bottom: National Museum of Wildlife Art; Million Dollar Cowboy Bar; Bin 22 restaurant

play zone for families with a pair of parallel alpine slides, a bungee trampoline, and the Treetop Adventure Park of high ropes and aerial thrills. A bouldering park is at the base of the mountain.

At **Jackson Hole Mountain Resort** (3275 W. Village Dr., 307/733-2292, www.jacksonhole.com), thrill seekers can tackle a guided mountain climbing experience on granite walls. On the **via ferrata** (9am-5pm daily mid-June-Sept., starts at $333/2 people, 2-6 hrs), you'll travel across suspended metal bridges, carved steps, ladders, and iron rungs. Reservations are recommended.

Golf

The golf season in Jackson Hole runs daily May through mid-October on two 18-hole courses ($80-200, advance reservations recommended). **Jackson Hole Golf and Tennis Club** (5000 Spring Gulch Rd., Jackson, 307/733-3111, www.jhgtc.com) is a redesigned course by Robert Trent Jones Jr. **Teton Pines Resort and Country Club** (3450 N. Clubhouse Dr., Wilson, 307/733-1005, www.tetonpines.com) is a course designed by Arnold Palmer and Ed Seay.

Nightlife

You'll find live music and crowds at two nightlife venues. The top stop is the **Million Dollar Cowboy Bar** (25 N. Cache St., 307/733-2207, www.milliondollarcowboybar.com, 11am-2am daily year-round), crowned with its neon cowboy on a horse. The bar is decked out with knobbled-pine trim, inlaid silver coins, and saddles with saddle blankets as stools. Jack Daniel's whiskey comes by the barrel. In the Wort Hotel, the **Silver Dollar Bar** (50 N. Glenwood St., 307/733-2190 or 800/322-2727, www.worthotel.com, 11am-2am daily year-round) mixes an authentic historic western ambience of oil paintings, murals, and bronzes with the bar counter inlaid with 2,032 uncirculated silver dollars from 1921.

Performing Arts

Near the Town Square, the **Jackson Hole Playhouse and Saddle Rock Saloon** (145 W. Deloney Ave., 307/733-6994, www.jacksonplayhouse.com, $25-40 shows only, $70-95 with dinner) puts on nightly theater performances of classic Broadway musicals in summer. **Off Square Theatre Company** (240 S. Glenwood St., 307/733-3021, www.offsquare.org) stages musicals and plays annually, put on by local actors.

Festivals and Events

In the early 1950s, elk antlers were used to build the first arch in the Jackson Town Square. Boy Scouts began collecting the antlers in the late 1950s; a decade later, they started the annual **Boy Scout Antler Auction** in the Town Square. Commonly known as **Elkfest**, the event takes place the Saturday before Memorial Day weekend. Registered bidders can purchase elk antlers collected from the National Elk Refuge; 75 percent of the proceeds go back to the refuge.

The **Jackson Hole Rodeo** (Teton County Fairgrounds, 447 Snow King Ave., 307/733-7927, www.jhrodeo.com, 8pm-10pm Wed. and Sat. late May-early Sept., Fri. July-Aug., $16-40) shows off local cowboys and cowgirls in bronc and bull riding, roping, and barrel racing. Kids can participate in a calf scramble to nab a ribbon off its tail. Three types of seating are available in the grandstands: reserved, roof-covered general admission, and uncovered general admission. Buy tickets in advance online to avoid lines at the rodeo grounds.

The **Teton County Fair** (Teton County Fairgrounds, 305 Snow King Ave., Jackson, 307/733-5289, www.tetoncountyfair.com, 5pm-midnight Wed.-Fri., 2pm-midnight Sat.-Sun. late July) hosts carnival rides, rodeos, farm animal shows, pig wrestling, food booths, and other county fair fun for 10 days in late July.

The **Grand Teton Music Festival** (Walk

Festival Hall, 3330 Cody Ln., Teton Village, 307/733-1128, gtmf.org, July-mid-Aug., $25-60) draws musicians, soloists, and conductors from top symphonies across the country. Concerts run five nights weekly. Single tickets go on sale in March online; order by phone or at the box office (10am-5pm Mon.-Sat.) in late June.

Shopping

More than 25 art galleries cluster in Jackson, mostly around the Town Square, convenient for art walks organized by **Jackson Hole Gallery Association** (jacksonholegalleryassociation.com). The galleries sell handmade jewelry, woodcarvings, furniture, bronze sculptures, photography, and crafts made by local artisans and internationally acclaimed artists. **MADE** (125 N. Cache St.., 307/690-7957, www.madejacksonhole.com, 10am-6pm daily) carries handcrafted art from more than 100 local and regional artists.

Valley Book Store (140 E. Broadway, 307/733-4533, www.valleybookstore. com, 9am-7pm Mon.-Sat., 10am-6pm Sun.) is an independent bookstore that carries a good collection of field guides, trail guides, and books about the region, national parks, natural history, and recreation. The store also has books by local authors.

For high-end outdoor clothing, go to **Stio** (10 E. Broadway, 307/201-1890, www. stio.com, 10am-7pm daily). You can also buy recycled gear through **Headwall Recycle Sports** (520 S. US 89, 307/734-8022, www.headwallsports.com, 9am-7pm daily). They carry hiking, camping, skiing, snowboarding, and biking gear.

Food
Jackson

Dining in Jackson is a culinary treat. But make reservations for dinner or you may have a very long wait. Restaurants are open year-round; some shorten hours or days in spring, fall, and winter. Expect spendy meal prices due to Jackson's resort town status.

Fine Dining

Order a bottle of fine wine to go with dinner at the **Blue Lion** (160 N. Millward St., 307/733-3912, bluelionrestaurant.com, 5:30pm-10pm daily, $20-46), where elk tenderloin or a rack of lamb can only be topped by the house mud pie.

To watch food artistry in action, gather around the open kitchen at the chef-owned **Trio** (45 S. Glenwood St., 307/734-8038, bistrotrio.com, 5:30am-10pm daily, $20-52). An eclectic menu offers grilled meats and fish. The wood-fired oven puts out pizzas and chicken.

Steakhouses

Chef-owned **Local** (55 N. Cache St., 307/201-1717, localjh.com, 5pm-9pm Mon.-Sat., $19-75) serves rib-eye and filet mignon with a contemporary flair along with tasty sides and sauces.

A block off the Town Square, **Snake River Grill** (84 E. Broadway, 307/733-0557, www.snakerivergrill.com, 5:30pm-10pm daily, $22-50) does creative Wagyu and Angus steaks, as well as fish and duck, artfully presented and cooked to perfection.

Tapas and Small Plates

At **Bin 22** (200 W. Broadway, 307/739-9463, bin22jacksonhole.com, 11:30am-10pm Mon.-Sat., 3pm-10pm Sun., $6-30), you'll think you're in a wine shop...which you are. Walk through the cases of wine to the back, where delightful tapas and small plates are served with wines and craft beers. Choose a spot at one of several big, shareable tables with stools that foster leisure conversations between strangers. Small-plate entrées are made to share: pancetta-wrapped dates, house-pulled mozzarella, and several Spanish dishes.

Pub Fare

Snake River Brewing (265 S. Millward St., 307/739-2337, snakeriverbrewing. com, 11am-11pm daily, $9-18) serves up pale ale, lager, and Zonker Stout along with unique bar bites, burgers, pizza, and pasta.

The eatery at **Roadhouse Brewing Company** (20 E. Broadway, 307/739-0700, roadhousebrewery.com, 11:30am-close Mon.-Sat., 11am-close Sun., $12-27) serves hefty tastes of their mountain-style IPA along with traditional pub fare, flatbreads, lobster rolls, and a few dishes with Asian twists.

Cookouts

Cowboyland means cookouts in summer. Advance reservations are required. First, you'll get to the **Bar T 5 Cookout** (812 Cache Creek Dr., 307/733-5386, www. bart5.com, Mon.-Sat. mid-May-Sept., $52 adults, $41 kids) via covered wagon. Then, cowhands cook a meal of Dutch-oven roast beef in an outdoor pavilion and a band plays western music. You'll take another ride in the wagon back to town.

The **Bar J Chuckwagon** (4200 W. Bar J Chuckwagon, Wilson, 800/905-2275, barjchuckwagon.com, gates 5:30pm, dinner 7pm daily late May-late Sept., $35-50 adults, $18 kids) serves a western dinner for 650 people in cattle-call fashion with the Bar J Wranglers playing twangy music and telling cowboy stories. Claim your seat and enjoy barbecued steak, chicken, or pork.

Burgers and Pizza

At **Liberty Burgers** (160 N. Cache St., 307/200-6071, jacksonholerestaurants. com, 11:30am-9pm daily, $6-15), indulge your burger cravings with eclectic ingredients like wild arugula, garlic aioli, avocado, and sauces. Order sides of kale salad, sweet potato fries, or roasted stuffed jalapeños.

Housed in the historic Teton Theater, **Hand Fire Pizza** (120 N. Cache St.,

307/733-7199, www.handfirepizza.com, 5pm-10pm daily, $10-30) creates healthy wood-fired pizzas made with organic, hormone- and nitrate-free, and mostly regional ingredients. Options include gluten-free crusts or dairy-free cheeses. Look for the weekly special or create your own combination.

Cafés

Two long-time staples serve top-notch meals with indoor and outdoor seating. **Persephone Cafe** (145 E. Broadway, 307/200-6708, persephonebakery.com, 7am-6pm Mon.-Sat., 7am-5pm Sun., $4-15) churns out rustic artisan breads, classic croissants, brioche, and scones, which serve as the backbone for breakfast and lunch. **Café Genevieve** (135 E. Broadway, 307/732-1910, genevievejh. com, 8am-10pm daily, $9-41) delivers foods with southern flair, including eggs Benedict with Cajun sausage. Their pig candy (candied bacon) appetizer works anytime.

Groceries

Jackson has two small, unique markets. For upscale items, check out **Pearl Street Market** (40 W. Pearl St., 307/733-1300, www.pearlstmarketjh.com, 7am-9pm daily). En route toward Grand Teton National Park, stop at **Creekside Market and Deli** (545 N. Cache St., 307/733-7926, creeksidejacksonhole.com, 6am-8pm daily) to grab picnic goodies.

Teton Village

Most restaurants in Teton Village are open late November to early April and mid-May to late September in conjunction with Jackson Hole Mountain Resort's lift operations. Make reservations for dinner; otherwise, you are guaranteed a long wait.

Teton Thai (7342 Granite Loop Rd., 307/733-0022, www.tetonthaivillage. com, 11:30am-9:30pm Mon.-Sat. mid-May-Sept. and late Nov.-early Apr., $22-28) serves classic recipes from Bangkok,

⮕ Side Trip: Teton Valley

The Teton Valley is on the less-traveled west side of the Teton Mountains in Idaho. It contains tiny towns like Victor and Driggs, which serve as gateways for four seasons of recreation. Teton Valley is the back door or west-side access into the Teton Mountains and, via hiking, into Grand Teton National Park. The Grand Targhee Resort has uncrowded slopes for skiing and snowboarding in winter. In summer, the resort morphs into a mountain biking destination.

The valley's claim to kitsch is the huge potato on the bed of a 1946 Chevy truck in front of the **Spud Drive-In** (2175 S. ID 33, Driggs, 208/557-3282, spuddrivein.com). The outdoor theater is between Victor and Driggs, and it shows double features.

Skiing and Snowboarding

Grand Targhee Resort (3300 Ski Hill Rd., Alta, WY, 307/353-2300 or 800/827-4433, www. grandtarghee.com, late Nov.-late Apr.) skis like a much bigger mountain and gains big views of the Grand Teton when weather permits. The resort has five lifts spread across 2,602 acres and 2,176 feet (663 m) of vertical, but much of its terrain is open glade skiing, prime on powder days. Targhee is known for dry, light powder snow. **Lift tickets** ($98-105) are more affordable than at Jackson Hole. The resort also has terrain parks, rentals, lessons, naturalist programs, restaurants, and lodging.

Mountain Biking

At Grand Targhee Resort, the **Grand Targhee Bike Park** (3300 Ski Hill Rd., Alta, WY, 307/353-2300 or 800/827-4433, www.grandtarghee.com, 10am-5pm daily mid-May-mid-Sept.) is becoming one of the most-lauded places to mountain bike in the Northern Rockies. Lifts service 13 miles (21 km) of downhill trails, plus flow trails, a skills park, and events. The resort has rentals ($60-80) and combo bike park and lift passes ($31-41). Surrounding the resort, Caribou-Targhee National Forest also has 47 miles (76 km) of cross-country multiuse single-track trails.

from pad Thai to roasted duck curry. They can do *hot* here!

Il Villaggio Osteria (Hotel Terra, 3335 W. Village Dr., 307/739-4100, www. jhosteria.com, 11:30am-close daily year-round, $20-45) brings Italy to the Wyoming slopes with house-made pastas, Italian wines, and an atmosphere that rings true to a bustling Italian eatery. They also do fresh takes on wood-fired pizza.

In the Four Seasons, the **Westbank Grill** (Four Seasons, 7680 Granite Loop Rd., 307/732-5000 or 307/732-5156, www. fourseasons.com/jacksonhole, 7am-11am, 11:30am-3pm, and 6pm-10pm daily May-Oct. and late Nov.-early Apr., $30-145) is a romantic place for sinking into a leisurely multicourse dinner spun around Wagyu beef and succulent game such as bison or venison.

Accommodations and Camping

Lodging properties have the highest prices of the year in summer and winter holidays. Visitors to Jackson Hole have considerable lodging choices, and prices for familiar chains will be inflated due to the resort nature of the town. To guarantee what you want, **book a year in advance.**

Jackson

Hotels and Inns

The historic **Wort Hotel** (50 N. Glenwood St, 307/733-2190 or 800/322-2727, www. worthotel.com, $330-1,100) is the place to stay if you like character. It's home to the famous Silver Dollar Bar. The 59 rooms come in nine different styles with one king or two queen beds (or a mix). Suites include sitting areas.

One block from the Town Square,

Food

For huge burgers, the **Brakeman American Grill** (27 N. Main St., Victor, 208/787-2020, www.brakemangrill.com, 11:30am-3:30pm and 5pm-8pm Tues.-Sun., $10-16) grinds their beef fresh daily and grills them to order.

The small **Forage Bistro and Lounge** (285 E. Little Ave., Driggs, 208/345-2858, www.forageandlounge.com, 11am-9pm Mon.-Fri., 10am-9pm Sat.-Sun., $10-20) serves small plates, unique salads, burgers, and sandwiches. By the same owners, **Citizen 33 Brewery** (364 N. Main St., Driggs, 208/357-9099, www.citizen33.com, 3pm-10pm daily, $10-15) is a craft brewery with pub fare.

Accommodations and Camping

Grand Targhee Resort (3300 Ski Hill Rd., Alta, WY, 307/353-2300 or 800/827-4433, www.grandtarghee.com, mid-May-mid-Sept. and late Nov.-late Apr., $120-700) has four lodging options: a two-bedroom tower condo, economy rooms, hotel rooms, and larger suites. Winter has the highest prices.

Caribou-Targhee National Forest (208/354-2312, www.fs.usda.gov) has three campgrounds (reservations 877/444-6777, www.recreation.gov, late May-late Sept., $12, $6 extra vehicle). East of Driggs, **Teton Canyon Campground** (20 sites) is on Teton Canyon Road. On ID 33 between Teton Pass and Victor are two roadside campgrounds: **Mike Harris Campground** (10 sites) and **Trail Creek Campground** (10 sites).

Getting There

From Jackson, WY 22 crosses scenic Teton Pass to become ID 33 in Idaho, going through Victor (25 mi/40 km, 40 min.) and Driggs (33 mi/53 km, 50 min.). To reach Alta and the Grand Targhee Resort from Driggs, take Ski Hill Road east for 13 miles (21 km), a 25-minute drive.

★ **Hotel Jackson** (120 N. Glenwood St., 307/733-2200, www.hoteljackson.com, $330-1,120) meets LEED building standards for its 55 luxurious rooms. Seven styles of rooms have two queens or one king bed. For a little more space, stay in one of four suites with decks. FIGS, the hotel's restaurant, serves breakfast, lunch, and dinner, plus hand-crafted cocktails.

The three-story **Wyoming Inn of Jackson Hole** (930 W. Broadway, 307/734-0035, www.wyominginn.com, $130-470) greets guests with a stone fireplace, wood carvings of bighorn sheep at the check-in desk, saddle-leather couches, and a moose paddle chandelier in the lobby. Rooms have one king or two queen beds and custom window seats; some have fireplaces. The hotel has an on-site restaurant that serves organic breakfasts, a fitness room, and guest laundry.

In downtown Jackson, the historic **Huff House** (240 E. Deloney Ave., 307/733-7141, www.huffhousejh.com, $190-480, 2-night min.) has 11 upscale rooms, suites, and cabins, all with private baths. Landscaped grounds feature a hot tub and patio with fireplace. Stays include hot breakfasts, afternoon cookies, off-street parking, and gracious hospitality.

Resorts

Perched on East Gros Ventre Butte with a commanding view of the Tetons, the **Amangani** (1535 NE Butte Rd., 307/734-4861, www.amanresorts.com, May-Oct. and late Nov.-Mar., $800-2,500, 2-night min. in summer) features floor-to-ceiling windows that capture the scenery. Enjoy the dining room, outdoor decks, pools, hot tubs, and patios, plus sumptuous guest suites featuring stone and wood styling, king beds, sitting areas, and spacious bathrooms.

Cowboy Village Resort (120 S. Flat Creek Dr., 307/733-3121 or 800/962-4988, www.townsquareinns.com, $100-310) has 82 log cabins with kitchenettes. Cabins have one or two queen beds (some in bunks) plus a sofa bed and small porches with picnic tables and barbecue grills. The resort has an indoor pool, hot tub, laundry, fitness center, and business center.

Guest Ranches

Guest ranches specialize in lodging with horseback riding. With panoramic views of the Teton Mountains, **Spring Creek Ranch** (1600 N. East Butte Rd., 307/733-8833 or 800/443-6139, www.springcreekranch.com, year-round, $275-1,400) offers an upscale cowboy experience. Lodging types range from hotel rooms to townhomes and condos. Amenities include an indoor hot tub, outdoor heated swimming pool, tennis courts, spa, and restaurant.

To get to remote **Flat Creek Ranch** (1 Upper Flat Creek Rd., Jackson, 307/733-0603, www.flatcreekranch.com, June-Sept., $2,700-8,950 pp for 3-9 nights) requires a 4WD-vehicle to handle the 15 miles (24 km) of bumpy back road across the National Elk Refuge. Five renovated, historic log cabins have a bedroom, living room, private bath with clawfoot tub, wood-burning stove, and porch. Solar rays power the electricity. Activities include horseback riding, fishing, hiking, and backcountry trips. Meals feature gourmet meats and fresh produce from the ranch garden.

Campgrounds

Reservations are a must for summer camping. In Jackson, the **Virginian RV Park** (750 W. Broadway, 307/733-7189 or 800/321-6982, virginianlodge.com, May-mid-Oct., $110 RV full hookup, no tents) is a large parking lot-style campground behind the Virginian Lodge. Campers have access to the lodge's restaurant,

saloon, outdoor pool, and hot tub. No tents are allowed.

South of Jackson on US 26/89/189/191, **Snake River Park KOA** (9705 S. US 89, 307/733-7078, www.snakeriverpark.com, mid-Apr.-Nov., $36-56 tents, $52-120 RVs) is tucked into a deep, narrow canyon between the busy two-lane highway and the Snake River. Tent sites line Horse Creek and the river. Back-in RV sites (30 ft/9 m maximum) are close together on a mowed lawn.

East of Moran Junction, **Fireside Buffalo Valley RV Park** (17800 US 287, Moran, 307/733-1980, yellowstonerv. com, year-round, $59-80 RVs) is a highway campground with wide-open views of the Teton Mountains and surrounded by the Buffalo Fork River. No tents are allowed here. About 190 sites have gravel pads.

Bridger-Teton National Forest (307/739-5500, www.fs.usda.gov/btnf) has **seven primitive campgrounds** (late May-Sept., $10-15 single site, $25 double site, $6-7 per extra vehicle) flanking the east side of Grand Teton National Park. The best are **Pacific Creek** (8 sites), **Turpin Meadow** (18 sites), **Atherton Creek** (20 sites), and **Curtis Canyon** (11 sites). They are all accessed via dirt or gravel forest roads, and no reservations are available.

Teton Village

Teton Village is the resort complex at the base of Jackson Hole Mountain Resort. It is home to upscale and luxury hotels, a hostel, and a couple of midrange hotels. Most hotels cluster around the base of the chairlifts, gondola, and Aerial Tram; for summer travelers, the lure is the village's proximity to Grand Teton National Park. Many lodges close in fall and spring.

Hostels

As the only hostel in Jackson Hole, **The Hostel** (3315 Village Dr., 307/733-3415, www.thehostel.us, year-round, $32-55) has snagged prime real estate. It has shared dorms with bunks, with both single and mixed gender rooms. The Hostel also offers private king and quad rooms ($80-170). Amenities include a washer, dryer, ski wax room, ski and board storage, and recreation room with refrigerator, microwave, freezer, and toaster.

Hotels

Hotel Terra (3335 W. Village Dr., 307/201-6065, www.hotelterrajacksonhole.com, mid-Nov.-early Apr. and mid-May-Oct., $270-560 rooms, $450-1,705 suites) uses eco-friendly features in its rooms, which range from Murphy-bed studios to suites with kitchens. All bathrooms have rain showers and air tubs. The hotel houses a spa, two hot tubs, and an outdoor infinity pool. Also on-site is Italian restaurant Il Villaggio Osteria and a café.

Resorts

Four Seasons Resort (7680 Granite Loop Rd., 307/732-5000 or 800.819-5053, www.fourseasons.com/jacksonhole, May-Oct. and late Nov.-early Apr., $370-970 rooms, $600-1,915 suites) has spacious guest rooms and suites with gas fireplaces and sitting areas; some face the mountain or valley. Suites and private residences ($2,700-3,900) have1-5 bedrooms. Concierge and valet services deliver seamless experiences for recreation. Amenities include year-round outdoor pools and three hot pools, clusters of outdoor fire pits, restaurants, a spa, fitness center, childcare, and ski and bike rentals.

Transportation and Services
Emergency Services

For medical emergencies, go to **St. John's Medical Center** (625 E. Broadway, 307/733-3636, www.stjohns.health).

Gas and Vehicle Charging Stations

Gas stations are common on the highways through Jackson and en route to Teton Pass at Wilson. (Wilson is west of Jackson and south of Teton Village.) Teton Village has a **Chevron** (3200 McCollister Dr.).

Electric vehicle charging stations are in Teton Village (3285 Village Dr.) and Jackson (7342 Granite Loop).

Cell Service and Internet Access

Cell service is available in all Jackson Hole towns, but not necessarily in the surrounding national forests. **Wireless internet** is widely available in accommodations, coffee shops, and some restaurants.

Getting Around
Bus

Teton County runs the **START Bus** (www.jacksonwy.gov, daily year-round, fares vary), which operates within Jackson's downtown core (6am-10pm, free) about every 30 minutes. Connections between Jackson, Wilson, and Teton Village (5am-11:30pm, $1-3 one-way) run at varied intervals with a transfer station at the Village Road Transit Center in Wilson. Be sure to have the exact fare in cash; drivers do not carry change. Maps and route schedules are available online.

Parking

Parking in downtown Jackson is difficult. It's best to walk from your hotel or hop on a START Bus. Find a large **visitor parking lot** with some pull-through RV spaces on the north side of the junction of Gill Avenue and Center Street.

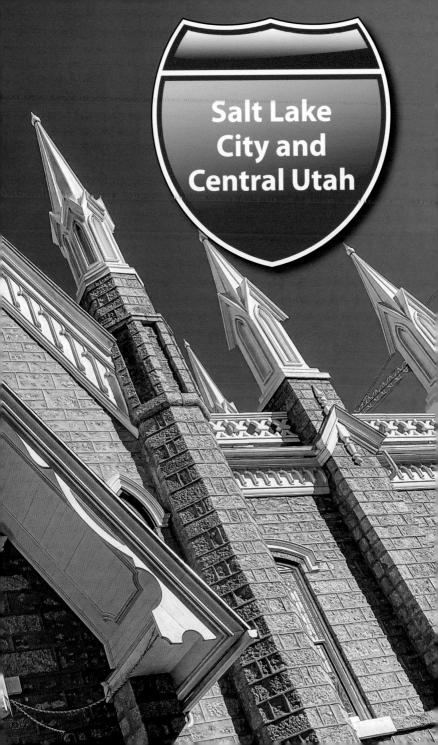

**Salt Lake
City and
Central Utah**

Highlights

★ **Leap back in time at Golden Spike National Historical Park:** Visit Promontory Summit, the site of the completion of the Transcontinental Railroad (page 481).

★ **Stroll through Temple Square:** In the epicenter of the Mormon faith, you can visit museums and public gardens and see eye-popping architecture (page 482).

★ **See the Great Salt Lake:** Get up close to this inland saltwater giant at **Antelope Island State Park** (page 484).

★ **Ride the tram at Snowbird Ski and Summer Resort:** Hop on a summertime tram that whisks you up high for top-of-the-world views (page 496).

★ **Play with the pros at Utah Olympic Park:** Watch Olympic hopefuls train for ski jumping. Better yet, get the ultimate thrill on a bobsled ride (page 501).

Salt Lake City

WEST VALLEY CITY

GLENDALE

3100 SOUTH

STONEBRIDGE GOLF CLUB

154

171

201

215

68

CALIFORNIA AVE

SALT LAKE INTERNATIONAL AIRPORT

80

215

REDWOOD RD

68

NORTH TEMPLE

RED IGUANA 2

RED IGUANA

13

89

To Ogden and Logan

CAPITOL HILL

Road Trip Route

1 km

1 mi

15

80

89

89

SOUTH SALT LAKE

71

2100 SOUTH

1700 SOUTH

1300 SOUTH

71

SUGARHOUSE BARBECUE

900 EAST

SALT LAKE CITY

400 WEST

THE STATE ROOM

TEMPLE SQUARE

600 SOUTH

800 SOUTH

186

SOUTH TEMPLE

89

BONNEVILLE BLVD

"DOWNTOWN" SEE MAP

CITY CREEK CANYON

City Creek Canyon Trail

Bonneville Shoreline Trail

To Provo and Alpine Loop Scenic Byway

5

15

THE AVENUES

PIONEER THEATRE COMPANY

1300 EAST

1500 EAST

MAZZA

80

3300 SOUTH

SUGAR HOUSE

SUNNYSIDE AVE

University of Utah

BONNEVILLE SHORELINE TRAIL

RED BUTTE GARDENS

NATURAL HISTORY MUSEUM OF UTAH

THIS IS THE PLACE HERITAGE PARK

HOGLE ZOO

EMIGRATION CANYON RD

Ulinta-Wasatch-Cache National Forest

WOODBRIDGE TERRACE

186

To Big Cottonwood Canyon, Brighton, Solitude, Little Cottonwood Valley, SNOWBIRD SKI AND SUMMER RESORT, and Alta

80

To Park City

To Mill Creek Canyon Trails

Salt Lake City enjoys a physical setting of great visual drama. The city lies on the broad valley floor and terraces once occupied by prehistoric Lake Bonneville. Great Salt Lake, the largest remnant of that ancient inland sea, lies just northwest of the city. Immediately to the east rises the Wasatch Range, a rugged spectacle with many peaks exceeding 11,000 feet (3,350 m). Cutting through its steep canyons are the streams that provide the area's and irrigation and drinking water.

This cosmopolitan city derives much of its identity from its Mormon heritage but has evolved into an outdoor paradise with year-round recreation. Modern Salt Lake City also offers an appealing mix of cultural activities, historic sites, varied architecture, elegant restaurants, and sophisticated hotels. On the edge of the city, walking trails and gardens get you in touch with nature and the Great Salt Lake is stunning in its immense size.

Visiting Salt Lake City is also about getting into the Wasatch Mountains. Just minutes from downtown are Park City and Little and Big Cottonwood Canyons, where you can ski some of the world's best powder in winter or hike among wildflowers in summer.

Planning Your Time

To see the sights in Salt Lake City and vicinity requires **two full days.** You could easily spend a day visiting just **Temple Square** and other city sights. A second day should be spent at **Antelope Island State Park** or **Park City.**

To the east of the city, it's best to pick an area—**Big Cottonwood Canyon, Little Cottonwood Canyon,** or **Park City**—and base yourself there for skiing, snowboarding, or summer fun. You don't need a car, especially in the Cottonwood Canyon areas. Park City has as much activity off the slopes as on. In summer, Park City and the canyons have cooler mountain air than Salt Lake City.

Seasonal Driving Concerns

Winter snow compounds the traffic snarls on Salt Lake City's interstates (I-15, I-80, I-215). State law requires carrying chains or having **mountain snow tires** (either studded or not). Snow tires are required November 1-May 1 with chains in the car for the Cottonwood Canyons and road to Park City. During extremely heavy snowstorms, the canyons may be temporarily restricted to vehicles with 4WD or chains.

Reservations

Getting campsites at the state parks and in the national forests surrounding Salt Lake City can be tough. Make camping reservations for **Utah state parks** (utah-stateparks.reserveamerica.com) 16 weeks in advance and for **Uinta-Wasatch-Cache National Forest** (877/444-6777 or www.recreation.gov) six months in advance.

Getting There

Car
From Grand Teton National Park
From **Grand Teton National Park,** the fastest route to Salt Lake City is 290 miles (465 km), which takes five hours. Head south from **Jackson,** Wyoming, on US 26/89/189/191 to Hoback Junction and then southwest onto US 26/89 to Alpine Junction. Take US 89 south to Brigham City and hop on I-15 south to reach Salt Lake City.

From Rocky Mountain National Park
From **Grand Lake,** Colorado, at the west

One Day in Salt Lake City

Morning
Spend the morning investigating **Temple Square,** the sacred center of the Mormon faith. Stroll the grounds, take a tour, and learn about the LDS religion and culture. Jump across the street for lunch at **Red Iguana 2.**

Afternoon
Stroll part of the **Bonneville Shoreline Trail** for views of the city below or hike in **Mill Creek Canyon.**

Evening
Dine at **The Copper Onion** before taking in an evening event: theater, music, or a drink at the **Tavernacle Social Club.**

With More Time
Add on a stay in **Park City** or camp in **Antelope Island State Park.**

entrance of **Rocky Mountain National Park,** two different routes head to Salt Lake City. Both require about 7.5 hours of driving.

The first route is 470 miles (760 km). Go south on US 34 to reach Granby before aiming northward on CO 125/WY 230. Next, take WY 130 to I-80, which crosses west through southern Wyoming to Salt Lake City.

The second route is 430 miles (690 km). It also starts by heading south on US 34 to Granby. Next, drive west on US 40 to reach I-80 west and Salt Lake City. A 34-mile (55-km) side trip to **Dinosaur National Monument** adds about 40 minutes.

From Denver
Driving from **Denver** to Salt Lake City takes about eight hours. There are two routes, both of which are mostly on interstates.

The first option is 520 miles (835 km) and follows I-80 through Wyoming. Drive north from Denver on I-25 to exit 269B at Larimer. Head northwest on CO 14 through Fort Collins to Laramie, Wyoming. Then follow I-80 west to Salt Lake City.

The second route is 525 miles (845 km) and follows I-70 through Colorado. Drive west on I-70 to exit 157, west of Green River. At Spanish Fork, head north on I-15 to Salt Lake City.

Air
Salt Lake City International Airport (SLC, 776 N. Terminal Dr., 801/575-2400, www. slcairport.com) is a major airline hub servicing most of the large U.S. carriers. It is the western hub for Delta.

The airport has three terminals; in each you'll find a ground-transportation information desk, food service, motel-hotel courtesy phones, and a ski-rental shop. Auto rentals are in the parking structure immediately across from the terminals.

Downtown is located less than 10 miles (16 km) west of the airport, a 10-minute drive. By far the easiest way to get downtown is via the **TRAX rail line** (801/743-3882, www.rideuta.com, 6am-11pm Mon.-Sat., 9:45am-10pm Sun., $2.50 one way), which runs between the airport and Salt Lake Central Station (300 S. 600 W.). Arriving travelers can take the shuttle from the ground level of the airport to the 1940 West Station/Temporary Airport Station, then continue on the Green Line to downtown SLC. Trains run every 15 minutes on weekdays, every 20 minutes on weekends.

Train

Amtrak (800/872-7245, www.amtrak. com) trains stop at the Salt Lake Central Station (300 S. 600 W.), which also serves as a terminus for local buses, light-rail, and commuter trains. The only Amtrak train that passes through the city is the California Zephyr, connecting three times a week to Reno and Oakland to the west and Denver and Chicago to the east.

Bus and Shuttle

Salt Lake City is at a crossroads of several major interstate highways and has good **Greyhound** (801/355-9579, www. greyhound.com) bus service. In summer, one bus daily leaves from Salt Lake Central Station (300 S. 600 W.) for Yellowstone National Park.

Mountain States Express (307/733-4629, www.mountainstatesexpress. com) runs daily shuttles to and from the airport in Salt Lake City to Jackson, Wyoming, near Grand Teton National Park. **Salt Lake Express** (877/714-6104, www.saltlakeexpress.com) shuttles also go between Salt Lake City's airport and Jackson, Wyoming.

Logan

Logan is surrounded by the lush dairy and farmlands of the Cache Valley and the lofty peaks of the Bear River Range. The town is east of I-15, at the junction of US 89 and US 191. Logan is built on terraces that mark the ancient shorelines of Lake Bonneville. People from all over Utah and the Intermountain West come to Logan to take in an opera, a chamber music concert, or an evening of theater in this scenic alpine valley. It's also enlivened by summer festivals.

The professional **Utah Festival Opera and Musical Company** (59 S. 100 W., 435/750-0300 or 800/262-0074, www. ufoc.org) takes over the beautifully restored **Ellen Eccles Theatre** (43 S. Main St.) from mid-July to early August. The

theater has excellent acoustics and a formal yet intimate atmosphere. Utah Festival Opera stages four operas and musicals, plus a number of music performances during its month-long festival season.

Just around the corner from the Ellen Eccles Theatre is the historic **Caine Lyric Theatre** (28 W. Center St., 435/797-8022, mid-June to mid-Aug.), where visiting equity actors lead a summer season of musicals, comedies, and dramas produced by Utah State University's drama department.

The **Cache Valley Visitors Bureau** (199 N. Main St., 435/755-1890, www. explorelogan.com) can fill you in on what's happening in the area.

Ogden

Located at the northern edge of the Wasatch Front urban area, Ogden remains its own city even as it is engulfed by suburbs. It was one of the West's most important rail hubs at the beginning of the 20th century. Downtown, the impressive Union Pacific Depot and grand architecture remain as vestiges of the city's affluence. It's worth exploring its museums and historic sites.

Union Station Museums

Travelers thronged into the cavernous **Union Station Building** (2501 Wall Ave., 801/629-8672, www.ogdencity.com/1562/ Union-Station) during the grand old days of railroading. Today, the depot is mostly known for its fine museums. A single ticket allows admission to all exhibitions (10am-5pm Mon.-Sat., $7 adults, $5 seniors, $3-4 kids).

The **Utah State Railroad Museum** comprises two rail exhibits. In the **Wattis Dumke Model Railroad** collection, highly detailed dioramas illustrate railroad scenes and construction feats. Eight HO-scale model trains roll through the Ogden rail yard and wind through a

★ Side Trip: Golden Spike National Historical Park

A treat for history and train buffs, the remote **Golden Spike National Historical Park** (6200 N. 22300 W., Corrinne, 435/471-2209, www.nps.gov/gosp, $20 per car, $15 motorcycles, $10 hiker or biker) preserves a segment of the original Transcontinental Railroad through the windy Promontory Mountains. It's where the last spike was driven into the rail line in 1869, connecting the United States from coast to coast. (The actual golden spike was a symbolic, commemorative creation to note this historic feat.) Today, two authentic replicas of the steam locomotives that met here travel on the park's short railway, about 1.7 miles (2.7 km) of track rebuilt on the original line.

Golden Spike National Historical Park

Sights and Tours

The **visitors center** (9am-5pm daily summer, 9am-5pm Thurs.-Mon winter) has indoor and outdoor exhibits, Junior Ranger programs, and maps for auto tours. It shows several films on the history of the Transcontinental Railroad and the process of building the locomotive replicas. Behind the center, you can walk a short interpretive trail to the **Last Spike Site** on the railroad tracks, where a polished wooden tie marks the spot.

The **replica locomotives,** the *Jupiter* and *No. 119*, go into action behind the visitors center in summer. **Train demonstrations** (daily except for boiler-flushing days, May-Sept.) bring the *Jupiter* down the track at 10am with *No. 119* following about 30 minutes later. Then the pair sits on display until 1pm when they both demonstrate a run before going on display again. At 4pm, *No. 199* heads back to the Engine House with *Jupiter* trailing about 30 minutes later.

Two self-guided **auto tours** (no RVs or trailers, weather permitting) explore the grades on either side of Promontory summit, traveling along 15 miles (24 km) of the original rail beds. The **East Auto Tour** (2 mi/3.2 km, year-round) follows the Union Pacific Railroad grade on a one-way unpaved road from the top to the bottom of the Big Fill where the railway company bypassed a rock arch, cut through solid rock, constructed trestles, and filled in the grade. The **West Auto Tour** (7 mi/11 km, late May-late Nov.) follows the Central Pacific Route uphill along the west grade where the "race" to the summit ensued.

You can view the working **Engine House** (10am-11:30am and 1pm-4pm, daily early May-mid-Oct., Thurs.-Mon. mid-Oct.-early May), where the locomotives receive maintenance and are stored for the winter. Guided tours are given on Saturdays (30-45 min., 11am, 1pm, 3pm, Oct.-May) when you can learn how steam powers the locomotives.

Getting There

The park sits at the north end of Great Salt Lake, where only one paved road reaches the site. The drive from Logan is 50 miles (80 km) and takes about an hour. From Salt Lake City, the drive is 90 miles (145 km) and takes about 1.5 hours.

model of the Salt Lake region. Exhibits and photos showcase great trains, such as the Big Boys, which weighed more than one million pounds and pulled heavy freight up the mountain ranges. You can also see a documentary film about the first transcontinental railroad. Outside, at the **Eccles Railroad Center,** you can visit giant diesel locomotives and some cabooses.

The **Browning-Kimball Classic Car Museum** displays a glittering collection of about a dozen antique autos, ranging from a 1-cylinder 1901 Oldsmobile to a 16-cylinder 1930 Cadillac sports sedan.

The **Myra Powell Gallery** displays paintings, sculpture, and photography in a former pigeon roost. Exhibitions rotate monthly.

Historic 25th Street

When Ogden was the railroad's main transport hub, 25th was the city's main street. Running between Washington Boulevard and the palatial Union Pacific Depot, the street boasts red brick buildings that housed many of the city's first businesses, which were run by immigrants attracted by the railroads.

After the dependency on the railway waned, this historic precinct fell into disrepair. But now, artists and small cafés have since reinvigorated the lovely historic buildings. It's a pleasant place for a stroll and many of the shops, galleries, and cafés are worth a detour. Pick up a brochure detailing building histories from the tourism office on Washington Boulevard.

On summer Saturdays, the **25th Street Farmers and Art Market** (25th St. and Grant Ave.) takes over Ogden Municipal Park. Also in the park, the **Ogden Amphitheater** (2549 Washington Blvd., 801/629-8000, ogdenamphitheater.com, early June-mid-Aug.) hosts free events, including movies and classical music concerts; check online for the schedule.

Salt Lake City

Sights

Although Salt Lake City is a sprawling urban area, the majority of visitor destinations are concentrated near the downtown core, making it easy to navigate. Excellent public transportation makes it simple to forgo driving: Just hop on the light-rail or a bus.

★ Temple Square

Temple Square (between North Temple St. and South Temple St., www.templesquare.com, 9am-9pm daily, free) has a special meaning for Mormons: It is the sacred center of the Church of Jesus Christ of Latter-day Saints (LDS). Founder Brigham Young chose this site in 1847. Later, the tabernacle, visitors centers, museums, genealogy center, and a host of other church administration buildings were added, with gardens, statues, and pools in between.

The square, which is surrounded by a wall, is open to the public. Visitors can enter through wrought-iron gates on the south, west, and north sides. All tours, exhibits, and concerts are free.

Temple Square Historical Tour

The free **Temple Square Historical Tour** (45 min.) begins every hour on the hour (usually 9am-8pm daily) at the North Visitors' Center. It offers an introduction to Salt Lake City's pioneers, the temple, the Tabernacle, the assembly hall, and historic monuments. Points of interest include a bell from the abandoned Nauvoo Temple; sculptures of Christ, church leaders, and handcart pioneers; an astronomy observation site; and a meridian marker (outside the walls at Main St. and South Temple St.) that surveyors used to map Utah. Although tour leaders don't normally proselytize, the guides give glimpses into their faith.

Downtown

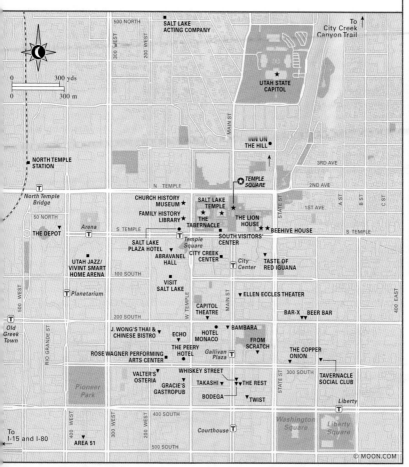

Salt Lake Temple and Gardens

Mormons hold sacred rites, such as, baptisms, marriages, and family-sealing ceremonies in the **Salt Lake Temple;** normal Sunday services take place in local stake or ward buildings. Only LDS members of good standing may enter the temple; non-Mormons are not allowed, but you can learn about it and see interior photos at the South Visitors' Center. You can also admire the temple's east facade from the Main Street gates and the adjacent manicured **gardens** with reflecting pools and fountains.

Tabernacle

Pioneers labored from 1863 to 1867 to construct the unique dome-shaped **Tabernacle.** Brigham Young's design took shape in massive latticed wooden beams resting on 44 supports of red sandstone. Wooden pegs and rawhide strips hold the structure together. The organ pipes resemble metal, balcony pillars appear to be marble, and the benches look like oak, yet all are painted pine. Its smooth arched ceiling and massive pipe organ with 12,000 pipes, five manuals, and one pedal keyboard contribute to phenomenal acoustics. **Daily recitals** (noon and 2pm Mon.-Sat., 2pm Sun., free) demonstrate the instrument's capabilities.

The renowned 360-member **Mormon Tabernacle Choir's rehearsals** (7:30pm-9:30pm Thurs., drop-ins welcome, free) and its **radio broadcast performances** (9:30am Sun., seating 8am-9:15am) welcome a public audience. Confirm the schedule (801/240-4150, www.mormontabernaclechoir.com) ahead of time, as sometimes the choir is on tour or holds performances at the nearby Conference Center.

Visitors Centers

Exhibits at the **North Visitors' Center** include films, an interactive map of Jerusalem, and interactive exhibits. A spiraling ramp leads to the upper level, where *Christus,* an 11-foot replica of a sculpture by Bertel Thorvaldsen, stands in a circular room with a wall mural depicting the universe.

Exhibits at the **South Visitors' Center** cover the building of the Salt Lake Temple and church history. A large baptismal font supported by 12 life-size oxen sculptures, representing the 12 tribes of Israel, is on display along with the metal plates inscribed with the Book of Mormon. The adjacent **Assembly Hall** holds concerts.

★ Great Salt Lake

A remnant of ancient Lake Bonneville, Great Salt Lake is the largest natural lake in the West. Because it has no outlet, it collects salt that is washed down feeder streams. Water evaporates, but not the salt. This giant inland sea is popular for sailing, kayaking, and pleasure boating, but cannot sustain fish due to its high salinity. (The high saline content also means you'll float easily in the lake.) Two

architectural detail at Temple Square

state parks are the best places to experience it.

Great Salt Lake State Park

Great Salt Lake State Park (14 mi/22.5 km west of Salt Lake City off I-80 exit 104, 801/250-1898 or 801/828-0787, stateparks.utah.gov, sunrise-sunset daily, $5 per vehicle) is the primary marina on the southern shore. It has paved boat launches and a beach. When lake waters are high enough, you can swim, wade, or just float right from the beach. Freshwater showers allow you to wash off the salty residue. A small parking lot-style **campground** (5 sites, reservations 800/322-3770, utahstateparks.reserveamerica.com, $35) is lakeside; it's best for RVs.

Antelope Island State Park

An ideal way to explore the Great Salt Lake is a visit to **Antelope Island** (4528 W. 1700 S., Syracuse, 801/773-2941, stateparks.utah.gov, 6am-7pm daily, $15 per car, $10 seniors, $3 bicycles and pedestrians), the largest of its 10 islands. The island's Frary Peak, rocky slopes, rolling grasslands, marshes, sand dunes, and lake views instill a sense of remoteness and rugged beauty.

The island is home to more than 600 free-ranging **bison** as well as deer, bighorn sheep, pronghorn, and other wildlife. The best place to see bison is usually on the east side, near the historic Fielding Garr Ranch. The yearly **bison roundup** (late Oct.) attracts visitors to watch the bison driven into corrals on the island's north end. Thanks largely to brine flies and shrimp, the island attracts a wide variety of **birds,** many that are migratory. Look for eared grebes, avocets, black-necked stilts, willets, sanderlings, long-billed curlews, burrowing owls, and raptors. The same no-see-ums that attract birds can attack visitors, especially May-June; come prepared to do battle.

The **visitors center** (9am-5pm daily summer, 10am-4pm daily winter) has exhibits on the island's natural and human history. Park trails are open to hiking, mountain biking, and horseback riding. The marina allows you to launch sailboats and kayaks. A white-sand beach in Bridger Bay is the best place to swim or float.

The park's dark skies create the perfect setting for overnighting with stargazing at one of three **campgrounds** ($20-40, includes day-use fees). They have pit toilets, tables, and fire pits. **Bridger Bay Campground** (26 sites, 3 wheelchair-accessible, tents or RVs), **White Rock Campground** (20 sites, tents or RVs) and **Lady Finger Campground** (5 sites, tents only) are all near Bridger Bay, which has potable water and showers. Make **reservations** (800/322-3770, utahstateparks.reserveamerica.com) 16 weeks in advance, especially for spring and fall.

To drive to Antelope Island from Salt Lake City, head north on I-15 and take Exit 332. Drive west on Antelope Drive to the park entrance. After the entrance gates, a paved road (7 mi/11 km, $2) crosses the lake on a causeway to reach the island. The park is about 40 miles (64 km) northwest of Salt Lake City, a one-hour drive.

Recreation
Hiking and Biking
Bonneville Shoreline Trail

The **Bonneville Shoreline Trail** (www.bonnevilleshorelinetrail.org) is a hiking, running, and bicycling path that skitters across the foothills of the Wasatch Range, overlooking the city below. The trail generally follows what was once the eastern shore of Lake Bonneville. It's a good trail for sunset views and spotting Antelope Island in Great Salt Lake. You can access segments of the trail from several locations; the nearest downtown segment (13.5 mi/21.7 km) runs from **Dry Gulch to Emigration Canyon** with several loops. Use the online map to find trailheads.

Mill Creek Canyon

Great mountain biking and many hiking trails lie along **Mill Creek Canyon,** just outside Salt Lake City. Reach it via Mill Creek Canyon Road from 3800 Wasatch Boulevard. You can bring your dog along, too, as this is one of the few canyons where pets are welcome. Odd-numbered days are designated leash-free days. Pick up trail maps at the entrance gate. A $3 fee is collected as you exit the canyon.

The **Desolation Trail** climbs 1,200 vertical feet (365 m) to **Salt Lake Overlook** (4.3 mi/6.9 km rt, 2.5 hours). You'll get big views of the canyon and Salt Lake Valley. Begin from the lower end of Box Elder Picnic Area (elev. 5,760 feet) on the south side of the road.

Bicycles are allowed in Mill Creek Canyon only on even-numbered days, the days when dogs must be leashed. Bikers can ride **Alexander Basin Trail** to the end of Mill Creek Canyon, then onto the **Big Water Trail.** You can then connect with a section of the **Great Western Trail**

Great Salt Lake from Antelope Island

and follow it to the ridgetop divide overlooking the Park City Mountain Resort. Turning south, the **Wasatch Crest Trail** cruises along the ridge around the head of the upper Mill Creek basin.

City Creek Canyon

In the city, a pleasant and relaxing route for a stroll or a jog follows **City Creek Canyon,** a shady stream-filled ravine just east of the state capitol.

Hikers and runners may travel on the road every day. In summer (Memorial Day–Sept. 30), bicyclists may enter only on odd-numbered days. Because City Creek is part of the city's water supply, no dogs are allowed. Motorized vehicles are allowed on holidays and on even-numbered days during summer. A gate at the edge of the ravine provides entry and supplies maps. A $3 charge applies if you drive through to the trailhead at the upper end.

From the trailhead at the road's end, hikers enjoy **City Creek Meadows.**

After 1.5 miles (2.4 km), you'll pass **Cottonwood Gulch,** where a side trail goes to an old mining area. Back on the main path, the trail grows steeper and winds through aspen groves to pass two shallow ponds. After the trail becomes indistinct, continue northeast to the meadows; maps and a compass will help. From the meadows, climb north up the ridge for splendid views of the Wasatch Range.

Golf

Salt Lake City claims to have the highest number of golf courses per capita in the nation, with more than a dozen in the metro area. There's a course for every level of expertise, from city-owned 9-hole courses for beginners to championship-level courses like the 27-hole private **Stonebridge Golf Club** (4415 Links Dr., West Valley City, 801/957-9000, www.golfstonebridgeutah.com) and the 36-hole par 71 or 72 public **Mountain Dell Golf Course** (I-80 exit 134, 801/582-3812, www.mountaindellgc.com), each offering challenging terrain and incredible mountain views.

Entertainment and Events

Salt Lake City offers a wide variety of high-quality arts and cultural institutions; classical and religious music venues are particularly noteworthy. Jazz, blues, and alternative music clubs and dance bars are also numerous.

Nightlife
Bars

For high-spirited, only-in-Salt-Lake fun, try **Twist** (32 Exchange Place, 801/322-3200, www.twistslc.com, nightly), with karaoke (Tues.) and live music (Wed.-Sat.). A good stop for drinks right downtown is **Bar X** (155 E. 200 S., 801/355-2287), one of SLC's oldest and most characterful bars. Right next door, sister establishment **Beer Bar** (161 E. 200 S., 801/355-3618) has a wall full of taps, more beer in bottles, good food, and board games. For a quiet cocktail and delicious nibbles in a stylish Western setting, **Whiskey Street** (323 S. Main St., 801/433-1371, whiskeystreet.com) has a 72-foot-long cherrywood bar, craft cocktails, and Parmesan truffle fries.

Area 51 (451 S. 400 W., 801/534-0819, www.area51slc.com) has three dance floors on two levels, plus theme nights (College, Alterna-Mash, Fetish, and more). **ECHO** (134 Pierpont Ave., no phone, www.echoslc.com) is one of the city's most popular spots for cocktails, DJs, theme parties, and events.

If you're into the speakeasy scene, check out **The Rest,** the underground bar beneath **Bodega** (331 S. Main St., 801/532-4042, www.bodega331.com, 5pm-11pm Tues.-Sat.). Make a reservation for this popular and very dark spot for inventive cocktails and good Mexican food.

Live Music

The **Tavernacle Social Club** (201 E. 300 S., 801/519-8900, www.tavernacle.com, 7pm-11pm Sun-Thurs., 5pm-1am Fri.-Sat.) is a Salt Lake original, a high-energy piano bar with an updated lounge act that features dueling pianos, sing-alongs, and karaoke (Thurs.-Tues.). To catch the flavor of local and regional bands, check out **Urban Lounge** (241 S. 500 E., 801/746-0557, www.theurbanloungeslc.com). Blues jams and jazz bands are featured at **Gracie's Gastropub** (326 S. W. Temple, 801/819-7565, www.graciesslc.com), which is also known for good food.

Touring national acts stop at **The Depot** (13 N. 400 W., 801/456-2800, www.depotslc.com), a nightclub in the cavernous Union Station. Big names such as the Decemberists and Jason Mraz play **The State Room** (638 S. State St., 801/596-3560, www.thestateroom.com), a more intimate venue.

Gay and Lesbian

Salt Lake City has a growing number of gay clubs. Start the evening at **Club Try-Angles** (251 W. 900 S., 801/364-3203, 4pm-1am Mon.-Fri., 6pm-1am Sat., 2pm-1am Sun, clubtry-angles.com), with a pleasant patio for drinks and sunning. The **Sun Trapp** (102 S. 600 W., 385/235-6786, thesuntrapp.com, 11am-midnight daily) is known for its friendly, welcoming, and laid-back atmosphere.

The Arts
Classical Music and Dance

From its modest beginnings in 1940, the **Utah Symphony** (tickets 801/533-6683, www.utahsymphony.org) has grown to become one of the best-regarded orchestras in the West. Each season, the symphony performs in the glittering **Abravanel Hall** (123 W. South Temple St.).

Capitol Theatre (50 W. 200 S.) is home to two companies. The **Utah Opera Company** (tickets 801/533-6683, www.utahopera.org) stages four operas during its October-May season. The versatile **Ballet West** (801/869-6900, balletwest.org) performs classical and contemporary works September-May.

The **Rose Wagner Performing Arts Center** (138 W. Broadway) features professional dance companies. The **Ririe-Woodbury Dance Company** (801/297-4241, www.ririewoodbury.com) includes mixed media, humor, and eye-catching choreography. The **Repertory Dance Theatre** (801/534-1000, www.rdtutah.org) focuses on classical American and contemporary dance.

Concerts

Temple Square (801/240-3323, www.templesquare.com) presents hundreds of free public performances a year, sponsored by the LDS Church. You might hear chamber music, a symphony, operatic selections, choral works, piano solos, a brass band, or a percussion ensemble. The **Temple Square Concert Series** presents hour-long concerts (7:30pm, Fri.-Sat., free) featuring local and international artists in the Assembly Hall. Held in the Brigham Young Historic Park,

Concerts in the Park (southeast corner of State St. and 2nd Ave., 7:30pm Tues. and Fri. June-Aug., free) are an outdoor affair.

The public is welcome to attend free performances and rehearsals in the Tabernacle. The renowned 360-voice **Mormon Tabernacle Choir** sings for its **radio broadcast** (9:30am Sun., be seated by 9:15am, remain seated for the entire performance) and **rehearsals** (8pm-9:30pm Thurs.). The **Mormon Youth Symphony** (8pm-9:30pm Wed.) and the **Youth Chorus** (8pm-9:30pm Tues.) also rehearses in the evenings. In June-August and December, rehearsals and broadcasts are held across the street in the Conference Center to accommodate the larger summer and Christmas season crowds. Organists demonstrate the sounds and versatility of the tabernacle's famous instrument in 30-minute **organ recitals** (noon and 2pm Mon.-Sat., 2pm Sun.).

Theater

Pioneer Theatre Company (300 S. 1400 E., 801/581-6961, www.pioneertheatre.org, Sept.-May), one of Salt Lake City's premier theater troupes, offers a seven-show season performing a mix of contemporary plays, classics, and musicals. The cutting-edge **Salt Lake Acting Company** (168 W. 500 N., 801/363-7522, www.saltlakeactingcompany.org, year-round) stages plays by local playwrights and new works from around the world.

Food
Family-Friendly

An excellent option for barbecue and soul food is **Sugarhouse Barbecue Co.** (880 E. 2100 S., 801/463-4800, www.sugarhousebbq.com, 11:30am-8pm Mon.-Thurs., 11:30am-9pm Fri.-Sat., noon-8pm Sun., $8-15), with Memphis-style slow-smoked ribs and Carolina pulled pork.

Tucked in the Gallivan Center complex at the heart of downtown, **From Scratch** (62 E. Gallivan Ave., 801/961-9000, www.

fromscratchslc.com, 11am-9pm Mon.-Thurs., 11am-10pm Fri., noon-10pm Sat., $13-18) takes its name seriously. The restaurant mills its own flour from local wheat and pretty much everything else on the menu is handmade. The pizzas are baked in a wood-fired oven but at lower temperatures than typical, resulting in a crisp but chewy slice.

International

Despite the building looking like a dive bar, ★ **Red Iguana** (736 W. North Temple St., 801/322-1489, http://rediguana.com, 11am-9pm Tues.-Sun., $10-17) offers excellent south-of-the-border cooking with a specialty in Mayan cuisine, mole, and regional foods. Best of all, flavors are crisp, fresh, and earthy. Arrive early, especially at lunch, to avoid the lines. You can get the same menu at **Red Iguana 2** (866 W. South Temple St., 801/214-6050) with the same hours. There's also the smaller **Taste of Red Iguana** (28 S. State St., 801/214-6350, 11am-7pm Mon.-Sat.) in the City Creek Center food court.

In the hip 15th and 15th neighborhood, ★ **Mazza** (1515 S. 1500 East, 801/484-9259, www.mazzacafe.com, 4pm-9pm Mon.-Sat., $8-25) has an excellent Lebanese menu that goes far beyond the usual kebabs. There's a second branch a few blocks southeast.

For the best and freshest sushi, go to **Takashi** (18 W. Market St., 801/519-9595, takashisushi.com, 11:30am-2pm and 4:30pm-9pm Mon.-Sat., $6-16). The Asian ribs are also excellent.

At **J. Wong's Thai & Chinese Bistro** (163 W. 200 S., 801/350-0888, jwongs.com, 11am-3pm and 5pm-10pm Mon.-Fri., noon-3pm and 5pm-10pm Sat., 4pm-9pm Sun., $12-28), you'll find beautifully prepared regional Chinese food and a good selection of Thai dishes in an upscale dining room.

Dress up for a visit to ★ **Valter's Osteria** (173 Broadway/300 S., 801/521-4583, valtersosteria.com, 5:30pm-10pm

Tues.-Sat., $16-35). Charming Valter's interpretations of his grandmother's Italian cooking can't be beat, especially the flavorful and delicate house-made pasta and the ravioli and gnocchi sampler. Attentive servers make every diner feel like a special friend.

Fine Dining

Emphasizing full-flavored New American cooking, ★ **The Copper Onion** (111 E. Broadway, 801/355-3282, thecopperonion.com, 5pm-9pm Wed.-Thurs., 5pm-10pm Fri., 10:30am-3pm and 5pm-10pm Sat., 10:30am-3pm Sun, $13-33) offers a choice of small and large plates, with such delights as a pork chop with farro, wild mushrooms, and pumpkin seeds. It always gets a mention when people talk about the best restaurants.

Bambara (202 S. Main St., 801/363-5454, bambara-slc.com, 5pm-9pm Tues.-Sat., $29-46), in the Hotel Monaco, emphasizes the freshest and most flavorful local meat and produce, with preparations in a wide-awake New American style that's equal parts tradition and innovation. This is easily one of the most beautiful dining rooms in the city.

Accommodations

Parking is tight in downtown SLC; expect to pay about $10-15 on top of room costs if you're parking a car at a downtown hotel. Note that pricing at these hotels is particularly dependent on convention traffic; if there's not much going on, it's pretty easy to find a room at SLC's finest for well under $200.

Hostels

The Avenues (107 F St. at 2nd Ave., 801/363-3855, www.saltlakehostel.com, $30 dorm, $90 private rooms) offers dorm rooms with use of a kitchen and laundry. You're likely to meet travelers from all over the world in this hostel that is a bit on the shabby side. Beds are in the dorm (sheets included) or in

original Red Iguana restaurant

private rooms, some of which have private baths.

Hotels and Inns

The first of SLC's historic hotels to be refurbished into a natty upscale lodging was the ★ **Peery Hotel** (110 W. 300 S., 801/521-4300, www.peeryhotel.com, $134-150). Its 1910 vintage style is preserved in the comfortable lobby, while the guest rooms are updated and nicely furnished. A restaurant is on the premises, with many others within a short walk.

Overlooking Temple Square, the **Salt Lake Plaza Hotel** (122 W. South Temple St., 801/521-0130 or 800/366-3684, plazahotel.com, $100-110) offers a pool and an on-site restaurant in addition to its great location.

Some of Salt Lake's grandest heritage homes sit on Capitol Hill, just below the state capitol. One of the most eye-catching is the red sandstone mansion now called the **Inn on the Hill** (225 N. State St., 801/328-1466, inn-on-the-hill.

com, $180-280). Built in 1906, the inn has 13 guest rooms decorated with period detail, but all with modern amenities such as private baths. Practically every room has views over Salt Lake City. Full gourmet breakfasts are included.

The ★ **Hotel Monaco** (15 W. 200 S., 801/595-0000 or 877/294-9710, www.monaco-saltlakecity.com, $177-280) occupies a grandly renovated historic building in a convenient spot in the middle of downtown, with Bambara, one of the most sophisticated restaurants in Utah. Guest rooms are sumptuously furnished with real élan. Expect wild colors and contrasting fabrics, lots of flowers, and excellent service. Facilities include an on-site fitness center, concierge, and valet services. Pets are welcome—and even invited to the nightly wine reception.

Transportation and Services
Emergency Services

Minor medical emergencies can be treated by **InstaCare Clinics** (389 S. 900 E., 801/282-2400, 9am-9pm daily), with more than 30 outlets in the greater Wasatch Front area. Hospitals with 24-hour emergency care include **Salt Lake Regional Medical Center** (1050 E. South Temple St., 801/350-4111, www.saltlakeregional.org), **LDS Hospital** (8th Ave. and C St., 801/350-4111, intermountainhealthcare.org), **St. Mark's Hospital** (1200 E. 3900 S., 801/268-7111, mountainstar.com), and **University Hospital** (50 N. Medical Dr./1900 E., 801/581-2121, healthcare.utah.edu).

Getting Around
Car Rental

All the major companies and many local outfits are eager to rent you a set of wheels. In winter you can find "skier-ized" vehicles with snow tires and ski racks ready to head for the slopes. Many agencies have an office or delivery service at the airport: Avis, Budget, Dollar, Enterprise, Hertz, National, and Payless.

Bike Sharing

The nonprofit **GREENbike** (801/333-1110, greenbikeslc.org) makes bikes available at over 45 stations in central Salt Lake City. Visitors can get a 24-hour pass ($7) or a 4-day pass ($15) that allow for unlimited 30-minute trips. Download the app to find stations and bike availability. You can take any bike from any station; when you're done, return your bike to any station. The bright green bikes have a basket large enough for a briefcase or knapsack, automatic front and rear LED lights, adjustable seats, and built-in cable lock.

Bus and Light-Rail

Utah Transit Authority (UTA, 801/287-4636, www.rideuta.com, 6am-7pm Mon.-Sat.) provides inexpensive bus and light-rail train service in town and to the airport, the University of Utah, and surrounding communities. TRAX light-rail trains connect the Vivint Smart Home Arena, the University of Utah, downtown Salt Lake City, the airport, and the southern suburbs. No charge is made for travel downtown within the Free-Fare Square area, generally bounded by North Temple Street, 500 South, 200 East, and 400 West; on TRAX, service is fare-free to Salt Lake Central Station at 600 West. A TRAX line connects Salt Lake City International Airport with Salt Lake Central Station.

During the winter ski season, skiers can hop on the Ski Bus Service to Solitude, Brighton, Snowbird, and Alta ski areas from downtown, the University of Utah, and other locations. A bus route map and individual schedules are online and at the ground transportation information desk at the airport, at the Salt Lake Convention and Visitors Bureau downtown, and at Temple Square visitors centers. Free transfers are provided on request when the fare is paid. On Sunday, only the airport, Ogden, Provo, and a few other destinations are served. UTA shuts down on holidays. Fares are $2.50 for two

TRAX light-rail in downtown Salt Lake City

hours of travel on both TRAX and the buses; a day pass is $5.

Taxi
City Cab (801/363-8400), **Ute Cab** (801/359-7788), and **Yellow Cab** (801/521-2100) have 24-hour service. Lyft and Uber are also available.

Big Cottonwood Canyon

With cliffs towering thousands of feet, Big Cottonwood Canyon has become a haven for skiers, snowboarders, and hikers. The gateway to the canyon is 15 miles (24 km) southeast of downtown Salt Lake City.

Getting There
From downtown Salt Lake City, take I-80 east to I-215 south. Take I-215 to exit 6 (6200 South) and follow 6200 South, which becomes Wasatch Boulevard.

Follow the signs to Big Cottonwood Canyon. Solitude is 14 miles (22.5 km) up Big Cottonwood Canyon and Brighton is at the road's end (16 mi/26 km).

UTA buses (801/743-3882, www.rideuta.com) and shuttles from **Canyon Transportation** (800/255-1841, canyontransport.com) serve all resorts.

Hiking
Because of water purity concerns, dogs are prohibited in this canyon.

Donut Falls
Distance: 1.5 miles (2.4 km) rt
Duration: 1 hour
Elevation gain: minimal
Effort: easy
Trailhead: 9 miles (14.4 km) up Big Cottonwood Canyon, at the end of the signed side road going to Jordan Pines Campground

The popular hike to **Donut Falls** follows a trail that's partly through the woods and partly an old dirt road. At the end, the waterfall spurts from a "doughnut hole" in a rock. Rockfall and erosion have actually made the doughnut-effect less prominent in recent years.

Brighton Lakes Trail
Distance: 6 miles (9.6 km) rt
Duration: 3 hours
Elevation gain: 1,200 feet (366 m)
Effort: moderate
Trailhead: behind the Brighton Lodge at Brighton

Brighton Lakes Trail winds through some of the prettiest land in the Wasatch Range. **Silver Lake,** with a boardwalk giving full access to fishing docks, is the first on the route. From there, the path follows **Big Cottonwood Creek** through stands of aspens and evergreens. The trail continues south across meadows filled with wildflowers, then climbs more steeply to **Brighton Overlook. Dog Lake,** surrounded by old mine dumps, lies to the south. Continue on the main trail to large, deep **Lake Mary,** below Mount Millicent. **Lake Martha** is farther up the trail. A final climb takes you to **Lake**

Catherine, bordered by a pretty alpine meadow to the north and the steep talus slopes of Sunset and Pioneer Peaks to the south.

Solitude Mountain Resort

The best thing about **Solitude Mountain Resort** (801/534-1400 or 800/748-4754, solitudemountain.com, 9am-4pm daily late Nov.-mid-Apr., lift tickets $115 adults, $85 seniors, $45-69 kids) is reflected in its name: It's rarely crowded. Recreation centers around a small European-style village with lodges.

Skiing and Snowboarding

Skiers and snowboarders have plenty of wide blue cruisers, eight lifts, and a terrain park. When conditions are favorable, gates open to expert terrain, including Honeycomb Canyon's ungroomed powder skiing. Day skiers generally head out from the Moonbeam base area, where a large day lodge has lockers, a café, and bar. Amenities include a ski school, rentals, and kids' programs. During peak holiday times, rates bump up $5-10, but you can save a few bucks by purchasing tickets online ahead of time.

Plenty of snow and nicely groomed tracks (12.4 mi/20 km) make Solitude's **Nordic Center** (Silver Lake Day Lodge, 801/536-5774, 8:30am-4:30pm daily mid-Nov.-mid-Apr., $20 ages 13-64, $10 seniors, $15 ages 5-12) one of the best places for both traditional cross-country skiers and skate skiers. Additional trails are groomed for **snowshoers** (6.2 mi/10 km, $8). Shuttles run daily from Solitude Village to the Nordic Center day lodge, which has rentals, instruction, and tours.

Summer Recreation

Solitude opens for **summer** (June-mid-Oct.), creating a leisurely place to get away for a day or more. Scenic **chairlift rides** (Fri.-Sun., $15 adults, $10 seniors and children) get you up high for views of Big Cottonwood Canyon and the Wasatch Range. Hiking trails depart from the top and bottom. The chair also services lift-accessed **mountain biking** ($30 for all day) and permits bikes on about 20 miles (32 km) of trails. An 18-hole **disc golf** course flanks the mountain. Activities are coordinated at the **Powderhorn Adventure Center,** where you can rent mountain bikes and discs.

Food

Snowshoe to the trailside **Yurt** (801/536-5765, 5:30pm Thurs.-Sat., 5pm Sun. winter, $145) for a five-course dinner. Snowshoes are provided and reservations are required; make them well in advance.

Outside the main resort complex, the **Silver Fork Lodge** (11332 E. Big Cottonwood Canyon, 801/533-9977, www.silverforklodge.com, 8am-8pm daily, $11-40) has a friendly atmosphere. Its restaurant is known for the 70-year-old sourdough starter used to make its pancakes. For dinner, go high-end with steak or blue-collar with meatloaf.

Accommodations

Most lodgings (801/534-1400 or 800/748-4754) at Solitude are in the European-style ski village owned and managed by the resort. Rates drop by at least half during the summer.

The **Inn at Solitude** ($308-370 winter, $149-179 summer) is a few steps from the base area lifts. The **Village at Solitude Condominiums** ($225-381) has units in three different developments. All have fireplaces, full kitchens, private decks, and come with 1-3 bedrooms.

Brighton Resort

Brighton (801/532-4731, www.brightonresort.com, 9am-4pm daily mid-Nov.-mid-Apr., lift tickets $119 adults, $74 seniors, $60 youths) is a longtime favorite with local families for the excellent skiing and friendly, unpretentious atmosphere. It's also the least expensive resort in the area.

Skiing and Snowboarding

With 66 runs, Brighton offers day and night skiing. It's the most snowboard-friendly of the Cottonwood resorts. Snowboarders looking for a challenge can head up the Crest Express quad to play around the My-O-My and Candyland terrain parks, plus the hill has two more terrain parks and a half-pipe. Brighton has a ski and snowboard school, rentals, ski shops, a couple of cafeterias, and a sit-down restaurant in the lodge. Solitude and Brighton are connected by the Sol-Bright run.

Food and Accommodations

Slope-side restaurants for lunch include the **Alpine Rose** cafeteria ($6-12) and the **Milly Chalet** ($6-12) at the base of the Millicent quad. **Molly Green's** ($10-18, 21 and over only) is a bar and grill with table service for dinner.

The resort's casual **Brighton Lodge** (855/201-7669, $169-249) offers accommodations with a heated outdoor pool and a spa. Much smaller than most ski-resort lodges, it has guest rooms, suites, and a few hostel rooms (twin beds or bunks, shared baths).

Camping

Uinta-Wasatch-Cache National Forest has two high-elevation campgrounds in Big Cottonwood Canyon. **Spruces Campground** (9.7 mi/15.6 km up the canyon, 92 sites, late May-mid-Oct., $26) is the largest. **Redman Campground** (13 mi/21 km up the canyon, 39 sites, mid-June-early Oct., $26) is located between Solitude and Brighton. Both have potable water during the summer. Make **advance reservations** (877/444-6777, www.recreation.gov). In order to protect the Salt Lake City watershed, dogs and other pets are not permitted; this is strictly enforced.

Little Cottonwood Canyon

The road through this glacial valley climbs steeply to the back of the canyon. Splendid peaks shoot upward on both sides, offering hiking, climbing, and winter skiing at two resorts.

Getting There

From downtown Salt Lake City, it's about a 40-minute drive (25 mi/40 km) to Snowbird and 45 minutes (27 mi/43 km) to Alta. Drive south on I-15 and east on I-215/Belt Route. Then go east on UT 190 and Wasatch Boulevard to UT 210 south and Little Cottonwood Road. Snowbird is 6 miles (9.7 km) up Little Cottonwood Road; Alta is 8 miles (12.9 km) up.

UTA buses (801/743-3882, www.rideuta.com) and shuttles from **Canyon Transportation** (800/255-1841, canyontransport.com) serve all resorts.

Hiking

Do not take a dog up Little Cottonwood Canyon. Because it's part of the Salt Lake City watershed, environmental regulations prohibit pets, even in the car.

White Pine, Red Pine, and Maybird Gulch

Length: 7-10.3 miles (11-16.6 km) rt
Duration: 3-5 hours
Elevation gain: 2,075-2765 feet (632-842 m)
Effort: strenuous
Trailhead: White Pine Trailhead, 5.3 miles (8.5 km) up Little Cottonwood Canyon and 1 mile (1.6 km) beyond Tanners Flat Campground

These heavily used trails lead to scenic alpine lakes. All three begin from the same trailhead and then diverge into separate valleys. You'll enjoy wildflowers and superb high-country scenery. After hiking on an old roadbed for a bit, you'll reach a junction. Turn sharply left at the junction for the trail to **White Pine Lake** (10.3 mi/16.6 km rt, 2,762 ft/842 m elevation), which is the most demanding. From the junction, the trail continues upward, eventually switchbacking up into meadows to reach the lake, which is set in a cirque.

For an easier hike, at the junction continue straight across the bridge over the stream for Red Pine Lake and Maybird Gulch. The **Red Pine Trail** (7 mi/11 km rt, 2,073 ft/823 m elevation) contours around a ridge, then parallels Red Pine Fork to the lake, a beautiful deep pool ringed by conifers and alpine meadows. Partway up the Red Pine Trail, the **Maybird Gulch Trail** (7.2 mi/11.6 km, 2,214 ft/675 m elevation) turns off to the right, leading to the two tiny **Maybird Lakes,** backed by Pfeifferhorn Peak.

Peruvian Gulch and Hidden Peak Trail

Length: 3.5 miles (5.6 km) one way
Duration: 2 hours
Elevation change: 3,240 feet (988 m)
Effort: strenuous
Trailhead: top or bottom of the Snowbird tram

These two Snowbird-area trails give you the advantage of hiking just one way by riding the **Snowbird tram** (adults $25-30, children and seniors $21-25). You can choose whether you want a lung-busting climb or a knee-pounding descent. From the top of **Hidden Peak** (11,000 ft/3,353 m), the trail crosses open rocky country on the upper slopes before dropping into spruce- and aspen-covered ridges lower down. Then the route joins an old mining road to descend **Peruvian Gulch** to the base area.

Catherine Pass

Length: 3 miles (4.8 km) rt
Duration: 2 hours
Elevation gain: 845 feet (258 m)
Effort: moderate
Trailhead: Catherine Pass Trailhead, on a dirt road 2 miles (3.2 km) beyond the large parking area near Alta's Snowpine Lodge; $8 road maintenance fee

The trek to **Catherine Pass** may be short, but it tops out at a high elevation (10,220 ft/3,115 m). The route ascends Albion Basin with views of Alta Ski Resort and levels out several times before climbing again. From the pass, three lakes spread out below the peaks of the Wasatch Range. For a longer trek, you can continue 5 miles (8 km) farther to Brighton.

Cecret Lake Trail

Length: 2 miles (3.2 km) rt
Duration: 1.5 hours
Elevation gain: 360 feet (110 m)
Effort: moderate
Trailhead: Cecret Lake, at the end of the dirt road that continues beyond the large parking area near Alta's Snowpine Lodge; $8 road maintenance fee

For a good family hike, follow this trail climbing glacier-scarred granite slopes to the pretty alpine **Cecret Lake,** set below Sugarloaf Mountain. Along the way, wildflowers put on colorful summer displays in Albion Basin. The idyllic lake sits in a bowl surrounded by meadows. Parking limited, so get an early start.

★ Snowbird Ski and Summer Resort

When you drive up Little Cottonwood Canyon, **Snowbird** (801/933-2222 or 800/232-9542, road and snow report 801/933-2100, www.snowbird.com) is the first resort you approach. In winter, it has outstanding skiing and snowboarding. In summer, scenic tram rides convey sightseers to the summit of Hidden Peak for huge views.

Skiing and Snowboarding

With a long ski season (mid-Nov.-May, lift tickets $110-155 adults, $110-123 seniors, $65-73 youths), Snowbird is known for its great snow, much of it classified as champagne powder. It's a big, fun place to ski or board, with varied terrain on the north faces of mountains in three distinct areas: Peruvian Gulch, Gad, and Mineral Basin on the back side. You can buy a special lift ticket that allows skiing between Snowbird and neighboring Alta. Plenty of lifts serve Snowbird, including six high-speed quads and an aerial tram.

The resort has lessons, rentals, guided tours, and restaurants.

Summer Recreation

In summer, Snowbird (June-mid-Oct.) offers tons of outdoor activities. The most popular one is taking a 10-minute scenic ride on the **Aerial Tram** (adults $25-30, children and seniors $21-25, includes chairlift) to the top of Hidden Peak. You can also hike from the top of the peak before catching a ride back down. Ride the **Peruvian chairlift** for more sightseeing and walk through a long tunnel into Mineral Basin for views or more hiking. Tickets allow you to take the lift up and the tram down or the other way around.

A plethora of thrill sports keep families entertained. Activities include zipping down the mountain on the **Mountain Coaster** or **Alpine Slide.** A bungee trampoline, climbing wall, tree climbs, and ropes courses challenge almost all ages, with mini versions for tiny kids. Rates and times vary.

Food

The eye-popping **Summit Restaurant** (9am-3pm daily, $11-19) is located at the top of the Hidden Peak tram. Its soaring all-windows structure houses an upscale cafeteria-style restaurant.

The ★ **Aerie** (5pm-9pm daily, $32-44) is the fancy 10th-floor restaurant at the Cliff Lodge, offering excellent steaks and pasta and fine sunset views of the mountains. If you'd like to partake of the scenery but aren't up for the splurge, check out the sandwiches and small plates menu in the lounge.

Accommodations

All of Snowbird's accommodations are run by the resort. Rates vary wildly according to season, day of week, and view, but are highest during the winter,

Top to bottom: Snowbird Ski and Summer Resort; view of Little Cottonwood Canyon; Alta Ski Area in Little Cottonwood Canyon

dropping by more than half during the summer.

The most upscale place to stay is the ski-in, ski-out ★ **Cliff Lodge,** with more than 500 guest rooms, four restaurants, retail shops, a year-round outdoor pool, and a top-notch spa. One very nice practical detail is the ground-floor locker, complete with boot dryer assigned to each guest. The Cliff is swanky without being snobbish or stuffy. Standard winter room rates run about $550, with many package deals available. During the summer, rates run around $150.

Getting Around
Snowbird provides free shuttle service between the different areas of the resort during skiing hours.

Alta Ski Area
Alta (801/359-1078, snow report 801/572-3939, www.alta.com) has a special mystique among skiers. A combination of deep powder, wide-open terrain, charming accommodations, and the polite but firm exclusion of snowboards make it special. Do not come to Alta expecting to do anything but ski. There is no shopping, no nightlife, no see-and-be-seen scene. Dogs are not permitted in the tiny town.

Skiing
Alta (mid-Nov.-Apr., lift tickets $141 adults, $72 kids) is for skiers only; snowboards aren't allowed. To keep the slopes from becoming too crowded, Alta limits the number of skiers allowed; this mostly happens during the holidays and on powder-filled weekends. Lifts include three high-speed quads, a high-speed triple, four slower chairlifts, and several tow ropes, offering access to 119 runs. Alta's **Alf Engen Ski School** (801/799-2271) has lessons, rentals, childcare, and guided snowcat skiing and snowboarding in the Grizzly Gulch backcountry.

Food
Almost all of Alta's lodges include breakfast and dinner for their guests. One restaurant of note is the **Shallow Shaft** (801-742-2177, www.shallowshaft. com, 5:30pm-8:30pm daily, $29-45). Although the place looks dubious from the outside, the interior has great views of the ski mountain. There's a fairly small menu of good steaks, fish, and pasta, along with a wine list as good as you'll find in Utah.

Accommodations
Although Alta's accommodations may be pricey, room rates include breakfast and dinner. In summer, rates drop by nearly half.

One of the most charming and central places to stay is the **Alta Lodge** (801/742-3500 or 800/707-2582, www.altalodge. com, dorm bed $127-157, standard room $358-540), which includes breakfast, afternoon tea, and dinner. It's an old-fashioned ski lodge that oozes authenticity with no-frills rooms and a relaxed atmosphere.

★ **Alta's Rustler Lodge** (801/742-4200, www.rustlerlodge.com, dorm bed $196, standard room $482-762) is laden with amenities, with a heated outdoor pool, a fine-dining restaurant, spa, and spacious guest rooms. Breakfast and dinner are included. Après-ski, it's common to see guests wandering the lobby swathed in their thick hotel bathrobes.

Getting Around

Parking can be difficult; pay attention to signs, as parking regulations are enforced. The **Alta Shuttle** (801/274-0223 or 866/274-0225, www.altashuttle.com, $43 one-way) runs to the airport and the **Alta Resort Shuttle** (8:30am-5:30pm daily winter, free) makes a continuous loop around lodges and the base area.

Camping

Uinta-Wasatch-Cache National Forest has two campgrounds in the canyon: **Tanners Flat Campground** (4.3 mi/6.9 km up Little Cottonwood Canyon, 34 sites, mid-May-mid-Oct., $26) and **Albion Basin Campground** (11 mi/17.7 km up the canyon and dirt road past Alta, 24 sites, late June-mid-Sept., $21). Both campgrounds have potable water and accept **reservations** (877/444-6777, www.recreation.gov).

Park City

With two ski areas, including one of the nation's largest, Park City is known worldwide for its snow sports. In summer, guests flock to the resorts to explore the scenic mountain landscapes. The well-heeled clientele that frequents the resorts has transformed this old mining town into the most sophisticated shopping, dining, and lodging center in Utah.

Getting There

From downtown Salt Lake City, it takes about 45 minutes (32 mi/52 km) to reach

Park City at dusk

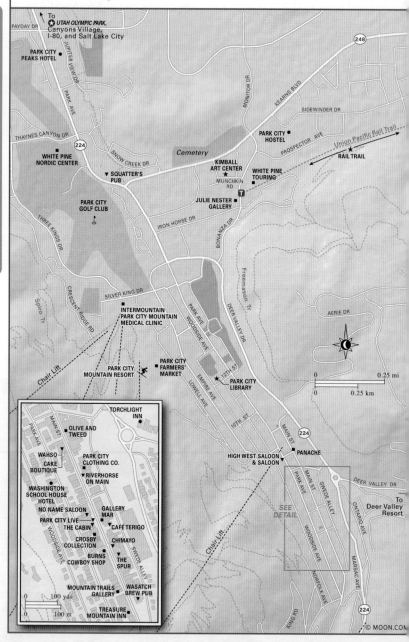

Park City

To **UTAH OLYMPIC PARK,** Canyons Village, I-80, and Salt Lake City

PAYDAY DR

PARK CITY PEAKS HOTEL

JUPITER VIEW DR

PARK AVE

248

KEARNS BLVD

MONITOR DR

SIDEWINDER DR

THAYNES CANYON DR

224

SNOW CREEK DR

PARK CITY HOSTEL

PROSPECTOR AVE

Union Pacific Rail Trail

RAIL TRAIL

WHITE PINE NORDIC CENTER

SQUATTER'S PUB

Cemetery

KIMBALL ART CENTER

MUNCHKIN RD

WHITE PINE TOURING

PARK CITY GOLF CLUB

JULIE NESTER GALLERY

IRON HORSE DR

BONANZA DR

THREE KINGS DR

Spiro Tr

CRESCENT RIDGE RD

SILVER KING DR

Freemason Tr

DEER VALLEY DR

AERIE DR

INTERMOUNTAIN PARK CITY MOUNTAIN MEDICAL CLINIC

PARK AVE

WOODSIDE AVE

Chair Lift

PARK CITY MOUNTAIN RESORT

PARK CITY FARMERS' MARKET

EMPIRE AVE

12TH ST

PARK CITY LIBRARY

0   0.25 mi

0   0.25 km

LOWELL AVE

10TH ST

MAIN ST

224

PANACHE

HIGH WEST SALOON & SALOON

DEER VALLEY DR

To Deer Valley Resort

PARK AVE

MAIN ST

SWEDE ALLEY

ONTARIO AVE

SEE DETAIL

WOODSIDE AVE

Chair Lift

NORFOLK AVE

MARSAC AVE

KING RD

224

© MOON.COM

Detail inset

TORCHLIGHT INN

OLIVE AND TWEED

MAIN ST

PARK AVE

WAHSO

CAKE BOUTIQUE

PARK CITY CLOTHING CO.

RIVERHORSE ON MAIN

WASHINGTON SCHOOL HOUSE HOTEL

NO NAME SALOON

GALLERY MAR

PARK CITY LIVE

THE CABIN

CAFÉ TERIGO

CROSBY COLLECTION

CHIMAYO

WOODSIDE AVE

BURNS COWBOY SHOP

THE SPUR

SWEDE ALLEY

MOUNTAIN TRAILS GALLERY

WASATCH BREW PUB

0   100 yds

0   100 m

TREASURE MOUNTAIN INN

Park City. Hop on I-80 east and then UT 224 south.

Sights
★ Utah Olympic Park

Built for the 2002 Olympics, **Utah Olympic Park** (3000 Bear Hollow Dr., near the Canyons Village, 435/658-4200, utaholympiclegacy.org, noon-4pm daily winter, noon-5pm daily spring., noon-6pm daily summer, free) was the site of the bobsled, skeleton, luge, and ski-jump competitions. Now aspiring Olympic athletes train here and visitors can often watch them. During the summer, freestyle skiers make acrobatic jumps, plunging into a huge swimming pool. Saturday afternoons feature a freestyle aerial show. For thrills, you can fly down the track on a professionally driven **bobsled** (summer $80, winter $175).

Recreation
Hiking

The ski areas open their trails to hikers in summer; pick up a trail map and just head out. **Deer Valley** (435/649-1000 or 800/424-3337, www.deervalley.com) and **Park City** (435/649-8111, www.parkcitymountain.com) both offer lift-assisted hiking that takes walkers up to the high country without a wind-sucking foot ascent; see individual resorts for information. From downtown Park City, follow trail signs to the slopes: Well-marked trails start just on the edge of town and head uphill. **Mountain Trails Foundation** (http://mountaintrails.org), a trail advocacy organization, has good interactive maps on their website.

Mountain Biking

With more than 350 miles (565 km) of mountain biking trails, Park City lures bikers of all skill levels. Both Park City ski resorts have at least one lift operating for lift-accessed mountain biking in summer.

For easy and family riding, the **Historic Union Pacific Rail Trail State Park** (435/649-6839, stateparks.utah.gov, dawn-dusk daily year-round, free) is a multiuse nonmotorized trail paralleling I-80 for 30 miles (48 km), from Deer Valley through Park City and the town of Coalville north to Evanston, Wyoming. Locate the trailhead and parking area behind the Park City Plaza. Rent a bike from **White Pine Touring** (1790 Bonanza Dr., 435/649-8710, 9am-7pm daily); their shop has easy access to the trail.

Golf

The Park City area has a number of 18-hole courses, including the **Park City Golf Club** (1541 Thaynes Canyon Dr., 435/615-5800, www.parkcitygolfclub.org, nonresidents $55-70). **Canyons Golf Course** (4000 Canyons Resort Dr., 435/615-4728, www.parkcitymountain.com, $100) is a 6,256-yard, par-70 course, designed by Gene and Casey Bates, with a number of holes built right on the ski runs of Park City Mountain Resort.

Entertainment and Events
Nightlife

Park City's nightlife centers on bars and dance clubs. The principal hangouts are on Main Street, although all the lodges and resorts and most of the larger hotels have bars and clubs of their own. Trendy **Park City Live** (427 Main St., 435/649-9123, http://parkcitylive.net, 8pm-2am daily) is the largest music venue in town, with long lines at the door, a crowded dance floor, and special VIP tables. The more down-home **No Name Saloon** (447 Main St., 435/649-6667, www.nonamesaloon.net, 11:30am-midnight Mon.-Thurs., 11:30am-1am Fri.-Sat., 10:30am-midnight Sun.) is a sports bar with food, including what's often called the town's best burger; head up to the rooftop to spy on Main Street action. Duck into **The Spur** (352 Main St., 435/615-1618, www.thespurbarandgrill.com, 10am-1am daily) for rock, acoustic folk, or bluegrass and a convivial atmosphere. Right across from Park City Live,

The Cabin (427 Main St., 435/565-2337, www.thecabinparkcity.com, noon-1am daily) has music every night and a good list of beers and cocktails.

The pubs are places to drink a microbrew and chat with friends. Try **Wasatch Brew Pub** (250 Main St., 435/649-0900, www.wasatchbeers.com, 3pm-8pm Thurs., noon-8pm Fri.-Sat., 11am-3pm Sun.). or **Squatters Pub** (1900 Park Ave., 435/649-9868, www.squatters.com, 10am-8pm daily).

Sundance Film Festival

Robert Redford began this noted festival in 1981 as a venue for independent films that otherwise had a difficult time reaching the screen or a mass audience. Since then, the **Sundance Film Festival** (435/658-3456, www.sundance.org) has become the nation's foremost venue for new and innovative cinema. The festival is held in the second half of January at the height of the ski season, packing Park City with the glitterati of New York and Hollywood. Make plans well in advance if you want to attend any of the screenings or activities.

Tickets to screenings can be hard to come by, especially for films with advance buzz or big stars; if you can't get tickets, put your name on waiting lists or join lines at theaters for canceled tickets. Tickets to less well-known films are usually available at the last minute. You can also get Park City packages through local hotels that include tickets.

Shopping

Historic **Main Street** is lined with upscale boutiques, gift shops, galleries, craft shops, and sporting goods stores.

Markets

The open-air **Park Silly Sunday Market** (435/714-4036, parksillysundaymarket. com, 10am-5pm Sun. early June-late Sept.) takes over the lower stretch of Main Street with arts and crafts, handmade clothing, food carts, and live music.

downtown Park City

The **Park City Farmers Market** (Silver King Lot, noon-5pm Wed. early June-Oct.) is held near the main base of Park City Mountain Resort.

Clothing

Panache (738 Main St., 435/649-7037, 10am-6pm daily) offers stylish high-end women's clothing and jewelry. **Olive & Tweed** (608 Main St., 435/649-9392, oliveandtweed.com, 10am-7pm Mon.-Thurs., 10am-9pm Fri.-Sun.) is an artisans co-op featuring women's clothing, jewelry, and lots of gifts. **Cake Boutique** (577 Main St., 435/649-1256, cakeparkcity.com, 10am-7pm Mon.-Sat., 11am-6pm Sun.) is a fashion-forward clothing store that veers toward designer hipster wear with lots of denim.

If you like the upscale Western look common in Park City, pick up some togs at **Park City Clothing Company** (558 Main St., 435/649-0555, 10am-9pm Mon.-Sat., 10am-6pm Sun.) with pearl-snap shirts, hats, boots, and jewelry amid the Coca-Cola memorabilia. For boots, check out **Burns Cowboy Shop** (363 Main St., 435/529-7484, 10am-6pm daily).

Galleries

Art galleries are a major scene in Park City, with lots of high-end art. Many galleries are along busy Main Street.

Gallery MAR (436 Main St., 435/649-3001, www.gallerymar.com, 11am-7pm Mon.-Thurs., 10am-9pm Fri.-Sat., 11am-6pm Sun.) represents a wide selection of mostly representational artists. **Julie Nester Gallery** (1280 Iron Horse Dr., 435/649-7855, www.julienestergallery.com, 11am-5pm Tues.-Sat.) represents a number of national contemporary artists, with more sophisticated works than you'd usually expect in a resort town. **Mountain Trails Gallery** (301 Main St., 435/615-8748, www.mountaintrailsgalleries.com, 10am-9pm daily) is Park City's top purveyor of Western and wildlife art, both painting and sculpture. For Indigenous art, antiques, and collectibles, go to the **Crosby Collection** (419 Main St., 800/960-3389, www.crosbycollection.com, 10am-6pm daily).

Park City's real jewel is the nonprofit **Kimball Arts Center** (401 Kearns Blvd., 435/649-8882, www.kimball-art.org, 10am-5pm Mon.-Fri., noon-5pm Sat.-Sun., donation). It's an arts education hub plus a sales and exhibition gallery focusing on the local arts community.

Food

Park City has the greatest concentration of good restaurants in Utah. The five blocks of historic Main Street alone offer many fine places to eat, and each of the resorts, hotels, and lodges offers more options. Note that many of the restaurants close in May and November. During ski-season weekends, dinner reservations are strongly recommended.

Chimayo (368 Main St., 435/649-6222, www.chimayorestaurant.com, 5pm-9pm Sun.-Thurs., 5pm-10pm Fri.-Sat. winter and summer, hours vary off-season,

$36-50) leads the area in contemporary Southwest cuisine such as trout fajitas seared with green pepitas and served with chipotle sour cream.

One of the most romantic restaurants in Park City is the stylish, slightly formal **Wahso** (577 Main St., 435/615-0300, www.wahso.com, 5pm-9pm Sun. and Wed.-Thurs., 5pm-10pm Fri.-Sat., $34-48). The name is a word in both Chinese and French (from *oiseau,* meaning "bird"), as is the cuisine: French sauces meet Chinese cooking techniques and vice versa.

The inspiration for the food at pleasant **Cafe Terigo** (424 Main St., 435/645-9555, www.cafeterigo.com, 11:30am-2:30pm and 5:30pm-9:30pm Mon.-Sat., $25-45) is Italian, but dishes such as pan-seared scallops with sweet corn risotto and red pepper puree show that ingredients and techniques have been substantially updated. The atmosphere, both inside and on the outside patio, is simultaneously calming and fun.

The classy **Riverhorse on Main** (540 Main St., 435/649-0799, riverhorse parkcity.com, 5pm-10pm Mon.-Fri., 11am-2pm and 5pm-10pm Sat.-Sun., $38-70) in the old Masonic building serves carefully prepared American standards with a few restrained flourishes. After a day of skiing, splurge on the trio of wild game (buffalo, venison, and elk).

Although ★ **High West Distillery and Saloon** (703 Park Ave., 435/649-8300, www.highwest.com, 11am-9pm daily, $18-52) is a great place to get an après-ski drink, it's also one of Park City's best restaurants. Try the three-bean bourbon chili topped with fried quinoa. Kids are welcome here, and there's a special menu with them in mind.

Accommodations

Park City is awash in condos, hotels, and B&Bs; guest capacity far exceeds the town's permanent population. Rates peak at dizzying heights during the ski season, when accommodations may also

lifts and ski runs at Park City Mountain Resort

be hard to find. Most lodgings have four different winter rates, which peak at the Christmas holidays, during the Sundance Film Festival, and in February-March; there are different rates for weekends and weekdays as well. Summer rates are usually about half what you will pay during these popular times. During ski season, many lodgings ask for minimum stays.

Hostels

A boon for budget travelers in a spendy town, the **Park City Hostel** (1781 Sidewinder Dr., 435/731-8811, www. parkcityhostel.com, dorm bed $65, private room $112-125) has shared dorm rooms, private rooms, and shared bathrooms. Facilities include an equipped kitchen.

Lodges, Inns, and Hotels

Park City's classic budget ski lodge, **Chateau Après Lodge** (1299 Norfolk Ave., 435/649-9372, www.chateauapres.com, men's dorm bed $50, private room $155,

winter), is a short walk from the Park City Mountain Resort base. Although the men's dorm is a barracks and regular guest rooms are far from elegant, this family-run lodge has a dedicated following among serious skiers. You can meet skiers from all over the world at the breakfast buffet.

A little way from downtown, the upscale **Park City Peaks Hotel** (2346 Park Ave., 435/649-5000 or 800/649-5012, www.parkcitypeaks.com, $254-324) is notable mainly because its summer rates are sometimes well under $100 a night.

Right downtown, the ★ **Treasure Mountain Inn** (255 Main St., 435/655-4501 or 800/344-2460, www.treasuremountain inn.com, $300-525) is a large complex of three buildings with several room types, all with kitchens. Large, refurbished guest rooms are beautifully furnished. Quiet rooms face the back pool and garden.

Just a block off Main Street, the landmark **Washington School House Hotel** (543 Park Ave., 435/649-3800 or 800/824-1672, www.washingtonschoolhouse.com, $1,188-5,400) was built from quarried limestone in1889 as the town's elementary school. It's now one of the most luxurious lodgings in Park City. Four large standard guest rooms and four suites are furnished with well-chosen antiques and art, an outdoor heated pool, hot tub, sauna, and ski lockers. During the summer it's possible to get a room for about $550.

Less vaunted but still quite luxurious, the **Torchlight Inn** (255 Deer Valley Dr., 435/612-0345 or 855/374-2329, www. torchlightinn.com, $389-560) is an extra-friendly B&B with full breakfast. It's on the edge of downtown.

Campgrounds

Park City RV Resort (2200 W. Rasmussen Rd., 435/649-2535, www.parkcityrv resort.com, tents $35, RVs $55-65) offers seasonal tent and year-round RV sites with full hookups. The campground, which has showers and a laundry, sits 6 miles (10 km) from town.

There's camping at two Utah state parks (stateparks.utah.gov) just outside Park City. On the Jordanelle Reservoir, **Jordanelle State Park** (UT 319, Heber City, 435/649-9540 or 435/782-3030) has RV campsites with electrical and water hookups ($45), drive-up or walk-in tent campsites ($30-35), and cabins ($100-130). **Wasatch Mountain State Park** (1281 Warm Springs Rd., Midway, 435/654-1791) has several campgrounds with RV hookups ($35-90), tent campsites ($14), and cabins ($70-85). Make **reservations** (800/322-3770, utahstateparks. reserveamerica.com) 16 months in advance.

Getting Around

Parking downtown can be extremely difficult. **Park City Transit** (435/615-5000, parkcity.org, free) operates a **trolley bus** that stops up and down Main Street about every 10 minutes daily. Several bus routes go to other parts of town, including every 10-20 minutes to the ski areas. Transit guides are online. Uber and Lyft also serve Park City.

Park City Mountain Resort

Part of Vail Resorts, **Park City Mountain Resort** (435/649-8111, www.parkcity mountain.com) is the second largest ski and snowboard resort in the United States. In total, the mega-resort has two major base areas, nine hotels, more than 24 restaurants, and 7,300 skiable acres encompassing a network of nearly 350 trails on 17 mountain peaks linked by 41 lifts.

Skiing and Snowboarding

The ski resort (mid-Nov.-mid-Apr.) has two base areas: **Park City** and **Canyons Village.** Both have ski schools, rentals, ski shops, day care, and restaurants on the slopes and in the base areas. The

Quicksilver Gondola, running both ways, connects the two ski areas via a mid-station atop Pine Cone Ridge; **free shuttle buses** run between them, too. Dynamic pricing for **lift tickets** (from $179 adults, $98 seniors, $91 ages 7-12) means prices change from day to day based on demand. It's a little cheaper to buy tickets online in advance.

From town, two lifts access the **Park City** ski area, where a fleet of high-speed six-passenger lifts, high-speed quads, and regular chairlifts carry up to 20,200 skiers per hour high onto the eastern slope of the Wasatch Range. It is loaded with natural half pipes, big bowls, and challenging terrain.

Canyons Village has lifts reaching nine separate peaks along the Wasatch Mountains and runs swooping down canyons in between. With large lodge hotels, restaurants, and shops, this area seems like its own small town.

Summer Recreation

Summer activities (July-early Sept.) take place out of the Park City base. Two chairlifts ($14-27) run for **scenic lift rides** or access to **hiking trails**. Lift-accessed **mountain biking** ($14-37) is possible along the resort's 35 miles (56 km) of trails, including fine downhills in the Canyons.

For thrills, you can sail down an elevated track on the **Mountain Coaster** ($14-29). An alternative sliding adventure whizzes down on an **Alpine Slide** ($14-24).

Food

Several midmountain eateries offer dining options for lunch in winter, from quick bites to heartier meals. But the best lunch spot is on the Canyons side at the top of the DreamCatcher and DreamScape lifts: **Cloud Dine** (435/615-2892, 10am-3:30pm daily, $15-30) serves sandwiches, flatbreads, pizza, and fresh donuts.

In the Grand Summit Hotel, **The Farm**

(435/615-8080, 11:30am-10pm Tues.-Sun., $28-52) uses locally sourced ingredients. For dinner you might have steelhead trout with pasta, wild mushrooms, and truffled leek cream—or just a burger and fries.

Accommodations

The enormous hotels in Canyon Village are built on a scale unlike any other lodgings in Park City. All have a mix of hotel rooms and condos. During ski season, expect to pay $500-750 for the most basic guest rooms, which are still luxurious. If you book **advance reservations** (855/680-3239) early enough, it's possible to find rooms in the $250-350 range. In summer, the same rooms are $145-250.

Facilities at the **Grand Summit** (4000 Canyons Resort Dr.), which directly fronts the gondola loading platform, include a full-service health club and a spa, with an indoor-outdoor pool, three on-site restaurants, a bar, and a brewpub. The **Sundial Lodge** (2025 Canyons Resort Dr.), a short walk from the gondola, has an outdoor heated pool, a hot tub, and an on-site exercise facility. Least expensive is the **Silverado** (2669 Canyons Resort Dr.), a few steps farther downhill, which still has the requisite outdoor heated pool, hot tub, and exercise room.

Deer Valley Resort

The poshest of the Utah ski areas is **Deer Valley Resort** (435/649-1000 or 800/424-3337, www.deervalley.com). You'll find upscale accommodations, gourmet dining, attentive service, and polished brass everywhere.

Skiing

With no snowboarding allowed, Deer Valley is just for skiers (early Dec.-early Apr.). The resort spans six mountains and two base areas: **Snow Park Lodge,** and 3 miles (5 km) higher, **Silver Lake Lodge** (parking is more limited). Free buses from town stop at both, which is easier than finding parking. Amenities include a ski school, ski shop, rentals, child-care service, and restaurants.

Deer Valley is famous for its meticulously groomed trails. The slopes are served by 21 lifts, 101 runs, and six bowls. To prevent overcrowded trails, the resort restricts ticket sales during holiday weeks. If you're planning on skiing then, reserve **lift tickets** ($199-229 adults, $140-160 seniors, $110-130 children) several days in advance.

Summer Activities

The resort opens for summer (10am-5pm daily late June-early Sept.) with a couple lifts in operation. **Scenic lift rides** ($12-25) go to mountaintops for big views and **hiking** trails. Lift-accessed **mountain biking**, rentals, lessons, and guided tours are available. The resort has 55 miles (89 km) of single- and double-track trails.

Food

Take a survey of lift riders and you'll find the most popular meal here is the seafood buffet at the **Snow Park Lodge** (435/645-6632, 6pm-9pm Thurs.-Sun. winter, $80 adults, $30 children). Both the quality and quantity of the food are unstinting.

The warm greeting equals the delicious eastern Mediterranean cooking at **Reefs** (Deer Valley Club, 7720 Royal St., 435/658-0323, www.reefsrestaurant.com, 4:30pm-10pm Tues.-Sun. winter, 4:30pm-10pm Tues.-Sat. summer, $14-36). You'll enjoy Lebanese- and Turkish-style standards in addition to poke and sashimi.

At the **Goldener Hirsch Inn** (Silver Lake Village, 435/649-7770, 11:30am-10pm daily, $29-56, reservations recommended), dishes reflect both an Austrian heritage and New World pizzazz. Wiener schnitzel is the house specialty and fondue is a popular après-ski option.

It's a treat to visit the elegant **Glitretind Restaurant** (435/645-6455, steinlodge.com, 7am-9pm daily, $28-58, reservations

⬡ Side Trip: Dinosaur National Monument

fossils at Quarry Exhibit Hall in Dinosaur National Monument

Straddling the Utah-Colorado border, **Dinosaur National Monument** (435/781-7700, www.nps.gov/dino, $25 per vehicle, $20 per motorcycle, $15 pedestrians and bicyclists) owes its name and fame to one of the world's most productive sites for dinosaur bones. River running allows a close look at the geology and wildlife of the area, with the bonus of thrilling rapids. The nearest services are available near the monument's headquarters at the **Canyon Visitor Center** (4545 E. US 40, Dinosaur, CO).

Dinosaur Quarry Area

On the western end of the monument, the **Dinosaur Quarry Area** has produced more complete skeletons, skulls, and juvenile specimens than any other site in the world. The first bones were discovered in the early 1900s. Once being carefully exposed, most of them were left in the soil just as they were found.

Start at the **Quarry Visitor Center** (UT 149, Jensen, 435/781-7700, 8am-6pm daily mid-May-mid-Sept., 9am-5pm daily mid-Sept.-mid-May). During the summer, a bus shuttles (9am-4:15pm daily) people every 15 minutes from the visitors center to the quarry site. The rest of the year, pick up a pass at the visitors center, then drive the steep 0.25 mi/0.4 km to

recommended), which serves contemporary cuisine alongside one of the state's largest wine lists.

Accommodations

Deer Valley has abundant lodging. However, it's hard to find a condo for under $800 or a hotel room for less than $350 per night. Summer rates are lower than winter.

Silver Lake

The luxurious **Stein Eriksen Lodge** (7700 Stein Way, 435/649-3700 or 866/996-0034, www.steinlodge.com, $700-4,100) is like a Norwegian castle built of log and stone. Guest rooms are exquisitely appointed. There's a day spa with a pool and a fitness room.

The small **Goldener Hirsch Inn** (7570 Royal St. E., 435/649-7770 or 800/252-3373, www.goldenerhirschinn.com, $800-1,250) has guest rooms furnished with gorgeous hand-carved beds imported from Austria. Hot tubs, a sauna, and underground parking are other perks. Shoulder-season rates can drop to about $250.

the quarry, where the fossils are. This is the **Quarry Exhibit Hall,** where approximately 1,500 bones of 11 different dinosaur species cover a rock face. You can actually touch the dinosaur bones. The exhibit hall also houses dinosaur reconstructions.

Harpers Corner Scenic Drive
The paved **Harpers Corner Scenic Drive** (64 mi/104 km rt, 2 hrs, mid-Apr.-Dec.) winds onto high ridges and canyon viewpoints in the heart of Dinosaur National Monument. It begins at the Canyon Visitor Center in Colorado and continues north past many overlooks of spectacular faulted and folded rock layers. Vegetation ranges from the cottonwoods along the rivers far below to the aspen and firs of the highlands.

River Running
Trips on the **Green and Yampa Rivers** take you down exciting rapids through spectacular canyons. Guided trips are best for first-time visitors. The most popular one-day commercial trips run on the **Green River** ($100-120 adults, $75-100 kids). Rafters bounce through the Class I-III rapids of Split Mountain Canyon for 9 miles (14.5 km). Several raft companies are authorized to guide one-day and multi-day trips down the rivers:

♦ **Adrift Adventures** (9500 E. 6000 S., Jensen, UT, 435/789-3600 or 800/824-0150, www.adrift.com)

♦ **OARS Dinosaur** (221 N. 400 E., Vernal, UT, 435/789-4316 or 800/342-8243, www.greenriverrafting.com)

♦ **Dinosaur Expeditions** (800/345-7238, www.dinosaurriverexpeditions.com)

Getting There
Quarry Visitor Center is a 190-mile (305-km) drive from Salt Lake City, taking a little more than three hours. Take I-80 east to US 189, then continue southeast on US 40 after Heber City. In Duchesne, continue east on US 40/191 through Vernal, then follow US 40 to Jensen. Take UT 149 north from Jensen to reach the visitors center.

Canyon Visitor Center is a 210-mile (335-km) drive from Salt Lake City, which takes about 3.5 hours. Follow the route to Quarry Visitor Center, but continue east from Jensen on US 40 until you cross into Colorado. The visitors center is just off the highway, a little past Dinosaur.

Snow Park
The Lodges at Deer Valley (435/645-6528 or 800/558-3337, www.deervalley.com, rooms $445-495, condos $675-1,000) has hotel rooms and full-kitchen condos, plus a year-round outdoor pool and hot tub. Shuttles ferry skiers to the lifts.

Near the base of the lifts, **The St. Regis Deer Valley** (2300 Deer Valley Drive East, 435/940-5700, www.marriott.com, $1,000-1,200) has beautifully outfitted rooms that mix rustic and stylish contemporary decor. Lift access is via a funicular.

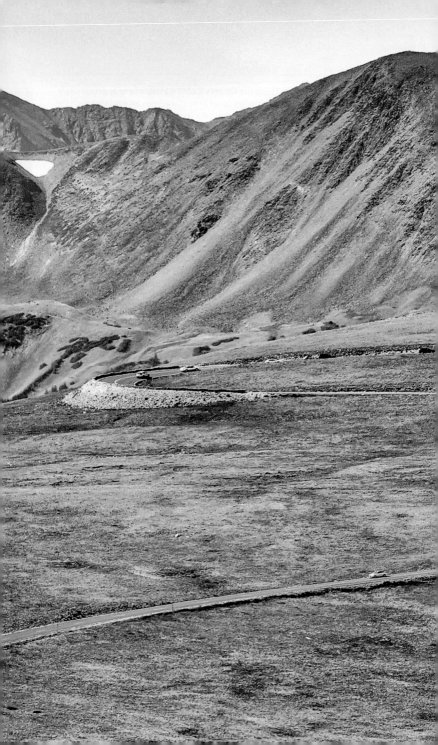

Rocky
Mountain
National Park

Highlights

★ **See the alluvial fan:** Follow the accessible path through a massive boulder field created by two floods— a testament to the power of water (page 520).

★ **Watch for wildlife:** Spot animals like elk, bighorn sheep, and moose as they bugle, mate, and care for their young (pages 521 and 524).

★ **Stroll around Lily Lake:** Circle this wildflower-rimmed lake on a wheelchair-accessible trail while enjoying views of the park's two tallest peaks (page 522).

★ **Drive Trail Ridge Road:** Drive to dizzying heights along this paved, top-of-the-world road, which crosses the Continental Divide (page 526).

★ **Peer into the depths at Forest Canyon Overlook:** The best overlook on Trail Ridge Road lets you look into a deep canyon (page 527).

★ **Appreciate Bear Lake Nature Trail:** Enjoy the scenery on an easy stroll around this glistening, tur-quoise lake (page 534).

★ **Hike to Nymph, Dream, and Emerald Lakes:** Follow the trail to these three sparkling gems (page 534).

★ **Traverse Lumpy Ridge Loop:** Circle Lumpy Ridge to see the weathered spires of the Twin Owls and inviting Gem Lake (page 537).

★ **Climb Longs Peak:** Making it to the summit of the park's highest peak is an adventure, but the rugged, high-elevation route isn't for everyone (page 543).

This alpine wonderland climbs to some of the highest points in the Rockies. Its rugged landscape is evidence of powerful tectonic plates and glaciers, which created a prominent vertical relief that shifts from meadowed valleys to alpine tundra.

This is one park where you can drive to extraordinary heights. You'll feel the altitude the moment you step out of your vehicle. At these elevations, breathing can be more labored; even taking a short uphill walk can feel like you're climbing Mount Everest. But the views are the ultimate reward: Mountains stretch for miles in all directions and scenic overlooks take in sweeping vistas that seem to go on forever.

Rocky Mountain National Park is a nature lover's dream. Hikers can find short trails to idyllic lakes or long treks into the backcountry. Backpackers can walk part of the Continental Divide Trail. Climbers can ascend the park's renowned fourteener, Longs Peak, or follow cracks up vertical rocks. Spring and early summer bring the chance to see spotted fawns and gangly moose calves. In fall, the bugles of bull elk resound through the air and bighorn sheep clash horns in displays of dominance.

Once covered by thick glaciers that sculpted peaks and ground out wide valleys, the park lands continue evolving today, shaped by the slow forces of snow, rain, and wind, as well as more dramatic events like floods and wildfires. Whatever the future brings, rich beauty and high adventure will be waiting in Rocky Mountain National Park.

Planning Your Time

Rocky Mountain National Park (970/586-1206, www.nps.gov/romo) is separated by the Continental Divide into east and west sides. These sides are only connected when **Trail Ridge Road** is open, from late May to mid October. Connecting the towns of Estes Park and Grand Lake, it's the highest continuous paved road in the United States. It takes about **four hours** to drive across without stops. The road provides access to hiking trails and the highest visitors center in all of the national parks.

Year-round, people visit the park mostly via the **east-side** entrances, which are closer to Denver. Due to the number of sights and trails on the east side, most visitors opt to stay **3-5 days. Bear Lake** is the most crowded region in the park, with a large web of trails. Especially in the summer, use the park's free shuttle system and plan hikes for early in the morning or late in the afternoon, when it's less crowded. North of Bear Lake, along the east flank of Trail Ridge Road, are **Moraine Park, Horseshoe Park,** and **Old Fall River Road. Estes Park** is the east side's bustling gateway town, with hotels, campgrounds, and restaurants. In the northeastern corner of the park, **Lumpy Ridge** is a rock climber's dream, with many bumpy geologic features to scale.

On the **west side** of the park, **Kawuneeche Valley,** home to the **Holzwarth Historic Site,** is also accessible to visitors year-round. In summer, you can camp at **Timber Creek Campground.** A few miles from the Kawuneeche Visitor Center, the small gateway town of **Grand Lake** has lodges and restaurants downtown, plus campgrounds on the lake. Many visitors spend just **one day** on

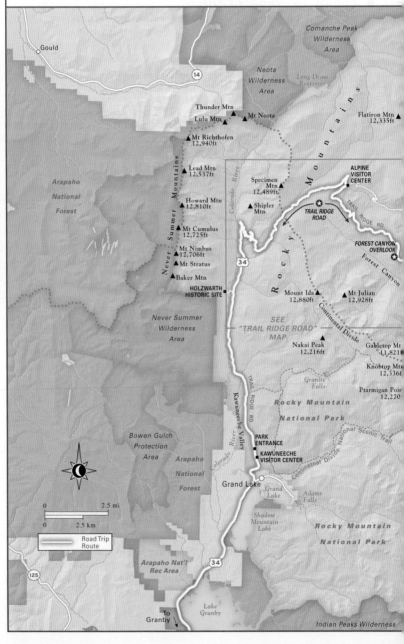

Rocky Mountain National Park

Gould

Comanche Peak Wilderness Area

Neota Wilderness Area

Long Draw Reservoir

Mountains

Flatiron Mtn 12,335ft

Thunder Mtn
Lulu Mtn ▲ ▲ Mt Neota

▲ Mt Richthofen 12,940ft

Never Summer Mountains

▲ Lead Mtn 12,537ft

Specimen Mtn 12,489ft

ALPINE VISITOR CENTER

TRAIL RIDGE RD

▲ Howard Mtn 12,810ft

▲ Shipler Mtn

TRAIL RIDGE ROAD

Colorado River

Rocky

FOREST CANYON OVERLOOK

Forest Canyon

▲ Mt Cumulus 12,725ft

Mt Nimbus ▲ 12,706ft
▲ Mt Stratus

▲ Baker Mtn

HOLZWARTH HISTORIC SITE

Arapaho National Forest

Mount Ida ▲ 12,880ft

▲ Mt Julian 12,928ft

Continental Divide

Never Summer Wilderness Area

SEE "TRAIL RIDGE ROAD" MAP

Gabletop Mt 11,821

Nakai Peak 12,216ft

Knobtop Mt 12,336f

Ptarmigan Poir 12,270

Granite Falls

Rocky Mountain National Park

National Scenic Trail

Bowen Gulch Protection Area

Arapaho National Forest

Kawuneeche Valley

Colorado River

TRAIL RIDGE RD

PARK ENTRANCE

KAWUNEECHE VISITOR CENTER

Continental Divide

Grand Lake

Grand Lake

Adams Falls

Shadow Mountain Lake

Rocky Mountain National Park

0   2.5 mi
0   2.5 km

Road Trip Route

Arapaho Nat'l Rec Area

125

34

To Granby

Lake Granby

Indian Peaks Wilderness

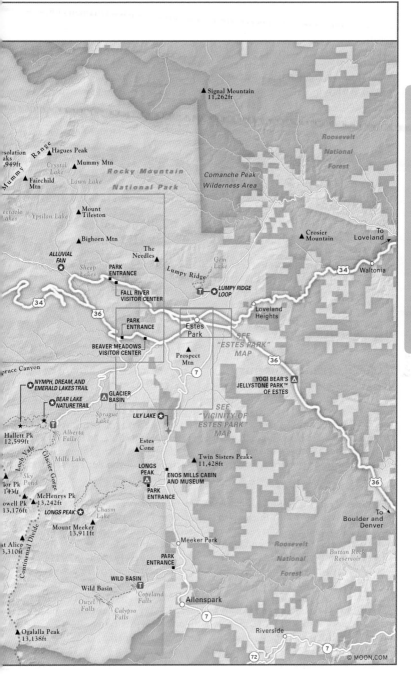

this side of the park, but it offers more breathing room for those looking to avoid crowds.

Longs Peak is considered one of the trickiest of Colorado's "fourteeners" (a mountain that's 14,000 feet or higher). For those who do not wish to summit Longs, gentler hikes are available in this area. A few miles north of the Longs Peak trailhead is **Lily Lake,** a delightful spot for picnicking, bird-watching, and relaxing. From the **Wild Basin trailhead,** it's a short hike to **Copeland Falls.**

While **summer** sees the best weather with all roads open, it also tallies up big crowds, especially in July. It's among the most-visited national park in the United States, with more than 4.5 million annual visitors.

On the east side, **shuttles** access the Bear Lake and Moraine Park areas. But the only way to access Horseshoe Park, Trail Ridge Road, and the west side of the park is by **private vehicle. RVs** can travel on all park roads, with the exception of Old Fall River Road.

Seasonal Driving Concerns

Most park roads are open and plowed year-round, with the exception of two roads: **Trail Ridge Road** is generally open from late May to mid-October (24 hours daily, weather permitting), though it can stay open later in unseasonably warm years. The **winter closure** spans from Many Parks Curve on the east side to the Colorado River Trail on the west side. When Trail Ridge Road is closed, you'll need to drop south of the park; allow an additional 2-3 hours each way to drive between Estes Park and Grand Lake. **Old Fall River Road** is typically open from early July until early October. Sometimes, it will close earlier in fall for maintenance.

For information about road closures, check the **park website** (www.nps.gov/romo) or call the **Trail Ridge Road status line** (970/586-1222). The **Colorado Division of Transportation** (511 or 303/639-1111, www.cotrip.org) has updates on roads that access the park.

Best Routes Through the Park

Trail Ridge Road tops the must-do list for any visitor to Rocky. From Estes Park, you can make a loop route to connect with it. From the Beaver Meadows entrance, tour through Moraine Park to connect with Trail Ridge Road. Go as far as Alpine Visitor Center before retracing your route back down to the junction with Horseshoe Park. Turn left and cruise through Horseshoe Park to exit via Fall River, then return to Estes Park.

Reservations and Where to Stay

In order to alleviate overcrowding, Rocky Mountain requires **timed entry tickets** for people visiting from **late May to early October.** Tickets, which are in two-hour windows, allow entry to either the whole park, including **Bear Lake Road** (5am-6pm daily) or all of the park except for Bear Lake Road (9am-3pm daily). Check the current ticketing policies on the park's website. **Reservations** (www.recreation.gov, $2/vehicle) are available 1-2 months in advance (with 25 percent of tickets held in reserve and released one day ahead). Even with a reservation, you'll still need to pay the park entry fee. If you have camping or activity reservations, you don't need a timed entry ticket.

There are **no lodges** inside the park. The park offers camping at Aspenglen, Moraine Park, Glacier Basin, Timber Creek, and Longs Peak Campgrounds. Of these, only Moraine Park is open year-round. **Reservations** (877/444-6777, www.recreation.gov) are accepted for Aspenglen, Glacier Basin, and Moraine Park. Make reservations six months in advance. **Sprague Lake Campground** has the only wheelchair-accessible wilderness campsite in the park.

Estes Park (on the east side) and **Grand Lake** (on the west side) are the

One Day in Rocky Mountain National Park

Morning

Pack a cooler for the day and get an early start through **Beaver Meadows Entrance Station.** Take Bear Lake Road to the **Bear Lake trailhead.** Just a few minutes' walk from the parking lot, you'll arrive at the banks of **Bear Lake,** where you can enjoy the short nature trail that follows the shore. Then, from the **Emerald Lake trailhead** (accessed from the same parking lot), hike to **Nymph, Dream, and Emerald Lakes** to see some of the best scenery in the park. Heading back down Bear Lake Road, stop at **Sprague Lake Picnic Area** for lunch.

Afternoon

Take in spectacular meadow views as you drive to **Moraine Park** from Bear Lake Road. Continue to **Old Fall River Road** and stop at the **alluvial fan.** Then drive up the scenic, one-way dirt portion of Old Fall River Road, which takes about an hour.

Admire the views from **Alpine Visitor Center** before heading down **Trail Ridge Road.** Along the way, stop to walk the **Alpine Communities Trail.** Next, pull over at the **Forest Canyon Overlook** to admire the landscape. Toward the end of your drive, take in the views from **Rainbow Curve** and **Many Parks Curve.**

Evening

At Deer Ridge Junction, drop down to **Sheep Lakes** in **Horseshoe Park** to spot some wildlife. Bide your time waiting for elk, moose, or bighorn sheep. Then head into **Estes Park** for a late dinner at local favorite **Smokin' Dave's BBQ & Brew.**

closest options for hotel or lodge accommodations. For summer and fall, aim to make reservations **9-12 months in advance.** For winter, you can often get last-minute accommodations, but if you want a particular spot, book six months in advance.

Getting There

Car

From Denver

From **Denver,** the drive to **Estes Park** and the east side of the park is 65 miles (104 km) and takes 1.5 hours. Take US 36 through Boulder and Lyons into Estes Park. If you're coming from the **Denver airport,** the drive is 75 miles (120 km) and takes about 1.5 hours. From the airport, go northeast on E 470 (toll road), then take I-25 north. Go west on CO 66 and continue to US 36 to Estes Park.

To get to **Grand Lake** and the park's west entrance from Denver, it's possible to take **Trail Ridge Road** through the

park in summer. The route is 115 miles (185 km) and takes at least three hours to drive. Take US 36 to Estes Park and follow Trail Ridge Road through the park to Grand Lake.

The other route to Grand Lake is 100 miles (161 km) from Denver and takes about two hours in good conditions. Take I-70 west to US 40. Continue north through Granby, then take US 34 to Grand Lake. In the winter, this route can take three hours to drive due to heavy traffic; I-70 is the main thoroughfare for many of Colorado's ski resorts.

From Grand Teton National Park

From **Jackson,** Wyoming, to **Estes Park** is 490 miles (790 km), about an eight-hour drive. Go south on US 191 to Hoback Junction and then southeast on US 191 to Rock Springs. Head east across southern Wyoming on I-80 to Laramie, then go south on US 287 to Fort Collins, Colorado. At Loveland, go west on US 34 to Estes Park.

The drive to **Grand Lake** from Jackson

is 465 miles (750 km) and takes a little less than eight hours. Follow US 191 south and east to I-80. Take I-80 east to WY 130. Head south on WY 130 and continue south on WY 230. This highway becomes CO 125 at the Colorado border. Continue south until you reach Granby, then take US 34 north into Grand Lake.

From Salt Lake City

There are two different routes to **Grand Lake** from **Salt Lake City,** Utah, both of which require about 7.5 hours to drive. The **northern route** is 470 miles (760 km) and follows I-80 east, then goes south on WY 130 and WY 230. WY 230 becomes CO 125 when it crosses the border into Colorado. Continue south to Granby, then take US 34 to Grand Lake.

The **southern route** is 430 miles (690 km) and follows I-80 east for a short distance before joining US 40 all the way to Granby. From there, take US 34 north to Grand Lake. On this route, you can add on a side trip to **Dinosaur National Monument,** which adds 35 miles (55 km) and 40 minutes to the drive time.

Air

The majority of people traveling to the Denver area by plane fly into **Denver International Airport** (DEN, 8500 Peña Blvd., 303/342-2000, www.flydenver.com). The airport, commonly referred to as DIA, is served by 23 airlines and features many restaurants, shops, and services. On-site is a rail station that transports passengers to Denver's downtown transit hub, **Union Station** (1701 Wynkoop St., www.unionstationindenver.com). To reach Rocky Mountain National Park, you can rent a car at the airport, schedule a pickup by the **Estes Park Shuttle** (970/586-5151, www.estesparkshuttle.com), or schedule transportation to Grand Lake with **Home James shuttle** (800/359-7536, www.homejamestransportation.com, summer only).

Train

At Denver's **Union Station** (1701 Wynkoop St., 303/592-6712, unionstationindenver.com), you can catch an **Amtrak train** (800/872-7245, www.amtrak.com) on the California Zephyr route. The train stops at a platform (not a full station) in Granby (438 Railroad Ave.). The train departs once daily. Amtrak has no service to Estes Park.

To continue to Grand Lake from Granby, you can rent a car from **Avalanche Car Rentals** (970/887-3908 or 888/437-4101, www.avscars.com).

Bus and Shuttle

Bustang (800/900-3011, ridebustang.com/estes-park, Sat.-Sun. July-early Oct., $5 one-way) is a weekend shuttle service that runs from Denver's Union Station with a pickup in Boulder to continue to the Estes Park Visitor Center. From there, you can connect with park shuttles to reach Bear Lake. The buses have bike racks. Buy tickets in advance online. Bustang riders will need to have a park entrance pass to continue into Rocky.

Greyhound (1055 19th St., Denver, 800/231-2222, www.greyhound.com) offers bus service between Denver and Granby once daily in each direction, with no transfers. From Granby, you will need to arrange transportation to Grand Lake and the park. Greyhound does not operate buses to Estes Park. To get from Granby to Grand Lake, you can rent a car from **Avalanche Car Rentals** (970/887-3908 or 888/437-4101, www.avscars.com).

Visiting the Park

Entrances and Fees

A one-day pass for an automobile is **$25;** a seven-day pass is **$35.** Individuals traveling by motorcycle or moped pay $25 for a one-day entrance pass and $30 for a seven-day pass. Bicyclists and pedestrians pay a $15 fee for a one-day visit and

$20 for seven days. An **annual pass** to the park costs $70.

There are three main, year-round entrances to the park. The busy **Beaver Meadows Entrance Station** (US 36), located on the east side nearest downtown Estes Park, is central to many park areas. Beaver Meadows can have long lines and sees double to triple the amount of people compared to other entrance stations.

Located on the east side, north of Estes Park, **Fall River Entrance Station** (US 34) provides easy access to Trail Ridge Road, Old Fall River Road, Aspenglen Campground, and Horseshoe Park.

Located 1.8 miles (2.9 km) north of Grand Lake, **Grand Lake Entrance Station** (US 34) serves the Kawuneeche Valley on the west side of the park and connects with the west side of Trail Ridge Road.

Additional entrances reach remote park zones. Off CO 7, south of Estes Park, spur roads go into the park at **Longs Peak** to reach the campground and trailhead. Farther south, another spur entrance goes into **Wild Basin.** Both are plowed in winter. These entrance stations are open year-round but are not staffed.

Visitors Centers

Rocky has four visitors centers that are open daily year-round. All visitors centers have information on ranger-led programs, trail conditions, road conditions, and weather. They also have restrooms. You can pick up Junior Ranger booklets for kids and shop the **Rocky Mountain Conservancy bookstores** (970/586-0121, rmconservancy.org) for books, maps, and souvenirs.

Beaver Meadows Visitor Center (1000 US 36, 970/586-1206, 8am-6pm daily summer, shorter hours fall-spring) serves as the park's headquarters. It's the closest visitors center to downtown Estes Park. You can see a park orientation film and examine the large topographical map of the park. Outside, you can see Longs Peak and watch elk in fall, winter, or spring. A short path drops to the **Wilderness Office** (970/586-1242, 7am-3:30pm daily), where you can get information and permits for backcountry camping.

Fall River Visitor Center (3450 Fall River Rd., 970/586-1206, 8am-5pm daily summer, shorter hours fall-spring) sits 4 miles (6.4 km) north of downtown Estes Park, just before the Fall River Entrance Station. It has wildlife displays and a kids' room for hands-on learning.

The **Alpine Visitor Center** (970/586-1206, 10:30am-4:30pm daily late May-mid-June, 9:30am-4:30pm daily mid-June-mid-Oct.) is at the junction of Old Fall River Road and Trail Ridge Road. It's the highest visitors center in the National Park Service. Its back windows have views into Fall River Cirque. Exhibits include displays about the alpine tundra and photos show the visitors center in winter. Several ranger-led interpretive walks and talks are offered.

The west side visitors center is located 1 mile (1.6 km) north of Grand Lake, after the entrance station. The **Kawuneeche Visitor Center** (16018 US 34, 970/627-3471, 9am-5pm daily summer, shorter hours fall-spring) shows a park film on request and has a topographical relief map of the park. The **Wilderness Office,** inside the visitors center, has permits and information for backcountry camping.

Sights

Horseshoe Park

Fall River cuts a path through **Horseshoe Park,** a glacier-carved valley. This is a great place to view the Mummy Range to the north and watch for wildlife. **Elk** meander through this montane meadow year-round; in the fall, it's a great spot to view the animals' mating rituals. In the summer, **bighorn sheep** have a proclivity for hanging out at **Sheep Lakes** on the western end. Sometimes, **moose** also visit the lakes. Near the lakes, the **Sheep Lakes Information Station** (US 34, 24

Tips to Avoid Crowds

During the summer and fall, visitors flood Rocky Mountain National Park every day from 10am to 3pm. You'll find long waits at entrance stations, congested visitors centers, full parking lots, heavily trafficked roads, and lines of hikers on trails. So what can you do if you want to beat the crowds?

♦ **Hiking:** Go very **early in the morning** or **late in the day.** This will help you get a parking spot at the trailhead while also making for fewer people on the trail.

♦ **Parking lots:** In July, August, and weekends in June and September, **parking lots fill** by the following times: Glacier Gorge Trailhead by 6am, Bear Lake by 8am, Park & Ride lot for Bear Lake shuttles by 9:15am, Wild Basin by 9:30am, and Alpine Visitor Center by 10am.

♦ **Road restrictions:** Some roads restrict vehicle access in summer. **Bear Lake Road** and **Wild Basin Road** usually begin restrictions at 9:30am.

♦ **Shuttles:** Ride the shuttles to avoid parking hassles and congested roads. They run every **30 minutes.**

♦ **West side:** Escape the east side crowds by visiting the west side of the park and hiking trails in **Kawuneeche Valley.**

hours daily year-round) has information on wildlife and is often staffed by rangers who give wildlife talks.

From the Fall River Entrance Station, drive west for 1.9 miles (3.1 km) on US 34 to the parking lot for Sheep Lakes. As US 34 sweeps around the lakes and climbs uphill to Deer Ridge Junction, you'll find three more pullouts.

★ Alluvial Fan

A testament to the power of water, the **alluvial fan** is the collection of dirt, sediment, and boulders left after two floods. First, in 1982, water rushed down from a failed dam at Lawn Lake, creating a massive boulder field. The flooding Roaring River carried rocks and debris 6 miles (10 km) down to the valley floor, where the water fanned out into Horseshoe Park. Some of the boulders weighed 2 tons (1,814 kg). Then in 2013, a storm dropped 12-14 inches (30-36 cm) of rain, causing a second flood in the same area, depositing layers of sediment amid the boulders.

From trailheads on the east and west sides of the alluvial fan, a paved, wheelchair-accessible trail extends for a half mile through the area. Lined with boulders for sitting and admiring the view, the trail crosses over Roaring River on a bridge, from where you can get a view of the boulder field and a waterfall upstream.

From US 34 on the west end of Horseshoe Park, turn onto Old Fall River Road. At the second and third parking lots on the right, you'll find the trailheads to either side of the Alluvial Fan.

Moraine Park

This valley takes its name from the glacial moraines that surround it. A moraine consists of natural materials that were put in place by the land-scouring action of a glacier. Several small glaciers converged in this area; with impressive force, they deposited mounds of rocks and dirt to the south, east, and north of the valley floor. The north and south moraines are lateral moraines—piles that form on the sides of a glacier—while the moraine at the foot of Eagle Cliff Mountain to the east is a terminal moraine—the spot

★ Wildlife-Watching Hot Spots

elk in Moraine Park

TOP EXPERIENCE

Dawn and dusk are usually the best times to spot wildlife. Do your part to **protect wildlife.** Follow the park's distance recommendations: 120 feet (36 m) from moose and bears and 75 feet (23 m) from elk and bighorn sheep. **Use binoculars** to get a close-up view. Do not feed wildlife any **human food.**

♦ **Bighorn sheep:** Spot bighorn sheep at **Sheep Lakes** in **Horseshoe Park,** most commonly May-mid-August. About 300-400 live in Rocky Mountain National Park.

♦ **Moose:** Keep your eyes open for moose along the **Colorado River** in **Kawuneeche Valley.** They often hang around willow thickets that provide good cover and winter food.

♦ **Elk:** Look around the fringes of meadows in **Horseshoe Park, Beaver Meadows,** and **Moraine Park** for the best places to spot elk year-round, but in summer you can also see them in the alpine tundra of **Trail Ridge Road.** The most dramatic season is fall, when bull elk bugle and spar during the rut.

♦ **Pika:** Walk the **Alpine Communities Trail** or look around talus and boulder piles in the higher elevations of the park roads. Listen for their call, an "eeeep" that functions as a warning to other pika.

♦ **Yellow-bellied marmot:** Peruse rocky areas flanked with meadows in the alpine tundra along **Trail Ridge Road,** especially around **Forest Canyon Overlook.** These burrowers can sometimes be seen sun-soaking on warm rocks.

where a glacier finally ceased its slide and melted away. Glaciers visited the area of Moraine Park more than once, retreating for the last time approximately 10,000 years ago.

Today, Moraine Park's expansive meadow is stunning in any season, even though portions of it as well as the surrounding forest burned in the 2020 East Troublesome Fire. Grasses and wildflowers will be the first foliage to return. It's especially beautiful in the summer, with the Big Thompson River curling through its verdant grasses. In the fall, this is a prime place to watch **bull elk** battle each other for mating rights with eligible cows. You can drive by the meadow, stop for a picnic lunch, book a horseback ride, or cast a line into the Big Thompson's waters. The Moraine Park Campground makes a great base for nearby activities.

To get to Moraine Park from the Beaver Meadows Entrance Station, travel west on US 36 to Bear Lake Road. Turn left (south) on Bear Lake Road and drive for 1.6 miles (2.6 km). There is a small parking lot and picnic table in on the eastern end of Moraine Park, good for taking in the views. Expect more great views on Fern Lake Road, which travels along this area's northern border.

Moraine Park Discovery Center

Busy **Moraine Park Discovery Center** (Bear Lake Rd., 1.5 mi/2.4 km from the Beaver Meadows Entrance Station, 970/586-8842, 9am-5pm daily late May-mid-Oct.) features interactive natural history exhibits and a small gift shop stocked with Rocky Mountain Conservancy items. The adjacent Moraine Park Amphitheater offers ranger programs. A short family-friendly interpretive **nature trail** starts just outside the steps of the front entrance; a self-guided trail tour booklet can be purchased for a small fee. Upstairs, a large picture window showcases the scenery. Park shuttles do not stop at the center.

★ Lily Lake

At 9,000 feet (2,743 m), **Lily Lake** is situated at a midline between two ecosystems: subalpine and montane. Fragrant ponderosa pines are abundant on the north side of lake, while the south is characterized by wetlands that are attractive to birds and resplendent with wildflowers in the summer. Watch for industrious

boulders and rubble in the Horseshoe Park alluvial fan

muskrats as they swim to and from small dams; they are easy to miss if you aren't looking for them.

The **nature trail** (0.8 mi/1.3 km, 0.5 hr) circling Lily Lake is flat, with a wide gravel and boardwalk surface good for wheelchairs. It's also great for families with small children and individuals with limited mobility. On a clear day, three nearby peaks are visible from various spots on the trail: Estes Cone, Mount Meeker, and Longs Peak. Restrooms are located at the trailhead.

The Lily Lake trailhead is a fee-free area of the park. From US 36 in Estes Park, drive 6.3 miles (10.1 km) south on CO 7 to the lake. There are two parking lots, one directly next to the lake and one on the other side of the highway. Be cautious at the crosswalk, as traffic can move fast.

Enos Mills Cabin Museum

Enos Mills (1870-1922) is best known for his role in lobbying Congress to officially create Rocky Mountain National Park in

1915. "The Father of Rocky Mountain National Park" moved to Colorado from Kansas, living by himself during the warm months in a one-room cabin that he built. It still stands today as the **Enos Mills Cabin Museum** (6760 CO 7, Estes Park, 970/586-4706, enosmills.com, year-round by appointment only, $20 adults, $10 children 6-12), operated by Elizabeth and Eryn Mills, a granddaughter and great-granddaughter team who lead tours of the National Historic Landmark. In addition to the classic cabin tour, there are winter **snowshoe tours** ($35 pp, includes snowshoe rental). Summer **nature walks** ($25 pp) come with an engaging narrative about local flora and fauna. By the time you leave, you will be filled with knowledge about this fascinating activist and nature lover who climbed Longs Peak more than 300 times and who once kept two grizzly cubs named Johnny and Jenny as pets.

Parking for the cabin is south of Lily Lake, at the Longs Peak Viewing Area on CO 7 (located just south of mile marker 8). Visitors who have made advance reservations are escorted onto the property. No restrooms are available and no pets are allowed.

Kawuneeche Valley

On the quieter west side of Trail Ridge Road, **Kawuneeche Valley** is flanked by the high Never Summer Mountains. The Upper Colorado River curves lazily through its forest and meadows, making the locale a perfect wildlife magnet. Around dawn and dusk, you can often spot moose around the willows along the river, and elk bed down in the meadow edges near the forest.

In 2020, the East Troublesome Fire swept through the southern half of Kawuneeche Valley and Grand Lake. Between Grand Lake Entrance Station and the Coyote Valley Trail, you'll see evidence of burned forest as smaller plants and wildflowers begin making a comeback.

★ Moose-Watching

Many people come to the Kawuneeche Valley specifically to spot **moose**. Positioning yourself near (but not *too* near) a moose's food source increases the likelihood of seeing one of these hulking creatures. The abundant willows on the valley floor are particularly delicious fare for moose. They also munch on grass, aquatic plants, aspen bark and leaves, and mosses. Some moose hot spots are near the **Kawuneeche Valley entrance sign,** around the **Holzwarth Historic Site,** and where the Continental Divide National Scenic Trail crosses US 34 (just north of the **Onahu trailhead**). The **Beaver Ponds Picnic Area** is another good place for observation. Any time of day is a good time to spot a moose. Don't be surprised if you stumble upon one taking a midafternoon bath. They feel right at home wading and even swimming in water.

Little Buckaroo Ranch Barn

Part of the park's Trail River Ranch property, **Little Buckaroo Ranch Barn** is a photographer's delight. Set in a meadow and backdropped by mountains, this gorgeous barn earned its spot on the National Register of Historic Places because of its unique architecture.

The Cajun-style barn was originally built in 1942 to house the horses of Frank and Mary Godchaux, a couple from Louisiana who summered here. Features include rustic log slab siding and a monitor roof—a raised structure on top of the ridge of a traditional roof. Today, this handsome structure stands vacant, surrounded by a grassy field. It's only possible to observe the barn from the **Bowen Gulch Trail.** Do not touch the exterior or make any attempt to enter.

From the Grand Lake Entrance Station, drive 4 miles (6.4 km) north on US 34/Trail Ridge Road. Turn left (west) on an unmarked dirt road. After less than half a mile, arrive at a small dirt parking

moose in Rocky Mountain National Park

area for the Bowen Gulch Trail. Park, walk over the bridge, go straight at the junction, and you will spot the barn to the left in the meadow. The dirt road is unplowed in the winter.

Holzwarth Historic Site

What's known today as the **Holzwarth Historic Site** was one of the first tourist operations in the Kawuneeche Valley. Homesteaders Sophie and John Holzwarth maintained it as a vacation lodge from 1920 to 1929, offering meals, accommodations, and guest ranch activities.

Although it no longer functions as guest ranch, there is still a major operation here in the summer. Approximately 30 volunteers facilitate a "step back in time" experience by offering drop-in **tours** (10:30am-4:30pm daily mid-June-Labor Day, free). The property includes multiple sleeping cabins, a taxidermy shop, a main house, an icehouse, and a woodshed. You'll find a mix of original

items from the ranch (including taxidermy animals), as well as other artifacts from the early 1920s.

The ranger-led **Old Ranch Campfire** (free) takes place on Fridays in the summer. Arrive at 7pm and enjoy a leisurely group walk to the crackling campfire, where songs and tall tales round out the evening. On occasion, the talented Grand Chorale Barbershop Chorus will perform a selection of songs. Pack layers, bug spray, and marshmallows to roast.

Holzwarth Historic Site's parking area is on US 34, about 7.5 miles (12.1 km) north of the Grand Lake Entrance Station. It's a flat and easy half-mile walk to the buildings. For people with mobility issues, complimentary transportation from the parking lot to the site is offered via a Park Service golf cart during the summer. Arrange a ride by stopping at the Fleshut Cabin, just steps from the parking lot. The cart is available from approximately 10:30am-4pm daily. From fall to spring, the buildings are closed, but you can still look around outside.

Colorado River

The **Colorado River** starts on the upper west side of Rocky and winds its way from north to south through the Kawuneeche Valley. The river and its tributaries are found in six other states besides Colorado—Wyoming, Utah, New Mexico, Arizona, Nevada, and California—and in Mexico. In its entirety, the river is 1,450 miles (2,330 km) long and provides water for drinking, hydroelectric power, agricultural use, and recreation. The **Coyote Valley Trail** (1 mi/1.6 km one-way) is a flat, wide dirt path along the Colorado River, one of the best locations for spotting wildlife and enjoying the river. It's also perfect for kids and those with mobility challenges. Find the trailhead 5 miles (8 km) north of the Kawuneeche Visitor Center.

Grand Lake

Grand Lake, in the town of the same

name, has a claim to fame as the largest and deepest of Colorado's natural lakes. You can admire it from **Lake Avenue.** To walk near the water, go to the small sandy public beach at **Lakefront Park** (Lake Ave. between Hancock St. and Ellsworth St.) or **Point Park Picnic Area** (710 Shadow Mountain Ln.), where views from the docks include Mount Craig in the background. In winter, the lake freezes and becomes a venue for pond hockey and ice fishing.

Headwaters Marina (Lake Ave. between Hancock St. and Ellsworth St., 970/627-5031, www.townofgrandlake.com/headwaters-marina.htm, daily summer, $20 adults, $10 kids) guides one-hour scenic boat tours departing at 10:30am, noon, and 2pm. On select evenings, they also offer sunset cruises.

Scenic Drives

TOP EXPERIENCE

★ Trail Ridge Road

Planners envisioned **Trail Ridge Road** (42 mi/68 km) as a drive that would showcase the area's most significant natural attractions. The route would travel east to west just south of Old Fall River Road, roughly following the Ute Trail (which still exists as a hiking trail alongside the road). Construction began in 1929 and the road opened to traffic in 1932. Today, it's traveled by hundreds of thousands of visitors each year and is a highlight of any park visit. Drive cautiously, as the road traces some steep cliffs without guardrails or retaining walls.

Trail Ridge Road typically opens by Memorial Day and is drivable until mid-October. However, the higher portions of the two-lane road can close at any time due to snow. The winter closure extends from Many Parks Curve on the east side to the Colorado River Trail on the west side.

The starting point for this driving tour is the **Beaver Meadows Entrance Station** on the east side; it ends at the **Grand Lake Entrance Station** on the west side. It's also possible to follow the route in reverse, starting in Grand Lake. Check the **park website** or call the **Trail Ridge Road status line** (970/586-1222) for road conditions. You'll need two hours, with stops, to drive to Alpine Visitor Center, which is about the halfway point. To drive the full road in one direction takes about four hours.

Hidden Valley

Many of the buildings of the park's past have been demolished or removed but still remain in people's memories. Perhaps no none is more mourned than **Hidden Valley Ski Resort,** which operated from 1955 until 1991. Consisting of a ski hill, a toboggan run, an ice-skating rink, and a lodge, Hidden Valley was a small but full-fledged resort. Though backcountry skiing is still an option here, the lack of lifts and groomed trails means less access for novice and intermediate skiers. Sledding is still popular here, too.

In summer, Hidden Valley is busy with picnickers. Young children take part in activities at the **Junior Ranger Headquarters,** located in a small building next to the parking lot. A half-mile **interpretive trail** starts behind Hidden Valley's buildings and makes a loop around Hidden Valley Creek. The turnoff to Hidden Valley is on the first major switchback after Deer Ridge Junction, where US 36 becomes US 34.

Many Parks Curve

At the next large switchback after Hidden Valley, the overlook at **Many Parks Curve** provides a great view of numerous wide mountain meadows. Upper Beaver Meadows, Horseshoe Park, and Moraine Park are also visible, as are the lengthy moraines that rise up next to these lush meadows. Along the bend in the road, a long boardwalk invites visitors out of their cars to gaze over the wide expanse of land below. There is also a small, rocky outcropping to scramble up to take photos. When winter comes, this is as high on Trail Ridge Road as visitors can go on the east side of the park before having to turn around.

Rainbow Curve
The prospect of traveling up Trail Ridge Road is thrilling for some, but anxiety inducing for others. After Many Parks Curve, the road twists and turns through a forested basin as it climbs to round a ridge; find **Rainbow Curve** at the north end of that ridge. This stop offers a happy medium for those whose nerves are rattled by steep drop-offs and absent guardrails. At 10,829 feet (3,301 m) in elevation, Rainbow Curve offers dramatic views, but the road is mostly tame. Many folks who are apprehensive choose this as a turnaround point, but leave feeling satisfied that they were still able to see something remarkable, whether it's bighorn sheep gathering in Horseshoe Park below or a rainbow after a thunderstorm. This is a particularly great vantage point for checking out the alluvial fan at the north end of Horseshoe Park. Directly west, Sundance Mountain has an easily visible glacial cirque on its east face.

★ Forest Canyon Overlook
After Rainbow Curve, the road climbs to **Forest Canyon Overlook.** A short path leads to an attractive rock wall perched atop a knoll. From this spot, the views of glacier-formed Forest Canyon are spectacular. An interpretive sign identifies specific landmarks, including pointed Hayden Spire and broad Terra Tomah Mountain. In the rocks around the base of the overlook, marmot sightings are almost guaranteed.

With stunning peaks all around, the last thing you might think to do here is to look down, but do it. Just beyond the edges of the easy paved trail, you will notice a geologic phenomenon called

patterned ground, the result of the continual freezing and thawing cycle found only in locations above the tree line. The shapes you see are rock fragments thrust above the soil into interesting patterns. Take care to stay on the walking path, since this location is designated as a Tundra Protection Area.

Rock Cut
As the road continues up past Forest Canyon Overlook, watch for elk and big horn sheep below. The road enters a cliff area and slices through the **Rock Cut.** This rocky outcropping posed a significant challenge during the construction of Trail Ridge Road. Using explosives, workers had to clear enough rock so that cars would be able to pass through. Because of the heavy labor involved and the ever-variable weather conditions above the tree line, this was one of the most difficult sections of the road to build. Admire their efforts as you drive along with sheer rock on either side.

Alpine Communities Trail
Immediately following the Rock Cut, both sides of the road are lined with parking spots for the **Alpine Communities Trail** (1 mi/1.6 km rt). This paved interpretive trail leads through the wildflowers and wildlife that live in the seemingly barren alpine tundra that dominates this elevation. You may see a pika skittering around the rocks and collecting plants. At the top, rocky outcroppings jut up from the tundra, lending a wildness to the landscape. Views extend north into the Mummy Range. Due to the elevation of 12,288 feet (3,745 m), this walk will seem tougher than it is. Stay on the pavement to protect the fragile vegetation.

Lava Cliffs Overlook
The road drops to Iceberg Pass, a lower point on Trail Ridge Road, before taking two big switchbacks up to **Lava Cliffs Overlook.** A common misconception is that the Lava Cliffs were once the site of

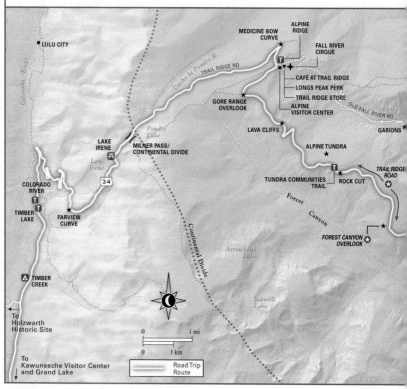

Trail Ridge Road

an active volcano. Not so: Experts have determined that this unique rock formation is actually the result of volcanic activity that occurred farther west in the Never Summer Mountains more than 20 million years ago. The cliffs are made up of volcanic ash that flowed from afar, settled, and hardened into rock. This is usually a brief stop, but avid birders will want to look for cavity-nesting birds, such as swallows, who love the many nooks and crannies of the cliffs.

Gore Range Overlook

After Lava Point, you'll top the highest elevation on Trail Ridge Road at 12,183 feet (3,713 m) and descend to **Gore Range Overlook.** On a clear day, there

are eye-popping views of nearby and far-away peaks, including the Gore Range, a stretch of impressive, jutting peaks approximately 50 miles (80 km) south-west of the park. To the west, the Never Summer Mountains rise, an implacable wall of peaks. Across Forest Canyon, the Continental Divide skitters across the top of the peaks.

Alpine Visitor Center

A short descent leads to the highest national park visitors center in the country. **Alpine Visitor Center** (Trail Ridge Rd. and Old Fall River Rd., 970/586-1206, 10:30am-4:30pm daily spring, 9:30am-4:30pm daily summer and fall) sits on Fall River Pass at a head-spinning 11,796

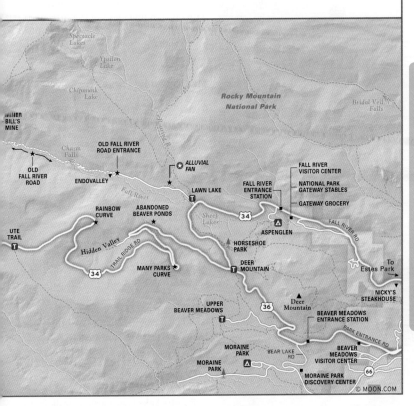

Spectacle Lakes

Ypsilon Lake

Chipmunk Lake

Rocky Mountain National Park

Bridal Veil Falls

MINER BILL'S MINE

Chasm Falls

OLD FALL RIVER ROAD ENTRANCE

ALLUVIAL FAN

FALL RIVER VISITOR CENTER

OLD FALL RIVER ROAD

ENDOVALLEY

Fall River

LAWN LAKE

FALL RIVER ENTRANCE STATION

NATIONAL PARK GATEWAY STABLES

GATEWAY GROCERY

RAINBOW CURVE

ABANDONED BEAVER PONDS

Sheep Lakes

34

FALL RIVER RD

UTE TRAIL

Hidden Valley

TRAIL RIDGE RD

ASPENGLEN

HORSESHOE PARK

To Estes Park

34

MANY PARKS CURVE

DEER MOUNTAIN

NICKY'S STEAKHOUSE

UPPER BEAVER MEADOWS

36

Deer Mountain

BEAVER MEADOWS ENTRANCE STATION

PARK ENTRANCE RD

MORAINE PARK

BEAR LAKE RD

BEAVER MEADOWS VISITOR CENTER

MORAINE PARK

66

MORAINE PARK DISCOVERY CENTER

© MOON.COM

feet (3,595 m) above sea level. Opened in June 1965, the structure is designed to withstand the extreme weather conditions typical at this elevation. Heavy logs crisscross the roof to prevent shingles from flying off in high winds. A diesel generator is the sole source of power and sewage must be hauled down the road daily during the summer. In the winter, the building gets buried under snow for around seven months.

Inside, there are educational displays, a Rocky Mountain Conservancy gift store, and restrooms. Large picture windows boast stunning views of the headwaters of the Fall River, dramatic peaks of the Mummy Range, and numerous other landmarks. Outside, patio overlooks yield the same views, making for great photographic fodder. Rangers field altitude-related questions and serve as a resource if you are feeling adverse effects from the elevation (shortness of breath, dizziness, headaches). They are also vigilant about tracking weather conditions and will warn visitors if lightning and thunder are imminent.

In a separate building, the **Café at Trail Ridge** (10am-4:30pm daily late May-mid-Oct., $5-10) serves up snacks and light meals while the **Trail Ridge Store** (970/586-2133, shop.trailridgegiftstore. com) sells souvenirs and gifts.

A short hike up the **Alpine Ridge Trail** (0.6 mi/1 km), aka "Huffer's Hill," begins next to the parking lot. You'll

breathe heavily while climbing the steep stairs, but at the top you'll be rewarded with outstanding views of the surrounding mountains. You can also take your photo with the sign that reads, "Elevation 12,000 feet."

Medicine Bow Curve

A quick drop from the visitors center leads to a pullout marking **Medicine Bow Curve.** On a clear day, some of the peaks of the 100-mile-long (160-km) Medicine Bow Mountain Range are visible to the north. This stop also provides an excellent vantage point of the Cache la Poudre River far below.

Milner Pass and the Continental Divide

Milner Pass sits at 10,759 feet (3,279 m). This spot also has a sign marking the **Continental Divide,** which runs north to south through the length of the park. It's one of only two places in the park where you can slip out of your car and instantly stand on top of the Divide (the other spot is La Poudre Pass in the northwest corner of the park). The Continental Divide creates two distinct drainages for snowmelt: One side drains into the Pacific Ocean, the other into the Atlantic Ocean.

Poudre Lake is just a short walk from the Continental Divide sign. From the lake, water narrows into the Cache la Poudre River, which flows east of the Continental Divide to the Great Plains, eventually leading into the Gulf of Mexico. The lake's primary activity is fishing. Many visitors also enjoy strolling a short portion of the Ute Trail along this grass-ringed lake.

Farview Curve

After Milner Pass, the road makes a sweeping turn at **Farview Curve.** The overlook takes in the Kawuneeche Valley

Top to bottom: Forest Canyon Overlook on Trail Ridge Road; pika on Alpine Communities Trail; Millner Pass on the Continental Divide

below, which includes the Colorado River snaking its way through the valley's vibrant green meadows. Shift your gaze west and you will see the Never Summer Mountains and the Grand Ditch. You might first mistake the Grand Ditch for a road carved into the mountainside, but it is actually a long canal used to divert snowmelt from the park's west side to its east side.

From Farview Curve, the road plunges down several sharp switchbacks to reach the floor of Kawuneeche Valley. After 15 miles (24 km), you'll reach the Grand Lake Entrance Station and the end of Trail Ridge Road.

Old Fall River Road

Before **Old Fall River Road** was built, the only way to cross the Continental Divide was on foot, on horseback, or by sled. (To carry heavy loads over these mountains, Indigenous people used a sled called a travois, which was commonly pulled by horses or dogs).

Old Fall River Road took seven years to build. The plan was to create a road from Estes Park to Grand Lake, following old Arapaho trails. The road finally opened in 1920. But it was a narrow roadway with steep grades, mud holes, and more than a dozen switchbacks that were difficult for cars to navigate. The dirt road served its purpose for a time, but was supplanted in 1932 by the improved Trail Ridge Road, which incorporated some of the original Old Fall River Road west of Fall River Pass.

Today, **Old Fall River Road** (9 mi/14.5 km) is a narrow dirt road traveling **one-way** from east to west, with a **speed limit of 15 mph** (24 kph). The road opens July 4 and closes in early October for winter. To reach the beginning of the road from Horseshoe Park, take the paved Fall River Road west for 1.8 miles (2.9 km) to a signed junction. The road heading to

the right serves as the entrance to Old Fall River Road. You'll need around an **hour** to drive the one-way length of road.

Chasm Falls

At a signed stop, a short, downhill path leads to picturesque **Chasm Falls.** Its water spills down between two narrow walls of granite and swirling into a pretty froth before rejoining Fall River. There is a fenced viewing platform at the bottom of the trail. In the Chasm Falls parking area, there are only spots for about 15 vehicles. Arrive in the early morning or later in the day for the best chance to secure a space.

Gabions

In an effort to protect Old Fall River Road and the surrounding landscape from erosion and slides, the park relies on an age-old civil engineering method: the use of **gabions** (French for "big cage"). In the switchbacks and along steep hillsides, you won't miss what appear to be long staircases. The "stairs" are made up of many individual wire cages filled with rocks that are secured together to form a retaining wall, holding back sodden soil during spring runoff. The park first installed the gabions in 1967. Up until that point, crews had to repair the road frequently after landslides and rock falls.

Fall River Cirque

On the last leg of the drive, the landscape opens up to reveal the stunning **Fall River Cirque,** the headwaters of the Fall River. There are no remnants of the glaciers that formed the cirque, but snow tends to collect in its bowl-like formation, remaining for most of the summer. Two sweeping switchbacks provide parking for viewing the cirque and the final segment of road, which climbs to Fall River Pass and the Alpine Visitor Center, where you can connect with Trail Ridge Road.

Recreation

Hiking

Colorado Wilderness Rides and Guides (720/242-9828, coloradowilderness-ridesandguides.com) leads hiking trips to several destinations, including Loch Vale and Sky Pond. Rates start at $185 per person. Custom trips are available. **Kirks Mountain Adventures** (230 E. Elkhorn Ave., Estes Park, 970/577-0790, www.kirksmountainadventures.com), a highly respected local outdoor shop, leads three-, six- and eight-hour hikes to waterfalls, lakes, and other natural attractions. Rates start at $105 per person.

Horseshoe Park

Lawn Lake

Distance: 12.4 miles (20 km) rt
Duration: 7 hours
Elevation gain: 2,249 feet (685 m)
Effort: very strenuous
Trailhead: Lawn Lake

Directions: From the Fall River Entrance Station, go 2.2 miles (3.5 km) west on US 34 to Fall River Rd. and turn right. The Lawn Lake trailhead is on the right side of the road.

The hike to Lawn Lake is a long one, which is why many visitors choose to split up the journey into two days. Two wilderness campsites (**Cutbank** and **Golden Banner**) are located along the trail. Two more can be found next to the lake (one of them is a wilderness stock campsite). If you are cranking out this hike in one day, get an early start. Be sure to wear sturdy boots, since some spots along the trail are rather rocky.

From the trailhead sign, start north along the **Lawn Lake Trail.** At approximately 1 mile (1.6 km), you will see extensive rubble from the Lawn Lake Flood of 1982, a landscape-changing event caused by the failure of a dam that once existed at the lake. At 1.4 miles (2.3 km), find a **junction** for the Ypsilon Lake Trail. Head straight to continue on to Lawn Lake. For the next 4 miles (6.4 km), the trail climbs

Old Fall River Road

steadily uphill through forest until it meets up with the **Black Canyon Trail**, which is another route to get to Lawn Lake.

From the junction, hike an additional 0.7 mile to **Lawn Lake**. Set in a subalpine basin, the lake has meadows and small stands of trees clustered around it. From the lake's banks, take in excellent views of Mummy Mountain, Hagues Peak, and Fairchild Mountain. Return the way you came.

Deer Ridge Junction
Deer Mountain

Distance: 6.2 miles (10 km) rt
Duration: 3 hours
Elevation gain: 1,083 feet (330 m)
Effort: moderate
Trailhead: Deer Mountain

The trek to the top of Deer Mountain is not excessively long nor extremely steep, but it is full of switchbacks. Do not short-cut the switchbacks as this causes harm to vegetation and soil.

After jumping on the **Deer Mountain Trail,** you will see a sign with two choices: Aspenglen Campground or Deer Mountain Summit. Follow the **North Deer Mountain Trail** straight (southeast) to the summit. The trail climbs through a grassy open landscape dotted with trees and within earshot of the highway below. The noise quickly fades as you forge on, climbing switchbacks for 2.2 miles (3.5 km) through the forest. Soon, the trail flattens and descends for roughly another 0.7 mile. At this point, a **spur trail** for the summit will appear; turn right (southwest) on the spur. The last 0.2-mile stretch is the steepest section of the trail but it is short. At the flat summit, you can see Estes Park, Lake Estes, Moraine Park, the park entrance, Glacier Basin Campground, and the YMCA of the Rockies. Snap a photo of the **USGS summit marker** as proof of your journey. You can return the way you came or turn the hike into a loop by continuing around the mountain on the Deer Mountain Trail and North Deer Mountain Trail for a hike that totals 10.8 miles (17.4 km) round-trip.

Fern Lake Road
Fern Lake and Odessa Lake

Distance: 9 miles (14.5 km) one-way
Duration: 5 hours
Elevation gain: 2,540 feet (774 m)
Effort: strenuous
Trailhead: Fern Lake

This shuttle-aided, one-way hike highlights gorgeous water features. If you opt to drive to Fern Lake Trailhead, plan to be there before 8am in the summer to get a parking spot. Otherwise, hop the Moraine Park Shuttle to the Fern Lake shuttle stop and walk to the trailhead (0.8 mi/1.3 km).

The 2020 East Troublesome Fire burned through the forest and meadows along this trail, but you will see wildflowers and grasses returning. The landscape reveals mounds of talus. After 1.2 mi (1.9 km), a group of granite boulders called

Arch Rocks appears, followed shortly after by a bridge above The Pool, the small, swirling eddy below the confluence of Fern Creek and Big Thompson River. Continuing west, pass the Old Forest Inn wilderness campsite and raucous Fern Falls. At Fern Lake (3.8 mi/6.1 km), you are likely to see anglers waist-deep in the water in the summer. Cast your gaze upward to view Little Matterhorn, with its resemblance to its namesake in the Swiss Alps.

From Fern Lake, continue on the flat path paralleling Fern Creek through a gorge to Odessa Lake for an even better vantage point of Little Matterhorn. After Odessa, keep an eye out for an unmarked social trail on your right, where the Fern Lake Trail makes a sharp, hairpin turn. At that bend, find the social trail to Lake Helene. After backtracking to the Fern Lake Trail, head east to a junction for Flattop Mountain. Bypass this junction in favor of the next trail junction for Bear Lake. Head south on the trail, passing the lake to return to its trailhead. Catch the Bear Lake Shuttle to the Park & Ride, where you can hop on the Moraine Park Shuttle back to the Fern Lake shuttle stop.

Bear Lake Road

In order to alleviate overcrowding, Rocky Mountain requires timed entry tickets for people visiting from late May to early October. There are two types of tickets; only one allows entry to Bear Lake Road along with the rest of the park. (The other type gives access to every part of the park except for Bear Lake Road.) Tickets, which are in two-hour windows, are available by reservation (www.recreation.gov, $2/vehicle) 1-2 months in advance, with some held back to release one day ahead. Check the current ticketing policies on the park's website.

★ Bear Lake Nature Trail
Distance: 0.5 mile (0.8 km) one-way
Duration: 20 minutes
Elevation gain: 20 feet (6 m)
Effort: easy
Trailhead: Bear Lake (Parking fills by 8am; arrive via shuttle.)

For a fun way to learn about the park's landscape and history, take the self-guided Bear Lake Nature Trail tour, suitable for all ages. The corresponding booklet is sold at visitors centers and the Bear Lake Ranger Station.

Head counterclockwise around the scenic lake and keep your eye out for bear paw prints mounted on wooden posts that correlate with facts in the tour booklet. Along the way, you will learn about natural phenomena such as "snow knees," tree trunks that have been bent into a knee-like shape after being pummeled with sliding, heavy snow year after year. Numerous benches around the lake are great for soaking up the scenery: placid water with a mountain backdrop. Most of the trail is level and wheelchair accessible; however, around bear paw marker 22, the path heads downhill and then uphill steeply. Take your time: The trail around Bear Lake is one to be strolled and savored, admiring various sights, sounds, and textures of the idyllic setting.

★ Nymph, Dream, and Emerald Lakes
Distance: 3.6 miles (5.8 km) rt
Duration: 2 hours
Elevation gain: 605 feet (184 m)
Effort: moderate
Trailhead: Emerald Lake (Parking fills by 8am; arrive via shuttle.)

A triple lineup of lakes and stunning glacier-carved scenery give this trail plenty of sights to ogle. But you will contend with loads of fellow hikers on this often-crowded trail. Go early or late in the day for thinner crowds. In summer, plan to arrive by 7:30am to get a parking spot or take the shuttle.

From the Emerald Lake Trailhead, the ascent begins in the forest, gaining steady elevation and rounding onto a shelf containing tiny Nymph Lake. In summer, the lake contains lily pads that bloom with large yellow flowers; their botanical name, *Nymphaea polysepala,* gives the lake its moniker. The trail arcs around the north side of the lake, affording several spots to stop for photos. You can turn around here to keep it a short hike (1 mi/1.6 km rt), but the scenery just gets better the farther you go.

Continuing on, you will break out of the forest onto a rocky hillside. The next ascent includes log steps for tread and small wooden bridges to cross streams. Summer wildflowers line the trail. You'll get glimpses of Longs Peak over your shoulder and Hallett Peak ahead. The trail wriggles into a narrow canyon, passing a junction for the Lake Haiyaya Trail, which heads left. A few steps farther, you'll reach **Dream Lake** (2.2 mi/3.5 km rt), which is much larger than Nymph. The trail follows the rocky north shore, affording many spots to enjoy the narrow blue-green lake flanked by mountains. This also makes a good turnaround point for a shorter hike. Strong hikers can add on the trail scrambling through the boulder fields to **Lake Haiyaya** in Chaos Canyon, for an additional 5.6 miles (9 km) round-trip.

The last steep shot of trail climbs steps and slabs amid wildflowers up into **Tyndall Gorge.** The path climbs across rocky areas above the boulder-strewn ravine housing Tyndall Creek. After a short drop, you reach **Emerald Lake,** which fills the steep-walled Tyndall Gorge, with Hallett Peak and Flattop Mountain as a dramatic backdrop. The remnant of **Tyndall Glacier** sits in a cirque to the right of Hallett Peak. Boulders rim the lake, making perfect places to sit and absorb the rugged glaciated scenery.

On a good weather day, you will be treated to impressive mountain views on the approach and the summit of Flattop Mountain on the Continental Divide. On a not-so-good day, a thick blanket of fog, a thunderstorm, or heavy precipitation might prevent you from attaining the summit. Plan for this hike when the weather forecast is fair. If conditions change once you are above the tree line, which they often do, turn around. The high elevation can be an issue for some hikers; if you are feeling symptoms of altitude sickness, turn around and head back down.

From the parking lot, walk toward Bear Lake and head right on the **Bear Lake Trail.** After just a few minutes, an **official trailhead sign** marks the start of the path, which is lined with aspen trees and large boulders. Continue to a **trail junction** for Mill Creek Basin. Turn left, then left again at a **second junction** for Odessa Lake to stay on the Flattop Mountain Trail. The trail ascends through forest, eventually arriving at the **Dream Lake overlook.**

The terrain will slowly start to change. Gnarled trees called krummholz appear close to the tree line. As the trees disappear behind you, you'll catch sight of **cairns** across the alpine tundra, which mark the route when visibility is low. After several switchbacks, the trail reaches the **Emerald Lake overlook.** Keep your eyes out for ptarmigan as you climb to a **horse hitch rack,** where great views of Tyndall Glacier unfold. Ascend to the summit atop the **Continental Divide** at a whopping elevation of 12,324 feet (3,756 m). Stop to savor the achievement. When you're ready, return the way you came.

Flattop Mountain

Distance: 8.8 miles (14.2 km) rt
Duration: 5.5 hours
Elevation gain: 2,850 feet (870 m)
Effort: very strenuous
Trailhead: Bear Lake (Parking fills by 8am; arrive via shuttle.)

Alberta Falls

Distance: 1.6 miles (2.6 km) rt
Duration: 45 minutes
Elevation gain: 160 feet (49 m)
Effort: easy
Trailhead: Glacier Gorge (Parking lot fills by 6am in summer; arrive via shuttle.)

The dynamic waters of Alberta Falls can be seen on the way to popular longer hikes such as Sky Pond, Mills Lake, and Black Lake. Alberta Falls is also an outstanding hike on its own. The **Glacier Gorge trailhead parking lot** routinely fills up by 6am in the summer, so plan to arrive via the free **park shuttle.**

The **Glacier Gorge Trail** starts in a forested area that is especially pretty at the peak of fall, when the aspens have turned brilliant yellow; even in late fall faded yellow leaves dust the trail. At the **trail junction** with Bear Lake, go left (south) toward **Alberta Falls.** The trail has a gentle grade. You'll soon reach an impressive **overlook of Glacier Creek.** Continue walking parallel to the creek until you reach a **small wooden sign** identifying **Alberta Falls** and the roaring cascade behind it. Wide slabs of rock are great for taking in the view and eating a snack or lunch before heading back the way you came.

Mills Lake

Distance: 5.6 miles (9 km) rt
Duration: 3 hours
Elevation gain: 700 feet (213 m)
Effort: moderate
Trailhead: Glacier Gorge (Parking lot fills by 6am in summer; arrive via shuttle.)

It is hard not to have high expectations when hiking to Mills Lake. This subalpine body of water is named after the "father" of Rocky Mountain National Park, Enos Mills, so it has to be impressive, right? Indeed, the scenery does not disappoint, especially on a warm, cloudless fall afternoon. The hike begins at the popular Glacier Gorge trailhead where parking is limited, so plan on taking the **park shuttle** if visiting in the summer.

Take the **Glacier Gorge Trail** south toward Alberta Falls, Mills Lake, and Loch Vale. After passing **Alberta Falls,** the **trail forks;** turn right (west) and follow the Glacier Gorge Trail south. This section has large open vistas and easy hiking, even descending gradually at one point.

At another fork, head left for **Mills Lake.** Walk through a forested area, then cross over two **footbridges** before reaching a section of rock slabs marked by **cairns.** Follow the cairns as views of Mills Lake unfold. It is worth heading a little farther along the trail that skirts the left side of the lake to explore various rocky fingers extending into the water and gain different vantage points of the surrounding mountains. From the lake, there are superb views in every direction, particularly of Longs Peak, Keyboard of the Winds, and Thatchtop Mountain. Return the way you came.

Loch Vale and Sky Pond

Distance: 9 miles (14.5 km) rt
Duration: 6 hours
Elevation gain: 1,650 feet (503 m)
Effort: strenuous
Trailhead: Glacier Gorge (Parking lot fills by 6am in summer; arrive via shuttle.)

Spectacular scenery awaits on the journey to Sky Pond. Adventurous souls will enjoy the final push, which includes a few minutes of rock scrambling.

Starting on the **Glacier Gorge Trail,** hike to **Alberta Falls.** Continue along a relatively flat section followed by a brief descent, after which the trail forks. Stay right (southwest) on the **Loch Vale Trail.** From here, the trail turns into a set of steeper switchbacks; heed the signs and don't shortcut the trail. You will arrive at **Loch Vale** in about 1.2 miles (1.9 km). As you wind around this gorgeous lake, there are plenty of nice spots to eat a snack or go fishing.

When you've had your fill, continue along the Loch Vale Trail. After crossing **two small bridges,** hike past the trail junction for **Andrews Glacier Trail.** The ground briefly becomes marshy; planks of wood aid hikers in crossing this sensitive area. Some steep rock steps plant you in the middle of a wide-open boulder field with great views in every direction. Continue hiking to a shelf amid the cliffs and boulders, where you can admire

Timberline Falls. A small **wooden sign** for Sky Pond points to the right.

Scramble up a set of rocks, which is easier going up than down. The climb can be tricky if the rocks are wet. Surrounded by rock slabs at the top is **Lake of Glass.** Continue following **cairns** along the rocky terrain and trail to reach **Sky Pond,** at 10,900 feet (3,322 m). The cliffs surrounding this lake, including the jagged edges of The Sharkstooth, are the most impressive feature. On the scramble back down, remove your backpack and hand it to someone below for better balance.

Lumpy Ridge
★ **Lumpy Ridge Loop**
Distance: 10.7 miles (17.2 km) rt
Duration: 5 hours
Elevation gain: 2,584 feet (788 m)
Effort: very strenuous
Trailhead: Lumpy Ridge
Directions: From US 34 heading toward Fall River Entrance Station, turn right onto MacGregor Ave., which curves into Devils Gulch Rd. Turn left onto Lumpy Ridge Rd. (1.9 mi/3 km from US 34) and continue to its terminus at the trailhead parking lot.

This versatile scenic loop can be enjoyed as a hike, a backpacking trip, or a challenging trail run. While these directions take you clockwise around the loop, the circuit can be traveled in either direction.

Starting from the Lumpy Ridge parking lot, follow the trailhead sign for **Twin Owls/Black Canyon Trail.** During this first stretch, you'll have great views of the Twin Owls, a pair of weathered spires. In the springtime, look for pasqueflowers on the sides of the trail. At the trail junction with an emergency telephone, follow the sign pointing west to Lawn Lake and climber access trails (called **Black Canyon Trail** on some maps), an easy stretch with views of MacGregor Ranch to the south and Lumpy Ridge's rock outcroppings to the north. Numerous paths on the right side divert to climbing areas.

At 2 miles (3.2 km), cross through a **green gate,** where the wide-open terrain changes to forest and climbs around the

back side of Lumpy Ridge. At approximately 3 miles (4.8 km) from the trailhead, you'll see debris from the **Colorado Flood of 2013:** uprooted trees and rocks that slid down the mountain. Continue climbing to a **trail junction** to go east on the **Dark Mountain Trail** toward the Peregrine and Cow Creek wilderness campsites. About 5.6 miles (9 km) from the trailhead, another trail junction points you east toward the **Cow Creek trailhead.** After passing **Rabbit Ears wilderness campsite,** another trail junction sends you right (south) on the **Gem Lake Trail,** which continues uphill through more flood debris.

Around 8 miles (12.9 km) into the loop, continue past a turnoff for the Balanced Rock Trail as you ascend on the Gem Lake Trail through the forest. The trail leads to tiny but inviting **Gem Lake.** From here to the parking lot (1.7 mi/2.7 km), the trek is downhill. En route, stop to admire the pile of rocks named **Paul Bunyan's Boot;** then take a left at the next junction to return to the trailhead.

For a **shorter excursion** (5.2 mi/8.4 km rt), head up the **Twin Owls/Black Canyon Trail.** At the junction, turn right, skirting below the Twin Owls and climbing past a second junction with another return trail to the parking lot. Continue ascending past **Paul Bunyan's Boot** and up the switchbacks to **Gem Lake.** After enjoying the lake, retrace your steps downhill to the nearest junction, turn left, and descend to the trailhead.

Lily Lake
Twin Sisters Western Summit
Distance: 7.4 miles (11.9 km) rt
Duration: 4.5 hours
Elevation gain: 2,253 feet (687 m)
Effort: strenuous
Trailhead: Twin Sisters (park pass not required)
Directions: Across from Lily Lake on CO 7, access a well-signed dirt road to the Twin Sisters trailhead. Park along the roadside.

Outstanding views await at the top of this challenging hike that travels

through the national park and Roosevelt National Forest. From the end of the dirt road, walk a short way to the **Twin Sisters trailhead sign.** Hike through forest until a break in the trees yields the first good glimpse of Longs Peak to the west. Ascend the trail until you arrive at the site of a huge **landslide** that was the result of the Colorado flood of 2013. The trail crosses directly over the slide, affording a good look at the rubble, after which the path turns into a **social trail** and is harder to follow. Look for **cairns,** broken branches, and logs that have been positioned along the route, guiding hikers rather steeply uphill to reconnect with the original trail through the forest.

Continue steadily ascending through the forest until you reach a **scree field** below the summit. Before you proceed, assess current weather conditions as the remaining terrain is exposed and not a place to be in a thunderstorm. Wind your way up the rocky path to a **saddle** between the two summits. Here you will find a **stone cabin** that used to serve as a housing facility for employees stationed at a fire lookout tower (long removed). Continue following the trail to the top of the **western summit.** If the skies are clear, you'll have a fantastic view of Longs Peak and Mount Meeker. Your options from here are to head back down to the saddle and follow cairns to the less-visited eastern summit or return the way you came.

Longs Peak
Chasm Lake

Distance: 8.4 miles (13.5 km) rt
Duration: 5.5 hours
Elevation gain: 2,380 feet (725 m)
Effort: strenuous
Trailhead: Longs Peak

This rugged trek climbs from forest into the rocky alpine zone to reach blue Chasm Lake, tucked right below the cliffs

Top to bottom: Twin Owls on Lumpy Ridge; Chasm Lake and Longs Peak; Ouzel Falls in Wild Basin

of Longs Peak. Before departing, check the forecast at the Longs Peak Ranger Station for afternoon thunderstorms. You'll likely need to arrive very early in the morning. Sometimes in summer the parking lot fills with climbers by 3am.

The **East Longs Peak Trail** ascends rapidly through the forest of **Pine Ridge,** up one long steep switchback passing the turnoff to Eugenia Mine Trail. At the next switchback, the trail runs above Alpine Brook and Goblins Forest wilderness campsite. The trail moderates slightly until a series of **short switchbacks** gain fast elevation.

After a **bridge,** the trail makes a huge switchback just below tree line. It's known as **Tishma's Corner,** a spot where winter and early season hikers can wander off trail due to lingering snow obscuring the way; many hikers have gotten lost. Keep a close eye on your map and the route, especially if there is snow. Above the corner, the vegetation changes: The forest thins, replaced by alpine tundra. Stay on the trail to protect the fragile tundra plants.

As you ascend, views open up to include Longs Peak and, behind you, Twin Sisters peaks, as well as the landslide from the 2013 flood. The trail crawls upward through rocky tundra interspersed with wildflowers to **Chasm Junction,** with an open-ceiling pit toilet nearby.

At Chasm Junction, crest **Mills Moraine** to traverse a steep wall under Mount Lady Washington. Below, **Peacock Pool** glimmers light blue; at the head of the cirque is **Columbine Falls.** The trail swings above the falls, passes a ranger cabin and pit toilet, and crosses through **Chasm Meadows.** The trail seems to disappear in a low-angled wall of rock; follow the **cairns** for a few hundred feet of scrambling over the crest to reach **Chasm Lake** at 11,760 feet (3,584 m).

Use **caution** on this hike. Turn around at Chasm Junction if the weather looks dicey. Hiking here July-mid-September is best, as a steep snowfield (requiring

crampons and ice axes) under Mount Lady Washington poses a hazard the rest of the year. The altitude can cause labored breathing, dizziness, and headaches; if you feel these symptoms, turn back.

Wild Basin

Wild Basin has limited parking. Plan to arrive before 9:30am in summer for a chance at a spot.

Copeland Falls

Distance: 0.6 mile (1 km) rt
Duration: 30 minutes
Elevation gain: 15 feet (4.6 m)
Effort: easy
Trailhead: Wild Basin

Copeland Falls is a perfect hike for families with wee ones and those on a tight schedule. This waterfall is a teaser for bigger attractions farther along the trail, but it is also great as a standalone outing. The water at the falls is swift; keep a safe distance.

Start at the **Wild Basin trailhead** and cross over Hunters Creek on the wooden **footbridge.** Head upstream on the wide dirt path, which has a gradual ascent. Lush foliage lines the trail. In 0.3 mile, a sign points toward the lower falls and upper falls. Take the **spur trail** to the **lower falls.** Rather than a tall waterfall, Copeland is a series of shorter cascades. To visit the **upper falls,** keep following the spur trail upstream. From its upper vantage point Copeland Falls appears bigger and gushier. To head back, you can either retrace your steps or continue upstream on a short path to reach the Wild Basin Trail. Then turn right to return to the trailhead.

Calypso Cascades

Distance: 3.6 miles (5.8 km) rt
Duration: 1.5 hours
Elevation gain: 700 feet (213 m)
Effort: easy to moderate
Trailhead: Wild Basin

With an abundance of water along the

trail and large trees providing cool shade, Calypso Cascades is a great destination for a warm summer day.

Take the Wild Basin Trail to **Copeland Falls,** continuing upstream through the forest, stepping over seeps of water. Look for several glacial **erratics** on the side of the trail. These enormous boulders were deposited by a long-forgotten glacier.

The trail gradually starts to ascend **rock steps.** Continue until you reach a sign for the **Pine Ridge wilderness campsite.** A few dozen paces later, you'll reach a junction for four additional wilderness campsites and the Calypso Cascades. Turn left (south) to cross a wooden **footbridge** with a torrent of water rushing below. Depending on the time of year, water might be covering a part of the steps in a section of trail just after the footbridge. If that's the case, take great care in negotiating the slippery rocks; turn around if you're not comfortable crossing. Otherwise, continue along the last part of the trail to **Calypso Cascades,** where **three long footbridges** provide places to admire the water. Return the way you came.

Ouzel Falls

Distance: 5.4 miles (8.7 km) rt
Duration: 3 hours
Elevation gain: 950 feet (290 m)
Effort: moderate
Trailhead: Wild Basin

The trail to Ouzel Falls provides a finale for a three-waterfall day: Tall (50 ft/15 m), bold, and raucous, it's one of the most memorable falls in the park. Its namesake, the ouzel, also known as the American dipper, is a dark bird known for vigorously plunging its body into the water as it gathers food. Keep an eye out and you might see one.

To get to the waterfall, hike west on the **Wild Basin Trail,** along the way enjoying **Copeland Falls** and **Calypso Cascades.** From the cascades, continue winding your way up through the forest at a moderate grade until you arrive at a wooden

footbridge for viewing. To see where the falls gush over a small cliff, follow a **social trail** up the left side of Ouzel Creek. Return the way you came.

Grand Lake
Cascade Falls

Distance: 7 miles (11.3 km) rt
Duration: 3 hours
Elevation gain: 300 feet (91 m)
Effort: moderate
Trailhead: North Inlet (park pass not required)
Directions: From Grand Lake, take West Portal Rd. to a junction, staying left. Take the Tonahutu/North Inlet spur road. Turn left and drive to another junction where a right turn reaches the North Inlet Trailhead.

The **North Inlet Trail** is flat and wide as it heads east. Much of the surrounding forest burned in the 2020 East Troublesome Fire. The trail runs along placid and mirrorlike North Inlet Creek, just to the south. After less than 1 mile (1.6 km), you'll reach the sprawling meadow of **Summerland Park.** Next, you will pass a privately owned house on the north side of the trail, followed by the **Summerland Park group campsite** on your right. Shortly thereafter, cross a small wooden footbridge and walk by the sign for the **Summerland wilderness site.**

Continue traveling upstream to another wilderness campsite, **Twinberry.** Soon, you will hear the rush of water on your right. Finally, at a **trail fork,** a stock-only path heads up, and another trail heads down to the falls. Walk along the short, rocky path down to **Cascade Falls,** tumbling and gushing over an impressive pile of granite. Take a seat on a nearby rock and look for dark birds called ouzels, also known as American dippers, frolicking in the spray of water. Head back west to your starting point.

Adams Falls

Distance: 0.6 mile (1 km) rt
Duration: 30 minutes
Elevation gain: 80 feet (24 m)
Effort: easy
Trailhead: East Inlet (park pass not required)

Directions: From Grand Lake, drive 2.3 miles (3.7 km) on West Portal Rd. to reach the trailhead.

The ease of reaching Adams Falls makes this trail a favorite among families. Expect to share the trail with many other visitors, especially on summer weekends.

Begin by ambling east through the forested area at a gentle grade. At a **signed fork,** swing right (south) and hike a short distance to a rock-walled **viewing platform.** There you'll see the cascades of **Adams Falls** squeezing through the gorge. (The park strongly discourages people from viewing the falls from points beyond the platform.) From the platform, return the way you came or continue east along a short loop trail for a view of the top of the falls. This route connects with the **East Inlet Trail.** Go left (west) to return to the trailhead.

Backpacking
Continental Divide Trail
27 miles (44 km)

In Rocky Mountain National Park, 27 miles (44 km) of existing park trails are part of the **Continental Divide National Scenic Trail** (CDT, 3,100 mi/4,990 km), the route of interconnected trails that stretches from Mexico to Montana and the Canadian border. This trek makes a loop from the **Green Mountain Trailhead** on the park's west side, taking **3-5 days.**

Link together the **Green Mountain Trail** with **Tonahutu Creek Trail** east to **Ptarmigan Pass** and **Flattop Mountain** for a long traverse above 12,000 feet (3,658 m) along the **Continental Divide.** Then descend the **North Inlet Trail** west to its trailhead and go north on the **Tonahutu Creek Trail** and west to end on **Green Mountain Trail.** Along the way, you'll enjoy Big Meadows, Granite Falls, Flattop Mountain, and Cascade Falls, plus the Continental Divide. Blue markers with the official CDT logo mark the trails.

On the Tonahutu Creek Trail, wilderness campsites include Sunset, Sunrise, Lower Granite Falls, Granite Falls, and Tonahutu Meadows, a high-elevation, scenic campsite. On the North Inlet Trail, go for Twinberry, Big Pool, Grouseberry, Porcupine, or July. July is closest to the high traverse along the Continental Divide. Parts of this zone burned in the 2020 East Troublesome Fire; some wilderness campsites were damaged and may be closed.

Lake Verna
28 miles (45 km)

On the west side of the park near Grand Lake, the **East Inlet Trailhead** leads to **Lake Verna** (10,255 ft/3,126 m) for a **three-day trip.** En route, the trail passes **Lone Pine Lake,** which makes a good place to camp on the ascent. Plan for two nights to include a hike to Lake Verna on day two.

North Inlet to Bear Lake
16.2 miles (26 km)

This hefty **two-day,** point-to-point romp crosses the Continental Divide at Flattop Mountain, topping out at 12,324 feet (3,756 m). From the **North Inlet Trailhead** near Grand Lake, hike the **North Inlet Trail** on the first day, aiming to camp at July Junction or North Inlet Junction. On the second day, slog up Flattop Mountain, then descend the Flattop Mountain Trail to Bear Lake, where you can catch shuttles to Estes Park.

Permits and Guides

Backpackers must have a **wilderness permit** ($30 per group) to camp overnight. Pick up permits from the main Wilderness Office at **Beaver Meadows Visitor Center** (970/586-1242) or the Wilderness Office at the **Kawuneeche Visitor Center** (970/627-3471). You can also request advance reservations beginning in early March by submitting the **Wilderness Campsite Reservation Request Application** on the **park website** (www.nps.gov/romo). Order maps through **Rocky Mountain Conservancy** (970/586-0121, rmconservancy.org).

RECREATION

Bear-resistant food storage cannisters are required.

Colorado Wilderness Rides and Guides (720/242-9828, coloradowildernessridesandguides.com) leads backpacking trips inside the park, including on the Continental Divide Loop. Trips run 2-5 days and start at $655 per person.

Climbing

Rocky Mountain is renowned for its hundreds of named climbing routes. **Traditional climbing** (using only removable hardware along the climbing route) is allowed in the park. Sport climbing (climbing with bolts or hardware permanently affixed to rocks) is prohibited.

Before heading out on an adventure, climbers should familiarize themselves with the park's climbing etiquette and rules, listed on the park website. A park entrance fee must be paid to access some climbing spots, although one of the most popular climbing areas, Lumpy Ridge, is fee-free. Those who plan to embark on overnight climbing trips must obtain a **bivouac permit** from the park's **Wilderness Office** (970/586-1242) at Beaver Meadows Visitor Center. Climbers should adhere to Leave No Trace principles and abide by raptor-nesting closures.

Guides

Several local guide services and outfitters based in Estes Park offer climbing instruction. They are authorized concessionaires for guiding climbs in the national park.

Colorado Mountain School (341 Moraine Ave., Estes Park, 720/387-8944, coloradomountainschool.com) teaches courses on technique and guides outings for more advanced climbers. On select dates in the summer, a group climb takes place: the **Lumpy Ridge Classic Climb.** Open to climbers with prior experience on multi-pitch routes, this full-day adventure includes a variety of routes along Lumpy Ridge.

Kent Mountain Adventure Center

traversing The Ledges on Longs Peak

(520 Steamer Dr., Estes Park, 970/586-5990, kmaconline.com) offers a variety of private, guided climbing experiences for everyone from novices to experts. **Colorado Wilderness Rides and Guides** (720/242-9828, coloradowildernessridesandguides.com) leads mountaineering trips on Mount Meeker and Longs Peak, among others.

★ Longs Peak: Keyhole Route

Distance: 15 miles (24 km) rt
Duration: 10-15 hours
Elevation gain: 5,000 feet (1,524 m)
Effort: very strenuous
Trailhead: East Longs Peak

The Keyhole Route is the most popular route to the summit of Longs Peak; thousands of people attempt it each year. The route is named for a large notch in the ridgeline that extends off the north side of Longs Peak. It's considered the least difficult path to the top and does not require technical gear (ropes, harnesses, protection). However, this ascent is for those who have experience in off-trail scrambling, as exposure, rockfall, and icy conditions pose extreme hazards. The route's popularity does not preclude climber injury or death. Every year people get into serious trouble on this climb. Weather is a major factor, but even on a bluebird day, climbers can encounter terrain slicked with ice or find themselves off-route due to snow. Altitude can also affect hiker judgment. Prepare in every way possible and expect to reevaluate your ability and conditions at various points en route.

When to Go

Longs Peak sees the most foot traffic **June-September.** The start of climbing season varies depending on the amount of snowfall the previous winter and how long the snow sticks to the mountain. Afternoon thunderstorms are typical June-August. For the most ideal time to attempt the climb, **late August-early September** usually see less afternoon rain and more blue skies. However, temperatures start dipping below freezing at night, causing areas of thin ice on the route, making for slick conditions. If possible, schedule your trip for a **weekday,** when the trails are less crowded.

To complete the route, which takes **10-15 hours,** most climbers **start at 1am-3am,** hiking by headlamp with fresh batteries. Aim to **arrive** at the Keyhole **around sunrise** so you can finish the climb down from the peak at or **before noon,** when foul weather can develop.

Spending the night at the **Boulderfield** is the best option for those who want to break up the journey into two days. However, the **nine wilderness campsites** there are in high demand and must be **reserved well in advance** through the **Wilderness Office** (970/586-1242).

East Longs Peak Trailhead

The most important stop before climbing is the **information kiosk** just in front of the **Longs Peak Ranger Station** at the

East Longs Peak Trailhead. Check the **weather report** and current **climbing conditions** and decide whether to go. An updated **Longs Peak Conditions Report** is also posted on the park's website; use this to assess the weather a few days out.

Just next to the ranger station, jump on the **East Longs Peak Trail,** then wind steadily uphill through forest for 0.5 mile until you reach your first **junction** with Eugenia Mine and Storm Pass. Continue to follow signs heading straight (west) to Longs Peak and Chasm Lake. Your climb continues through dense forest; you will encounter switchbacks along the way. The trail plateaus just before you hit the wilderness campsite of **Goblins Forest** and then stays fairly level for the next 0.5 mile before turning into switchbacks again. The next landmark is a footbridge that some call **Lightning Bridge** because it comes right before a sign warning of lightning danger just ahead. The bridge crosses Alpine Brook.

Tishma's Corner

After the bridge, the trail makes a huge switchback, first heading south and then northwest. The switchback, just below the tree line, is informally known as **Tishma's Corner.** While still a maintained trail, it's a spot where winter and early season hikers can get discombobulated. Snow hangs on longer on this section, so hikers on many occasions have accidentally dropped down into nearby basins off-trail and become lost.

At this point, the landscape changes quickly. The trees become stouter; the terrain rockier. You are in the transition zone between subalpine and alpine and will soon be entirely above the tree line. After several sets of switchbacks, a sign for the **Battle Mountain wilderness campsite** appears. Head straight (west), following the sign that says **Longs Peak Summit**. You are now 4 miles (6.4 km) from the peak. Shortly after leaving this signpost, you will get your first good look at the east face of Longs. Continue along

the trail until you reach **Chasm Junction** (3.3 mi/5.3 km from the trailhead).

Chasm Junction

At **Chasm Junction,** there's a small meadow where hikers tend to briefly congregate, hydrate, and refuel (as well as a public toilet). When you are ready to forge on, head northwest on the **East Longs Peak Trail** to the Boulderfield/Longs Peak summit (traveling southwest will take you to Chasm Lake). For 0.8 mile, the trail slowly ascends and skirts the east side of Mount Lady Washington until it reaches **Granite Pass.** Follow the trail marker left (southwest) and travel along a series of switchbacks that leads you to the **Boulderfield.** You are now 6 miles (9.7 km) from the trailhead.

The Boulderfield to the Keyhole

Once you arrive at the **Boulderfield,** expect to find big views, perhaps a ptarmigan or two, and lots of rocky terrain. Say good-bye to the maintained trail about halfway through the Boulderfield en route to Rocky's established **wilderness campsites.** Next to the horse **hitching post and privies,** there is a sign for the Keyhole Route. **Cairns** mark the way thereafter. Spending the night at the Boulderfield is the best option for hikers who want to break up their journey into two days. However, these nine wilderness campsites are in high demand and must be **reserved well in advance** through the wilderness office (970/586-1242). You can generally find **water to filter** within a few hundred yards of the established campsites.

This vast valley of rocks, ranging in size from small talus to boxcar-sized boulders, is where the trickier part of the journey begins. The Boulderfield is a slow, gradual uphill stretch. At any point, rocks can wobble and teeter underfoot; twisting your ankle is a real possibility. As you approach the Keyhole, there is some **Class Two** climbing involved. The rocks become bigger, and you will use your hands to gain upward momentum. While there is no doubt as to where you are headed—the large notch in the rock up ahead—navigating the path of least resistance to your destination will take some thought and consideration.

The **Keyhole,** a long ridge that extends off the north side of Longs Peak, is a game changer. From here on out, the pace of the trek changes, and exposure presents itself, much to the chagrin of acrophobes. Swift, unforgiving gusts of wind combined with steep drop-offs make this a **turnaround point** for many travelers. One of the many reasons to exercise good caution in this spot is that the rocks here may be covered in veriglass—thin layers of **ice.** If you choose to continue and walk through the Keyhole, a heady view of Glacier Gorge a few thousand feet below opens up. **Yellow and red bull's-eyes** painted on rocks from here to the summit prove helpful for many hikers. Understand that these markers do not guarantee safety and should not be followed if unforeseen hazards present themselves along the way. The bull's-eyes are not always apparent if there is snow on the route.

Many people turn back for the parking lot at the Keyhole. Making it to the Keyhole alone is without question a huge accomplishment. If you wonder if you should continue onward, consider this: The Keyhole is the **halfway point** in your journey to the peak. Even though the summit is only 1 mile (1.6 km) or so away as the crow flies, you should expect to take just as long to reach the top as you did to get to this point. Expect increasingly difficult terrain ahead.

As you poke your body on the other side of the Keyhole, the next challenge ahead is the **Ledges.**

The Ledges

In this next section, you will navigate across a series of slabbed **rock ledges.** The trail is relatively flat, but the terrain drops off steeply to the west. This is historically a **problematic spot** for climbers and not a place you want to slip or trip. You will encounter a piece of rebar sticking out from the rocks and some steps chiseled into the rock. While the sight of the rebar provides some climbers with a feeling of security, the metal is surprisingly slick from polishing by thousands of boots; take serious caution. Use all four limbs to navigate this section; a **bottleneck of climbers** waiting for their turn is common.

The Trough

The **Trough** is an approximately 0.3-mile-long gully, a scree-filled couloir. This is another spot where climbers assess their strength and might decide to turn around. Though the summit is close, there is somewhere around **1,000 vertical feet** (305 m) to climb in the Trough, and the presence of loose rocks can be maddening. Follow the **bull's-eyes,** but always be aware of who is above and below you. Make a point not to climb directly under another person, or you might find pebbles and rocks raining down on you.

The Narrows

The **Narrows** is a stretch of rock a little less than the width of a sidewalk, which would be relatively tame if it weren't for some serious exposure on the right-hand side. At this point you are at the **technical crux** of the route. There is a **large boulder** in this section that gives some people serious pause. Climbers usually end up making an awkward step-around between the wall and the rock. Be aware that this spot becomes **bottlenecked** with people; it is basically one in, one out. After the Narrows, it is time to press on to the Homestretch.

The Homestretch

The last section past the narrows is appropriately named the **Homestretch.** It is several hundred feet of **Class Two** slabs to the top. The rocks tend to be a little wet, and slicker than regular wet rock, because so many people have climbed them. Climbers usually find this spot much more challenging going down than coming up.

The Summit

The top of Longs is magnificent because of its spectacular views and its size. The **summit** is wide and flat, the size of several football fields. On a clear day, you can see Wyoming to the north, Pikes Peak to the south, Grays and Torreys peaks to the west, and the sprawl of Denver to the east. One hundred or more people could fit in this spot. While it is feasible to find yourself alone at the top, you should expect to have company, especially if you are climbing in high season. People have been known to lug some interesting items to the top—juggling balls and violins among them. Some cook up a celebratory sausage on their camp stove before heading down.

At minimum, swig some water, have a snack, and sign the **summit register** to make your achievement official. There are **no toilets** at the top of Longs Peak. Plan to use the toilets at the Boulderfield or a waste collection bag (offered at the Longs Peak Ranger Station). Save your personal business for places other than the mountaintop.

Heading Down

Though climbers are often awash with relief at having made it to the top, it is still 7.5 miles (12.1 km) back to the parking lot. Down-climbing from the peak to the Boulderfield is where accidents can and do happen. Stay focused, stay hydrated, and keep on keeping on until you are back where you started.

Lumpy Ridge

Lumpy Ridge is the park's most popular rock-climbing destination, offering variety, challenge, and superb views, but it isn't swarming with people. It first gained attention in the 1950s; since then, thousands of people have tested their climbing chops on its grand granite cracks and faces.

Lumpy Ridge allows only traditional or **trad climbing.** Climbers must place and remove their own protection as they climb; there are no bolts in the rock; you cannot permanently attach bolts or other equipment. Many climbers also enjoy **bouldering** on low rocks at Lumpy Ridge, using a crash pad but no ropes and harnesses. The granite here is coarse to the touch, with lumps and bumps that can scrape you. Be aware that closures occur March-July for raptor nesting.

Routes

Easier climbs on Lumpy Ridge include **Batman and Robin** and **Magical Chrome-Plated Semiautomatic Enema Syringe** or "Chrome-Plated" for short. More advanced climbers will be challenged by **Pear Buttress** on **The Book** formation. **The 37th Cog in Melvin's Wheel** is another great climb with a moderate amount of difficulty. If you are an expert climber, consider adding **Fat City** or **Crack of Fear** on the Twin Owls to your short list.

To access Lumpy Ridge's climbing features, park at the Lumpy Ridge trailhead. Hike north to the Black Canyon Trail (0.6 mi/1 km). Various spur trails along the Black Canyon Trail take climbers directly to the rock. These spur trails are not indicated on the park's free handout map; however, wooden signs direct climbers to some of the most popular areas, including the **Twin Owls, Batman, Checkerboard, The Book, The Pear,** and **Sundance.**

Road Biking

Due to summer vehicular traffic, cyclists aiming to ride **Bear Creek Road** or **Trail Ridge Road** should plan to ride at dawn or after 4pm for a safer and more pleasant experience. Bicycles are not permitted on trails in the park.

You can also enjoy the climb up **Old Fall River Road** and the flying descent down **Trail Ridge Road**—although you'll have to dodge potholes and rumble across washboards on the old dirt section. The climb, which starts on a 10 percent grade on Old Fall River Road, is about 4,000 feet (1,219 m) in a mere 9 miles (14.5 km). When traffic picks up, kicked-up dust can be an added factor. The best time of year to ride Old Fall River Road is **spring,** when it opens to cyclists in both directions for about 2-4 weeks before it opens to cars.

Estes Park Mountain Shop (2050 Big Thompson Ave., 970/586-6548, www. estesparkmountainshop.com, 8am-9pm daily summer, 8am-8pm daily winter) rents road bikes ($30-75) and mountain bikes ($25-70).

Horseback Riding

Jackson Stables (2515 Tunnel Rd., Estes Park, 970/586-3341, ext. 1140/1149 summer, 970/586-6748 winter, www. jacksonstables.com, early May-late Oct., 1-5 hrs, $60-140) is on the YMCA property adjacent to the national park. Popular trips go to Moraine Park, Beaver Meadows, Bierstadt Lake, and Glacier Basin.

Just outside the Fall River Entrance, adjacent to the Fall River Visitor Center, **National Park Gateway Stables** (4600 Fall River Rd., 970/586-5269, www.skhorses. com, May-Sept., $80-240) guides trail rides for two, four, or six hours to eastside park locations along Fall River, including Deer Mountain and the alluvial fan.

Reservations are recommended for all rides. Wear long pants and sturdy shoes or cowboy boots. Helmets are provided but not required.

Fishing

A **Colorado fishing license** must be obtained before fishing park streams or lakes. You can purchase licenses online or by phone through **Colorado Parks and Wildlife** (800/244-5613, cpw.state.co.us) and at fly shops in Estes Park and Grand Lake.

Different rules apply to lakes and rivers in the national park. Pick up the park's official **fishing brochure** or look online for possession limits, closed waters, and catch-and-release requirements. Bear Lake is completely off-limits to fishing. While hiking into a high mountain lake might sound appealing for solitude, not all lakes have fish; check at visitors centers or look online for a list of lakes containing fish.

The **east side** has dozens of great spots to cast a line, some busier than others. The **Big Thompson River** in **Moraine Park** lures scads of anglers because it is easily accessible from the main entrance. Plus, you can simultaneously watch for wildlife, particularly elk. **Fall River** along US 34 often offers more secluded fishing, especially near the turnoff to Old Fall River Road. During the elk rut (Sept.-Oct.), sections of Fall River and Big Thompson River are inaccessible 5pm-7am, and the park restricts foot traffic to Horseshoe Park, Moraine Park, and Upper Beaver Meadows.

Fly-fishing aficionados love **Kawuneeche Valley**'s streams. Favorite spots include the **North Inlet, East Inlet,** and **Tonahutu Creek.** Do not expect to catch monsters, but the fishing is good for brook trout. You can also catch brookies and other trout in the **Colorado River,** most easily accessed at the **Coyote Valley Trail** and **Holzwarth Historic Site.** To cast for native Colorado River cutthroat trout, try **Lake Nanita** or **Timber Lake.** During the **elk rut** (Sept.-Oct.), anglers cannot access certain sections of the Colorado River 5pm-7am; foot traffic to Harbison Meadow and the Holzwarth Historic Site meadow is also restricted.

Guides and Fly Shops

Guided trips in Rocky Mountain National Park are usually wade-fishing and either fly-fishing or spin-casting. Trips run 2-8 hours. Rates start at $150 for two hours for one person. Typically included in the price are your guide's expertise, gear (including waders, flies, rods, and reels), transportation, snacks, and/or lunch. A Colorado fishing license must be purchased separately. Plan on 15-20 percent gratuity.

In Estes Park, licenses, gear, flies, and guides are available at **Kirks Fly Shop** (230 E. Elkhorn Ave., 970/577-0790, www.kirksflyshop.com, 7am-8pm daily summer, shorter hours off-season), **Estes Angler** (338 Riverside Dr., 970/586-2110, www.estesangler.com, 9am-5pm daily, shorter hours off-season), and **Scot's Sporting Goods** (870 Moraine Ave., 970/586-2877, www.scotssportinggoods. com, 8am-8pm daily summer, shorter hours off-season). **Sasquatch Fly Fishing** (970/586-3341 summer, 303/601-8617 winter, www.sasquatchflyfishing.com), based out of the YMCA of the Rockies, offers fly-fishing trips in summer.

In Grand Lake, **Kirks Fly Shop Grand Lake** (612 Grand Ave., 970/627-5021, www.kirksflyshopgrandlake.com, 7am-5pm daily) guides fly-fishing trips and sells licenses, gear, and tackle.

Boating and Paddling

Lake Estes is the largest body of water in Estes Park, attracting locals and visitors alike for boating, paddling, and trout fishing (swimming is not permitted). You can launch your own watercraft (no Jet Skis) at the designated boat launch adjacent to the **Lake Estes Marina** (1770 Big Thompson Ave., 970/586-2011, May-mid-Sept.). You must also purchase a Lake Estes **boating permit** ($5) from the marina store and pay the **day-use fee** ($5).

The marina also rents pontoon boats and motorized fishing boats ($50-70/hour). Anglers can rent a rod and reel ($2/hour). Paddlers can rent canoes, kayaks, and paddleboards ($25-30/hour). You can also rent a four-person paddle boat ($35/hour). Fuel and life jackets are included in rates. Boating permits are not required for rentals and day-use fees are waived.

With **Grand Lake** and **Shadow Mountain Lake** so close and **Lake Granby**

farther south, water sports abound west of the park. To launch your own watercraft, go to the **boat ramp at Grand Lake** near the East Inlet Trailhead parking lot. Non-motorized hand-carried boats can launch at **Point Park.** For Shadow Mountain Lake, drive to the south end for the **Green Ridge Boating Site.**

On Grand Lake, **marinas** and **paddling businesses** have rentals in summer (mid-May-mid-Sept.) lined up along Lake Avenue. Hourly rates for motorized boats start around $65 for small boats and $115 for larger boats. Paddling crafts go from $23 per hour. **Grand Lake Marina & Boater's Choice** (1132 Lake Ave., 970/627-9273, www.glmarina.com) rents pontoon boats, sport boats, canoes, paddleboards, and single and double kayaks. **Headwaters Marina** (on Lake Ave. between Hancock St. and Ellsworth St., 970/627-5031, www.townofgrandlake. com/headwaters-marina.htm) rents pontoon boats, runabouts, and pedal boats. **Mountain Paddlers** (1030 Lake Ave., 970/531-6334, www.mountainpaddlers. com) rents single and double kayaks. **Rocky Mountain SUP** (1005 Lake Ave., 970/557-5150, rmsup.com) rents paddleboards.

On Shadow Mountain Lake, **Trail Ridge Marina** (12634 US 34, 970/627-3586, trailridgemarina.com) rents fishing boats, pontoon boats, paddleboards, and single or double kayaks.

Food

Inside the Park

Rocky Mountain National Park is a good place to take along a cooler or daypack with lunch, water, and snacks; most park locales lack food services. Stock up on supplies in Estes Park or Grand Lake.

The park has only one restaurant: the **Café at Trail Ridge** (Trail Ridge Rd. and Old Fall River Rd., www. trailridgegiftstore.com, 10am-4:30pm daily late May-mid-Oct., $5-10). The café serves typical lunch fare of burgers, hot dogs, chili, and soup, including a couple vegetarian options. It also has a variety of snacks.

Picnic Areas

Rocky has many designated picnic areas with tables, toilets, and sometimes fire grates (bring your own firewood; gathering is illegal). You'll also find scattered picnic tables without additional facilities in a few locations along roads and at trailheads.

On the east side, **Bear Lake Road** has a few of the best picnic areas. These include **Sprague Lake, Hollowell Park,** and **Upper Beaver Meadows.** The first two are open year-round, while you can only drive to the Upper Beaver Meadows picnic area in summer and fall. On Fall River Road, **Endovalley picnic area** is the largest in the park; it makes a good place to share a meal before a scenic drive up the road. On CO 7 south of Estes Park, a picnic at **Lily Lake** pairs well with a hike around the lake.

On Trail Ridge Road, you can picnic at **Hidden Valley** as a way to experience the old ski area located on the east side. West of Milner Pass and the Continental Divide, **Lake Irene** also has a picnic area.

On the west side, smaller picnic areas cluster in Kawuneeche Valley on the lower elevations of Trail Ridge Road. Find the best ones at **Coyote Valley Trailhead**, where you can also walk the trail, and **Hozwarth Historic Site**, where you can tour the area. Both offer opportunities for spotting moose.

Outside the Park
Estes Park
Barbecue

Pig, chicken, and cow tchotchkes are found throughout **Smokin' Dave's BBQ & Brew** (820 Moraine Ave., 907/577-7427, smokindavesbbq.com, opens 11am daily, closing times vary, $9-28), a cheerful and bustling restaurant that is a favorite among locals and visitors. With your belt loosened and shirtsleeves rolled way up, dig into heaping plates of tender, melt-in-your-mouth smoked meats doused in your choice of homemade sauces. Comforting sides like spiced apples and Southern green beans taste as though they were lovingly prepared in a family kitchen.

Steakhouses

The **Rock Inn Mountain Tavern** (1675 CO 66, 970/586-4116, www.rockinnestes. com, opens 4pm daily, closing times vary, $10-35) feels every bit an authentic old-style tavern with its hearty fare, rich wood-and-rock interior, and barstools that don't sit unoccupied for long. It has a less touristy vibe than many other restaurants in town, making it a great place to unwind after a day of outdoor adventure. The steaks are delicious—juicy and thick-cut—and a pot of locally blended tea is a sublime way to top off a meal. There's live music most evenings in the summer. The Rock does not take reservations.

Fine Dining

Bird & Jim (915 Moraine Ave., 970/586-9832, www.birdandjim.com, 11am-9pm Mon.-Sat., 10:30am-9pm Sun., $11-40) sets itself apart with modern decor, a heavy emphasis on farm-to-table cuisine, and seasonal menu items that are vegan, vegetarian, and gluten-free. Paleo diet followers will rejoice in seeing bone broth on the menu; buy it by the cup or quart. The spacious restaurant boasts an open kitchen and lots of natural light. Find silverware wrapped in colorful, uniquely patterned cloth napkins on the tables and eye-catching chandeliers overhead. The restaurant's name is a nod to adventurer Isabella Bird and her friend Rocky Mountain Jim.

Chef-owned ★ **Seasoned-An American Bistro** (205 Park Ln., 970/586-9000, www.seasonedbistro.com, 3pm-7pm Wed.-Thurs., 11am-7pm Fri.-Sun., $10-46) serves both small and full dinner plates, with suggested wine and local

ESTES PARK

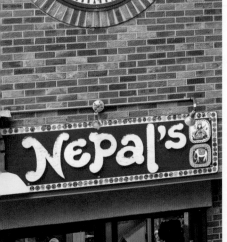

craft beer pairings. The creative menu changes seasonally based on what's fresh; new dishes are inspired by cuisines from across the Americas. The atmosphere is intimate indoors, perfect for celebratory events and romantic dining. The outside patio has views of Prospect Mountain and downtown. Make reservations, especially on weekends.

Southeast Asian

Comforting and warm, ★ **Nepal's Café** (184 E. Elkhorn Ave., 970/577-7035, 11am-9pm daily, $11-20) is a lovely treat anytime, but especially when the damp and chilly Rocky Mountain weather moves in. A dozen or so tables are packed in the cozy dining room amid the hum of conversation and clattering of dishes from the kitchen. The delicious food includes curries, kormas, noodle dishes, and flatbreads with various levels of spiciness. For a sweet treat, accompany your meal with a glass of mango saffron lemonade.

Pizza

Sometimes when you get off the trail, you just need a slice of pizza. **Antonio's Real New York Pizza** (1560 Big Thompson Ave., 970/586-7275, noon-8pm Tues.-Sun., $8-40) hits the spot. You can get classic or eclectic pies here, including one with chicken wings. If you have a large hungry group, try sharing the huge Hell's Kitchen variety pie. Calzones topped with house-made sauces range in size from single-serving to monstersized. Top off meals with tiramisu or New York cheesecake.

Cafés

You may have to wait in line for seat at the ★ **Notchtop Bakery and Café** (Stanley Village, 459 E. Wonderview Ave. #5, 970/586-0272, thenotchtop.com,

Top to bottom: sign entering Estes Park; breakfast at the Notchtop Bakery and Café; Nepal's Café

7am-3pm daily, $9-15), where the huge breakfast and lunch menus feature meaty dishes as well as gluten-free, vegetarian, and vegan options. The lure is fresh-baked pastries, unique eggs Benedict toppings, espressos, paninis, protein bowls, and hot sandwiches. The kitchen uses natural ingredients mostly from local farms. Add on exquisite morning cocktails like mimosas and margaritas.

For family-friendly but healthy options, the **Egg of Estes** (393 E. Elkhorn Ave., 970/586-1173, eggofestes.com, 7am-2pm daily, $9-15) serves breakfast and lunch with a homestyle flair. Get your eggs done any style: omelets, Benedicts, scrambles, hashes, skillets, frittatas, or sandwiches. Lunch offers more traditional sandwiches.

Grand Lake

At ★ **Cork on the Water** (1007 Lake Ave., 970/798-8059, 11am-10pm daily summer, $10-15), the small-plates menu and overall atmosphere are geared toward a decidedly adult crowd. Great for date night or an evening out with friends, it's a fine spot to settle in with a charcuterie board and a glass of wine. There's indoor and outdoor seating, but most patrons naturally gravitate to a table on the deck because of the lake views. The vibe is relaxed, with mellow music playing and lanterns at each table providing soft lighting after the sun sets. Try the grilled street corn; it's heavenly.

When a special occasion is on the calendar, **The Historic Rapids Lodge and Restaurant** (210 Rapids Ln., 970/627-3707, www.rapidslodge.com, dinner daily late May-late June, lunch and dinner daily late June-Labor Day, limited days off season, $25-50) delivers. The dimly lit dining room in this historic hotel is comfortable and attractive, with an original stone fireplace from the early 1900s and large windows showcasing the Tonahutu Creek just outside. The menu features game, seafood, and poultry

dishes, all impeccably prepared and presented. The bar specializes in flavored martinis. On sunny days, sit riverside on the patio.

The reliable **Sagebrush BBQ & Grill** (1101 Grand Ave., 970/627-1404, www.sagebrushbbq.com, 8am-9pm Sun.-Thurs., 8am-10pm Fri.-Sat., $7-30) remains open year-round, even when most other establishments are closed for the season. Expect a menu of satisfying favorites, including ribs, burgers, steaks, and sandwiches. A bucket of peanuts is complimentary at each table; you're invited to brush the shells onto the floor. The Sagebrush is located on the site of the original Grand County jail; in the front dining room, cell bars dating back to the late 1800s are part of the decor.

If you're craving burgers, head to family-friendly **Squeaky B's** (1000 Grand Ave., 970/798-8221, squeakybs.com, 11am-7pm daily summer, $10-15). Natural ingredients from Colorado (and the owner's family ranch) are homemade into craft burgers, farm-fresh salads, and milkshakes, which come in boozy versions for adults. Order boxed meals to go for excursions into Rocky or out on Grand Lake.

Accommodations and Camping

There are **no overnight lodgings** in Rocky Mountain National Park. For lodges, hotels, and cabins, you must go to **Estes Park,** the larger town flanking the east side, or **Grand Lake,** the smaller town to the west.

Inside the Park
Campgrounds

Camping is the only option for overnighting inside the park. All campsites have picnic tables and firepits with grates; some have tent pads and bear boxes for food storage. Campgrounds have potable

Estes Park

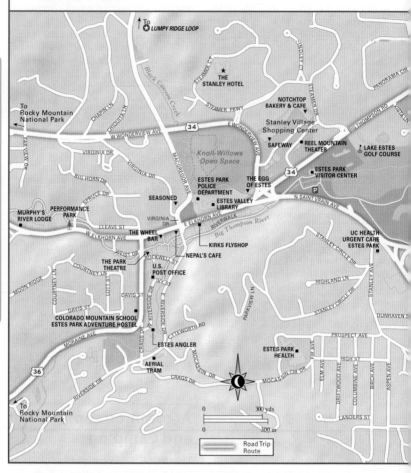

water, flush or vault toilets, and firewood sales. Dump stations for RVs are at Moraine Park, Glacier Basin, and Timber Creek. Hookups are not available inside the park. Campgrounds do not have cell reception. **Reservations** (877/444-6777, www.recreation.gov) are accepted six months in advance for Moraine Park, Glacier Basin, and Aspenglen Campgrounds. Timber Creek and Longs Peak Campgrounds are first come, first served.

East Side
Moraine Park Campground (Bear Lake Rd., 2.5 mi/4 km from the Beaver Meadows Entrance Station, 244 sites summer, 77 sites winter, RV limit 40 ft/12 m, $20-30) is the busiest campground in the park. Although you can make reservations for summer, winter is first come, first served (no water). Most sites are pleasantly shaded under a canopy of trees spared from the 2020 East Troublesome Fire. Nearby are hiking trails, ranger-led

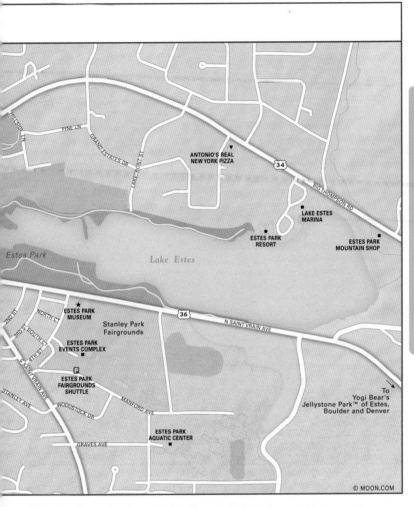

ANTONIO'S REAL
NEW YORK PIZZA

34

BIG THOMPSON RD

LAKE ESTES
MARINA

ESTES PARK
RESORT

ESTES PARK
MOUNTAIN SHOP

Estes Park

Lake Estes

ESTES PARK
MUSEUM

NORTH CT

Stanley Park
Fairgrounds

ESTES PARK
EVENTS COMPLEX

P
ESTES PARK
FAIRGROUNDS
SHUTTLE

36

N SAINT VRAIN AVE

WOODSTOCK DR

MANFORD AVE

STANLEY AVE

ESTES PARK
AQUATIC CENTER

GRAVES AVE

To
Yogi Bear's
Jellystone Park™ of Estes,
Boulder and Denver

HILLSIDE LN

PINE LN

GRAND ESTATES DR

LAKE FRONT ST

© MOON.COM

evening programs at the outdoor amphitheater, and shuttle stops. Four campsites—A39, A40, A41, and A42—are wheelchair-accessible.

The effects of bark beetle infestation are obvious in **Glacier Basin Campground** (Bear Lake Rd., 6 mi/9.7 km south from the Beaver Meadows Entrance Station, 150 sites, late May-early Sept., RV limit 35 ft/11 m, $30), where the trees have been wiped out in the campground's C, D, and group loops, leaving no shade. Campsites

A33, A35, B60, and B61 are wheelchair-accessible. A shuttle stop is located at the campsite entrance and the Park & Ride is across Bear Lake Road. On the east side of the campground, a hiking trail leads to Sprague Lake, Storm Pass, and other destinations. Ranger-led programs take place in the amphitheater most nights. **Group sites** (tents only, $40-60) lack trees, so there's not much privacy.

Aspenglen Campground (US 34 west of the Fall River Entrance Station, 53

Vicinity of Estes Park

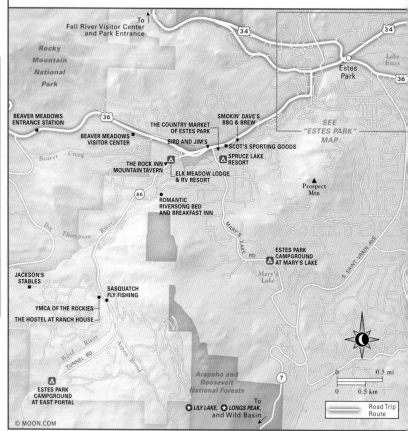

To
Fall River Visitor Center
and Park Entrance

Rocky
Mountain
National
Park

34

34

Lake
Estes

Estes
Park

36

BEAVER MEADOWS
ENTRANCE STATION

36

SMOKIN' DAVE'S
BBQ & BREW

THE COUNTRY MARKET
OF ESTES PARK

BEAVER MEADOWS
VISITOR CENTER

BIRD AND JIM'S

SCOT'S SPORTING GOODS

SEE
"ESTES PARK"
MAP

Beaver   Creek

THE ROCK INN
MOUNTAIN TAVERN

SPRUCE LAKE
RESORT

ELK MEADOW LODGE
& RV RESORT

66

ROMANTIC
RIVERSONG BED
AND BREAKFAST INN

Prospect
Mtn

Big   Thompson   River

MARY'S   LAKE   RD

ESTES PARK
CAMPGROUND
AT MARY'S LAKE

S SAINT VRAIN AVE

JACKSON'S
STABLES

SASQUATCH
FLY FISHING

Mary's
Lake

YMCA OF THE ROCKIES

THE HOSTEL AT RANCH HOUSE

Wind   River

TUNNEL RD

Aspen   Brook

Arapaho and
Roosevelt
National Forests

7

0   0.5 mi

ESTES PARK
CAMPGROUND
AT EAST PORTAL

To
LILY LAKE, LONGS PEAK,
and Wild Basin

0   0.5 km

Road Trip
Route

© MOON.COM

sites, late May-late Sept., RV limit 30 ft/9m, $30) has a more private feel than Moraine Park or Glacier Basin. Most sites have partial shade. Flanking Horseshoe Park, the campground is only a five-minute drive to Sheep Lakes, so it's easy to make dawn or dusk trips for wildlife-watching. Two campsites are wheelchair-accessible and five are walk-in tent sites.

It's tough to get a campsite at forested **Longs Peak Campground** (Longs Peak Rd., 26 sites, late June-early Sept., no RVs, $30), but it's the best locale for spending the night before climbing Longs Peak.

Campers tuck into their tents as early as 8pm; alarms buzz at 1am, sending people stumbling around in the dark packing up their gear. Sometimes sleep is fitful due to the elevation. To get to the campground from Estes Park, take CO 7 south for 9 miles (14.5) km, then drive 1 mile (1.6 km) west on Longs Peak Road.

Sprague Lake (Sprague Lake Rd. off Bear Lake Rd., year-round) is home to one **wheelchair-accessible wilderness campsite** ($30 per group). From the southwest side of the lake, take the level hard-packed gravel path (0.5 mi/0.8 km) to a short spur trail that is about 120 yards (110 m) long and dead-ends at the campsite. Tucked back in the trees, this is the only campsite at Sprague Lake, affording a good deal of privacy. Up to 12 people, including five wheelchair users (at least one required, motorized wheelchairs are OK), may camp here for up to three nights. Make reservations through the **Wilderness Office** (next to the Beaver Meadows Visitor Center, 970/586-1242). The campsite is equipped with accessible picnic tables, two large tent pads, a bear box, a storage locker for non-food items, and an accessible vault toilet. Water must be collected from the lake's inlet and purified. The site also features a charcoal grill and firepit; wood must be carried in.

West Side

The west side's only campground, 10 miles (16 km) north of Grand Lake, is **Timber Creek Campground** (US 34, 98 sites, late May-late Sept., $30). Shade is sparse, as mountain pine beetles did a number on the trees and most were removed. The first-come, first-served campground has an amphitheater for ranger-led programs. A few minutes' walk takes campers down to the shores of the Colorado River for fishing or relaxing.

Outside the Park
Estes Park

Estes Park is loaded with hotels, boutique inns, and cabins. You can find popular chain motels, too. Summer has the highest rates of the year followed by slightly lower rates in fall; prices drop further for rooms in winter and spring.

Hostels

One of the better budget options in town is a bunk at the Colorado Mountain School's **Estes Park Adventure Hostel** (341 Moraine Ave., 720/387-8944, coloradomountainschool.com, $45). The facility features 16 beds with linens in three rooms, with a large shared kitchen,

showers, bathrooms, and lounge space. Beds can be reserved online for one or more nights. Downtown Estes Park is walking distance from the hostel.

The Hostel at Ranch House (YMCA of the Rockies, 2515 Tunnel Rd., 970/586-3344, reservations 888/613-9622, ymcarockies.org, $30) has 17 beds in five dorms with shared bathrooms, a living room, and kitchen. Stays include linens and towels. The historic house is part of YMCA of the Rockies, so guests have access to activities and programs, some of which are included with the stay.

Bed-and-Breakfasts

You'll crush hard on the ★ **Romantic RiverSong Bed & Breakfast Inn** (1766 Lower Broadview Rd., 970/586-4666, www.romanticriversong.com, from $235), with 27 acres of manicured lawns, hiking trails, and riverside seating; you'll fall head over heels in love when you see your quarters: generously sized, luxurious, and full of whimsical details. Indeed, the stage is set perfectly for romance. Every room has its own theme and unique touches. The Cowboy's Delight is cozy and inviting, with barnwood walls and red plaid accents throughout; the Meadow Bright room boasts a massive rock fireplace next to a two-person jetted tub. Breakfast is served in a dining room bathed in sunlight and features such favorites as Giddyup Grits and Mountain Man Stuffed French Toast. Your choices for lazy afternoon activities include lawn chess and a streamside massage.

Hotels

History may have shaped ★ **The Stanley Hotel** (333 Wonderview Ave., 970/577-4000 or 800/976-1377, www.stanleyhotel.com, from $259) but today it is a collection of properties, including a boutique lodge neighboring the main hotel, extended-stay accommodations, nearby condominiums, and a lodge that is a 10-minute drive from the main grounds. To stay in the historic hotel is to be in the

center of everything (everything paranormal and ghostly, that is). Standard rooms are outfitted with handsome wood furniture and beds are comfortable, with bright white sheets and soft blankets. Reserve rooms well ahead of a visit, especially if you have plans to arrive in October, the busiest month at the hotel. Room 217, the room where Stephen King stayed when he was inspired to write his novel *The Shining*, usually books up for October 31 several years in advance. Plan to sip one of the 1,000 expressions of whiskey at the whiskey bar (10am-1:30am) in the **Cascades Restaurant.** Pooches are not allowed in the hotel but are treated like royalty in the boutique rooms and suites of **The Lodge at Stanley Hotel** (from $349) next door.

Lodges
Murphy's River Lodge (481 W. Elkhorn Ave., 970/480-5081, www.murphysriverlodge.com, from $140) has the luxury of being right on Fall River, where you can enjoy a walk along the water as you go into town for dinner. Appealing mountain modern rooms come in many configurations, plus condos, and can match the needs of single travelers, couples, and families. It also has accessible rooms, dog-friendly accommodations, and several vacation homes. Picnic areas have barbecues and firepits. The indoor pool is great for the kids; adults will also enjoy the hot tub.

Resorts
★ **YMCA of the Rockies** (2515 Tunnel Rd., 970/586-3344, reservations 888/613-9622, ymcarockies.org, lodge rooms from $155, cabins from $170) spreads across an immense property adjacent to Rocky Mountain National Park with mountain views and tons of activities. It's centered around a historic log lodge,

Top to bottom: Asplenglen Campground; Timber Creek Campground; lodge at YMCA of the Rockies

Stanley Hotel

The Stanley Hotel in Estes Park

When you drive into Estes Park, there is no missing **The Stanley Hotel** (333 Wonderview Ave., 970/577-4000 or 800/976-1377, www.stanleyhotel.com). With a brilliant white exterior, red roof, dome-topped cupola, and grand veranda, the multistory, Georgian-style hotel is eye-catching.

The founder of The Stanley was Freelan Oscar Stanley, who was better known as F. O. He and his twin brother, Francis Edgar (F. E.) invented the Stanley Steamer steam car, developed their own highly coveted line of violins, and created a piece of photographic equipment purchased by the Eastman Kodak Company.

After he received a diagnosis of tuberculosis in 1903, F. O. traveled from the East Coast to Estes Park to experience the reportedly curative properties of high-altitude air. He bounced back from ill health in a short time and subsequently became active in the community. The Stanley, which opened for business in 1909, first served as luxurious accommodations for F. O. and his wife Flora's high-society East Coast friends. The hotel thrived for many decades but started showing signs of age in the 1970s. Enter author Stephen King in 1974. After spending just one night at the hotel, he was inspired to pen his now famous book, *The Shining*. From its early days, there was anecdotal evidence that The Stanley might be haunted, but King put the property on the map as a paranormal hot spot. Today, people from all over the world stay at The Stanley in hopes of hearing, seeing, smelling, or feeling something unusual in its rooms and hallways. The 4th floor of the hotel, in particular, is noted for ghostly occurrences. There is even a resident psychic in the building. Night tours and elaborate Halloween celebrations (all open to the public, not just overnight guests) routinely sell out.

Advance reservations for any activity, meal, or overnight stay at The Stanley are highly recommended. Those without reservations can still stroll the hotel grounds for free—don't miss *The Shining*-inspired hedge maze out front—and wander about the lobby, where an old Stanley steam car is parked.

with a quiet location outside town that provides opportunities to watch wildlife. The complex has hotel-style rooms in nine different two-story lodges and more than 250 cabins with 2-4 bedrooms and full kitchens. Both the rooms and cabins have private bathrooms; all cabins have gas or wood fireplaces. None of the facilities have air-conditioning. For June-November stays, you can make reservations for lodge rooms starting January 1; you'll need to wait until the first Wednesday in April to book cabins. For December-May stays, you can reserve lodge rooms starting July 1 and cabins starting the first Wednesday in October. Amenities include an indoor swimming pool, restaurant, café, dog park, and walking paths. Spring through fall, outdoor activities include a climbing wall, archery, hiking, yoga, horseback riding, fishing, kids and family programs, tennis, mini-golf, volleyball, and basketball. Activities change seasonally; some are included in the rate.

For anyone spending time boating or paddling Lake Estes, **The Estes Park Resort** (1700 Big Thompson Ave., 970/577-6400 or 855/377-3778, www. theestesparkresort.com, from $263) is utterly convenient. It sits right on the waterfront next to the marina that rents pontoon boats and paddleboards. The resort has 54 rooms and suites, some with lake views. Clusters of wooden Adirondack chairs circle two gas fire pits where you can enjoy sunsets over the lake and mountain views. A biking and hiking trail departs from the hotel to circle Lake Estes. You can rent cruiser bikes from the marina.

Campgrounds

Just half a mile from the Beaver Meadows Visitor Center, **Elk Meadow Lodge & RV Resort** (1665 CO 66, 970/586-5342, elk-meadowrv.com, early May-early Oct., tent sites $40-44, RVs $75-81) offers the RV hookups closest to the national park. Amenities include a swimming pool and live entertainment on most weekends in the lodge.

Estes Valley Recreation and Park District (evrpd.colorado.gov, late May-mid-Oct., $45-65) operates two campgrounds for tents and RVs. Partial and full hookups are available, as are accessible campsites. Showers are coin-operated and there are accessible bathrooms. Make **reservations** (800/964-7806, www. reserveamerica.com) 180 days prior to arrival. You can count on lots of sun exposure at **Estes Park Campground at Marys Lake** (2120 Marys Lake Rd., 970/577-1026, 120 sites), which has a swimming pool, small store, and a playground.

Estes Park Campground at East Portal (3420 Tunnel Rd., 970/586-4188, 68 sites, late May-late Sept., RV limit 22 ft/6.7 m, tents $45, RVs $55-80) has some shaded sites for tents or RVs. Amenities include a playground; ice and firewood are for sale. You can make reservations six months in advance via Reserve America (www.reserveamerica.com).

Spruce Lake Resort (1050 Marys Lake Rd., 970/586-2889, sprucelakerv.com, May-early Oct., $73-80) sits on a lake stocked with rainbow trout. There's a mini-golf course, heated outdoor swimming pool, and hot tub. The 123 RV sites have partial or full hookups. There are no tent sites.

You will feel like you're at summer camp all over again at **Yogi Bear's Jellystone Park of Estes Campground** (5495 US 36, 970/586-4230, www. jellystoneofestes.com, early May-early Oct., $65-98), several miles southeast of downtown Estes Park. The impressive list of family-friendly activities offered in the summer includes wagon rides, scavenger hunts, and movie nights. Tent sites and RV sites line up in rows, nose to tail, along the edges of the campground's roads.

Grand Lake

Grand Lake lodgings are packed in summer, so make reservations **6-12 months** in advance.

Lodges and Cabins

The Historic Rapids Lodge and Restaurant (210 Rapids Ln., 970/627-3707, www.rapidslodge.com) appeals to a wide range of visitors. The century-old lodge consists of a collection of guest rooms ($98-232) and suites ($99-178). Each unit has unique decor, ranging from vintage to contemporary furnishings. The Tonahutu guest room is a favorite, with its large windows; it's also the only lodge room with a king bed. Occupying the entire top floor of the main building is the Treehouse Suite, a cozy retreat with raspberry-hued carpeting. The lodge is **adults only.** The North Inlet trailhead is less than a 10-minute walk from the lodge.

Bordered by Rocky on three sides with a stop-you-in-your-tracks view of the lake, the classic ★ **Grand Lake Lodge** (15500 US 34, 970/627-3967, www.highwaywestvacations.com, late May-mid-Oct., $145-380) has served guests since 1920. Right outside the west entrance to the park, the lodge was once a vacation spot for Henry Ford. The cabin he stayed in, one of 70 on the property, is named for him; it has some of the nicest furnishings of any of the accommodations. There's a beautiful outdoor swimming pool. Other on-site recreational pursuits include horseshoes, volleyball, table tennis, and billiards. Breakfast, lunch, and dinner are served seven days a week. Cabins can book up a year in advance for summer.

Ten minutes south of Grand Lake, you can stay in restored historic log cabins with **Colorado Cabin Adventures** (12082 US 34, 970/509-0810, year-round, from $318). Seven cabins have 1-3 bedrooms. While the exteriors may be rustic, the interiors have gas fireplaces, modern kitchens, and private bathrooms. The biggest perk is the North Fork of the Colorado River, which abuts the property. You can also enjoy barbecue grills, picnic tables, and outdoor games.

Campgrounds

There are no RV hookups in the national park, but two campgrounds outside downtown Grand Lake can meet your RV needs. **Elk Creek Campground and RV Resort** (143 County Road 48, 970/627-8502, www.elkcreekcamp.com, Apr.-early Oct.) has 12 tent sites ($32), 50 RV sites with partial or full hookups ($56-62), 14 cabins ($75-85), and one tepee ($50) for overnight stays. On-site amenities include a trout pond, arcade, shower room, and dump service for RVs.

Winding River Resort (1447 County Road 491, 970/627-3215, www.windingriverresort.com, late May-Sept.) has 27 tent-only sites ($42), 40 RV sites with partial or full hookups ($55-63), four small camping cabins ($75), four larger cabins ($270-375), two lodge rooms ($135-170), and two Conestoga covered wagons ($135). The resort offers a number of unique recreational opportunities. Among them is a small museum where you can ogle sleighs and carriages that date back to the 1800s. The facility also hosts "cowboy church" on Sundays next to the Colorado River; bring your own lawn chairs.

Arapahoe National Recreation Area (970/887-4100, www.fs.usda.gov, May-early Oct., $23-39) has a few campgrounds farther afield on Shadow Mountain Lake and Granby Lake. These ultra-popular campgrounds see heavy use in summer. They have sites for tents or RVs, restrooms, and potable water. They also offer boating, paddling, and fishing access from the campground or nearby. Day-use fees ($5) are required. **Reservations** (877/444-6777, www.recreation.gov) can be made six months in advance for June-late September. **Green Ridge** (77 sites, RV limit 35 ft/11 m) is on the southern end of Shadow Mountain Lake near the dam. On Granby Lake, **Stillwater** (108 sites, 21 electrical sites, RV limit 40 ft/12 m) is on the west shore just off US 34; **Arapaho**

Bay (84 sites, RV limit 35 ft/11 m) is on the southeast arm of Grand Lake. **Sunset Point** (25 sites, RV limit 50 ft/15 m) is on the south shore of Granby Lake. Sunset Point's sites are first come, first served.

Transportation and Services

Emergency Services

Emergency phones are located at the Timber Creek Campground on the west side, the Aspenglen Campground on the east side, and the Lawn Lake trailhead on Fall River Road. In an emergency, call 911 or the park's **dispatch center** (970/586-1203).

On the west side, the closest hospital to Grand Lake is the **Middle Park Medical Center-Granby Campus** (1000 Granby Park Dr. S., Granby 970/887-5800, www. middleparkhealth.org), which is 15 miles (24 km) south in Granby.

For medical emergencies on the east side, go to urgent care in Estes Park: **Estes Park Health** (420 Steamer Dr., 970/577-4500, eph.org) or **UCHealth Urgent Care-Estes Park** (Timberline Medical Center, 131 Stanley Ave., Ste. 202, 970/586-2343, www.uchealth.org). Estes Park Health also has an **emergency room** (555 Prospect Ave., 970/586-2317).

Gas

There are no gas stations inside the park. There are numerous places to fill up in Estes Park and Grand Lake.

Cell Service

Cell service is unreliable along Trail Ridge Road and Old Fall River Road. Coverage is nonexistent along CO 7, from Lily Lake south to the town of Lyons, and at all park campgrounds. For Verizon subscribers, cell phone coverage is usually good in Grand Lake. Reception with other carriers can be inconsistent.

Tours

Wildside 4x4 Tours (970/586-8687, www. wildside4x4.com, year-round) offers Trail Ridge Road, wildlife, sunset, and winter photo tours.

Yellow Wood Guiding (303/775-5484, www.ywguiding.com, year-round) specializes in private nature, sightseeing, wildlife safaris, and photography tours.

Thomas Mangan Photography (303/517-5325, www.thomasmangan. com), a well-known landscape photographer, offers private photo tours and instruction for up to three participants.

Tour Estes Park (303/260-8134, tour-estespark.com, year-round, from $50) is a local one-man operation led by Bruce Davies. Tours may be custom-tailored to include sightseeing, hiking, fishing, or snowshoeing around Estes Park.

Getting Around
Shuttles

From late spring until early fall, the best (and most eco-friendly) mode of transport on the east side is the park's **shuttle bus** system, which runs. This **free service** helps reduce traffic congestion at trailheads and also makes some great one-way hikes possible. The park's shuttle service is only offered in the **Bear Lake** region.

The **Hiker Shuttle Express Route** (7:30am-8pm daily late May-mid-Sept., weekends only mid-Sept.-mid-Oct.) runs from the Estes Park Visitor Center to the Park & Ride. A park pass is needed to ride into the park from town.

The **Bear Lake Route** (7am-7:30pm daily late May-mid-Oct.) takes passengers to the Park & Ride, Bierstadt Lake trailhead, Glacier Gorge trailhead, and Bear Lake.

The **Moraine Park Route** (7am-7:30pm daily late May-mid-Oct.) makes stops at the Park & Ride, Sprague Lake, Glacier Basin Campground, Hollowell Park, Tuxedo Park, Moraine Park Campground C Loop, Cub Lake trailhead, and Fern Lake Bus Stop.

Outside the Park

The **Estes Park Free Shuttle System** (970/577-9900, www.visitestespark.com, 9am-8:30pm daily July-early Oct.) operates a fleet of buses and a street trolley that make more than 55 stops throughout town on five routes. Locations include campgrounds, hotels, Lake Estes, restaurants, and the Estes Valley Community Center. All shuttles originate from the Estes Park Visitor Center (500 Big Thompson Ave.). Once in town, pick up a copy of the shuttle schedule and map from the visitors center or check the website.

Mountain Transit Adventures (MTA, 970/888-1227, www.mtagrandlake. wordpress.com, year-round) provides on-demand shuttle service in 40-passenger buses and 12-passenger vans for visitors to Grand Lake. Pricing varies based on distances and number of riders. MTA shuttles passengers around Grand Lake, Rocky Mountain National Park, and to and from the Amtrak station in Granby.

Highlights

★ **Stroll down the 16th Street Mall:** Enjoy the vibe of this bustling street that blends historic and modern architecture in a pedestrian-friendly zone with shops and restaurants (page 568).

★ **Visit the Denver Art Museum:** This striking arrowhead-shaped museum houses a massive collection that includes Indigenous art (page 568).

★ **Admire the flowers at the Denver Botanic Gardens:** Relish this urban oasis teeming with 34,000 different plants (page 572).

★ **Wander through City Park:** This large park is home to a zoo, a museum, two lakes, free jazz concerts, and some of the best views in town (page 573).

★ **Rock out at Red Rocks Amphitheatre:** Beneath a circle of stones, enjoy an unforgettable concert with perfect acoustics (page 577).

★ **See a show at the Denver Center for the Performing Arts:** Attend an evening performance of one of Colorado's renowned companies of dance, music, opera, and theater (page 577).

★ **Browse the shops at Larimer Square:** Wander this spirited shopping district with colorful art galleries and exclusive boutiques (page 579).

★ **Hike or climb the Flatirons:** These rocky spires shoot up from the forested hillside above Boulder, attracting hikers, climbers, and those who just want to admire them from town (pages 585, 592, and 593).

★ **Ramble through Chautauqua:** This historic complex has views of the Flatirons and lots of paths for strolling (page 585).

★ **Have an adventure at Eldorado Canyon State Park:** Hike, climb, or picnic in this spectacular canyon surrounded by panoramic views (page 589).

Denver and Boulder

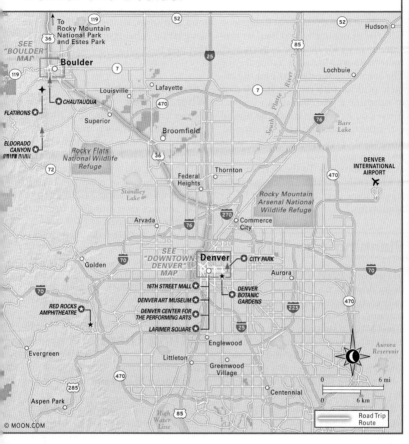

© MOON.COM

The Mile High City is Colorado's cosmopolitan core. A gateway to the mountains, Denver sprawls vibrantly along the foothills. The city's river network is the basis for its metropolitan trail system, which makes it easy to travel between fascinating attractions, trendy restaurants, chic shopping districts, and thriving art outlets. Nearby, the foothills hold the incomparable outdoor Red Rocks Amphitheatre, where the famed rock formations make for outstanding acoustics.

The city core, an architectural mix of ornate historical buildings adjacent to modern glass skyscrapers, bustles from morning until well after dark. Shopping, dining, and nightlife lend a vibrancy to the streets, with pedestrian blocks adding even more attraction. The nationally acclaimed Denver Performing Arts Complex serves as the hub for music, dance, opera, and plays. Everywhere you walk, street art appears, tantalizing the mind and entertaining the spirit.

North of Denver, the Front Range foothills rise dramatically, and Boulder provides a center for outdoor recreation en route to Rocky Mountain National Park. The scenery is spectacular and the climate is ideal, with more than 300 days of sunshine a year. Bohemian Boulder thrives on its reputation as the brainiest, fittest, and foodiest city around. Restaurants, brewpubs, and concerts are just steps away from college campuses and tech start-ups. To the west, though, is what truly sets these cities apart: the jagged, snow-covered peaks of the Rocky Mountains.

Planning Your Time

In Denver, **1-2 days** will suffice to see the major downtown attractions, sample locally crafted beers, enjoy innovative restaurants, and stroll along the busy 16th Street Mall. In **summer,** which draws the most visitors, the days can be hot, but the heat is usually broken by midafternoon thunderstorms. Temperatures are usually mild in **spring** and **fall,** both great times to visit with the perk of lower prices for lodging. In **winter,** which sees the fewest crowds, Denver's weather can be cold and icy.

If you've got the time to spare, **three days** in Boulder is ideal. Crowds descend in **summer,** especially on holiday weekends. For hiking, visit in **autumn,** when the weather is most stable. September and October are ideal, with warm, sunny days followed by crisp nights and the aspen and cottonwoods slowly turning to gold.

Seasonal Driving Concerns

Be ready for winter conditions from fall through spring. Occasional **blizzards** can disrupt transportation even during fall and spring. In winter, **storms** deliver snow and ice. Colorado has a traction law

that requires one of the following during winter storms: a 4WD or AWD vehicle; carrying **chains;** or having tires with a **mud and snow, winter,** or **all-weather** designation. Chains or alternative traction may be required as a last resort before highways close.

Reservations and Where to Stay

Denver and Boulder are just 30 miles apart, so you can base yourself in either city and easily hop back and forth between them. If you want city vibes, stay in Denver. If you want quicker access to trails for hiking or mountain biking, stay in Boulder. In either case, it's wise to make advance reservations for summer **six months in advance.**

To **camp at Colorado state parks,** you'll need to make reservations. The booking window for any given date opens **six months** to the day ahead. Sites in summer go quickly. Book by phone (800/244-5613) or online (www.cpwshop.com).

Getting There

Car
From Rocky Mountain National Park

US 36 is the shortest route from Rocky's eastern gateway of **Estes Park** to downtown Denver. The drive, which goes through Boulder, is 60 miles (94 km) and takes 1.5 hours.

If you're coming to Denver from the park's western gateway of **Grand Lake,** the drive is 100 miles (160 km) and can take 2-3 hours. From US 34, head to US 40, then take I-70 east into Denver. In the winter, and especially on weekends, I-70 routinely becomes clogged with traffic because it's the main thoroughfare for many of Colorado's ski resorts.

From Grand Teton National Park

From **Jackson,** Wyoming, outside Grand Teton National Park, the drive to Denver

One Day in Denver

Pack in bustling city experiences on your day in Denver. It's possible to follow this entire itinerary on foot.

Morning
Start with breakfast at the **Delectable Egg.** Afterward, walk 10 minutes south to the **Denver Art Museum** to take in the exhibits, especially the Indigenous art.

Afternoon
Head a short distance north to the **16th Street Mall.** After grabbing lunch at an outdoor café, spend the afternoon strolling the promenade, shopping, and admiring the city's architecture. You can also stop at nearby **Larimer Square** and admire historic **Union Station.**

Evening
Dine early at **Bistro Vendome** before taking in an evening of opera, theater, ballet, or symphonic music at the **Denver Center for the Performing Arts.**

With More Time
Spend a day in **Boulder,** hiking the **Flatirons,** picnicking at **Eldorado Canyon State Park,** and sipping tea at the **Boulder Dushanbe Teahouse.**

---

is 510 miles (820 km) and takes 8.5 hours. Go south on US 189/191 to Hoback Junction, then stay left on US 191 to Rock Springs. From there, jump east onto I-80 to Laramie and then south on US 287 to Fort Collins, where CO 14 connects with I-25 to continue south to Denver.

Air

One of the busiest airports in the country, **Denver International Airport** (DEN, 8500 Peña Blvd., 303/342-2000 or 800/247-2336, www.flydenver.com) is serviced by 20 airlines and acts as a hub for United, Southwest, and Great Lakes Airlines. It sits about 30 minutes (25 mi/40 km) east of downtown.

All of the major **car rental companies** have depots at or near the airport. Most require you to first visit their desk on Level 5, then ride a shuttle a short distance to the depot. Shuttles pick up and drop off from Level 5, Island 4, outside doors 505-513 on the east side and 504-512 on the west side. Denver also has several **car-share companies,** including **eGo** (1536 Wynkoop St., #101, 303/720-1185,

carshare.org), with multiple locations for vehicle pickup.

Airport Transportation
Operated by **RTD** (303/299-6000, www.rtd-denver.com), the **University of Colorado A-Line train** ($10.50 one-way) takes about 35 minutes to travel between the airport and downtown Denver's **Union Station** (1701 Wynkoop St.), the main transportation hub. Most trains run every 15 minutes. The train picks up at the Transit Center on the south side of the main terminal. Train tickets are available for purchase from kiosks.

Several hotels offer **shuttle service** from the airport (Level 5, Island 3). Shuttles usually visit both east and west terminal locations before departing. **Taxis** pick up and drop off from Level 5, Island 1.

Train
Amtrak (800/872-7245, www.amtrak.com) offers daily service to Denver's **Union Station** (1701 Wynkoop St.) along the California Zephyr route. Tickets are

available online or in person at the station. The route originates in Chicago in the east and in the San Francisco Bay Area in the west.

Bus

Greyhound (www.greyhound.com) and the Colorado Department of Transportation's **Bustang** (800/900-3011, www.ridebustang.com) offer regional service between **Union Station** (1701 Wynkoop St.) and locations such as Colorado Springs, Vail, and Estes Park, on the eastern boundary of Rocky Mountain National Park.

The **Regional Transportation District** (303/299-6000, www.rtd-denver.com, from $3) operates **buses** and **light-rail trains** that transport passengers throughout Denver and connects with regional bus lines to Boulder and Fort Collins. The concourse at **Union Station** (1701 Wynkoop St.) serves 16 routes, including the four Flatirons Flyer routes to Boulder and the free MetroRide and 16th Street MallRide.

Sights

Downtown
Museum of Contemporary Art Denver

Right away, the **Museum of Contemporary Art Denver** (1485 Delgany St., 303/298-7554, mcadenver.org, noon-7pm Tues.-Fri., 10am-5pm Sat.-Sun., $10) hits you with an eye-catching "bleeding heart" sculpture, *Toxic Schizophrenia,* mounted beside the museum's entrance. Everything about this museum is modern, from its sleek, glassy exterior to its thought-provoking exhibits by mostly Colorado artists. The museum's rooftop café is a great place to enjoy amazing city views along with lunch or cocktails.

Black American West Museum & Heritage Center

Originally founded to tell the story of the West's Black cowboys, the **Black American West Museum & Heritage Center** (3091 California St., 720/242-7428, www.bawmhc.org, 10am-2pm Fri.-Sat., $7-10) has broadened its scope to teach about the many crucial roles filled by African Americans during the United States' westward expansion. Exhibits cover the Buffalo Soldiers, Black military units that played a crucial role in settling the West; Dr. Justina Ford, Denver's first female doctor of the early 20th century; and Henry Parker, one of the first miners to discover gold in Colorado.

★ 16th Street Mall

Along the mile-long pedestrian promenade of the **16th Street Mall,** you'll find outdoor cafés, bars, restaurants, and shops. The space is adorned with public art and small gardens. One notable sight is the 1909 **D & F Tower,** a partial replica of the famous Campanile of St. Mark's in Venice. After dark, millions of lights wrapping the trees blink on, adding vibrancy to the bustling scene.

Up and down 16th Street, electric **MallRide buses** (www.rtd-denver.com, daily, free) run every few minutes and stop at every corner. Horse-drawn carriages and a few pedi-cabs are also available (for a fee).

Union Station

In LoDo (Lower Downtown), **Union Station** (1701 Wynkoop, 303/592-6712, unionstationindenver.com) is one of the best people-watching places. Restaurants and bars, both indoors and outdoors, amp up the food scene, and small shops offer places to browse for books, local crafts, jewelry, souvenirs, and gifts. Periodic live music and other events add to the fun. The century-old landmark also still functions as a train station serving light-rail and Amtrak.

Capitol Hill
★ Denver Art Museum

The **Denver Art Museum** (100 W. 14th

Ave., 720/865-5000, denverartmuseum.org, 10am-5pm Tues.-Thurs. and Sat.-Sun., 10am-8pm Fri., $8-10) is best known for its striking, geometric Frederic C. Hamilton Building, designed by architect Daniel Libeskind. Completed in 2006, this metallic, arrowhead-shaped complex houses contemporary, African, and Oceanic art collections. The museum typically displays more than a dozen rotating exhibits at any given time, as well as portions of its permanent collections, including an American Indian gallery whose holdings represent more than 100 Indigenous North American groups. The museum also has an extensive Western American art collection that includes *In the Enemy's Country* by Charles M. Russell, Frederic Remington's *The Cheyenne,* and *Long Jakes,* an oil painting by Charles Deas, as anchors.

U.S. Mint

Denver's branch of the **U.S. Mint** (320 W. Colfax Ave., 303/405-4761 or 800-872-6468, www.usmint.gov) is one of the federal government's four official places where it makes money—more than 50 million coins per day! Established in 1863 as an assay office, this branch makes all denominations of circulating coins and stores silver bullion. The 45-minute **tour** (8am-3:30pm Mon.-Thurs., free) covers the mint's long history and all of the steps involved in manufacturing coins. The gift shop sells commemorative coins. Register online for tours far in advance, as space is limited. Weekday mornings have the most availability.

Molly Brown House Museum

The beautiful home of *Titanic* survivor Margaret "Molly" Brown is now the **Molly Brown House Museum** (1340 Pennsylvania St., 303/832-4092, www.mollybrown.org, 11am-4pm daily, closed Mon. in winter, $12-16). After Molly

Top to bottom: D & F Tower on the 16th Street Mall; historic Union Station; Denver Art Museum

DENVER

Downtown Denver

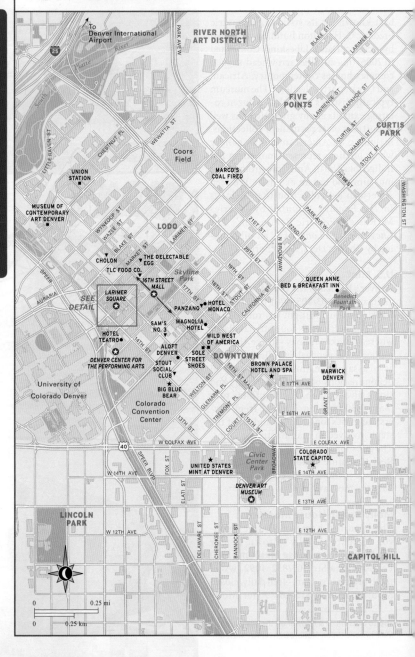

To Denver International Airport

RIVER NORTH ART DISTRICT

PARK AVE W

FIVE POINTS

CURTIS PARK

Coors Field

MARCO'S COAL FIRED

UNION STATION

MUSEUM OF CONTEMPORARY ART DENVER

LODO

QUEEN ANNE BED & BREAKFAST INN

Skyline Park

CHOLON
THE DELECTABLE EGG
TLC FOOD CO.
16TH STREET MALL

LARIMER SQUARE

SEE DETAIL

PANZANO
HOTEL MONACO

SAM'S NO. 3
MAGNOLIA HOTEL

HOTEL TEATRO

WILD WEST OF AMERICA

DENVER CENTER FOR THE PERFORMING ARTS

ALOFT DENVER
SOLE STREET SHOES

DOWNTOWN

STOUT SOCIAL CLUB

BROWN PALACE HOTEL AND SPA

WARWICK DENVER

University of Colorado Denver

BIG BLUE BEAR

Colorado Convention Center

W COLFAX AVE

E 17TH AVE

E 16TH AVE

E COLFAX AVE

UNITED STATES MINT AT DENVER

Civic Center Park

COLORADO STATE CAPITOL

E 14TH AVE

W 14TH AVE

DENVER ART MUSEUM

E 13TH AVE

LINCOLN PARK

W 12TH AVE

E 12TH AVE

CAPITOL HILL

0   0.25 mi

0   0.25 km

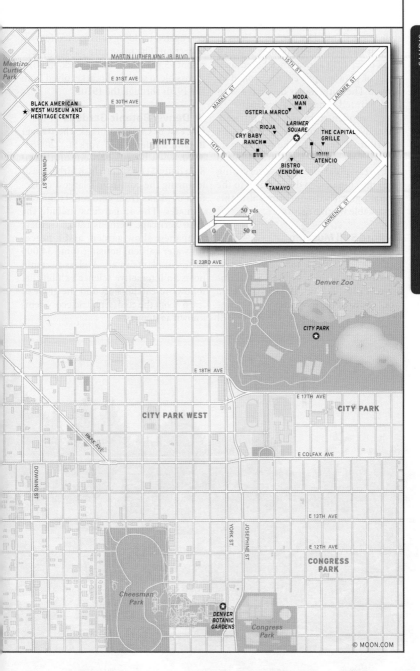

MARTIN LUTHER KING JR BLVD

Mestizo-Curtis Park

E 31ST AVE

★ BLACK AMERICAN WEST MUSEUM AND HERITAGE CENTER

E 30TH AVE

WHITTIER

DOWNING ST

Inset map (Larimer Square area):

15TH ST

MARKET ST

LARIMER ST

▼ MODA MAN

OSTERIA MARCO ▼

RIOJA ▼

LARIMER SQUARE ✪

14TH

CRY BABY RANCH ■

THE CAPITAL GRILLE

JOHN ATENCIO ■

■ VE

BISTRO VENDÔME ▼

▼ TAMAYO

LAWRENCE ST

0   50 yds

0   50 m

E 23RD AVE

Denver Zoo

CITY PARK ✪

E 18TH AVE

CITY PARK WEST

E 17TH AVE   CITY PARK

PARK AVE

E COLFAX AVE

DOWNING ST

E 13TH AVE

YORK ST

JOSEPHINE ST

E 12TH AVE

CONGRESS PARK

Cheesman Park

✪ DENVER BOTANIC GARDENS

Congress Park

© MOON.COM

and her husband, mining engineer J. J. Brown, struck it rich in the Little Johnny Mine, they purchased this Queen Anne-style home flanked by two stone lions in 1894. It has been painstakingly restored to its circa-1910 appearance based on a series of photographs commissioned by Brown. The entryway is decorated with gold-painted Anaglypta wallpaper, a grand wooden staircase, and intricate stained-glass windows. The Browns entertained guests in the formal parlor, with its magnificent grand piano and fuzzy polar-bear rug. Everything from the china-laden dining table to the emerald-green bedroom brings alive this remarkable woman's story.

Clyfford Still Museum

The **Clyfford Still Museum** (1250 Bannock St., 720/354-4880, clyffordstill-museum.org, 10am-5pm Tues.-Sat., 11am-5pm Fri., $6-10) features the iconoclastic work of one of the most important painters of the 20th century. Clyfford Still pioneered abstract expressionist art in the years following World War II. More than 3,100 paintings are displayed in a corrugated building constructed for this collection. The museum's paintings represent 95 percent of Still's work, making it possible to see how his art evolved from the 1920s through the 1970s.

★ Denver Botanic Gardens

Just east of Cheesman Park, the **Denver Botanic Gardens** (1007 York St., 720/865-3500, www.botanicgardens.org, 9am-8pm daily, $11-15) are a lush, urban oasis featuring the continent's largest collection of plants from cold and temperate climates. The 45 gardens include the 1986 Xeriscape Demonstration Garden, a Japanese show garden, and a peaceful water garden, housing some 34,000 different plants in all. A glass pyramid hosts an interactive science exhibit that follows researchers around the globe to learn about the cold, semiarid ecosystems known as steppes.

Denver Botanic Gardens

Greater Denver
★ City Park

One of the city's oldest public spaces, **City Park** (2001 Colorado Blvd., www. denvergov.org) is a beautiful place to relax, picnic, and enjoy mountain views. The largest of Denver's many parks, it's best known for hosting the Denver Zoo and the Denver Museum of Nature and Science. It acts a recreation hub with the Mile High Loop, a tree-lined, walking and running path, a golf course, tennis courts, fountains, flower beds, and a lake where you can rent kayaks and pedal boats.

Denver Zoo

The **Denver Zoo** (2300 Steele St., 720/337-1400, denverzoo.org, 9am-4pm daily, $10-15) houses more than 4,000 animals from all corners of the globe. The zoo pioneered the use of natural-looking enclosures rather than cages to contain the animals. The enormous Elephant Passage can host up to 12 elephants along with other creatures like Indian rhinos, clouded leopards, Malayan tapirs, and agile gibbons swinging in the trees.

Denver Museum of Nature and Science

The **Denver Museum of Nature and Science** (2001 Colorado Blvd., 303/370-6000, www.dmns.org, 9am-5pm daily, $15-20) is filled with natural wonders, from sparkling crystals and golden nuggets found in Colorado to ancient Egyptian mummies. Displays include two fantastic permanent exhibits. *Space Odyssey,* where you can pilot a space shuttle and view a Martian canyon, and *Prehistoric Journeys,* which travels through 3.5 billion years of Earth history to trace the evolution of life. Part of the exhibit is a laboratory where many of the fossils on display were prepared, including the diplodocus skeleton that's locked in battle with a stegosaurus. Kids love the hands-on Discovery Zone. The museum charges extra fees ($4-9) for the planetarium, IMAX, and special exhibits.

Wings Over the Rockies Air & Space Museum

Housed in a 1930s-era hangar on the grounds of a former air force base, the **Wings Over the Rockies Air & Space Museum** (7711 E. Academy Blvd., 303/360-5360, wingsmuseum.org, 10am-5pm Mon.-Sat., noon-5pm Sun., $10-17) is a highlight for space and science buffs. The museum features models of moon-landing equipment, a real moon rock, and four dozen space and aircraft, including a 1966 F-4E Phantom II jet, a 1964 F-104C Starfighter, and—for *Star Wars* fans—an X-Wing fighter that George Lucas used to promote his *Star Wars* trilogy.

Recreation

Multiuse Trails

On the edge of LoDo, several paths for walkers, runners, and bikers radiate out from **Confluence Park** (2250 15th St.), where Cherry Creek and the South Platte River join. Close to the park, you can rent bikes from **Confluence Kayaks** (2301 7th St., 303/433-3676, www.confluencekayaks. com, 10am-7pm Mon.-Fri., 10am-6pm Sat., noon-5pm Sun., from $25).

The **Cherry Creek Trail** (24.6 mi/39.6 km) is a mostly paved path from Confluence Park south through **Cherry Creek State Park** (4201 S. Parker Rd., Aurora, cpw.state.co.us, 303/690-1166, 5am-10pm daily). The paved **South Platte River Trail** follows the South Platte River south through downtown Denver to the suburb of Sheridan (10 mi/16 km) and north to Commerce City (10 mi/16 km). From the intersection of Hampden Avenue and South Santa Fe Boulevard,

the trail also connects with the **Bear Creek Bike Trail** (14.5 mi/23.3 km), which heads west to the town of Morrison in the Denver foothills.

Paddling

Paddlers congregate along the South Platte River, which flows from the reservoir in **Chatfield State Park** (11500 Roxborough Rd., Littleton, 303/791-5555, cpw.state.co.us, $10/vehicle) through the city. In addition to kayaking, you can also boat and fish in Chatfield Lake.

The South Platte River has multiple access points for paddlers, including **Overland Park** (Florida Ave. and S. Platte River Dr.) and **Confluence Park** (2250 15th St.), next to the REI store. Close to Confluence Park, **Confluence Kayaks** (2301 7th St., 303/433-3676, www.confluencekayaks.com, 10am-7pm Mon.-Fri., 10am-6pm Sat., noon-5pm Sun., from $40) rents tubes, white-water and inflatable kayaks, and stand-up paddleboards.

Ferril Lake at City Park

At City Park, **Ferril Lake** is the place to paddle flat water. You can rent canoes, single and double kayaks, paddleboards, and paddleboats on-site from **Wheel Fun Rental** (2001 Steele St., 720/984-8881, wheelfunrentals.com, late May-Oct., $15-30/hr).

Golf

Denver has scads of golf courses, most of which have rentals, driving ranges, putting greens, and restaurants. Two are city-owned (www.cityofdenvergolf.com, $26-48): the par 72, 18-hole **City Park Golf Course** (3181 E. 23rd Ave., 720/865-3410) at City Park, and **Willis Case Golf Course** (4999 Vrain St., 720/865-0700), northeast of downtown with great mountain views.

South of Denver, the **Fox Hollow Golf Course** (13410 W. Morrison Rd., Lakewood, 303/986-7888, www.lakewood.org, $55-86) has 27 holes on three very different nines: The Meadow features creekside fairways, The Links is a Scottish-style course, and The Canyon plunges down a narrow gulch. The 18-hole par-72 championship **Foothills Golf Course** (3901 S. Carr St., Littleton, 303/409-2400, www.foothillsgolf.org, $36-50) is a treed parkland course.

About 20 miles (32 km) south, the **Ridge at Castle Pines North** (1414 Castle Pines Pkwy., Castle Pines, 303/688-4301, www.playtheridge.com, $85-165) is an upscale course which frequently gets recognized in golf magazines.

Spectator Sports

Seeing the **Denver Broncos** play football is a high-octane experience: 76,125 orange-and-blue-clad fans toss beach balls, make waves, and scream at the top of their lungs. Dress for the weather, which can be a sunny 70°F (21°C) or a below-freezing blizzard. Games take place at **Sports Authority Field at Mile High** (1701 Bryant St., 720/258-3000, www.sportsauthorityfieldatmilehigh.com), an enormous glass-and-metal stadium. Tickets are extremely hard to get; your best bet is **Ticketmaster** (www.ticketmaster.com), which guarantees ticket authenticity. The city's Major League Lacrosse team, the **Denver Outlaws** (www.denveroutlaws.com), also plays at the stadium.

The **Colorado Rockies** play baseball at LoDo's **Coors Field** (2001 Blake St., 303/292-0200, colorado.rockies.mlb.com). A row of purple seats in the upper deck marks the mile-high elevation, making it by far the highest Major League Baseball park. You can buy cheap seats in "The Rockpile," a central section of bleachers, and drop in at the Coors-operated brewery behind the right-field stands.

The **Colorado Avalanche** (www.coloradoavalanche.com) play hockey at the **Ball Arena** (1000 Chopper Cir., 303/405-1100, www.pepsicenter.com; tickets 866/461-6556, www.altitudetickets.com).

Entertainment and Events

Nightlife

Bars and Breweries

With its 125 breweries and taprooms, it's hard to go anywhere in Denver without finding the perfect spot for a pint of craft beer. Bars and brewpubs are clustered in several hot spots, especially LoDo and Cherry Creek.

Downtown and LoDo

Outside of Union Station, **Wynkoop Brewing Company** (1634 18th St., 303/297-2700, www.wynkoop.com, 11am-close daily) was Colorado's first brewpub. One of the founding partners was John Hickenlooper, who later went on to become Denver's mayor, then the governor of Colorado. Today, Wynkoop is one of the state's largest breweries and still known for its innovative beers, which have included some unusual ingredients like green chile and gummy bears.

Denver's oldest Irish tavern, the red-doored **Nallen's Irish Pub** (1429 Market St., 303/527-0667, www.nallenspub.com, 2pm-2am daily) serves up countless pints of dark, foamy Guinness and hosts special festivities, including bagpipers and Irish dancers on St. Paddy's Day. **Blake Street Tavern** (2301 Blake St., 303/675-0505, www.blakestreettavern.com, 11am-2am Mon.-Fri., 9am-2am Sat., 10am-2am Sun.) is one of Denver's best sports bars, with 60 big-screen TVs and an underground level where you can play shuffleboard, Skee Ball, darts, and even Pac-Man and other 1980s video games.

Near Coors Field, the **Falling Rock Tap House** (1919 Blake St., 303/293-8338, fallingrocktaphouse.com, 11am-2am daily) has a large patio and 2,200 bottles of beer lining the inside walls. The enormous list of beers includes more than 75 on tap and 130 different bottled brands. Nearby, the **Star Bar** (2137 Larimer St., 720/328-2420, www.thestarbardenver.com, 4pm-1:30am daily) serves sophisticated cocktails made with top-shelf liquors, as well as canned wine made nearby at **The Infinite Monkey Theorem** (www.theinfinitemonkeytheorem.com).

Cherry Creek

In addition to a menu of Colorado-grown and raised food, **Historians Ale House** (24 Broadway, #102, 720/479-8505, historiansalehouse.com, 11am-midnight Mon.-Thurs., 11am-2am Fri., 10am-2am Sat., 10am-midnight Sun.) has 40 beers on tap.

Modeled after a German biergarten, **Lowry Beer Garden** (7577 E. Academy Blvd., 303/366-0114, lowrybeergarden.com, 11am-9pm Sun.-Mon., 11am-10pm Tues.-Thurs., 11am-11pm Fri.-Sat.) is a relaxed spot. The immense outdoor patio has communal tables plus foosball and table tennis.

Dance Clubs

Denver's hottest nightlife area is the **South of Colfax ("SoCo") Nightlife District** (bounded by Colfax Ave., Speer Blvd., and Lincoln St., https://coclubs.com). One admission gets you into seven different clubs, where you can dance to music ranging from reggae and Top 40 to R&B and hip-hop. **Milk** (1037 Broadway, 303/832-8628, 9pm-2am Wed.-Sat.) has live jazz and dancing on the rooftop lounge with panoramic city views. Upscale **Club Vinyl** (1082 Broadway, 303/860-8469, 9pm-2am Thurs.-Sat.) has four levels of dance floors and a rooftop patio. Inside a former place of worship, **The Church** (1160 N. Lincoln St., 303/832-2383, 9pm-2am Fri.-Sat.) is a unique dance club with stained-glass windows, multiple dance floors, a blasting sound system, a sushi bar, and a loyal "congregation."

LGBTQ

Blush and Blu (1526 E. Colfax Ave., 303/484-8548, blushbludenver.com, 4pm-midnight Mon.-Tues., 2pm-2am

★ Red Rocks Amphitheatre

Red Rocks Amphitheatre

In the foothills of the Rocky Mountains, **Red Rocks Amphitheatre** (18300 W. Alameda Pkwy., Morrison, 720/865-2494, redrocksonline.com, sunrise-sunset daily) blends dramatic scenery with outstanding acoustics. The outdoor venue can host almost 10,000 people for a unique concert experience with massive vertical slabs of red rock as a backdrop. This iconic concert venue regularly attracts top music stars from around the world. Big-name acts like The Beatles, Bruce Springsteen, Jimi Hendrix, Stevie Nicks, and John Legend have all performed here.

The surrounding **Red Rocks Park** has a **visitors center** (7am-7pm daily Apr.-Oct., 8am-4pm daily Nov.-Mar.) with displays about its musical history and the geologic events that created this remarkable setting. You can see the fossilized fragments of a sea serpent and flying reptiles, view dinosaur tracks, and get up-close looks at the amphitheater's two main rock slabs, Ship Rock and Creation Rock, which are both about 300 feet (90 m) tall.

To learn more about Colorado's impressive musical legacy, stop by the **Colorado Music Hall of Fame** at the park's **Trading Post** (17900 Trading Post Rd., 303/672-1273, cmhof.org, 10am-5pm daily, by donation). A series of exhibits focus on music stars with connections to the state alongside displays of historical artifacts.

Wed., noon-2am Thurs.-Fri., 11am-2am Sat.-Sun.) is part coffeehouse and part bar. It's a predominantly lesbians crowd, although everyone is welcome. Evenings feature karaoke, games, and open mic nights. **X Bar** (629 E. Colfax Ave., 303/832-2687, www.xbardenver.com, 3pm-11pm daily) has two dance floors and an outdoor patio. **Tracks** (3500 Walnut St., 303/863-7326, tracksdenver.com, 5pm-10pm Fri., 11am-10pm Sat.) is an inclusive dance and nightclub spot where allies are welcome. It features

a sound and light show, a Saturday drag brunch, and limited VIP bottle service by reservation (480/735-4691).

The Arts
★ Denver Center for the Performing Arts

The centerpiece of the city's culture and entertainment, the **Denver Center for the Performing Arts** (1400 Curtis St., 720/865-4220, www.artscomplex.com) is one of the largest performing arts centers in the country. The four-block

complex contains 10 theaters with more than 10,000 seats. It houses the opera house, the Boettcher Concert Hall, and the Buell Theatre. With a massive domed glass ceiling covering the venues, the complex dominates downtown even on nights when no shows are scheduled. The center hosts regular performances by the **Colorado Ballet** (303/837-8888, www.coloradoballet.org), **Opera Colorado** (303/468-2030, www.operacolorado.org), and the **Colorado Symphony Orchestra** (303/623-7876, coloradosymphony.org). The **Denver Center Theatre Company,** the region's largest professional theater company, produces classical and contemporary dramas, as well as a large number of world premieres. The center also features many traveling Broadway musicals, Pulitzer Prize-winning plays, and family-friendly performances. The **box office** (14th and Curtis Sts., 303/893-4100, www.denvercenter.org) sells tickets for many of these events. South of the complex, the adjoining sculpture park is worth a walk to admire *The Dancers,* a pair of 50-foot-high (15.2-m) sculptures.

Denver has some other notable troupes and diverse venues, including **Su Teatro Cultural and Performing Arts Center** (721 Santa Fe Dr., 303/296-0219, suteatro.org), which highlights Latinx cultures. The center hosts the annual **Chicano Music Festival** (July) and the **Shadow Theatre Company** (720/375-0115, thesourcedenver.org), which features African American theater.

Festivals and Events

The **Denver March Pow Wow** (www.denvermarchpowwow.org, Mar.) is a traditional social gathering that honors Indigenous heritage with workshops, intertribal and competitive dances, handmade crafts, and drumming.

With collaborative murals, a kids' art

Top to bottom: Denver Center for the Performing Arts; Larimer Square; Tattered Cover Book Store

station, seven performance stages, and dozens of art booths, the **Cherry Creek Arts Festival** (www.cherryarts.org, July) is the nation's top outdoor arts festival.

At the **Great American Beer Festival** (www.greatamericanbeerfestival.com, Oct.), visitors from around the globe flock to Denver to sample and celebrate American craft beer.

For the holiday season, Denver's Skyline Park is transformed into **Christkindl Market** (christkindlmarketdenver.com, mid-Nov.-Dec. 25), a German outdoor holiday market, complete with serenading musicians, food and craft booths, and hot mulled wine.

Shopping

Shopping Districts
★ Larimer Square
Denver's most historic block, **Larimer Square** (14th and 15th Sts. at Larimer St., www.larimersquare.com) was where miners first built after they settled along the South Platte River. Most of the square's restored buildings date to the 1880s. They house a variety of shops and restaurants, most of which are independently owned.

Eve (1413 Larimer St., 720/932-9382, www.eveinc.net, 10am-7pm Mon.-Fri., 10am-6pm Sat., noon-5pm Sun.) focuses on stylish women's clothing and accessories, including products from Papillon, Capote, and Trina Turk.

From boots and buckles to belts and bolos, **Cry Baby Ranch** (1421 Larimer St., 303/623-3979, www.crybabyranch.com, 10am-7pm Mon.-Fri., 10am-6pm Sat., noon-5pm Sun.) sells anything your inner cowgirl (or boy) might crave. **Moda Man** (1459 Larimer St., 303/862-5949, www.modaman.com, 10am-7pm Mon.-Thurs., 10am-8pm Fri.-Sat., noon-5pm Sun.) features contemporary-casual men's clothing by top fashion designers. **John Atencio** (1440 Larimer St., 303/534-4277, johnatencio.com, 10am-6pm Mon.-Fri., 10am-5pm Sat.) designs and sells beautiful, handcrafted jewelry. His shop features a sparkling selection of beautiful rings, signature pendants, and gold and silver bracelets, crosses, and earrings.

16th Street Mall
The **16th Street Mall** (Wynkoop St. to Broadway) is known for its pedestrian-friendly shopping. It's easy to stroll between the several hundred stores; if you get tired, hop on the **MallRide** (www.rtd-denver.com, daily, free), a free electric bus that stops at every block along the mall between Civic Center and Union Station.

The mall consists primarily of chain stores, especially casual clothing outlets. Scattered in between are a few more unique options. **Sole St. Shoes** (716 16th St., 303/893-5280, 10am-8pm Mon.-Sat., 10am-7pm Sun.) is a "sneaker boutique" with retro options as well as standard brands like Nike and New Balance. **Wild West of America** (715 16th St., 303/446-8640, 9am-7pm daily) sells moccasins, key chains, and dozens of other knickknacks.

In a historic LoDo building, **Tattered Cover Book Store** (1628 16th St., www.tatteredcover.com, 303/436-1070, 10am-6pm daily) carries just about every kind of book you might want, from bestsellers to Denver history and outdoor guidebooks. It often hosts author appearances. Find satellite locations in Union Station and the airport.

Cherry Creek Mall
Denver's ritziest shopping district is just east of the Denver Country Club and south of Speer Boulevard. In this area are two upscale shopping areas: the indoor **Cherry Creek Mall** (3000 E. 1st Ave., 303/388-3900, www.shopcherrycreek.com, 11am-7pm Mon.-Sat., 11am-6pm Sun.), Denver's largest, and the outdoor **Cherry Creek North** (299 Milwaukee St., Ste. 201, 303/394-2904, cherrycreeknorth.com, 10am-6pm Mon.-Sat., 11am-5pm

Sun.), which has more character and correspondingly higher prices.

Cherry Creek Mall features mostly high-end chains, including Louis Vuitton, Ralph Lauren, Tiffany & Co., and Neiman Marcus. Cherry Creek North is a more spread-out shopping and restaurant district with a great selection of fun and fashionable shops. **Little Feet** (201 University Blvd., 303/388-9535, www.littlefeetdenver.com, 10am-6pm Mon.-Sat., 11am-5pm Sun.) is a family-owned store that specializes in kids' shoes. **Title Nine** (158 Steele St., 303/321-4001, www.titlenine.com, 11am-5pm daily) features comfortable women's sportswear and casual clothing. The colorful and eclectic **Artisan Center** (2757 E. 3rd Ave., 303/333-1201, www.artisancenterdenver.com, 10am-5:30pm daily) sells cards, candles, chimes, jewelry, and scarves made by mostly local artists.

Camping and Outdoor Gear

Perched on the bank above Confluence Park is the **Denver Flagship REI** (1416 Platte St., 303/756-3100, www.rei.com, 9am-9pm Mon.-Sat., 9am-7pm Sun.). The huge brick warehouse has an enormous selection from bikes and kayaks to windbreakers, gloves, and freeze-dried backpacking meals. The flagship store includes a climbing wall, a third-floor play area for kids, and a Starbucks with a nice deck.

Food

Fine Dining

With its lion-flanked exterior and a posh, dark-wood-paneled interior, **The Capital Grille** (1450 Larimer St., 303/539-2500, www.thecapitalgrille.com, 11am-10pm Mon.-Sat., 4pm-9pm Sun., $32-76) serves up some of the fanciest food in town, including fresh Maine lobster, veal chops, and, of course, plenty of porterhouse and rib eye steak. The large wine cellar is overseen by advanced sommelier Brian Phillips.

The Hotel Monaco's restaurant **Panzano** (909 17th St., 303/296-3525, www.panzano-denver.com, 4pm-8pm Tues.-Thurs., 5pm-9pm Fri.-Sat., $26-58) has earned numerous accolades. With impeccable service, an award-winning wine list, and a diverse menu of northern Italian cuisine built around seasonal and local ingredients, Panzano is a contemporary place for happy hour, a romantic dinner, or a post-theater splurge.

Named one of the country's top restaurants by Zagat, **Beatrice & Woodsley** (38 S. Broadway, 303/777-3505, beatriceandwoodsley.com, 5pm-close daily, 9am-2pm brunch Sat.-Sun., $24-36), whose name comes from a local story about two lovebirds, focuses on local, seasonal, and conscientious ingredients. Their rustic menu, which includes veggie, dairy-free, and gluten-free options, showcases a variety of carefully prepared small and large plates, including grilled heirloom

carrots, drunken duck, and pan-seared barramundi.

International

Named for the largest Chinese market in Ho Chi Minh City, Vietnam, **CholLon Modern Asian Bistro** (1555 Blake St., 303/353-5223, www.cholon.com, 4pm-8:30pm Wed.-Thurs., 4pm-9pm Fri.-Sat., $12-20) was a 2011 James Beard finalist for best new restaurant. It's the passion of executive chef Lon Symensma, whose colorful dishes are works of art. Main plates include fresh and flavorful combos like lobster crepes and crunchy Thai shrimp rolls served with umami mayo.

Modeled after the Place Vendome in Paris, the chic ★ **Bistro Vendome** (1420 Larimer St., 303/825-3232, www.bistrovendome.com, 4:30pm-10pm Mon.-Fri., 10am-2:30pm and 4:30pm-10pm Sat.-Sun., $21-32) is widely praised as Denver's best French restaurant. Its short menu includes classic options like *poisson entier* (whole-fried fish), hearty

bouillabaisse stew made with prawns, mussels, clams, and English peas, and decadent chocolate soufflé to top off your exquisite meal. Brunch is served on weekends.

For a quick, casual bite while you're walking the mall, you can't beat **TLC Food Co.** (16th St. Mall and Larimer St., www.tlcfoodco.com, 11am-4pm Mon.-Sat., $9), a small cart that sells gyros, brisket, sausages, and other Armenian, Greek, and Italian foods. For more upscale Mediterranean, try ★ **Rioja** (1431 Larimer St., 303/820-2282, www.riojadenver.com, 4pm-10pm Mon.-Fri., 10am-2:30pm and 4pm-10pm Sat.-Sun., $20-34). Executive chef and owner Jennifer Jasinski was named a James Beard Foundation semifinalist in 2016. The carefully culled menu changes seasonally but typically features handmade pastas as well as a few seafood entrées like a tuna-octopus duet. Brunch is served on weekends.

Osteria Marco (1453 Larimer St.,

Bistro Vendome in Larimer Square

303/534-5855, www.osteriamarco.com, 11:30am-9pm Sun.-Thurs., 11:30am-10pm Fri.-Sat., $10-36) is a great, informal place to gather, although it can be a touch too loud. The fabulous menu includes rabbit, handcrafted pizzas with unusual ingredients like figs and goat cheese, and on Sunday nights, slow-roasted suckling pig. **Marco's Coal Fired** (2129 Larimer St., 303/296-7000, www.marcoscfp.com, 11am-10pm Sun.-Thurs., 11am-11pm Fri.-Sat., $11-19) is known for its mouthwatering Neapolitan-style pizzas made by hand with imported Italian ingredients. The cozy booths, brick walls, and pizza oven make it an especially comfortable place to enjoy their signature limoncello chicken wings and meatball sliders or to share a decadent Nutella-stuffed pizza. They also serve gluten-free and vegan options.

Part of celebrity chef Richard Sandoval's restaurant empire, **Tamayo** (1400 Larimer St., 720/946-1433, www.eattamayo.com, 11am-8pm Sun.-Thurs., 11am-9pm Sat.-Sun., $13-30) features fresh Mexican fare in creative combinations like crab and shrimp enchiladas and adobo pork tacos. The establishment has an enormous rooftop deck, a great place to enjoy one of the 100 tequilas. Brunch is served on weekends.

Pub Fare

A casual place with a slightly upscale vibe, ★ **Stout Social Club** (1400 Stout St., 720/214-9100, stoutsocial.com, noon-10pm daily, $7-20) has more than 40 taps that rotate craft brews, including regional ones, to go with their giant soft pretzels, big sandwiches, and burgers. The house specialty is green chili mac and cheese. They also get inventive with signature cocktails, shared plates, and even sushi. Fridays and Saturdays bring on fresh oysters.

Cafés

Part of a small Denver-based chain, **Snooze** (1701 Wynkoop St., 303/825-3536, snoozeeatery.com, 7am-2pm Mon.-Fri., 6:30am-2:30pm Sat.-Sun., $8-15) is known for its friendly service, fun atmosphere, and inventive menu with treats like shrimp and grits, pineapple upside down pancakes, and Goldilocks' porridge as well as dirty drunken chai and other potent morning cocktails. On Market Street, the **Delectable Egg** (1642 Market St., 303/572-8146, www.delectableegg.com, 7am-2pm daily, $7-16) has been a local breakfast and lunch tradition since 1982, thanks to its diverse menu with several French toast options (like peanut butter crunch), frittatas, eggs Benedicts, and quiche Lorraine crepes.

Consistently ranked as one of Denver's best breakfast spots, **Sam's No. 3** (1500 Curtis St., 303/534-1927, samsno3.com, 7am-2pm Sun.-Tues., 7am-8pm Wed.-Sat., $7-23) is a popular diner serving up huge portions of tasty food. Choose from classic egg dishes or fluffy pancakes to smothered "Big as Your Head" two-pound breakfast burritos.

Accommodations

Denver sees its highest rates for lodging during summer, holidays, and dates surrounding sporting events. The city has loads of chain hotels.

Hostels

Denver has two hostels near downtown. Both have shared bunk rooms (linens included) and women-only or co-ed options. Amenities include bed outlets for charging phones, shared bathrooms, and communal kitchens. Within a 10-minute walk from many downtown sights, **Hostel Fish** (1217 20th St., 303/954-0962, hostelfish.com, $38-65) has bunk beds in dorms that sleep 4-10. On Capitol Hill, the **Ember Hostel** (857 Grant St., 303/942-1633, www.emberhostels.com, $38-65) has dorm rooms with 4-16 bunks, a large patio with a firepit, and a large hot tub.

Hotels

Near the Convention Center, the **Warwick Denver** (1776 Grant St., 303/861-2000, warwickhotels.com, $199-300) has generously sized rooms and suites with a mix of classic and contemporary decor. Amenities include a gym with floor-to-ceiling windows and stunning views, a rooftop pool, and complimentary cruiser bikes.

Inside Denver's landmark Union Station, **The Crawford Hotel** (1701 Wynkoop St., 720/460-3700, www.thecrawfordhotel.com, $280-622) features three floors of unique rooms. Each room represents a different era of the station's history—from the art deco Pullman Room to the Victorian Classic to the upstairs Loft Rooms with tall ceilings, original beams, and brick walls. Bathrooms vary, with amenities ranging from freestanding claw-foot tubs to modern rain showers.

★ **The Oxford Hotel** (1600 17th St., 303/628-5400, www.theoxfordhotel.com, $240-565) is a LoDo property filled with historic charm. Prominent guests such as the Dalai Lama and Hillary Clinton have stayed in the classically designed rooms, which feature upgraded beds as well as timeless touches like antique headboards, full drapery, and claw-foot tubs. Luxury amenities include a full-service spa and fitness center, an art deco martini bar, and a steakhouse.

With both comfort and historical charm, ★ **Hotel Teatro** (1100 14th St., 888/727-1200, www.hotelteatro.com, $249-460) provides nice views and an excellent location just steps from Larimer Square and the performing arts complex. The 110 rooms and suites feature lofty ceilings, in-room coffeemakers, thick mattresses, and plush terrycloth robes. In addition to a relaxed coffee lounge lined with floor-to-ceiling bookcases, the hotel has an upscale restaurant.

The **Magnolia Hotel** (818 17th St., 303/607-9000, www.magnoliahotels.com, $269-350) has been restored to reflect its original appearance as the historic American National Bank Building. The large boutique property features 297 stylish rooms with either two queen beds or one king bed and oversize baths with a choice of tub or a walk-in shower. Large windows give each room a bright and spacious appearance. Another plus is its great central location just steps from the 16th Street Mall.

The city's most luxurious accommodation in 1892, the ★ **Brown Palace Hotel** (321 17th St., 303/297-3111, www.brownpalace.com, $279-699) remains a venerable downtown institution. Many things have not changed, including the 26 stone medallions carved with images of Colorado wildlife on the building's exterior and the eight-story atrium with cast-iron railings and ornate grillwork panels. The renovated guest rooms sport a modern Victorian look; rooms come with queen- or king-size beds, and suites are named for famous guests, including presidents Roosevelt, Eisenhower, and Reagan. The popular Beatles Suite includes framed records and a custom jukebox. The hotel has an on-site spa and several dining options, including a tavern with a classic pub vibe and an upscale restaurant.

Aloft Denver (800 15th St., 303/623-3063, www.aloftdenverdowntown.com, $200-300) looks like a piece of modern art, with its strikingly angular roof and a high-ceilinged, industrial-chic lobby decorated with contemporary art and brassy throw pillows. The sparsely furnished rooms include one king or two queen beds, high-speed Wi-Fi, flat-screen TVs, and minifridges. You can't beat the location just a block from the Convention Center and the 16th Street Mall.

From the attentive staff to the ornate and intricately painted lobby ceiling, the experience at the **Kimpton Hotel Monaco Denver** (1717 Champa St., 303/296-1717, www.monaco-denver.com, $199-670) is memorable. The upscale rooms are playfully decorated with geometric patterns and brightly colored accents. Standard rooms have oversize working areas and a choice of bed configurations; larger rooms and suites are also available. Amenities range from a fitness center to unusual perks like yoga mats in every room.

Inns and Bed-and-Breakfasts

On the eastern edge of the downtown, the ★ **Queen Anne Bed & Breakfast Inn** (2147 Tremont Pl., 303/296-6666, www.queenannebnb.com, $175-250) is an eco-friendly establishment with four "local artist" suites and nine bright and colorful rooms. Some rooms overlook the peaceful garden, where the owners grow more than 100 varieties of fruits, herbs, and vegetables. It's a great place to lounge with coffee in the morning before the organic breakfast is served.

Transportation and Services

Emergency Services

Denver has a number of excellent hospitals, including the **University of Colorado Hospital** (12605 E. 16th Ave., Aurora, 720/848-0000, www.uchealth.org), **St. Anthony Central** (11600 W. 2nd Place, Lakewood, 720/321-0000, www.stanthonyhosp.org), **Denver Health** (777 Bannock St., 303/436-6000, www.denverhealth.org), and **Presbyterian/St. Luke's Medical Center** (1719 E. 19th Ave., 720/754-6000, pslmc.com). The **Children's Hospital Colorado** (www.childrenscolorado.org) also has several metro-area locations, including a large campus in Aurora (13123 E. 16th Ave., Aurora, 720/777-1234).

Downtown Denver has a number of urgent care facilities, including one operated by **Concentra** (1730 Blake St., 303/296-2273, www.concentra.com, 8am-6pm Mon.-Fri.) and one at the **Denver Health** location.

Getting Around
Bus and Light-Rail

The **Regional Transportation District** (www.rtd-denver.com, $2.60-10.50) operates a network of buses and light-rail trains that transports passengers throughout Denver and connects with regional buses to Boulder and Fort Collins. **Union Station** (1701 Wynkoop St.) serves 16 bus routes, including the four Flatirons Flyer routes to Boulder and the free MetroRide and 16th Street MallRide.

Taxi

Local taxi companies include **Yellow Cab** (303/777-777, www.denveryellowcab.com), **Metro Taxi** (303/333-3333, www.metrotaxidenver.com), and **Union Taxi Cooperative** (303/922-2222, www.uniontaxidenver.net).

Boulder

In the foothills of the Rockies, Boulder benefits from an eye-popping backdrop of pointed rock fins and snowcapped summits. Residents enthusiastically embrace all the town has to offer—not just the landscape, but organic food at the local farmers market, farm-to-table restaurants, Buddhist meditation centers, and a vibrant performing arts scene.

The town core forms a rectangle with the foothills to the west, the University of Colorado (CU) campus to the south, Pearl Street to the north, and the Twenty Ninth Street Mall to the east. You can get around easily by foot, bus, or bike, although it's easiest to get to Chautauqua Park and other foothills sights by car.

Getting There
Car
From Denver

From downtown **Denver** to Boulder, the drive is 30 miles (48 km) and usually takes about 45 minutes; it can take substantially longer during rush hour or inclement weather. In downtown, merge onto I-70 west and then continue west on I-270. Take US 36 west to Boulder.

From Rocky Mountain National Park

From **Estes Park** on the eastern border of Rocky Mountain National Park, follow US 36 southwest to Boulder. The drive is 35 miles (56 km) and takes about an hour.

Bus

The **Regional Transportation District** (303/299-6000, www.rtd-denver.com) operates a network of buses from Denver, Nederland, and Fort Collins. Boulder is an easy hour-long bus ride from Denver International Airport or Union Station in downtown Denver. Buses arrive at two hubs: the downtown **RTD Bus Station** (1800 14th St., 303/299-6000, 7am-6:30pm Mon.-Fri.) or the **Boulder Junction at Depot Square Station** (3175 Pearl Pkwy., 303/299-6000, 9am-1pm and 2pm-6pm Mon.-Fri.).

Sights
★ Flatirons

As Boulder's most recognizable landmark, the 300-million-year-old **Flatirons** jutting up from the ponderosa forest are within view from most parts of town. Their name comes from their resemblance to pioneer irons. Lined up in a row, these five red-brown slabs of sandstone tilt against Green Mountain, part of the **City of Boulder Open Space and Mountain Parks** (303/441-3440, www.osmp.org). Trails loop around the Flatirons. Climbers ascend their cracks. For non-hikers, one of the best places to enjoy them is strolling Chautauqua Park.

★ Chautauqua

Tucked beneath the Flatirons, **Chautauqua** originally had nearly 100 cottages as part of the Chautauqua adult education movement in the late 19th and early 20th centuries. Today, the nonprofit **Colorado Chautauqua Association** (303/442-3282, www.chautauqua.com) offers artistic performances, scholarly lectures, and films, just as it did in 1898, when the complex first opened. Many events are held in the **Chautauqua Auditorium,** a large wooden structure with great acoustics. A large, green lawn on the complex's northern side is a favorite summer hangout and picnic spot. On the complex's western edge is the jewel of Boulder's extensive open-space system, gorgeous **Chautauqua Park** (900 Baseline Rd., www.bouldercolorado. gov), where grassy meadows dotted with spring wildflowers rise to meet the serrated Flatirons. Open year-round, Chautauqua has about 40 miles (64 km) of hiking trails, 58 rental cottages, and a general store.

Go early in the morning on a weekday to find a parking spot. On summer weekends, the city offers a **Park-to-Park shuttle** (bouldercolorado.gov, 8am-8pm Sat.-Sun. late May-early Sept., free) to Chautauqua from downtown Boulder.

University of Colorado Boulder

From humble beginnings in the 19th century, the **University of Colorado Boulder** has grown into a tier-one research university. **Old Main,** CU's first building, includes the **CU Heritage Center** (Old Main Building, 1600 Pleasant St., 303/492-6329, cuheritage.org, 10am-4pm Mon.-Sat., free), with exhibits relaying the school's history and a Lego model of the flagship campus. Of special interest are the exhibits about alumnus Glen Miller and the **Space Exploration Gallery,** which includes a moon rock collected by Apollo 15 astronauts and equipment used by some of the 20 astronaut alumni.

On the south side of campus, the renovated **Fiske Planetarium** (2414 Regent Dr., 303/492-5002, fiske.colorado.edu, 8am-5pm Mon.-Fri. while school is in session) has a high-definition IMAX-sized screen and a state-of-the-art Megastar projector for its 360-degree star shows, movies, lectures, and popular late-night laser shows. On a clear Friday night, you

Boulder

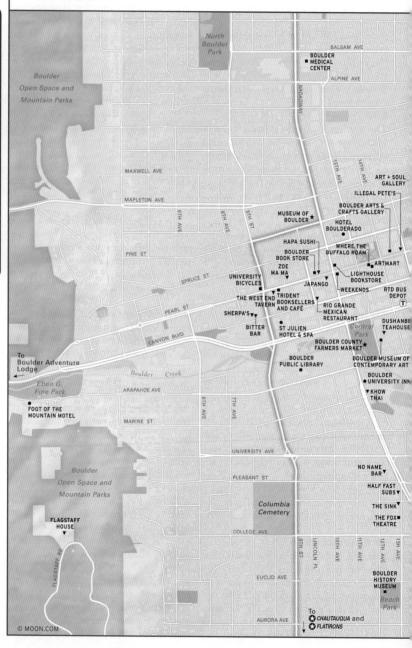

North Boulder Park

Boulder Open Space and Mountain Parks

BALSAM AVE

BOULDER MEDICAL CENTER

ALPINE AVE

BROADWAY

13TH AVE

14TH AVE

MAXWELL AVE

ART + SOUL GALLERY

MAPLETON AVE

ILLEGAL PETE'S

6TH AVE

8TH ST

9TH ST

MUSEUM OF BOULDER

BOULDER ARTS & CRAFTS GALLERY

HOTEL BOULDERADO

PINE ST

HAPA SUSHI

BOULDER BOOK STORE

WHERE THE BUFFALO ROAM

ARTMART

ZOE MA MA

SPRUCE ST

UNIVERSITY BICYCLES

JAPANGO

LIGHTHOUSE BOOKSTORE

TRIDENT BOOKSELLERS AND CAFÉ

WEEKENDS

RTD BUS DEPOT

THE WEST END TAVERN

PEARL ST

SHERPA'S

RIO GRANDE MEXICAN RESTAURANT

DUSHANBE TEAHOUSE

BITTER BAR

ST JULIEN HOTEL & SPA

Central Park

CANYON BLVD

BOULDER COUNTY FARMERS MARKET

BOULDER MUSEUM OF CONTEMPORARY ART

To Boulder Adventure Lodge

Boulder Creek

BOULDER PUBLIC LIBRARY

Eben G. Fine Park

ARAPAHOE AVE

6TH AVE

7TH AVE

BOULDER UNIVERSITY INN

KHOW THAI

FOOT OF THE MOUNTAIN MOTEL

MARINE ST

UNIVERSITY AVE

PLEASANT ST

NO NAME BAR

HALF FAST SUBS

Boulder Open Space and Mountain Parks

Columbia Cemetery

THE SINK

THE FOX THEATRE

FLAGSTAFF HOUSE

COLLEGE AVE

9TH ST

LINCOLN PL

10TH AVE

11TH AVE

12TH AVE

13H AVE

FLAGSTAFF RD

EUCLID AVE

BOULDER HISTORY MUSEUM

Beach Park

AURORA AVE

To CHAUTAUQUA and FLATIRONS

© MOON.COM

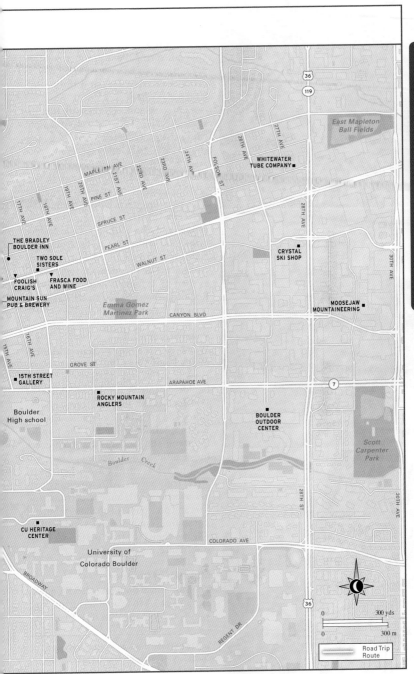

- WHITEWATER TUBE COMPANY ■
- East Mapleton Ball Fields
- THE BRADLEY BOULDER INN ●
- TWO SOLE SISTERS ▼
- CRYSTAL SKI SHOP ■
- FOOLISH CRAIG'S ■
- FRASCA FOOD AND WINE ▼
- MOUNTAIN SUN PUB & BREWERY ▼
- MOOSEJAW MOUNTAINEERING ■
- Emma Gomez Martinez Park
- 15TH STREET GALLERY ■
- ROCKY MOUNTAIN ANGLERS ■
- Boulder High school
- BOULDER OUTDOOR CENTER ■
- Boulder Creek
- Scott Carpenter Park
- CU HERITAGE CENTER ■
- University of Colorado Boulder

Streets: 17TH AVE, 18TH AVE, 19TH AVE, 20TH AVE, 21ST AVE, 22ND AVE, 23RD AVE, 24TH AVE, MAPLE AVE, PINE ST, SPRUCE ST, PEARL ST, WALNUT ST, FOLSOM ST, 26TH AVE, 27TH AVE, 28TH AVE, 28TH ST, 30TH AVE, CANYON BLVD, GROVE ST, ARAPAHOE AVE, COLORADO AVE, BROADWAY, REGENT DR, 16TH AVE, 15TH AVE

Route markers: 36, 119, 7

0   300 yds
0   300 m

Road Trip Route

can catch Fiske's evening star show, then walk next door to the **Sommers-Bausch Observatory** (outreach.colorado.edu, 8pm fall-spring, 9pm summer, weather permitting) for a free stargazing session using their telescopes and the world's largest star wheel.

CU's social hub is **University Hill,** the student-centered district west of campus with a compact collection of offbeat indie shops, cafés, bars, and restaurants covering several blocks between University and College Avenues. Although the establishments frequently change, a few have persevered, including the historic 1926 **Fox Theatre,** a popular live music venue, and **The Sink,** a classic college pizza joint with autographs, newspaper clippings, and cartoons of illustrious customers like President Obama, as well as their most famous employee, Robert Redford, who swabbed the floors while working here as a student in 1955.

Pearl Street Mall

Wandering the four pedestrian blocks of the **Pearl Street Mall** (Pearl St. between 11th and 15th Sts., www.boulderdowntown.com) is a highlight of Boulder. Visitors and locals browse bookstores and art galleries; families flock to see the Balloon Man and the pop-jet fountain; and students and tech execs linger at the many coffee shops.

Summer evenings are when Pearl Street truly bustles. Alfresco dining venues overflow with hungry patrons, and bars and brewpubs fill up. Entertainment ranges from outdoor movies and Boulder Theater shows to street performers who sing, dance, and juggle fire.

Museum of Boulder

The **Museum of Boulder** (2205 Broadway St., 303/449-3464, boulderhistory.org, 9am-5pm Mon. and Wed.-Fri., 10am-5pm

---

Top to bottom: the Flatirons above Boulder; Chautauqua Park; rock climbing in Eldorado Canyon State Park

Sat.-Sun., $10) displays thousands of artifacts donated by Boulder-area citizens since 1944, including a horse-drawn sleigh and carriage and historic microscopes and chemistry sets. You can also see artifacts once belonging to Chief Niwot, leader of the local Arapaho people, who was fatally wounded at the tragic Sand Creek Massacre.

Boulder Museum of Contemporary Art

The renovated **Boulder Museum of Contemporary Art** (1750 13th St., 303/443-2122, bmoca.org, 11am-5pm Tues.-Sun., $2) features three rotating exhibits by nationally and internationally renowned artists in a historic 1906 redbrick warehouse. It's adjacent to Central Park, a grassy area with a concrete bunker-like band shell, and the beautiful Boulder Dushanbe Teahouse.

National Center for Atmospheric Research

On the city's southwestern fringe is the **National Center for Atmospheric Research** (NCAR, 1850 Table Mesa Dr., 303/497-1000, ncar.ucar.edu, 8am-5pm Mon.-Fri., 9am-4pm Sat.-Sun. and holidays, free), one of Boulder's three federal labs, which conducts cutting-edge atmospheric research and explores its human implications using some of the nation's fastest supercomputers. Built in a spectacular setting, high on a flat-topped mesa, this blocky, concrete complex was designed to look like part of the landscape by the famous architect I. M. Pei, whose plans were inspired by the Mesa Verde cliff dwellings. Tours and exhibits in the lobby let you feel a cloud, steer a hurricane, examine the sun, and learn more about the research happening here. You can also visit two galleries that highlight the connection between art and science, eat in the cafeteria, and walk the easy, outdoor Weather Trail, where signs describe phenomena like mountain wave clouds, climate zones, and cold fronts.

★ Eldorado Canyon State Park

Eldorado Canyon State Park (9 Kneale Rd., Eldorado Springs, cpw.state.co.us, 6am-8pm daily, $10/vehicle) is best known for its technical rock climbing, hiking, and angling. More than 40 picnic spots are available, many along the creek. Eldorado Springs, a natural artesian spring, continuously feeds the refreshing and cold **Eldorado Swimming Pool** (294 Artesian Dr., 303/499-9640, www.eldoradosprings.com, 10am-6pm daily Memorial Day-Labor Day, prices vary). The refurbished historic site was part of a resort in the early 1900s that hosted luminaries from around the world.

Hiking trails abound in the park. From the Rattlesnake Gulch Trailhead, the flat **Fowler Trail** (2 mi/3.2 km one-way) passes directly behind the Bastille, a rock formation named for the notorious French prison. From the same trailhead, you can ascend the **Rattlesnake Gulch Trail** (3.5 mi/5.6 km rt, 1,200 ft/365 m elevation gain), a steep loop that climbs past the burned ruins of a historic hotel to views of the snowcapped Continental Divide. The out-and-back **Eldorado Canyon Trail** (7 mi/11.3 km rt) ascends a well-graded path to patches of peaceful pines, then descends to the **Walker Ranch Loop,** where you can enjoy a well-deserved picnic lunch by a small waterfall before retracing your steps.

South of Boulder, the park is just beyond the community of Eldorado Springs. Boulder County runs the **Eldo Shuttle** (www.bouldercounty.org, 8am-7pm Sat.-Sun. summer, free) on summer weekends. The route runs from the university, with several stops along CO 93, to the park about every 15 minutes.

Scenic Drives
Flagstaff Mountain

Flagstaff Road (4.2 mi/6.7 km one way, 20 minutes) climbs west up a series of impressive switchbacks to ascend **Flagstaff Mountain,** a gem in Boulder's extensive Open Space and Mountain

◈ Side Trip: Peak-to-Peak Highway

Nederland on the Peak-to-Peak Highway

Of the many scenic mountain roads in Colorado, one of the most famous is the **Peak-to-Peak Highway** (55 mi/89 km, 2-3 hrs), running from Longs Peak in Rocky Mountain National Park to Mount Evans in the south. Colorado's oldest scenic byway offers some of the most stunning views the Front Range has to offer. Jagged peaks and their rugged, bowl-shaped cirques, where glaciers once lay, are front and center as you drive (or bike) at a leisurely pace through evergreen forests and sunlit groves of quaking aspen stretching along a string of pretty mountain communities. This route also parallels the Continental Divide.

The route is bookended by the towns of **Estes Park** in the north and **Black Hawk** in the south. Along the way, the road winds past old mine tailings, ghost towns, and several quaint communities. About midway is **Nederland,** which was established in the 1850s

Parks. **Panorama Point,** the first parking area on the right, and the **Sunrise Amphitheater** at the summit offer incredible views of the city. The Denver skyline, the red-roofed CU campus, and the pancake-flat plains stretch to the east. Start the drive on Baseline Road at Chautauqua Park.

Atop the mountain is the iconic **Flagstaff House** (1138 Flagstaff Rd., 303/442-4640, www.flagstaffhouse.com, 5:30pm-9pm Sun. and Tues.-Thurs., 5pm-9:30pm Fri.- Sat. Jan.-May, 5:30pm-9pm Sun.-Thurs., 5pm-9:30pm Fri.- Sat. June-Dec., $90), one of Colorado's best restaurants, which is celebrated for its stunning views, its 16,000-bottle wine cellar, and its exceptional food and service.

Boulder Canyon

West of town, **Boulder Canyon Drive** (CO 119, 16 mi/26 km one way, 35 minutes) snakes through Boulder Canyon, a scenic stretch of curvy road below granite rock formations. The route follows Middle Boulder Creek through Arapahoe and Roosevelt National Forests west to Barker Meadows Reservoir and the small town of **Nederland.** You can turn around here or connect midway with the Peak-to-Peak Scenic Byway to make a loop. En route, stop to walk up some stairs to **Boulder Falls,** a 70-foot (21-m) flume that splits around a rock to plunge down into a pool. Go early in the morning or later in the evening to avoid heavy traffic.

as a trading post between European settlers and the Ute people. Tiny **Allenspark** was named for Alonzo Allen, a miner from Wisconsin who built a cabin here. The road also passes **Ward,** an isolated community of self-described recluses and misfits. The drive ends with the mining-turned-gambling towns of **Black Hawk** and **Central City.**

As its name implies, peaks flank this highway. You can see **Longs Peak** when driving past Rocky Mountain National Park. Mountains in the **Indian Peaks Wilderness** and **James Peak Wilderness** are visible near Nederland. **Mount Meeker** and **Chiefs Head Mountain** appear around Allenspark. Rivaling the beauty of the mountains, golden aspen leaves attract road-trippers during the busy September leaf-peeping season.

The Peak-to-Peak also accesses some of the region's best recreation. In summer and early autumn, **Brainard Lake** and the **Fourth of July Trailhead** offer hiking, angling, wildlife spotting, and more tremendous views. In winter, you can cross-country ski to Brainard Lake, snowshoe through sunny glades in the serene **Peaceful Valley,** or ski and snowboard at **Eldora Ski Resort.** North of Ward, the Civilian Conservation Corps-built **Camp Dick,** along the Middle St. Vrain Creek, offers fly-fishing, while the nearby **Buchanan Pass** and **Sourdough Trails** are ideal for hiking and mountain biking.

From Boulder

From Boulder, you can create a **loop** that tours the entire Peak-to-Peak. Drive US 36 northwest to Estes Park. From there, drive south along the Peak-to-Peak Scenic Byway (CO 7, 72, and 119) to Black Hawk. Continue east on CO 119 and 93 via Golden back to Boulder. The total trip is 135 miles (215 km) and takes about five hours with stops. You can also access the Peak-to-Peak midway at Nederland via Boulder Canyon Drive (CO 119).

From Denver

From Denver, drive I-25 north and US 36 northwest to Estes Park. From there, drive south along the Peak-to-Peak Scenic Byway (CO 7, 72, and 119) to Black Hawk. Turn right toward Central City and follow the Central City Parkway south to I-70. Go east on I-70 and US 6, then north on I-25 to Denver. The total trip is 160 miles (260 km) and takes about six hours with stops.

Recreation
Hiking

The **City of Boulder Open Space and Mountain Parks** (303/441-3440, www.osmp.org) has trail maps and up-to-date information on dog regulations, seasonal wildlife restrictions, and trail closures. The **Chautauqua Ranger Cottage** (9am-4pm daily May-Sept., 9am-4pm Sat.-Sun. Oct.-Apr.) also has maps, weather info, and trail conditions and closures.

Mesa Trail

Distance: 7.3 miles (11.7 km) one way
Duration: 4 hours
Elevation change: 1,085 feet (331 m)
Effort: moderate-strenuous
Trailhead: South Mesa Trailhead (4111 Eldorado Springs Dr.)

The crown jewel of Boulder's extensive trail system is the gorgeous **Mesa Trail,** a north-south route that parallels the base of the Flatirons. The trail is point-to-point, not a loop, so you'll either need to hike it out and back, plan a shuttle, or hike one section and side trail at a time. You can also use it to connect with side trails to various destinations.

From the South Mesa Trailhead, the route climbs steadily through the grasslands up to the mesa. It then undulates through lush forests humming with birds and other wildlife like the black Abert's squirrel, only found in Southwestern ponderosa pine forests. The trail skirts in and out of multiple canyons with views of the Flatirons and mountains before descending to **Chautauqua.**

Side trails along the way include the **Fern Canyon Trail** (2.8 mi/4.5 km one-way), a classic uphill hike that ascends Bear Peak, Boulder's highest summit. The trail ends on an exposed, craggy summit with panoramic views from the high peaks to the plains. From the top, either retrace your steps down Fern Canyon or descend the longer and more moderate **West Ridge Trail** on Bear Peak's western side, where ghostly stumps left from a 2012 wildfire still loom above the path. After 2 miles (3.2 km), West Ridge joins up with **Bear Canyon Trail**, which intersects the Mesa Trail.

★ Flatirons Loop

Distance: 2.2 miles (3.5 km) rt
Duration: 2 hours
Elevation gain: 715 feet (218 m)
Effort: moderate
Trailhead: Chautauqua Trailhead

Hike this loop to get up close to the Flatirons; for more of a challenge, take one or both of the side trips. Junctions are well signed but take a map from the Chautauqua Cottage at the trailhead just in case. Plan to get a parking spot by 8am or take the free bus. Expect to encounter crowds, especially on weekends.

Start on the paved **Chautauqua Trail** that climbs to a junction with the Bluebell-Baird Trail. En route, you'll enter a ponderosa forest and follow a creek drainage. Continue left at the junction onto the **Second-Third Flatiron Trail.**

You'll soon reach a junction with the first optional side trip up the **First-Second Flatiron Trail** (add 1.4 mi/2.3 km rt, 960 ft/293 m elevation gain, 1.5 hrs). This out-and-back trail switchbacks up a steep talus slope in between the First and Second Flatirons with views of both. It ends at a saddle in between the First Flatiron and a smaller knob known as **Sunset Rock.** From here, return down to the main Flatiron Trail.

Turn right to continue farther on the Second-Third Flatiron Trail. From the junction with the Bluebell-Baird Trail

Royal Arch rock formation at the Flatirons

(before the First-Second Flatiron Trail), the **Second-Third Flatiron Trail** (0.5 mi/0.8 km one way) goes to the junction with the Royal Arch Trail. This segment crosses a talus slope to the pass below the base of the Second Flatiron, where you may see rock climbers. The trail then drops passing a climber's trail to the Third Flatiron, and views of the slab, before reaching the Royal Arch Trail.

From this junction, another optional side trip follows the out-and-back **Royal Arch Trail** (add 1.4 mi/2.3 km rt, 1,500 ft/457 m elevation gain, 1.5 hrs) for a strenuous climb through Bluebell Canyon. The trail leads up switchbacks and stairs to a ridge and then drops to **Tangen Spring** and the **Royal Arch** rock formation. Returning requires climbing back over the ridge.

From the junction at the beginning of the Royal Arch Trail, turn right to complete the loop back to the trailhead. At the intersection with Bluebell Road, turn left to get on the Bluebell-Baird Trail

and right onto the Bluebell Mesa Trail. At the end of that trail, turn right onto the Chautauqua Trail to return to the trailhead.

★ Rock Climbing

Boulder lures rock climbers from across North America. Some locales have seasonal closures to protect nesting raptors (early Feb.-late July). The **Flatirons** have hundreds of routes and multi-pitch ascents with the easiest access via **Chautauqua.** Routes on the first and third Flatirons are of varied difficulty with 4-10 pitches.

In **Boulder Canyon,** short trails from CO 119 go to more than 20 granite crags that vary from easy to challenging. The canyon entices climbers of all skill levels for top-roping, sport, and trad pitches.

Eldorado Canyon State Park (9 Kneale Rd., Eldorado Springs, cpw.state.co.us, 6am-8pm daily, $10/vehicle) attracts rock climbers to crimp tiny edges on their way up the vertical sandstone cliffs. More than 500 trad routes grace the golden canyon walls, including classic multi-pitch routes like **Bastille Crack** (5.7), **Yellow Spur** (5.9), and the famous **Naked Edge fingercrack** (5.11b), a normally full-day route that a team of Colorado speedsters climbed and descended in less than 25 minutes.

If you want to learn to climb or hire a guide, **Colorado Wilderness Rides and Guides** (720/242-9828, coloradowildernessridesandguides.com, $210-495) has full-day trips, which include all the necessary rock-climbing gear. **Colorado Mountain School** (720/387-8922, coloradomountainschool.com) also guides climbs in the Flatirons.

Bicycling

Boulder is a cycling town. You can rent bikes from two shops. **University Bicycles** (839 Pearl St., 303/444-4196, ubikes.com, 10am-6pm Mon.-Sat., 11am-5pm Sun.) rents road, mountain, snow, town, and kids bikes. **Boulder Cycle Sport**

(4580 Broadway, 303/444-2453, www.bouldercyclesport.com, 10am-6pm Mon.-Fri., 10am-5pm Sat., 10am-4pm Sun., $35-50/day) rents road and mountain bikes. Both shops can provide directions and advice for rides.

Road Biking

The canyons around Boulder make great road biking routes. North of Boulder, **Lefthand Canyon Drive** (8 mi/12.9 km one way) is one of the most popular canyon rides for its gentle grade on a quiet road to tiny Jamestown. A more **challenging ride** (16.5 mi/27 km one way, 3,500 ft/1,067 m elevation gain) starts on the same road but turns left to begin the climb up to the hippie enclave of Ward, where you can refuel at the tiny **Ward General Store** (62 Utica St., 303/459-1010, hours vary).

Scenic Flagstaff Road climbs **Flagstaff Mountain** (4 mi/6.4 km, one-way) starting off steady but amping up the pitch to Panorama Point for the first views. Winding switchbacks lead to a spur road and the summit at Sunrise Amphitheater, with views of the plains.

Mountain Biking

The best beginner mountain bike trail offers views of the northern foothills and plains. From the Boulder Valley Ranch Trailhead, the **Eagle Trail** (3 mi/4.8 km one way, 400 ft/122 m elevation gain) has one short but steep section that reaches a 15 percent grade. At the second junction with the **Sage Trail,** turn right to return to the trailhead.

For foothill rides through ponderosa pines, head to the **Betasso Preserve** (377 Betasso Rd., Sun.-Tues. and Thurs.-Fri.), where the most popular rides are the moderate **Benjamin Loop** (7.5 mi/12 km) and the more challenging **Betasso-Canyon Loop** (6 mi/9.7 km).

South of town are two flatter rides. The **Marshall Mesa Trailhead** (5258 Eldorado Springs Dr.) is the start of the **Dirty Bismark Route** (15 mi/24 km, 1,500 ft/457

top-rope climbing in Boulder Canyon

m elevation gain), a fun dirt loop with great views and climbing. The **Doudy Draw Trailhead** provides access to the **Doudy Draw Double Lollipop Loop** (10.4 mi/16.7 km), as well as the **Super Loop** (22 mi/35 km), which combines the best of the foothills and the flats.

Water Sports

Anglers try their luck in **Walden and Sawhill Ponds** (75th St., 1 mi/1.6 km north of Valmont Dr.), a group of ponds that contains both smallmouth and largemouth bass. For information about guided fishing trips, equipment, river reports, and expert advice, stop by **Rocky Mountain Anglers** (1904 Arapahoe Ave., 303/447-2400, rockymtanglers.com, 7am-7pm Mon.-Sat., 8am-6pm Sun.).

During spring runoff, Boulder Creek is popular with white-water kayakers. Near the mouth of Boulder Canyon is the **Boulder Kayak Playpark** (Eben G. Fine Park, 101 Arapahoe Ave.). The Class-II stretch (0.5 mi/0.8 km) starts with an

exciting 6-foot (1.8-m) plunge into a large pool. The **Boulder Outdoor Center** (2525 Arapahoe Ave., #E4-228, 303/444-8420, boc123.com) is the best source for local boating information.

On summer afternoons after the high-water levels have dropped, **Boulder Creek** is a popular spot for tubing. You can rent single or double tubes at **Boulder Nordic Sport** (629 S. Broadway, Ste. K, 877/267-7547, www.bouldernordic.com, 10am-6pm Mon.-Fri., 10am-5pm Sat., 10am-4pm Sun., $20-30) or **Whitewater Tube Co.** (2709 Spruce St., 720/239-2179, www.whitewatertubing.com, 10am-6pm daily mid-May-mid-Sept., $17-24), which also offers shuttles.

The best outdoor swim spot is **Boulder Reservoir** (5565 N. 51st St., 303/441-3461, www.bouldercolorado.gov, $7-11). The complex is a popular summer hangout and a recreation hot spot, with sailing, canoeing, waterskiing, and fishing. The picnic area has tables, a grill, horseshoes, and a volleyball court, while the dirt path around the lake is a favorite running and cycling spot.

Golf

The county has two courses with mountain views: the **Flatirons Golf Course** (5706 Arapahoe Ave., 303/442-7851, www.flatironsgolf.com, greens fees $38-45), which is operated by the city of Boulder, and the **Indian Peaks Golf Course** (2300 Indian Peaks Trl., 303/666-4706, www.indianpeaksgolf.com, greens fees $44-61), to the east in Lafayette.

Skiing

When there's enough snow, the open-space trails are great for snowshoeing and cross-country skiing. Between November and March, as conditions allow, the non-profit **Boulder Nordic Club** (bouldernordic.org) grooms trails in **North Boulder Park** (9th St. and Cedar Ave.). **Crystal Ski Shop** (1933 28th St., 303/449-7669, www.crystalskishop.com, 7am-8pm daily) rents snowshoes and cross-country skis.

Entertainment and Events
Nightlife
Boulder's clubs and bars are concentrated in two clusters: downtown and Uni Hill, but there are also taverns and breweries scattered all around town.

Downtown
The Pearl Street area offers the highest concentration of bars, breweries, and clubs. For a summer sundown drink, head to the fabulous rooftop decks at two locales. **West End Tavern** (926 Pearl St., 303/444-3535, www.thewestendtavern.com, 11:30am-close daily) pours 25 craft beers on tap. The **Rio Grande Mexican Restaurant** (1101 Walnut St., 303/444-3690, www.riograndemexican.com, 11am-9pm Sun.-Thurs., 11am-10pm Fri.-Sat.) serves a rainbow of margaritas.

For happy hour deals, try the **Bitter Bar** (835 Walnut St., 303/442-3050, www.thebitterbar.com, 5pm-close daily), a hip lounge serving creative cocktails with fun names like Birds and the Bees and Kiss the Sky. **Japango** (1136 Pearl St., 303/938-0330, www.boulderjapango.com, 11am-10pm daily) has a daily afternoon happy hour that includes hot sake and Sapporo Draft to sip on the outdoor patio.

University Hill
Up on "the Hill" next to CU, **The Sink** (1165 13th St., 303/444-7465, thesink.com, noon-9pm daily) is a true Boulder institution, with walls covered with retro artwork and ceilings filled with scribbled signatures dating back decades. In addition to serving up heavily topped pizza and the "best burger in Boulder," the city's oldest bar and restaurant is legendary for its daily themed happy hours.

A block away, **Half Fast Subs** (1215 13th St., 303/449-0404, www.halffastsubs.com, 10:30am-11pm Mon.-Wed., 10:30am-12:30am Thurs.-Fri., 11am-12:30am Sat., 11am-10pm Sun.) has an outdoor patio where you can sip potent Hurricanes and Bombers from the brief drink menu. A couple blocks north, the inconspicuous **No Name Bar** (1325 Broadway St., 4pm-1am daily) truly has no name, but it does have live music and a good selection of craft beer and infused tequilas.

Breweries
Boulder's 20 breweries are scattered all across town, so have a fun night or two following part of the **Boulder Beer Trail** (www.bouldercoloradousa.com).

Downtown, a perennial favorite is **Mountain Sun Pub & Brewery** (1535 Pearl St., 303/546-0886, www.mountainsunpub.com, 11am-1am daily), a laid-back spot with delicious food and a large selection of house and seasonal ales, including the not-too-sweet Blackberry Wheat and the popular Isadore Java porter.

Sanitas Brewing (3550 Frontier Ave., #A, 303/442-4130, www.sanitasbrewing.com, 2pm-6pm Mon.-Sat., noon-5pm Fri.-Sun.), named for a summit in Boulder's spectacular backdrop, has a large outdoor patio with Flatirons views and bocce ball. Its industrial-chic tap-room has a great selection of IPAs and fruity farmhouse ales.

Live Music
Boulder's best-known live music venue is **The Fox Theatre** (1135 13th St., 303/786-7030, foxtheatre.com). Originally constructed on the Hill as a movie theater in 1926, the building was eventually converted into a funky concert hall. The 625-seat venue is known for its great sound, as well as its diverse calendar of up-and-coming acts, great local musicians, and renowned national acts. The historic **Boulder Theater** (2032 14th St., 303/786-7030, www.bouldertheater.com), housed in a 1906 art deco opera building, offers 250 events a year, from headline speakers and film festivals to performances by well-known names like Lyle Lovett and local hit band Big Head Todd and the Monsters.

Art Galleries

One of the best places to pick up an affordable gift or a Colorado souvenir is **Artmart** (1326 Pearl St., 303/443-8248, www.artmartgifts.com, 10am-9pm daily), which features the work of more than 300 artists, many of them local. Much of their inventory is Boulder- and Colorado-centric, including handmade jewelry, wall signs, and other decor.

One of the oldest artist-owned cooperatives in the United States, **Boulder Arts & Crafts Gallery** (1421 Pearl St., 303/443-3683, boulderartsandcrafts. com, 11am-6pm Wed.-Sun.) is a bright and cheerful shop filled with beautiful artwork in many mediums—ceramics, fiber, wood, glass, and paint—plus photography and jewelry. Pearl Street also hosts a number of traditional fine art galleries, each with its own distinct style. **Art + Soul Gallery** (1505 Pearl St., 303/544-5803, www.artandsoulboulder. com, 11am-5pm Tues.-Sat., 11am-4pm Sun.) highlights contemporary creativity in its fine art and diverse selection of designer jewelry. The **15th Street Gallery** (1708 15th St., 303/447-2841, www.15thstreetgalleryboulder.com, 10am-6pm Mon.-Fri., 10am-5pm Sat.) is a swanky contemporary gallery showcasing work by established artists in a wide range of mediums, including etchings, woodcuts, sculpture, and acrylic and oil paintings.

Festivals and Events

The acclaimed **Colorado Shakespeare Festival** (303/492-8008, www. coloradoshakes.org, June-Aug., $18-95) performs in CU's **Mary Rippon Theatre** (1030 Broadway St.), an open-air amphitheater, plus three other campus theaters. The **Colorado Music Festival** (303/440-7666, coloradomusicfestival.org, late June-early Aug., $15-70) is a series of classical and chamber performances held each summer at the Chautauqua Auditorium (900 Baseline Rd.). It features both traditional and contemporary artists in instrumental and vocal performances, as well as a patriotic family concert around the Fourth of July.

What started in 1979 as a few hundred people running through the streets of Boulder has grown into the largest 10K footrace in the United States. Held each Memorial Day, the **Bolder Boulder** (303/444-7223, www.bolderboulder. com, registration $54-89) begins near the Twenty Ninth Street Mall and ends at CU's Folsom Field stadium. The 50,000-plus participants start in 100 waves with wheelchair racers first, followed by the next 30 waves of serious runners, who must qualify for these spots. Next come 70 more waves of runners, with walkers starting last, many of whom dress up in wacky costumes. Dozens of live bands are scattered along the route.

Shopping

Boulder is known for its eclectic mix of funky boutiques, indie bookstores, and local chains. **Pearl Street** is lined with trendy clothing and jewelry shops, specialty food stores, and outdoor clothing chains. Just east is the **Twenty Ninth Street Mall,** an open-air retail center filled with upscale chains and practical stores.

Clothing and Accessories

Two Sole Sisters (1703 Pearl St., 303/442-0404, www.twosolesisters.com, 11am-5pm Tues.-Sun.) is named for the two sisters who founded this local indie store. The shabby-chic boutique sells fun and funky handbags and jewelry and lots of stylish shoes, from high-heeled sandals to all-weather boots.

Weekends (1200 Pearl St., 303/444-4231, weekendsboulder.com, 10am-6pm Mon.-Sat., 11am-5pm Sun.) is one of Pearl Street's largest retailers. The locally owned shop has a large selection of casual men's and women's shoes and clothing from brands like Frye Shoes, Shinola, and Rebecca Taylor. Denim clothing from fashion-forward designers like rag & bone, J Brand, and KATO is a specialty.

Where the Buffalo Roam (1320 Pearl St., 303/938-1424, wherethebuffaloroam. com, 11am-6pm daily) is a souvenir shop that has T-shirts and CU apparel.

Outdoor Gear

The city has a good selection of outdoor equipment stores. For gear and clothing for every activity and season, locals head to **Moosejaw Mountaineering** (1755 29th St., Unit 1092, 720/452-2432, www.moosejaw. com, 10am-7pm Mon.-Sat., 11am-6pm Sun.) and **Neptune Mountaineering** (633 S. Broadway, 303/499-8866, www. neptunemountaineering.com, 10am-7pm Mon.-Fri, 9am-6pm Sat.-Sun.), opened by local Gary Neptune in 1973. **REI** (1789 28th St., 303/583-9970, www. rei.com, 9am-9am-8pm Mon.-Sat., 10am-6pm Sun.) is also a good choice for climbing and camping gear, maps, and kayaks.

Bookstores

A local landmark since 1973, **Boulder Book Store** (1107 Pearl St., 303/447-2074, www.boulderbookstore.net, 10am-10pm Mon.-Sat., 10am-8pm Sun.) is crammed full of recent releases and used classics. Three stories are divided into helpful sections, which include separate children's and teens areas, travel guides, local reads, and lots of periodicals.

To get into the New Age spirit, visit the **Lighthouse Bookstore** (1201 Pearl St., 303/939-8355, www. lighthousebookstoreofboulder.com, 10am-6pm Mon.-Sat., 11am-6pm Sun.), which specializes in metaphysical, spiritual, and magick books as well as runes and tarot cards.

Trident Booksellers and Café (940 Pearl St., 303/443-3133, www.tridentcafe. com, 7am-8pm daily) has been a local hangout since 1980, selling new and collectible books focused on philosophy, religion, metaphysics, and history.

Food

Dining is one of Boulder's many great pleasures. The city offers a disproportionately large variety of cuisines and high-quality establishments. Most locals take advantage of this diversity, as well as the abundance of fresh, local, and organic ingredients creatively combined by local chefs. Pearl Street offers the highest concentration of options, including many award-winning restaurants, but it's worth exploring away from the city center to discover some of Boulder's other culinary gems.

International

Khow Thai (1600 Broadway St., 303/447-0273, khow-thai.com, noon-9:30pm Mon.-Sat., 5pm-9:30pm Sun., $12-17) is a small, no-frills establishment that looks like a cafeteria but smells heavenly. Their peanut-topped pad thai with shrimp or veggies is perfectly spiced. The piquant green papaya salad, with lime juice and fish sauce, is a great break from traditional green salads.

Tiny **Zoe Ma Ma** (2010 10th St., 303/545-6262, www.zoemama.com, 11am-9pm daily, $7-14) features a simple menu of street food inspired by the owner's mother's cooking. Its best-selling *za jiang mian* (a pork noodle dish) was featured on the Food Network's *Cheap Eats*. The long outdoor booth and cafeteria-style tables are always overflowing.

A bit more upscale is **Hapa Sushi** (1117 Pearl St., 303/578-3071, hapasushi.com, 11am-10pm daily, $9-20), whose name is derived from a Hawaiian word meaning a harmonious blend of American and Asian cultures. The food is a similar combination of traditional Japanese cooking and creative outside influences. The menu features a variety of sushi rolls and a large selection of sashimi, with good vegetarian and vegan options and several types of sake.

★ **Sherpa's** (825 Walnut St., 303/440-7151, sherpas-restaurant.com, 11am-9:30pm daily, $10-22) has Boulder's best

Nepalese and Tibetan food, made from authentic recipes by chef Jangbu Sherpa, who has summited Mount Everest an astounding 10 times without using supplemental oxygen. Located in an old house with one of Boulder's best outdoor seating areas, the restaurant is divided into many small rooms. It's a relaxed atmosphere, with photos of Himalayan peaks tacked to the walls. The menu includes Himalayan staples like *dal baht* and Tibetan *momos* (steamed or fried dumplings with veggies or meat) and spicy yak stew. Add an order of freshly baked naan and a cold pint for a very satisfying meal.

A multiple-year semifinalist for the prestigious James Beard Award, **Frasca Food & Wine** (1738 Pearl St., 303/442-6966, www.frascafoodandwine.com, 5pm-9pm Wed.-Sun.) features northern Italian food from the Friuli-Venezia Giulia region, made with local ingredients and paired with top-flight wines. Frasca's wine list boasts more than 200 varieties. The menu offers choose-your-own multicourse dinners ($95) as well as a five-course Friulano tasting dinner ($130) paired with an optional wine flight ($98) by master sommelier Bobby Stuckey and chef Lachlan Mackinnon-Patterson. Make reservations up to two months in advance.

The only Persian-style teahouse in the Western Hemisphere, the ★ **Boulder Dushanbe Teahouse** (1770 13th St., 303/442-4993, boulderteahouse.com, 11am-8pm Tues.-Fri., 10am-8pm Sat.-Sun., $14-24) is a work of art created by more than 40 Tajik artisans. The teahouse is built around a central fish pool, encircled by copper sculptures of seven maidens who were the subjects of a popular 12th-century poem. The brightly painted wooden beams and recessed ceiling panels are painted with vibrant flowers, entangled vines, and colorful geometric designs, while hand-embossed wooden pillars support the ceiling. Seating is at low Tajik tables and chairs including *topchans* (platforms with low tables

encircled by cushions) or regular tables and chairs. Sip a cup of fragrant, house-made chai or one of the dozens of loose-leaf teas. The afternoon tea service, with a three-tiered tray filled with sweet and savory pastries, tea sandwiches, sweets, and fresh fruit, is also a fun way to celebrate. The teahouse menu varies by season with choices like Persian chickpea *kufteh* or spicy Indonesian peanut noodles. Reservations are required for afternoon tea and recommended for dinner.

Cafés

Foolish Craig's (1611 Pearl St., 303/247-9383, www.foolishcraigs.com, 8am-2pm daily, $8-15) is best known for crepes with funny names like The Homer (D'oh!), which is stuffed with Mediterranean veggies and topped with sour cream. Others include the Fahgeddaboudit and the hangover favorite, The Altitude Adjustment.

Accommodations

Although Boulder has some great places to stay overnight, none are cheap. Prices spike around big CU events like graduation and football games, as well as during summer. Rates are often lower in winter.

Hostels and Motels

Up Fourmile Canyon, the **Boulder Adventure Lodge** (A-Lodge, 91 Fourmile Canyon Dr., 303/444-0882, a-lodge.com, dorm $65, rooms $109-240) is an older motel and campground for budget-conscious travelers. It's a little rough around the edges, but has Boulder's only hostel-style shared bunk room for all genders. Small motel rooms have queens and bunk beds. The complex also has a few tent campsites ($50) and an outdoor patio, pool, and hot tub.

While the rustic, red-trimmed log cabins at the family run **Foot of the Mountain Motel** (200 W. Arapahoe Ave., 303/442-5688, www.footofthemountainmotel. com, $95-225) are dark and pretty basic, they are also clean, comfortable, and in an ideal location along Boulder Creek. They have tubing, hiking, and biking right outside the door and are within walking distance of Pearl Street.

Inns, Bed-and-Breakfasts, and Cottages

The renovated **Boulder University Inn** (1632 Broadway St., 303/417-1700, www.boulderuniversityinn.com, $152-249) is ideally situated between CU and downtown, just steps from Boulder Creek. Although some guests complain of noise, especially from rooms closest to Broadway, it's a comfortable stop for travelers, with all the other expected amenities.

Just one block from Pearl Street, **The Bradley Boulder Inn** (2040 16th St., 303/545-5200, www.thebradleyboulder.com, $245-290) is a refined bed-and-breakfast with 12 stylish rooms with a variety of amenities, from baths with jetted tubs to balconies with mountain views. The cozy sitting room features a large stone fireplace surrounded by plush chairs. With a wine-and-cheese hour each evening, a home-cooked breakfast, and nearby health club privileges, you'll want to stay for a very long time. Kids under 14 are not allowed and second-floor access is by stairs only.

★ **The Colorado Chautauqua Association** (900 Baseline Rd., 303/442-3282, www.chautauqua.com, $200-325) rents out 58 of its historic cottages nestled beneath the Flatirons at the edge of gorgeous Chautauqua Park. The quaint (and sometimes a bit run-down) cottages are available in studio, 1-, 2-, and 3-bedroom configurations, all with fully equipped kitchens, screened porches, and front door access to many of Boulder's best hiking trails. During the busy summer season, a minimum four-night stay is required. Two lodges (mid-June-Aug., $130-175), one of which has apartment-style rooms, have rooms available in summer.

Hotels

Just south of the Pearl Street Mall, the luxurious, 201-room **St Julien Hotel & Spa** (900 Walnut St., 720/406-9696, stjulien.com, $289-610) has plush pillow-top beds, oversize bathrooms with soaking tubs, and stunning views of Boulder's mountain backdrop from some of the more expensive rooms. The hotel also has an upscale restaurant and bar, and sponsors fun events like Saturday afternoon tea, when hot or iced tea and champagne cocktails are served alongside dainty tea sandwiches and scones.

Just a two-minute walk from Pearl Street, the landmark ★ **Hotel Boulderado** (2115 13th St., 303/442-4344, www.boulderado.com, $179-449) is housed in a historic brick building with bright-green awnings. Local businesspeople raised the funds to build it as the city's first upscale hotel, which opened on Near Year's Day in 1909. Since then, many well-known guests have stayed in the stylish Victorian rooms, including conservationist Enos Mills, Helen Keller, Louis Armstrong, and Robert Frost. Of special note is the lobby's stunning stained-glass ceiling, which was restored in the late 1970s after the original Italian glass was destroyed during a particularly heavy late-season snowstorm in 1959.

Transportation and Services
Emergency Services

The city's main hospitals are **Boulder Community Health** (4747 Arapahoe Ave., 303/415-7000, www.bch.org) and **Boulder Medical Center** (2750 Broadway St., 303/440-3000, and 4750 Arapahoe Ave., Ste. 200, 303/938-4700, www.bouldermedicalcenter.com). Urgent care facilities include **Rocky Mountain Urgent Care** (4800 Baseline Rd., #106, 303/529-8379, www.rockymountainurgentcare.com, 8am-7pm Mon.-Fri., 9am-4pm Sat.-Sun.) and **Concentra Urgent Care** (3300 28th St., 303/541-9090, www.concentra.com, 8am-5pm Mon.-Fri.).

Getting Around

The **Regional Transportation District** (www.rtd-denver.com, $3-11 one-way) operates a network of buses throughout the city and connects with regional buses to Denver, Nederland, and Fort Collins. The Boulder service features brightly painted buses with fun names like **Hop,** which runs between CU, downtown, and the Twenty Ninth Street Mall; **Skip,** which runs along Broadway Street; and **Jump,** which runs east-west along Arapahoe Avenue.

Purchase tickets at one of the two RTD hubs: the downtown **RTD Bus Station** (1800 14th St., 303/299-6000, 7am-6:30pm Mon.-Fri.) or the **Boulder Junction at Depot Square Station** (3175 Pearl Pkwy., 303/299-6000, 9am-1pm and 2pm-6pm Mon.-Fri.). Many Safeway and King Soopers stores also sell 10-packs of single-fare passes. You can also pay on the bus with exact change.

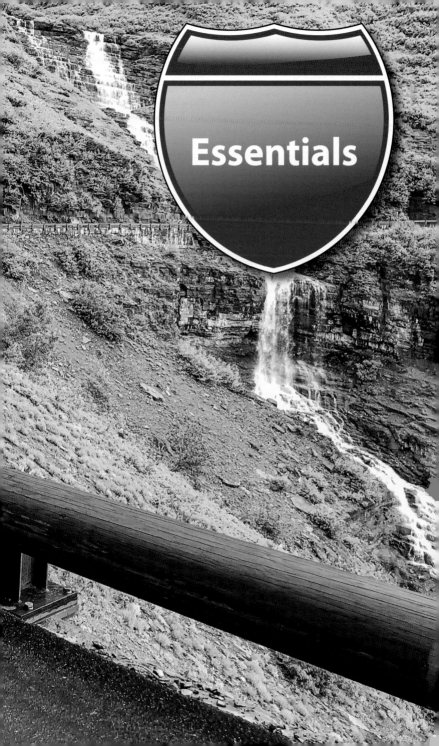

Getting There

Calgary, Alberta
Air

Northeast of downtown, **Calgary International Airport** (YYC, 403/735-1200 or 877/254-7427, www.yyc.com) is Canada's fourth-busiest airport, served by 25 airlines, including Air Canada and WestJet. Arrivals are on the lower level, where passengers are greeted by volunteers who are dressed in traditional Western attire and can answer questions about the airport, transportation, and the city. Across from the baggage carousels is an information desk. Airport shuttles connect with downtown, hotels, car rental agencies, and the Greyhound bus terminal. The desks for all major rental car companies are across the road.

It's a 1.5-hour drive from the airport to Banff National Park. To Kootenay, it's a little under two hours; to Yoho, it's a little more than two hours. It takes 3 hours to drive to Waterton Lakes National Park and 3.5 hours to drive to Jasper from the Calgary airport.

Downtown Calgary is a 15-minute drive from the airport. **Taxis** are available, or you can hop the **Calgary Transit bus** (403/537-7777, www.calgarytransit. com, 5am-midnight daily, $11). Once you reach downtown, your ticket includes unlimited transit network rides for the remainder of the day. The airport bus runs every 30 minutes.

Bus

Rider Express (no phone, riderexpress. ca) offers the only service connecting cities in British Columbia, Alberta, and Saskatchewan, including long-distance routes between Vancouver and Lake Louise, Banff, and Calgary.

Red Arrow (403/531-0350 or 800/232-1958, www.redarrow.ca) provides bus service to Calgary from Lethbridge, Edmonton, Red Deer, and Fort McMurray.

Flathead Valley, Montana
Air

Fly into Flathead Valley through **Glacier Park International Airport** (FCA, 4170 US 2, 406/257-5994, www.iflyglacier. com), which is centrally located between the four towns of Whitefish, Kalispell, Columbia Falls, and Bigfork. Rental cars are available. From the airport, it's just a half-hour drive to Glacier's west entrance, but you'll need three hours to drive north to Waterton Lakes National Park in Canada.

Train

The Empire Builder train, run by **Amtrak** (800/872-7245, www.amtrak.com), stops at the **Whitefish station** (500 Depot St., Whitefish) twice daily. Reservations are a must in summer. The westbound route originates in Chicago, stopping at Milwaukee, St. Paul-Minneapolis, and Fargo, then continues to East Glacier (summer only), Essex, and West Glacier along the park's southern boundary on its way to Whitefish. The ride from Chicago to Whitefish takes more than 30 hours. Eastbound trains starting in Seattle and Portland join in Spokane to reach Whitefish in a little more than 15 hours.

Bus

Greyhound (800/231-2222, www.grey hound.com) services Whitefish and Kalispell. Connections to larger cities are via Billings and Spokane, Washington.

Bozeman, Montana
Air

Bozeman Yellowstone International Airport (BZN, 850 Gallatin Field Rd., Belgrade, 406/388-8321, www. bozemanairport.com) has more flights than the Glacier airport. Rental cars are available. Bozeman is located 10 miles (16 km) and 15 minutes east of the airport on I-90. It's a little less than a two-hour drive to Yellowstone National Park's West Entrance. You can reach the North Entrance in 1.5 hours.

Bus

Greyhound (800/231-2222, www. greyhound.com) services Missoula, Butte, and Bozeman. Connections to larger cities are via Billings and Spokane, Washington. Buses run once daily to Missoula, where a transfer is required to reach Bozeman.

Jackson, Wyoming
Air

Jackson Hole Airport (JAC, 1250 E. Airport Rd, Jackson, 307/733-7682, www.jacksonholeairport.com) is actually inside Grand Teton National Park, just north of Jackson. Major cities across the country have direct flights to Jackson Hole, but some flights run seasonally in winter or summer. Flights to Jackson Hole are usually more expensive than to other area airports. The airport is a 90-minute-drive from Yellowstone's South Entrance.

A two-hour drive from both Yellowstone and Grand Teton National Parks, **Idaho Falls Regional Airport** (IDA, 2140 N. Skyline Dr., Idaho Falls, 208/612-8221, www.idahofallsidaho.gov) often has cheaper options than flying into Jackson Hole. Some flights are daily, while others are weekly or summer only.

Bus

Mountain States Express (307/733-4629, www.mountainstatesexpress.com) runs daily shuttles to and from the airport in Salt Lake City, Utah, to Jackson. Salt Lake Express (877/714-6104, www. saltlakeexpress.com) services connect riders with Salt Lake City Airport or Idaho Falls Airport and Jackson.

Salt Lake City, Utah
Air

Salt Lake City International Airport (SLC, 776 N. Terminal Dr., 801/575-2400, www. slcairport.com) is a major airline hub servicing most of the large U.S. carriers. It is the western hub for Delta. The airport has three terminals; in each you'll find

a ground-transportation information desk, food service, motel-hotel courtesy phones, and a ski-rental shop. Auto rentals are in the parking structure immediately across from the terminals.

From the airport, it's a five-hour drive to both Yellowstone (via the West Entrance) and Grand Teton National Parks. It's a 7.5-hour drive to the western entrance of Rocky Mountain National Park, in Grand Lake, Colorado.

Downtown SLC is located less than 10 miles (16 km) west of the airport, a 10-minute drive via North Temple or I-80. By far the easiest way to get from the airport to downtown is via the **TRAX rail line** (801/743-3882, www.rideuta. com, 6am-11pm Mon.-Sat., 9:45am-10pm Sun., $2.50 one way), which runs between the airport and Salt Lake Central Station. Arriving travelers can take the shuttle from the ground level of the airport to the 1940 West Station/Temporary Airport Station, then continue on the Green Line to downtown SLC. Trains run every 15 minutes on weekdays, every 20 minutes on weekends.

Train

Amtrak (800/872-7245, www.amtrak. com) trains stop at the **Salt Lake Central Station** (300 S. 600 W.), which also serves as a terminus for local buses, light-rail, and commuter trains. The only Amtrak train that currently passes through the city is the California Zephyr, connecting three times a week to Reno and Oakland to the west and Denver and Chicago to the east.

Bus

Salt Lake City is at a crossroads of several major interstate highways and has good **Greyhound** (801/355-9579, www. greyhound.com) service. In summer, one bus daily leaves from **Salt Lake Central Station** (300 S. 600 W.) for Yellowstone National Park.

Mountain States Express (307/733-4629, www.mountainstatesexpress.com)

Coronavirus in the U.S. and Canadian Rockies

At the time of writing in 2021, the U.S, and Canadian Rockies had been variably impacted by the effects of the coronavirus. Some areas are beginning to recover, while others are still experiencing high infection and hospitalization rates. The restrictions on crossing the U.S./Canadian border were beginning to loosen, but the situation is constantly evolving. Now more than ever, Moon encourages its readers to be courteous and ethical in their travel. Be respectful to local residents and mindful of the situation in your chosen destination when planning your trip.

Before You Go

♦ Check websites (listed below) for local restrictions and the overall health status of the destination and your point of origin. If you're traveling to or from an area that is currently a COVID-19 hotspot, you may want to reconsider your trip. Moon encourages travelers to get vaccinated if their health status allows and to take a coronavirus test with enough time to receive the results before departure if possible. Some destinations may require proof of vaccination or a negative COVID test result before arrival, along with other tests and/or a self-quarantine period after arrival. Check local requirements and factor these into your plans.

♦ If you plan to fly, check with your airline and the local health authorities for updated travel requirements. Some airlines may be taking more steps to help you travel safely, such as limiting occupancy; check their websites before buying your ticket. Flights may be more infrequent, with increased cancellations.

♦ Pack hand sanitizer, a thermometer, and plenty of face masks. Consider packing snacks, bottled water, a cooler, or anything else you might need to limit the number of stops along your route. Be prepared for possible closures and reduced services over the course of your travels.

runs daily shuttles to and from the airport in Salt Lake City to Jackson, Wyoming, near Grand Teton National Park. **Salt Lake Express** (877/714-6104, www.saltlakeexpress.com) shuttles also connect Salt Lake City's airport and Jackson, Wyoming.

Denver, Colorado
Air
One of the busiest airports in the country, **Denver International Airport** (DEN, 8500 Peña Blvd., 303/342-2000 or 800/247-2336www.flydenver.com) is serviced by 20 airlines and is a hub for United, Southwest, and Great Lakes Airlines. It sits about 30 minutes (25 mi/40 km) east of downtown. From the airport, it's a 1.5-hour drive to Estes Park, the gateway town on the eastern side of Rocky Mountain National Park.

Train
Amtrak (800/872-7245, www.amtrak.com) offers daily service to Denver's **Union Station** (1701 Wynkoop St.) along the California Zephyr route. Tickets are available online or in person at the station. The route originates in Chicago in the east and in the San Francisco Bay Area in the west.

Bus
Greyhound (www.greyhound.com) and the Colorado Department of Transportation's **Bustang** (800/900-3011, www.ridebustang.com) offer regional service between **Union Station**

♦ Assess the risk of entering crowded spaces, joining tours, and taking public transit.

♦ Expect general disruptions. Events may be postponed or cancelled. Some national park, tours, and private venues may require reservations, enforce capacity limits, or operate during different hours than the ones listed. Other venues may be closed entirely, and food venues may be take-out only.

Resources

♦ **World Health Organization:** www.who.int/emergencies/diseases/novel-coronavirus-2019/travel-advice

♦ **International Air Transport Organization:** www.iatatravelcentre.com/world.php

♦ *New York Times* **Coronavirus Map:** www.nytimes.com/interactive/2020/world/coronavirus-maps.html

♦ **CDC:** www.cdc.gov/coronavirus/2019-ncov/travelers

♦ **U.S. State Department:** https://travel.state.gov/content/travel/en/traveladvisories/ea/covid-19-information.html

♦ **U.S. National Park Service COVID-19 landing page:** www.nps.gov/aboutus/news/public-health-update.htm

♦ **Parks Canada COVID-19 landing page:** www.pc.gc.ca/en/voyage-travel/securite-safety/covid-19-info

(1701 Wynkoop St.) and locations such as Colorado Springs, Vail, and Estes Park, on the eastern boundary of Rocky Mountain National Park.

Train Services

On **Via Rail** (888/842-7245, www.viarail.ca), The Canadian service connects Toronto, Winnipeg, Edmonton, Jasper, Kamloops, and Vancouver. Unfortunately, the tracks pass far north of Calgary and Banff. The Canadian runs each direction three times per week May-mid-October. The remainder of the year, service drops to two times per week. Economy class offers the cheapest travel with a reclining seat and no meals included. Meals and snacks are available for purchase. Three sleeper options include varied levels of privacy from shared berth

rooms to private rooms and all meals in the dining car. Via Rail runs on freight lines, which can often cause delays and late trains.

The **Rocky Mountaineer** (877/460-4200 Canada & U.S. or 604/606-7245 international, www.rockymountaineer.com, mid-Apr.-mid-Oct.) offers luxury train travel with glass-domed viewing cars. Offered one-way or round-trip, this guided train tour includes gourmet meals and overnights in hotels en route, so you can see all the scenery during the day. One historic, two-day route links Vancouver with Lake Louise or Banff, departing 2-3 times per week. The train chugs through the spiral tunnels in Yoho National Park. Other options connect Vancouver with Jasper on different routes that take 2-3 days; these depart

Other Airports

Billings, Montana
Billings Logan International Airport (BIL, 1901 Terminal Circle, 406/247-8609, www.flybillings.com) is serviced by seven carriers. From the airport, you can drive to Yellowstone National Park's North Entrance year-round in less than three hours. It's a little more than three hours to the Northeast Entrance. Due to winter road closures, this route is only possible late May-mid-October.

Cody, Wyoming
Yellowstone Regional Airport (COD, 2101 Roger Sedam Dr., 307/587-5096, http://flyyra.com) is only serviced by United Airlines from Denver. To reach the East Entrance of Yellowstone National Park takes 1.25 hours of driving. It's almost two hours to the Northeast Entrance. Due to winter road closures, these routes are only open May-October.

Cranbrook, Alberta
Canadian Rockies International Airport (YXC, 1-9370 Airport Access Rd., 250/426-7913, flyyxc.com), serviced by two airlines, connects with flights from Vancouver and Calgary. You'll need 1.5 hours to drive to Kootenay National Park, or 3 hours to reach Yoho National Park.

Edmonton, Alberta
Edmonton International Airport (YEG, 1000 Airport Rd NW, Nisku, AB, flyeia.com), which is serviced by 15 airlines, is a four-hour drive to Jasper National Park or the north end of Banff National Park.

Great Falls, Montana
Great Falls International Airport (GTF, 2800 Terminal Dr., 406/727-3404, flygtf.com), serviced by four airlines, requires 2.5 hours to drive to Glacier National Park, 3.5 hours to Waterton Lakes National Park, and 4 hours to the West Entrance or North Entrance of Yellowstone National Park.

Missoula, Montana
Missoula International Airport (MSO, 5225 US 10 W., 406/728-4381, flymissoula.com), serviced by six airlines, is a 2.5-hour drive from Glacier National Park and a 5-hour drive from Waterton Lakes National Park.

West Yellowstone, Montana
Yellowstone Airport (WYS, 607 Airport Rd., West Yellowstone, 406/646-7631, www.yellowstoneairport.org) operates early May-mid October just outside of West Yellowstone and is only two miles from the West Entrance to Yellowstone National Park. Delta is the only airline operating here, with flights from Salt Lake City.

twice weekly. Some packages include activities at destinations.

Amtrak (800/872-7245, www.amtrak.com) has two lines that service the Rocky Mountain states. Reclining coach seats are the economy option; business class (when offered) has extra perks thrown in. Food and beverages are available for purchase. You can upgrade to private rooms or roomettes for sleeping, which include meals in the dining car. Amtrak runs on freight lines, which often cause delays and late trains.

- The Empire Builder runs daily, linking Chicago, St. Paul-Minneapolis, Spokane, Seattle, and Portland with stops at towns in the vicinity of Glacier

National Park. The train stops at three Montana towns bordering the park: East Glacier (summer only), Essex, and West Glacier. The trail also stops at Whitefish in Flathead Valley.

- The California Zephyr has service daily between Chicago, Omaha, Denver, Salt Lake City, and San Francisco (Emeryville). It stops at two smaller Colorado towns closer to Rocky Mountain National Park: Granby is about a 30-minute drive from the west entrance to the park, while Nederland is about a one-hour drive from the east entrance at Estes Park.

Major Highways and Interstates
Canada
Three major highways slice east-west through Canada and the Canadian Rockies. **CA 16** (Yellowhead Hwy.) runs through Alberta, connecting Edmonton, Jasper, and Jasper National Park. Further south, **CA 1** (Trans-Canada) goes through Calgary, Canmore, Banff, Lake Louise, Banff National Park, and Yoho National Park, BC. **BC 3** is the farthest south, zig-zagging north of the international border; this gets you closest to Waterton Lakes National Park.

For north-south roads, **AB 2** runs along the eastern front of the mountains in Alberta, dropping through Edmonton, Calgary, and Fort Macleod to the international border crossing at Piegan-Carway into Montana, where it turns into US 89. **BC 93** cuts right through the Canadian Rockies from Jasper National Park to southwest Montana. En route, it follows the Icefields Parkway into Banff National Park, then continues into British Columbia through Kootenay National Park and the Columbia Valley to the international border crossing at Roosville, where it becomes US 93 in Montana.

United States
Major east-west interstates bisect the Rocky Mountains in the United States.

I-90 is the furthest north. It passes south of Glacier National Park. The Montana towns of Billings, Bozeman, Butte, and Missoula all sit on I-90. **I-80** crosses southern Wyoming south of Grand Teton and north of Rocky Mountain National Park to go through Salt Lake City, Utah. South of Salt Lake City, **I-70** cruises across Utah on the boundary between the mountains and desert canyons into Colorado to reach Denver, passing south of Rocky Mountain National Park.

Interstate arteries for north-south travel go on the east or west side of the Rocky Mountains. From the international border crossing at Sweetgrass (AB-4), **I-15** drops through Montana east of Glacier and goes through Great Falls, Helena, and Butte, crossing the Rockies. It continues south through eastern Idaho, Idaho Falls, and then to Salt Lake City, Utah. From I-15, routes to Yellowstone or Grand Teton take 2-3 hours. On the plains of eastern Wyoming, **I-25** drops from I-90 at Buffalo through Casper and Cheyenne to enter Colorado and reach Denver. I-25 passes east of Yellowstone, Grand Teton, and Rocky Mountain National Parks.

Road Rules

Car Rentals
Across North America, car rental companies maintain desks in most airports. They either have their cars on site or take you by shuttle to their **off-site lots** to pick up your vehicle. At smaller seasonal airports, the number of companies may be limited. Larger cities have rental car outlets; some towns surrounding the national parks also have car rentals.

Reservations are ideal, especially for summer travel. Be aware that **one-way rentals** usually incur additional fees. Most companies offer discounts for weekly rentals or longer. If you are a member of the Canadian Automobile Association (CAA) or the American

Automobile Association (AAA), check on available discounts. When you make your reservation, it's imperative that you ask about taking the car **across the border;** you'll also need to show your rental agreement at the border.

RV Rentals

RVs are a popular way to travel around the Rocky Mountains. Make **advance reservations** to ensure you can get the vehicle that's right for your trip. When you make your reservation, ask about **crossing the international border** to be sure you can do so. If you are planning a **one-way trip,** ask about additional costs.

Cruise America/Cruise Canada (800/671-8042, www.cruiseamerica. com) rents RVs in Denver, Salt Lake City, and Calgary, as well as in multiple cities in Montana (Billings, Bozeman, Missoula), plus larger cities in both countries. **Canadream** (www.canadream.com, 888/948-9576 Canada, 888/948-9576 international) has rental outlets in Calgary and Edmonton. In the United States, **RVShare** (rvshare.com) is a web-based rental service that links up renters with individual RV owners.

Some **national parks** have **limitations** on what roads and campgrounds RVs can access:

- **Glacier National Park** in Montana has the most roads that restrict RV access. The narrow, curvy **Going-to-the-Sun Road** bans RVs and trailer combos longer than 21 feet (6.4 m), wider than 8 feet (2.4 m), and taller than 10 feet (3 m). Several **remote dirt roads** elsewhere in the park also have length and trailer restrictions.

- In **Rocky Mountain National Park, Old Fall River Road** doesn't allow vehicles with trailers or RVs longer than 25 feet (7.6 m).

- Two secondary roads in **Grand Teton National Park** ban RVs entirely: the **Moose-Wilson Road** and **Signal Mountain Road.**

- In **Yoho National Park,** the **Yoho Valley Road** specifies no trailers but does not limit RV size. However, there are two tight, challenging switchbacks that require RVs to ascend backwards through the middle of the drive.

Many national park **campgrounds** also have length limits for RVs. Most are rustic and lack hookups for RVs. Generator hours are usually restricted, too. If possible, make advance reservations for all of your campsites to ensure your RV will fit. If you require hookups, you may want to camp in the small towns surrounding the national parks, where full hookups are common.

Driving Rules and Etiquette

Driver's Licenses and International Permits

A current driver's license from a U.S. state or Canadian province is valid for driving in North America for up to six months. Because rules are inconsistent between states, drivers from outside North America should get an **International Driving Permit (IDP)** to use in tandem with your driver's license from home. Contact your country's department of motor vehicles and driver's licenses to get an IDP **before you depart from home.** Once in the United States or Canada, you cannot get an IDP.

Insurance

All drivers in Canada and the United States must have insurance and carry **proof of insurance** in the vehicle. Drivers from other countries should bring documentation and check with their home insurance about coverage amounts. You can also purchase insurance when you rent a car or RV. You may also have rental insurance through a motor club membership, your personal insurance policy, or the credit card used to reserve the rental; know your options before arrival.

Cell Phones

Rules on the use of electronic devices

while driving vary by town, county, and state in the United States. In general, the best and safest policy is to stick to **hands-free use** when driving at all times. The provinces of British Columbia and Alberta are stricter, with a complete ban on the use of hand-held cell phones or electronic devices while driving.

Seat Belts

Wearing seat belts is **mandatory** in the United States and Canada. Each state and province has varying regulations on safety seats for **babies and children,** based on age and weight. Most require infants to ride in rear-facing car seats and children (over 40 lbs/18 kg) to use booster seats and restraints.

Speed Limits and Traffic Signals

Speed limits differ in Canada and the United States. Canada follows the metric system, so speeds will appear in **kilometers per hour (kph).** The United States follows the imperial system, so speeds will appear in **miles per hour (mph).** Highway speeds vary, but are generally between 50-65 mph (80-100 kph).

Across the Rocky Mountain provinces (AB and BC) and states (MT, WY, UT, and CO), motorists are allowed to **turn right after stopping at a red light.** As you pull out, look for both traffic and pedestrians. Signs at the intersection will indicate if right turns on red lights are prohibited.

Driving Hazards
Road Conditions

Check current road conditions before launching for the day. In Canada, information on construction delays and current weather is available; you can often see current conditions via webcams. Consult traveler information for **British Columbia** (800/5504997 in North America, www.driveBC.ca) or **Alberta** (call 511 toll free in province, www.511Alberta.ca). Smartphone apps

are available for both provinces: **BC Highways** and **511 Alberta.**

For road conditions in the United States, including construction delays, current weather, and webcams, resources may vary by state:

- **Montana:** call 511, www.mdt.mt.gov/travinfo/; smartphone app **MDT Travel Info**
- **Wyoming:** call 511 or 888/996-7623 toll free nationwide, www.wyoroad.info; smartphone app **Wyoming 511**
- **Utah:** call 511, udot.traffic.utah.gov; smartphone app **UDOT Traffic**
- **Colorado:** www.cdot.gov/travel or www.cotrip.org; smartphone app **CDOT Colorado Road Conditions**

Mountain Roads

Roads in the Rocky Mountains tend to be **curvy** and sometimes **narrow.** In cliffside areas, they may not have **guardrails** or have them only in certain spots. Mountain roads tend to be isolated with **minimal services** and no streetlights. Use caution when driving, and always check the weather.

Weather

Rocky Mountain weather is finicky. **Storms** can move in fast; what begins as a blue-sky day can shift quickly. with afternoon **lightning, hail, rain,** or **fog.** At high elevations, it can even **snow in summer,** although it usually melts fast. Check the weather forecast frequently to be prepared.

From **October to mid-April,** snow and ice are common in the Rocky Mountains. Snow is also common at **low elevations** in the Rocky Mountain states and provinces.

Winter Travel

Many roads require **snow plowing** to keep them open through winter. Others, particularly high-elevation roads in national parks, **close in winter** due to voluminous snow. If visibility is difficult and snow accumulation heavy, some roads close temporarily until the storm passes and they can be plowed to reopen.

For safety, your vehicle should have **winter tires** for better traction. They are required during winter on many of the mountain highways in the Rockies. Road signs may say "must carry chains or traction devices." You must be prepared with **chains** when they are required, so be sure to carry a pair with you. They are not a replacement for winter tires, but an additional requirement. Know how to put chains on your tires; chain-up areas are usually signed pullovers before mountain passes. **Studded tires** are an acceptable alternative to chains. Do not attempt to drive snowy or icy roads with summer tires.

Many of the mountain zones are prone to avalanches. **Do not stop in avalanche paths** due to the risk of snow slides. Sometimes roads will close during avalanche control work.

Wildlife

Wildlife poses a driving hazard in the Rocky Mountains. Animals can dash onto roadways with little warning, and it's difficult at moderate speeds to brake safely without causing an accident or injury to the animal or your car. **Dawn and dusk** are particularly difficult times for spotting wildlife ready to jump onto the road. Stay alert: The entire Rocky Mountain area is essentially one huge wildlife crossing, with minimal warning signage. You will see some overpasses, fencing, and underpasses built specifically for **wildlife crossing** in Banff and Kootenay National Parks.

Wildlife-watching also poses a hazard, causing **animal jams.** Rather than stopping in the road and blocking traffic, **pull over** onto the side to watch the animals. Be cautious about getting out of your car to snap photos. You'll want to be aware of other cars around you, many of whose drivers are gawking instead of paying attention to driving. You'll also want to maintain distance from wildlife: Stay about three bus lengths (120 ft/35 m) away from bison, elk, deer, bighorn sheep, and mountain goats. Maintain 100 yards (100 m) from bears and wolves.

Emergencies and Roadside Assistance

In Canada and the United States, call **911** in case of emergency. Your call will automatically reach the appropriate dispatch for police, ambulance, and fire. Stay at the scene of car accidents until the police dismiss you. You may also find on many mountainous roads that **cell phones** do not get reception; in an emergency, flag down a passerby who can call for assistance at the nearest town or ranger station.

In the Rocky Mountains, where long distances of remote roads can stretch forever, it's wise to have the assurance of a **roadside assistance program.** Some insurance programs provide them. Otherwise, get roadside assistance through the **Canadian Automobile Association** (www.caa.ca) or **American Automobile Association** (www.aaa.com).

Maps and GPS

In the United States, national parks distribute maps from the entrance stations and visitors centers. These work well for road trips, but are not exceptionally detailed for assessing road steepness or topographical changes. Each park also has an association that sells maps and guidebooks. Members of the **American Automobile Association** (www.aaa.com) can get driving maps for states, provinces, and smaller regions.

In Canada, the best driving maps for the Canadian Rockies come from **Gem Trek** (403/762-3095, gemtrek.com), a local company in Banff. The maps also include trail descriptions. Members of **Canadian Automobile Association** (www.caa.ca) can get driving maps for provinces, states, and smaller regions.

In the Rocky Mountains, do not rely solely on a GPS for route-finding on roads, especially secondary roads. Double check GPS-suggested routes against a **hard-copy map** and information on seasonal road closures. In mountain states and provinces, it's not uncommon for GPS directions to send drivers up closed roads or longer-than-necessary routes.

Gas

Gas in Canada is sold by the **liter.** In the United States, it is sold by the **gallon.** These two measurements are not remotely close. One liter of gas in Canada equals 0.26 gallons; 1 gallon of gas in the U.S. equals 3.79 liters. So don't be fooled into thinking that gas prices look pretty good for drivers going from Montana into Alberta or British Columbia. In general, gas in the United States is a little cheaper than gas in Canada.

Be sure to gas up just before entering the national parks, as not all have gas stations; do not expect to find fuel inside **Kootenay, Glacier,** or **Rocky Mountain National Parks.** The other national parks have gas stations, but they are sometimes spaced far from each other.

Parking

Inside national parks, you'll find **free parking** in designated lots at visitors centers, lodges, trailheads, and attractions. However, in peak season (summer), lots often fill early in the morning. Expect to pay to park in the towns inside the Canadian national parks, such as Jasper, Lake Louise, and Banff. During peak season, parking can be difficult to find streetside or in downtown areas. Larger cities and resort towns will often have fee-based lots and streetside meters or kiosks.

Motorcycles

Motorcyclists are quite common in the Rocky Mountains. Scenery, fresh air, and the open road are big lures. The **Icefields Parkway** in Banff and Jasper,

Glacier's **Going-to-the-Sun Road,** and Rocky Mountain's **Trail Ridge Road** are the major draws for motorcyclists.

Helmets are required for motorcycle riders in British Columbia and Alberta. In the United States, helmet laws vary by state. In Montana, Idaho, Wyoming, and Colorado, helmets are only required for riders under 18 years old. In Utah, only those under 21 years old must wear helmets.

Visas and Officialdom

Passports and Visas
Entering the United States

International travelers entering the United States must have **passports.** One exception applies to travelers from Canada and countries in the Western Hemisphere Travel Initiative, who may use **passport cards, NEXUS cards,** or **enhanced driver's licenses. Visas** may also be required for some countries; check travel.state.gov for countries with visa waivers, visa applications, and fees.

Entering Canada

International travelers entering Canada must have **passports.** The one exception is travelers from the United States and Western Hemisphere Travel Initiative countries, who may use **passport cards, NEXUS cards,** or **enhanced driver's licenses. Visas** are not required for visitors from the United States and many other countries. Find the list of visa-exempt countries and visa requirements at www.cic.gc.ca.

Border Crossings

The international boundary between Canada and the United States has several border crossings in eastern British Columbia and Alberta, which all cross into Montana. The borders are controlled by **Canada Border Services Agency** (CBSA, www.cbsa-asfc.gc.ca) and **U.S. Customs and Border Protection** (CBP, www.cbp.gov/travel).

Roosville

The **Roosville border crossing** (BC 93/US 93) sits on the west side of the Rocky Mountains between eastern British Columbia and northwest Montana, on the route from Banff and Kootenay National Parks to Glacier National Park. It is open 24 hours daily year-round.

Chief Mountain

A **seasonal** port of entry on Chief Mountain International Highway (AB 6/MT 17), the **Chief Mountain border crossing** is open daily from mid-May through September. During the height of the season, from June through early September, the border is open 7am-10pm. In May and the rest of September, it's open 9am-6pm. This is the fastest link between Waterton Lakes National Park and Glacier National Park.

Piegan-Carway

Farther east of Waterton-Glacier and the Chief Mountain crossing is the **Piegan-Carway border crossing** (AB 2/US 89), which is open year-round (7am-11pm daily). This is the fastest route between Calgary and Glacier National Park or Flathead Valley.

Goat Haunt, USA

Two national parks share the international boundary: **Waterton Lakes National Park** in Canada and **Glacier National Park** in the United States. Together, they serve as the world's first **International Peace Park.** Special border rules allow passengers to cross the border (without the need of a passport) via a **boat tour** from Waterton Lake to Goat Haunt, USA, a summer-only outpost in Glacier. You can also **hike** across this border with a passport and registration in Waterton (using CBP ROAM kiosks or the CBP ROAM app). You'll still need to take appropriate **passports** or **passport cards.** For further information on hiking across the border, call the **Roosville Port of Entry** (406/889-3865) for hiking into the United States or the **Canada Border Services Agency** (403/653-3535) for hiking into Canada.

U.S. and Canadian Customs

In general, Canada and the United States have similar customs laws: **no plants, controlled substances, firewood,** or **live bait** can cross the border. Some fresh meats, poultry products, fruits, and vegetables are restricted. **Pets** are permitted to cross the border with a certificate of rabies vaccination dated within 30 days prior to crossing. To find out what can and can't go across the border, consult the **Canada Border Services Agency** (CBSA, www.cbsa-asfc.gc.ca) or **U.S. Customs and Border Protection** (CBP, www.cbp.gov/travel).

Be aware of two major differences in customs rules between the countries. While **marijuana** is legal in Canada, it is illegal under U.S. federal law and therefore considered criminal to bring it across the border into the United States. Most **firearms and weapons** are illegal in Canada; this classification includes **bear spray.** An exception is made for bear spray that's labeled as **USEPA-approved** or with an indication that it's intended for use on bears; these can be carried across the border.

Travel Tips

Alcohol and Smoking Laws

Alcohol and smoking laws vary in Canada. The **legal age** for purchasing alcohol, cannabis, or tobacco products is **19** in British Columbia and **18** in Alberta. Smoking is not permitted in public indoor spaces, including restaurants and bars. Parks Canada has a **liquor and cannabis curfew** from 11pm to 7am.

In the United States, the legal age for buying alcohol and tobacco products is **21.** Smoking is generally banned in public spaces indoors. While marijuana is still federally banned (and cannot be brought across the international border), a patchwork of states, including **Montana** and **Colorado,** have legalized it. Recreational marijuana use remains illegal in **Utah** and **Wyoming.** However, be aware that possession and use of **marijuana is illegal in the U.S. national parks** and all other federal lands.

Time Zones

Most of the Rocky Mountain provinces and states—and all of the national parks in this guide—are on **Mountain Standard Time** (MST). Most of British Columbia is on Pacific Standard Time (PST), with the exception of the southeastern portion of the province, which is on MST. (This area of BC includes the towns of Cranbrook and Radium Hot Springs, as well as Kootenay National Park.) All the Rocky Mountain provinces and states observe **Daylight Saving Time,** which moves clocks forward one hour from early March to early November; exact dates vary from year to year.

Access for Travelers with Disabilities

Travelers with disabilities can find accessible accommodations, restaurants, campgrounds, restrooms, visitors centers, and sightseeing attractions throughout the Rocky Mountains, although not everything is barrier-free. Many of the national parks have been improving accessibility on **trails** to make them barrier-free and meet the need for stable walking or wheelchair surfaces. In general, the national parks in the U.S. and Canadian Rockies tend to have **accessible visitors center, lodge rooms,** and **campsites** (at some campgrounds).

Wheelchair Getaways (www.accessible vans.com) rents accessible vans for traveling from multiple U.S. locations. **Wheelchair Traveling** (http://wheelchairtraveling.com) has travel advice for a few national parks in the Rockies. **DisabledTravelers.com** (www.

disabledtravelers.com) has a broad range of accessibility information.

U.S. National Parks

Many of the parks offer detailed accessibility brochures, **captioned** or **audio-described videos,** and **large-print** or **braille brochures.** Glacier and Rocky Mountain have **accessible shuttles.** Qualified **service dogs** are allowed in the parks anywhere that visitors can go.

The best **accessible trails** are in Glacier (Trail of the Cedars), Grand Teton (Jenny Lake Discovery Trail), and Rocky Mountain (Lily Lake). Yellowstone has the most accessible trails overall; additionally, some Xanterra **tours** (www. yellowstonenationalparklodges.com) can accommodate wheelchairs. In Grand Teton, **rafting trips** through Grand Teton Lodging Company (www.gtlc.com) can accommodate some wheelchairs.

Check out the **National Park Service accessibility page** (www.nps.gov/aboutus/accessibility.htm) for links to specifics on individual parks.

Canadian National Parks

Service dogs are allowed, but they must be leashed. **Jasper** has the most accessible features, including **accessible tours** of Maligne Lake and the Columbia Icefield's Skywalk. (See the park website for more information. Look under Plan Your Trip/Facilities and Services for Accessible Park Facilities.) The trail around Annette Lake is paved and wheelchair-accessible.

In Banff, the Banff Gondola and ROAM buses are wheelchair-accessible, as is a portion of the Johnston Canyon catwalk trail. The Lake Minnewanka **boat cruise** can accommodate wheelchairs. Yoho has two **accessible trails** with outstanding scenery: Emerald Lake and Takakkaw Falls. In Waterton, the Lakeshore Trail is accessible from Peach Park to Cameron Creek. For soaking in hot springs, Miette (in Jasper), Radium Hot Springs (in Kootenay), and Banff

Upper Hot Springs have **submersible wheelchairs.**

Online information on accessibility varies by park. For information on accessibility in Banff, Yoho, Kootenay, and Waterton, the best bet is to call the park's visitors centers. You can also get additional information from **Banff Lake Louise Tourism** (www.banfflakelouise. com/accessibility) and **Kootenay Rockies** (www.kootenayrockies.com), which covers both Yoho and Kootenay.

Passes and Discounts

In the United States, citizens and permanent residents who are blind or have permanent disabilities can get a **free lifetime Access Pass** for entry to all U.S. national parks and other federal sites. The pass admits the holder plus three other adults in the same vehicle. Pass holders also get 50 percent discounts on federally run tours and campgrounds. Get these passes in person at entrance stations with proof of medical disability or eligibility for receiving federal benefits. It's also possible to apply for a pass online (https://store.usgs.gov/access-pass) but note that there's a processing fee ($10) for the application.

Senior Travelers

U.S. citizens and permanent residents age 62 or over can buy the **lifetime Senior Pass** ($80, which provides entrance to all national parks and federal lands, plus gives discounts for federally operated campgrounds and tours. To purchase one, bring proof of age (state driver's license, birth certificate, or passport) in person to any national park entrance station or apply online (https://store.usgs.gov/senior-pass, $10 processing fee). Seniors from other countries can purchase the **Senior Annual Pass** ($20).

In Canada, all seniors can purchase a discounted **Discovery Pass** ($60), valid for 12 months. You must be at least 65 years old, but do not have to be a Canadian citizen.

Seniors looking for educational group travel should check out **Road Scholar** (www.roadscholar.org), which offers multiple programs that visit individual national parks in the Canadian and U.S. Rockies as well as a few that stitch together multiple parks. **AARP** (www.aarp. org) has travel information for seniors that includes tips for road trips and outdoor adventures in several national parks in the U.S. Rockies. Seniors can also get **travel insurance** through AARP.

Traveling with Children

National parks are great destinations for kids, especially when they can be active: hiking, biking, paddling, swimming, watching wildlife, and roasting marshmallows around a campfire. To ensure a successful hike, choose age-appropriate distances and pack along water, snacks, extra layers, sunscreen, and bug repellant.

Junior Rangers and Xplorers

In U.S. national parks, kids can earn a unique **Junior Ranger** badge at each park by completing self-guided activities in booklets (some have small fees), available at all visitors centers. This is a great way to learn about each park. Most activities are geared toward kids ages 6-12.

At Canadian national parks, the **Xplorers Program** is included in the park entry fee. Each park has a unique booklet (available at visitors centers) with activities to teach kids about the individual parks. Upon completion, kids receive a small token souvenir.

Ranger-Led Family Programs

Most of the parks offer ranger-led programs intended for families with kids. These include hikes, wildlife talks with props, games, night sky telescope viewing, and evening campground programs. Schedules are online, at visitors centers, and sometimes on campground bulletin boards.

Traveling with Pets

In national parks, **pets must be leashed at all times** to prevent conflicts with wildlife. Dogs can stress wild animals and even trigger aggressive reactions. Some dog parks in towns outside the parks allow for off-leash running. Be considerate of wildlife and other visitors by keeping your pet under control and disposing of waste in garbage cans. Avoid leaving pets unattended in a car anywhere. All of the national parks levy steep fines for breaking pet-related regulations.

In U.S. national parks, pets are allowed in limited areas: **campgrounds, parking lots,** and **roadside pullouts.** They are not allowed on trails, beaches, in the backcountry, or at many park lodges. Outside the parks, you can find pet-friendly lodging.

In Canadian national parks, **some trails** allow dogs on leashes while others do not. Find out the rules for specific trails ahead of time to avoid a hefty fine. Some **lakes** permit dogs, even in canoes. Many park lodges have **pet-friendly accommodations** for an extra fee. Banff, Lake Louise, and Jasper have **dog nannies** or **kennels** if you want to explore without your pooch.

Travelers of Color

The population in the Rocky Mountain corridor states and provinces range between 83-93 percent white. But larger cosmopolitan cities such as Edmonton, Calgary, Salt Lake City, and Denver tend to be more diverse, with up to 30 percent of the population identifying as nonwhite. Banff, Jasper, and Yellowstone attract the most international travelers in the Rocky Mountain national parks.

The national parks are striving to employ a more diverse staff and tell more inclusive stories. Both Parks Canada and the U.S. National Park Service have plans in the works to improve diversity and inclusion in the coming years. In the Rocky Mountain parks, this includes increasing representation of the Indigenous cultures that extend as much as 10,000 years back, long before white explorers arrived.

Some of the parks have programs that highlight cultures from First Nations in Canada and Native Americans in the United States. Glacier offers the acclaimed **Native America Speaks** program that features local Indigenous people sharing their stories. Launched in 2021, the podcast *Parks* (www.parkspodcast.com), by Mary Mathis and Cody Nelson, features Indigenous voices telling the story of Yellowstone.

One of the best resources for travelers of color visiting national parks is **Diversify Outdoors** (www.diversifyoutdoors.com), a coalition of bloggers and social media personalities who are passionate about the outdoors and strive for equity, inclusion, and access for all.

LGBTQ Travelers

Much of the Rocky Mountain area is made up of small rural towns and farming communities, which are often conservative places. However, some of the cities in this region have active and welcoming LGBTQ communities. You can find gay-friendly dining and nightlife spots in Calgary, Banff, Denver, Salt Lake City, and a few of the smaller cities, including Jasper. These same places also have pride festivals, parades, and celebrations.

Calgary is home to *Gay Calgary Magazine* (www.gaycalgary.com), where you can find events and inclusive businesses. **Pride Foundation** (pridefoundation.org) offers resources for the Northwest region of the United States, including Montana and Idaho. For Wyoming-based resources, visit **Wyoming Equality** (www.wyomingequality.org).

For a queer-focused podcast on the U.S. national parks, check out the travels of Dusty Ballard and Michael Ryan on *Gaze at the National Parks* (gazeatthe-nationalparks.com). **Hello Ranger** (hellorangercommunity.com) is an inclusive group of national park fans with information on traveling in the U.S. national parks.

Mister B&B (www.misterbandb.com) and **Purple Roofs** (www.purpleroofs.com) list LGBTQ-friendly and queer-owned accommodations around some of the national parks in the Rockies. International Gay and Lesbian Travel Association (www.iglta.org) is a trade organization with listings of gay-friendly hotels, tour operators, and safety information.

Reservations

National parks are extremely popular, so be prepared to book **lodges, campgrounds,** and **tours** as soon as reservations are available. Most park lodges take reservations at least **one year** in advance; some accept them up to **18 months** in advance. Each park concessionaire has its own reservation policy, so check with them for the specifics.

Canadian national park campgrounds (877/737-3783 North America or 519/826-5391 outside North America, reservation. pc.gc.ca) usually begin taking reservations in January for the year ahead, but the exact dates for different parks are staggered. Most **U.S. national park campgrounds** (877/833-6777, www. recreation.gov) take reservations six months in advance. For **Yellowstone National Park,** contact **Xanterra** (866/439-7375 or 307/344-7311, www. yellowstonenationalparklodges.com), the concessionaire, **12-18 months** in advance.

Travelers without reservations may be able to nab last-minute rooms by calling the park lodging companies. Otherwise, head to gateway towns on the perimeter of the park in question to find lodging. Campers should head to first-come, first-served campgrounds, but plan to be there early in the morning to claim a spot that opens.

Cell Phone Service and Internet Access

Cell service and internet connectivity in the Rocky Mountains is limited. The high mountains block reception for cell phones and only limited places inside the national park connect to Wi-Fi. Most lodges provide Wi-Fi access to guests, but speeds may be slow. Slow internet connectivity and limited cell service often prevents large downloads. Before you leave home, download all apps, music, documents, maps, and anything else you might want for your trip.

Some national park **visitors centers** have public Wi-Fi. However, the systems are extremely limited and crowded. You can usually check email and look up information online, but sending photos and large files may not work.

Plan to be out of reach while you travel inside the parks, where cell service is nonexistent on many roads, trails, campgrounds, picnic areas, and some lodges. For safety and assurance, let people know you will not be reachable and when you can reconnect with them.

If you have an emergency on a road where there is no service, flag down a car to get a message to the nearest ranger station or visitors center. Be specific about where you are located and the exact help you need. Hikers should be prepared to self-rescue; otherwise, send someone in your party out for help. Before you go to the backcountry, be prepared with enough supplies to stay warm and nourished in the time it may take to get help.

Cell Phone Etiquette

Many people visit national parks to escape the stresses of their lives. Be conscientious and kind to those around you in national parks by adhering to common courtesies:

- **Turn off the ringer.** Phone noise catapults park visitors back into the hubbub of modern life. Ringing phones can distract or startle birds and other wildlife. If you put your phone in **airplane mode,** you'll also save more power for taking photos and videos.

- **Turn your phone off.** On trails or in the backcountry, refrain from using your phone in hearing distance of other hikers. It's good for the psyche to cut the technological cord from time to time. You might hear birds singing, elk bugling, or a wolf howling.

- **Separate yourself.** If you must make a call, move away from campsites, beaches, and other visitors.

Health and Safety

Emergencies

In an emergency, call **911** to reach police, fire, or ambulance services 24 hours per day in all Rocky Mountain provinces and states—including within the national parks. In Canada, for non-emergency medical needs 24 hours per day, you can also call **811.** In British Columbia, the call will connect with **HealthLink BC** (www.healthlinkbc.ca). In Alberta, it will reach **Alberta's Health Link** (www. albertahealthservices.ca).

If you need help in a park but don't have cell services, get to the nearest ranger station or visitors center. If you can't get there yourself, flag down a car or hiker that can do so for you.

Health Insurance

Before you depart on your trip, check your health insurance to see if it will cover you while traveling outside your home network and/or into another country. If it provides no coverage or only partial coverage, purchase **supplemental travel insurance.** Most policies must be purchased before you leave on your trip, not while you are en route.

Supplemental travel insurance is available through organizations like **AARP** (www.aarp.org), **AAA** (www.aaa. com), and **CAA National** (www.caa.

ca). You can also get it through **Allianz Travel Insurance** (888/360-7805, www. allianztravelinsurance.com).

Wilderness Safety
Water Hazards

In the natural world, water can be swift, frigid, unforgiving, and sometimes lethal. The number-one cause of death in the Rocky Mountains is drowning, often after a fall into water. Be extremely cautious around lakes, fast-moving streams, and waterfalls, where slick moss and algae cover the rocks and there may be submerged obstacles.

Giardia

Lakes and streams can carry parasites like *Giardia lamblia.* If ingested, it causes cramping, nausea, and severe diarrhea for up to six weeks. Avoid giardia by **boiling water** (for one minute, plus one minute for each 1,000 ft/305 m of elevation above sea level) or using a one-micron **filter.** Bleach also works (add two drops per quart/liter and wait 30 minutes). Tap water in campgrounds, hotels, and picnic areas has been treated; you'll taste the chlorine in some places.

Dehydration

Many first-time hikers to the Rocky Mountains are surprised to find they drink more water than at home. Winds, altitude, and lower humidity can quickly lead to dehydration. It manifests first as a headache. Drink lots of water, even more than you normally would, especially while hiking. Monitor children's fluid intake. Take electrolytes with water to prevent dehydration in the first place. Hammer Nutrition's Edurolytes Fizz or Nuun tablets are easy to drop in a water bottle and both can be bought online.

Altitude

Some visitors from sea level locales feel the effects of altitude at high elevations. Watch for lightheadedness, headaches, or shortness of breath. To **acclimatize,** slow down your hiking pace and drink lots of fluids. If symptoms spike, descend in elevation as soon as possible. Higher altitudes also increase your UV radiation exposure: To prevent **sunburn,** use a strong sunscreen and wear sunglasses and a hat.

Ice and Snow

While glacial ice often looks solid to step on, it often hides unseen caverns beneath it. Buried **crevasses** (large vertical cracks) are difficult to see and **snow bridges** can collapse as you're crossing them. Keep safe by staying off the ice unless you are on a guided **ice tour** or **glacier tour.** Steep snowfields also pose a danger from falling. Use an ice axe to steady yourself—or stay off them entirely. Only slide on the snow where you can have a safe run away from rocks and trees.

Hypothermia

Exhausted hikers are at risk for hypothermia. The body's inner core loses heat, reducing mental and physical functions. Watch for uncontrolled shivering, poor judgment, fumbling, mumbling, incoherence, and slurred speech. Avoid becoming hypothermic by staying dry. Don rain gear and warm moisture-wicking layers, rather than cotton, which won't dry and fails to retain heat. Get hypothermic hikers into dry clothing and shelter. Give warm nonalcoholic and noncaffeinated liquids. If the victim cannot regain body heat, get into a sleeping bag with the victim, both stripped for skin-to-skin contact.

Blisters

Incorrect socks and ill-fitting shoes cause most blisters. Cotton socks absorb sweat from the feet while you're hiking and hold onto it, providing a surface for friction. Synthetic or wool-blend socks wick water away from the skin. To prevent blisters, recognize "hot spots" or rubs, applying moleskin or New-Skin to sensitive areas. In a pinch, slap duct tape on

trouble spots. Once a blister occurs, apply specialty blister bandages or Second Skin, a product developed for burns that cools blisters and cushions them. Cover Second Skin with moleskin to avoid future rubbing.

Hantavirus

Hantavirus infection, with flu-like symptoms, is contracted by inhaling dust from deer mice droppings. Avoid burrows and woodpiles thick with rodents. Store all food in rodent-proof containers. If you find rodent dust in your gear, disinfect it with water and bleach (1.5 cups/355 milliliters bleach to one gallon/7.79 liters water). If you contract the virus, seek immediate medical attention.

Mosquitoes and Ticks

Insects can carry diseases such as West Nile virus and Rocky Mountain spotted fever. Protect yourself by wearing long sleeves and pants as well as using insect repellent in spring and summer, when mosquitoes and ticks are common. If you are bitten by a tick, remove it, disinfect the bite, and see a doctor if lesions or a rash appears.

Wildlife

For your safety and to prevent animals from acclimating to humans, maintain your distance at all times. Do not approach wild animals. Stay 100 yards (100 m) away from wolves, coyotes, mountain lions (cougars), and bears. That's the length of a U.S. football field, 10 bus lengths, or almost the length of a soccer field. With all other wildlife, stay at a distance of 75 feet (30 m), or the length of three buses. Even though animals like bison or moose look docile, they can injure you swiftly. Park visitors are responsible for keeping wildlife wild and other humans safe. Avoid contributing to the food conditioning of wild animals: Do not feed wildlife. Properly dispose of garbage to prevent it from attracting animals. Do not disturb or harass wildlife;

Bear Safety

The Rocky Mountains have a high density of **grizzly bears** and **black bears.** Food is the biggest bear attractant. Proper use, storage, and handling of food and garbage prevents bears from being conditioned to humans and turning aggressive. With strict food and garbage rules, the parks have minimized aggressive bear encounters and avoided both human and bear deaths. Take precautions to keep yourself (and the bears) safe.

Be conscious of food: Bears are dangerous around food, be it a carcass in the woods, a pack on a trail, or a cooler in a campsite. Protecting yourself also protects bears. Start by paying attention to food wrappers and crumbs. Food dropped along the trail attracts wildlife, as do "biodegradable" apple cores and other food remnants. Pick up what you drop and **pack out all your garbage** to dispose of it properly.

Camp safely: Use low-odor foods and keep food and cooking gear out of sleeping sites in the backcountry. Hang your food or store it in provided bear boxes. Keep a clean camp to avoid attracting wildlife. In frontcountry campgrounds, put all food, cooking gear, garbage, pet food and bowls, coolers, and scented products (such as shampoo, toothpaste, citronella candles, dish soap, sunscreen, lip balm, and even dish towels) in vehicles.

Hike safely: Avoid surprising a bear on the trail by making noise in the form of **talking, clapping, hooting,** and **hollering.** You may feel silly at first, but everyone does it. Jingling bells are sold in gift shops as "bear bells." Many hikers hate them and locals call them "dinner bells." Bells fail to carry sound the way a human voice does. Bear bells are best kept as souvenirs. Always stay 100 yards (100 m) away from bears.

Carry pepper spray: Its capsicum derivative deters bear attacks without injuring the bears or humans. Do not use bear sprays on your body, in tents, or on gear; it is to be sprayed directly at the bear. Wind and rain may reduce its effectiveness. Small purse-size pepper sprays are too small to deter bears; buy an 8-ounce (237-ml) can. Practice how to use it, but be sure to still make noise on the trail as a preventive measure. Carry it on the front of your pack for quick access, not inside your pack. Pepper spray is generally not allowed on airplanes. Some visitors centers, stores, park hotels, backcountry permit offices, and ranger stations accept used canisters of bear spray for recycling.

this includes making loud sounds or abrupt movements.

Recreation

Hiking

Hiking at the high elevations in the Rocky Mountains may be much harder than the same distance through your neighborhood park back home. Choose appropriate routes for mileage and elevation gain with this in mind. Always carry hiking essentials.

When you're out on the trail, follow Leave No Trace principles at all times. Stay on established trails and boardwalks to avoid damaging fragile ecosystems.

Trail Status

Conditions on mountain trails vary significantly depending on the season, elevation, recent weather, and bear activity. Swinging and plank bridges across rivers and creeks are installed in late May-June. Most years, higher passes are snowbound until mid-July. Steep snowfields often inhibit hiking on some trails. To find out about trail conditions before hiking, stop at ranger stations or visitors centers for updates or consult trail status reports on park websites. Bear or fire closures are also listed online.

Signage

All national park trailheads and junctions have excellent signage, at least compared to national forests and wilderness areas. Some signs show both kilometers and miles, especially in Glacier and Waterton; otherwise, Canadian parks show kilometers and U.S. parks show miles. Be prepared to convert kilometers to miles (or vice versa) in your head by brushing up your math skills. To convert kilometers to miles, multiply the kilometers listed by 0.6 (example: 3 km x 0.6 = 1.8 miles). To convert miles to kilometers, multiply the miles by 1.6 (example: 2 miles x 1.6 = 3.2 km). These calculations are easy approximations for the trail. For more precise conversions, multiply by 0.62 for kilometers to miles or 1.61 for miles to kilometers.

Backpacking

Permits or wilderness passes are required for backpacking or backcountry camping in all national parks in the Rockies. In most areas, specific campgrounds are assigned. You can usually pick up permits up to 24-48 hours in advance, depending on the park. Fees run $3-10 per person per night, although some parks charge a flat rate. During July and August, lines usually form at the backcountry permit offices at least an hour before opening.

Many parks accept **advance reservations** for permits. Most Canadian parks start allowing reservations in January for the rest of the year; most U.S. parks launch reservations in January, March, or April for the year ahead. Advance reservations usually require a fee up to $40 if the park is able to fill your request. July and August have the most competition for permits. Be online as soon as possible when reservations open.

Banff, Jasper, Kootenay, and Yoho National Parks allow do-it-yourself **online reservations** (877/737-3783 reservation.pc.gc.ca). In the U.S. national parks, most reservations are submitted as requests; rangers fill spaces and notify applicants of the permit status.

Biking

National parks in the Rocky Mountains attract cyclists for day-long rides and long-distance trips. **Helmets** are mandatory for all riders in British Columbia. Alberta, Montana, and Utah only require helmets for cyclists younger than 18 years. Wyoming and Colorado have no helmet requirements. For safety, it's best to wear a helmet at all times, regardless of local regulations.

You may also want to wear **bright colors** for visibility, as many drivers are gawking at the scenery or wildlife. You will need to contend with large RVs whizzing past your elbows on many roads that have minimal shoulders. Bring **spare tubes** and **brake pads,** a **pump,** and equipment to make minor repairs yourself; bike shops are infrequent. The national parks have designated shared **hiker-biker campsites** where you pay a per-person rate.

In a few of the national parks, **spring** brings on a unique opportunity: Plows open the road to cyclists while they remain closed to car traffic for a few weeks or months. Find these outstanding bicycling experiences in Banff, Waterton Lakes, Glacier, Yellowstone, Grand Teton, and Rocky Mountain National Parks. Glacier National Park's Going-to-the-Sun Road has limited hours for cyclists in summer, as well.

The epic **Great Divide Bike Trail** (3,084 mi/4,962 km) is one of the country's most scenic mountain bike rides, weaving together a route from Jasper, Alberta, to Antelope Well, New Mexico. While the trail mostly travels outside the national parks, it still covers spectacular terrain in the Rocky Mountains. It does cut briefly through Banff and Grand Teton National Parks. Segments combine gravel and dirt roads, rail trails, single-track bike trails, and bits of paved roads. Most riders take two months or so to complete the trail. Get planning information and maps from **Adventure Cycling** (www.adventurecycling.com).

Mountain Hiking Essentials

Unpredictable weather in the mountains can shift a warm summer day into wintry conditions in hours. Be prepared.

♦ **Extra Clothing:** Rain pants and jackets can double as wind protection, while gloves and a warm, lightweight hat can save fingers and ears from frostbite. Carry at least one extra water-wicking layer for warmth. Avoid cotton fabrics, which stay soggy and fail to retain body heat.

♦ **Extra Food and Water:** Take snacks like high-energy protein bars. Always carry extra water: Most visitors find they drink more at these high elevations than they do at home. Avoid drinking directly from streams or lakes due to the possibility of giardia and other illness-inducing bacteria, filter or treat water first.

♦ **Map and Compass or GPS Device:** Although national park trails are extremely well signed, it's still good to take a topographical map to help keep from getting lost. Compasses or GPS devices will also help, but only if you know how to use them.

♦ **Flashlight:** Carry a small flashlight or headlamp for after-dark emergencies. Take extra batteries, too.

♦ **First-Aid Kit:** Carry a fully equipped first-aid kit with blister remedies. Don't forget to add personal items like bee-sting kits and allergy medications.

♦ **Sun Protection:** Altitude, snow, ice, and lakes all increase ultraviolet radiation. Protect yourself with a minimum SPF 30 sunscreen, sunglasses, and a sun hat or brimmed cap.

♦ **Emergency Toilet Supplies:** Not every trail has a conveniently placed pit toilet. To accommodate an alfresco toilet stop, carry a small trowel, toilet paper, a small bottle of hand sanitizer, and plastic baggies for used toilet paper.

♦ **Menstrual Products:** Carry heavy-duty zippered baggies and pack out tampons, pads, and everything else.

♦ **Insect Repellent:** Summer can be abuzz with mosquitoes and blackflies at any elevation. Insect repellents that contain 50 percent DEET work best. Purchase applications that rub or spray at close range rather than aerosols that go airborne onto other people, plants, and animals.

♦ **Pepper Spray:** In case of bear encounters, carry pepper spray on the front of your pack. (But only bring it if you know how to use it effectively.)

♦ **Miscellaneous:** A knife may come in handy, as can a few feet of nylon cord and a bit of duct tape (wrap a few feet around something small like a flashlight handle or water bottle to avoid bringing the whole heavy roll). Many hikers have repaired boots and packs with duct tape and a little ingenuity.

Leave No Trace

To keep the national parks pristine, you'll need to take an active role in maintaining them. Practice Leave No Trace principles to ensure the parks are in the same (or better) condition when you depart. For more information, visit www.LNT.org.

♦ **Travel and camp on durable surfaces.** Camp only in designated sites. Protect fragile plants by staying on trails, refusing to cut switchbacks, and walking single file. If you must walk off the trail, step on rocks, snow, or dry grasses rather than wet soil and delicate plants.

♦ **Leave what you find.** Flowers, rocks, and fur tufts on shrubs are protected park resources, as are historical cultural items. For lunch stops and camping, sit on rocks or logs where you find them rather than moving them to accommodate comfort.

♦ **Properly dispose of waste.** Pack out whatever you bring, including all garbage. If toilets are not available, pack out toilet paper. Urinate on rocks, logs, gravel, or snow to protect soils and plants from salt-starved wildlife, and bury feces 6-8 inches (15-20 cm) deep at least 200 feet (61 m) from water.

♦ **Minimize campfire impacts.** Where permitted, make fires in designated fire pits only, not on beaches. Use small pieces of wood (the diameter of your wrist) that's dead and downed, not live branches. Be aware: Collecting firewood is not permitted in many places in the parks. Purchase local firewood instead.

♦ **Respect wildlife.** Bring binoculars, spotting scopes, and telephoto lenses to aid in watching wildlife. Keep your distance. Do not feed any wildlife, even ground squirrels. Once fed, they become more aggressive.

♦ **Be considerate of other visitors.** Be aware of cell phones and how their noise cuts into the natural soundscapes of the parks.

They have a four-map series for the whole route, plus a guidebook. You can also get a four-part GPX data to load into a GPS device to help keep you on the right route.

Climbing and Mountaineering

National parks in the Rocky Mountains are renowned for rock, ice, and glacier climbing opportunities, plus ski mountaineering. These exciting activities can become deadly, especially with fast-changing mountain weather. Do not go on your own unless you have the proper equipment and training. The safest option is to go with a guide service. Jasper, Banff, Yoho, Grand Teton, and Rocky Mountain National Parks all allow approved concessionaires to guide climbing

and mountaineering trips; the type varies from park to park.

Water Sports
Watercraft Inspections and Permits

The Rocky Mountain states, provinces, and national parks are on heightened alert to prevent **Aquatic Invasive Species (AIS)** or **Aquatic Nuisance Species (ANS)** from getting into pristine mountain lakes. For that reason, your watercraft may be required to pass an inspection upon entering these areas. Before you arrive, **clean, drain, and dry** all motorized watercraft, trailers, and paddle crafts (kayaks, canoes, paddleboards, rafts).

Some national parks, such as **Glacier** and **Waterton Lakes,** require boat and trailer **quarantines** to prevent AIS

Local Websites for Boating and Fishing Info

Province or State	Boating Regulations/Fees	Fishing Regulations/Fees
Alberta	tc.canada.ca	albertaregulations.ca
British Columbia	tc.canada.ca	www2.gov.bc.ca
Montana	fwp.mt.gov	fwp.mt.gov
Wyoming	wgfd.wyo.gov	wgfd.wyo.gov
Utah	stateparks.utah.gov	wildlife.utah.gov
Colorado	cpw.state.co.us	cpw.state.co.us

contamination. The quarantine lengths (30-90 days) mean boating is not feasible for casual visitors. Other parks limit activity on certain lakes or ban trailers from entering the water, effectively permitting only hand-carried watercraft. Most parks also require permits for watercraft. Check each park's restrictions online before you travel, so you know what to expect.

Boating, Paddling, and Rafting

In Canada, boaters must have their motorized watercraft licensed by the federal government and be in possession of a **Pleasure Craft Operator Card (PCOC).** Licensing and PCOC rules are waived for visiting boaters to Canada staying less than 45 days. Non-motorized watercraft are exempt. Canadian Rockies national parks do not charge an additional fee for boating.

In the United States, boat licensing is overseen by each state and national park, with different requirements and fees for motorized and non-motorized watercraft. In addition, some states require an AIS/ANS certification (fee required). Visitors are exempt, but the duration varies by state. Only Yellowstone ($5-10) and Grand Teton ($5-30) charge boating fees for motorized and non-motorized watercraft.

Fishing

Fishing in most places requires a **license or permit,** and regulations vary regarding limits, type of fish, lures, and where you can fish. Before you fish, pick up copies of the local regulations or get them online. In most **provinces and states,** you can purchase licenses from sporting goods stores, angling shops, or online. Rates vary depending on age and residency.

Most **national parks** have their own rules, permits, licenses, and fees. They also have their own regulations, so pick them up at visitors centers before casting a line.

- **Canadian national parks** all have the same fishing permit fee: $10 for a single-day permit and $35 for an annual permit. Regulations vary between parks. Purchase these permits and pick up regulations at visitors centers.

- In **U.S. national parks,** fishing fees vary by park: Permits in Glacier are free. Yellowstone charges $40 for a three-day permit and $55 for a week-long permit. In Grand Teton and Rocky Mountain, there's no park-specific permit or fee, but you'll need to obtain a state license before fishing in either park. You can buy licenses or permits at visitors centers, unless the park requires a state license.

Resources

Internet Resources
National Parks
Parks Canada
www.pc.gc.ca
The official website of Parks Canada, which manages Canada's national parks and national historic sites has information on each park and historic site, including fees, camping, and wildlife.

U.S. National Park Service
www.nps.gov
The official website of the National Park Service, which manages the U.S. national parks and other federal locales. It has information on each park, including fees, camping, things to do, wildlife, and safety alerts.

Alberta
Banff & Lake Louise Tourism
www.BanffLakeLouise.com
This is the official tourism organization for the towns of Banff and Lake Louise. It also covers activities in Banff National Park. You can find tips on trip planning as well as information on lodging, dining, events, and activities.

Tourism Calgary
www.visitcalgary.com
The official tourism organization for Calgary includes information on lodging, dining, activities, tours, and events.

Tourism Jasper
www.jasper.travel
The official tourism organization for the town of Jasper also incorporates some information on park activities on its website. You can also find info on lodging, dining, activities, events, and tours.

Travel Alberta
www.travelalberta.com
Learn more about the province, plan your travels, and order tourism literature. The site also includes information on Banff, Jasper, and Waterton Lakes National Parks.

Waterton Lakes Chamber of Commerce
https://mywaterton.ca
The official website for Waterton Townsite contains dining, lodging, recreation, visitor services, and camping information for Waterton. Some services adjacent to the park are also included.

British Columbia
Destination British Columbia
www.destinationbc.ca
The official tourism website for the province of British Columbia includes information for Kootenay and Yoho National Parks as well as surrounding towns.

Field, BC Tourism
www.field.ca
This website has information on lodging, dining, and activities in and around Field, including parts of Yoho National Park.

Kootenay Rockies Tourism
www.kootenayrockies.com
This is the official tourism website for the Columbia River Valley and the towns of Golden and Radium Hot Springs. It has trip-planning details, plus information on lodging and activities, including in Kootenay and Yoho National Parks.

Tourism Radium Hot Springs Association
www.radiumhotsprings.com
This official tourism website has information on activities and lodging for the town of Radium Hot Springs, as well as trip-planning tips.

Colorado
Boulder Convention and Visitors Bureau
www.bouldercoloradousa.com
This tourism website has info on restaurants, lodging, and events in Boulder.

Colorado Tourism
www.colorado.com
The most comprehensive travel website about Colorado has information on historic sites, ski resorts, visitor centers, and recreation areas.

Visit Denver
www.denver.org
The official guide to Colorado's largest city and surrounding regions has a plethora of information.

Visit Estes Park
www.visitestespark.com
The official website for Estes Park is replete with information about the town and Rocky Mountain National Park. Check out this site for information about lodging, activities, restaurants, and events.

Montana
Bozeman Convention
and Visitors Bureau
www.bozemancvb.com
This official tourism website features information on lodging, restaurants, events, activities, and places to go around Bozeman.

Flathead Valley Convention
and Visitors Bureau
www.fcvb.org
The Flathead Valley's tourism board covers info on Kalispell, Columbia Falls, Whitefish, Bigfork, Lakeside, Flathead Lake, and ski resorts. It covers recreation, lodging, dining, and special events.

Gardiner Chamber of Commerce
www.visitgardinermt.com
The official tourism website for Gardiner covers visitor services, lodging, dining, and places to go.

Montana Office of Tourism
www.visitmt.com
The official travel website for Montana.

You'll find access to the state's activities, lodging, dining, and recreation by location or activity.

West Yellowstone
Chamber of Commerce
https://destinationyellowstone.com
The official website for West Yellowstone covers lodging, dining, and activities, plus tours into Yellowstone.

Whitefish Convention
and Visitors Bureau
https://explorewhitefish.com
The official travel website covering recreation, lodging, dining, and special events in the town of Whitefish and at Whitefish Mountain Resort.

Utah
Utah Office of Tourism
www.visitutah.com
The official tourism site for Utah covers places to visit, things to do, and trip-planning information.

Visit Salt Lake City
www.visitsaltlake.com
Find the scoop on all aspects of visiting Salt Lake City, including accommodations (sometimes with special deals), events, and activities ranging from genealogical research to bird-watching. It's also a good place to find special deals on ski passes.

Wyoming
Jackson Hole Chamber of Commerce
www.jacksonholechamber.com
Find businesses, activities, entertainment, lodging, and restaurants for Jackson Hole.

Wyoming Travel and Tourism
www.travelwyoming.org
This site offers info on state-wide lodging, dining, and recreation options.

INDEX

LIST OF MAPS

PHOTO CREDITS

ACKNOWLEDGMENTS

A huge thank you goes out to the National Park Service and Parks Canada for all of their work in protecting and preserving national parks. It's through their labors that we can enjoy such beautiful and unique places.

Thanks also go to my parents for introducing me as a child to the outdoors and national parks. Our family expeditions for hiking, backpacking, camping, and skiing shaped a way of life for me. Those experiences and the exposure to nature are priceless gifts.

My hiking, camping, and skiing buddies provide amazing support on trips. Most of all, they are always fun on trails and always up for adventures.

Lastly, a huge thank you goes to Leah Gordon for her editing work on this book, to Albert Angulo for creating the maps, and to Darren Alessi for his eye for photos.

U.S. CIVIL RIGHTS TRAIL

A TRAVELER'S GUIDE TO THE PEOPLE, PLACES, AND EVENTS THAT MADE THE MOVEMENT

Deborah D. Douglas • Foreword by Bree Newsome Bass

MOON

the OPEN ROAD

50 BEST ROAD TRIPS in the USA

From Weekend Getaways to Cross-Country Adventures

JESSICA DUNHAM

MOON

Road Trip USA

25th ANNIVERSARY EDITION

CROSS-COUNTRY ADVENTURES ON AMERICA'S TWO-LANE HIGHWAYS

Jamie Jensen

MOON

BASEBALL Road Trips

TIMOTHY MALCOLM

THE COMPLETE GUIDE TO ALL THE BALLPARKS, WITH BEER, BITES, AND SIGHTS NEARBY

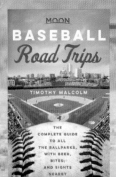

MOON

BLUE RIDGE PARKWAY Road Trip

WITH SHENANDOAH & GREAT SMOKY MOUNTAINS NATIONAL PARKS

JASON FRYE

MOON

CALIFORNIA Road Trip

SAN FRANCISCO, YOSEMITE, LAS VEGAS, GRAND CANYON, LOS ANGELES, & THE PACIFIC COAST HIGHWAY

STUART THORNTON

MOON

NASHVILLE TO NEW ORLEANS Road Trip

NATCHEZ TRACE PARKWAY • MEMPHIS • TUPELO • MISSISSIPPI BLUES TRAIL

MARGARET LITTMAN

MOON

NEW ENGLAND Road Trip

SEASIDE SPOTS, MAJESTIC MOUNTAINS & FALL FOLIAGE, COZY GETAWAYS

MILES HOWARD

MOON

NORTHERN CALIFORNIA Road Trips

DRIVES ALONG THE COAST, REDWOODS, AND MOUNTAINS WITH THE BEST STOPS ALONG THE WAY

STUART THORNTON & KAYLA ANDERSON

MORE ROAD TRIP GUIDES FROM MOON

MOON
OREGON TRAIL
Road Trip

HISTORIC SITES, SMALL TOWNS, AND
SCENIC LANDSCAPES ALONG THE LEGENDARY
WESTWARD ROUTE

KATRINA EMERY

MOON
PACIFIC COAST HIGHWAY
Road Trip

CALIFORNIA,
OREGON & WASHINGTON

IAN ANDERSON

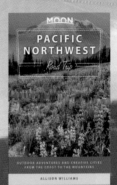

MOON
PACIFIC NORTHWEST
Road Trip

OUTDOOR ADVENTURES AND CREATIVE CITIES
FROM THE COAST TO THE MOUNTAINS

ALLISON WILLIAMS

MOON
ROUTE 66
Road Trip

JESSICA DUNHAM

MOON
SOUTH FLORIDA & THE KEYS
Road Trip

WITH MIAMI, WALT DISNEY WORLD, TAMPA &
THE EVERGLADES

JASON FERGUSON

MOON
SOUTHERN CALIFORNIA
Road Trip

DRIVES ALONG THE BEACHES, MOUNTAINS, AND DESERTS
WITH THE BEST STOPS ALONG THE WAY

IAN ANDERSON

MOON
SOUTHWEST
Road Trip

LAS VEGAS, ZION & BRYCE, MONUMENT VALLEY,
SANTA FE & TAOS, AND THE GRAND CANYON

TIM HULL

MOON
VANCOUVER & CANADIAN ROCKIES
Road Trip

VICTORIA, BANFF, JASPER, CALGARY,
THE OKANAGAN, WHISTLER &
THE SEA-TO-SKY HIGHWAY

CAROLYN B. HELLER

MOON
YELLOWSTONE TO GLACIER NATIONAL PARK
Road Trip

JACKSON HOLE, CODY, THE GRAND TETONS
& THE ROCKY MOUNTAIN FRONT

CARTER G. WALKER

MOON.COM | @MOONGUIDES

MOON
USA NATIONAL PARKS
THE COMPLETE GUIDE TO ALL
62 PARKS
BECKY LOMAX

Craft a personalized journey through the top National Parks in the U.S. and Canada with Moon!

MOON
ACADIA
NATIONAL PARK
HILARY NANGLE

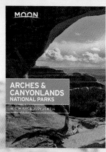

MOON
ARCHES &
CANYONLANDS
NATIONAL PARKS
W.C. McRAE & JUDY JEWELL

MOON
BANFF
NATIONAL PARK
HIKE · CAMP
SEE WILDLIFE
ANDREW HEMPSTEAD

DEATH VALLEY
NATIONAL PARK
JENNA BLOUGH

MOON
GLACIER
NATIONAL PARK
HIKING · CAMPING
LAKES & PEAKS
BECKY LOMAX

MOON
GRAND
CANYON
HIKE · CAMP
RAFT THE
COLORADO RIVER
TIM HULL

MOON
MOUNT RUSHMORE
& THE BLACK HILLS
Including the Badlands
LAURAL A. BIDWELL

MOON
ROCKY
MOUNTAIN
NATIONAL PARK
HIKE · CAMP
SEE WILDLIFE
ERIN ENGLISH

MOON
SEQUOIA &
KINGS CANYON
HIKING · CAMPING
WATERFALLS & BIG TREES
LEIGH BERNACCHI

In these books:

Coverage of gateway cities and towns

Suggested itineraries from one day to multiple weeks

Advice on where to stay (or camp) in and around the parks

MOON

GREAT SMOKY MOUNTAINS
NATIONAL PARK

HIKING · CAMPING
SCENIC DRIVES

JASON FRYE

MOON

**JOSHUA TREE
& PALM SPRINGS**

ERIN SLOUGH

MOON

**YELLOWSTONE
& GRAND TETON**

HIKE, CAMP
SEE WILDLIFE

BECKY LOMAX

MOON

**YOSEMITE
SEQUOIA &
KINGS CANYON**

ANN MARIE BROWN

MOON

**ZION &
BRYCE**

W. C. MCRAE, JUDY JEWELL

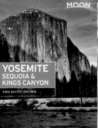

Get inspired for your next adventure

Follow @**moonguides** on Instagram or subscribe to our newsletter at **moon.com**

#TravelWithMoon

MAP SYMBOLS

═════ Highway	○ City/Town	ⓘ Information Center	⚑ Golf Course
═════ Primary Road	⊙ State Capital	🅿 Parking Area	✦ Unique Feature
═════ Secondary Road	⊛ National Capital	⛪ Church	✦ Unique Feature Hydro
======= Unpaved Road	● Highlight	🍇 Winery/Vineyard	🖐 Waterfall
---------- Trail	★ Point of Interest	⛺ Trailhead	◮ Camping
············ Ferry	• Accommodation	🚊 Train Station	▲ Mountain
-•-•-•- Railroad	▼ Restaurant/Bar	✈ International Airport	⚡ Ski Area
━━━ Pedestrian Walkway	■ Other Location	✈ Regional Airport	🦪 Glacier
▥▥▥▥ Stairs		⚶ Park	

CONVERSION TABLES

°C = (°F - 32) / 1.8
°F = (°C x 1.8) + 32
1 inch = 2.54 centimeters (cm)
1 foot = 0.304 meters (m)
1 yard = 0.914 meters
1 mile = 1.6093 kilometers (km)
1 km = 0.6214 miles
1 fathom = 1.8288 m
1 chain = 20.1168 m
1 furlong = 201.168 m
1 acre = 0.4047 hectares
1 sq km = 100 hectares
1 sq mile = 2.59 square km
1 ounce = 28.35 grams
1 pound = 0.4536 kilograms
1 short ton = 0.90718 metric ton
1 short ton = 2,000 pounds
1 long ton = 1.016 metric tons
1 long ton = 2,240 pounds
1 metric ton = 1,000 kilograms
1 quart = 0.94635 liters
1 US gallon = 3.7854 liters
1 Imperial gallon = 4.5459 liters
1 nautical mile = 1.852 km

°FAHRENHEIT	°CELSIUS
230	110
220	
210	100 WATER BOILS
200	
190	90
180	80
170	
160	70
150	
140	60
130	50
120	
110	40
100	
90	30
80	
70	20
60	
50	10
40	
30	0 WATER FREEZES
20	-10
10	
0	-20
-10	
-20	-30
-30	
-40	-40

MOON U.S. & CANADIAN ROCKY MOUNTAINS ROAD TRIP

Avalon Travel
Hachette Book Group
1700 Fourth Street
Berkeley, CA 94710, USA
www.moon.com

Editor and Series Manager: Leah Gordon
Acquiring Editor: Nikki Ioakimedes
Copy Editors: Kimberly Ehart, Kathryn Ettinger, and
  Kevin McLain
Production and Graphics Coordinator:
  Darren Alessi
Cover Design: Erin Seaward-Hiatt
Interior Design: Darren Alessi
Moon Logo: Tim McGrath
Map Editor: Albert Angulo
Cartographer: John Culp
Indexer: Rachel Kuhn

ISBN-13: 9781640498051
Printing History
1st Edition — February 2022
5 4 3 2 1

Text © 2022 by Becky Lomax, Andrew Hempstead,
  W. C. McRae, Judy Jewell, Erin English, and Terri
  Cook.
Maps © 2022 by Avalon Travel.

Front cover photo: Moraine Lake in the Valley of
the Ten Peaks, Banff National Park © Bill Brooks /
Alamy Stock Photo

Printed in Malaysia for Imago